An Introduction to Sociolinguistics

Blackwell Textbooks in Linguistics

The books included in this series provide comprehensive accounts of some of the most central and most rapidly developing areas of research in linguistics. Intended primarily for introductory and post-introductory students, they include exercises, discussion points, and suggestions for further reading.

1. Liliane Haegeman — *Introduction to Government and Binding Theory* (Second Edition)
2. Andrew Spencer — *Morphological Theory*
3. Helen Goodluck — *Language Acquisition*
4. Ronald Wardhaugh — *Introduction to Sociolinguistics* (Fifth Edition)
5. Martin Atkinson — *Children's Syntax*
6. Diane Blakemore — *Understanding Utterances*
7. Michael Kenstowicz — *Phonology in Generative Grammar*
8. Deborah Schiffrin — *Approaches to Discourse*
9. John Clark and Colin Yallop — *An Introduction to Phonetics and Phonology* (Second Edition)
10. Natsuko Tsujimura — *An Introduction to Japanese Linguistics*
11. Robert D. Borsley — *Modern Phrase Structure Grammar*
12. Nigel Fabb — *Linguistics and Literature*
13. Irene Heim and Angelika Kratzer — *Semantics in Generative Grammar*
14. Liliane Haegeman and Jacqueline Guéron — *English Grammar: A Generative Perspective*
15. Stephen Crain and Diane Lillo-Martin — *An Introduction to Linguistic Theory and Language Acquisition*
16. Joan Bresnan — *Lexical-Functional Syntax*
17. Barbara A. Fennell — *A History of English: A Sociolinguistic Approach*
18. Henry Rogers — *Writing Systems: A Linguistic Approach*
19. Benjamin W. Fortson IV — *Indo-European Language and Culture: An Introduction*
20. Liliane Haegeman — *Thinking Syntactically: A Guide to Argumentation and Analysis*

An Introduction to Sociolinguistics
FIFTH EDITION

Ronald Wardhaugh

Blackwell
Publishing

BLACKWELL PUBLISHING
350 Main Street, Malden, MA 02148-5020, USA
9600 Garsington Road, Oxford OX4 2DQ, UK
550 Swanston Street, Carlton, Victoria 3053, Australia

First published 1986 by Basil Blackwell Ltd
Second edition (1992), third edition (1998), and fourth edition (2002) published by Blackwell Publishers Ltd
Fifth edition published 2006 by Blackwell Publishing Ltd

4   2008

Library of Congress Cataloging-in-Publication Data

Wardhaugh, Ronald.
 An introduction to sociolinguistics / Ronald Wardhaugh. — 5th ed.
  p. cm. — (Blackwell textbooks in linguistics ; 4)
 Includes bibliographical references and index.
 ISBN: 978-1-4051-3559-7 (pbk. : alk. paper)
 1. Sociolinguistics. I. Title. II.
Series.
P40.W27 2006
306.44—dc22
                                                              2005019312

A catalogue record for this title is available from the British Library.

Set in 10/12pt Sabon
by Graphicraft Limited, Hong Kong
Printed and bound in Singapore
by C.O.S. Printers Pte Ltd

For further information on
Blackwell Publishing, visit our website:
www.blackwellpublishing.com

Contents

Preface

This book is intended to provide students with a sound, basic coverage of most of the topics dealt with in courses described as either 'Sociolinguistics' or 'The Sociology of Language.' It assumes very little previous knowledge of linguistics, anthropology, or sociology, and so should prove to be most useful in a first-level course. It may also be used as a supplementary text in a higher-level course that deals with a narrow range of topics but in which the instructor wants students to become familiar with topics not treated in that course. Each of the sub-topics covered here concludes with a 'Discussion' section. The material in these sections is designed to encourage further discussion and research; it may also lead to assignments of various kinds.

It is obvious that a book of this kind draws on a variety of sources. The breadth of the published sources can be seen in the bibliographic information that is included. I owe a considerable debt to the sources mentioned there. During the many years I taught, my students also provided me with numerous insights into what works in the classroom and what does not. My thanks go once again to Judy Morris and Angie Camardi for all their secretarial assistance with the first edition. For this edition, as for the previous editions, my thanks go to all those who provided comments to me in various ways over the years. It is certainly satisfying to see a fifth edition. I hope it continues to reflect what is happening in this most interesting area of linguistics, one that seemed for a time to be coming apart at the seams because of its rapid evolution and success. However, any deeper examination shows that sociolinguistics is still clearly unified through its concern with how people use language to create and express identities, relate to one another in groups, and seek to resist, protect, or increase various kinds of power.

R.W.

Acknowledgments

I am grateful for permission to use the following tables:

Table 3.1 (p. 82), from Roger T. Bell, *Sociolinguistics*; copyright © 1976 by Roger T. Bell, published by B. T. Batsford Ltd.

Table 6.3 (p. 160), Table 7.5 (p. 171), Table 8.5 (p. 207), from Peter Trudgill, *Sociolinguistics: An Introduction to Language and Society*, third edition; copyright © 1995 by Peter Trudgill, published by Penguin Books.

Table 7.6 (p. 173), from Peter Trudgill, *The Social Differentiation of English in Norwich*; copyright © 1974 by Cambridge University Press.

Table 7.8 (p. 179), Table 8.6 (p. 216), Table 9.1 (p. 231), from R. A. Hudson, *Sociolinguistics*, second edition; copyright © 1996 by Cambridge University Press.

Table 8.4 (p. 202), from Peter Trudgill, 'Sex, Covert Prestige and Linguistic Change in the Urban British English of Norwich,' *Language in Society*; copyright © 1972 by Cambridge University Press.

Table 9.2 (p. 234), from Robbins Burling, *Man's Many Voices: Language in its Cultural Context*; copyright © 1970 by Holt, Rinehart and Winston, reprinted by permission of CBS Publishing.

Tables 11.2 and 11.3 (p. 278), from Clifford Geertz, *The Religion of Java*; copyright © 1960 by The Free Press, a division of Macmillan, Inc.

1 Introduction

Any discussion of the relationship between language and society, or of the various functions of language in society, should begin with some attempt to define each of these terms. Let us say that a *society* is any group of people who are drawn together for a certain purpose or purposes. By such a definition 'society' becomes a very comprehensive concept, but we will soon see how useful such a comprehensive view is because of the very different kinds of societies we must consider in the course of the various discussions that follow. We may attempt an equally comprehensive definition of language: a *language* is what the members of a particular society speak. However, as we will see, speech in almost any society can take many very different forms, and just what forms we should choose to discuss when we attempt to describe the language of a society may prove to be a contentious matter. Sometimes too a society may be plurilingual; that is, many speakers may use more than one language, however we define language. We should also note that our definitions of language and society are not independent: the definition of language includes in it a reference to society. I will return to this matter from time to time.

Knowledge of Language

When two or more people communicate with each other in speech, we can call the system of communication that they employ a code. In most cases that code will be something we may also want to call a language. We should also note that two speakers who are bilingual, that is, who have access to two codes, and who for one reason or another shift back and forth between the two languages as they converse by code-switching (see chapter 4) are actually using a third code, one which draws on those two languages. The system (or the *grammar*, to use a well-known technical term) is something that each speaker 'knows,' but two very important issues for linguists are just what that knowledge is knowledge of and how it may best be characterized.

In practice, linguists do not find it at all easy to write grammars because the knowledge that people have of the languages they speak is extremely hard to describe. It is certainly something different from, and is much more considerable than, the kinds of knowledge we see described in most of the grammars we find on library shelves, no matter how good those grammars may be. Anyone who knows a language knows much more about that language than is contained in any grammar book that attempts to describe the language. What is also interesting is that this knowledge is both something which every individual who speaks the language possesses (since we must assume that each individual knows the grammar of his or her language by the simple reason that he or she readily uses that language) and also some kind of shared knowledge, that is, knowledge possessed by all those who speak the language. It is also possible to talk about 'dead' languages, e.g., Latin or Sanskrit. However, in such cases we should note that it is the speakers who are dead, not the languages themselves, for these may still exist, at least in part. We may even be tempted to claim an existence for English, French, or Swahili independent of the existence of those who speak these languages.

Today, most linguists agree that the knowledge speakers have of the language or languages they speak is knowledge of something quite abstract. It is a knowledge of rules and principles and of the ways of saying and doing things with sounds, words, and sentences, rather than just knowledge of specific sounds, words, and sentences. It is knowing what is *in* the language and what is not; it is knowing the possibilities the language offers and what is impossible. This knowledge explains how it is we can understand sentences we have not heard before and reject others as being *ungrammatical*, in the sense of not being possible in the language. Communication among people who speak the same language is possible because they share such knowledge, although how it is shared – or even how it is acquired – is not well understood. Certainly, psychological and social factors are important, and genetic ones too. Language is a communal possession, although admittedly an abstract one. Individuals have access to it and constantly show that they do so by using it properly. As we will see, a wide range of skills and activities is subsumed under this concept of 'proper use.'

Confronted with the task of trying to describe the grammar of a language like English, many linguists follow the approach which is associated with Chomsky, undoubtedly the most influential figure in late twentieth-century linguistics. Chomsky has argued on many occasions that, in order to make meaningful discoveries about language, linguists must try to distinguish between what is important and what is unimportant about language and linguistic behavior. The important matters, sometimes referred to as *language universals*, concern the learnability of all languages, the characteristics they share, and the rules and principles that speakers apparently follow in constructing and interpreting sentences; the less important matters have to do with how individual speakers use specific utterances in a variety of ways as they find themselves in this situation or that.

Chomsky has also distinguished between what he has called *competence* and *performance*. He claims that it is the linguist's task to characterize what speakers know about their language, i.e., their competence, not what they do with their language, i.e., their performance. The best-known characterization of this distinction comes from Chomsky himself (1965, pp. 3–4) in words which have been extensively quoted:

Linguistic theory is concerned primarily with an ideal speaker–listener, in a completely homogeneous speech-community, who knows its language perfectly and is unaffected by such grammatically irrelevant conditions as memory limitations, distractions, shifts of attention and interest, and errors (random or characteristic) in applying his knowledge of the language in actual performance. This seems to me to have been the position of the founders of modern general linguistics, and no cogent reason for modifying it has been offered. To study actual linguistic performance, we must consider the interaction of a variety of factors, of which the underlying competence of the speaker–hearer is only one. In this respect, study of language is no different from empirical investigation of other complex phenomena.

From time to time we will return to this distinction between competence and performance. However, the knowledge we will seek to explain involves more than knowledge of the grammar of the language for it will become apparent that speakers know, or are in agreement about, more than that. Moreover, in their performance they behave systematically: their actions are not random; there is order. Knowing a language also means knowing how to use that language since speakers know not only how to form sentences but also how to use them appropriately. There is therefore another kind of competence, sometimes called *communicative competence*, and the social aspects of that competence will be our concern here.

Discussion

1. Hymes (1964b, p. 16) presents the following two instances of behavior which the participants, speakers of Ojibwa, an American Indian language, describe as language behavior:

    > An informant told me that many years before he was sitting in a tent one afternoon during a storm, together with an old man and his wife. There was one clap of thunder after another. Suddenly the old man turned to his wife and asked, 'Did you hear what was said?' 'No,' she replied, 'I didn't catch it.' My informant, an acculturated Indian, told me he did not at first know what the old man and his wife referred to. It was, of course, the thunder. The old man thought that one of the Thunder Birds had said something to him. He was reacting to this sound in the same way as he would respond to a human being, whose words he did not understand. The casualness of the remark and even the trivial character of the anecdote demonstrate the psychological depth of the 'social relations' with other-than-human beings that becomes explicit in the behavior of the Ojibwa as a consequence of the cognitive 'set' induced by their culture.
    >
    > A white trader, digging in his potato patch, unearthed a large stone similar to the one just referred to. He sent for John Duck, an Indian who was the leader of the *wábano*, a contemporary ceremony that is held in a structure something like that used for the Midewiwin (a major ceremony during which stones occasionally had animate properties such as movement and opening of a mouth). The trader called his attention to the stone, saying that it must belong to his pavilion. John Duck did not seem pleased at this. He bent down and spoke to the boulder in a low voice, inquiring whether it had ever been in his pavilion. According to John the stone replied in the negative.

It is obvious that John Duck spontaneously structured the situation in terms that are intelligible within the context of Ojibwa language and culture. . . . I regret that my field notes contain no information about the use of direct verbal address in the other cases mentioned (movement of stone, opening of a mouth). But it may well have taken place. In the anecdote describing John Duck's behavior, however, his use of speech as a mode of communication raises the animate status of the boulder to the level of social interaction common to human beings. Simply as a matter of observation we can say that the stone was treated *as if* it were a 'person,' not a 'thing,' without inferring that objects of this class are, for the Ojibwa, necessarily conceptualized as persons.

Hymes argues that 'in general, no phenomenon can be defined in advance as never to be counted as constituting a message.' How does this observation apply to the above examples? Can you think of possible examples drawn from your own experience? Note that a basic assumption here is that 'messages,' whatever they are, require a 'language.' Should every 'language' in which you can send 'messages' be of equal interest to us as sociolinguists, e.g., the 'language' of flowers, semaphore signaling, dress codes, and road signs? If not, what principles should guide us in an attempt to constrain our interests? And how do you view the 'languages' of logic, mathematics, and computers?

2. What obstacles do you see in an attempt to define English as a language when you consider that such a definition must cover all of the following (and much more): both Cockney and Jamaican English; the speech of two-year-olds; fast colloquial speech; the language of formal written documents such as real estate transfers; formulaic expressions such as *How do you do?* and *It never rains but it pours*; completely novel sentences, i.e., sentences you have not heard or seen before (e.g., just about any sentence in this book); and slips of the tongue, e.g., *queer dean* for *dear Queen*? What kind of abilities must you yourself have in order even to consider attempting such a task?

Variation

The competence–performance distinction just mentioned is one that holds intriguing possibilities for work in linguistics, but it is one that has also proved to be quite troublesome, particularly when much of the variety we experience within language is labeled 'performance' and then put to one side by those who consider 'competence' to be the only valid concern of linguists. The language we use in everyday living is remarkably varied. Some investigators believe that this variety throws up serious obstacles to all attempts to demonstrate that each language is truly a homogeneous entity, and that it is possible to write a complete grammar for a language which makes use of *categorical rules*, i.e., rules which specify exactly what is – and therefore what is not – possible in the language. Everywhere we turn we seem to find at least a new wrinkle or a small inconsistency with regard to any rule we might propose. When we look closely at any language, we will discover time and time again that there is considerable internal variation and that speakers make constant use of the many different possibilities offered to them. No one speaks the same way all the time and people constantly exploit the nuances of the languages they speak for a wide variety of purposes. The consequence is a kind of paradox: while many linguists would like to view any language as a homogeneous entity and each speaker of that language as controlling only a single style, so that they can make the strongest possible theoretical generalizations, in actual fact that language will exhibit considerable internal variation, and single-style speakers will not be found (or, if found, will appear to be quite 'abnormal' in that respect, if in no other!).

A recognition of variation implies that we must recognize that a language is not just some kind of abstract object of study. It is also something that people use. Can we really set aside, at any point in our study of language, this fact of use? It is not surprising therefore that a recurring issue in linguistics in recent years has been the possible value of a linguistics that deliberately separates itself from any concern with the use, and the users, of language. Following Chomsky's example, many linguists have argued that we should not study a language in use, or even how the language is learned, without first acquiring an adequate knowledge of what language itself is. In this view, linguistic investigations should focus on developing this latter knowledge. The linguist's task should be to write grammars that will help us develop our understanding of language: what it is, how it is learnable, and what it tells us about the human mind. This kind of linguistics is sometimes referred to as 'theoretical linguistics' and it has claimed a privileged position for itself within the overall discipline of linguistics. Investigations of language use have little to offer us in such a view.

Many sociolinguists have disagreed, arguing that an *asocial* linguistics is scarcely worthwhile and that meaningful insights into language can be gained only if such matters as use and variation are included as part of the data which must be explained in a comprehensive theory of language; such a theory of language must have something to say about the uses of language. This is the view I will adopt here. However, while doing so, from time to time I will voice some skepticism about the claims of other investigators that we should pursue certain ideological ends in investigating such use (see chapters 13–15). Detachment and objectivity are essential requirements of serious scientific inquiry.

We will see that there is considerable variation in the speech of any one individual, but there are also definite bounds to that variation: no individual is free to do just exactly what he or she pleases so far as language is concerned. You cannot pronounce words any way you please, inflect or not inflect words such as nouns and verbs arbitrarily, or make drastic alterations in word order in sentences as the mood suits you. If you do any or all of these things, the results will be unacceptable, even gibberish. The variation you are permitted has limits and these limits can be described with considerable accuracy. Individuals know the various limits (or norms), and that knowledge is both very precise and at the same time almost entirely unconscious. It is also difficult to explain how individual speakers acquire knowledge of these norms of linguistic behavior, for they appear to be much more subtle than the norms that apply to such matters as social behavior, dress, and table manners. This is another issue to which we will return from time to time. Our task will be one of trying to specify the norms of linguistic behavior that exist in particular groups and then trying to account for individual behavior in terms of these norms. This task is particularly interesting because most people have no conscious awareness that we can account for much of their linguistic behavior in this way.

People have also learned such behavior. We must be concerned with that learning. Why does speaker X behave this way but speaker Y behave that way? To answer that question we must look at such issues as identity, group membership, power, and socialization.

Each of us has an identity (or, perhaps more accurately, a set of identities). That identity has been constructed from interaction with others and it is the sense of self each of us has achieved, the result of our socialization, i.e., our experiences with the outside world as we have dealt with that world in all its complexity. Consequently, any of many factors might have affected it: race, ethnicity, gender, religion, occupation, physical location, social class, kinship, leisure activities, etc. Identity is created in dealing with such factors and in dealing with members of groups for whom these factors are their identifying characteristics. An identity may also change for identities can sometimes be quite malleable, but, of course, it may also stay fixed if change is not allowed or if a fixed identity is to be maintained at all costs.

Identity is very important: individual identity and group identity. It will be a recurrent theme in the pages that follow. Much of what we find in linguistic behavior will be explicable in terms of people seeking to negotiate, realize, or even reject identities through the use of language. In fact, as we will see, language is a profound indicator of identity, more potent by far than cultural artifacts such as dress, food choices, and table manners.

Groups, too, have identities, their ways of achieving a sense of solidarity among members, so we will be interested in the linguistic characteristics of both individuals and groups. Concepts such as 'community' (see chapter 5), 'social network' (see pp. 129–30), and 'community of practice' (see p. 127) will be found in the pages that follow. These are useful in referring to groups of various kinds, for it is within groups that individuals form relationships or reject such a possibility. However, groups, like individuals, are complex entities so we must never forget that any reference made in the following pages to 'middle class,' 'women,' 'speakers of Haitian Creole,' 'teenagers,' etc. in reality subsumes a variety of individual identities each in its own way just as complex as the whole.

Finally, in all the above we must recognize that 'power' plays a significant role in everything that happens. Some forces in society are stronger than others and produce real effects, among them linguistic effects that have consequences for the lives we live. Bourdieu (1991) conceives of languages as symbolic marketplaces in which some people have more control of the goods than others because certain languages or varieties have been endowed with more symbolic power than others and have therefore been given a greater value, e.g., standard languages, certain accents, a particular gendered style of speaking, a specific type of discourse. Power and some of the various responses to it will also find frequent mention in the pages that follow.

Discussion

1. I have said that languages contain a great deal of variety. What evidence can you cite to show some of the variety? Consider, for example, how many different ways you can ask someone to open a window or seek permission to open the window yourself because the room you are in is too warm. How many ways can you pronounce variants of *and, have, do, of,* and *for*? When might *Did you eat yet?* sound like *Jeechet*? What did you do with the words and sounds? Do you speak the same way to a younger sibling at home over the breakfast table as you would to a distinguished public figure you meet at a ceremonial dinner? If you do not, and it is almost certain that you do not, what are the differences in the linguistic choices you make? Why do you make them?

2. An individual can use language in a variety of ways and for many different purposes. What might cause a speaker to say each of the following? When would each be quite inappropriate?

   a. Do you think it's cold in here?
   b. The airport, as fast as you can.
   c. I do.
   d. I leave my house to my son George.
   e. Do you love me?
   f. How strange!
   g. Can we have some silence at the back?
   h. What a beautiful dress!
   i. Cheers!
   j. Will you marry me?
   k. Do you come here often?
   l. Keep to the right, please.
   m. Damn!
   n. You don't love me any more.

   Do you know of any grammar book that tells you when to use (or not to use) each of the above? Would you describe your knowledge of when to use (or not to use) each as a matter of competence or of performance? (In thinking about this you might consult just about any discussion of Chomsky's work on linguistic theory.)

3. Do you always agree with people you know about the 'correct' choice to make of certain linguistic forms? What do you, and they, regard as the correct completions of the *tag questions* found in the following examples? (The first is done for you.)

   a. He's ready, *isn't he?*
   b. I have a penny in my purse, _____ ?
   c. I may see you next week, _____ ?
   d. I'm going right now, _____ ?
   e. The girl saw no one, _____ ?

f.   No one goes there any more, _____ ?
g.   Everyone hates one another here, _____ ?
h.   Few people know that, _____ ?
i.   The baby cried, _____ ?
j.   Either John or Mary did it, _____ ?
k.   Each of us is going to go, _____ ?

What kinds of difficulties did you find in completing this task? What kinds
of agreements and disagreements do you find when you compare your
responses to those of others? What do the standard grammars have to say
about correctness here? How would you advise an adult learning English as
a foreign language concerning this particular problem?

4.   Describe some aspects of your own speech which show how it varies from
the speech of certain other people you know. Do you pronounce words
differently, use different word forms, choose different words, or use different grammatical structures? How do you view, i.e., judge, the speech of
those who speak differently from you?

5.   Hudson (1996, p. 12) says that we may be impressed by the amount of
agreement that is often found among speakers. This agreement goes well
beyond what is needed for efficient communication. He particularly points
out the conformity we exhibit in using irregular forms, e.g., *went* for the
past tense of *go*, *men* as the plural of *man*, and *best* as the superlative of
good. This *irregular morphology* is somewhat inefficient; all it shows is our
conformity to rules established by others. How conformist do you consider
yourself to be so far as language is concerned? What 'rules' do you obey?
When do you 'flout the rules,' if you ever do?

Scientific Investigation

The scientific study of language, its uses, and the linguistic norms that people
observe poses a number of problems. Such a study must go a long way beyond
merely devising schemes for classifying the various bits and pieces of linguistic
data you might happen to observe. That would be a rather uninteresting activity,
a kind of butterfly collecting. A more profound kind of theorizing is called for:
some attempt to arrive at an understanding of the general principles of organization that surely must exist in both language and the uses of language. It is
just such an attempt that led Saussure (1959) to distinguish between *langue*
(group knowledge of language) and *parole* (individual use of language); Bloomfield
(1933) to stress the importance of *contrastive distribution* (since *pin* and *bin* are
different words in English, /p/ and /b/ must be contrastive units in the structure
of English); Pike (1967) to distinguish between *emic* and *etic* features in language
(/p/ and /b/ are contrastive, therefore *emic*, units, but the two pronunciations of
p in *pin* and *spin* are not contrastive, therefore *etic*); and Sapir (1921) and, much
later, Chomsky (1965) to stress the distinction between the 'surface' characteristics

of utterances and the 'deep' realities of linguistic form behind these surface characteristics. A major current linguistic concern is with matters such as language universals, i.e., the essential properties and various typologies of languages (see Comrie, 1989, and Cook and Newson, 1996), the factors that make languages learnable by humans but not by non-humans (see Pinker, 1994), and the conditions that govern such matters as linguistic change (see Labov, 1994, and McMahon, 1994).

There is not just one way to do linguistics, although it is true to say that some linguists occasionally behave as though their way is the only way. It is actually quite possible for two linguists to adopt radically different approaches to both language and linguistic theorizing in their work while still doing something that many consider to be genuine linguistics. Perhaps nowhere can such differences of approach be better observed than in attempts to study the relationship of language to society. Such attempts cover a very wide range of issues and reveal the diversity of approaches: different theories about what language is; different views of what constitute the data that are relevant to a specific issue; different formulations of research problems; different conceptions of what are 'good' answers, the 'significance' or 'interest' of certain findings, and the generalizability of conclusions; and different interpretations of both the theoretical and 'real-world' consequences of particular pieces of research, i.e., what they tell us about the nature of language or indicate we might do to change or improve the human condition.

Discussion

1. Find out what you can about Saussure's distinction between *langue* and *parole* and about Pike's *etic–emic* distinction. How might these distinctions relate to any study of language use in society?
2. Bloomfield's views on contrastive distribution are very important. Be sure you know what is meant by the concept of 'contrast' in linguistics. You might test out your knowledge of the concept by trying to find out how many contrastive consonant and vowel sounds you have in the variety of English you speak. If you find the number of consonant sounds to be any other than 24 and the number of vowel sounds to be far different from 14, you may be on the wrong track.

Language and Society

In the following chapters we will look at many ways in which language and society are related. The possible relationships have long intrigued investigators. Indeed, if we look back at the history of linguistics it is rare to find investigations of any language which are entirely cut off from concurrent investigations of the history of that language, or of its regional and/or social distributions, or of its relationship to objects, ideas, events, and actual speakers and listeners in the 'real' world. That is one of the reasons why a number of linguists have found Chomsky's asocial view of linguistic theorizing to be a rather sterile type of activity, since it explicitly rejects any concern for the relationship between a language and those who use it.

We must acknowledge that a language is essentially a set of items, what Hudson (1996, p. 21) calls 'linguistic items,' such entities as sounds, words, grammatical structures, and so on. It is these items, their status, and their arrangements that language theorists such as Chomsky concern themselves with. On the other hand, social theorists, particularly sociologists, attempt to understand how societies are structured and how people manage to live together. To do so, they use such concepts as 'identity,' 'power,' 'class,' 'status,' 'solidarity,' 'accommodation,' 'face,' 'gender,' 'politeness,' etc. A major concern of this book is to examine possible relationships between 'linguistic items' on the one hand and concepts such as 'power,' 'solidarity,' etc. on the other. We should note that in doing so we are trying to relate two different kinds of entities in order to see what light they throw on each other. That is not an easy task. Linguistic items are difficult to define. Try, for example, to define exactly what linguistic items such as sounds, syllables, words, and sentences are. Then try to define precisely what you understand by such concepts as 'social class,' 'solidarity,' 'identity,' 'face,' and 'politeness.' Finally, try to relate the two sets of definitions within some kind of theory so as to draw conclusions about how items in these two very different classes relate to each other. Do all this while keeping in mind that languages and societies are constantly changing. The difficulties we confront are both legion and profound.

There are several possible relationships between language and society. One is that social structure may either influence or determine linguistic structure and/or behavior. Certain evidence may be adduced to support this view: the *age-grading* phenomenon whereby young children speak differently from older children and, in turn, children speak differently from mature adults; studies which show that the varieties of language that speakers use reflect such matters as their regional, social, or ethnic origin and possibly even their gender; and other studies which show that particular ways of speaking, choices of words, and even rules for conversing are in fact highly determined by certain social requirements.

A second possible relationship is directly opposed to the first: linguistic structure and/or behavior may either influence or determine social structure. This is the view that is behind the Whorfian hypothesis (see chapter 9), the claims of Bernstein (see chapter 14), and many of those who argue that languages rather than speakers of these languages can be 'sexist' (see chapter 13). A third possible relationship is that the influence is bi-directional: language and society may influence each other. One variant of this approach is that this influence is dialectical in nature, a Marxist view put forward by Dittmar (1976), who argues (p. 238) that 'speech behaviour and social behaviour are in a state of constant interaction' and that 'material living conditions' are an important factor in the relationship.

A fourth possibility is to assume that there is no relationship at all between linguistic structure and social structure and that each is independent of the other. A variant of this possibility would be to say that, although there might be some such relationship, present attempts to characterize it are essentially premature, given what we know about both language and society. Actually, this variant view appears to be the one that Chomsky himself holds: he prefers to develop an asocial linguistics as a preliminary to any other kind of linguistics, such an asocial approach being, in his view, logically prior.

We must therefore be prepared to look into various aspects of the possible relationships between language and society. It will be quite obvious from doing so that correlational studies must form a significant part of sociolinguistic work. Gumperz (1971, p. 223) has observed that sociolinguistics is an attempt to find correlations between social structure and linguistic structure and to observe any changes that occur. Chambers (2002, p. 3) is even more direct: 'Sociolinguistics is the study of the social uses of language, and the most productive studies in the four decades of sociolinguistic research have emanated from determining the social evaluation of linguistic variants. These are also the areas most susceptible to scientific methods such as hypothesis-formation, logical inference, and statistical testing.' However, as Gumperz and others have been quick to indicate, such studies do not exhaust sociolinguistic investigation, nor do they always prove to be as enlightening as one might hope. It is a well-known fact that a correlation shows only a relationship between two variables; it does not show ultimate causation. To find that X and Y are related is not necessarily to discover that X causes Y (or Y causes X), for it is also quite possible that some third factor, Z, may cause both X and Y (or even that some far more subtle combination of factors is involved). We must always exercise caution when we attempt to draw conclusions from such relationships.

A worthwhile sociolinguistics, however, must be something more than just a simple mixing of linguistics and sociology which takes concepts and findings from the two disciplines and attempts to relate them in simple ways. It certainly must go beyond Horvath's view (1998, p. 448) that sociolinguists should just pick and choose freely from sociology: 'What my kind of sociolinguists do is go periodically to sociology and find "social networks" or "the linguistic market place"... and we find [these concepts] terribly useful in understanding the patterns that emerge from our data. However, we are not engaged in the sociologists' struggles over the importance of social networks *vis-à-vis* other ways of dealing with the structure of society and may remain blissfully unaware of whether or not these models have become contentious within the home discipline.' A serious scientific approach is incompatible with 'blissful unawareness' in an essential part of its underpinnings. Hymes (1974, p. 76) has pointed out that even a mechanical amalgamation of standard linguistics and standard sociology is not likely to suffice in that in adding a speechless sociology to a sociology-free linguistics we may miss what is important in the relationship between language and society. Specific points of connection between language and society must be discovered, and these must be related within theories that throw light on how linguistic and social structures interact.

Holmes (1992, p. 16) says that 'the sociolinguist's aim is to move towards a theory which provides a motivated account of the way language is used in a community, and of the choices people make when they use language.' For example, when we observe how varied language use is we must search for the causes.

'Upon observing variability, we seek its social correlates. What is the purpose of the variation? How is it evaluated in the community? What do its variants symbolize?' (Chambers, 2003, p. 226). For Chambers these questions 'are the central questions of sociolinguistics.' Chambers is not alone in holding such views. Others too believe that sociolinguistics is the study of language variation and that the purpose of such study is to find out what variation tells us about language and speakers' 'knowledge' of language, in this case their unconscious knowledge of subtle linguistic differences.

We will also see that there is some opposition to this idea that sociolinguistic investigations should be confined to fairly straightforward correlational studies of this kind. Critics such as Cameron (1997) claim that these studies do not provide very satisfactory explanations for linguistic behavior because of inadequacies with social theory – sometimes there is none at all – and failure to appreciate the difficulties in using social concepts. Any conclusions are likely to be suspect. What is needed, according to Cameron (p. 62), is more social engagement so that socio-linguistics would 'deal with such matters as the production and reproduction of linguistic norms by institutions and socializing practices; how these norms are apprehended, accepted, resisted and subverted by individual actors and what their relation is to the construction of identity.' Milroy (2001, pp. 554–5) makes a somewhat similar claim in discussing the processes of standardization and change: 'Social patterns are adduced only in so far as they may elucidate pat-terns of language by exhibiting co-variation with linguistic variables . . . and as long as internal analyses are quite strongly biased in favor of linguistic, rather than social, phenomena, the quantitative paradigm will be to that extent impeded in its attempts to explain the social "life" of language and the social origins of language change.' I have already mentioned this idea of necessary social engagement and I will return to it later. However, one point is clear in the above disagreement: sociolinguistics, whatever it is, is about asking important questions concerning the relationship of language to society. In the pages that follow I will try to show you some of those questions.

Discussion

1. To convince yourself that there are some real issues here with regard to the possible relationships between language and society, consider your responses to the following questions and compare them with those of others.

    a. Does an Inuit 'see' a snowscape differently from a native of Chad visiting the cold north for the first time because the Inuit must be using a language developed to deal with the surrounding snowscape?
    b. If men and women speak differently, is it because the common language they share has a gender bias, because boys and girls are brought up differently, or because part of 'gender marking' is the linguistic choices one can – indeed, must – make?
    c. Is language just another cultural artifact, like property, possessions, or money, which is used for the expression of power and/or as a medium of exchange?

d. If language is an essential human attribute and humans are necessarily social beings, what problems and paradoxes do you see for theoretical work in sociolinguistics if the latter is to grapple with the relationships between linguistic and social factors?

2. One aspect of the power of professionals is said to be the way they are able to use language to control others. How do physicians, psychiatrists, lawyers, social workers, teachers, priests, police officers, etc. use language to control others? Does this same power principle apply to parents (in relation to children), men (in relation to women), upper social classes (in relation to lower social classes), speakers of standard languages (in relation to speakers of nonstandard varieties of those languages), and so on?

Sociolinguistics and the Sociology of Language

Some investigators have found it appropriate to try to introduce a distinction between *sociolinguistics* or *micro-sociolinguistics* and the *sociology of language* or *macro-sociolinguistics*. In this distinction, sociolinguistics is concerned with investigating the relationships between language and society with the goal being a better understanding of the structure of language and of how languages function in communication; the equivalent goal in the sociology of language is trying to discover how social structure can be better understood through the study of language, e.g., how certain linguistic features serve to characterize particular social arrangements. Hudson (1996, p. 4) has described the difference as follows: sociolinguistics is 'the study of language in relation to society,' whereas the sociology of language is 'the study of society in relation to language.' In other words, in sociolinguistics we study language and society in order to find out as much as we can about what kind of thing language is, and in the sociology of language we reverse the direction of our interest. Using the alternative terms given above, Coulmas (1997, p. 2) says that 'micro-sociolingustics investigates how social structure influences the way people talk and how language varieties and patterns of use correlate with social attributes such as class, sex, and age. Macro-sociolinguistics, on the other hand, studies what societies do with their languages, that is, attitudes and attachments that account for the functional distribution of speech forms in society, language shift, maintenance, and replacement, the delimitation and interaction of speech communities.'

The view I will take here is that both sociolinguistics and the sociology of language require a systematic study of language *and* society if they are to be successful. Moreover, a sociolinguistics that deliberately refrains from drawing conclusions about society seems to be unnecessarily restrictive, just as restrictive indeed as a sociology of language that deliberately ignores discoveries about language made in the course of sociological research. So while it is possible to do either kind of work to the exclusion of the other, I will be concerned with looking at both kinds. My own views are essentially in agreement with those of Coulmas (1997, p. 3), expressed as follows:

There is no sharp dividing line between the two, but a large area of common concern. Although sociolinguistic research centers about a number of different key issues, any rigid micro–macro compartmentalization seems quite contrived and unnecessary in the present state of knowledge about the complex interrelationships between linguistic and social structures. Contributions to a better understanding of language as a necessary condition and product of social life will continue to come from both quarters.

Consequently, I will not attempt to make the kinds of distinctions found in Trudgill (1978). He tries to differentiate those studies that he considers to be clearly sociolinguistic in nature from those that clearly are not, for, as he says, 'while everybody would agree that sociolinguistics has *something* to do with language and society, it is clearly also not concerned with everything that could be considered "language and society".' The problem, therefore, lies in the drawing of the line between *language and society* and *sociolinguistics*. Different scholars draw the line in different places (p. 1). Trudgill argues that certain types of language studies are almost entirely sociological in their objectives and seem to fall outside even the sociology of language. Included in this category are ethnomethodological studies (see chapter 10) and work by such people as Bernstein (see chapter 14). For Trudgill, such work is definitely not sociolinguistics, however defined, since it apparently has no linguistic objectives.

According to Trudgill, certain kinds of work combine insights from sociology and linguistics. Examples of such work are attempts to deal with the structure of discourse and conversation (see chapter 12), speech acts (see chapter 12), studies in the ethnography of speaking (see chapter 10), investigations of such matters as kinship systems (see chapter 9), studies in the sociology of language, e.g., bilingualism, code-switching, and diglossia (see particularly chapter 4), and certain 'practical' concerns such as various aspects of teaching and language behavior in classrooms. While Trudgill considers all such topics to be genuinely sociolinguistic, he prefers, however, to use that term in a rather different and somewhat narrower sense. Elsewhere (1995, p. 21), he says that such concerns are perhaps better subsumed under anthropological linguistics, geolinguistics, the social psychology of language, and so on.

For Trudgill there is still another category of studies in which investigators show a concern for both linguistic and social matters. This category consists of studies which have a linguistic intent. 'Studies of this type are based on empirical work on language as it is spoken in its social context, and are intended to answer questions and deal with topics of central interest to linguists' (1978, p. 11). These studies are just another way of doing linguistics. Included in this category are studies of variation and linguistic change (see chapters 6–8), and the seminal figure is Labov. According to Trudgill, Labov has addressed himself to issues such as the relationship between language and social class, with his main objective not to learn more about a particular society or to examine correlations between linguistic and social phenomena, but to learn more about language and to investigate topics such as the mechanisms of linguistic change, the nature of linguistic variability, and the structure of linguistic systems. Trudgill's view is that 'all work in this category is aimed ultimately at improving linguistic theory and at developing our understanding of the nature of language' (1978, p. 11). For him this is genuine sociolinguistics. Chambers (2002, 2003) voices a similar view and Downes (1998, p. 9) echoes it: 'sociolinguistics is that branch of linguistics which studies just those properties of language and languages which *require* reference to social, including contextual, factors in their explanation.' However, in reviewing research on language and society, Downes' reach far exceeds that of Trudgill, even that of his glossary of terms (2003, p. 123), where he characterizes sociolinguistic research as 'work which is intended to achieve a better understanding of the nature of human language by studying language in its *social context* and/or to achieve a better understanding of the nature of the relationship and interaction between language and society.'

(A word of warning may be in order. Trudgill, Chambers, Downes, and I – and many others we will come across – approach sociolinguistics from a background in linguistics rather than in sociology – or psychology, or feminist studies, or . . . Readers should always keep that fact in mind when assessing what we say.)

As I have already indicated in referring earlier to Cameron's views (1997), there is also a growing amount of work within a broadly defined sociolinguistics that takes what I will call an 'interventionist' approach to matters that interest us. This work has been called 'linguistics with a conscience and a cause, one which seeks to reveal how language is used and abused in the exercise of power and the suppression of human rights' (Widdowson, 1998, p. 136). Two of its main exponents are Fairclough (1995, 2001) and van Dijk (1993), who champion an approach called 'critical discourse analysis.' This work focuses on how language is used to exercise and preserve power and privilege in society, how it buttresses social institutions, and how even those who suffer as a consequence fail to realize how many things that appear to be 'natural' and 'normal' are not at all so. They are not so because it is power relations in society that determine who gets to say what and who gets to write what. The claim is that politics, medicine, religion, eduation, law, race, gender, and academia can only be understood for what they really are within the framework of critical discourse analysis: as systems that maintain an unequal distribution of wealth, income, status, group membership, education, and so on. Fairclough (2001, p. 6) expresses what he sees as the failure of sociolinguistics to deal with such matters as follows: 'Sociolinguistics is strong on "what?" questions (what are the facts of variation?) but weak on "why?" and "how?" questions (why are the facts as they are?; how – in terms of the development of social relationships of power – was the existing sociolinguistic order brought into being?; how is it sustained?; and how might it be changed to the advantage of those who are dominated by it?).'

This is very much an ideological view. Its proponents maintain that all language use is ideological as are all investigations, i.e., that there is no hope of an 'objective' or 'neutral' sociolinguistics. Consequently, critical discourse analysis is ideological and judgmental. It claims the high ground on issues; it is 'a resource for people who are struggling against domination and oppression in its linguistic forms' (Fairclough, 1995, p. 1). We might well exercise caution in assessing any claims we find: appeals to what is right tend to short-circuit genuine scientific inquiry. In chapters 13–15 we will see examples of sociolinguistic studies which are definitely interventionist in approach.

Discussion

1. Ethnomethodology (see chapter 10) is the study of commonsense knowledge
    and practical reasoning. To convince yourself that you have such knowledge
    and do employ such reasoning, see what happens if you react 'literally'
    when someone next addresses you with such formulaic expressions as
    How do you do? or *Have a nice day.* For example, you can respond *What do
    you mean, 'How do I do?'* or *How do you define 'a nice day'?* (Be careful!)
    You should find that commonsense knowledge tells you not to take every-
    thing you hear literally. So far as practical reasoning is concerned, collect
    examples of how people actually do reach conclusions, give directions, and
    relate actions to consequences or 'causes' to 'effects.' Do they do this in
    any 'scientific' manner?
2. Bernstein, a British sociologist, has claimed that some children acquire a
    somewhat limited exposure to the full range of language use as a result of
    their upbringing, and may consequently be penalized in school. What kinds
    of evidence would you consider to be relevant to confirming (or disconfirming)
    such a claim?
3. Conversations are not simple matters. What can you say about each of the
    conversations that follow? Do you see anything you might call 'structural' in
    some that you do not see in others? How, in particular, does the last 'fail'?

    a. A. Excuse me!
        B. Yes.
        A. Gotta match?
        B. Sorry!
        A. Thanks.
    b. A. Gotta match?
        B. Nope?
    c. A. Excuse me, gotta match?
        B. Yes. (offer)
        A. (silence)

4. Labov (1970, p. 30) has described the sociology of language as follows:

    > It deals with large-scale social factors, and their mutual interaction with lan-
    > guages and dialects. There are many open questions, and many practical prob-
    > lems associated with the decay and assimilation of minority languages, the
    > development of stable bilingualism, the standardization of languages and the
    > planning of language development in newly emerging nations. The linguistic
    > input for such studies is primarily that a given person or group uses language
    > X in a social context or domain Y.

    What are some of the 'questions' and 'problems' you see in your society, either
    broadly or narrowly defined, that fall within such a sociology of language?
5. As a further instance of a topic that might be covered in the sociology of
    language, consider who speaks English in the world, where, and for what

purposes? You might also contrast what you can find out about the uses of English with what you can find out about the uses of Latin, Swahili, French, Haitian Creole, Basque, and Esperanto.

6. Studies of linguistic variation make use of the concept of the 'linguistic variable.' One simple linguistic variable in English is the pronunciation of the final sound in words like *singing, running, fishing*, and *going* (*-ing* or *-in'*) in contexts such as 'He was singing in the rain,' 'Running is fun,' 'It's a fishing boat,' and 'Are you going?' and on various occasions (e.g., in casual conversation, in formal speech making, or in reading individual words out aloud). What do you find? How might you try to explain any differences you find?

Methodological Concerns

Sociolinguistics should encompass everything from considering 'who speaks (or writes) what language (or what language variety) to whom and when and to what end' (Fishman, 1972b, p. 46), that is, the social distribution of linguistic items, to considering how a particular linguistic variable (see above) might relate to the formulation of a specific grammatical rule in a particular language or dialect, and even to the processes through which languages change. Whatever sociolinguistics is, it must be oriented toward both data and theory: that is, any conclusions we come to must be solidly based on evidence. Above all, our research must be motivated by questions that can be answered in an approved scientific way. Data collected for the sake of collecting data are of little interest, since without some kind of focus – that is, without some kind of non-trivial motive for collection – they can tell us little or nothing. A set of random observations about how a few people we happen to observe use language cannot lead us to any useful generalizations about behavior, either linguistic or social. We cannot be content with 'butterfly collecting,' no matter how beautiful the specimens are! We must collect data for a purpose and that purpose should be to find an answer, or answers, to an interesting question. Questions phrased in ways that do not allow for some kind of empirical testing have no more than a speculative interest.

Those who seek to investigate the possible relationships between language and society must have a twofold concern: they must ask good questions, and they must find the right kinds of data that bear on those questions. We will discover how wide the variety of questions and data in sociolinguistics has been: correlational studies, which attempt to relate two or more variables (e.g., certain linguistic usages to social-class differences); implicational studies, which suggest that if X, then Y (e.g., if someone says *tess* for *tests*, does he or she also say *bes'* for *best*?); microlinguistic studies, which typically focus on very specific linguistic items or individual differences and uses and seek possibly wide-ranging linguistic and/or social implications (e.g., the distribution of *singing* and *singin'*); macrolinguistic studies, which examine large amounts of language data to draw broad conclusions about group relationships (e.g., choices made in language planning – see chapter 15); and still other studies, which try to arrive at generalizations about certain universal characteristics of human communication, e.g., studies of conversational structure.

Since sociolinguistics is an empirical science, it must be founded on an adequate database. As we will see, that database is drawn from a wide variety of sources. These include censuses, documents, surveys, and interviews. Some data require the investigator to observe 'naturally occurring' linguistic events, e.g., conversations; others require the use of various elicitation techniques to gain access to the data we require and different varieties of experimental manipulation, e.g., the matched-guise experiments referred to in chapters 4 and 14. Some kinds of data require various statistical procedures, particularly when we wish to make statements about the typical behavior of a group, e.g., a social class; other kinds seem best treated through such devices as graphing, scaling, and categorizing in non-statistical ways, as in dialect geography (see chapter 6) or the study of kinship systems (see chapter 9).

A bona fide empirical science sets stringent demands so far as data collecting and analysis are concerned, demands involving sampling techniques, error estimation, and the confidence level, or the *level of significance* with which certain statements can be made, particularly when arguments are based on numbers, e.g., averages, percentages, or proportions. As we will see (chapters 6–7), sociolinguists try to meet these statistical demands when they are required. However, many of the conclusions we can draw from sociolinguistic studies are of a non-statistical nature and leave no element of doubt. This is because much of language use is categorical (i.e., something is or is not) rather than statistical (i.e., some phenomenon occurs with this or that probability). A recurring concern, then, must be with considering the certainty with which we can draw our conclusions in sociolinguistics. What is the theoretical framework? What are the relevant data? What confidence can we have in the gathering of the data, and in the analysis? What do the results really show? How should they be interpreted in relation to such concepts as 'identity,' 'power,' 'solidarity,' 'class,' 'gender,' etc.? What do we mean by such concepts? How useful are they in trying to achieve an understanding of how people function in society? What kind of social theory do we subscribe to? In these respects sociolinguistics is like all other sciences, so we should expect no less than that these requirements be met.

As part of an attempt to work out a set of principles, or axioms, which sociolinguistic investigations should follow, Bell (1976, pp. 187–91), drawing extensively on the work of Labov, has suggested eight as worthy of consideration:

1. *The cumulative principle.* The more that we know about language, the more we can find out about it, and we should not be surprised if our search for new knowledge takes us into new areas of study and into areas in which scholars from other disciplines are already working.
2. *The uniformation principle.* The linguistic processes which we observe to be taking place around us are the same as those which have operated in the past, so that there can be no clean break between *synchronic* (i.e., descriptive and contemporary) matters and *diachronic* (i.e., historical) ones.

3. *The principle of convergence.* The value of new data for confirming or interpreting old findings is directly proportional to the differences in the ways in which the new data are gathered; particularly useful are linguistic data gathered through procedures needed in other areas of scientific investigation.

4. *The principle of subordinate shift.* When speakers of a non-standard (or subordinate) variety of language, e.g., a dialect, are asked direct questions about that variety, their responses will shift in an irregular way toward or away from the standard (or superordinate) variety, e.g., the standard language, so enabling investigators to collect valuable evidence concerning such matters as varieties, norms, and change.

5. *The principle of style-shifting.* There are no 'single-style' speakers of a language, because each individual controls and uses a variety of linguistic styles and no one speaks in exactly the same way in all circumstances.

6. *The principle of attention.* 'Styles' of speech can be ordered along a single dimension measured by the amount of attention speakers are giving to their speech, so that the more 'aware' they are of what they are saying, the more 'formal' the style will be.

7. *The vernacular principle.* The style which is most regular in its structure and in its relation to the history of the language is the vernacular, that relaxed, spoken style in which the least conscious attention is being paid to speech.

8. *The principle of formality.* Any systematic observation of speech defines a context in which some conscious attention will be paid to that speech, so that it will be difficult, without great ingenuity, to observe the genuine 'vernacular.'

The last principle accounts for what Labov has called the 'observer's paradox.' He points out (1972b, pp. 209–10) that the aim of linguistic research is to find out how people talk when they are not being systematically observed, but the data are available only through systematic observation. Somehow speakers must have their attention diverted away from the fact that they are being observed so that the vernacular can emerge. This can happen when speakers become emotional. Labov found that a question like 'Have you been in a situation where you were in serious danger of being killed?' nearly always produces a shift of style away from careful speech toward the vernacular, thus providing the linguist with the kinds of data being sought.

The above principles are fundamental to studies in language variation. Other kinds of studies will require other kinds of principles. Trying to make these explicit will be one of the tasks I hope to accomplish in the chapters that follow.

Discussion

1. The uniformation principle mentioned above proposes that there is a relationship between *synchronic* (i.e., descriptive) and *diachronic* (i.e., historical) statements made about a language. There has been a long advocacy in linguistics for separating the two (see Saussure, 1959, Bloomfield, 1933, and just about any introductory linguistics text written prior to the mid-1970s).

Try to discover the reasons that are usually given for such an insistence on separation.

2. To convince yourself that there are no 'single-style' speakers, try for an hour or two not to vary your speech style as circumstances change. For example, try to speak to your cat (or dog), your close friends, your teachers, and complete strangers with exactly the same degree of formality (or informality), principles of word choice, precision of articulation, and method of address (e.g., *John, Mr Smith, Sir*). Report what happened and how you felt about what you were doing as the setting and participants changed. How did others react? (Be careful: you might run into difficulties!)

3. For Labov and other sociolinguists the *vernacular* is very important. What do you understand by this term? When do you use such a variety? How easy or difficult is self-observation of that variety?

4. On the whole we will be concerned with the spoken varieties of languages rather than the written varieties. What are some of the essential differences between the two? What do linguists mean when they say that the spoken language is 'primary' and the written language is 'secondary'? How do most people relate the spoken and written varieties?

Overview

Sociolinguistics brings together linguists and sociologists to investigate matters of joint concern but they are not the only researchers involved in studies of language in society. Scholars from a variety of other disciplines have an interest too, e.g., anthropologists, psychologists, educators, and planners. We will see, for example, that a number of anthropologists have done work which we can describe as sociolinguistic in nature, for example in the exploration of kinship systems. The same may be said of certain psychologists, particularly those concerned with the possible effects of linguistic structure on social and psychological behavior. Many educators too must make decisions about matters involving language, such as the teaching of standard languages and the skills of literacy. As we will discover in the latter case, some sociolinguists have been quite active in trying to influence educators in their attitudes toward certain kinds of linguistic behavior or varieties of language spoken by specific groups of children, such as the English spoken by certain black inhabitants of many cities in the northern United States, a variety sometimes referred to as African American Vernacular English (see chapter 14). Language planners obviously need a considerable amount of linguistic knowledge in making sound decisions about, for example, which language or language variety to encourage in certain circumstances, or in any attempts to standardize a particular language or variety, or to change existing relationships between languages or varieties. We will observe that there are many interconnections between sociolinguistics and other disciplines and also between concerns which are sometimes labeled *theoretical* and others which are said to be *practical*. At the very least, sociolinguistics is a socially relevant variety of linguistics, but it is probably much more. You will be able to form your own views on both issues as we proceed through the various topics treated in the chapters that follow.

These chapters are organized within four general topics. However, there will be considerable moving back and forth with cross-referencing within topics and among topics. Inter-relationships are everywhere and I make no apology for that.

Part I, *Languages and Communities*, deals with some traditional language issues: trying to separate languages from dialects and looking at types of re-gional and social variation within languages (chapter 2); reviewing the phenomena of pidgins and creoles (chapter 3); conceiving of languages as codes (chapter 4); and trying to figure out what kinds of 'groups' are relevant when we study language use (chapter 5).

Part II, *Inherent Variety*, is sometimes regarded as 'core' sociolinguistics. Here the concerns are factors in language variation (chapters 6–7) and what these might show us about how languages change (chapter 8).

Part III, *Words at Work*, is concerned with some traditional social and cul-tural issues: language as a possible shaper of culture (chapter 9); speech in a broad social context (chapter 10); terms of address and expressions of politeness and what they mean (chapter 11); and certain essential characteristics of every-day language, i.e., how utterances can be acts and how conversation works (chapter 12).

Part IV, *Understanding and Intervening*, looks into three areas of life in which sociolinguistics offers us some hope of understanding pressing problems (and which some sociolinguists argue require our deliberate intervention). Gender, one of the great 'growth areas' in language study, is the first of these (chapter 13). Education, particularly because certain practices seem to 'advantage' some students and 'disadvantage' others, is the second (chapter 14). Language plan-ning issues, as well as the spread of English and the 'death' of many languages, are the third (chapter 15). Chapter 16 provides a few concluding remarks.

Further Reading

The basic texts, going from roughly less difficult to more difficult, are Spolsky (1998), Trudgill (1995), Montgomery (1995), Holmes (1992), Romaine (2000), Hudson (1996), Mesthrie et al. (2000), and Downes (1998). Fasold (1984, 1990) is a two-volume treatment, and Ammon et al. (1987), Coulmas (1997), and Mesthrie (2001) attempt to provide comprehensive overviews. Murray (1998) discusses a variety of theoretical issues.

Foley (1997) and Duranti (1997) are good anthropologically oriented treat-ments of many of the topics that we will deal with. Edwards (1985) is concerned with a variety of sociological matters and Fairclough writes about power (2001) and discourse (1995). Cook and Newson (1996) and Seuren (2004) discuss Chomsky's linguistic ideas, and Smith (1999) both his linguistic and political ideas. Crystal (1997) is a very readable reference book on language; Crystal

(2003a) and McArthur (1992) have lots of interesting observations about English, and Asher and Simpson (1993) and Bright (1992) are encyclopedic in scope.

Recent books of readings are the two volumes of Trudgill and Cheshire (1998) and Cheshire and Trudgill (1998), the more comprehensive Coupland and Jaworski (1997), and Paulston and Tucker (2003).

The basic journals are *Language in Society*, *Journal of Sociolinguistics*, and *International Journal of the Sociology of Language*.

Duranti (2001), Trudgill (2003), and Swann et al. (2004) offer useful coverage of terms found in the sociolinguistic literature.

Part I Languages and Communities

In language there are only differences.

Ferdinand de Saussure

Strange the difference of men's talk.

Samuel Pepys

Choice words, and measured phrase, above the reach
Of ordinary men, a stately speech.

William Wordsworth

Correct English is the slang of prigs who write history and essays.

George Eliot

Language is by its very nature a communal thing; that is,
it expresses never the exact thing but a compromise – that which
is common to you, me and everybody.

T. E. Hulme

I include 'pidgin-English' . . . even though I am referred to in that
splendid language as 'Fella belong Mrs Queen.'

Prince Philip

2 Languages, Dialects, and Varieties

I stated in the introductory chapter that all languages exhibit internal variation, that is, each language exists in a number of varieties and is in one sense the sum of those varieties. But what do we mean by *variety*? Hudson (1996, p. 22) defines a variety of language as '*a set of linguistic items with similar distribution*,' a definition that allows us to say that all of the following are varieties: Canadian English, London English, the English of football commentaries, and so on. According to Hudson, this definition also allows us 'to treat all the languages of some multilingual speaker, or community, as a single variety, since all the linguistic items concerned have a similar social distribution.' A variety can therefore be something greater than a single language as well as something less, less even than something traditionally referred to as a dialect. Ferguson (1972, p. 30) offers another definition of variety: 'any body of human speech patterns which is sufficiently homogeneous to be analyzed by available techniques of synchronic description and which has a sufficiently large repertory of elements and their arrangements or processes with broad enough semantic scope to function in all formal contexts of communication.' Note the words 'sufficiently homogeneous' in this last quotation. Complete homogeneity is not required; there is always some variation whether we consider a language as a whole, a dialect of that language, the speech of a group within that dialect, or, ultimately, each individual in that group. Such variation is a basic fact of linguistic life.

Hudson and Ferguson agree in defining *variety* in terms of a specific set of 'linguistic items' or 'human speech patterns' (presumably, sounds, words, grammatical features, etc.) which we can uniquely associate with some external factor (presumably, a geographical area or a social group). Consequently, if we can identify such a unique set of items or patterns for each group in question, it might be possible to say there are such varieties as Standard English, Cockney, lower-class New York City speech, Oxford English, legalese, cocktail party talk, and so on. One important task, then, in sociolinguistics is to determine if such unique sets of items or patterns do exist. As we proceed we will encounter certain difficulties, but it is unlikely that we will easily abandon the concept of 'variety,' no matter how serious these difficulties prove to be.

Discussion

1. I have just suggested that, although a concept like 'variety' is difficult to define, it may still be useful in sociolinguistic work. Linguists have found such concepts as 'sound,' 'syllable,' 'word,' and 'sentence' equally difficult to define (in contrast to lay usage, in which they are just assumed to be obvious and uncontroversial). In one sense, linguistics is all about trying to provide adequate definitions for words such as *sound, syllable, word, sentence*, and *language*. What are some of the problems you are aware of concerning the linguist's difficulty with these words and the associated concepts? What parallels do you see, if any, between these problems and the sociolinguist's problem with *variety* (and the other terms to be used in the remainder of this chapter)?

2. Hymes (1974, p. 123) has observed that language boundaries between groups are drawn not on the basis of the use of linguistic items alone, because attitudes and social meanings attached to those items also count. He says:

   > Any enduring social relationship or group may come to define itself by selection and/or creation of linguistic features, and a difference of accent may be as important at one boundary as a difference of grammar at another. Part of the creativity of users of languages lies in the freedom to determine what and how much linguistic difference matters.

   How does this inter-relationship between linguistic items and the social evaluations of such items apply in how we regard each of the following pronunciations?

   a. butter, budder, bu'er
   b. fishing, fishin'
   c. farm, fahm
   d. width pronounced like wit, like with
   e. Cuba pronounced as Cuber
   f. ate pronounced like eight, like et
   g. been pronounced like bean, like bin
   h. mischievous pronounced with four syllables (i.e., as mischievious)
   i. aluminum, aluminium
   j. pólice, gúitar, Détroit (with the stress as indicated)

   And each of the following utterances?

   a. He hurt hisself.
   b. He done it.
   c. He dove in.
   d. He run away last week.
   e. It looks like it's going to rain.
   f. To whom did you give it?
   g. She's taller than me now.

    h.   Yesterday he laid down after lunch for an hour.
    i.   Can I leave the room?
    j.   He ain't got no money left.
    k.   Try and do it soon.
    l.   Between you and me, I don't like it.
    m.   There's twenty dollars for you to spend.
    n.   She invited Sally and I to the party.
    o.   I wants it.
    p.   You done it, did you?
    q.   Stand over by them boys.
    r.   Is he the one what said it?
    s.   They don't learn you nothing there.

Language and Dialect

For many people there can be no confusion at all about what language they speak. For example, they are Chinese, Japanese, or Korean and they speak Chinese, Japanese, and Korean respectively. It is as simple as that; language and ethnicity are virtually synonymous (Coulmas, 1999). A Chinese may be surprised to find that another person who appears to be Chinese does not speak Chinese, and some Japanese have gone so far as to claim not to be able to understand Caucasians who speak fluent Japanese. Just as such a strong connection between language and ethnicity may prove to be invaluable in nation-building, it can also be fraught with problems when individuals and groups seek to realize some other identity, e.g., to be both Chinese and American, or to be Canadian rather than Korean-Canadian. As we will see (p. 368), many Americans seem particularly reluctant to equate language with ethnicity in their own case: although they regard English as the 'natural' language of Americans, they do not consider American to be an ethnic label. The results may be the same; only the reasons differ.

Most speakers can give a name to whatever it is they speak. On occasion, some of these names may appear to be strange to those who take a scientific interest in languages, but we should remember that human naming practices often have a large 'unscientific' component to them. Census-takers in India find themselves confronted with a wide array of language names when they ask people what language or languages they speak. Names are not only ascribed by region, which is what we might expect, but sometimes also by caste, religion, village, and so on. Moreover, they can change from census to census as the political and social climate of the country changes.

While people do usually know what language they speak, they may not always lay claim to be fully qualified speakers of that language. They may experience difficulty in deciding whether what they speak should be called a *language* proper or merely a *dialect* of some language. Such indecision is not surprising: exactly how do you decide what is a language and what is a dialect of a language? What criteria can you possibly use to determine that, whereas variety X is a language, variety Y is only a dialect of a language? What are the essential differences between a language and a dialect?

Haugen (1966a) has pointed out that *language* and *dialect* are ambiguous terms. Ordinary people use these terms quite freely in speech; for them a dialect is almost certainly no more than a local non-prestigious (therefore powerless) variety of a real language. In contrast, scholars often experience considerable difficulty in deciding whether one term should be used rather than the other in certain situations. As Haugen says, the terms 'represent a simple dichotomy in a situation that is almost infinitely complex.' He points out that the confusion goes back to the Ancient Greeks. The Greek language that we associate with Ancient Greece was actually a group of distinct local varieties (Ionic, Doric, and Attic) descended by divergence from a common spoken source with each variety having its own literary traditions and uses, e.g., Ionic for history, Doric for choral and lyric works, and Attic for tragedy. Later, Athenian Greek, the *koiné* – or 'common' language – became the norm for the spoken language as the various spoken varieties converged on the dialect of the major cultural and administrative center. Haugen points out (p. 923) that the Greek situation has provided the model for all later usages of the two terms with the resulting ambiguity. *Language* can be used to refer either to a single linguistic norm or to a group of related norms, and *dialect* to refer to one of the norms.

The situation is further confused by the distinction the French make between *un dialecte* and *un patois*. The former is a regional variety of a language that has an associated literary tradition, whereas the latter is a regional variety that lacks such a literary tradition. Therefore *patois* tends to be used pejoratively; it is regarded as something less than a dialect because of its lack of an associated literature. Even a language like Breton, a Celtic language still spoken in parts of Brittany, is called a *patois* because of its lack of a strong literary tradition and the fact that it is not some country's language. However, *dialecte* in French, like *Dialekt* in German, cannot be used in connection with the standard language, i.e., no speaker of French considers Standard French to be a dialect of French. In contrast, it is not uncommon to find references to Standard English being a dialect – admittedly a very important one – of English.

Haugen points out that, while speakers of English have never seriously adopted *patois* as a term to be used in the description of language, they have tried to employ both *language* and *dialect* in a number of conflicting senses. *Dialect* is used both for local varieties of English, e.g., Yorkshire dialect, and for various types of informal, lower-class, or rural speech. 'In general usage it therefore remains quite undefined whether such dialects are part of the "language" or not. In fact, the dialect is often thought of as standing outside the language. . . . As a social norm, then, a dialect is a language that is excluded from polite society' (pp. 924–5). It is often equivalent to *nonstandard* or even *substandard*, when such terms are applied to language, and can connote various degrees of inferiority, with that connotation of inferiority carried over to those who speak a dialect.

We can observe too that questions such as 'Which language do you speak?' or 'Which dialect do you speak?' may be answered quite differently by people who appear to speak in an identical manner. As Gumperz (1982a, p. 20) has pointed out, many regions of the world provide plenty of evidence for what he calls 'a bewildering array of language and dialect divisions.' He adds: 'socio-historical factors play a crucial role in determining boundaries. Hindi and Urdu in India, Serbian and Croatian in Yugoslavia [of that date], Fanti and Twi in West Africa, Bokmål and Nynorsk in Norway, Kechwa and Aimara in Peru, to name just a few, are recognized as discrete languages both popularly and in law, yet they are almost identical at the level of grammar. On the other hand, the literary and colloquial forms of Arabic used in Iraq, Morocco, and Egypt, or the Welsh of North and South Wales, the local dialects of Rajasthan and Bihar in North India are grammatically quite separate, yet only one language is recognized in each case.'

The Hindi–Urdu situation that Gumperz mentions is an interesting one. Hindi and Urdu are the same language, but one in which certain differences are becoming more and more magnified for political and religious reasons. Hindi is written left to right in the Devanagari script, whereas Urdu is written right to left in the Arabic–Persian script. Whereas Hindi draws on Sanskrit for its borrowings, Urdu draws on Arabic and Persian sources. Large religious and political differences make much of small linguistic differences. The written forms of the two varieties, particularly those favored by the elites, also emphasize these differences. They have become highly symbolic of the growing differences between India and Pakistan. (We should note that the situation in India and Pakistan is in almost direct contrast to that which exists in China, where mutually unintelligible Chinese languages (called 'dialects' by the Chinese themselves) are united through a common writing system and tradition.)

Gumperz (1971, pp. 56–7) points out that everyday living in parts of India, particularly in the large cities and among educated segments of those communities, requires some complex choices involving the distinction between Hindi and Urdu:

> Since independence Hindi has become compulsory in schools, but Urdu continues to be used extensively in commerce, and the Ghazal, the best known form of Urdu poetry, is universally popular. If we look at the modern realist Hindi writers, we find that they utilize both Sanskrit and Persian borrowings. The juxtaposition of the two styles serves to express subtle shades of meaning and to lend reality to their writings. Similarly on the conversational level the use of Hindi and Urdu forms is not simply a matter of birth and education. But, just as it is customary for individuals to alternate between dialect and standard depending on the social occasion, so when using the standard itself the speaker may select from a range of alternatives. Hindi and Urdu therefore might best be characterized not in terms of actual speech, but as norms or ideal behavior in the sociologist's sense. The extent to which a speaker's performance in a particular communication situation approximates the norm is a function of a combination of factors such as family background, regional origin, education and social attitude and the like.

So far as everyday use is concerned, therefore, it appears that the boundary between the spoken varieties of Hindi and Urdu is somewhat flexible and one that changes with circumstances. This is exactly what we would expect: there is considerable variety in everyday use but somewhere in the background there is an ideal that can be appealed to, proper Hindi or proper Urdu.

In the first of the two quotations from Gumperz there is a reference to Yugoslavia, a country now brutally dismembered by the instruments of ethnicity, language, and religion. Within the old Yugoslavia Serbs and Croats failed to agree on most things and after the death of President Tito the country, slowly at first and then ever more rapidly later, fell into a fatal divisiveness. Slovenians and Macedonians excised themselves most easily, but the Serbs and the Croats were not so lucky. Linguistically, Serbo-Croatian is a single South Slav language but one used by two groups of people, the Serbs and Croats, with somewhat different historical, cultural, and religious backgrounds. There is a third group in Bosnia, a Muslim group, who also speak Serbo-Croatian, and their existence further compounded the problems and increased the eventual bloodshed. Finally, there is a very small Montenegrin group. The Serbian and Croatian varieties of Serbo-Croatian are known as *srpski* and *srpskohrvatski* respectively. The actual differences between them involve different preferences in vocabulary rather than differences in pronunciation or grammar. That is, Serbs and Croats often use different words for the same concepts, e.g., Serbian *varos* and Croatian *grad* for 'train.' The varieties are written in different scripts (Roman for Croatian and Cyrillic for Serbian), which also reflect the different religious loyalties of Croats and Serbs (Catholic and Orthodox). As conflict grew, differences became more and more important and the country and the language split apart. Now in Serbia people speak Serbian just as they speak Croatian in Croatia. Serbo-Croatian no longer exists as a language of the Balkans. And now that there is a separate Bosnia the Bosnians call their variety *bosanski* and Montenegrins call their variety *crnogorski* (Carmichael, 2002, p. 236, and Greenberg, 2004).

In direct contrast to the above situation, we can observe that the loyalty of a group of people need not necessarily be determined by the language they speak. Although the majority of the people in Alsace are speakers of a variety of German insofar as the language of their home-life is concerned, their loyalty is unquestionably toward France. They look west not east for national leadership and they use French, not German, as the language of mobility and higher education. However, everyday use of Alsatian is a strong marker of local identity; it is an important part of being Alsatian in France. We can contrast this situation with that in another area of France. In Brittany a separatist movement, that is, a movement for local autonomy if not complete independence, is centered on Breton, a language which, unfortunately for those who speak it, is in serious decline. Breton identity no longer has the support of widespread use of the language.

The various relationships among languages and dialects discussed above can be used to show how the concepts of 'power' and 'solidarity' help us understand what is happening. Power requires some kind of asymmetrical relationship between entities: one has more of something that is important, e.g. status, money, influence, etc., than the other or others. A language has more power than any of its dialects. It is the powerful dialect but it has become so because of non-linguistic factors. Standard English and Parisian French are good examples. Solidarity, on the other hand, is a feeling of equality that people have with one another. They have a common interest around which they will bond. A feeling of solidarity can lead people to preserve a local dialect or an endangered language to resist power, or to insist on independence. It accounts for the persistence of local dialects, the modernization of Hebrew, and the separation of Serbo-Croatian into Serbian and Croatian.

The language–dialect situation along the border between the Netherlands and Germany is an interesting one. Historically, there was a continuum of dialects of one language, but the two that eventually became standardized as the languages of the Netherlands and Germany, Standard Dutch and Standard German, are not *mutually intelligible*, that is, a speaker of one cannot understand a speaker of the other. In the border area speakers of the local varieties of Dutch and German still exist within that *dialect continuum* (see p. 45) and remain largely intelligible to one another, yet the people on one side of the border say they speak a variety of Dutch and those on the other side say they speak a variety of German. The residents of the Netherlands look to Standard Dutch for their model; they read and write Dutch, are educated in Dutch, and watch television in Dutch. Consequently, they say they use a local variety, or dialect, of Dutch in their daily lives. On the other side of the border, German replaces Dutch in all equivalent situations. The interesting linguistic fact, though, is that there are more similarities between the local varieties spoken on each side of the border than between the one dialect (of Dutch?) and Standard Dutch and the other dialect (of German?) and Standard German, and more certainly than between that dialect and the south German, Swiss, and Austrian dialects of German. However, it is also of interest to note (Kremer, 1999) that younger speakers of Dutch in this area of the Netherlands are more conscious of the standard language border than older speakers. Apparently, their Dutch identity triumphs over any linguistic connections they have with speakers of the same dialect over the national border.

Gumperz has suggested some of the confusions that result from popular uses of the terms *language* and *dialect*. To these we can add the situation in Scandinavia as further evidence. Danish, Norwegian (actually two varieties), and Swedish are recognized as different languages, yet if you speak any one of them you will experience little difficulty in communicating while traveling in Scandinavia (excluding, of course, Finland, or at least the non-Swedish-speaking parts of that country). Danish and Norwegian share much vocabulary but differ considerably in pronunciation. In contrast, there are considerable vocabulary differences between Swedish and Norwegian but they are similar in pronunciation. Both Danes and Swedes claim good understanding of Norwegian. However, Danes claim to comprehend Norwegians much better than Norwegians claim to comprehend Danes. The poorest mutual comprehension is between Danes and Swedes and the best is between Norwegians and Swedes. These differences in mutual intelligibility appear to reflect power relationships: Denmark long dominated Norway, and Sweden is today the most influential country in the region and Denmark the least powerful.

A somewhat similar situation exists in the relationship of Thai and Lao. The Laos understand spoken Thai and hear Thai constantly on radio and television. Educated Laos can also read written Thai. However, Thais do not readily understand spoken Lao nor do they read the written variety. Lao is a low-prestige language so far as Thais are concerned; in contrast, Thai has high prestige in Laos. Thais, therefore, are unwilling to expend effort to understand Lao, whereas Laos are willing to make the extra effort to understand Thai.

If we turn our attention to China, we will find that speakers of Cantonese and Mandarin will tell you that they use the same language. However, if one speaker knows only Cantonese and the other only Mandarin, they will not be able to converse with each other: they actually speak different languages, certainly as different as German and Dutch and even Portuguese and Italian. If the speakers are literate, however, they will be able to communicate with each other through a shared writing system. They will almost certainly insist that they speak different *dialects* of Chinese, not different *languages*, for to the Chinese a shared writing system and a strong tradition of political, social, and cultural unity form essential parts of their definition of *language*.

The situation can become even more confused. A speaker of Cockney, a highly restricted London variety of English, may find it difficult to communicate with natives of the Ozark Mountains in the United States. Do they therefore speak separate languages? Is there one English language spoken in Britain and another, American, spoken in the New World? The American writer Mencken (1919) had very definite views that the varieties spoken on the two sides of the Atlantic were sufficiently distinctive to warrant different appellations. It is also not unusual to find French translations of American books described on their title pages as translations from 'American' rather than 'English.' Is there a bona fide separate Scottish variety of English? There was before the crowns and parliaments were united several centuries ago. However, today there is no clear answer to that question as the power relationship between England and Scotland fluctuates and the issue of language differences is but one of many that must be dealt with. Is the French of Quebec a dialect of Standard (continental) French, or should we regard it as a separate language, particularly after a political separation of well over two centuries? Is Haitian Creole (see p. 84) a variety of French, or is it an entirely separate language, and if so in what ways is it separate and different? How do the different varieties of English spoken in Jamaica (see p. 81) relate to other varieties of English? Or is that question really answerable? What, above all, is English? How can we define it as something apart from what Speaker A uses, or Speaker B, or Speaker C? If it is something A, B, and C share, just what is it that they do share?

We undoubtedly agree that this book is written in English and that English is a language, but we may be less certain that various other things we see written or hear spoken in what is called *English* should properly be regarded as English rather than as dialects or varieties of English, perhaps variously described as Indian English, Australian English, New York English, West Country English, African American Vernacular English, nonstandard English, BBC English, and so on. A language then would be some unitary system of linguistic communication which subsumes a number of mutually intelligible varieties. It would therefore be bigger than a single dialect or a single variety. However, that cannot always be the case, for some such systems used by very small numbers of speakers may have very little internal variation. Yet each must be a language, for it is quite unlike any other existing system. Actually, neither the requirement that there be internal variation nor the 'numbers game,' i.e., that a language must somehow be 'bigger' than a dialect, offers much help. Many languages have only a handful of speakers; several have actually been known to have had only a single remaining speaker at a particular point in time and the language has 'died' with that speaker.

Still another difficulty arises from the fact that the terms *language* and *dialect* are also used in an historical sense. It is possible to speak of languages such as English, German, French, Russian, and Hindi as Indo-European dialects. In this case the assumption is that there was once a single language, Indo-European, that the speakers of that language (which may have had various dialects) spread to different parts of the world, and that the original language eventually diverged into the various languages we subsume today under the *Indo-European family* of languages. However, we should also be aware that this process of divergence was not as clean-cut as this classical *neo-grammarian* model of language differentiation suggests. (In such a model all breaks are clean, and once two varieties diverge they lose contact with each other.) Processes of convergence must also have occurred, even of convergence among entirely unrelated languages (that is, languages without any 'family' resemblance). For example, Indo-European and Dravidian languages have influenced each other in southern India and Sri Lanka, and in the Balkans there is considerable evidence of the spread of common features across languages such as Albanian, Greek, Turkish, and several Slavic languages. In such situations, language and dialect differences become further obscured, particularly when many speakers are also likely to be multilingual.

Perhaps some of the difficulties we have with trying to define the term *language* arise from trying to subsume various different types of systems of communication under that one label. An alternative approach might be to acknowledge that there are different kinds of languages and attempt to discover how languages can differ from one another yet still be entities that most of us would want to call languages rather than dialects. It might then be possible to define a dialect as some sub-variety of one or more of these entities.

One such attempt (see Bell, 1976, pp. 147–57) has listed seven criteria that may be useful in discussing different kinds of languages. According to Bell, these criteria (standardization, vitality, historicity, autonomy, reduction, mixture, and *de facto* norms) may be used to distinguish certain languages from others. They also make it possible to speak of some languages as being more 'developed' in certain ways than others, thus addressing a key issue in the language–dialect distinction, since speakers usually feel that languages are generally 'better' than dialects in some sense.

Standardization refers to the process by which a language has been codified in some way. That process usually involves the development of such things as grammars, spelling books, and dictionaries, and possibly a literature. We can often associate specific items or events with standardization, e.g., Wycliffe's and Luther's translations of the Bible into English and German, respectively, Caxton's establishment of printing in England, and Dr Johnson's dictionary of English published in 1755. Standardization also requires that a measure of agreement be achieved about what is in the language and what is not. Once we have such a codification of the language we tend to see it as almost inevitable, the result of some process come to fruition, one that has also reached a fixed end point. Change, therefore, should be resisted since it can only undo what has been done so laboriously. Milroy (2001, p. 537) characterizes the resulting ideology as follows: 'The canonical form of the language is a precious inheritance that has been built up over the generations, not by the millions of native speakers, but by a select few who have lavished loving care upon it, polishing, refining, and enriching it until it has become a fine instrument of expression (often these are thought to be literary figures, such as Shakespeare). This is a view held by people in many walks of life, including plumbers, politicians and professors of literature. It is believed that if the canonical variety is not universally supported and protected, the language will inevitably decline and decay.'

Once a language is standardized it becomes possible to teach it in a deliberate manner. It takes on ideological dimensions – social, cultural, and sometimes political – beyond the purely linguistic ones. In Fairclough's words (2001, p. 47) it becomes 'part of a much wider process of economic, political and cultural unification . . . of great . . . importance in the establishment of nationhood, and the nation-state is the favoured form of capitalism.' According to these criteria, both English and French are quite obviously standardized, Italian somewhat less so, and the variety known as African American Vernacular English (see chapter 14) not at all.

Haugen (1966a) has indicated certain steps that must be followed if one variety of a language is to become the standard for that language. In addition to what he calls the 'formal' matters of codification and elaboration, the former referring to the development of such things as grammars and dictionaries and the latter referring to the use of the standard in such areas as literature, the courts, education, administration, and commerce, Haugen says there are important matters to do with 'function.' For example, a norm must be selected and accepted because neither codification nor elaboration is likely to proceed very far if the community cannot agree on some kind of model to act as a norm. That norm is also likely to be – or to become – an idealized norm, one that users of the language are asked to aspire to rather than one that actually accords with their observed behavior.

Selection of the norm may prove difficult because choosing one vernacular as a norm means favoring those who speak that variety. It also diminishes all the other varieties and possible competing norms, and those who use those varieties. The chosen norm inevitably becomes associated with power and the rejected alternatives with lack of power. Not surprisingly, it usually happens that a variety associated with an elite is chosen. Attitudes are all-important, however. A group that feels intense solidarity may be willing to overcome great linguistic differences in establishing a norm, whereas one that does not have this feeling may be unable to overcome relatively small differences and be unable to agree on a single variety and norm. Serbs and Croats were never able to agree on a norm, particularly as other differences reinforced linguistic ones. In contrast, we can see how Indonesia and Malaysia are looking for ways to reduce the differences between their languages, with their common Islamic bond a strong incentive.

The standardization process itself performs a variety of functions (Mathiot and Garvin, 1975). It unifies individuals and groups within a larger community while at the same time separating the community that results from other communities. Therefore, it can be employed to reflect and symbolize some kind of identity: regional, social, ethnic, or religious. A standardized variety can also be used to give prestige to speakers, marking off those who employ it from those who do not, i.e., those who continue to speak a nonstandard variety. It can therefore serve as a kind of goal for those who have somewhat different norms; Standard English and Standard French are such goals for many whose norms are dialects of these languages. However, as we will see (particularly in chapters 6–8), these goals are not always pursued and may even be resisted.

It still may not be at all easy for us to define *Standard English* because of a failure to agree about the norm or norms that should apply. For example, Trudgill (1995, pp. 5–6) defines Standard English as follows (note his use of 'usually' and 'normally' in this definition):

> Standard English is that variety of English which is usually used in print, and which is normally taught in schools and to non-native speakers learning the language. It is also the variety which is normally spoken by educated people and used in news broadcasts and other similar situations. The difference between standard and nonstandard, it should be noted, has nothing in principle to do with differences between formal and colloquial language, or with concepts such as 'bad language.' Standard English has colloquial as well as formal variants, and Standard English speakers swear as much as others.

Historically, the standard variety of English is based on the dialect of English that developed after the Norman Conquest resulted in the permanent removal of the Court from Winchester to London. This dialect became the one preferred by the educated, and it was developed and promoted as a model, or norm, for wider and wider segments of society. It was also the norm that was carried overseas, but not one unaffected by such export. Today, Standard English is codified to the extent that the grammar and vocabulary of English are much the same everywhere in the world: variation among local standards is really quite minor, being differences of 'flavor' rather than of 'substance,' so that the Singapore, South African, and Irish varieties are really very little different from one another so far as grammar and vocabulary are concerned. Indeed, Standard English is so powerful that it exerts a tremendous pressure on all local varieties, to the extent that many of the long-established dialects of England and the Lowlands English of Scotland have lost much of their vigor. There is considerable pressure on them to converge toward the standard. This latter situation is not unique to English: it is also true in other countries in which processes of standardization are under way. It does, however, sometimes create problems for speakers who try to strike some kind of compromise between local norms and national, even supranational, ones.

Governments sometimes very deliberately involve themselves in the standardization process by establishing official bodies of one kind or another to regulate language matters or to encourage changes felt to be desirable. One of the most famous examples of an official body established to promote the language of a country was Richelieu's establishment of the Académie Française in 1635. Founded at a time when a variety of languages existed in France, when literacy was confined to a very few, and when there was little national consciousness, the Académie Française faced an unenviable task: the codification of French spelling, vocabulary, and grammar. Its goal was to fashion and reinforce French nationality, a most important task considering that, even two centuries later in the early nineteenth century, the French of Paris was virtually unknown in many parts of the country, particularly in the south. Similar attempts to found academies in England and the United States for the same purpose met with no success, individual dictionary-makers and grammar-writers having performed much the same function for English. Since both French and English are today highly standardized, one might question whether such academies serve a useful purpose, yet it is difficult to imagine France without the Académie Française: it undoubtedly has had a considerable influence on the French people and perhaps on their language.

Standardization is sometimes deliberately undertaken quite rapidly for political reasons. In the nineteenth century Finns developed their spoken language to make it serve a complete set of functions. They needed a standardized language to assert their independence from both Swedes and Russians. They succeeded in their task so that now the Finnish language has become a strong force in the nation's political life and a strong marker of Finnish identity among Germanic tongues on the one side and Slavic tongues on the other. In the twentieth century the Turks under Atatürk were likewise successful in their attempt to both standardize and 'modernize' Turkish. Today, we can see similar attempts at rapid standardization in countries such as India (Hindi), Israel (Hebrew), Papua New Guinea (Tok Pisin), Indonesia (Bahasa Indonesia), and Tanzania (Swahili). In each case a language or a variety of a language had to be selected, developed in its resources and functions, and finally accepted by the larger society. As we have seen, standardization is an ideological matter. Williams (1992, p. 146) calls it 'a sociopolitical process involving the legitimisation and institutionalisation of a language variety as a feature of sanctioning of that variety as socially preferable.' It creates a preferred variety of a language, which then becomes the winner in a struggle for dominance. The dispreferred varieties are losers.

The standardization process occasionally results in some languages actually achieving more than one standardized variety. Norwegian is a good example with its two standards, Nynorsk and Bokmål. In this case there is a special problem, that of trying to unify the two varieties in a way that pleases everyone. Some kind of unification or amalgamation is now official government policy (see pp. 373–4). Countries with two or more competing languages that cannot possibly be unified may tear themselves apart, as we saw in Yugoslavia, or periodically seem to come very close to doing that, as with Belgium and Canada (see chapter 15).

Standardization is also an ongoing matter, for only 'dead' languages like Latin and Classical Greek are standardized for all time. Living languages change and the standardization process is necessarily an ongoing one. It is also one that may be described as more advanced in languages like French or German and less advanced in languages like Bahasa Indonesia and Swahili.

Hindi is still in the process of being standardized in India. That process is hindered by widespread regional resistance to Hindi out of the fear that regional languages may be submerged or, if not submerged, quite diminished. So far as standardization is concerned, there are problems with accepting local varieties, and with developing and teaching the existing standard as though it were a classical language like Sanskrit and downplaying it as a living language. Hindi is still often taught much like Latin in schools in the West; it is in many places an underused second language at best; children are not encouraged 'to play in Hindi,' and teachers rarely employ Hindi as a language of instruction. Likewise, the kinds of literature available in Hindi are still very limited, there being shortages of everyday reading materials that might appeal to the young, e.g., comic books, mystery stories, and collections of folk tales. Consequently, the process of the standardization of a 'living' Hindi is proving to be a slow one.

The standardization process is also obviously one that attempts either to reduce or to eliminate diversity and variety. However, there may well be a sense in which such diversity and variety are 'natural' to all languages, assuring them of their vitality and enabling them to change (see chapter 8). To that extent, standardization imposes a strain on languages or, if not on the languages themselves, on those who take on the task of standardization. That may be one of the reasons why various national academies have had so many difficulties in their work: they are essentially in a no-win situation, always trying to 'fix' the consequences of changes that they cannot prevent, and continually being compelled to issue new pronouncements on linguistic matters. Unfortunately, those who think you can standardize and 'fix' a language for all time are often quite influential. They often find ready access to the media, there to bewail the fact that English, for example, is becoming 'degenerate' and 'corrupt,' and to advise us to return to what they regard as a more perfect past. They may also resist what they consider to be 'dangerous' innovations, e.g., the translation of a sacred book into a modern idiom or the issue of a new dictionary. Since the existence of internal variation is one aspect of language and the fact that all languages keep changing is another, we cannot be too sympathetic to such views.

Vitality, the second of Bell's seven criteria, refers to the existence of a living community of speakers. This criterion can be used to distinguish languages that are 'alive' from those that are 'dead.' Two Celtic languages of the United Kingdom are now dead: Manx, the old language of the Isle of Man, and Cornish. Manx died out after World War II, and Cornish disappeared at the end of the eighteenth century, one date often cited being 1777, when the last known speaker, Dorothy Pentreath of Mousehole, died. Many of the aboriginal languages of the Americas are also dead. Latin is dead in this sense too for no one speaks it as a native language; it exists only in a written form frozen in time, pronounced rather than spoken, and studied rather than used.

Once a language dies it is gone for all time and not even the so-called revival of Hebrew contradicts that assertion. Hebrew always existed in a spoken form as a liturgical language, as did Latin for centuries. Modern Hebrew is an outgrowth of this liturgical variety. It is after all 'Modern' Hebrew and the necessary secularization of a liturgical language to make it serve the purposes of modern life has not been an easy and uncontroversial matter. Many languages, while not dead yet, nevertheless are palpably dying: the number of people who speak them diminishes drastically each year and the process seems irreversible, so that the best one can say of their vitality is that it is flagging. For example, the French dialects spoken in the Channel Islands of Jersey, Guernsey, and Sark are rapidly on their way to extinction. Each year that passes brings a decrease in the number of languages spoken in the world (see pp. 378–9).

We should note that a language can remain a considerable force even after it is dead, that is, even after it is no longer spoken as anyone's first language and exists almost exclusively in one or more written forms, knowledge of which is acquired only through formal education. Classical Greek and Latin still have considerable prestige in the Western world, and speakers of many modern languages continue to draw on them in a variety of ways. Sanskrit is important in the same way to speakers of Hindi; Classical Arabic provides a unifying force and set of resources in the Islamic world; and Classical Chinese has considerably influenced not only modern Chinese but also Japanese and Korean. Such influences cannot be ignored, because the speakers of languages subject to such influences are generally quite aware of what is happening: we can even say that such influence is part of their knowledge of the language. We can also periodically observe deliberate attempts to throw off an influence perceived to be alien: for example, Atatürk's largely successful attempt to reduce the Arabic influence on Turkish, and periodic attempts to 'purify' languages such as French and German of borrowings from English. While in the case of Hebrew, a language used only in a very restricted way for religious observances was successfully expanded for everyday use, we should note that a similar attempt to revitalize Gaelic in Ireland has been almost a complete failure.

Historicity refers to the fact that a particular group of people finds a sense of identity through using a particular language: it belongs to them. Social, political, religious, or ethnic ties may also be important for the group, but the bond provided by a common language may prove to be the strongest tie of all. In the nineteenth century a German nation was unified around the German language just as in the previous century Russians had unified around a revitalized Russian language. Historicity can be long-standing: speakers of the different varieties of colloquial Arabic make much of a common linguistic ancestry, as obviously do speakers of Chinese. It can also, as with Hebrew, be appealed to as a unifying force among a threatened people.

Autonomy is an interesting concept because it is really one of feeling. A language must be felt by its speakers to be different from other languages. However, this is a very subjective criterion. Ukrainians say their language is quite different from Russian and deplored its Russification when they were part of the Soviet Union. Some speakers of African American Vernacular English (see chapter 14) maintain that their language is not a variety of English but is a separate language in its own right and refer to it as *Ebonics*. In contrast, speakers of Cantonese and Mandarin deny that they speak different languages: they maintain that Cantonese and Mandarin are not autonomous languages but are just two dialects of Chinese. As we will see (chapter 3), creole and pidgin languages cause us not a few problems when we try to apply this criterion: how autonomous are such languages?

Reduction refers to the fact that a particular variety may be regarded as a sub-variety rather than as an independent entity. Speakers of Cockney will almost certainly say that they speak a variety of English, admit that they are not representative speakers of English, and recognize the existence of other varieties with equivalent subordinate status. Sometimes the reduction is in the kinds of opportunities afforded to users of the variety. For example, there may be a reduction of resources; that is, the variety may lack a writing system. Or there may be considerable restrictions in use; e.g., pidgin languages are very much reduced in the functions they serve in society in contrast to standardized languages.

Mixture refers to feelings speakers have about the 'purity' of the variety they speak. This criterion appears to be more important to speakers of some languages than of others, e.g., more important to speakers of French and German than to speakers of English. However, it partly explains why speakers of pidgins and creoles have difficulty in classifying what they speak as full languages: these varieties are, in certain respects, quite obviously 'mixed,' and the people who speak them often feel that the varieties are neither one thing nor another, but rather are debased, deficient, degenerate, or marginal varieties of some other standard language.

Finally, having *de facto norms* refers to the feeling that many speakers have that there are both 'good' speakers and 'poor' speakers and that the good speakers represent the norms of proper usage. Sometimes this means focusing on one particular sub-variety as representing the 'best' usage, e.g., Parisian French or the Florentine variety of Italian. Standards must not only be established (by the first criterion above), they must also be observed. When all the speakers of a language feel that it is badly spoken or badly written almost everywhere, that language may have considerable difficulty in surviving; in fact, such a feeling is often associated with a language that is dying. Concern with the norms of linguistic behavior, 'linguistic purism' (see Thomas, 1991), may become very important among specific segments of society. For example, so far as English is concerned, there is a very profitable industry devoted to telling people how they should behave linguistically, what it is 'correct' to say, what to avoid saying, and so on (see Baron, 1982, Cameron, 1995, and Wardhaugh, 1999). As we will see (chapters 7–8), people's feelings about norms have important consequences for an understanding of both variation and change in language.

If we apply the above criteria to the different varieties of speech we observe in the world, we will see that not every variety we may want to call a language has the same status as every other variety. English is a language, but so are Dogrib, Haitian Creole, Ukrainian, Latin, Tok Pisin, and Chinese. Each satisfies a different sub-set of criteria from our list. Although there are important differences among them, we would be loath to deny that any one of them is a language. They are all equals as languages, but that does not necessarily mean that all languages are equal! The first is a linguistic judgment, the second a social one.

As we have just seen, trying to decide whether something is or is not a language or in what ways languages are alike and different can be quite troublesome. However, we usually experience fewer problems of the same kind with regard to dialects. There is usually little controversy over the fact that they are either regional or social varieties of something that is widely acknowledged to be a language. That is true even of the relationship of Cantonese and Mandarin to Chinese if the latter is given a 'generous' interpretation as a language.

Some people are also aware that the standard variety of any language is actually only the preferred dialect of that language: Parisian French, Florentine

Italian, or the Zanzibar variety of Swahili in Tanzania. It is the variety that has been chosen for some reason, perhaps political, social, religious, or economic, or some combination of reasons, to serve as either the model or norm for other varieties. It is the empowered variety. As a result, the standard is often not called a dialect at all, but is regarded as the language itself. It takes on an ideological dimension and becomes the 'right' and 'proper' language of the group of people, the very expression of their being. One consequence is that all other varieties become related to that standard and are regarded as dialects of that standard with none of the power of that standard. Of course, this process usually involves a complete restructuring of the historical facts. If language X^1 differentiates in three areas to become dialects XA, XB, and XC, and then XA is elevated to become a later standard X^2, then XB, and XC are really historical variants of X^1, not sub-varieties of X^2. What happens in practice is that XB and XC undergo pressure to change toward X^2, and X^2, the preferred variety or standard, exerts its influence over the other varieties.

We see a good instance of this process in Modern English. The new standard is based on the dialect of the area surrounding London, which was just one of several dialects of Old English, and not the most important for both the western and northern dialects were once at least equally as important. However, in the modern period, having provided the base for Standard English, this dialect exerts a strong influence over all the other dialects of England so that it is not just first among equals but rather represents the modern language itself to the extent that the varieties spoken in the west and north are generally regarded as its local variants. Historically, these varieties arise from different sources, but now they are viewed only in relation to the standardized variety.

A final comment seems called for with regard to the terms *language* and *dialect*. A dialect is a subordinate variety of a language, so that we can say that Texas English and Swiss German are, respectively, dialects of English and German. The language name (i.e., *English* or *German*) is the superordinate term. We can also say of some languages that they contain more than one dialect; e.g., English, French, and Italian are spoken in various dialects. If a language is spoken by so few people, or so uniformly, that it has only one variety, we might be tempted to say that *language* and *dialect* become synonymous in such a case. However, another view is that it is inappropriate to use *dialect* in such a situation because the requirement of subordination is not met. Consequently, to say that we have dialect A of language X must imply also the existence of dialect B of language X, but to say we have language Y is to make no claim about the number of dialect varieties in which it exists: it may exist in only a single variety, or it may have two (or more) subordinate dialects: dialects A, B, and so on.

Finally, two other terms are important in connection with some of the issues discussed above: *vernacular* and *koiné*. Petyt (1980, p. 25) defines the former as 'the speech of a particular country or region,' or, more technically, 'a form of speech transmitted from parent to child as a primary medium of communication.' If that form of speech is Standard English, then Standard English is the vernacular for that particular child; if it is a regional dialect, then that dialect is the child's vernacular. A *koiné* is 'a form of speech shared by people of different vernaculars – though for some of them the *koiné* itself may be their vernacular.' A koiné is a common language, but not necessarily a standard one. Petyt's examples of koinés are Hindi for many people in India and Vulgar Latin (*vulgar*: 'colloquial' or 'spoken') in the Roman Empire. The original koiné was, of course, the Greek koiné of the Ancient World, a unified version of the Greek dialects, which after Alexander's conquests (*circa* 330 BCE) became the lingua franca of the Western world, a position it held until it was eventually superseded, not without a struggle, by Vulgar Latin.

Discussion

1. A survey of the following kind might prove quite revealing. Ask a variety of people you know questions such as these, and then try to organize their responses in a systematic way:

    a. Which language(s) do you speak?
    b. Do you speak a dialect of X?
    c. Where is the best X spoken?
    d. What is your native language (or mother tongue)?
    e. Do you speak X with an accent? If so, what accent?

    Try also to get definitions from your informants for each of the terms that you use.
2. A question found on many national census forms concerns the language or languages spoken (or known). It may ask respondents either to check one or more language names or to volunteer a name or names. What problems do you see in collecting data in such a way? Think of countries like China, the United States, Canada, India, France, Spain, and Norway.
3. Is Afrikaans a dialect of Dutch or a different language? To attempt an answer to this question you will have to consider a variety of issues: What is the origin of Afrikaans? Are Afrikaans and Dutch mutually intelligible? How different are the orthographies (i.e., systems of spelling), sounds, vocabularies, and grammars? How important is the factor of the national consciousness of those who speak Afrikaans? Is the initial question clearly answerable from the kinds of theories and data that are currently available to us?
4. Speakers of Faroese are said to understand speakers of Icelandic but not vice versa. Danes seem to understand Norwegians better than Norwegians understand Danes. Monolingual speakers of Mandarin and Cantonese cannot communicate with each other in speech. What do such facts have to say about using the criterion of mutual intelligibility in deciding whether we are dealing with a single language, with two dialects of one language, or with two separate languages? Consider the following pieces of evidence in arriving at your answer. Speakers of Isoko in Nigeria say they cannot understand those who speak other Urhobo languages/dialects; but these others apparently understand them. This situation seems to have developed concurrently with demands for greater political autonomy and ethnic self-sufficiency.

5.   Standard languages are usually based on an existing dialect of the language. For example, the British variety of English is based, historically at least, on the dialect of the area surrounding London, Continental French on the dialect of Paris, and Italian on the dialect of Florence or Tuscany (although Rome and Milan became important influences in the late twentieth century). In other countries the situation is not so clear-cut. What can you find out about the difficulties of choosing a variety for standardization in Denmark, Indonesia, Greece, China, Haiti, and the Arab world?

6.   Old English, the language spoken a thousand years ago in England, was a west-country variety of English, West Saxon. The court was located at Winchester and the literature and documents of the period were written in West Saxon (or sometimes in Latin). By 1400 the English court was well established in London, which became the center of social, political, and economic power. It also became the literary center of the country, particularly after the development of printing. The variety of English spoken in and around London, including Oxford and Cambridge (which were important intellectual centers), became predominant. How would you use facts such as these to argue that no variety of a language is intrinsically better than another and that what happens to a language is largely the result of the chance interplay of external forces? Can you think of other examples which might support such a conclusion?

7.   Mencken wrote a series of books under the general title *The American Language*. Why did he choose this particular title? Why not *The English Language in America*? If the English of the United States is properly regarded as a separate language, how about the varieties found in Canada, Australia, South Africa, and Singapore? You might read Lilles (2000) for a strongly expressed dismissal of 'Canadian English,' as a 'fiction [without] any value linguistically, pragmatically, socially, or politically' (p. 9). (See Clyne, 1992, for a discussion of what he calls 'pluricentric languages.')

8.   One of the goals Dr Johnson set himself in compiling his *Dictionary* of 1755 was to 'fix,' i.e., standardize, English. What does Johnson say in the Preface to that dictionary about his success in meeting that goal?

9.   The publication in 1961 of *Webster's Third New International Dictionary* caused a tremendous stir in North America, being regarded by many critics as an attack on prevailing language standards. What were the issues? (See Sledd and Ebbitt, 1962, Finegan, 1980, and Wardhaugh, 1999.)

10. Writing of the codification of Standard English, Leith (1997, pp. 56–7) says that 'by analyzing "correct" usage in terms that only a tiny minority of educated people could command, the codifiers ensured that correctness remained the preserve of an elite. The usage of most people was wrong, precisely because it was the usage of the majority.' There appear to be both advantages and disadvantages to having a 'standard language.' Is it possible to make an objective assessment of these? Or is any judgment inherently ideological?

11. If Scotland continues to devolve from England, what might this mean for the variety of English spoken there? How might Scots become unequivocally a distinctive variety of English?

12. Arabs have a particular historical view of Arabic and Turks of Turkish. Try to find out something about these views. How do they help Arabs and Turks to maintain their languages? Hindi and Urdu are now viewed as rather different by those who speak these languages. How is each language being reshaped to conform to these views?

13. How would you evaluate each of the following languages according to the criteria stated above (standardization, vitality, historicity, autonomy, reduction, mixture, and *de facto* norms); that is, for each criterion, does the language possess the stated characteristic or lack it: Haitian Creole, Provençal, Singapore English, Old English, Pitcairnese, African American Vernacular English, Tok Pisin, Cockney, Ukrainian, and the language of Shakespeare's plays?

14. Find out what you can about Basic English. In what ways is it a reduced form of Standard English? Do the kinds of reductions introduced into Basic English make it 'simpler' to learn and use? (You will have to define 'simpler.')

15. From time to time certain users of languages such as French and German have objected to borrowings, in particular borrowings from English. What Anglicisms have been objected to? What kinds of native resources have been suggested as suitable alternative sources of exploitation in order to develop and/or purify the language? What motivates the objections?

16. Some Chinese scholars are concerned with developing the vocabulary of Chinese to make it usable for every kind of scientific and technical endeavor. They reject the idea that such vocabulary should be borrowed from other languages. What do you think they hope to gain by doing this? Do they lose anything if they are successful?

17. 'A language is a dialect with an army and a navy' is a well-known observation. (Today we would add an 'airforce'!) True? And, if so, what are the consequences?

18. In the *UNESCO Courier* of April, 2000, a writer makes the following observation: 'Languages usually have a relatively short life span as well as a very high death rate. Only a few, including Basque, Egyptian, Chinese, Greek, Hebrew, Latin, Persian, Sanskrit, and Tamil have lasted more than 2000 years.' How is this statement at best a half-truth?

19. Are the Australian, New Zealand, Canadian, and other national varieties of English 'new dialects' of English, or autonomous languages, or possibly even both? (See Hickey, 2004, Gordon et al., 2004, and Trudgill, 2004.)

Regional Dialects

Regional variation in the way a language is spoken is likely to provide one of the easiest ways of observing variety in language. As you travel throughout a wide geographical area in which a language is spoken, and particularly if that language has been spoken in that area for many hundreds of years, you are almost certain to notice differences in pronunciation, in the choices and forms of words, and in syntax. There may even be very distinctive local colorings in the language which you notice as you move from one location to another. Such distinctive varieties are usually called *regional dialects* of the language. As we saw earlier (p. 28), the term *dialect* is sometimes used only if there is a strong tradition of writing in the local variety. Old English and to a lesser extent Middle English had dialects in this sense. In the absence of such a tradition of writing the term *patois* may be used to describe the variety. However, many linguists writing in English tend to use *dialect* to describe both situations and rarely, if at all, use *patois* as a scientific term. You are likely to encounter it only as a kind of anachronism, as in its use by Jamaicans, who often refer to the variety of English spoken on the island as a 'patois.'

The *dialect–patois* distinction actually seems to make more sense in some situations, e.g., France, than in others. In medieval France, a number of languages flourished and several were associated with strong literary traditions. However, as the language of Paris asserted itself from the fourteenth century on, these traditions withered. Parisian French spread throughout France, and, even though that spread is still not yet complete (as visits to such parts of France as Brittany, Provence, Corsica, and Alsace will confirm), it drastically reduced the importance of the local varieties: they continue to exist largely in spoken forms only; they are disfavored socially and politically; they are merely *patois* to those who extol the virtues of Standard French. However, even as these varieties have faded, there have been countervailing moves to revive them as many younger residents of the areas in which they are spoken see them as strong indicators of identities they wish to preserve.

There are some further interesting differences in the use of the terms *dialect* and *patois* (Petyt, 1980, pp. 24–5). *Patois* is usually used to describe only rural forms of speech; we may talk about an *urban dialect*, but to talk about an *urban patois* seems strange. *Patois* also seems to refer only to the speech of the lower strata in society; again, we may talk about a *middle-class dialect* but not, apparently, about a *middle-class patois*. Finally, a dialect usually has a wider geographical distribution than a *patois*, so that, whereas *regional dialect* and *village patois* seem unobjectionable, the same cannot be said for *regional patois* and *village dialect*. However, as I indicated above, many Jamaicans refer to the popular spoken variety of Jamaican English as a *patois* rather than as a dialect. So again the distinction is in no way an absolute one.

This use of the term *dialect* to differentiate among regional varieties of specific languages is perhaps more readily applicable to contemporary conditions in Europe and some other developed countries than it would have been in medieval or Renaissance Europe or today in certain other parts of the world, where it was (and still is) possible to travel long distances and, by making only small changes in speech from location to location, continue to communicate with the inhabitants. (You might have to travel somewhat slowly, however, because of the necessary learning that would be involved!) It has been said that at one time a person could travel from the south of Italy to the north of France in this manner. It is quite clear that such a person began the journey speaking one language and ended it speaking something entirely different; however, there was no one point at which the changeover occurred, nor is there actually any way of determining how many intermediate dialect areas that person passed through. For an intriguing empirical test of this idea, one using recent phonetic data from a continuum of Saxon and Franconian dialects in the Netherlands, see Heeringa and Nerbonne (2001). They conclude that the traveler 'perceives phonological distance indirectly' (p. 398) and that there are 'unsharp borders between dialect areas' (p. 399).

Such a situation is often referred to as a *dialect continuum*. What you have is a continuum of dialects sequentially arranged over space: A, B, C, D, and so on. Over large distances the dialects at each end of the continuum may well be mutually unintelligible, and also some of the intermediate dialects may be unintelligible with one or both ends, or even with certain other intermediate ones. In such a distribution, which dialects can be classified together under one language, and how many such languages are there? As I have suggested, such questions are possibly a little easier to answer today in certain places than they once were. The hardening of political boundaries in the modern world as a result of the growth of states, particularly nation-states rather than multinational or multi-ethnic states, has led to the hardening of language boundaries. Although residents of territories on both sides of the Dutch–German border (within the West Germanic continuum) or the French–Italian border (within the West Romance continuum) have many similarities in speech even today, they will almost certainly tell you that they speak dialects of Dutch or German in the one case and French or Italian in the other. Various pressures – political, social, cultural, and educational – serve to harden current state boundaries and to make the linguistic differences among states more, not less, pronounced. Dialects continue therefore to disappear as national languages arise. They are subject to two kinds of pressure: one from within, to conform to a national standard, and one from without, to become different from standards elsewhere.

When a language is recognized as being spoken in different varieties, the issue becomes one of deciding how many varieties and how to classify each variety. *Dialect geography* is the term used to describe attempts made to map the distributions of various linguistic features so as to show their geographical provenance. For example, in seeking to determine features of the dialects of English and to show their distributions, dialect geographers try to find answers to questions such as the following. Is this an *r*-pronouncing area of English, as in words like *car* and *cart*, or is it not? What past tense form of *drink* do speakers prefer? What names do people give to particular objects in the environment, e.g., *elevator* or *lift*, *petrol* or *gas*, *carousel* or *roundabout*? Sometimes maps are drawn to show actual boundaries around such features, boundaries called *isoglosses*, so as to distinguish an area in which a certain feature is found from areas in which it is absent. When several such isoglosses coincide, the result is sometimes called a *dialect boundary*. Then we may be tempted to say that speakers on one side of that boundary speak one dialect and speakers on the other side speak a different dialect.

As we will see when we return once again to this topic in chapter 6, there are many difficulties with this kind of work: finding the kinds of items that appear to distinguish one dialect from another; collecting data; drawing conclusions from the data we collect; presenting the findings; and so on. It is easy to see, however, how such a methodology could be used to distinguish British, American,

Australian, and other varieties of English from one another as various dialects of one language. It could also be used to distinguish Cockney English from Texas English. But how could you use it to distinguish among the multifarious varieties of English found in cities like New York and London? Or even among the varieties we observe to exist in smaller, less complex cities and towns in which various people who have always resided there are acknowledged to speak differently from one another?

Finally, the term *dialect*, particularly when it is used in reference to regional variation, should not be confused with the term *accent*. Standard English, for example, is spoken in a variety of accents, often with clear regional and social associations: there are accents associated with North America, Singapore, India, Liverpool (Scouse), Tyneside (Geordie), Boston, New York, and so on. However, many people who live in such places show a remarkable uniformity to one another in their grammar and vocabulary because they speak Standard English and the differences are merely those of accent, i.e., how they pronounce what they say.

One English accent has achieved a certain eminence, the accent known as *Received Pronunciation* (or RP), the accent of perhaps as few as 3 percent of those who live in England. (The 'received' in Received Pronunciation is a little bit of old-fashioned snobbery: it means the accent allows one to be received into the 'better' parts of society!) This accent is of fairly recent origin (see Mugglestone, 1995), becoming established as prestigious only in the late nineteenth century and not even given its current label until the 1920s. In the United Kingdom at least, it is 'usually associated with a higher social or educational background, with the BBC and the professions, and [is] most commonly taught to students learning English as a foreign language' (Wakelin, 1977, p. 5). For many such students it is the only accent they are prepared to learn, and a teacher who does not use it may have difficulty in finding a position as a teacher of English in certain non-English-speaking countries in which a British accent is preferred over a North American one. In fact, those who use this accent are often regarded as speaking 'unaccented' English because it lacks a regional association within England. Other names for this accent are *the Queen's English*, *Oxford English*, and *BBC English*. However, there is no unanimous agreement that the Queen does in fact use RP, a wide variety of accents can be found among the staff and students at Oxford University, and regional accents are now widely used in the various BBC services. As Bauer (1994, pp. 115–21) also shows, RP continues to change. One of its most recent manifestations has been labeled 'Estuary English' (Rosewarne, 1994) – sometimes also called 'Cockneyfied RP' – a development of RP along the lower reaches of the Thames reflecting a power shift in London toward the world of finance, banking, and commerce and away from that of inherited position, the Church, law, and traditional bureaucracies. Trudgill (1995, p. 7) has pointed out what he considers to be the most interesting characteristics of RP: 'the relatively very small numbers of speakers who use it do not identify themselves as coming from any particular geographical region'; 'RP is largely confined to England' and there it is a *'non-localized* accent'; and 'it is . . . not necessary to speak RP to speak Standard English' because 'Standard English can be spoken with any regional accent, and in the vast majority of cases normally is.' It is also interesting to observe that the 1997 *English Pronouncing Dictionary* published by Cambridge University Press abandoned the label RP in favor of BBC English even though this latter term is not unproblematic as the BBC itself has enlarged the accent pool from which it draws its newsreaders.

The development of Estuary English is one part of a general leveling of accents within the British Isles. The changes are well documented; see, for example, Foulkes and Docherty (1999), who review a variety of factors involved in the changes that are occurring in cities. One feature of Estuary English, the use of a glottal stop for *t* (Fabricus, 2002), is also not unique to that variety but is spreading widely, for example to Newcastle, Cardiff, and Glasgow, and even as far north as rural Aberdeenshire in northeast Scotland (Marshall, 2003). Watt (2000, 2002) used the vowels in *face* and *goat* to show that Geordie, the Newcastle accent, levels toward a regional accent norm rather than toward a national one, almost certainly revealing a preference for establishing a regional identity rather than either a very limited local identity or a wider national one.

The most generalized accent in North America is sometimes referred to as *General American* or, more recently, as *network English*, the accent associated with announcers on the major television networks. Other languages often have no equivalent to RP: for example, German is spoken in a variety of accents, none of which is deemed inherently any better than any other. Educated regional varieties are preferred rather than some exclusive upper-class accent that has no clear relationship to personal achievement.

As a final observation I must reiterate that it is impossible to speak English without an accent. There is no such thing as an 'unaccented English.' RP is an accent, a social one rather than a regional one. However, we must note that there are different evaluations of the different accents, evaluations arising from social factors not linguistic ones. Matsuda (1991, p. 1361) says it is really an issue of power: 'When . . . parties are in a relationship of domination and subordination we tend to say that the dominant is normal, and the subordinate is different from normal. And so it is with accent. . . . People in power are perceived as speaking normal, unaccented English. Any speech that is different from that constructed norm is called an accent.' In the pages that follow we will return constantly to linguistic issues having to do with power.

Discussion

1. What regional differences are you aware of in the pronunciation of each of the following words: *butter, farm, bird, oil, bag, cot, caught, which, witch, Cuba, spear, bath, with, happy, house, Mary, merry, marry*?
2. What past tense or past participle forms have you heard for each of the following verbs: *bring, drink, sink, sing, get, lie, lay, dive*?
3. What are some other variants you are aware of for each of the following sentences: 'I haven't any money,' 'I ain't done it yet,' 'He be farmer,' 'Give it me,' 'It was me what told her'? Who uses each variant? On what occasions?
4. What other names are you aware of for objects sometimes referred to as *seesaws, cobwebs, sidewalks, streetcars, thumbtacks, soft drinks, gym shoes, elevators*? Again, who uses each variant?

5. What do you yourself call each of the following: *cottage cheese, highway, first grade, doughnuts, griddle cakes, peanuts, spring onions, baby carriage, chest of drawers, faucet, frying pan, paper bag, porch, sitting room, sofa, earthworm*?

6. Each of the following is found in some variety of English. Each is comprehensible. Which do you yourself use? Which do you not use? Explain how those utterances you do not use differ from those you do use.

   a. I haven't spoken to him.
   b. I've not spoken to him.
   c. Is John at home?
   d. Is John home?
   e. Give me it.
   f. Give it me.
   g. Give us it.
   h. I wish you would have said so.
   i. I wish you'd said so.
   j. Don't be troubling yourself.
   k. Coming home tomorrow he is.

7. How might you employ a selection of items from the above questions (or similar items) to compile a checklist that could be used to determine the geographical (and possibly social) origins of a speaker of English?

8. A local accent may be either positively or negatively valued. How do you value each of the following: a Yorkshire accent; a Texas accent; the accents of the Queen of England, the Prime Minister of the United Kingdom, and the President of the United States? Think of some others. Why do you react the way you do? Is it a question of being able to identify with the speaker or not; of social class; of education; or stereotyping; or what? How appropriate would each of the following be: RP in a Tyneside working-class pub; network English at a Black Power rally in Harlem; and Parisian French at a hockey game at the Montreal Forum?

9. A. S. C. Ross, in *Noblesse Oblige* (Mitford, 1956), a book which discusses somewhat lightheartedly, but not un-seriously, differences between 'U' (upper-class) and 'non-U' (not upper-class) speech in the United Kingdom, observes (pp. 75–6):

   > Many (but not all) U-speakers make *get* rhyme with *bit*, *just* (adverb) with *best*, *catch* with *fetch*. . . . U-speakers do not sound the *l* in *golf*, *Ralph* (which rhymes with *safe*), *solder*; some old-fashioned U-speakers do not sound it in *falcon*, *Malvern*, either, but it is doubtful how far this last survives. . . .
   >
   > *Real*, *ideal* have two, respectively, three syllables in U speech, one, respectively, two in non-U speech (note, especially, non-U *really*, rhyming with *mealie*). . . . Some U-speakers pronounce *tyre* and *tar* identically (and so for many other words, such as *fire* – even going to the length of making *lion* rhyme with *barn*).

Ross makes numerous other observations about differences between the two varieties. Do you consider such differences to be useful, unnecessary, snobbish, undemocratic, inevitable, or what?

10. There may have been a recent fall-off in the high social prestige associated with RP in England and elsewhere. How might you establish whether such is the case?

11. Differences in the accent one uses to speak a standard variety of a language may be more important in some parts of the world than others. Are differences in accent as important within the United States, Canada, and Australia as they appear to be in the British Isles? Do speakers of German from Hanover, Berlin, Vienna, and Zürich view differences in German accent in the same way as speakers of English? What factors appear to account for the different evaluations of accents?

12. The fact that Standard English can be spoken with a variety of accents often poses certain difficulties for the teaching of English in non-English-speaking countries. What are some of the problems you might encounter and how might you try to solve them?

13. Preston (1989) has demonstrated that speakers of English (in this case in the United States) have certain perceptions about regional varieties of English other than their own, i.e., what they are like and how their own variety differs. Try to describe what you believe to be the characteristics of another variety of English and then check out the facts. Try to account for any differences you find between the two, between beliefs and facts. (See also Preston, 1999, 2002, and Long and Preston, 2003.)

Social Dialects

The term *dialect* can also be used to describe differences in speech associated with various social groups or classes. There are social dialects as well as regional ones. An immediate problem is that of defining *social group* (see chapter 5) or *social class* (see chapter 6), giving proper weight to the various factors that can be used to determine social position, e.g., occupation, place of residence, education, 'new' versus 'old' money, income, racial or ethnic origin, cultural background, caste, religion, and so on. Such factors as these do appear to be related fairly directly to how people speak. There is a British 'public-school' dialect, and there is an 'African American Vernacular English' dialect found in cities such as New York, Detroit, and Buffalo. Many people also have stereotypical notions of how other people speak, and, as we will see in chapter 7 in particular, there is considerable evidence from work of investigators such as Labov and Trudgill that social dialects can indeed be described systematically.

Whereas regional dialects are geographically based, social dialects originate among social groups and are related to a variety of factors, the principal ones apparently being social class, religion, and ethnicity. In India, for example, caste, one of the clearest of all social differentiators, quite often determines which variety of a language a speaker uses. In a city like Baghdad the Christian, Jewish, and Muslim inhabitants speak different varieties of Arabic. In this case the first two groups use their variety solely within the group but the Muslim variety serves as a lingua franca, or common language, among the groups. Consequently, Christians and Jews who deal with Muslims must use two varieties: their own at home and the Muslim variety for trade and in all inter-group relationships. Ethnic variation can be seen in the United States, where one variety of English has become so identified with an ethnic group that it is often referred to as African American Vernacular English (AAVE). Labov's work in New York City shows that there are other ethnic differences too: speakers of Jewish and Italian ethnicity differentiate themselves from speakers of either the standard variety or AAVE. On occasion they actually show *hypercorrective* tendencies in that they tend to overdo certain imitative behaviors: Italians are inclined to be in the vanguard of pronouncing words like *bad* and *bag* with a vowel resembling that of *beard* and Jews in the vanguard of pronouncing words like *dog* with a vowel something like that of *book*. A possible motivation for such behavior is a desire to move away from the Italian and Yiddish vowels that speakers could so easily use in these words but which would be clear ethnic markers; however, the movement prompted by such avoidance behavior goes beyond the prevailing local norm and becomes an ethnic characteristic that serves as an indicator of identity and solidarity.

Studies in *social dialectology*, the term used to refer to this branch of linguistic study, confront many difficult issues, particularly when investigators venture into cities. Cities are much more difficult to characterize linguistically than are rural hamlets; variation in language and patterns of change are much more obvious in cities, e.g., in family structures, employment, and opportunities for social advancement or decline. Migration, both in and out of cities, is also usually a potent linguistic factor. Cities also spread their influence far beyond their limits and their importance should never be underestimated in considering such matters as the standardization and diffusion of languages.

In later chapters (particularly chapters 6–8) we will look closely at the importance of language variation in cities and see how important such variation is in trying to understand how and why change occurs in languages. In this way we may also come to appreciate why some sociolinguists regard such variation as being at the heart of work in sociolinguistics.

Discussion

1. Gumperz (1968) maintains that separate languages maintain themselves most readily in closed tribal systems in which kinship dominates all activities; on the other hand, distinctive varieties arise in highly stratified societies. He points out that, when social change causes the breakdown of traditional social structures and the formation of new ties, linguistic barriers between varieties also break down. Can you think of any examples which either confirm or disconfirm this claim?

2. If some social dialects may properly be labeled *nonstandard*, Labov (1970, p. 52) raises a very important issue in connection with finding speakers who can supply reliable data concerning such varieties. He says:

> We have not encountered any non-standard speakers who gained good control of a standard language, and still retained control of the non-standard verna-cular. Dialect differences depend upon low-level rules which appear as minor adjustments and extensions of contextual conditions, etc. It appears that such conditions inevitably interact, and, although the speaker may indeed appear to be speaking the vernacular, close examination of his speech shows that his grammar has been heavily influenced by the standard. He may succeed in convincing his listeners that he is speaking the vernacular, but this impression seems to depend upon a number of unsystematic and heavily marked signals.

If Labov's observation is correct, what must we do to gain access to any information we seek about 'the non-standard vernacular'? What difficulties do you foresee?

3. How are language norms established and perpetuated in rather isolated rural communities, e.g., a small village in the west of England, or in north-ern Vermont, or in the interior of British Columbia? How different do you think the situation is in London, New York, or Vancouver? Are there any similarities at all? How are language norms established overall in England, the United States, and Canada?

Styles, Registers, and Beliefs

The study of dialects is further complicated by the fact that speakers can adopt different *styles* of speaking. You can speak very formally or very informally, your choice being governed by circumstances. Ceremonial occasions almost invariably require very formal speech, public lectures somewhat less formal, casual conversation quite informal, and conversations between intimates on matters of little importance may be extremely informal and casual. (See Joos, 1962, for an entertaining discussion.) We may try to relate the level of formality chosen to a variety of factors: the kind of occasion; the various social, age, and other differences that exist between the participants; the particular task that is involved, e.g., writing or speaking; the emotional involvement of one or more of the participants; and so on. We appreciate that such distinctions exist when we recognize the stylistic appropriateness of *What do you intend to do, your majesty?* and the inappropriateness of *Waddya intend doin', Rex?* While it may be difficult to characterize discrete levels of formality, it is nevertheless possible to show that native speakers of all languages control a range of stylistic vari-eties. It is also quite possible to predict with considerable confidence the stylistic features that a native speaker will tend to employ on certain occasions. We will return to related issues in chapters 4, 7, and 11.

Register is another complicating factor in any study of language varieties. Registers are sets of language items associated with discrete occupational or social groups. Surgeons, airline pilots, bank managers, sales clerks, jazz fans, and pimps employ different registers. As Ferguson (1994, p. 20) says, 'People participating in recurrent communication situations tend to develop similar vocabularies, similar features of intonation, and characteristic bits of syntax and phonology that they use in these situations.' This kind of variety is a register. Ferguson adds that its 'special terms for recurrent objects and events, and formulaic sequences or "routines," seem to facilitate speedy communication; other features apparently serve to mark the register, establish feelings of rapport, and serve other purposes similar to the accommodation that influences dialect formation. There is no mistaking the strong tendency for individuals and co-communicators to develop register variation along many dimensions.' Of course, one person may control a variety of registers: you can be a stockbroker and an archeologist, or a mountain climber and an economist. Each register helps you to express your identity at a specific time or place, i.e., how you seek to present yourself to others.

Dialect, style, and register differences are largely independent: you can talk casually about mountain climbing in a local variety of a language, or you can write a formal technical study of wine making. You may also be judged to speak 'better' or 'worse' than other speakers who have much the same background. It is quite usual to find some people who are acknowledged to speak a language or one of its varieties better or worse than others. In an article on the varieties of speech he found among the 1,700 or so speakers of Menomini, an Amerindian language of Wisconsin, Bloomfield (1927) mentioned a variety of skills that were displayed among some of the speakers he knew best: a woman in her sixties who spoke 'a beautiful and highly idiomatic Menomini'; her husband, who used 'forms which are current among bad speakers' on some occasions and 'elevated speech,' incorporating forms best described as 'spelling pronunciations,' 'ritualistic compound words and occasional archaisms' on others; an old man who 'spoke with bad syntax and meagre, often inept vocabulary, yet with occasional archaisms'; a man of about forty with 'atrocious' Menomini, i.e., a small vocabulary, barbarous inflections, threadbare sentences; and two half-breeds, one who spoke using a vast vocabulary and the other who employed 'racy idiom.'

Value judgments of this kind sometimes emerge for reasons that are hard to explain. For example, there appears to be a subtle bias built into the way people tend to judge dialects. Quite often, though not always, people seem to exhibit a preference for rural dialects over urban ones. In England the speech of Northumbria seems more highly valued than the speech of Tyneside and certainly the speech of Liverpool seems less valued than that of northwest England as a whole. In North America the speech of upstate New York does not have the negative characteristics associated with much of the speech of New York City. Why such different attitudes should exist is not easy to say. Is it a preference for things that appear to be 'older' and 'more conservative,' a subconscious dislike of some of the characteristics of urbanization, including uncertainty about what standards should prevail, or some other reason or reasons?

Sometimes these notions of 'better' and 'worse' solidify into those of 'correctness' and 'incorrectness.' We may well heed Bloomfield's words (1927, pp. 432–3) concerning the latter notions:

> The popular explanation of 'correct' and 'incorrect' speech reduces the matter to one of knowledge versus ignorance. There is such a thing as correct English. An ignorant person does not know the correct forms; therefore he cannot help using incorrect ones. In the process of education one learns the correct forms and, by practice and an effort of will ('careful speaking'), acquires the habit of using them. If one associates with ignorant speakers, or relaxes the effort of will ('careless speaking'), one will lapse into the incorrect forms . . . there is one error in the popular view which is of special interest. The incorrect forms cannot be the result of ignorance or carelessness, for they are by no means haphazard, but, on the contrary, very stable. For instance, if a person is so ignorant as not to know how to say *I see it* in past time, we might expect him to use all kinds of chance forms, and, especially, to resort to easily formed locutions, such as *I did see it*, or to the addition of the regular past-time suffix: *I seed it*. But instead, these ignorant people quite consistently say *I seen it*. Now it is evident that one fixed and consistent form will be no more difficult than another: a person who has learned *I seen* as the past of *I see* has learned just as much as one who says *I saw*. He has simply learned something different. Although most of the people who say *I seen* are ignorant, their ignorance does not account for this form of speech.

Many people hold strong beliefs on various issues having to do with language and are quite willing to offer their judgments on issues (see Bauer and Trudgill, 1998, Niedzielski and Preston, 1999, and Wardhaugh, 1999). They believe such things as certain languages lack grammar, that you can speak English without an accent, that French is more logical than English, that parents teach their children to speak, that primitive languages exist, that English is degenerating and language standards are slipping, that pronunciation should be based on spelling, and so on and so on. Much discussion of language matters in the media concerns such 'issues' and there are periodic attempts to 'clean up' various bits and pieces, attempts that Cameron (1995) calls 'verbal hygiene.' Most linguists studiously avoid getting involved in such issues having witnessed the failure of various attempts to influence received opinions on such matters. As I have written elsewhere (1999, p. viii), 'Linguists . . . know that many popular beliefs about language are false and that much we are taught about language is misdirected. They also know how difficult it is to effect change.' Language beliefs are well entrenched as are language attitudes and language behaviors. Sociolinguists should strive for an understanding of all three because all affect how people behave toward others.

As we have seen, many varieties of language exist and each language exists in a number of guises. However, languages do not vary in every possible way. It is still quite possible to listen to an individual speaker and infer very specific things about that speaker after hearing relatively little of his or her speech. The interesting problem is accounting for our ability to do that. What are the specific linguistic features we rely on to classify a person as being from a particular place, a member of a certain social class, a representative of a specific profession, a social climber, a person pretending to be someone he or she is not, and so on? One possible hypothesis is that we rely on relatively few cues, e.g., the presence or absence of certain linguistic features. We are also sensitive to the consistency or inconsistency in the use of these cues, so that on occasion it is not just that a particular linguistic feature is always used but that it is used such and such a percent of the time rather than exclusively or not at all (see chapter 7). However, we may actually perceive its use or non-use to be categorical, i.e., the feature to be totally present or totally absent. This last hypothesis is an interesting one in that it raises very important questions about the linguistic capabilities of human beings, particularly about how individuals acquire the ability to use language in such ways. If you must learn to use both linguistic feature X (e.g., *-ing* endings on verbs) and linguistic feature Y (e.g., *-in'* endings on verbs) and how to use them in different proportions in situations A, B, C, and so on, what does that tell us about innate human abilities and the human capacity for learning?

The existence of different varieties is interesting in still another respect. While each of us may have productive control over only a very few varieties of a language, we can usually comprehend many more varieties and relate all of these to the concept of a 'single language.' That is, our *receptive* linguistic ability is much greater than our *productive* linguistic ability. An interesting problem for linguists is knowing how best to characterize this 'knowledge' that we have which enables us to recognize something as being in the language but yet marked as 'different' in some way. Is it part of our *competence* or part of our *performance* in the Chomskyan sense? Or is that a false dichotomy? The first question is as yet unanswered but, as the second suggests, it could possibly be unanswerable. I will have more to say on such matters as we look further into the various relationships between language and society.

Discussion

1. When might each of the following sentences be stylistically appropriate?

    a. Attention!
    b. I do hereby bequeath . . .
    c. Our Father, which art in Heaven . . .
    d. Been to see your Dad recently?
    e. Get lost!
    f. Now if we consider the relationship between social class and income . . .
    g. Come off it!
    h. Take care!
    i. Haven't we met somewhere before?

2. What stylistic characteristics do you associate with each of the following activities: talking to a young child; writing an essay for a professor; playing a board game with a close friend; approaching a stranger on the street

to ask for directions; attending a funeral; talking to yourself; getting stopped for speeding; burning your finger?

3. One of the easiest ways of persuading yourself that there are registers associated with different occupations is to read materials associated with different callings. You can quickly compile register differences from such sources as law reports, hairdressing or fashion magazines, scholarly journals, recipe books, sewing patterns, instruction manuals, textbooks, and so on. The supply is almost inexhaustible! You might compile lists of words from various sources and find out how long it takes one of your fellow students to identify the particular 'sources' as you read the lists aloud.

4. Hudson (1996, p. 46) says 'your dialect shows who (or what) you *are*, whilst your register shows what you are *doing*.' He acknowledges that 'these concepts are much less distinct than the slogan implies'; however, you might use them to sort out what would be dialect and register for a professor of sociology from Mississippi; a hairdresser from Newcastle working in London; a British naval commander; a sheep farmer in New Zealand; and a 'street-wise' person from any location you might choose.

5. Wolfram and Fasold (1974, p. 20) offer the following working definitions of what they called *standard*, *superstandard* (or *hypercorrect*) and *substandard* (or *nonstandard*) speech. They say of someone that:

> If his reaction to the *form* (not the content) of the utterance is neutral and he can devote full attention to the meaning, then the form is standard for him. If his attention is diverted from the meaning of the utterance because it sounds 'snooty,' then the utterance is superstandard. If his attention is diverted from the message because the utterance sounds like poor English, then the form is substandard.

What are your reactions to each of the following?

a. Am I not?
b. He ain't got none.
c. May I leave now?
d. Most everyone says that.
e. It is I.
f. It was pretty awful.
g. Lay down, Fido!
h. He wanted to know whom we met.
i. Between you and I, . . .
j. I seen him.
k. Are you absolutely sure?
l. Who did you mention it to?

Try to apply Wolfram and Fasold's definitions.

6. What judgments might you be inclined to make about a person who always clearly and carefully articulates every word he or she says in all

circumstances? A person who insists on saying both *between you and I* and *It's I*? A person who uses malapropisms? A person who, in speaking rapidly in succession to a number of others, easily shifts from one variety of speech to another?

7. What do you regard as the characteristics of a 'good' speaker of English and of a 'poor' speaker? Consider such matters as pronunciation, word choice, syntactic choice, fluency, and style.

8. There seems to be evidence that many people judge themselves to speak 'better' than they actually do, or, if not better, at least less casually than they do. Do you know of any such evidence? If it is the case that people do behave this way, why might it be so?

9. Find some articles or books on 'good speaking,' on 'how to improve your speech,' or on 'how to impress others through increasing your vocabulary,' and so on. How valuable is the advice you find in such materials?

10. If you had access to only a single style and/or variety of language, what difficulties do you think you might encounter in trying to express different levels of formality as the social situation changed around you, or to indicate such things as seriousness, mockery, humor, respect, and disdain? Is the kind of variation you need a resource that more than compensates for the difficulties that result in teaching the language or arriving at some consensus concerning such concepts as 'correctness' or 'propriety'?

11. Hudson (1996, p. 21) says that 'lay people' sometimes ask linguists questions such as 'Where is real Cockney spoken?' They assume such questions are meaningful. (Another is 'Is Jamaican creole a kind of English or not?') Hudson says that such questions 'are not the kind of questions that can be investigated scientifically.' Having read this chapter, can you think of some other questions about language which are frequently asked but which might also be similarly unanswerable? How about the following: Who speaks the best English? Where should I go to learn perfect Italian? Why do people write and talk so badly these days? Explain why each is unanswerable – by a linguist at least!

12. Cameron (1996, p. 36) includes the following practices under 'verbal hygiene': ' "prescriptivism," that is, the authoritarian promotion of elite varieties as norms of correctness, . . . campaigns for Plain English, spelling reform, dialect and language preservation, non-sexist and non-racist language, Esperanto and the abolition of the copula, . . . self-improvement activities such as elocution and accent reduction, Neurolinguistic Programming, assertiveness training and communication skills training.' How helpful – or harmful – do you consider such activities?

13. Mugglestone (1995, p. 330) writes as follows: 'The process of standardization . . . can and will only reach completion in a dead language, where the inviolable norms so often asserted by the prescriptive tradition (and the absolutes of language attitudes) may indeed come into being.' If variation sets limits to language standardization, why do some people still insist that rigid standards should be prescribed (and followed)?

Further Reading

Chambers and Trudgill (1998), Davis (1983), and Petyt (1980) provide introductions to the study of dialects. Wolfram and Fasold (1974) focus specifically on social dialectology. English dialects are the concern of Hughes and Trudgill (1996), Trudgill (1999), Upton and Widdowson (1996), Wakelin (1977), and Wells (1982). Joseph (1987) discusses the standardization of languages and Grillo (1989) the dominant positions of Standard English and Standard French. Rai (1991) discusses the origins of the Hindi–Urdu split and Vikør (1993) provides useful information on the language situation in Scandinavia. Milroy and Milroy (1999) deals with issues of 'authority' and standardization and Bex and Watts (1999) with issues surrounding Standard English. Bailey and Görlach (1982), Strevens (1972), and Trudgill and Hannah (2002) discuss the different varieties of English found in various parts of the world. Joos (1962) is a classic account of stylistic differences, and Biber and Finegan (1994) deals with register. Bauer and Trudgill (1998), Cameron (1995), and Wardhaugh (1999) deal with various aspects of beliefs about and attitudes toward language. Schieffelin et al. (1998) focuses on various language ideologies.

3 Pidgins and Creoles

Among the many languages of the world are a few often assigned to a somewhat marginal position: the various lingua francas, pidgins, and creoles. To the best of our knowledge all have existed since time immemorial, but, in comparison with what we know about many 'fully fledged' languages, we know comparatively little about them. There is a paucity of historical records; the history of serious study of such languages goes back only a few decades; and, because of the circumstances of their use, they have often been regarded as being of little intrinsic value or interest. Until recently, pidgins and creoles have generally been viewed as uninteresting linguistic phenomena, being notable mainly for linguistic features they have been said to 'lack,' e.g., articles, the copula, and grammatical inflections, rather than those they possess, and those who speak them have often been treated with disdain, even contempt.

Hymes (1971, p. 3) has pointed out that before the 1930s pidgins and creoles were largely ignored by linguists, who regarded them as 'marginal languages' at best. (Some linguists were even advised to keep away from studying them lest they jeopardize their careers!) He points out that pidgins and creoles 'are marginal, in the circumstances of their origin, and in the attitudes towards them on the part of those who speak one of the languages from which they derive.' They are also marginal 'in terms of knowledge about them,' even though 'these languages are of central importance to our understanding of language, and central too in the lives of some millions of people. Because of their origins, however, their association with poorer and darker members of a society, and through perpetuation of misleading stereotypes . . . most interest, even where positive, has considered them merely curiosities.' He adds that much 'interest and information, scholarly as well as public, has been prejudicial. These languages have been considered, not creative adaptations, but degenerations; not systems in their own right, but deviations from other systems. Their origins have been explained, not by historical and social forces, but by inherent ignorance, indolence, and inferiority.' As languages of those without political and social power, literatures, and 'culture,' they could be safely and properly ignored, for what could they possibly tell us about anything that English and French or even Greek, Latin, and Sanskrit could not?

Fortunately, in recent years such attitudes have changed and, as serious attention has been given to pidgins and creoles, linguists have discovered many interesting characteristics about them, characteristics that appear to bear on fundamental issues to do with all languages, 'fully fledged' and 'marginal' alike. Moreover, pidgins and creoles are invaluable to those who use them. Not only are they essential to everyday living but they are also frequently important markers of identity. In an interview in 1978 a schoolboy in Belize had this to say about his language: 'Well, usually in Belize you find the language, the main language you know is this slang that I tell you about, the Creole. And you'd recognize them by that, you know. They usually have this, you know, very few of them speak the English or some of them usually speak Spanish' (Le Page and Tabouret-Keller, 1985, p. 216). The study of pidgins and creoles has become an important part of linguistic and, especially, sociolinguistic study, with its own literature and, of course, its own controversies. With pidgins and creoles we can see processes of language origin and change going on around us. We can also witness how people are attracted to languages, how they exploit what linguistic resources they have, and how they forge new identities. We do not have to wait a millennium to see how a language changes; a few generations suffice. To some extent, too, the speakers of such languages have benefited as more and more of them have come to recognize that what they speak is not just a 'bad' variety of this language or that, but a language or a variety of a language with its own legitimacy, i.e., its own history, structure, array of functions, and the possibility of winning eventual recognition as a 'proper' language.

Lingua Francas

People who speak different languages who are forced into contact with each other must find some way of communicating, a *lingua franca*. In a publication concerned with the use of vernacular languages in education published in Paris in 1953, UNESCO defined a lingua franca as 'a language which is used habitually by people whose mother tongues are different in order to facilitate communication between them.' A variety of other terms can be found which describe much the same phenomenon. Samarin (1968, p. 661) lists four: a *trade language* (e.g., Hausa in West Africa or Swahili in East Africa); a *contact language* (e.g., Greek koiné in the Ancient World); an *international language* (e.g., English throughout much of our contemporary world); and an *auxiliary language* (e.g., Esperanto or Basic English). They usually develop as a consequence of population migration (forced or voluntary) or for purposes of trade. Still another kind of lingua franca is a *mixed language*. Bakker (1997) describes one such language, Michif, a mixture of Cree and French spoken mainly in Canada by well under a thousand people of *métis* (aboriginal and French) ancestry. Michif is sometimes characterized as a language that mixes Cree verbs and French nouns but probably more accurately is one that uses Cree grammar and French vocabulary. It is a clear marker of group identity for those who use it and emerged to express 'a new ethnic identity, mixed Cree and French. A new language was needed to express that identity. The most obvious way to form a new language was through mixing the two community languages, Cree and French' (Bakker and Papen,

1997, p. 355). Winford (2003, p. 206) adds that the Michif are an example of 'newly emerged social groups who wanted a language of their own . . . [and] who saw themselves as distinct from either of the cultural groups from which they descended.'

At one time or another, Greek koiné and Vulgar Latin were in widespread use as lingua francas in the Mediterranean world and much of Europe. Sabir was a lingua franca of the Mediterranean (and later far beyond); originating in the Middle Ages and dating back at least to the Crusades, it survived into the twentieth century. In other parts of the world Arabic, Mandarin, Hindi, and Swahili have served, or do serve, as lingua francas. Of these, Arabic was a lingua franca associated with the spread of Islam. Today, English is used in very many places and for very many purposes as a lingua franca, e.g., in travel and often in trade, commerce, and international relations (see pp. 379–80).

A lingua franca can be spoken in a variety of ways. Although both Greek koiné and Vulgar Latin served at different times as lingua francas in the Ancient World, neither was a homogeneous entity. Not only were they spoken differently in different places, but individual speakers varied widely in their ability to use the languages. English serves today as a lingua franca in many parts of the world: for some speakers it is a native language, for others a second language, and for still others a foreign language. However, in the last two categories abilities in the language may vary widely from native-like to knowledge of only some bare rudiments. This is certainly the case in India, where even though Hindi is the official language, English, spoken in all kinds of ways, is widely used as a lingua franca. Swahili is a lingua franca of East Africa. On the coast it has long been spoken as a native language. As Swahili spread inland in Tanzania, it was simplified in structure, and even further inland, in Zaïre, it underwent still further simplification. Such simplification was also accompanied by a reduction in function, i.e., the simplified varieties were not used for as many purposes as the fuller variety of the coast. In rural northern parts of Zaïre even more simplification resulted so that the Swahili spoken there became virtually unintelligible to coastal residents. While the existence of this variety demonstrates that Swahili was being used as a lingua franca, what many people were actually using was a pidginized form, Zaïre Pidgin Swahili. In this respect, those who used that variety were not unlike many today who use English as a lingua franca: they use local pidginized versions of English, not Standard English. Today, that Zaïre Pidgin English has become a creole, Restructured Swahili, and it is considerably different from the Swahili of the coast (see Holm, 1989, pp. 564–7).

In North America, Chinook Jargon was used extensively as a lingua franca among native peoples of the northwest, from British Columbia into Alaska, during the second half of the nineteenth century. ('Jargon' is one of the original derogatory terms for a pidgin.) Speakers of English and French also learned it. Today Chinook Jargon is virtually extinct. Its vocabulary came from various sources: principally, Nootka, Chinook, Chehalis (all Amerindian languages), French, and English. The sound system tended to vary according to the native language of whoever spoke Chinook Jargon. The grammar, ostensibly Chinook, was extremely reduced so that it is really quite difficult to say with conviction that it is more Chinook than anything else. Even though today hardly anyone can use Chinook Jargon, a few words from it have achieved limited use in English: e.g., *potlach* ('lavish gift-giving'), *cheechako* ('greenhorn'), and possibly *high mucky-muck* ('arrogant official') (see Taylor, 1981). There is an interesting distributional relationship between Chinook Jargon and another lingua franca used widely by native peoples, Plains Sign Language: Chinook Jargon is basically a coastal phenomenon and Plains Sign Language an interior one on the plateau. Hymes (1980, pp. 416–17) has observed that we do not know why the plateau developed a sign language and the coast a jargon. Perhaps the reason was slavery or the amount of slavery. The Chinook held slaves in considerable numbers, mostly obtained by purchases from surrounding peoples, but also secondarily through raiding parties. It seems likely that the slaves learned a reduced form of Chinook and that this reduced form was used between them and their owners. As we will see, it is in observations such as these that we may find clues as to the origin and spread of pidgins and creoles and come to realize how important social factors have been in their development.

Discussion

1. A particularly interesting lingua franca is Plains Sign Language used by aboriginal peoples in North America (see Taylor, 1981, for a description of this and other aboriginal lingua francas). Try to find out in what ways Plains Sign Language must be distinguished from American Sign Language, i.e., the communication system that many deaf people use.
2. Esperanto and Basic English have both been proposed for use as auxiliary languages, i.e., as lingua francas. What advantages are claimed for each? Do you see any disadvantages? (There are numerous other proposals for auxiliary languages, so you might care to extend your inquiry to these too.)

Definitions

A *pidgin* is a language with no native speakers: it is no one's first language but is a *contact language*. That is, it is the product of a multilingual situation in which those who wish to communicate must find or improvise a simple language system that will enable them to do so. Very often too, that situation is one in which there is an imbalance of power among the languages as the speakers of one language dominate the speakers of the other languages economically and socially. A highly codified language often accompanies that dominant position. A pidgin is therefore sometimes regarded as a 'reduced' variety of a 'normal' language, i.e., one of the aforementioned dominant languages, with simplification of the grammar and vocabulary of that language, considerable phonological variation, and an admixture of local vocabulary to meet the special needs of the contact group. Holm (1988, pp. 4–5) defines a pidgin as:

a reduced language that results from extended contact between groups of people with no language in common; it evolves when they need some means of verbal communication, perhaps for trade, but no group learns the native language of any other group for social reasons that may include lack of trust or of close contact.

The process of pidginization probably requires a situation that involves at least three languages (Whinnom, 1971), one of which is clearly dominant over the others. If only two languages are involved, there is likely to be a direct struggle for dominance, as between English and French in England after 1066, a struggle won in that case by the socially inferior language but only after more than two centuries of co-existence. When three or more languages are involved and one is dominant, the speakers of the two or more that are inferior appear to play a critical role in the development of a pidgin. They must not only speak to those who are in the dominant position, but they must also speak to each other. To do this, they must simplify the dominant language in certain ways, and this process of simplification may or may not have certain universal characteristics. We may argue, therefore, that a pidgin arises from the simplification of a language when that language comes to dominate groups of speakers separated from each other by language differences. This hypothesis partially explains not only the origin of pidgins in slave societies, in which the slaves were deliberately drawn from a variety of language backgrounds, but also their origin on sea coasts, where a variety of languages might be spoken but the language of trade is a pidgin. It also helps to explain why pidginized varieties of languages are used much more as lingua francas by people who cannot speak the corresponding standard languages than they are used between such people and speakers of the standard varieties. For example, Pidgin Chinese English was used mainly by speakers of different Chinese languages, and Tok Pisin is today used as a unifying language among speakers of many different languages in Papua New Guinea.

A common view of a pidginized variety of a language, for example, Nigerian Pidgin English, is that it is some kind of 'bad' English, that is, English imperfectly learned and therefore of no possible interest. Consequently, those who speak a pidgin are likely to be regarded as deficient in some way, almost certainly socially and culturally, and sometimes even cognitively. Such a view is quite untenable. Pidgins are not a kind of 'baby-talk' used among adults because the simplified forms are the best that such people can manage. Pidgins have their own special rules, and, as we will see, very different pidgins have a number of similarities that raise important theoretical issues having to do with their origin. Individual pidgins may be ephemeral, e.g., the pidgin German of the *Gastarbeiters* ('guest-workers') in Germany that developed in the 1970s and 1980s in cities such as Berlin and Frankfurt among workers from countries such as Turkey, Greece, Italy, Spain, and Portugal. The phenomenon, however, is persistent and between 2 and 12 million people in the world are estimated to use one or other of them. Furthermore, they are used for matters which are very important to those concerned, even self-government in Papua New Guinea. They are highly functional in the lives of those who use them and are important for that reason alone if for no other.

In contrast to a pidgin, a *creole* is often defined as a pidgin that has become the first language of a new generation of speakers. As Aitchison (1994, p. 3177) says, 'creoles arise when pidgins become mother tongues.' A creole, therefore, is a 'normal' language in almost every sense. Holmes (1992, p. 95) says that 'A creole is a pidgin which has expanded in structure and vocabulary to express the range of meanings and serve the range of functions required of a first language.' In practice it is not always easy to say whether we have a pidgin rather than a creole. Tok Pisin and some of the West African pidgins such as Nigerian Pidgin English probably exist as both pidgins and creoles. They have speakers who use them only as second languages in an expanded form and also speakers for whom they are first languages. Such expanded varieties are often characteristic of urban environments in which there is likely to be considerable contact among speakers of different languages and are sometimes referred to as extended pidgins. Winford (2003, p. 307) says that 'creoles constitute a motley assortment of contact vernaculars with different histories and lines of development, though of course they still have much in common . . . [and] there are no structural characteristics that all creoles share . . . [and] no structural criteria that can distinguish creoles from other types of language.'

Just like a pidgin, a creole has no simple relationship to the usually standardized language with which it is associated. If a variety of pidgin English has a complex relationship to Standard English, so Haitian Creole, which is French-based, has a complex relationship to Standard French. As we will see, the latter relationship is quite different in still another way from the relationship between Jamaican Creole, which is English-based, and Standard English. However, speakers of creoles, like speakers of pidgins, may well feel that they speak something less than normal languages because of the way they and others view those languages when they compare them with languages such as French and English. The result is that the many millions of people who speak almost nothing but creole languages – the estimates range from a low of 6–7 million to as many as 10–17 million – are likely to feel a great sense of inferiority about their languages. In fact, as mentioned above, it was only very recently that linguists themselves – those who try to be most objective and least oriented toward making value judgments on linguistic matters – have found creoles worthy of serious scholarly attention.

If we look at the actual processes involved in *pidginization* and *creolization*, we can see that they are almost diametrically opposed to each other in certain important ways. Pidginization generally involves some kind of 'simplification' of a language, e.g., reduction in morphology (word structure) and syntax (grammatical structure), tolerance of considerable phonological variation (pronunciation), reduction in the number of functions for which the pidgin is used (e.g., you usually do not attempt to write novels in a pidgin), and extensive borrowing of words from local mother tongues. Winford (2003, p. 302) points out that 'pidginization is really a complex combination of different processes of change, including reduction and simplification of input materials, internal innovation, and regularization of structure, with L1 influence also playing a role.' On the other hand, creolization involves expansion of the morphology and syntax, regularization of the phonology, deliberate increase in the number of functions in which the language is used, and development of a rational and stable system for increasing vocabulary. But even though the processes are different, it is still not always clear whether we are talking about a pidgin, an expanded pidgin, or a creole in a certain situation. For example, the terms *Hawaiian Pidgin English* and *Hawaiian Creole English* may be used by even the same creolist (Bickerton, 1977, 1983) to describe the same variety. Likewise, Tok Pisin is sometimes called a pidgin and sometimes a creole. In the absence of evidence for the existence of initial pidgins, Caribbean creoles such as Haitian Creole may also have come into existence through abrupt creolization, new languages created in as little as two generations. Mauritian creole may be another example. Creolists do unite about one important matter. They 'generally accept that creole formation was primarily a process of second language acquisition in rather unusual circumstances. Moreover, children may have played a role in regularizing the developing grammar' (Winford, 2003, p. 356).

Within pidgin and creole studies there is actually some controversy concerning the terms *pidginization* and *creolization*. Winford (1997a) has pointed out that these terms cover a wide variety of phenomena that are not well understood. He suggests *pidgin formation* and *creole formation* as alternatives so that investigators would focus on the specific linguistic inputs and processes that are involved: 'we should be asking ourselves . . . which kinds of linguistic processes and change are common to all . . . contact situations and which are not, and how we can formulate frameworks to account for both the similarities and differences in the types of restructuring found in each case' (p. 138). Thomason (2001) acknowledges that pidgins and creoles arise from contact between and among languages but stresses how varied these types of contact are so that they may well resist efforts to analyze, explain, or classify the language varieties that emerge.

Recognizing how difficult it is to achieve agreement on what exactly constitutes pidgins and creoles, DeCamp (1977, pp. 4–5) has offered descriptions of what he regards as 'clear-cut' examples of one of each of these. He says that:

> Everyone would agree that the Juba Arabic spoken in the southern Sudan is a pidgin. In most communities it is not the native language of any of its speakers but functions as an auxiliary interlingua for communication between speakers of the many mutually unintelligible languages spoken in that region. It is a new language, only about a hundred years old. It has a small vocabulary, limited to the needs of trade and other interlingual communication, but this restricted vocabulary is supplemented, whenever the need arises, by using words from the various native languages or from normal Arabic. It has a very simple phonology with few morphophonemic processes. The complicated morphological system of Arabic (which includes, for example, suffixes on the verb to indicate tense, negation, and the person, number, and gender of both the subject and the direct and indirect objects) has been almost entirely eliminated. Such grammatical information is indicated by word order, by separate uninflected pronouns or auxiliaries, or else is simply missing. Yet Juba Arabic is a relatively stable language in its own right, with its own structure, not just half-learned or baby-talk Arabic. It is easier for an Arabic speaker to learn than for an English speaker, but the Arabic speaker still must learn it as a foreign language; he cannot simply improvise it.
>
> Similarly, everyone agrees that the vernacular language of Haiti is a creole. It is the native language of nearly all Haitians, though standard French is also spoken by some people and is the official language, and one also hears many varieties

intermediate between the standard and the creole. Historically it probably evolved from pidginized varieties of French at the time when these began to be acquired as a native language. Because it is a native language and must perform a wide range of communicative and expressive functions, it has an extensive vocabulary and complex grammatical system comparable to that of a so-called normal language. In fact, scholars disagree on whether there are any formal characteristics by which we could identify Haitian as a creole if we did not know its history. Although its vocabulary is largely French, the phonology and syntax are so different that most varieties are mutually unintelligible with standard French. In some ways its grammatical structure is more similar to creole Portuguese, creole Spanish, and even to creole English than to standard French, and most creolists object to calling it a dialect of French.

These two descriptions succinctly describe most of the defining features of pidgins and creoles. I will turn to some of these features in more detail in the following section and discuss some of the implications of others in succeeding sections.

Discussion

1. If someone told you that pidginized varieties of a language are 'corrupt' and 'ungrammatical,' and indicated that their speakers are either 'lazy' or 'inferior,' how might you try to show that person how wrong he or she is? What kinds of evidence would you use?
2. The 'stripped-down' nature of pidgins has led them to being called 'reduced' or 'minimal' languages. They have even been compared to forms of 'baby-talk.' A different view is that they are 'optimal' communication systems, perfectly appropriate to the circumstances of their use. Do you see any merit in this latter view?
3. While there is little dispute about the origin of the term 'creole' when used to describe a type of language, there is some dispute about the origin of the term 'pidgin.' What can you find out about the origins of the two terms, particularly about the origin of the latter? (See especially Todd, 1990, pp. 22–4, Romaine, 1988, pp. 12–13, and Aitchison, 1994, p. 3177.)

Distribution and Characteristics

Pidgin and creole languages are distributed mainly, though not exclusively, in the equatorial belt around the world, usually in places with direct or easy access to the oceans. Consequently, they are found mainly in the Caribbean and around the north and east coasts of South America, around the coasts of Africa, particularly the west coast, and across the Indian and Pacific Oceans. They are fairly uncommon in the more extreme northern and southern areas of the world and in the interiors of continents. Their distribution appears to be fairly closely related to long-standing patterns of trade, including trade in slaves. A basic source on their distribution is Hancock (1977), a survey that was intended to list each language that had been treated as either a pidgin or a creole whether or not Hancock himself agreed with the classification. The list includes Maltese and Hindi for example, languages which Hancock believes should not be included. More recently Holm (1989) provides a useful survey of pidgins and creoles, and Smith (1995) lists 351 pidgins and creoles along with 158 assorted mixed languages.

Hancock lists 127 pidgins and creoles. Thirty-five of these are English-based. These include such languages as Hawaiian Creole, Gullah or Sea Islands Creole (spoken on the islands off the coasts of northern Florida, Georgia, and South Carolina), Jamaican Creole, Guyana Creole, Krio (spoken in Sierra Leone), Sranan and Djuka (spoken in Suriname), Cameroon Pidgin English, Tok Pisin, and Chinese Pidgin English (now virtually extinct). Another fifteen are French-based, e.g., Louisiana Creole, Haitian Creole, Seychelles Creole, and Mauritian Creole. Unlike English-based creoles, French-based creoles (both Caribbean and Pacific varieties) are mutually intelligible. Fourteen others are Portuguese-based, e.g., Papiamentu (used in Aruba, Bonaire, and Curaçao), Guiné Creole, Senegal Creole, and Saramaccan (spoken in Suriname); seven are Spanish-based, e.g., Cocoliche (spoken by Italian immigrants in Buenos Aires); five are Dutch-based, e.g., US Virgin Islands Dutch Creole (or Negerhollands), now virtually extinct, and Afrikaans (here said to have been creolized in the seventeenth century); three are Italian-based, e.g., Asmara Pidgin (spoken in parts of Ethiopia); six are German-based, e.g., Yiddish and whatever still remains of Gastarbeiter Deutsch; and the rest are based on a variety of other languages, e.g., Russenorsk (a Russian–Norwegian contact language, now extinct), Chinook Jargon (a virtually extinct contact language of the Pacific Northwest of the United States and Canada), Sango (extensively used in the Central African Republic), various pidginized forms of Swahili (a Bantu language) used widely in East Africa, and varieties of Hindi, Bazaar Malay (a variety of Malay in widespread use throughout Malaysia, Singapore, and Indonesia), and Arabic. Of the one hundred-plus attested living pidgins and creoles, the majority are based on one or other of the European languages, but several, e.g., Chinook Jargon and Sango, show little or no contact with a European language. We will see that this lack of contact is an important factor when considering the possible origins of pidgins and creoles or attempting to form hypotheses to account for their various shared characteristics.

The Caribbean area is of particular interest to creolists because of the many varieties of language found there. There are countries or areas that are almost exclusively Spanish-speaking and have no surviving pidgins or creoles as a result of their settlement histories, e.g., the Dominican Republic, Cuba, and Puerto Rico. Others have only English-based creoles, e.g., Antigua, Barbados, Grenada, Jamaica, and Guyana. Still others have only French-based ones, e.g., Martinique, Guadeloupe, St Lucia, and Haiti. Some have both, e.g., Dominica and Trinidad. Aruba, Bonaire, and Curaçao have Portuguese-based creoles, and one, the US Virgin Islands, has a virtually extinct Dutch-based creole. The official language in each case can be quite different: it is English in all of the above except Martinique, Guadeloupe, and Haiti, where it is French, and Aruba, Bonaire, and Curaçao, where it is Dutch. In the southern United States, there are different versions of French in Louisiana (Louisiana Creole, the Cajun French of Acadians from Nova Scotia, and even a very little Standard French), Gullah, and possibly the variety of English now usually referred to as African American Vernacular English (see pp. 342–5).

Suriname, the former Dutch Guiana, a country on the northeast coast of South America, is particularly interesting linguistically. The official language of Suriname is Dutch, but that language is the native tongue of less than 2 percent of the population. However, two English-based creoles, Sranan and Djuka, are spoken. Sranan, spoken in the coastal areas, is said to be a 'conservative' English creole that bears little resemblance any more to English. Inland, Djuka, the most important of a group of creoles known collectively as 'Bush Negro,' is descended from a pidginized variety of English used by runaway slaves. It is a creole, but it is also found in pidginized varieties among the native Indians of the interior of Suriname for whom it has become a lingua franca. Also found in inland Suriname is another creole, Saramaccan, which is sometimes regarded as Portuguese-based and sometimes as English-based. It seems to have been undergoing a process which we will refer to as *relexification* (see pp. 76–7), when those who spoke it were cut off from contact with England after England ceded the colony to Holland in 1667.

The language distribution of this whole Caribbean area reflects its social and political history. That is the only way you can explain why a French-based creole is spoken in St Lucia, which now has English as its official language; why the former island of Hispaniola contains both the Spanish-speaking Dominican Republic and the French-creole-speaking Haiti; why the people of Dutch Curaçao speak Papiamentu, which is a Portuguese-based creole (or perhaps Portuguese with a little Spanish, there being some controversy on this matter); and why Suriname, officially Dutch-speaking, has two (or perhaps three) English-based creoles.

Other parts of the world are no less complicated linguistically. Sierra Leone has both pidginized and creolized Englishes. The pidgin is West African Pidgin English, widely used as a trading language in West Africa and to that extent indigenous to the country. The creole, Krio, is found in and around the capital, Freetown, and appears to have originated among the slaves who returned to Africa from Jamaica and Britain. It is not a creolized version of West African Pidgin English. In addition, Standard English is spoken in Freetown but with two norms, one deriving from the British Isles and the other locally based. Consequently, it is possible in Freetown to hear even the simplest of propositions expressed in a variety of ways according to who is speaking and the occasion: Standard (British) English, Standard Sierra Leone English, Krio, and West African Pidgin English.

In describing the linguistic characteristics of a pidgin or creole it is difficult to resist the temptation to compare it with the standard language with which it is associated. In certain circumstances such a comparison may make good sense, as in the linguistic situations in Jamaica and Guyana; in others, however, it seems to make little sense, as in Haiti. In the brief discussion that follows some such comparisons will be made, but they are not meant to be invidious to the pidgin or creole. Each pidgin or creole is a well-organized linguistic system and must be treated as such: you cannot speak Tok Pisin by just 'simplifying' English quite arbitrarily: you will be virtually incomprehensible to those who actually do speak it, nor will you comprehend them. You will instead be using

Tok Masta, a term used by Papua New Guineans to describe the attempt which certain anglophones make to speak Tok Pisin. To use Tok Pisin properly you have to learn it, just as you must learn German or Chinese in order to speak these languages properly; you might find Tok Pisin easier to learn than those two languages, but that is another matter, something of the same order as being likely to find German easier to learn than Chinese.

The sounds of a pidgin or creole are likely to be fewer and less complicated in their possible arrangements than those of the corresponding standard language. For example, Tok Pisin makes use of only five basic vowels and also has fewer consonants than English. No contrast is possible between words like *it* and *eat*, or *pin* and *fin*, or *sip*, *ship*, and *chip*: the necessary vowel and consonant distinctions (contrasts) are not present. Speakers of Tok Pisin distinguish a ship from a sheep by calling the first a *sip* and the second a *sipsip*. It is also because of the lack of the /p/–/f/ distinction that some written versions of Tok Pisin record certain words with *p* spellings, whereas others record the same words with *f* spellings. So far as speakers of Tok Pisin are concerned, it does not make any difference if you say *wanpela* or *wanfela* ('one'); you will be judged to have said the words in the same way, any difference being no more important to speakers of Tok Pisin than the difference to us between typical North American and British English pronunciations of the middle consonant sound in *butter*. While the numbers of sounds used in pidgins and creoles may be smaller than in the corresponding standard languages, they also tend to 'vary' more as to their precise quality.

One additional point is worth stressing. A language like English often has complicated phonological relationships between words (or *morphemes*, the small bits of meaning in words) that are closely related, e.g., the first vowel in *type* and *typical*, the *c* in *space* and *spacious*, and the different sounds of the 'plural' ending in *cats, dogs*, and *boxes*. The technical term for this is *morphophonemic variation*. Such variation is not found in pidgins, but the development of such variation may be one characteristic of *creolization*, the process by which a pidgin becomes a creole.

In pidgins and creoles there is likely to be a complete lack of inflection in nouns, pronouns, verbs, and adjectives. Nouns are not marked for number and gender, and verbs lack tense markers. Transitive verbs, that is, verbs that take objects, may, however, be distinguished from intransitive verbs, that is, those that do not take objects, by being marked, e.g., by a final *-im* in Tok Pisin. Pronouns will not be distinguished for case, so there will be no *I–me, he–him* alternations. In Tok Pisin *me* is either 'I' or 'me.' The equivalent of 'we' is either *mipela* ('I and other(s) but not you') or *yumi* ('I and you'). *Yu* is different from *yupela* ('singular' versus 'plural'), and *em* ('he,' 'she,' or 'it') is distinguished from *ol* ('they' or 'them'). In Tok Pisin there are few required special endings on words, and two of these are actually homophones: *-pela*, a suffix on adjectives, as in *wanpela man* ('one man'), and *-pela*, a plural suffix on pronouns, as in *yupela* ('you plural'). Another is *-im*, the transitive suffix marker on verbs that is mentioned above.

We should not be surprised that there is such a complete reduction of inflection in pidgins. Differences like *one book–two books, he bakes–he baked*, and *big–*

bigger are quite expendable. No one seems to have any interest in maintaining them, and alternative ways are found to express the same concepts of number, time, and comparison. In contrast, we should note how important inflectional endings and changes are in a language like English, particularly irregular ones such as *go–went*, *good–better*, and *drink, drank, drunk*. They are used as one of the indicators of regional and social origin. Which set of inflections you acquire is almost entirely an accident of birth, but if it is not the socially preferred set the accident can prove to be a costly one. Pidgins do comfortably without inflections, but it is not surprising that some people view their absence as a sign of deficiency and inferiority in both languages and speakers in much the same way as they view acquisition of a set which is dispreferred.

Syntactically, sentences are likely to be uncomplicated in clausal structure. The development of embedded clauses, e.g., of relative clauses, is one characteristic of the process of creolization: pidgins do not have such embedding. The use of particles, that is, usually small isolated words, is also quite frequent. Negation may be achieved through use of a simple negative particle *no* in the English-based Krio, e.g., *i no tu had* ('It's not too hard') and *pa* in the French-based Seychelles Creole, e.g., *i pa tro difisil* ('It's not too difficult'). One particularly interesting feature is the use of pre-verbal particles to show that an action is continuing, i.e., to show 'continuous aspect.' We can see this in the use of *de, ape*, and *ka* in the following examples taken respectively from English, French, and Portuguese creoles: *a de go wok* ('I'm going to work' in Krio); *mo ape travaj* ('I'm working' in Louisiana French); and *e ka nda* ('He's going' in St Thomas). What we can see from even these few examples is that creoles associated with quite different standard languages apparently use identical syntactic devices. This phenomenon has intrigued many creolists and, as we will see in the following section, has led to the formulation of certain hypotheses about the origins of pidgins and creoles.

The vocabulary of a pidgin or a creole has a great many similarities to that of the standard language with which it is associated. However, it will be much more limited, and phonological and morphological simplification often leads to words assuming somewhat different shapes. As noted above in the example of *sip* and *sipsip*, it is sometimes necessary to use this *reduplicative* pattern to avoid possible confusion or to express certain concepts, e.g., 'repetition' or 'intensification.' Consequently, we find pairs like *talk* ('talk') and *talktalk* ('chatter'), *dry* ('dry') and *drydry* ('unpalatable'), *look* ('look') and *looklook* ('stare'), *cry* ('cry') and *crycry* ('cry continually'), *pis* ('peace') and *pispis* ('urinate'), and *san* ('sun') and *sansan* ('sand'). Certain concepts require a somewhat elaborate encoding: for example, in Tok Pisin 'hair' is *gras bilong het*, 'beard' is *gras bilong fes*, 'feathers' is *gras bilong pisin*, 'moustache' is *gras bilong maus*, 'my car' is *ka bilong me*, and 'bird's wing' is *han bilong pisin*. A pidgin or creole may draw on the vocabulary resources of more than one language. Tok Pisin draws primarily from English but also from Polynesian sources, e.g., *kaikai* ('food'), and even German, because of historical reasons, e.g., *rausim* ('throw out' from the German *heraus*, 'outside'). The source may not always be a 'polite' one, e.g., Tok Pisin *bagarap* ('break down') is from the English *bugger up*. So *ka bilong mi i bagarap* is 'My car broke down.' In examples like *pikinini man* ('boy' or 'son'), *pikinini meri* ('girl' or 'daughter'), *pikinini dok* ('puppy'), and *pikinini pik* ('piglet'), we can see not only the process of showing 'diminutives' through this use of *pikinini* but also a connection to the Portuguese word *pequeño* ('little'). In the Caribbean varieties, there is also often a noticeable African element in the vocabulary (e.g., see Turner, 1949, on Gullah). Still another source of vacabulary will be innovation. A good example from Winford (2003, p. 322) is '*as* (< Engl. *arse*) means not just "buttock," but also "cause, foundation." Similarly, *bel* means not just "belly," but also "seat of the emotions".'

Discussion

1. Pidgins and creoles have been said to have 'the grammar of one language and the vocabulary of another.' In what sense is such a statement true, false, or a bit of both?

2. Examine the following example of British Solomon Islands Pidgin (from Trudgill, 1995, p. 158) with its English gloss. Describe as many of its grammatical features as you can.

    > Mifɛlə i-go go lɔŋ sɔlwater, lʊkautɪm fɪš, nau wɪn i-kəm. Nau mifɛlə i-go ɔləbaut lɔŋ kinú, nau bɪgfɛlə wɪn i-kəm nau, mifɛlə i-fafasi ɔləbautə, rɔŋ tuməs.

    > We kept going on the sea, hunting for fish, and a wind arose. Now we were going in canoes, and an immense wind arose now, and we were thrown around and were moving very fast.

3. Mühlhäusler (1982, pp. 462–3) offers the following two versions of Mark 5: 1–5, one in Tok Pisin and the other in Solomon Islands Pidgin. (On p. 463 he gives a third version in New Hebrides (now Vanuatu) Bichelamar.) Compare these versions to each other and to the original. According to Mühlhäusler it takes a speaker of the Solomon Islands variety about three months to master Tok Pisin. What kinds of differences appear to account for this?

    ### Tok Pisin

    > Ol i kamap long hapsait bilong raunwara, long graun bilong ol Gerasa. Em i lusim bot pinis, na kwiktaim wanpela man i gat spirit doti i stap long en, em i kam painim Jisas. Dispela man i stap nabaut long ples matmat na i kam. Em i save slip long ples matmat. Na i no gat wanpela man inap long pasim em. Sen tu i no inap. Planti taim ol i bin pasim em long hankap na sen. Tasol em i save brukim sen na hankap tu. Em i strongpela tumas, na i no gat man inap long holim pas em. Oltaim long san na long nait em i stap long matmat na long maunten. Na em i save singaut nogut na katim skin bilong em yet long ston. [*Tok Pisin Nupela Testamen*, Canberra and Port Moresby: The British and Foreign Bible Society, 1969]

    ### Solomon Islands Pidgin English

    > Bihaen olketa i go long narasaet long big wata Galili. Desfala haf ia olketa i go soa long hem, i haf bulong oketa pipol long Gerasa. Steretwe taem Jisas

i go soa, wanfala man wea i stap long berigiraon i kamaot fo mitim hem. Desfala man ia devol nogud i stap long hem. Ples bulong hem nao long berigiraon. Bikos hem i karangge tumas, no man i save taemapim. Plande taem olketa i hankapem han an lek bulong hem, bat hem i smasing olgeta nomoa. No man i storong fitim fo holem. De an naet hem i no save stap kwait. Hem i waka long go olabaot long melewan berigiraon an olketa hil. Hem i waka tu long singaot karangge an katem bodi bulong hem wetem ston. [From an unpublished translation by T. Faifu under the auspices of the Roman Catholic, Anglican, and United and South Seas Evangelical Church]

4. The Nigerian writer Chinua Achebe uses local varieties of English in his novels. The following extract is from *A Man of the People* (1975a, pp. 14–15). What characteristics of pidgins and creoles do you find in it?

> The same man who had drawn our attention to the Minister's humility was now pointing out yet another quality. I looked at him closely for the first time and noticed that he had one bad eye – what we call a cowrie-shell eye.
> 'You see how e de do as if to say money be san-san,' he was saying. 'People wey de jealous the money gorment de pay Minister no sabi say no be him one de chop am. Na so so troway.'
> Later on in the Proprietor's Lodge I said to the Minister: 'You must have spent a fortune today.'
> He smiled at the glass of cold beer in his hand and said:
> 'You call this spend? You never see some thing, my brother. I no de keep anini for myself, na so so troway. If some person come to you and say "I wan' make you Minister" make you run like blazes comot. Na true word I tell you. To God who made me.' He showed the tip of his tongue to the sky to confirm the oath. 'Minister de sweet for eye but too much katakata de for inside. Believe me yours sincerely.'
> 'Big man, big palaver,' said the one-eyed man.
> It was left to Josiah, owner of a nearby shop-and-bar to sound a discordant, if jovial, note.
> 'Me one,' he said, 'I no kuku mind the katakata wey de for inside. Make you put Minister money for my hand and all the wahala on top. I no mind at all.'
> Everyone laughed. Then Mrs John said:
> 'No be so, my frien'. When you done experience rich man's trouble you no fit talk like that again. My people get one proverb: they say that when poor man done see with him own eye how to make big man e go beg make e carry him poverty de go je-je.'

5. Hall (1966, p. 157) cites the following utterances from the French-based Dominican Creole (from Taylor, 1951a). He employs a *phonemic* (i.e., broad phonetic) writing system. What parts of the creole are French, and what are not? Would the use of a spelling system based on Standard French (rather than this kind of spelling) make these sentences easier to comprehend, or would it suggest similarities that are not really there? What might such a spelling look like in this case? You might compare responses of people who know some French with those who do not in answering the preceding questions.

mun sot.	People [are] stupid.
nu fē.	We [are] hungry.
u pa-las sottiz.	You [are] not tired [of] stupidity.
per esit.	[The] priest [is] here.
u se-madam li.	You are his wife.
ri duvā plere deyer.	Laughter ahead, weeping behind.
parol ā-buš pa-šay.	Words in [the] mouth [are] not [a] load [*that is*, Fine talk is no guarantee of deeds or intentions].
nu gade jo.	We looked at them.
jo gade nu.	They looked at us.
pa-pale sot.	Don't talk nonsense!
žordi mwē malad.	Today I [am] sick.
i-pa-ākor malad āpil.	He (she) [is] not yet very sick.
i-pa malad āpil ākor.	He (she) [is] no longer very sick.
i-ramase jo a-ter.	He picked them up off [the] ground.
mwē ba žanin sēk predjal pu-i-gāje pē ba mwē.	I gave Jeannine five 'predials' [15 cents] for her [to] buy bread for me.
ba mwē i vit.	Give it to me quickly.
u ža di mwē listwer sa.	You already told me that story.
jo vini esit kote mwē.	They came here beside me.
es jo maše?	[Did] they walk? [Have] they walked?
puci u pa-vini ā-travaj ijer?	Why didn't you come to work yesterday?
mwē te-ni mal dā.	I had tooth-ache.
se-su u te-su.	It's drunk you were!
nu prā šimē par bwa, se-la solej kuše nu.	We took [the] path by [the] woods, it's there [the] sun laid us [down] [*that is*, It's there darkness overtook us].
šjē epi šat pa-ka-dakor.	Dogs and cats don't agree.
tu-le-žu kalbas kaj laivjer, jō, i-ni pu-rete la.	Every day [a, the] calabash goes [to the] river, one day it has to remain there.

6. Webster (1960) cites the following as an example of Korean Bamboo English, a pidginized variety of English that flourished for a brief while during the Korean War in the early 1950s. He cautions as follows (p. 261): 'I would surmise it was written by a relatively sophisticated soldier,' and 'is a good bit more fluent than the general speech used in talking to Koreans.' Is this a typical pidgin? (Certain words are glossed for you.)

The Story of Cinderella-San

Taksan years ago, skoshi [little] Cinderella-san lived in hootchie [house] with sisters, poor little Cinderella-san ketchee no fun, have-no social life. Always washee-washee, scrubee-scrubee, make chop-chop [food]. One day Cinderella-san sisters ketchee post cardo from Seoul. Post cardo speakie so: one prince-san have big blowout, taksan [big] kimchi [Korean food], taksan beeru, play 'She Ain't Go No Yo Yo.' Cindy-san sisters taksan excited, make Cinderella-san police up clothes.

Sisters go blackmarket, ketchee fatigues, new combat boots, bring to hootchie and Cinderella-san cut down fatigues, shine-shine boots. Come night of big shindig, sisters speak sayonara, leave Cindy-san by fire.

Eiiiii . . . is appearing fairy Godmother-san. She speak: 'Cindy-san, worry hava-no, I ketchee you number one outfit and you go to hoedown number one prince.' Godmother-san speak Cindy-san ketchee one mouse and one mouse-trap. Godmother-san waving wand and mousetrap and mouse becoming streamlined oxcart. Then wave wand again one time and old rubber shoes changee into polished Corcoran jump boots. 'Meda-meda [look],' say Cindy-san. 'Number one.'

'One thing, kiddee,' speak fairy Godmother-san, 'knock it off by 2400. I gotta get these clothes back to QM warehouse.'

'Hokay,' speak Cindy-san, taksan happy, and rush off to Seoul to hootchie of number one prince. Cindy-san ketchee big hit at barn dance. All rest jo-sans [girls] bags by Cindy-san. Number one prince is on make, ketchee beeru and Spam sandwiches for Cindy-san and dance to 'I Ain't Got No Yo Yo' eight times.

Suddenly clock starts to strike 2400. Cindy-san has skoshi time, can speak only sayonara to number one prince before chogeying [going] to oxcart pool to go home. She hubba-hubba [hurry] home but lose Corcoran jump boot. Time to stop hava-no and number one prince ketchee.

Next day big bulletin go out: Number-one prince meda-meda for jo-san who has foot to fit Corcoran jump boot, ketchee and marry, make number one jo-san in Korea.

Prince try taksan feet in boot – all time no fit. Finally come to hootchie of Cinderella-san. Sisters all shook up, sit and giggle on straw mat as prince tries on number twelve feet.

'Never hatchie,' he speak. 'Who is jo-san who do washee-washee?' Sisters laugh. 'Ugly Cinderella-san,' they speak. 'Nevah hoppen [impossible].' 'What to lose,' speak Prince. 'Edewa [come] shipsho [hurry] bali-bali [quick] ugly jo-san.'

Cindy-san grins. She ketchee five aces in this deal, all time know jump boot fit. Boot slide on skoshi foot with number one fit.

'Kid, you dai jobu [OK],' he speak. 'Come on my house, be number one princess.'

'Sayonara, old bags,' speak Cindy-san to sisters, and go home with number one prince. Taksan happy ever after.

Origins

Linguists who have studied pidgins and creoles have long been intrigued by the similarities they have found among them. Pidgins from very different parts of the world exhibit remarkable similarities in structure even when the standard languages with which they are associated are quite different. Furthermore, pidgins and creoles based on the same standard language but found in places far distant from one another may have a high degree of mutual intelligibility, e.g., the various pidginized and creolized varieties of French found geographically as far apart as the Caribbean, the Indian Ocean, and the South Pacific. How can we account for these similarities?

One theory about the origins of pidgins is easily dismissed. This is the idea that pidgins arise because the people among whom they are found lack the ability to learn the standard languages with which the pidgins are associated. Such a view may sometimes be associated with another one, that European languages are somehow 'better' than others and that many people speak 'primitive' languages, i.e., languages that are 'deficient' in certain respects. Such deficiencies may then be cited as evidence that the people themselves are inferior. We must note that linguists have been unable to locate a single such 'primitive language,' that claims about associated intellectual deficiencies are largely 'racist,' and that this theory about the origins of pidgins ignores many important facts.

There is no evidence either for any *'foreigner-talk'* or *'baby-talk'* theory (see Bloomfield, 1933, pp. 472–3) for the origin of pidgins and creoles, i.e., that they result from Europeans deliberately simplifying their languages in order to communicate with others. According to this theory, these simplified forms then serve to provide pidgins with their basic structures and vocabularies. There are too many structural similarities among pidgins and creoles associated with very different European languages to make such a theory of origin plausible, e.g., between the English-based creole of Jamaica and the French-based one of Haiti. If there is evidence of simplification, it is evidence of some very different process at work than any kind of 'talking down,' 'baby-talk,' or 'mimicry' can explain. Moreover, pidgins are far less frequently used between Europeans and non-Europeans than among non-Europeans. In fact, many Europeans who must deal regularly with pidginized varieties of their languages speak them very badly indeed, failing to understand some of the basic structural characteristics of the pidgins. Finally, there is plenty of evidence that it is Europeans who learn the pidgins from non-Europeans rather than the opposite, although the use of so much European vocabulary may tend to conceal that fact.

One theory, the theory of *polygenesis*, is that pidgins and creoles have a variety of origins; any similarities among them arise from the shared circumstances of their origins. For example, speakers of English have had to make themselves understood for the purposes of trade and those trading with them have had to be understood. Consequently, certain simplified forms of English have developed independently in a number of places, giving rise to varieties of pidgin English. Because in every case the target language is English, these local varieties will have certain similarities. In this view a 'pidgin X' or 'creolized Y' is a variety of X or Y, much as Cockney English is a variety of English. Then, more generally, since English, French, Spanish, and Portuguese are really not so different – they are all Indo-European languages – we might expect similarities. We can go even further to claim that a 'simplification' process for any language would produce much the same results everywhere: a simpler set of sounds, no inflections, basic word order patterns, short uncomplicated utterances, and so on. Various other explanations have been offered for the resulting similarities including the similar social contexts of their origin, the similar communicative needs of those who use them, and, most plausible of all, a shared *substratum*.

This last idea seems particularly appropriate to explain many similarities among the Atlantic Ocean and possibly certain Indian Ocean pidgins and creoles on the one hand and Pacific Ocean pidgins and creoles on the other. The former are said to have an African substrate and the latter an Oceanic one, i.e., each contains certain language characteristics of the native ancestral languages of their speakers. In this view Atlantic pidgins and creoles retain certain characteristics of ancestral African languages. African slaves were often multilingual, spoke languages of similar structure but different vocabulary, and tended to treat English and French, and to a lesser extent Portuguese, in the same way. Therefore, the pidgins and creoles are European-language-based and were freshly created in different places. What similarities they have they owe to this fusion of European and African components (see Holm, 1988, 2004, and Winford, 2003, pp. 16–17).

We can contrast such *polygenetic* views with *monogenetic* ones. One such view of the similarities among Atlantic pidgins and creoles requires us to examine the very beginnings of the pidginization process. For example, according to McWhorter (1995, 2000), their similarities can be accounted for if we look back to the beginnings of the slave trade and the existence of English and French slave forts on the West African Coast. In these forts contact languages developed, with the most important of these from this point of view being West African Pidgin Portuguese. These contact languages provided the bases for most of the pidgins and creoles that later developed across the Atlantic. This is his Afrogenesis hypothesis concerning origin. McWhorter points to the relative paucity of Spanish-based creoles in the New World as evidence which supports this claim as well as to the fact that such creoles are also missing from places we might expect to find them, e.g., Puerto Rico and Cuba. (The Spanish creoles that do exist, e.g., Papiamentu, are relexified (see following pages) Portuguese ones.) McWhorter points out that Spain came late to the sugar industry, did not use labor-intensive cultivation systems, sometimes took areas from Portugal, and did not have large slave forts and settlements in Africa. This view of the development of pidgins and creoles is a monogenetic view, claiming as it does that a single source accounts for the perceived similarities among the varieties we find.

Another variant of such a monogenetic theory is that the similarities among pidgins and creoles might be attributable to a common origin in the language of sailors in some kind of nautical jargon. It is a well-known fact that the crews of ships were – and sometimes still are – often drawn from a variety of sources. For example, Nelson's flagship *Victory* is said to have been crewed by sailors of fourteen different nationalities. A common shipboard lingua franca, or nautical jargon, developed among the members of the sailing community. In this view, it was that lingua franca, rather than a pidginized variety of a standard language, that was carried along the shipping routes. However, the evidence for this theory is weak, consisting of a few sea-based terms in different pidgins. Moreover, it almost completely ignores the more serious structural similarities among existing pidgins and creoles, similarities that seem to require a more profound explanation.

The theory of *relexification* is an attempt to offer such an explanation. According to this theory, all the present European-language-based pidgins and creoles derive from a single source, a lingua franca called Sabir used in the Mediterranean in the Middle Ages. In the fifteenth and sixteenth centuries the Portuguese *relexified* this language; that is, they introduced their own vocabulary into its grammatical structure, so that a Portuguese-based pidgin came into widespread use as a trade language. Later, this pidgin was in turn relexified into pidginized French, English, and Spanish. In each case the underlying grammatical structure remained largely unaffected, but a massive shift occurred in vocabulary as replacement words were imported from the *lexifier language* to produce a conspicuous *superstratum*. It is also argued that Portuguese relics still remain after relexification, e.g., *savvy* and *piccaninny* (from Portuguese *saber*, 'know,' and *pequeño*, 'little'), in English-based creoles.

Such a theory attempts to provide a serious explanation for the fact that pidgins and creoles associated with different standard languages have certain common structural features but quite different vocabularies. In this view a pidgin English is therefore an Anglicized version of the original pidgin and a pidgin French is a Gallicized version. The theory leads creolists such as Todd (1990) to go so far as to use a version of the classical comparative method of reconstruction in an attempt to show how various pidgins and creoles have descended from a Portuguese-based ancestor. Todd provides a family-tree type model (p. 37) for pidgins and creoles, which shows them originating in Sabir. Sabir then becomes Proto-Portuguese Pidgin, which in turn splits into two distinct branches, Atlantic Portuguese Pidgin and Indo-Pacific Portuguese Pidgin. The former has sub-branches with Portuguese varieties (e.g., Guiné Crioule), Hispanic varieties (e.g., Papiamentu), Anglicized varieties (e.g., Jamaican), and Gallicized ones (e.g., Louisiana, Haitian); the latter has its sub-branches too – Gallicized ones (e.g., Seychelles), Nederlandized ones (e.g., Afrikaans), and Anglicized ones (e.g., Tok Pisin).

The theory of relexification is not without its problems. One is that pidgins are so stripped down that they lack most of the features that linguists usually rely on to relate one language to another. The similarities among them are very general, and it is quite possible that some alternative theory may better explain them, e.g., some general principles of language acquisition. Relexification also asks us to believe that, in learning a language, people somehow can learn the grammar quite independently of the vocabulary and that they do indeed learn the first but completely replace the second during the process of learning. We might also expect more Portuguese to have survived.

Lefebvre (1998), after more than twenty years of study of Haitian Creole, answers some of these objections. He says (pp. 10–11) that there are important factors in the creation of a creole. Adults relexify to communicate: 'creole languages [are] created by adult speakers with a mature lexicon.' A process of dialect leveling follows, which 'operates on the variation resulting from the relexification of the various substratum lexicons,' there usually being several of these. Finally, speakers reanalyze the resulting language in 'a mental process whereby a particular form which signals one lexical entry becomes the signal of another lexical entry.' In other words relexification is the starting point of a larger process.

There is some good evidence that relexification has occurred. If we look at Saramaccan, it seems to be a pidgin in the process of relexification from Portuguese to English (hence the disagreement I noted earlier about its classification). It was 'frozen' in this intermediate, transitional stage when its speakers were cut off from England in 1667 when the colony became a Dutch possession. There is also evidence that in parts of West Africa such kinds of replacement do occur, that people know the vocabularies of different languages but use a kind of common grammar in speaking them so that when they come across a new language they employ the 'new' vocabulary in the 'old' grammatical framework and manage to make themselves understood. We could argue, however, that all we have in this case is a reintroduction of the substratum theory in a new and subtle form; in any case, such a theory seems inadequate on other grounds. There is also no apparent relexification possible for varieties such as Pitcairnese (spoken by descendants of the *Bounty* mutiny of 1790), Sango, and Chinook Jargon. At least some pidgins and creoles cannot owe their origin to this process.

One of the severest condemnations of relexification comes from Bickerton (1977, p. 62), who argues that: 'We are asked to believe that an original contact language could be disseminated round the entire tropical zone, to peoples of widely differing language background, and still preserve a virtually complete identity in its grammatical structure wherever it took root, despite considerable changes in its phonology and virtually complete changes in its lexicon.' Bickerton considers that relexification asks us to accept too many improbabilities. Instead, he offers (1981) an alternative theory to account for the similarities we find: his Language Bioprogram hypothesis.

Bickerton (1983) claims that only this hypothesis adequately explains the similarities among creoles: universal principles of first language acquisition are involved. Jespersen (1922, p. 234) had previously pointed out certain similarities between pidgins and creoles and children's language. Bickerton argues that it is better to focus on what pidgins and creoles *have* and *do* than on what they *lack*. Typically, creoles are developed by children who find themselves born into a multilingual environment in which the most important language for peer contact is a pidgin. Children are compelled to develop that language because each child has a bioprogram to develop a full language. Children use this bioprogram in the same way wherever they happen to be and the consequence is that 'the grammatical structures of creoles are more similar to one another than they are to the structures of any other language' (p. 121). Bickerton further develops this thesis, claiming that children have certain innate language abilities that they are actually forced to suppress as they learn languages like English and French. 'It [is] only in pidgin-speaking communities, where there [is] no grammatical model that could compete with the child's innate grammar, that the innate grammatical model [is] not eventually suppressed' (p. 121). It is in just these circumstances that creoles arise. Bickerton says that the essential difference between pidginization and creolization is that pidginization is second-language learning with restricted input and creolization is first-language learning, also with restricted input. There has been much discussion of Bickerton's ideas but they have found only luke-warm support; they are said to give too much weight to the role of children in the development of creoles and too little to the role of expanded pidgins, the diversity found in creoles, and the amount of time the creolization process usually requires. However, at the same time we will see in various chapters that follow that there is considerable evidence showing that children play an import-ant role in how languages change.

Discussion

1. Hall (1966, p. 122) points out that 'English has been extensively relexified, in the last thousand years, with morphemes [i.e., words and parts of words with meaning] . . . from French, Latin, and Greek; yet it is still to be clas-sified as a Germanic, not a Romance, language' because of its basic struc-tural features, which are Germanic. In what ways is this kind of relexification similar to and different from the kind discussed in this chapter?
2. Bickerton (1977, p. 49) says that, essentially, 'pidginization is second-language learning with restricted input, and . . . creolization is first-language learning with restricted input.' How valid do you think Bickerton's claim is?
3. Bickerton (1983, p. 116) claims that there is now an impressive body of evidence to support the following claim: 'between the ages of two and four the child born into a community of linguistically competent adults speaks a variety of language whose structure bears a deep resemblance to the structure of creole languages.' Assess this claim. You should consult Bickerton (1990).

From Pidgin to Creole

Whatever their origins, it is generally acknowledged that a pidgin is almost always involved in the earliest stage of a creole. The pidgin comes about from the need to communicate, particularly when those who need to communicate speak a variety of languages and the speakers of the 'target' language are 'superior' in some sense and perhaps transient too. Thus, pidginization seems to have happened – and seems still to happen – repeatedly, for it is one of the basic means by which linguistic contact is made among speakers of different lan-guages who find themselves in an asymmetrical social relationship, i.e., one in which there is a serious imbalance of power. The fact that is especially interest-ing is how similar the results are from place to place and from time to time.

Not every pidgin eventually becomes a creole, i.e., undergoes the process of creolization. In fact, very few do. Most pidgins are lingua francas, existing to meet temporary local needs. They are spoken by people who use another lan-guage or other languages to serve most of their needs and the needs of their children. If a pidgin is no longer needed, it dies out. It may also be the case that the pidgin in a particular area must constantly be 'reinvented'; there is no reason to believe, for example, that either Cameroonian Pidgin English or Hawaiian Pidgin English have had uninterrupted histories.

Creolization occurs only when a pidgin for some reason becomes the variety of language that children must use in situations in which use of a 'full' language is effectively denied them. A creole is the native language of some of its speakers. We can see how this must have happened in Haiti when French was effectively denied to the masses and the African languages brought by the slaves fell into disuse. We can also see how, while many of the guest workers in Germany developed pidginized varieties of German to communicate when necessary with one another, their children did not creolize these varieties but, with varying success, acquired Standard German, since they had to go to school and be educated in German. A full language was available to them so they had no need to creolize Gastarbeiter Deutsch.

The example of Tok Pisin is useful in considering how a pidgin expands and develops into a creole. It was not until the 1960s that the pidgin was nativized, i.e., children began to acquire it as a first language, and, therefore, becoming for them a creole (while remaining an extended pidgin for previous generations). Mühlhäusler (1982) has noted that in Tok Pisin grammatical categories such as time and number have become compulsory, a word-formation component has been developed, devices for structuring discourse are now present, and there are opportunities for stylistic differentiation (p. 449). So far as functions are concerned, Tok Pisin has become symbolic of a new culture; it is now used in many entirely new domains, e.g., government, religion, agriculture, and aviation; it is employed in a variety of media; and it is supplanting the vernaculars and even English in many areas (pp. 448–9). Aitchison (1991) has also noted what is happening to Tok Pisin. She points out four kinds of change. One of these is that people speak creoles faster than pidgins and they do not speak them word by word. Consequently, processes of assimilation and reduction can be seen at work in Tok Pisin: *ma bilong mi* ('my husband') becomes *mamblomi*. A second change is the expansion of vocabulary resources: new shorter words are formed, so that *paitman* ('fighter') exists alongside *man bilong pait* ('man of fight'). There is also much borrowing of technical vocabulary from English. A third change is the development of a tense system in verbs. *Bin* is used as a past time marker and *bai*, from *baimbai* ('by and by'), as a future time marker. Finally, greater sentence complexity is now apparent. Some speakers are now able to construct relative clauses because *we* (from 'where') is developing as an introductory marker. In ways such as these, the original pidgin is quickly developing into a fully fledged language, which we call a creole only because we know its origin.

This last point is important: it is only because we know the origins of creoles that we know they are creoles. Hall (1966, pp. 122–3) has observed that:

> All the evidence available so far indicates that the type of linguistic change and the mechanisms involved – sound-change, analogy, borrowing of various kinds – are the same for pidgins and creoles as they are for all other languages. The only difference lies in the rate of change – far faster for a pidgin (because of the drastic reduction in structure and lexicon) than for most languages. When a pidgin has

become nativized, the history of the resultant creole is, in essence, similar to that of any other language. Hence, whereas a pidgin is identifiable at any given time by both linguistic and social criteria, a creole is identifiable only by historical criteria – that is, if we know that it has arisen out of a pidgin. There are no structural criteria which, in themselves, will identify a creole as such, in the absence of historical evidence.

Hall adds that the kinds of changes we associate with creolization normally take thousands of years in languages for which we have good historical data.

Recent intensive study of pidgins and creoles has revealed how quickly such languages can and do change. Pidginization can occur almost 'overnight.' Relexification also seems to be a rapid process. Creolization can take as little as two generations. The particular combination of language and social contact that gives rise to pidgins and creoles seems also to have occurred frequently in the history of the human species.

What this suggests is that many now traditional views about how languages change may need revision. Such change may not be slow and regular at all, or it may be so only in the absence of certain kinds of language contact. Since contact situations appear to hasten change, the study of pidgins and creoles offers important clues to the kinds of changes that you might seek to discover. For example, does a contact situation lead to a reduction in inflectional morphology? Does it favor the development of a fixed word order in sentences? Finding answers to questions such as these may provide interesting insights into how languages change.

Because a creole can be related to some other dominant (or superordinate) language a *creole* (or *post-creole*) *continuum* can arise. For example, an English-based creole can develop a number of varieties when it is in contact with Standard English. As the range of these varieties increases, Standard English may more and more influence them so that some varieties will come to resemble Standard English. This process has become known as *decreolization*. However, Winford (1997b) points out that there are various kinds of continua and 'Each creole continuum is unique in its own way' (p. 311). Consequently, much research is still needed to discover how the varieties arise and relate to one another.

In discussing the creole continuum that exists in Guyanese English, Bickerton (1975, p. 24) has proposed a number of terms that may be used to refer to its different parts. He uses the term *acrolect* to refer to educated Guyanese English, a variety which really has very few differences from other varieties of Standard English. He uses the term *basilect* to refer to the variety at the other extreme of the continuum, the variety that would be least comprehensible to a speaker of the standard, perhaps even incomprehensible. *Mesolects* are intermediate varieties. However, these are not discrete entities, for one important characteristic of these intermediate mesolects is that they blend into one another to fill the 'space' between the acrolect and the basilect.

As we might expect, there is considerable social stratification involved in such a situation. Bickerton cites Allsopp (1958) to show how the following Guyanese varieties of the Standard English sentence *I told him* may be pronounced in the various parts of the continuum:

1. ai tɔuld hɪm
2. ai toːld hɪm
3. ai toːl ɪm
4. ai tɛl ɪm
5. a tɛl ɪm
6. ai tɛl ɪ
7. a tɛl i
8. mi tɛl i
9. mi tɛl am

The first three varieties (1–3) exemplify middle-class usage and are typical acrolect forms. The next four (4–7) are mesolect forms found in the lower-middle and urban working classes. Item 8 is found in the rural working class, and item 9 is used by old and illiterate rural laborers: these are typical basilect forms.

Additional evidence on the Guyanese continuum is provided by Bell (1976, p. 136), who produces the sentences found in table 3.1. He uses information supplied by Cave (1973) to show how, in the Guyanese continuum, there are eighteen different ways of rendering a sentence like *I gave him one*. In this continuum the 'highest' acrolect sentence is [aɪ geɪv hɪm wʌn], the 'lowest' basilect sentence is [mɪ giː æm wan], and there are intermediate mesolect sentences such as 8 [a dɪd gɪv iː wan], and 13 [mɪ di gɪ hiː wan].

Writing of the continuum that exists in Jamaica, DeCamp (1977, p. 29) has observed that particular speakers control a span of the spectrum, not just one discrete level within it. He says that the breadth of the span depends on the breadth of the speaker's social activities:

> A labor leader, for example, can command a greater span of varieties than can a sheltered housewife of suburban middle class. A housewife may make a limited adjustment downward on the continuum in order to communicate with a market woman, and the market woman may adjust upward when she talks to the housewife. Each of them may then believe that she is speaking the other's language, for the myth persists in Jamaica that there are only two varieties of language – standard English and 'the dialect' – but the fact is that the housewife's broadest dialect may be closer to the standard end of the spectrum than is the market woman's 'standard.'

What is particularly important here, though, is the additional observation that Jamaicans do not perceive the existence of a continuum. Instead, they perceive what they say and hear only in relation to the two ends and make any judgments and adjustments in terms of the two extremes, Standard English or 'the dialect,' 'patois,' or 'Quashie,' as it is sometimes referred to. Patrick (1999) points out that at least in Kingston the continuum is much more complicated: multi-dimensional rather than uni-dimensional. The idea of a simple continuum may therefore be little more than a neat theoretical concept, since the variation found in everyday language use requires taking into consideration many other explanatory factors.

A continuum can arise only if the two extreme varieties are varieties of the same language, as with standard X and creolized X (e.g., Standard English and Jamaican

Table 3.1 A Guyanese continuum

1	aɪ				wʌn
2				him	
3		geɪv		ɪm	
4				i:	
5				hɪm	
6	a	gɪv		ɪm	
7					
8		dɪd	gɪv	i:	
9		dɪ			
10		dɪd	gɪ		wan
11			gi:		
12					
13		dɪ	gɪ	hi:	
14					
15	mɪ			i:	
16		bɪn			
17			gi:	æm	
18					

Source: Bell (1976, p. 136)

Creole English). When different languages are involved there can be no continuum, as between Sranan, an English-based creole, and Dutch in Suriname. If the total society is highly stratified, so that there is little or no contact between the groups who speak the creolized and superordinate varieties, and/or if these two varieties have separate and distinct functions in the lives of people, then there will be no continuum. We will have a *diglossic* situation (see chapter 4), as in

Haiti between Haitian Creole and French. A continuum appears to require that there be some kind of continuity in society among the various sub-groups. It arises from the development of varieties intermediate between the original pidgins and the superordinate variety. The different linguistic situations in Jamaica and Haiti would therefore suggest that the social situations in these countries are very different, a suggestion which seems to have some validity.

It is also important to note that not only Patrick (1999) but others such as Le Page and Tabouret-Keller (1985) reject the idea of the continuum as being altogether too simplistic. They claim that it results from simplifying and manipulating data rather than trying to confront the evidence in all its complexity. It is too simplistic to explain the linguistic choices that speakers make. It is essentially a uni-dimensional approach to a situation in which all the factors suggest that only a multi-dimensional approach can offer an appropriate account of speakers' linguistic behavior. There is considerable merit to this view.

According to theorists such as Rickford (1977) and Dillard (1972), the process of decreolization can also be observed in the United States in what has happened in the linguistic history of the black slave population that was brought to work the cotton plantations. The original slaves brought with them a number of West African languages, but many must also have arrived with some knowledge of Portuguese-based or English-based pidgins, the trading lingua francas of the African coast. Slave owners deliberately chose slaves from different language backgrounds to discourage rebellion. Such circumstances fostered the development of English-based pidgins and the process of creolization. So long as whites and blacks kept a considerable distance apart, physically and socially, there was little opportunity for decreolization. We can see that this was the case with Gullah, geographically isolated on the Sea Islands off the southeast coast and still today the most distinctive indigenous black speech in the United States, particularly because of its large African vocabulary (see Mufwene, 1993). However, as blacks began to win more and more recognition of equality under the law and opportunities for various kinds of advancement increased, Standard English began to exert a strong influence on the original creole, so that today a genuine continuum exists. In fact, this continuum is so strong that many people, both whites and blacks, regard any characteristics which seem to mark the speech of US blacks as being instances of either 'southern' speech or 'lower-class' speech. In other words, AAVE, the modern reflex of the original creole, is now regarded as either a regional or social variant of the standard language. There are, however, other explanations of the origins of AAVE. We will return to these and related matters in chapter 14 because of some of the consequences that arise in resolving certain educational issues.

A *diglossic* situation is one in which the creole and the standard lack continuity so far as functions are concerned, and that functional discontinuity is generally strongly supported by severe social stratification. Haitian Creole and Standard French differ almost as much as two quite unrelated languages; there are no intermediate varieties in Haiti, and the two are kept socially and functionally apart. In Haiti one possible solution to such a diglossic situation would seem to be the elevation of the creole to 'full' language status through the process of standardization. However, the socially and politically elite in Haiti, even though they themselves use Haitian Creole in certain circumstances, officially disdain any language other than Standard French and the general populace find little or no encouragement for thinking well of the creole. On the other hand, Afrikaans, of possible creole origin, has been developed into a 'full' language in South Africa, Bahasa Indonesia has been developed out of certain varieties of Malay, and Tok Pisin is now used in Papua New Guinea as a unifying language.

As Bell (1976, pp. 160–1) has pointed out, various things can happen to a creole. It can reach a quite stable relationship with the language or languages of the community, as in the current relationship between Haitian Creole and French. It may for one reason or another be extinguished by the standard language: for example, in the Dutch West Indies, Dutch has virtually extinguished Negerhollands, and English is severely cutting into Gullah in the Sea Islands. A creole may in some cases become a standard language, with possible examples being Afrikaans, Swahili, Bahasa Indonesia, and Maltese. A creole continuum, as for example in Jamaica and Guyana, is another possibility.

The different linguistic situations create different social and educational problems for speakers of the pidgins and creoles. In a diglossic situation such as in Haiti there are traditional power relationships exemplified in the distributions of the two varieties of language, e.g., Haitian Creole and the local variety of French. Everyone speaks the former, but those at the 'upper' levels of Haitian society also speak French. There are also varieties of the creole, the *kreyòl fransize* ('French creole') or *kreyòl swa* ('smooth creole') of the educated, urban, bilingual upper class and the *gwo kreyòl* ('vulgar creole') or *kreyòl rèk* ('rough creole') of the rest of the people. The creole is associated with ignorance, poverty, and inferiority, even by those who speak it, but at the same time it is a marker of Haitian solidarity: it is what makes Haitians distinctively Haitians. French, though quite alien to well over three-quarters of the population, is the preferred language of education and it also provides access to the outside world (although recently English has been making inroads). Those who have knowledge of French regard it as the language of culture even though, by the standards of Continental French, the Haitian variety of French tends to be grandiose, flowery, and archaic. The result, predictably, is that little or no progress is made in Haiti in solving pressing social and educational problems. Many of these are directly related to linguistic matters so it is not surprising that they should be as severe as they are if we remember that the creole is said to have no grammar, that the elite have long resisted literacy campaigns (there was only 20 percent literacy in 1984!), and that it was not until 1961 that the creole gained any limited official recognition at all and not until 1979 that it became the medium of instruction for the first four years of schooling (see also pp. 91–2).

Jamaica might appear to offer more hope that a unified language will evolve. However, the subtle gradations that exist in a continuum can also be put to use to classify people. The people who use the two ends of the Jamaican continuum are almost as far apart socially as those Haitians who speak only Haitian Creole are from those who are completely bilingual in the creole and French. Some varieties of Jamaican English are clearly felt to be 'superior' and others clearly 'inferior,' so the particular span of varieties a Jamaican uses serves as a clear social class marker. DeCamp (1977, p. 26) has pointed out some of the serious educational consequences of such attitudes. He says that in Jamaica 'most educators persist in treating the "dialect problem" as if it were a problem of speech correction, attributing it to careless, slovenly pronunciation. . . . The creole is inseparably associated with poverty, ignorance, and lack of moral character.' There is a strong social prejudice against the creole, a prejudice which inhibits even the middle class, many of whom 'lead lives of desperate linguistic anxiety, loudly proclaiming the superiority of their own "standard" English while nursing inward doubts about whether their English is really sufficiently standard.'

Wassink's study (1999) of speakers from the semi-rural community of Gordon Town outside Kingston, Jamaica, revealed that some of the negative attitudes toward the existence of a continuum may be weakening. There is still considerable ambivalence about what locals call the *patois*: for example, respondents were more willing to hear it used by others than they were to use it themselves. Young people were also more accepting than old. 'Gordon Town respondents maintained reservations about JC [Jamaican Creole] but they also indicated that it has great social value to them . . . [it] being more expressive than English' (p. 85).

This problem is no longer unique to Jamaica. In recent decades there has been considerable emigration from Jamaica (and from other countries in which the same kind of continuum is normal), so that a further dimension has been added to the continuum: a new standard is superposed on the previous Jamaican one, e.g., British English or Canadian English. How best to deal with the social and educational factors associated with a continuum is no longer a problem unique to certain places where creoles have developed, but is now a problem for educators in cities like London, Toronto, and New York. Edwards (1986) and Hewitt (1986, 1989) have pointed out how in England black youths of West Indian origin not only learn the local variety of English but often too a particular variety of Caribbean English that differs from that of their parents. Edwards says that they deliberately *recreolize* the English they use in an attempt to assert their ethnic identity and solidarity because of the social situation in which they find themselves (Edwards, 1986, p. 111). Sebba (1993) offers further evidence of this phenomenon. He shows how some young British African Caribbeans create London Jamaican English forms that are clearly different from Jamaican Jamaican English (JJE) forms, e.g., *fru* for *through* (JJE *tru*). For these youngsters this type of creole has covert prestige with its images of solidarity, Black Britishness, and distinctiveness from other varieties of English: it is deliberately, oppositionally, and nonlegitimately different. We will see too (in chapter 14) that claims have been advanced that the speech of certain blacks in the United States may now be diverging from that of the wider society.

Creating a new 'full' language from a creole also has its own special problems. Bahasa Indonesia has to be standardized and taught to speakers of many different languages. Afrikaans has already been standardized. Both states have found that a strong unifying 'national' consciousness among potential speakers has been of immense value. To some extent Tok Pisin relies on the same motivation, but in this case the numbers in support of a new language are small and the price to pay in terms of linguistic isolation, which must be added to the geographic isolation that already exists, is high. Currently Tok Pisin is rapidly being creolized, particularly in urban areas, and attempts are being made to standardize the emerging creole. Its uses are being extended in a variety of ways, e.g., in the House of Assembly as an official language alongside English, in broadcasting, in newspapers, and in primary education. However, the process has not been without its problems. One is the growth of varieties of the language, so that there are now both rural and urban varieties, a situation which threatens Tok Pisin's development as a lingua franca. Another is that there has been wholesale borrowing into Tok Pisin of English words rather than the exploitation of native sources. If Tok Pisin were to become more and more recognizably 'English,' we might anticipate the development of a creole continuum with all the attendant problems, not the least of which, of course, is the threat that such a development poses to the native creole, as in Jamaica, Guyana, and Nigeria, placing, as it does, that creole in an even more unfavorable light in the eyes of those who speak it. Tok Pisin could fall into jeopardy if this should happen.

Discussion

1. While all linguists believe that all languages change over time, some believe that they change at a fairly fixed rate, particularly over very long periods of time. This belief enables them not only to reconstruct protolanguages (i.e., common ancestral languages) but also to attempt to date these. What problems might the existence of creoles pose for such views?

2. Hall (1972, p. 151) has commented that the major factor that brings about a change of status for a pidgin or a creole is 'political, i.e., pressure effectively exerted by or on behalf of the population which uses it, for its recognition.' He adds that the 'correlation between political factors and status-achievement, for pidgins and creoles, is so close that we may expect to see other such languages rise to the status of standards only where the areas where they are spoken gain political independence or autonomy, and use the local tongue as a symbol of nationality.' If Hall is correct, what do you think will happen to the many pidgins and creoles that exist today? Are there any countervailing forces which must also be recognized?

3. Saville-Troike (1989) quotes the following from a letter to the editor of the Trinidad *Guardian*. A report on a Language Arts syllabus had recognized that most Trinidadians spoke a creole and that English was not their native language. The letter writer protests as follows:

> If the language of the barrack yard and the market is to be the accepted mode of expression in the school-room . . . there would be no need for teachers . . . we could save the high wages of these experts and set them free to go and plant peas . . . where they can give full vent to this dialect stuff . . . What, if not broken English, is this dialect? . . . I feel that such discussions should be banned from our news media as a most damaging . . . exercise.

What might you say in a follow-up letter to the editor of the *Guardian*?

4. Many Jamaicans speak disparagingly of Jamaican creole or 'the patois.' The language of education in Jamaica is Standard English. However, much of the teaching of Standard English proves to be ineffective. Why might this be the case?

5. Todd (1990, p. 83) takes Whinnom (1971, p. 110) severely to task for saying the following:

> I feel that . . . modern linguists . . . have been dangerously sentimental about creole languages, which, with only a few notable exceptions, constitute in most communities a distinct handicap to the social mobility of the individual, and *may* also constitute a handicap to the creole speaker's personal intellectual development.

Read what each has to say on this matter and try to reach some conclusion about the issues.

Further Reading

Very useful introductory texts on pidgins and creoles are Holm (1988, 1989, 2000, 2004), Mühlhäusler (1997), Romaine (1988), Todd (1990), Sebba (1997), Arends et al. (1995), Kaye and Tosco (2001), and Singh (2000). Aitchison (1994) is an excellent brief account. Le Page and Tabouret-Keller (1985) and Morgan (1994) deal with interesting issues of identity in creole situations. Winford (2003) enlightens on all kinds of language contact, and Lefebvre (2004) discusses many of the most pressing issues in pidgin–creole linguistics. Two collections of papers illuminate some of the controversies in pidgin and creole studies: Spears and Winford (1997) and Thomason (1997).

The *Journal of Pidgin and Creole Languages* is an important journal.

4 Codes

As I indicated in chapter 2, it is possible to refer to a language or a variety of a language as a *code*. The term is useful because it is neutral. Terms like *dialect*, *language*, *style*, *standard language*, *pidgin*, and *creole* are inclined to arouse emotions. In contrast, the 'neutral' term *code*, taken from information theory, can be used to refer to any kind of system that two or more people employ for communication. (It can actually be used for a system used by a single person, as when someone devises a private code to protect certain secrets.) All of the above, then, are codes by this, admittedly loose, definition. What is interesting is the factors that govern the choice of a particular code on a particular occasion. Why do people choose to use one code rather than another, what brings about shifts from one code to another, and why do they occasionally prefer to use a code formed from two other codes by switching back and forth between the two or even mixing them?

Such questions as these assume that there are indeed few single-code speakers; people are nearly always faced with choosing an appropriate code when they speak. Very young children may be exceptions, as may learners of a new language (for a while at least) and the victims of certain pathological conditions. In general, however, when you open your mouth, you must choose a particular language, dialect, style, register, or variety – that is, a particular code. You cannot avoid doing so. Moreover, you can and will shift, as the need arises, from one code to another. Within each code there will also be the possibility of choices not all of which will have the same import because some will be more marked than others, i.e., will be more significant. The various choices will have different social meanings. What are some of the factors that influence the choices you make?

We will look mainly at the phenomenon of *code-switching* in bilingual and multilingual situations. However, many of the issues that we will see there will also arise with those codes which can be called sub-varieties of a single language, e.g., dialects, styles, and registers. In particular, we will examine the so-called *diglossic* situation in which clear functional differences between the codes govern the choice. Following a brief look at some types of bilingual situations, we will consider code-switching as a phenomenon that requires serious explanation.

Discussion

1. Use of the term *code* allows us to use derivative terms like *codification* and *recodification*. Writing systems are said to be codifications of speech. How do the English and Chinese writing systems differ as codifications of their respective languages?
2. A recodification is a further manipulation of a code. Morse Code and Pig Latin are two simple recodifications. What are the principles behind each?
3. Some codifications or recodifications have very clear social functions. You might care to look at the following from such a perspective: Walbiri 'upside-down talk' (Hale, 1971); Hanunóo 'love play' (Conklin, 1959); and glossolalia (Samarin, 1973).

Diglossia

A *diglossic* situation exists in a society when it has two distinct codes which show clear functional separation; that is, one code is employed in one set of circumstances and the other in an entirely different set. Ferguson (1959, p. 336) has defined diglossia as follows:

> DIGLOSSIA is a relatively stable language situation in which, in addition to the primary dialects of the language (which may include a standard or regional standards), there is a very divergent, highly codified (often grammatically more complex) superposed variety, the vehicle of a large and respected body of written literature, either of an earlier period or in another speech community, which is learned largely by formal education and is used for most written and formal spoken purposes but is not used by any sector of the community for ordinary conversation.

In the same article he identifies four language situations which show the major characteristics of the diglossic phenomenon: Arabic, Swiss German, Haitian (French and Creole), and Greek. In each situation there is a 'high' variety (H) of language and a 'low' variety (L). Each variety has its own specialized functions, and each is viewed differently by those who are aware of both.

In the Arabic situation the two varieties are Classical Arabic (H) and the various regional colloquial varieties (L). In Switzerland they are Standard German (H) and Swiss German (L). In Haiti the varieties are Standard French (H) and Haitian Creole (L). In Greece they are the Katharévousa (H) and Dhimotiki, or Demotic (L), varieties of Greek. In each case the two varieties have coexisted for a long period, sometimes, as in the case of Arabic, for many centuries. Consequently, the phenomenon of diglossia is not ephemeral in nature; in fact, the opposite is true: it appears to be a persistent social and linguistic phenomenon.

A key defining characteristic of diglossia is that the two varieties are kept quite apart in their functions. One is used in one set of circumstances and the other in an entirely different set. For example, the H varieties may be used for delivering sermons and formal lectures, especially in a parliament or legislative body, for giving political speeches, for broadcasting the news on radio and television, and for writing poetry, fine literature, and editorials in newspapers. In contrast, the L varieties may be used in giving instructions to workers in low-prestige occupations or to household servants, in conversation with familiars, in 'soap operas' and popular programs on the radio, in captions on political cartoons in newspapers, and in 'folk literature.' On occasion, a person may lecture in an H variety but answer questions about its contents or explain parts of it in an L variety so as to ensure understanding.

You do not use an H variety in circumstances calling for an L variety, e.g., for addressing a servant; nor do you usually use an L variety when an H is called for, e.g., for writing a 'serious' work of literature. You may indeed do the latter, but it may be a risky endeavor; it is the kind of thing that Chaucer did for the English of his day, and it requires a certain willingness, on the part of both the writer and others, to break away from a diglossic situation by extending the L variety into functions normally associated only with the H. For about three centuries after the Norman Conquest of 1066, English and Norman French coexisted in England in a diglossic situation with Norman French the H variety and English the L. However, gradually the L variety assumed more and more functions associated with the H so that by Chaucer's time it had become possible to use the L variety for a major literary work.

The H variety is the prestigious, powerful variety; the L variety lacks prestige and power. In fact, there may be so little prestige attached to the L variety that people may even deny that they know it although they may be observed to use it far more frequently than the H variety. Associated with this prestige valuation for the H variety, there is likely to be a strong feeling that the prestige is deserved because the H variety is more beautiful, logical, and expressive than the L variety. That is why it is deemed appropriate for literary use, for religious purposes, and so on. There may also be considerable and widespread resistance to translating certain books into the L variety, e.g., the Qur'an into one or other colloquial varieties of Arabic or the Bible into Haitian Creole or Demotic Greek. (We should note that even today many speakers of English resist the Bible in any form other than the King James version.)

This last feeling concerning the natural superiority of the H variety is likely to be reinforced by the fact that a considerable body of literature will be found to exist in that variety and almost none in the other. That literature may also be regarded as reflecting essential values about the culture and, when parts of it are classical literature, deemed worthy of recalling by allusion and quotations on occasions suitable for the employment of H. Speakers of Arabic in particular gain prestige from being able to allude to classical sources. The folk literature associated with the L variety will have none of the same prestige; it may interest folklorists and it may be transmuted into an H variety by writers skilled in H, but it is unlikely to be the stuff of which literary histories and traditions are made in its 'raw' form.

Another important difference between the H and L varieties is that all children learn the L variety. Some may concurrently learn the H variety, but many do not learn it at all; e.g., most Haitians have no knowledge at all of Standard French but all can speak some variety of Haitian Creole, although some, as I have said, may deny that they have this ability. The H variety is also likely to be learned in some kind of formal setting, e.g., in classrooms or as part of a religious or cultural indoctrination. To that extent, the H variety is 'taught,' whereas the L variety is 'learned.' Teaching requires the availability of grammars, dictionaries, standardized texts, and some widely accepted view about the nature of what is being taught and how it is most effectively to be taught. There are usually no comparable grammars, dictionaries, and standardized texts for the L variety, and any view of that variety is likely to be highly pejorative in nature. When such grammars and other aids do exist, they have in many cases been written by outsiders, e.g., 'foreign' linguists. They are also likely to be neither well known to the people whose linguistic usage they describe nor well received by those people, since such works are unlikely to support some of the myths that accompany diglossia, particularly the myth that the L variety lacks any kind of 'grammar.'

The L variety often shows a tendency to borrow learned words from the H variety, particularly when speakers try to use the L variety in more formal ways. The result is a certain admixture of H vocabulary into the L. On other occasions, though, there may be distinctly different pairs of words, i.e., doublets, in the H and L varieties to refer to very common objects and concepts. Since the domains of use of the two varieties do not intersect, there will be an L word for use in L situations and an H word for use in H situations with no possibility of transferring the one to the other. So far as the pronunciation of the two varieties is concerned, the L system will often appear to be the more 'basic.' However, actual circumstances can vary. Whereas the two varieties of Greek have very similar sound systems, there is a considerable difference between Classical Arabic and the colloquial varieties and a still greater difference between High German and Swiss German.

Diglossia is a widespread phenomenon in the world, well attested in both space (e.g., varieties of Tamil in the south of India) and time (e.g., Latin in Europe in the Middle Ages). According to Ferguson (1959, p. 338), it is likely to come into being when (1) 'there is a sizable body of literature in a language closely related to (or even identical with) the natural language of the community . . . [and when (2)] literacy in the community is limited to a small elite, [and] . . . a suitable period of time, of the order of several centuries, passes from the establishment of (1) and (2).' People living in a diglossic community do not usually regard diglossia as a 'problem.' It becomes a problem only when there is a growth of literacy, or when there is a desire to decrease regional and/or social barriers, or when a need is seen for a unified 'national' language.

In Haiti, any attempt to develop literacy had to confront directly the issue of whether to increase the amount of Standard French taught or to 'elevate' the L variety, Haitian Creole, into a national language. Haitian Creole was eventually recognized as a national language in 1983, with prestigious French, of course, the other. Both languages were made official in 1987. There has been an ongoing debate about the most appropriate orthography (spelling system) for Haitian Creole: about the use of certain letters and accents, and about whether the differences between French and Haitian Creole should be minimized in the orthography for Haitian Creole or whether that orthography should be as trans-parent as possible in relating letters to sounds, particularly the sounds of the most widespread variety of Haitian Creole. French, though not widely used, has such prestige that, according to Schieffelin and Doucet (1998, p. 306) virtually any proposal for an othography for kreyòl has created 'resistance both to the adoption of the orthography and to the use of kreyòl as a medium of instruction in school. The double resistance comes from both the masses and the educated elite minority. The masses see the officialization of written and spoken kreyòl in school as limiting their access to French and, consequently, their social and economic mobility. The elites, who already know kreyòl, do not see the point of teaching it, in any form, in school.'

The Greeks have still not entirely solved the problems associated with their two varieties: 'conservative' Greeks want to resolve any differences in favor of the H variety, but 'liberals' favor the L variety. (It was at one time said that you could judge a Greek's social and political attitudes by the way he or she declined third-declension nouns!) The twentieth century witnessed a long and sometimes bitter struggle between supporters of the two varieties. Religious authorities condemned a 1921 translation of the New Testament into Demotic Greek and this action led to rioting in the streets of Athens. One consequence of the language disagreement was that, when the 'liberal' government of the 1960s was overthrown by the 'colonels' in 1967, the former government's program to extend the uses of Dhimotiki was superseded by restoration of use of the H variety, Katharévousa, for example in education, and the suppression of Dhimotiki because of its association with 'left-wing' views. With the return to constitutional government in 1975 the H was superseded in turn by the L, Dhimotiki was declared the official language of Greece in 1976, and Katharévousa disappeared almost entirely from public view. The new model for Greece seems to be based on the variety spoken in Athens. Today, the opponents of this new Greek language based on the L variety attack it for being impoverished and cut off from its roots, which are said to be the former H variety and Ancient Greek (Frangoudaki, 1992). Tseronis (2002) says that the two most recent Greek dictionaries, the *Dictionary of Modern Greek Language* (DOMGL) and the *Dictionary of Common Modern Greek* (DOCMG) show that the process of standardization continues. The DOMGL finds its roots in Katharévousa and the DOCMG in Dhimotiki. However, both point to eventual unification around the variety spoken in Athens and an end to the H–L division.

The linguistic situations in Haiti and Greece are intimately tied to power relationships among social groups. Traditionally, in each country the H variety has been associated with an elite and the L variety with everyone else. Diglossia reinforces social distinctions. It is used to assert social position and to keep people in their place, particularly those at the lower end of the social hierarchy. Any move to extend the L variety, even in the case of Haiti to make the population literate in any variety, is likely to be perceived to be a direct threat to those who want to maintain traditional relationships and the existing power structure.

The following example from Trudgill (1995, pp. 101–2) shows how different the Zürich variety of Swiss German is from High German:

Low variety – Swiss German

En Schwyzer isch er zwaar nie woorde, weder en papiirige na äine im Hëërz ine; und eebigs häd mer syner Spraach aagmërkt, das er nüd daa uufgwachsen ischt. Nüd nu s Muul häd Ussländer verraate, au syni Möödteli. Er häd lieber mit syne tüütsche Landslüüte weder mit de Yhäimische vercheert, und ischt Mitgliid und Zaalmäischter von irem Veräin gsy.

High variety – Standard German

Ein Schweizer ist er zwar nie geworden, weder auf dem Papier noch im Herzen; und man hat es seine Sprache angemerkt, dass er nicht dort aufgewachsen ist. Nicht nur die Sprache hat den Ausländer verraten, sondern auch seine Gewohnheiten. Er hat lieber mit seinen deutschen Landsleuten als mit den Einheimischen verkehrt, und ist Mitglied und Zahlmeister ihres Vereins gewesen.

English

He never actually became Swiss, neither on paper nor in his heart; and you could tell from his language that he had not grown up there. It was not only his language that showed that he was a foreigner – his way of life showed it too. He preferred to associate with his German compatriots rather than with the natives, and was a member and the treasurer of their society.

Swiss German diglossia has its own stabilizing factors. Switzerland is a multilingual country, with German, French, and Italian its three official languages. Strong constitutional protection is provided for German, the H variety of which is taught in the schools and used in official publications, newspapers, literature, and church services. This allows the German Swiss to communicate with speakers of German elsewhere in Europe and gives them access to everything written in Standard German. However, the Germans in Switzerland can also assert their independence of other Germans through use of their L variety. This is their own distinctive unifying spoken variety of German, one in which they take a special pride. The continuation of the High German–Swiss diglossic situation depends every much on the continued effectiveness of educating Swiss German children to use High German in the schools so as to encourage diglossia there. Some Swiss do worry that such teaching of High German may not always produce the desired results and that any quest for identity through increased use of Swiss German might lead to growing cultural isolation from other users of German.

In much the same way, the people of Luxembourg have achieved a certain distinctiveness with their own diglossic – or better still, triglossic – situation (see Newton, 1996). In this case Luxemburgish, called *Lëtzebuergesch*, a variety of German, is the L variety and Standard German is the H variety. The following examples are from Trudgill (1995, p. 103):

Luxemburgish

Wéi de Rodange 1872 säi Buch drécke gelooss huet, du bluf hien drop sëtzen. En hat e puer Leit ze luusség op d'Zéiwe getrëppelt, déi dat net verquësst hun. Eréischt eng Generation doerno huet de Rodange uge-faang séng giedléch Plaz ze kréien.

Séng Kanner hu wéinstens nach erlieft, wéi 1927 eng Grimmel vun deem gutt gemaach guf, wat un him verbrach gi wor!

Standard German

Als Rodange 1872 sein Buch drucken liess, hatte er keinen Erfolg damit. Mit zuviel List war er ein paar Leuten auf die Zehen getreten, und die konnten ihm das nicht verzeihen. Erst eine Generation später begann Rodange, seinen ihm zustehenden Platz zu erhalten. Seine Kinder haben es wenigstens noch erlebt, dass 1927 ein wenig von dem gut gemacht wurde, was an ihm verbrochen worden war!

English

When Rodange had his book printed in 1872 he had no success with it. With too much intrigue he had trodden on some people's toes, and they could not forgive him that. Only a generation later did Rodange begin to receive his rightful place. His children at least experienced the making good, in 1927, of some of the wrong that had been done him.

However, the situation is a little more complicated in Luxembourg than in Switzerland because still another language, French, is involved. All three languages – German, French, and Luxemburgish – have been official languages since 1984. Inhabitants of Luxembourg not only use Luxemburgish (e.g., in ordinary conversation) and Standard German (e.g., in letter writing, books, and newspapers), but they also use French (e.g., in parliament and higher education) – see Clyne (1984, pp. 20–1). Moreover, they frequently borrow words from French for use in Luxemburgish. Consequently, it is not unusual for a speaker of Standard German who goes to live in Luxembourg to feel that Luxemburgish is a variety of French rather than a variety of German! French is highly regarded in Luxembourg and is also the most widely used language (by 96 percent of residents), although 81 percent can speak German and 80 percent can speak Luxemburgish (Fehlen, 2002, p. 91). However, the clear marker of Luxembourg identity among Luxembourgers is their use of Luxemburgish; it is a solidarity marker just as is the use of Swiss German among Swiss Germans.

The Arabic situation is very different again. There are a number of flourishing regional varieties of the L and many Arabs would like to see the Arab-speaking world unify around one variety. They acknowledge the highly restricted uses of the H variety, but also revere it for certain characteristics that they ascribe to it: its beauty, logic, and richness. Classical Arabic is also the language of the Qur'an. Ferguson has pointed out that choosing one colloquial variety of Arabic to elevate above all others poses a number of problems. Almost certainly, any Arab will tell you that the variety he or she speaks is the 'best,' so there would be considerable disagreement about where one should begin any attempt to standardize modern Arabic on a single colloquial variety. There is, however, a consensus among Arabs that any standard that may eventually emerge will be a version of the H variety developed to meet modern needs and purged of regional peculiarities and foreign impurities.

While acknowledging that diglossic situations are essentially stable, Ferguson did predict (1959, p. 340) what he thought the future held for the situations he examined. He regarded the situation in Switzerland as relatively stable. The Arabic one seemed to point to the development of several regional standard varieties of Arabic, each using a considerable amount of vocabulary drawn from Classical Arabic. In Haiti, there would be a slow development of Haitian Creole based on the L variety of the capital, Port-au-Prince. Finally, in Greece the standard would be based on the L variety of Athens with considerable admixture of vocabulary from Katharévousa.

What Ferguson describes are 'narrow' or 'classic' diglossic situations. They require the use of very divergent varieties of the same language and there are few good examples. Fishman has broadened or extended the term to include a wider variety of language situations. For Fishman (1980, p. 3) diglossia is '*an enduring societal arrangement*, extending at least beyond a three generation period, such that two "languages" each have their secure, phenomenologically legitimate and widely implemented functions.' By acknowledging that his use of the term *language* also includes sub-varieties of one language, Fishman includes Ferguson's examples. He does add, though, that in the case of two varieties of the same language, they be 'sufficiently different from one another that, without schooling, the elevated variety cannot be understood by speakers of the vernacular' (p. 4). Fishman's proposal extends the concept of 'diglossia' to include bilingual and multilingual situations in which the different languages have quite different functions. For example, one language is used in one set of circumstances and the other in an entirely different set and such difference is felt to be normal and proper. Fishman gives examples such as Biblical Hebrew and Yiddish for many Jews, Spanish and Guaraní in Paraguay, and even Standard English and Caribbean Creole. I will have more to say about code choices in such situations in the following sections.

Discussion

1. In what ways was the relationship between Classical Latin and the vernacular Romance languages, particularly the languages presently known as French, Italian, Spanish, and Portuguese, a diglossic one for a number of centuries? At which point did diglossia cease? Can we answer this last question with any great degree of precision?
2. The history of English in the three centuries after 1066 is of considerable interest. The Norman Conquest established Norman French as the H variety and English as the L variety. What caused English eventually to triumph and French to be eliminated from use in England (except as a clearly marked 'foreign' language)? Where did Latin fit into the overall picture?
3. There was, and still is, among certain ultra-orthodox sects in Israel resistance to the use of Biblical Hebrew as a vernacular language, that is, as a language of everyday living, because they regard such use as 'profane.' How different are Biblical and Modern Hebrew?
4. If someone were to tell you that diglossia is but a simple reflection of the social, cultural, or political oppression of a people, how might you answer?

5. How 'diglossic' are classroom situations in which children who come to school speaking only a regional or social variety of English well removed from the standard variety are taught the standard variety and its various uses, particularly its use in writing?

Bilingualism and Multilingualism

Monolingualism, that is, the ability to use only one language, is such a widely accepted norm in so many parts of the Western world that it is often assumed to be a world-wide phenomenon, to the extent that bilingual and multilingual individuals may appear to be 'unusual.' Indeed, we often have mixed feelings when we discover that someone we meet is fluent in several languages: perhaps a mixture of admiration and envy but also, occasionally, a feeling of superiority in that many such people are not 'native' to the culture in which we function. Such people are likely to be immigrants, visitors, or children of 'mixed' marriages and in that respect 'marked' in some way, and such marking is not always regarded favorably.

However, in many parts of the world an ability to speak more than one language is not at all remarkable. In fact, a monolingual individual would be regarded as a misfit, lacking an important skill in society, the skill of being able to interact freely with the speakers of other languages with whom regular contact is made in the ordinary business of living. In many parts of the world it is just a normal requirement of daily living that people speak several languages: perhaps one or more at home, another in the village, still another for purposes of trade, and yet another for contact with the outside world of wider social or political organization. These various languages are usually acquired naturally and unselfconsciously, and the shifts from one to another are made without hesitation.

People who are bilingual or multilingual do not necessarily have exactly the same abilities in the languages (or varieties); in fact, that kind of parity may be exceptional. As Sridhar (1996, p. 50) says, 'multilingualism involving balanced, nativelike command of all the languages in the repertoire is rather uncommon. Typically, multilinguals have varying degrees of command of the different repertoires. The differences in competence in the various languages might range from command of a few lexical items, formulaic expressions such as greetings, and rudimentary conversational skills all the way to excellent command of the grammar and vocabulary and specialized register and styles.' Sridhar adds: 'Multilinguals develop competence in each of the codes to the extent that they need it and for the contexts in which each of the languages is used.' Context determines language choice. In a society in which more than one language (or variety) is used you must find out who uses what, when, and for what purpose if you are to be socially competent. Your language choices are part of the social identity you claim for yourself.

In the previous paragraph I have referred to varieties as well as languages in discussing the issues that concern us. This is a consequence of the difficulties of trying to distinguish languages from dialects and among dialects themselves. Consequently, attempts to distinguish people who are *bilingual* from those who are *bidialectal* may fail. There may be some doubt that very many people are actually bi- or even multi-dialectal. They may speak varieties which are distinctly different, but whether each separate variety is genuinely a dialect depends on how one defines *dialect*, which, as we saw in chapter 2, is not at all an easy matter to decide. So it sometimes is too with deciding who is or who is not bilingual. Is someone who speaks both Hindi and Urdu bilingual, who speaks both Serbian and Croatian, Nynorsk and Bokmål, or Russian and Ukrainian? Such speakers may well tell you they are. But, on the other hand, a Chinese who speaks both Mandarin and Cantonese will almost certainly insist that he or she speaks only two dialects of Chinese, just as an Arab who knows both a colloquial variety and the classical, literary variety of Arabic will insist that they are only different varieties of the same language. In some cases, then, the bilingual–bidialectal distinction that speakers make reflects social, cultural, and political aspirations or realities rather than any linguistic reality. What we will concern ourselves with, then, are unequivocal cases in which there can be no doubt that the two languages, or codes, are mutually unintelligible.

An interesting example of multilingualism exists among the Tukano of the northwest Amazon, on the border between Colombia and Brazil (Sorensen, 1971). The Tukano are a multilingual people because men must marry outside their language group; that is, no man may have a wife who speaks his language, for that kind of marriage relationship is not permitted and would be viewed as a kind of incest. Men choose the women they marry from various neighboring tribes who speak other languages. Furthermore, on marriage, women move into the men's households or longhouses. Consequently, in any village several languages are used: the language of the men; the various languages spoken by women who originate from different neighboring tribes; and a widespread regional 'trade' language. Children are born into this multilingual environment: the child's father speaks one language, the child's mother another, and other women with whom the child has daily contact perhaps still others. However, everyone in the community is interested in language learning so most people can speak most of the languages. Multilingualism is taken for granted, and moving from one language to another in the course of a single conversation is very common. In fact, multilingualism is so usual that the Tukano are hardly conscious that they do speak different languages as they shift easily from one to another. They cannot readily tell an outsider how many languages they speak, and must be suitably prompted to enumerate which languages they speak and to describe how well they speak each one.

Multilingualism is a norm in this community. It results from the pattern of marriage and the living arrangements consequent to marriage. Communities are multilingual and no effort is made to suppress the variety of languages that are spoken. It is actually seen as a source of strength, for it enables the speakers of the various linguistic communities to maintain contact with one another and provides a source for suitable marriage partners for those who seek them. A man cannot marry one of his 'sisters,' i.e., women whose mother tongue is the same as his. People are not 'strangers' to one another by reason of the fact that they cannot communicate when away from home. When men from one village visit another village, they are likely to find speakers of their native language. There will almost certainly be some women from the 'home' village who have married into the village being visited, possibly even a sister. The children of these women, too, will be fluent in their mothers' tongue. Many others also will have learned some of it because it is considered proper to learn to use the languages of those who live with you.

Somewhat similar attitudes toward multilingualism have been reported from other parts of the world. For example, Salisbury (1962) reports that among the Siane of New Guinea it is quite normal for people to know a number of languages. They choose the most appropriate one for the particular circumstances in which they find themselves. Moreover, they prize language learning, so that, when someone who speaks a language they do not know enters a community, people in the community will try to learn as much as they can about the language and to find occasions to use their learning. Salisbury specifically mentions the interest taken in pidgin English when a group of laborers returned from service on the coast; almost immediately a school was established so that the rest of the village males could learn the pidgin.

We have no reason to assume that such situations as these are abnormal in any way. In many parts of the world people speak a number of languages and individuals may not be aware of how many different languages they speak. They speak them because they need to do so in order to live their lives: their knowledge is instrumental and pragmatic. In such situations language learning comes naturally and is quite unforced. Bilingualism or multilingualism is not at all remarkable. To be a proper Tukano or Siane you must be multilingual and a skilled user of the languages you know; that is an essential part of your Tukano or Siane identity.

A different kind of bilingual situation exists in Paraguay (see Rubin, 1968). Because of its long isolation from Spain and the paucity of its Spanish-speaking population, an American Indian language, Guaraní, has flourished in Paraguay to the extent that today it is the mother tongue of about 90 percent of the population and a second language of several additional percent. Guaraní is recognized as a national language. On the other hand, Spanish, which is the sole language of less than 7 percent of the population, is the official language of government and the medium of education, although in recent years some use has been made of Guaraní in primary education. In the 1951 census just over half the population were bilingual in Guaraní and Spanish. These figures indicate that the lesser-known language in Paraguay is Spanish. The capital city, Asunción, is almost entirely bilingual, but the further one goes into the countryside away from cities and towns the more monolingually Guaraní-speaking the population becomes.

Spanish and Guaraní exist in a relationship that Fishman (1980) calls 'extended diglossic' in which Spanish is the H variety and Guaraní the L variety. Spanish is the language used on formal occasions; it is always used in government business, in conversation with strangers who are well dressed, with foreigners, and in most business transactions. People use Guaraní, however, with friends, servants, and strangers who are poorly dressed, in the confessional, when they tell jokes or make love, and on most casual occasions. Spanish is the preferred language of the cities, but Guaraní is preferred in the countryside, and the lower classes almost always use it for just about every purpose in rural areas.

Parents may attempt to help their children improve their knowledge of Spanish by using Spanish in their presence, for, after all, Spanish is the language of educational opportunity and is socially preferred. But between themselves and with their children absent they will almost certainly switch to Guaraní. In the upper classes males may well use Guaraní with one another as a sign of friendship; upper-class females prefer Spanish in such circumstances. Outside Paraguay, Paraguayans may deliberately choose to converse in Guaraní to show their solidarity, particularly when among other South American Spanish-speaking people. Males may drink in Guaraní but use more and more Spanish as they feel the influence of alcohol, for Spanish is the language of power. Spanish may also be the language they choose to use when addressing superiors, and there may be some conflict in choosing between Spanish and Guaraní in addressing parents or grandparents. In such situations solidarity tends to win over power and Guaraní is often the choice. Courtship may begin in Spanish but, if it goes anywhere, it will proceed in Guaraní. Men tell jokes and talk about women and sports in Guaraní, but they discuss business affairs in Spanish.

We can see, therefore, that the choice between Spanish and Guaraní depends on a variety of factors: location (city or country), formality, gender, status, intimacy, seriousness, and type of activity. The choice of one code rather than the other is obviously related to situation. Paraguay identity requires you to be attuned to the uses of Spanish and Guaraní, to be aware that they 'mean' different things, and that it is not only what you say that is important but which language you choose to say it in.

In Papua New Guinea there are many languages and an increasingly used lingua franca, Tok Pisin. Many people are plurilingual. The Yimas of Papua New Guinea use their own language in traditional pursuits and Tok Pisin for topics from the encroaching outside world. Domestic matters and local food provision, largely the province of females, call for Yimas just as do mortuary feasts, the province of males. But matters to do with government, trade, and travel require Tok Pisin. Language choice among the Yimas is dependent on occasion: Yimas to perform traditional practices and Tok Pisin to establish identity within a wider community.

What I have tried to stress in this section is that bilingualism and multilingualism are normal in many parts of the world and that people in those parts would view any other situation as strange and limiting. There is a long history in certain Western societies of people actually 'looking down' on those who are bilingual. We give prestige to only a certain few classical languages (e.g., Greek and Latin) or modern languages of high culture (e.g., English, French, Italian, and German). You generally get little credit for speaking Swahili and, until recently at least, not much more for speaking Russian, Japanese, Arabic, or Chinese. Bilingualism is actually sometimes regarded as a problem in that many bilingual individuals tend to occupy rather low positions in society and knowledge of another language becomes associated with 'inferiority.' Bilingualism is sometimes seen as a personal and social problem, not something that has strong positive connotations. One unfortunate consequence is that some Western societies go to great lengths to downgrade, even eradicate, the languages that immigrants bring with them while at the same time trying to teach foreign languages in schools. What is more, they have had much more success in doing the former than the latter. I will return to this issue in chapter 15, specifically in connection with certain recent developments in the United States.

A bilingual, or multilingual, situation can produce still other effects on one or more of the languages involved. As we have just seen, it can lead to loss, e.g., language loss among immigrants. But sometimes it leads to diffusion; that is, certain features spread from one language to the other (or others) as a result of the contact situation, particularly certain kinds of syntactic features. This phenomenon has been observed in such areas as the Balkans, the south of India, and Sri Lanka. Gumperz and Wilson (1971) report that in Kupwar, a small village of about 3,000 inhabitants in Maharashtra, India, four languages are spoken: Marathi and Urdu (both of which are Indo-European) and Kannada (a non-Indo-European language). A few people also speak Telugu (also a non-Indo-European language). The languages are distributed mainly by caste. The highest caste, the Jains, speak Kannada and the lowest caste, the untouchables, speak Marathi. People in different castes must speak to one another and to the Telugu-speaking rope-makers. The Urdu-speaking Muslims must also be fitted in. Bilingualism or even trilingualism is normal, particularly among the men, but it is Marathi which dominates inter-group communication. One linguistic consequence, however, is that there has been some convergence of the languages that are spoken in the village so far as syntax is concerned, but vocabulary differences have been maintained (McMahon, 1994, pp. 214–16). It is vocabulary rather than syntax which now serves to distinguish the groups, and the variety of multilingualism that has resulted is a special local variety which has developed in response to local needs.

Discussion

1. A distinction is sometimes made between communities in which there is *stable bilingualism* and those in which there is *unstable bilingualism*; Switzerland, Canada, and Haiti are cited as examples of the former, and the linguistic situations found in cities like New York or among many immigrant peoples as examples of the latter. Why are the terms *stable* and *unstable* useful in such circumstances?

2. The term *bilingual* is used in describing countries such as Canada, Belgium, and Switzerland (also *multilingual* in this case). What kind of bilingualism (or multilingualism) is this?

3. A speaker of English who wants to learn another language, particularly an 'exotic' one, may find the task difficult. Speakers of that other language may insist on using what little English they know rather than their own language, and there may also be compelling social reasons that prevent the would-be learner from achieving any but a most rudimentary knowledge of the target language. What factors contribute to this kind of situation? How might you seek to avoid it?

4. Is it possible to have a society in which everyone is completely bilingual in the same two languages and there is no diglossia? How stable would such a situation be?

5. Some communities regard bilingualism as a serious threat; it has even been referred to as a 'Trojan horse,' initially attractive but ultimately fatal. Why might this be so? (Consider the experience of migration and also the sorry state of many minority languages in the world.)

Code-Switching

I have observed that the particular dialect or language that a person chooses to use on any occasion is a code, a system used for communication between two or more parties. I have also indicated that it is unusual for a speaker to have command of, or use, only one such code or system. Command of only a single variety of language, whether it be a dialect, style, or register, would appear to be an extremely rare phenomenon, one likely to occasion comment. Most speakers command several varieties of any language they speak, and bilingualism, even multilingualism, is the norm for many people throughout the world rather than unilingualism. People, then, are usually required to select a particular code whenever they choose to speak, and they may also decide to switch from one code to another or to mix codes even within sometimes very short utterances and thereby create a new code in a process known as *code-switching*. Code-switching (also called code-mixing) can occur in conversation between speakers' turns or within a single speaker's turn. In the latter case it can occur between sentences (inter-sententially) or within a single sentence (intra-sententially). Code-switching can arise from individual choice or be used as a major identity marker for a group of speakers who must deal with more than one language in their common pursuits. As Gal (1988, p. 247) says, 'codeswitching is a conversational strategy used to establish, cross or destroy group boundaries; to create, evoke or change interpersonal relations with their rights and obligations.' We will now look more closely at this phenomenon.

In a multilingual country like Singapore, the ability to shift from one language to another is accepted as quite normal. Singapore has four official languages: English, the Mandarin variety of Chinese, Tamil, and Malay, which is also the national language (see also pp. 371–2). However, the majority of its population are native speakers of Hokkien, another variety of Chinese. National policy promotes English as a trade language, Mandarin as the international 'Chinese' language, Malay as the language of the region, and Tamil as the language of one of the important ethnic groups in the republic. What this means for a 'typical' Chinese child growing up in Singapore is that he or she is likely to speak Hokkien with parents and informal Singapore English with siblings. Conversation with friends will be in Hokkien or informal Singapore English. The languages of education will be the formal variety of Singapore English and Mandarin. Any religious practices will be conducted in the formal variety of Singapore English if the family is Christian, but in Hokkien if Buddhist or Taoist. The language of government employment will be formal Singapore English but some Mandarin will be used from time to time; however, shopping will be carried on in Hokkien, informal Singapore English, and the 'bazaar' variety of Malay used throughout the region. (See Platt and Platt, 1975, pp. 91–4, for a fuller discussion.) The linguistic situation in Singapore offers those who live there a wide choice among languages, with the actual choice made on a particular occasion determined by the kinds of factors just mentioned. (It may even be possible to characterize the total linguistic situation in Singapore as a complicated diglossic one if we accept Fishman's view of diglossia.)

We may also ask what happens when people from a multilingual society, people who are themselves multilingual, meet in a 'foreign' setting: what language or languages do they use? Tanner (1967) reports on the linguistic usage of a small group of Indonesian graduate students and their families living in the United States. Among them these students knew nine different languages, with nearly everyone knowing Indonesian (Bahasa Indonesia), Javanese, Dutch, and English. They tended to discuss their academic work in English but used Indonesian for most other common activities. Unlike Javanese, 'Indonesian . . . , whether the official or the daily variety, is regarded as a neutral, democratic language. A speaker of Indonesian need not commit himself to any particular social identity, nor need he impute one to those with whom he converses' (p. 134). The students also used Dutch, but mainly as a resource, e.g., for vocabulary, or because of the place it necessarily held in certain fields of study, e.g., Indonesian studies. Local languages like Javanese tended to be used only with intimates when fine shades of respect or distance were necessary, particularly when in the presence of important older people. Tanner's findings conform to an earlier prediction made by Geertz (1960, p. 259): 'Indonesian appeals to those whose sense of political nationality as Indonesians rather than as Javanese is most developed, to those who are interested in the cultural products of the new Indonesia's mass media . . . and those who wish to take leadership positions in government and business.' He adds that, 'although the use of Indonesian for everyday conversation is still mostly confined to the more sophisticated urbanites, and its use suggests something of an air of "public speaking" for most Javanese, it is rapidly becoming more and more an integral part of their daily cultural life and will become even more so as the present generation of school children grows to adulthood.' Javanese will continue to be used 'in certain special contexts and for certain special purposes.'

Situations such as those just described are not uncommon. In Kenya, local languages, Swahili, and English all find use and choosing the right language to use on a particular occasion can be quite a delicate matter. Whiteley (1984, pp. 74–5) describes the kind of situation that can occur between a member of the public and members of the government bureaucracy:

> A man wishing to see a government officer about renewing a licence may state his request to the girl typist in Swahili as a suitably neutral language if he does not know her. To start off in English would be unfortunate if she did not know it, and on her goodwill depends his gaining access to authority reasonably quickly.

She may reply in Swahili, if she knows it as well as he does and wishes to be co-operative; or in English, if she is busy and not anxious to be disturbed; or in the local language, if she recognises him and wishes to reduce the level of formality. If he, in return, knows little English, he may be put off at her use of it and decide to come back later; or, if he knows it well, he may demonstrate his importance by insisting on an early interview and gain his objective at the expense of the typist's goodwill. The interview with the officer may well follow a similar pattern, being shaped, on the one hand, by the total repertoire mutually available, and on the other by their respective positions in relation to the issue involved.

Trudgill (1995, pp. 108–10) describes a situation in Kampala, the capital of Uganda, which is similar in many respects.

The actual choice of code in a setting clearly marked as bilingual can be a difficult task. As Heller (1982) has observed, language plays a symbolic role in our lives, and when there is a choice of languages the actual choice may be very important, particularly when there is a concurrent shift in the relationship between the languages, as is occurring in Montreal between English and French. In such circumstances, as Heller observes, 'negotiation in conversation is a playing out of a negotiation for position in the community at large' (p. 109). Heller studied the uses of the two languages in a Montreal hospital during the summer of 1977. Which language was used varied as circumstances changed. What is particularly interesting is that the pattern that has evolved of asking which language someone wishes to use in a public service encounter ('English or French, Anglais ou Français?') is not very effective. The reason is that too many other factors are involved to make the choice that simple (p. 118):

> the negotiation of language has to do with judgments of personal treatment, that is, how one expects to be treated in such a situation. But such judgments are dependent upon social knowledge, knowledge about group relations and boundaries and ways of signalling them, and knowledge about other social differences, e.g., status differences.
> . . . This negotiation itself serves to redefine the situations in the light of ongoing social and political change. In the absence of norms, we work at creating new ones. The conventionalization of the negotiating strategies appears to be a way of normalizing relationships, of encoding social information necessary to know how to speak to someone (and which language to speak is but one aspect of this).

Most of Heller's examples show how the conventionalization to which she refers – i.e., asking the other which language is preferred – often does not work very well in practice. Social and political relationships are too complicated to be resolved by such a simple linguistic choice.

We can see still other examples of how a speaker may deliberately choose to use a specific language to assert some kind of 'right.' A bilingual (in French and English) French Canadian may insist on using French to an official of the federal government outside Quebec, a bilingual (Catalan and Spanish) resident of Barcelona may insist on using Catalan, a bilingual (Welsh and English) resident of Wales may insist on using Welsh, and so on. In these cases code choice becomes a form of political expression, a move either to resist some other power, or to gain power, or to express solidarity.

We are therefore turning to the issue of what brings a speaker to choose variety X of a language A rather than variety Y, or even language A rather than language B. What might cause a speaker to switch from variety X to variety Y or from language A to language B? A number of answers have been suggested, including solidarity, accommodation to listeners, choice of topic, and perceived social and cultural distance. In other words, the motivation of the speaker is an important consideration in the choice. Moreover, such motivation need not be at all conscious, for apparently many speakers are not aware that they have used one particular variety of a language rather than another or sometimes even that they have switched languages either between or within utterances.

Equating in this instance code with language, we can describe two kinds of code-switching: situational and metaphorical. *Situational code-switching* occurs when the languages used change according to the situations in which the conversants find themselves: they speak one language in one situation and another in a different one. No topic change is involved. When a change of topic requires a change in the language used we have *metaphorical code-switching*. The interesting point here is that some topics may be discussed in either code, but the choice of code adds a distinct flavor to what is said about the topic. The choice encodes certain social values. Linguists have found it very difficult to explain precisely when, linguistically and socially, code-switching occurs, i.e., what all the constraints are. However, there is broad agreement about the general principles that are involved.

Instances of situational code-switching are usually fairly easy to classify for what they are. What we observe is that one variety is used in a certain set of situations and another in an entirely different set. However, the changeover from one to the other may be instantaneous. Sometimes the situations are so socially prescribed that they can even be taught, e.g., those associated with ceremonial or religious functions. Others may be more subtly determined but speakers readily observe the norms. This kind of code-switching differs from diglossia. In diglossic communities the situation also controls the choice of variety but the choice is much more rigidly defined by the particular activity that is involved and by the relationship between the participants. Diglossia reinforces differences, whereas code-switching tends to reduce them. In diglossia too people are quite aware that they have switched from H to L or L to H. Code-switching, on the other hand, is often quite subconscious: people may not be aware that they have switched or be able to report, following a conversation, which code they used for a particular topic.

As the term itself suggests, metaphorical code-switching has an affective dimension to it: you change the code as you redefine the situation – formal to informal, official to personal, serious to humorous, and politeness to solidarity. In a number of places Gumperz (particularly 1982a) cites examples of metaphorical code-switching from three sets of languages (Hindi and English, Slovenian and German, and Spanish and English) to show how speakers employ particular languages to convey information that goes beyond their actual words, especially to define social situations. What happens in each case is that one language expresses a *we*-type solidarity among participants, and is therefore deemed suitable for in-group and informal activities, whereas the other language is *they*-oriented and is considered appropriate to out-group and more formal relationships, particularly of an impersonal kind. The *we–they* distinction is by no means absolute, so fine-shading is possible in switching; i.e., certain topics may be discussed in either code, and the particular choice made itself helps to define the social situation or to shift that definition, as the case may be. Woolard (1989) provides a good example of this kind of shift from Barcelona. Catalans use Catalan only to each other; they use Castilian to non-Catalans and they will even switch to Castilian if they become aware that the other person is speaking Catalan with a Castilian accent. Catalan is only for Catalans. It also never happens that one party speaks Catalan and the other Castilian even though such a conversation is theoretically possible since all Catalans are bilingual.

A particular group of people may employ different kinds of code-switching for different purposes. In their account of how the population of Hemnesberget, a small Norwegian town of 1,300 inhabitants located close to the Arctic Circle, use a local northern dialect of Norwegian, Ranamål, and one of the standard varieties, Bokmål, Blom and Gumperz (1972) show how both situational and metaphorical code-switching are used. Situational switching occurs when a teacher gives some kind of formal lecture in Bokmål but the discussion that follows is in Ranamål. Metaphorical switching is a more complicated phenomenon. One type tends to occur when government officials and local citizens transact business together. Although the variety generally used in such circumstances is Bokmål, it is not unusual for both parties to use the occasional Ranamål expression for special effect. Blom and Gumperz also discovered that, while most locals thought they used Ranamål exclusively in casual conversations and reserved Bokmål for use in school and church and on formal occasions, such was not the case. Tape recordings revealed switches to Bokmål to achieve certain effects. Moreover, the participants were not conscious of these switches, and even after such switching to Bokmål was pointed out to them and they declared they would not do it again, they continued to do so, as further tapings revealed.

Such persistence suggests that metaphorical code-switching in such situations is deeply ingrained and that it serves subtle but strong functions. Not only do natives of Hemnesberget find the existence of two varieties of Norwegian useful to them in demonstrating *we*-ness (Ranamål) and *they*-ness (Bokmål), but they also are able to employ both varieties together in such ways as to express fine gradations of feeling for others, involvement with the topic, politeness to strangers, and deference to officials.

Gumperz (1982a, pp. 44–58) also reports on an interesting situation in the Gail Valley of Austria near the borders of the former Yugoslavia and Italy, which shows how two languages (Slovenian and German) are used, what kinds of code-switching occur, and what changes appear to be in progress. Slovenian has long been spoken in the valley, but the valley is part of Austria so German is the prestige language. The Slovenians of the village are bilingual. However, the bilingual population tends to use Slovenian and German for quite different purposes. Gumperz explains (p. 47) that there are 'three speech varieties: a formal style of standard Austrian German, the regional German dialect, and the village variety of Slovenian. To interact in accordance with the village communicative conventions, a speaker must control all three of these.' Children are encouraged to learn Standard German in school so as to maximize their opportunities for employment. It is regarded 'as impolite or even crude to use Slovenian in the presence of German-speaking outsiders, be they foreigners or monolingual Germans from the region.' Slovenian itself is reserved mainly for use in the family and informal local friendship circles. However, 'there is by no means a one-to-one relationship between extralinguistic context and language use.'

Gumperz's analysis of code-switching in the community reveals that the situation is quite complex because of the number of possibilities that are available, with the 'right' choice highly dependent on the social context and intent of the speaker. A further complication is that the need to maintain the in-group (Slovenian) versus out-group (German) difference has weakened considerably in recent years, mainly as a result of economic development brought about by increased tourism in the area. The use of Slovenian is decreasing. The young use less and less Slovenian and code-switch much less than their elders, preferring to use German almost exclusively among themselves. While older bilinguals do not speak German exactly like monolingual Germans, many young bilinguals do. There is therefore a shift in progress in the functions of the two languages, one which also affects code-switching since it involves the values attached to the languages and therefore a change in norms.

Code-switching is not a uniform phenomenon; i.e., the norms vary from group to group, even within what might be regarded as a single community. Gumperz (1982a, p. 68) has pointed out, for example, that:

> In a relatively small Puerto Rican neighborhood in New Jersey, some members freely used code-switching styles and extreme forms of borrowing both in everyday casual talk and in more formal gatherings. Other local residents were careful to speak only Spanish with a minimum of loans on formal occasions, reserving code-switching styles for informal talk. Others again spoke mainly English, using Spanish or code-switching styles only with small children or with neighbors.

He adds that 'each communicating subgroup tends to establish its own conventions with respect to both borrowing and code-switching,' and that factors such as region of origin, local residence, social class, and occupational niche are involved in defining the norms. Moreover, bilinguals in such communities are aware not only of the norms that apply within their own sub-groups but also of some of the norms that other bilinguals observe (p. 69):

> Residents of such large Spanish–English-speaking communities as San Francisco or New York, which include immigrants from many Latin American regions, in fact claim that they can tell much about a person's family background and politics from the way that person code-switches and uses borrowings. What the outsider sees as almost unpredictable variation becomes a communicative resource for members. Since bilingual usage rules must be learned by living in a group, ability to speak appropriately is a strong indication of shared background assumptions. Bilinguals, in fact, ordinarily do not use code-switching styles in their contact with other bilinguals before they know something about the listener's background and attitudes. To do otherwise would be to risk serious misunderstanding.

The following example from Chinua Achebe's novel *No Longer at Ease* (1975b, pp. 66–7) shows how code-switching can be used within a situation involving a creole to imply wrong-doing. Obi is a British-educated Nigerian and Joseph a minister in the government. Clara is a friend of both.

> When Obi got back to Joseph's room it was nearly eleven o'clock. Joseph was still up. In fact he had been waiting all the afternoon to complete the discussion they had suspended last night.
> 'How is Clara?' he asked . . .
> 'She is fine,' he said. 'Your Nigerian police are very cheeky, you know.'
> 'They are useless,' said Joseph, not wanting to discuss the police.
> 'I asked the driver to take us to the Victoria Beach Road. When we got there it was so cold that Clara refused to leave her seat. So we stayed at the back of the car, talking.'
> 'Where was the driver?' asked Joseph.
> 'He walked a little distance away to gaze at the lighthouse. Anyway, we were not there ten minutes before a police car drew up beside us and one of them flashed his torch. He said: "Good evening, sir." I said: "Good evening." Then he said: "Is she your wife?" I remained very cool and said: "No." Then he said: "Where you pick am?" I couldn't stand that, so I blew up. Clara told me in Ibo to call the driver and go away. The policeman immediately changed. He was Ibo, you see. He said he didn't know we were Ibos. He said many people these days were fond of taking other men's wives to the beach. Just think of that. "*Where you pick am?*"'
> 'What did you do after that?'
> 'We came away. We couldn't possibly stay after that.'

In addition to the police officer's switch from the standard *Is she your wife?* to the creole *Where you pick am?*, we have the reported shift to the use of Ibo, which has the immediate effect of changing the police officer's attitude because he too speaks Ibo. Further on in the novel (p. 100), Achebe describes the speech of still another character in the following way:

> Whether Christopher spoke good or 'broken' English depended on what he was saying, where he was saying it, to whom and how he wanted to say it. Of course that was to some extent true of most educated people, especially on Saturday nights. But Christopher was rather outstanding in thus coming to terms with a double heritage.

(The 'double heritage' referred to is the local combination of African and British influences.)

On p. 85, I pointed out a kind of code-switching that occurs among certain young people of Caribbean descent in England. These youngsters speak the local variety of English natively but also have a creole-based variety of their own which they switch to for purposes of solidarity. What is interesting is that on certain occasions they will allow youths of their acquaintance from other ethnic groups to switch to that variety too, as they show their willingness to extend some kind of solidarity to them. Rampton (1995) discusses some of the consequences of this 'crossing' behavior of members of these other groups, i.e., their deliberate adoption of stigmatized linguistic forms.

Code-switching itself may meet with certain kinds of resistance. Numerous instances have been reported of speakers of various languages refusing to allow others to code-switch and instead insisting on using the other's language, even if sometimes such use provided a poorer means of communication. In colonial times Europeans have been known to use a local language very badly with servants rather than let them use English, French, and so on, in order to maintain social distance. In other circumstances knowledge of the second code must be suppressed, i.e., code-switching is disallowed. Certain social situations may require that one code be used rather than another, even though that second code is known to all participants but the first only to some. For example, a head of state may be required to use the official language of that state when addressing another head of state, at least in public. On many public occasions in Canada it is obligatory for officials to say a few words in the official language that they are not using, e.g., introduce some French sentences into an otherwise all-English speech. The ability to code-switch may even be regarded with suspicion or disfavor in certain circumstances: speakers of English do not usually give much credit to their fellows who speak 'exotic' languages, such ability being regarded quite often as 'strange' in some way. As I have indicated, certain English-speaking societies find difficulty in coming to terms with immigrants who speak other languages, the resulting multilingualism often being viewed as creating a 'problem.'

There can also be a switch of codes within a simple utterance without any associated topic change. Pfaff (1979) provides the following examples of this kind of code-switching (sometimes called intra-sentential code-switching, or code-mixing) among Spanish–English bilinguals:

No van a bring it up in the meeting.
'They are not going to bring it up in the meeting.'

Todos los Mexicanos were riled up.
'All the Mexicans were riled up.'

Estaba training para pelear.
'He was training to fight.'

Some dudes, la onda is to fight y jambar.
'Some dudes, the in thing is to fight and steal.'

Another example, this time of a long utterance, spoken quite flowingly by a New York Puerto Rican speaker, comes from Labov (1971, p. 457):

Por eso cada, you know it's nothing to be proud of, porque yo no estoy proud of it, as a matter of fact I hate it, pero viene Vierne y Sabado yo estoy, tu me ve haci a mi, sola with a, aqui solita, a veces que Frankie me deja, you know a stick or something, y yo equi solita, queces Judy no sabe y yo estoy haci, viendo television, but I rather, y cuando estoy con gente yo me . . . borracha porque me siento mas, happy, mas free, you know, pero si yo estoy com mucha gente yo no estoy, you know, high, more or less, I couldn't get along with anybody.

Bilinguals often switch like this, primarily as a solidarity marker and this kind of mixture has become an established community norm in the Puerto Rican community in New York City. However, a speaker who mixes codes in this way in conversation with a friend or acquaintance will almost certainly shift entirely to English when addressing a monolingual English-speaking person or entirely to Spanish when addressing a complete stranger who is obviously of Spanish origin.

Nishimura (1997) reports on the language choices of several Niseis (second-generation Japanese immigrants) living in Toronto as they conversed with a variety of friends in private homes. These Niseis spoke Japanese to native Japanese, English to fellow Niseis, and a mixture of Japanese and English to mixed groups of Japanese and Niseis. However, their Japanese contained some English words – mainly when they did not know the Japanese equivalents – and their English made 'sporadic use of Japanese phrases and sentences symboliz[ing] the speaker's identity as a Nisei' (p. 156). However, all three types of use clearly show a speaker's identity as a Nisei and his or her solidarity with other Niseis. Winford (2003, p. 41) says that the ability to code-mix Alsatian and French in Strasbourg symbolizes ethnic identity and solidarity. He contrasts Strasbourg with Brussels where, especially among young people, the mixing of French and Dutch is no longer seen as a marker of Brussels identity.

Monolinguals are likely to be very critical of the new codes that result. They may even use derogatory terms to describe what they hear, e.g., *Franglais* (French and English in Quebec), *Fragnol* (French and Spanish in Argentina), *Spanglish* (Cuban Spanish and English in the USA), and *Tex-Mex* (English and Mexican Spanish in Texas). Such dismissal of the phenomenon demonstrates serious misunderstanding. What we have here is not just a haphazard mixing of two languages brought about by laziness or ignorance or some combination of these. What we have are conversants with a sophisticated knowledge of both languages who are also acutely aware of community norms. These norms require that both languages be used in this way so that conversants can show their familiarity or solidarity. The ability to mix codes in this way is now often a source of pride, e.g., the ability to use *pocho* or *caló*, the names that many Spanish-speaking North Americans give to these varieties.

As I indicated earlier, a fundamental difficulty in understanding the phenomenon of code-switching is accounting for a particular choice or switch on a particular occasion. In order to provide such an account we must look at the total linguistic situation in which the choice is made, e.g., the linguistic situation in New York City, Brussels, Luxembourg, Kampala, Hemnesberget, or Papua New Guinea. This task is no different, except perhaps quantitatively, from the task of trying to account for an individual's choice of one variety of a language in one set of circumstances and of another in a different set. Such a task is not an easy one. Sankoff (1972), for example, has quite clearly demonstrated how difficult it is to account for code choice in Papua New Guinea: prediction appears to be out of the question, but even accounting for choices after they have been made is difficult.

Myers-Scotton (1993b, and Scotton, 1983) has tried to account for code-switching by proposing that speakers have unmarked and marked choices available to them when they speak. These choices vary by situation. It is an unmarked choice for a citizen to address an inquiry to an official in Bokmål in Hemnesberget, for a teacher to speak Standard German to a visitor in a school in the Gail Valley, and for a police officer to speak English to someone in a good car in Nigeria. Corresponding marked choices for initial encounters between people who do not know each other in each of the above encounters would be Ranamål, Slovenian, and one of the indigenous Nigerian languages. However, the unmarked choices are these latter languages when locals converse socially in each of these places. Quite often, in fact, local solidarity requires the use of a non-prestige language or variety; it may even require a mixing of two languages. These last observations are important: the unmarked–marked distinction is quite independent of any High–Low, standard–nonstandard, language–dialect, or pure–mixed distinctions. It is entirely dependent on situation. Myers-Scotton (1993a) has further developed her views to try to account for some of the actual linguistic consequences of code-switching. Her Matrix Language Frame model says that in code-switching one language acts as a dominant or matrix language and the other as a subordinate or embedded language. She says that it is the basic word structure of the matrix language that determines what happens to words in the embedded language.

Myers-Scotton has provided us with a good explanation for the variety of code-switching behaviors we have observed. Speakers choose, not always consciously by any means, how they say what they want to say. They are generally aware of the power dimensions in the situations they find themselves in and they also know who they want to be identified with, the solidarity dimension. They have some idea too of how they want to appear to others and how they want others to behave toward them, both of these matters of 'face,' another concept we will have occasion to use (see p. 276). When speakers have two or more codes available to them, they increase their possible range of language behaviors. (The problems they have in communicating therefore become easier or more difficult, depending on how you view what communication is!) Code-switching can allow a speaker to do many things: assert power; declare solidarity; maintain a certain neutrality when both codes are used; express identity; and so on.

In situations in which several languages or language varieties coexist, choices have consequences. Bailey (2005) describes how Dominican American high-school students in Providence, Rhode Island negotiate their way among other students of different language backgrounds, mainly other Hispanics and African Americans. They share a language with the former and color and social-class characteristics with the latter. However, they seek to assert their own separate identity. Consequently, they have developed a code that 'includes distinctive alternation of forms indexing a Dominican American identity. Most salient of these, perhaps, is the alternation between English and Spanish in code-switching' (p. 259). They actually do use some speech characteristics of the African American students but such use does not make them 'black' since their ability to use Spanish, their Spanish ethnolinguistic identity, triumphs over any common identity derived from African descent (p. 263). While they continue to speak their varieties of Spanish and English, they maintain at least for now their separate identity. However, Bailey adds (pp. 270–1), if succeeding generations of students fail to continue to do so, this could have serious consequences for maintaining a separate Dominican American identity.

In this chapter we have seen numerous examples of the power and solidarity dimensions. Gardner-Chloros (1991) in a study of language use in Strasbourg shows among other things how switching between codes, in this case Standard French and Alsatian German, can be an effective neutral compromise for some locals. They can employ code-switching when use of French alone might appear to be too snobbish and Alsatian alone to be too rustic. It is also often necessary when several generations of a family are present and allows for accommodation across the generations. Another investigation (Gardner-Chloros, 1997) focused on the use of the two languages in three department stores in Strasbourg: Printemps, a branch of the famous chic Paris store, Magmod, old-fashioned and less luxurious, and Jung, quite provincial in comparison to either of the others. In other words, there is a kind of prestige hierarchy with Printemps at the top, Magmod in the middle, and Jung at the bottom. One would assume that in Printemps French would be the language most likely to be used by shoppers and shop assistants alike and that Jung would attract most use of Alsatian; Magmod would be somewhere in the middle. Gardner-Chloros found that young French-speaking shoppers in Jung and older Alsatian-speaking shoppers in Printemps code-switched to the other language. There was least code-switching in Magmod. Code-switching goes in both directions: 'up' in Printemps and 'down' in Jung. As Gardner-Chloros says (p. 374), it 'is clear . . . that the . . . assumption that switching reveals a desire to converge to the prestige norm is inadequate. The group which switches more than any other appears to do so in order to fit in with its surroundings, since it is made up of people who are more at ease in the prestige norm, French, than in Alsatian. Accommodation would therefore appear to be as relevant a motive as prestige.' We will look more closely below at this concept of 'accommodation' for its usefulness in explaining what appears to be happening here.

In a study of code-switching within Chinese–English bilingual families in Tyneside, England Li (1995) and Li and Milroy (1995) show how effective a switch from the unmarked variety, in this case Chinese, to the marked variety, in this case English, can be when a mother asks her 12-year-old son in English rather than Chinese, why he has not finished his homework. English is the preferred language of the boy but Chinese that of his mother and the unmarked choice in parent–child talk. As Li and Milroy (p. 257) say, 'the mother knows that by choosing the preferred language of the child instead of her own preferred language, she is turning a simple question into an indirect request for the child to do his homework before playing with the computer.' Moreover, the child correctly interprets the question as a request.

A further example comes from Fiji (Siegel, 1995) and it shows how the unmarked–marked distinction can be used for humorous effect. Fiji is split almost equally on racial lines with half the population speaking Fijian and the other half, of Indian descent, speaking Fijian Hindi, an immigrant language derived from contact among different varieties of Hindi and English. The two groups use English in most contact situations and English is also the language of government, education, and business. Fijians often know some Fijian Hindi and sometimes use it among themselves in code-switching situations but only for purposes of joking. They introduce Fijian Hindi words into their utterances so as to direct some kind of mild humor at a fellow Fijian. As Siegel says (p. 101), 'In the Fiji situation, Hindi is not normally used for communication among Fijians; so when a Fijian switches to Hindi among other Fijians, it is a marked choice. For the listener(s), it is almost always a clear signal that the speaker is joking.'

Code choices can have still another important dimension. You can try to adopt a code used by others. Actors do this all the time, but how often do we try to imagine ourselves in the shoes of some other or others, or, in some cases, actually try them on? The linguistic term for this kind of code choice is *crossing* (sometimes *styling*) (see Rampton, 1995, 2001). Sweetland (2002) describes how a young white woman in the United States uses linguistic features generally associated with African American Vernacular English (AAVE) in order to achieve membership in a group of blacks, helped in this case by her growing up in an overwhelmingly black neighborhood. Bucholtz (1999) describes a similar case of a white male student in a California high school where 'an ideologically defined black–white dichotomy . . . structures students' social worlds. Yet many European American students symbolically cross this divide through linguistic and other social practices that index their affiliation with African American youth culture, and especially hip hop' (p. 445). This student drew on features of AAVE to identify the group he wished to claim some kind of honorary membership in, particularly through his use of a black-influenced speech style. (We should also remember that we are being asked to perform a variety of crossing when we are urged to abandon one language or dialect in favor of another. Crossing is difficult at the best of times and often the results fall far short of the promises that are made or the hopes that are raised.)

As we have seen, your choice of code also reflects how you want to appear to others, i.e., how you want to express your identity and/or how you want others to view you. This is apparent from various *matched-guise* experiments that certain social psychologists have conducted. If person A is perfectly bilingual in languages X and Y, how is he or she judged as a person when speaking X? How do the same judges evaluate A when A is speaking language Y? In matched-guise experiments the judges are unaware that they are judging A twice and that the only variable is that A is using language X on one occasion and language Y on the other, and using each for the same purpose. Their judgments, therefore, really reflect their feelings about speakers of X and Y, feelings about such matters as their competence, integrity, and attractiveness.

Lambert, a Canadian social psychologist, developed this technique in order to explore how listeners react to various characteristics in speech. Listeners were asked to judge particular speech samples recorded by bilingual or bidialectal speakers using one language or dialect (one guise) on one occasion and the other language or dialect (the other guise) in identical circumstances. The judgments sought are of such qualities as intelligence, kindness, dependability, ambition, leadership, sincerity, and sense of humor. Since the only factor that is varied is the language or dialect used, the responses provide group evaluations of speakers of these languages and dialects and therefore tap *social stereotypes*. In one such study Lambert (1967) reported the reactions of Canadian men and women, both English and French speakers, to subjects who spoke English on one occasion and French on another. Both English and French listeners reacted more positively to English guises than French guises. Among 80 English Canadian (EC) and 92 French Canadian (FC) first-year college-age students from Montreal, he found (pp. 95–7) that:

> the EC listeners viewed the female speakers more favorably in their French guises while they viewed the male speakers more favorably in their English guises. In particular, the EC men saw the FC lady speakers as more intelligent, ambitious, self-confident, dependable, courageous and sincere than their English counterparts. The EC ladies were not quite so gracious, although they, too, rated the FC ladies as more intelligent, ambitious, self-confident (but shorter) than the EC women guises. Thus, ECs generally view FC females as more competent and the EC men see them as possessing more integrity and competence. . . . FC men were not as favorably received as the women were by their EC judges, EC ladies like EC men, rating them as taller, more likeable, affectionate, sincere, and conscientious, and as possessing more character and a greater sense of humor than the FC version of the same speakers. Furthermore, the EC male judges also favored EC male speakers, rating them as taller, more kind, dependable and entertaining. Thus, FC male speakers are viewed as lacking integrity and as being less socially attractive by both EC female, and, to a less marked extent, EC male judges.
>
> . . . The reactions to Continental French (CF) speakers are generally more favorable although less marked. The EC male listeners viewed CF women as slightly more competent and CF men as equivalent to their EC controls except for height and religiousness. The EC female listeners upgraded CF women on sociability and self-confidence, but downgraded CF men on height, likeability and sincerity. Thus, EC judges appear to be less concerned about European French people in general than they are about the local French people; the European French are neither downgraded nor taken as potential social models to any great extent. . . .
>
> . . . the FC listeners showed more significant guise differences than did their EC counterparts. FCs generally rated European French guises *more* favorably and Canadian French guises *less* favorably than they did their matched EC guises. One important exception was the FC women who viewed FC men as more competent and as more socially attractive than EC men.

What is surprising in all of this is that the French Canadians had such a poor valuation of themselves, apparently viewing their own linguistic and cultural group as somewhat inferior to both the English Canadian and the Continental French groups, with this preference apparently stronger in French Canadian males than females. (This study is now nearly forty years old; it would be surprising if a replication done today would show the same results, in view of the many changes that have occurred in Quebec in recent decades.)

Other investigators have used the matched-guise technique (see chapter 14) and report results which clearly indicate that listeners are affected by code choices when they judge what speakers say to them. Certain codes are deemed more appropriate for certain messages than other codes. Code and message are inseparable. Consequently, when a choice between codes exists (and such a choice nearly always does exist), you must exercise that choice with great care since it can affect what happens to the message you wish to communicate. Giles and

Coupland (1991, p. 58) conclude their summary of the work done up to 1990 on the matched-guise technique with the observation that, 'Listeners can very quickly stereotype others' personal and social attributes on the basis of language cues and in ways that appear to have crucial effects on important social decisions made about them.'

One important consequence from all that I have said above is that speakers often try to accommodate to the expectations that others have of them when they speak. *Accommodation* is one way of explaining how individuals and groups may be seen to relate to each other. One individual can try to induce another to judge him or her more favorably by reducing differences between the two. An individual may need to sacrifice something to gain social approval of some kind, for example, shift in behavior to be more like the other. This is *convergence* behavior. Alternatively, if one desires to be judged less favorably the shift in behavior is away from the other's behavior. This is *divergence* behavior. The particular behaviors involved may be of various kinds, not necessarily speech alone: types of dress, choices of cultural pursuits, etc. There is also always a cost–benefit aspect to any kind of accommodation. We see convergence when a speaker tries to adopt the accent of a listener or that used within another social group or even in extreme cases gives up a particular accent, dialect, or language completely. As a group phenomenon this last choice may 'kill' a minority language. Divergence is behind exaggerating differences, e.g., recreolization (p. 85), Paraguayans using Guaraní rather than Spanish when abroad (p. 99), and many efforts in language planning (see chapter 15).

Giles and Coupland (pp. 60–1) explain speech accommodation as 'a multiply-organized and contextually complex set of alternatives, regularly available to communicators in face-to-face talk. It can function to index and achieve solidarity with or dissociation from a conversational partner, reciprocally and dynamically.' Le Page (1997, p. 28) extends this definition to put even more emphasis on the speaker's creation of his or her identity (Le Page's italics): '*we do not necessarily adapt to the style of the interlocutor, but rather to the image we have of ourselves in relation to our interlocutor.*' Speaking is not merely a social act that involves others; it is also a personal act in that it helps create the identity one wishes to be seen as having in a particular set of circumstances.

One type of convergent behavior is said to be motivated by how speakers often attempt to deal with listeners through *audience design*, i.e., by orienting their speech toward others through code choices (Bell, 1984, 2001). Bell goes so far as to declare that '*Speakers design their style primarily for and in response to their audience*' (2001, p. 143: italics in the original) or occasionally by reference to a third party (*referee design*) as when the speech of an absent reference group influences language choices. He says that audience design applies to all codes and all speakers, who have what he calls '*a fine-grained ability*' (p. 146) to do this. 'Individual speakers use style – and other aspects of their language repertoire – to represent their identity or to lay claim to other identities' (p. 163). Style shifts constantly, but 'a person is more than an ever-shifting kaleidoscope of personas created in and by different situations, with no stable core' (p. 164). We are what we are, but we do have the ability to present ourselves in different ways. We have control over what is sometimes called *speaker design*: the use of language 'as a resource in the actual creation, presentation, and re-creation of speaker identity' (Schilling-Estes, 2002, p. 388). Everything we say to others recognizes those others; an individual's speech is not a series of monologs for it is shaped toward and tailored by what others say and do.

Johnson-Weiner (1998) uses accommodation theory to explain differences in language choice between some Old Order Amish and Old Order Mennonite communities in the northeastern United States (mainly New York and Pennsylvania) and Ontario and other New Order communities. The main difference is that the Old Order communities adhere strictly to use of different varieties of German – Low Pennsylvania German, High Pennsylvania German, and 'Bible German' – and English according to circumstances. They use the varieties of German exclusively within the communities and use English as a contact language with the outside world. Within the New Order communities such as the Beachy Amish and Horning Mennonites there has been a complete shift to English. However, all groups follow strict rules – although not always the same ones – about dress and use (or non-use) of automobiles, electricity, and telephones. Johnson-Weiner says that for the Old Order communities the maintenance of German shows a desire for deliberate divergence from the outside world to the point of rejection. Its use of English accommodates to a necessity to keep that world at bay; it is a way of dealing with that world so as to preserve each community's isolation from it. For communities such as the Beachy Amish and Horning Mennonites the use of English paradoxically provides both inclusion (convergence) and exclusion (divergence) in that it enables both communication with the outside world and a clear expression to that world of the values of each community, particularly its strong religious beliefs.

We find another example of this accommodation process at work in Yau's account (1997) of language use in the Hong Kong Legislative Council between 1991 and 1995, i.e., in the years approaching the return of Hong Kong to China (1997). The council was a mixed group of establishment appointees and democratically elected members. Its working languages were English and Cantonese with the first having long historic use in the council and the second being the language of Hong Kong, although almost completely ignored in the higher administration of the colony. During the period of the investigation there was a decrease in the amount of English used in the council and an increase in the use of Cantonese and in the amount of code-switching to Cantonese. Yau hypothesizes that during these years the council became increasingly aware that the total Hong Kong community was following its actions closely and that councilors and the government officials brought before the council increased their use of Cantonese as a consequence. They were accommodating to the power shift that was to take place in 1997. What little code-switching there was to English was found mainly in Cantonese-speaking councilors' dealings with the anglophone president of the council, another type of accommodation. Evans and Green (2001, 2003) report that after 1997 writing and particularly reading in English continue to play an important role in the lives of Chinese professionals with such use directly related to status. However, it is still too early to predict future directions since geopolitical and economic forces will largely determine what will happen.

The code we choose to use on a particular occasion indicates how we wish others to view us. If we can comfortably control a number of codes, then we would appear to have an advantage over those who lack such control. Speaking several of the languages can obviously be distinctly advantageous in a multilingual gathering. Finlayson et al. (1998) provide an interesting example. They show that by code-switching in a conversation, a speaker can both access different identities and accommodate to others. Code-switching allows a speaker to meet someone else half-way, establish common ground, and show flexibility and openness. Such qualities are extremely important in the particular social environment they discuss, a black South African township home to various languages: 'people in the townships are prepared to accommodate each other and believe that it is important to do so because the issue of communication is at stake. Multilingualism is an accepted fact of life by the residents of Tembisa who speak different languages' (p. 403). Code-switching shows one to be a 'cooperative person, someone who can recognize that everyone does not have the same background' (p. 417). It reduces possibilities of conflict in situations which otherwise might be fraught with danger.

In the last few pages I have been using code and style almost interchangeably since style is one aspect of code: style is how you choose to code what you want to say on a particular occasion. It 'is the implementation, at any given time, of a combination of features from many varieties . . . registers . . . and performance genres . . . at [the] speaker's disposal . . . it is continuously modulated as it is accomplished, co-produced by audience, addressees, and refereees, sensitive to characteristics of these as well as to delicate contextual factors such as presence of an overhearer' (Mendoza-Denton, 2001, p. 235). Bernsten (1998) investigated the shop talk of sixty-four employees in an automobile plant in Flint, Michigan. Workers and supervisors used language differently and each had certain expectations of what language uses were appropriate and inappropriate. Workers deemed supervisors who were too polite to be ineffective and sometimes their use of questions such as 'Aren't you going to fix that?' to be ambiguous. The styles of both workers and supervisors actually favored the use of bald imperatives without politeness markers as each group sought to assert or resist power within a basically adversarial relationship.

Mishoe (1998) investigated two styles of speaking in Cedar Falls in rural North Carolina using evidence from a single family. She calls one style 'home style,' used for in-group communication in the community, and the other style the 'local standard,' the local approximation of Standard American English. 'What I need me is some time and some money, but I ain't got neither one right now' is home style, and 'I don't go to saloons to eat – even if they have good food, I don't want that kind of environment' is local standard. She found that the local standard was used in very limited circumstances, e.g., for answering the telephone, claiming some kind of expertise, exerting some other kind of power, or talking about sad things. Such uses were clearly marked and most conversations proceeded in home style. Mishoe concludes that the 'ultimate reason for style shifting is to promote ones [sic] self in the most positive light, and here we see ordinary people negotiating language in their home, showing themselves to be linguistic virtuosos' (p. 177).

Finally, Barrett (1998) looked closely at how African American professional drag queens performing in gay bars in Texas switch styles during their stage performances. He defines style as the 'set of linguistic variables that are characteristic of a given dialect, register, or genre' (p. 142). The drag queens control three styles: 'an AAVE style, a gay male style, and a style based on stereotypes of white women's speech' (p. 145). The styles are deliberate stereotypes. Abrupt style-shifting allows the performers to make observations about such issues as ethnicity, sexuality, gender, or class, and also about a drag queen's own loyalties and identities – they are after all gay, black males not heterosexual, white females – and to 'undermine assumptions concerning the personal identity of the performer' (p. 158).

Code-switching can be a very useful social skill. The converse of this, of course, is that we will be judged by the code we choose to employ on a particular occasion. People have distinct feelings about various codes: they find some accents 'unpleasant,' others 'beautiful'; some registers 'stuffy'; some styles 'pedantic'; some languages or kinds of language 'unacceptable' or their speakers 'less desirable'; and so on. We cannot discount such reactions by simply labeling them as instances of *linguistic prejudice*. Linguistic prejudice, either for or against particular accents, dialects, or languages, is a fact of life, a fact we must recognize. However, we must also remember that it is often all too easy to think that someone who uses learned words, beautifully constructed sentences, and a prestige accent must be saying something worthwhile and that someone who uses common words, much 'slurring,' and a regional accent cannot have anything of interest to say!

Discussion

1. Using the example of what he calls a 'hypothetical government functionary' in Belgium, Fishman (1972a) explains how topic and domain influence linguistic choice. The domain may be social, cultural, or psychological in nature and will involve a consideration of such matters as role relationships and locales. Fishman offers the following account of the linguistic behavior of his functionary (p. 16):

    > A government functionary in Brussels arrives home after stopping off at his club for a drink. He *generally* speaks standard French in his office, standard Dutch at his club, and a distinctly local variant of Flemish at home. In each instance he identifies himself with a different speech network to which he belongs, wants to belong, and from which he seeks acceptance. All of these networks – and more – are included in his overarching speech community, even though each is more commonly associated with one variety than with another. Nevertheless, it is not difficult to find occasions at the office in which he speaks or is spoken to in one or another variety of Flemish. There are also occasions at the club when he speaks or is addressed in French; finally, there are occasions at home when he communicates in standard Dutch or even French.

Show how Fishman's explanation is relevant to this account. Are you aware of any similar kinds of linguistic behavior in your own environment?

2.   When you visit a foreign country whose language you know either well or poorly, when do you use that language and when do you not? What factors govern your choice?

3.   The claim is sometimes made (e.g., Gumperz, 1982a, p. 61) that in conversational code-switching 'participants immersed in the interaction itself are often quite unaware which code is used at any one time.' How would you propose to investigate such a claim? Gumperz says that this is also the case with metaphorical code-switching (p. 62). He writes as follows (p. 70):

> Code-switching occurs in conditions of change, where group boundaries are diffuse, norms and standards of evaluation vary, and where speakers' ethnic identities and social backgrounds are not matters of common agreement. Yet, if it is true that code-switching styles serve as functioning communicative systems, if members can agree on interpretations of switching in context and on categorizing others on the basis of their switching, there must be some regularities and shared perceptions on which these judgments can be based.

Elaborate on the various factors Gumperz mentions in the first of these two sentences. Discuss the implications of the second sentence for any theory which attempts to explain linguistic and/or communicative competence in humans.

4.   Code-switching and borrowing are different phenomena. Try to distinguish between the two.

Further Reading

The 'classic' essay on diglossia is Ferguson (1959); Hudson (1992) is a good bibliography. Fishman (1972a, 1972b) and Gumperz (1971, 1982a, 1982b) are older sources. Heller (1988), Myers-Scotton (1993a, 1993b, 1998), Milroy and Muysken (1995), Auer (1998), and Eckert and Rickford (2001) are good sources for code-switching and stylistic choices. Scotton (1986) discusses both diglossia and code-switching. Much of Lambert's work has employed the matched-guise technique to examine aspects of bilingualism, and the paper cited (Lambert, 1967) provides a good introduction. See Giles and Powesland (1975) and Giles and Coupland (1991) for accommodation.

5 Speech Communities

Language is both an individual possession and a social possession. We would expect, therefore, that certain individuals would behave linguistically like other individuals: they might be said to speak the same language or the same dialect or the same variety, i.e., to employ the same code, and in that respect to be members of the same *speech community*, a term probably derived from the German *Sprachgemeinschaft*. Indeed, much work in sociolinguistics is based on the assumption that it is possible to use the concept of 'speech community' without much difficulty. Hudson (1996, p. 29) rejects that view: 'our sociolinguistic world is not organized in terms of objective "speech communities," even though we like to think subjectively in terms of communities or social types such as "Londoner" and "American." This means that the search for a "true" definition of the speech community, or for the "true" boundaries around some speech community, is just a wild goose chase.' We will indeed discover that just as it is difficult to define such terms as *language*, *dialect*, and *variety*, it is also difficult to define *speech community*, and for many of the same reasons. That difficulty, however, will not prevent us from using the term: the concept has proved to be invaluable in sociolinguistic work in spite of a certain 'fuzziness' as to its precise characteristics. It remains so even if we decide that a speech community is no more than some kind of social group whose speech characteristics are of interest and can be described in a coherent manner.

Definitions

Sociolinguistics is the study of language use within or among groups of speakers. What are groups? 'Group' is a difficult concept to define but one we must try to grasp. For our purposes, a group must have at least two members but there is really no upper limit to group membership. People can group together for one or more reasons: social, religious, political, cultural, familial, vocational, avocational, etc. The group may be temporary or quasi-permanent and the purposes of its members may change, i.e., its *raison d'être*. A group is also more than its members for they may come and go. They may also belong to other groups and may or may not meet face-to-face. The organization of the group may be tight or loose and the importance of group membership is likely to vary among individuals within the group, being extemely important to some and of little consequence to others. An individual's feelings of identity are closely related to that person's feelings about groups in which he or she is a member, feels strong (or weak) commitment (or rejection), and finds some kind of success (or failure).

We must also be aware that the groups we refer to in various research studies are groups we have created for the purposes of our research using this or that set of factors. They are useful and necessary constructs but we would be unwise to forget that each such group comprises a set of unique individuals each with a complex identity (or, better still, identities). Consequently, we must be careful in drawing conclusions about individuals on the basis of observations we make about groups. To say of a member of such a group that he or she will always exhibit a certain characteristic behavior is to offer a *stereotype*. Individuals can surprise us in many ways.

The kind of group that sociolinguists have generally attempted to study is called the *speech community*. (See Patrick, 2002, for a general survey.) For purely theoretical purposes, some linguists have hypothesized the existence of an 'ideal' speech community. This is actually what Chomsky (1965, pp. 3–4) proposes, his 'completely homogeneous speech community' (see p. 3). However, such a speech community cannot be our concern: it is a theoretical construct employed for a narrow purpose. Our speech communities, whatever they are, exist in a 'real' world. Consequently, we must try to find some alternative view of speech community, one helpful to investigations of language in society rather than necessitated by abstract linguistic theorizing.

Lyons (1970, p. 326) offers a definition of what he calls a 'real' speech community: 'all the people who use a given language (or dialect).' However, that really shifts the issue to making the definition of a language (or of a dialect) also the definition of a speech community. If, as we saw in chapter 2, it proves virtually impossible to define *language* and *dialect* clearly and unambiguously, then we have achieved nothing. It is really quite easy to demonstrate that a speech community is not coterminous with a language: while the English language is spoken in many places throughout the world, we must certainly recognize that it is also spoken in a wide variety of ways, in speech communities that are almost entirely isolated from one another, e.g., in South Africa, in New Zealand, and among expatriates in China. Alternatively, a recognizably single speech community can employ more than one language: Switzerland, Canada, Papua New Guinea, many African states, and New York City.

Furthermore, if speech communities are defined solely by their linguistic characteristics, we must acknowledge the inherent circularity of any such definition in that language itself is a communal possession. We must also acknowledge that using linguistic characteristics alone to determine what is or is not a speech community has proved so far to be quite impossible because people do not necessarily feel any such direct relationship between linguistic characteristics A, B, C, and so on, and speech community X. What we can be sure of is that speakers do use linguistic characteristics to achieve group identity with, and group differentiation from, other speakers, but they use other characteristics as well: social, cultural, political and ethnic, to name a few. Referring to what they call *speech markers*, Giles, Scherer, and Taylor (1979, p. 351) say:

> through speech markers functionally important social categorizations are discrim-inated, and ... these have important implications for social organization. For humans, speech markers have clear parallels ... it is evident that social categories of age, sex, ethnicity, social class, and situation can be clearly marked on the basis of speech, and that such categorization is fundamental to social organization even though many of the categories are also easily discriminated on other bases.

Our search must be for criteria other than, or at least in addition to, linguistic criteria if we are to gain a useful understanding of 'speech community.'

For very specific sociolinguistic purposes we might want to try to draw quite narrow and extremely precise bounds around what we consider to be a speech community. We might require that only a single language be spoken (and employ a very restrictive definition of language in doing so), and that the speakers in the community share some kind of common feeling about linguistic behavior in the community, that is, observe certain linguistic norms. This appeal to norms forms an essential part of Labov's definition of speech community (1972b, pp. 120–1):

> The speech community is not defined by any marked agreement in the use of language elements, so much as by participation in a set of shared norms; these norms may be observed in overt types of evaluative behavior, and by the uniform-ity of abstract patterns of variation which are invariant in respect to particular levels of usage.

This definition shifts the emphasis away from an exclusive use of linguistic criteria to a search for the various characteristics which make individuals feel that they are members of the same community. Milroy (1987a, p. 13) has indicated some consequences of such a view:

> Thus, all New York speakers from the highest to lowest status are said to consti-tute a single speech community because, for example, they agree in viewing pres-ence of post vocalic [r] as prestigious. They also agree on the social value of a large number of other linguistic elements. Southern British English speakers cannot be said to belong to the same speech community as New Yorkers, since they do not attach the same social meanings to, for example, (r): on the contrary, the highest prestige accent in Southern England (RP) is non-rhotic. Yet, the Southern British speech community may be said to be united by a common evaluation of the vari-able (h); *h*-dropping is stigmatized in Southern England ... but is irrelevant in New York City or, for that matter, in Glasgow or Belfast.

In this sense, 'speech community' is a very abstract concept, one likely to create not a few problems, because the particular norms that a community uses may or may not be exclusively linguistic in nature, and even the linguistic norms them-selves may vary considerably among small sub-groups. For example, speakers of Hindi will separate themselves entirely from speakers of Urdu; most Ukrainians will separate themselves from most Russians (but possibly not vice versa); and most Chinese will see themselves as members of the same community as all other Chinese, even though speakers of Cantonese or Hokkien might not be able to express that sense of community to a speaker of Mandarin or to each other except through their shared writing system.

The single-language, or single-variety, criterion is also a very dubious one. Gumperz (1971, p. 101) points out that 'there are no *a priori* grounds which force us to define speech communities so that all members speak the same language.' As I observed in the previous chapter, many societies have existed and still exist in which bilingualism and multilingualism are normal. For example, early in the year 2000 London was judged to be the most 'international' of all cities in the world based on the number of different languages spoken there – over 300. It is such considerations as these which lead Gumperz (p. 101) to use the term *linguistic community* rather than speech community. He proceeds to define that term as follows:

> a social group which may be either monolingual or multilingual, held together by frequency of social interaction patterns and set off from the surrounding areas by weaknesses in the lines of communication. Linguistic communities may consist of small groups bound together by face-to-face contact or may cover large regions, depending on the level of abstraction we wish to achieve.

In this definition, then, communities are defined partially through their relationships with other communities. Internally, a community must have a certain social cohesiveness; externally, its members must find themselves cut off from other communities in certain ways. The factors that bring about cohesion and differentiation will vary considerably from occasion to occasion. Individuals will therefore shift their sense of community as different factors come into play. Such a definition is an extension of the one that Bloomfield (1933, p. 42) uses to open his chapter on speech communities: 'a speech community is a group of people who interact by means of speech.' The extension is provided by the insistence that a group or community is defined not only by what it is but by what it is not: the 'cut-off' criterion.

Gumperz (1971, p. 114) offers another definition of the speech community:

> any human aggregate characterized by regular and frequent interaction by means of a shared body of verbal signs and set off from similar aggregates by significant differences in language usage.
>
> Most groups of any permanence, be they small bands bounded by face-to-face contact, modern nations divisible into smaller subregions, or even occupational associations or neighborhood gangs, may be treated as speech communities, provided they show linguistic peculiarities that warrant special study.

Not only must members of the speech community share a set of grammatical rules, but there must also be regular relationships between language use and social structure; i.e., there must be norms which may vary by sub-group and social setting. Gumperz adds (p. 115):

Wherever the relationships between language choice and rules of social appropriateness can be formalized, they allow us to group relevant linguistic forms into distinct dialects, styles, and occupational or other special parlances. The sociolinguistic study of speech communities deals with the linguistic similarities and differences among these speech varieties.

Furthermore, 'the speech varieties employed within a speech community form a system because they are related to a shared set of social norms' (p. 116). Such norms, however, may overlap what we must regard as clear language boundaries. For example, in Eastern Europe many speakers of Czech, Austrian German, and Hungarian share rules about the proper forms of greetings, suitable topics for conversation, and how to pursue these, but no common language. They are united in a *Sprachbund*, 'speech area,' not quite a 'speech community,' but still a community defined in some way by speech. As we can see, then, trying to define the concept of 'speech community' requires us to come to grips with definitions of other concepts, principally 'group,' 'language' (or 'variety'), and 'norm.'

Hymes (1974, p. 47) disagrees with both Chomsky's and Bloomfield's definitions of a speech community. He claims that these simply reduce the notion of speech community to that of a language and, in effect, throw out 'speech community' as a worthwhile concept. He points out that it is impossible to equate language and speech community when we lack a clear understanding of the nature of language. He insists that speech communities cannot be defined solely through the use of linguistic criteria (p. 123). The way in which people view the language they speak is also important, that is, how they evaluate accents; how they establish the fact that they speak one language rather than another; and how they maintain language boundaries. Moreover, rules for using a language may be just as important as feelings about the language itself. He cites the example of the Ngoni of Africa. Most Ngoni no longer speak their ancestral language but use the language of the people they conquered in Malawi. However, they use that language in ways they have carried over from Ngoni, ways they maintain because they consider them to be essential to their continued identity as a separate people. Hymes adds that analogous situations may be observed among some native groups in North America: they use English in special ways to maintain their separate identities within the dominant English-speaking community. As we saw too in the previous chapter code-switching can be used to achieve a shared identity and delimit a group of speakers from all others.

For Hymes, the concept of 'speech community' is a difficult one to grasp in its entirety, for it depends on how one defines 'groups' in society. He also distinguishes (pp. 50–1) between participating in a speech community and being a fully fledged member of that community:

> To participate in a speech community is not quite the same as to be a member of it. Here we encounter the limitation of any conception of speech community in terms of knowledge alone, even knowledge of patterns of speaking as well as of grammar, and of course, of any definition in terms of interaction alone. Just the matter of accent may erect a barrier between participation and membership in one case, although be ignored in another. Obviously membership in a community depends

upon criteria which in the given case may not even saliently involve language and speaking, as when birthright is considered indelible.

However, he reaffirms (p. 51) an earlier (1962, pp. 30–2) definition of speech community: 'a local unit, characterized for its members by common locality and primary interaction.' He is prepared to 'admit exceptions cautiously.'

Brown and Levinson (1979, pp. 298–9) point out that:

> Social scientists use the word 'group' in so many ways, as for example in the phrases *small group, reference group, corporate group, ethnic group, interest group*, that we are unlikely to find any common core that means more than 'set'. Social scientists who adopt the weak concept of structure . . . are likely to think of groups in relatively concrete terms, as independently isolable units of social structure. . . . On the other hand, social theorists who adopt the stronger concept of structure are more likely to think of groups as relative concepts, each group being a unit that is relevant only in relation to units of like size that for immediate purposes are contrasted with it. Thus for a man who lives in Cambridge, his territorial identification will be with Cambridge when contrasted with Newmarket, with Cambridgeshire when contrasted with Lancashire, with England when contrasted with Scotland, with the United Kingdom when contrasted with Germany, and so on.

'Group' is therefore a relative concept and 'speech community' must also be relative. You are a member of one speech community by virtue of the fact that on a particular occasion you identify with X rather than Y when apparently X and Y contrast in a single dimension. This approach would suggest that there is an English speech community (because there are French and German ones), a Texas speech community (because there are London and Bostonian ones), a Harvard speech community (because there are Oxford and Berkeley ones), a Chicano speech community (because there are Spanish and English ones), and so on. An individual therefore belongs to various speech communities at the same time, but on any particular occasion will identify with only one of them, the particular identification depending on what is especially important or contrastive in the circumstances. For any specific speech community, the concept 'reflects what people do and know when they interact with one another. It assumes that when people come together through discursive practices, they behave as though they operate within a shared set of norms, local knowledge, beliefs, and values. It means that they are aware of these things and capable of knowing when they are being adhered to and when the values of the community are being ignored . . . it is fundamental in understanding identity and representation of ideology' (Morgan, 2001, p. 31).

Discussion

1. Try to label yourself according to what kind(s) of English you speak. Explain why you choose the specific terms you use and any connotations these terms have for you, e.g., *Bristol English, Texas English, educated Tyneside English*.

2. To show that very small changes in linguistic behavior can serve to disaffiliate you from other members of the same speech community, make deliberate adjustments in your speech on some occasion: that is, become more formal or less formal than seems to be required by the occasion; introduce technical or learned vocabulary when it is not called for; employ slang or coarse expressions; shift your accent (perhaps even to mimic another person); or switch to a distinct regional dialect. (Be careful!) What happens? How do such shifts affect your relationship to your listeners and any feelings you or they have about a common identity?

3. In what respects do (or did) the following pairs of people belong to the same speech communities or to different ones: Presidents J. F. Kennedy and Lyndon Johnson; Indira Gandhi and Margaret Thatcher; the Pope and the Archbishop of Canterbury; Professor Henry Higgins and Eliza Doolittle; Elizabeth II and John Lennon; Geoffrey Chaucer and George Bernard Shaw.

4. Describe the linguistic uses of some bilinguals with whom you are familiar. When do they use each of the languages? If you are bilingual yourself, in what ways do you identify with people who show the same range of linguistic abilities? A different range?

5. In what respects does the language which is characteristic of each of the following groups, if there is such a characteristic language, mark each group off as a separate speech community: adolescents; stockbrokers; women; linguists; air traffic controllers; priests; disk jockeys? How useful is the concept of 'speech community' in cases such as these?

6. Le Page and Tabouret-Keller (1985) and Trudgill (1986, pp. 85–6) distinguish between *focused* and *diffuse* languages and communities, the main difference being the degree to which people agree about the shared features of the language or community. In this view the English public schools would be highly focused but Kingston, Jamaica, would be quite diffuse. Try to apply this distinction to other situations of which you are aware.

Intersecting Communities

The fact that people do use expressions such as *New York speech*, *London speech*, and *South African speech* indicates that they have some idea of how a 'typical' person from each place speaks, that is, of what it is like to be a member of a particular speech community somewhat loosely defined. Such a person may be said to be typical by virtue of observing the linguistic norms one associates with the particular place in question. But just what are these norms? I have already noted (p. 49) the work of Preston (1989, 1999, 2002), which shows that a person's perceptions of the language characteristics of particular areas do not always accord with linguistic facts. Rosen (1980, pp. 56–7) has also indicated some of the problems you find in trying to call a city like London a speech community and in describing exactly what characterizes its speech. He says that such cities 'cannot be thought of as linguistic patchwork maps, ghetto after ghetto, not only because languages and dialects have no simple geographical distribution but also because interaction between them blurs whatever boundaries might be drawn. Both a geographical model and a social class model would be false, though each could contribute to an understanding.' In such places, 'dialects and languages are beginning to influence each other. Urbanization is a great eroder of linguistic frontiers.' The result is:

> the creation of thousands of bilingual and to a certain extent bidialectal speakers on a scale and of a diversity unprecedented in our history. Which dialect of English they learn depends in the main on their social class position in this country. It is common practice to talk of the 'target language' of a second-language learner. In London it will be a moving target, though undoubtedly most by virtue of their social position will have as their chief model London working-class speech.

London is a community in some senses but not in others; however, with its 300 languages or more it is in no sense a single speech community (see Baker and Eversley, 2000). It is just too big and fragmented. On the other hand, if we say it must be a composite of small speech communities, we may not be any better off. Are these smaller communities geographical, social, ethnic, religious, or occupational in orientation? That is, how do any linguistic factors we might isolate relate to such social factors? Are the communities static or fluid? If they are static, how do they maintain themselves, and if they are fluid, what inferences must we draw concerning any concept we might have of 'speech community'? Are their boundaries strong and clear or are they weak and permeable? Moreover, London is no different from most large cities anywhere in the world, a world which is increasingly a world of large cities, heterogeneously populated.

We can easily see how difficult it is to relate the concept of 'speech community' directly to language or languages spoken and even to groups and norms if we refer back to the linguistic situation among the Tukano described in the previous chapter (p. 97). In that situation, which requires one to take as a marriage partner someone who speaks an entirely different language and furthermore requires the female to join the male's household, multilingualism is endemic and normal. However, each residential community has its unique multilingual mix and no language equates in distribution to a specific residential community. Such a situation is not unique. Many other parts of the world would have some of the same multilingual characteristics; e.g., the Balkans, large areas of the Indian subcontinent, and Papua New Guinea. The actual equation of language to community is perhaps most easily seen in certain modern states which have insisted that language be used to express some concept of 'nationhood' and, in doing so, have tried to standardize and promote a particular language (or particular languages) at the expense of competitors. But such solutions are not always lasting or uncontroversial, as we can see in countries such as Germany, France, the United Kingdom, Canada, and the United States, all of which have recently had to acknowledge in one way or another the presence of people who do not speak the standard variety (or varieties) but who are, nevertheless, very much part of the larger communities.

Perhaps the concept of 'speech community' is less useful than it might be and we should return to the concept of 'group' as any set of individuals united for a common end, that end being quite distinct from ends pursued by other groups. Consequently, a person may belong at any one time to many different groups depending on the particular ends in view.

We can illustrate this approach as follows. At home, a person may live in a bilingual setting and switch easily back and forth between two languages. She – let this be a female person – may shop in one of the languages but work in the other. Her accent in one of the languages may indicate that she can be classified as an immigrant to the society in which she lives, an immigrant, moreover, from a specific country. Her accent in the other language shows her to be a native of region Y in country Z. Outside country Z, however, as she now is, she regards herself (and others from Z agree with her) as speaking not a Y variety of Z but as speaking Z itself. She may also have had extensive technical training in her new country and in her second language and be quite unable to use her first language in work related to this specialty. In the course of the day, she will switch her identification from one group to another, possibly even, as we saw in the preceding chapter, in the course of a single utterance. She belongs to one group at one moment and to a different one at another. But to how many altogether?

The concept must be flexible because individuals find it advantageous to shift their identities quite freely. As Bolinger (1975, p. 333) says,

> There is no limit to the ways in which human beings league themselves together for self-identification, security, gain, amusement, worship, or any of the other purposes that are held in common; consequently there is no limit to the number and variety of speech communities that are to be found in a society.

Saville-Troike (1996, p. 357) places even more importance on the need for individuals to identify themselves with various others but her views are essentially the same as those of Bolinger: 'Individuals may belong to several speech communities (which may be discrete or overlapping), just as they may participate in a variety of social settings. Which one or ones individuals orient themselves to at any given moment – which set of social and communicative rules they use – is part of the strategy of communication. To understand this phenomenon, one must recognize that each member of a community has a repertoire of social identities and that each identity in a given context is associated with a number of appropriate verbal and nonverbal forms of expression.'

A very interesting variant of this notion is the idea that speakers participate in various *communities of practice*. Eckert and McConnell-Ginet (1998, p. 490) define a community of practice as 'an aggregate of people who come together around mutual engagements in some common endeavor. Ways of doing things, ways of talking, beliefs, values, power relations – in short, practices – emerge in the course of their joint activity around that endeavor.' A community of practice is at the same time its members and what its members are doing to make them a community: a group of workers in a factory, an extended family, an adolescent gang, a women's fitness group, a classroom, etc. They add (p. 490): 'Rather than seeing the individual as some disconnected entity floating around in social space, or as a location in a network, or as a member of a particular group or set of groups, or as a bundle of social characteristics, we need to focus on communities of practice.' (See Meyerhoff, 2002, particularly pp. 527–30, for additional details.) It is such communities of practice that shape individuals, provide them with their identities, and often circumscribe what they can do. Eckert used this concept in her research (see p. 212).

If there is no limit to the ways in which individuals can classify themselves and speakers must constantly create and recreate social identities for themselves, then it may be almost impossible to predict which group or community an individual will consider himself (or herself) to belong to at a particular moment. The group chosen to identify with will change according to situation: at one moment religion may be important; at another, regional origin; and at still another, perhaps membership in a particular profession or social class. An individual may also attempt to bond with others because all possess a set of characteristics, or even just a single characteristic, e.g., be of the same gender, or even because all lack a certain characteristic, e.g., not be of white skin color. The bonding can therefore be positive, as when the individuals share some feature or features, or negative, as when the individuals lack some feature or features. Language bonding appears to be no different. In one case command of a particular dialect or language may provide a bond and therefore a sense of community or solidarity with others; in another case the lack of such command may exclude you from a community of speakers, e.g., of RP users or speakers of Yoruba if all you speak is Brooklynese. But even sharing the same dialect might be of no significance: if the circumstances require you to discuss astrophysics and you lack the language of astrophysics, you will not be able to enter the community of astrophysicists. Speakers of Yoruba may also find themselves with speakers of Japanese and Arabic within an English-speaking foreign-student speech community at a North American or European university.

Each individual therefore is a member of many different groups. It is in the best interests of most people to be able to identify themselves on one occasion as members of one group and on another as members of another group. Such groups may or may not overlap. One of the consequences of the intersecting identifications is, of course, linguistic variation: people do not speak alike, nor does any individual always speak in the same way on every occasion. The variation we see in language must partly reflect a need that people have to be seen as the same as certain other people on some occasions and as different from them on other occasions.

Discussion

1. Try to determine in what respects the following countries are both single speech communities and complexes of intersecting speech communities: the United States, Singapore, the People's Republic of China, Australia, Switzerland, Haiti, and India.
2. Explain the idea that a community or group must be defined partly in relation to some other community or group and to circumstances. Show how this helps to explain what is likely to happen in such situations as the following:

a. In a 'jam' in Turkey, you find someone who also speaks English. That someone is (i) a Turk who speaks it badly; (ii) a Turk who speaks it well; (iii) someone from another part of the English-speaking world who speaks Turkish well.

b. While sightseeing by yourself in Nepal, you, from Dubuque, Iowa, meet someone from (i) Glasgow, (ii) Boston, (iii) Iowa, (iv) Dubuque.

c. When stopped by a police officer for speeding in a large city, you hear the officer begin speaking to you in the strong regional accent that you yourself have.

d. You overhear someone discussing you quite unfavorably in an 'exotic' language which you, by reason of foreign birth, happen to speak like a native.

Networks and Repertoires

Another way of viewing how an individual relates to other individuals in society is to ask what *networks* he or she participates in. That is, how and on what occasions does a specific individual A interact now with B, then with C, and then again with D? How intensive are the various relationships: does A interact more frequently with B than with C or D? How extensive is A's relationship with B in the sense of how many other individuals interact with both A and B in whatever activity brings them together? If, in a situation in which A, B, C, D, and E are linked in a network, as in figure 5.1, are they all equally linked as in (1) in that illustration; strongly linked but with the link through A predominant, as in (2); weakly linked, with the link to A providing all the connections, as in (3); or, as in (4), is the link from A to E achieved through C?

You are said to be involved in a *dense* network if the people you know and interact with also know and interact with one another. If they do not the network is a *loose* one. You are also said to be involved in a *multiplex* network if the people within it are tied together in more than one way, i.e., not just through work but also through other social activities. People who go to school together, marry each other's siblings, and work and play together participate in dense multiplex networks. In England these are said to be found at the extremes of the social-class structure. Such networks indicate strong social cohesion, produce feelings of solidarity, and encourage individuals to identify with others within the network. On the other hand, middle-class networks are likely to be loose and simplex; therefore, social cohesion is reduced and there are weaker feelings of solidarity and identity.

Dubois and Horvath (1999, p. 307) acknowledge that while the concept of social networks seems to be useful in studying language behavior in urban settings, its effectiveness in nonurban settings, in their case among English–French bilingual Cajuns in rural Louisiana, is not so clear. They say: 'The notion of network is strongly conditioned by the effects of scale and place. Being a member of an open or closed network is quite different if you live in New

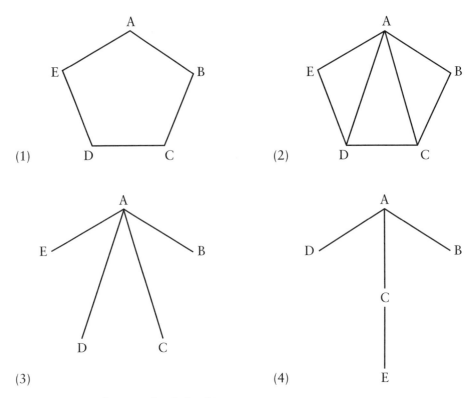

Figure 5.1   Simple network relationships

Orleans . . . , Lafayette . . . , Eunice . . . , or Iota. . . . We do not wish to imply that the notion of network loses its methodological importance in nonurban settings, but only that the linguistic effect of closed and open networks is intimately related to the type of community under study.'

Much linguistic behavior seems explicable in terms of network structure and we will see in chapters 7 and 8 how valuable the concept of 'social network' is when we consider matters of language variation and change (see Milroy, 2002, for additional details). Milroy and Gordon (2003, p. 119) also point out that the 'concepts of network and community of practice are . . . closely related, and the differences between them are chiefly method and focus. Network analysis typically deals with structural and content properties of the ties that constitute *egocentric* personal networks . . . [but] cannot address the issues of how and where linguistic variants are employed . . . to construct local social meanings. Rather, it is concerned with how informal social groups . . . support local norms or . . . facilitate linguistic change.'

It is quite apparent that no two individuals are exactly alike in their linguistic capabilities, just as no two social situations are exactly alike. People are separated from one another by fine gradations of social class, regional origin, and occupation; by factors such as religion, gender, nationality, and ethnicity; by psychological differences such as particular kinds of linguistic skills, e.g., verbality or literacy; and by personality characteristics. These are but some of the more obvious differences that affect individual variation in speech.

An individual also has a *speech repertoire*; that is, he or she controls a number of varieties of a language or of two or more languages. Quite often, many individuals will have virtually identical repertoires. In this case it may be possible to argue, as Platt and Platt (1975, p. 35) do, that 'A speech repertoire is the range of linguistic varieties which the speaker has at his disposal and which he may appropriately use as a member of his speech community.'

The concept of 'speech repertoire' may be most useful when applied to individuals rather than to groups. We can use it to describe the communicative competence of individual speakers. Each person will then have a distinctive speech repertoire. Since the Platts find both a community's speech repertoire and an individual's speech repertoire worthy of sociolinguistic consideration, they actually propose the following distinction (p. 36):

> We . . . suggest the term *speech repertoire* for the repertoire of linguistic varieties utilized by a speech community which its speakers, as members of the community, may appropriately use, and the term *verbal repertoire* for the linguistic varieties which are at a particular speaker's disposal.

In this view each individual has his or her own distinctive verbal repertoire and each speech community in which that person participates has its distinctive speech repertoire; in fact, one could argue that this repertoire is its defining feature.

Focusing on the repertoires of individuals and specifically on the precise linguistic choices they make in well-defined circumstances does seem to offer us some hope of explaining how people use linguistic choices to bond themselves to others in very subtle ways. A speaker's choice of a particular sound, word, or expression marks that speaker in some way. It can say 'I am like you' or 'I am not like you.' When the speaker also has some kind of range within which to choose, and that choice itself helps to define the occasion, then many different outcomes are possible. A particular choice may say 'I am an X just like you' or it may say 'I am an X but you are a Y.' It may even be possible that a particular choice may say 'Up till now I have been an X but from now on you must regard me as a Y,' as when, for example, someone pretends to be something he or she is not and then slips up. However, it also seems that it is not merely a simple matter of always choosing X rather than Y – for example, of never saying *singin'* but always saying *singing*. Rather, it may be a matter of proportion: you will say *singin'* a certain percent of the time and *singing* the rest of the time. In other words, the social bonding that results from the linguistic choices you make may depend on the quantity of certain linguistic characteristics as well as their quality.

We have seen that 'speech community' may be an impossibly difficult concept to define. But in attempting to do so, we have also become aware that it may be just as difficult to characterize the speech of a single individual. Perhaps that second failure follows inevitably from the first. We should be very cautious therefore about definitive statements we may be tempted to make about how a particular individual speaks, the classic concept of 'idiolect.' Just what kinds of data should you collect? How much? In what circumstances? And what kind of claims can you make? We will need to find answers to questions such as these before we can proceed very far. Any attempt to study how even a single individual speaks in a rather limited set of circumstances is likely to convince us rather quickly that language is rather 'messy' stuff. For certain theoretical reasons it might be desirable to ignore a lot of that mess, as Chomsky insists that we do; but it would be unwise for sociolinguists always to do so since that is, in one sense, what sociolinguistics is all about: trying to work out either the social significance of various uses of language or the linguistic significance of various social factors. The following three chapters will address some of these issues.

Discussion

1. Try to construct a network of your linguistic relationships in an attempt to represent the different varieties of language you use and the relative proportions of use among those varieties. What are some of the difficulties you encounter in doing so? (The latter will probably have to do with taking into account external factors such as place, occasion, participants, and so on. A multi-dimensional network may seem necessary, something next to impossible to represent on a two-dimensional surface.)
2. Blom and Gumperz (1972), Gal (1978, 1979), and Milroy (1980, 1987a) all use the concept of 'network' in their investigations. What similarities and differences do you find in their uses?
3. Keep a log of your linguistic usage over a day. Record such factors as the time spent talking versus listening, reading versus writing, conversing, lecturing, gossiping, asking and answering, complaining, requesting, stating, deliberately being silent, singing, humming, being formal and being informal, and so on. What are some of the difficulties you encounter in trying to do this kind of thing? (Again, one of them is likely to be the difficulty of devising a multi-dimensional system of classification.)
4. Most of us know someone who has a repertoire of linguistic abilities that we admire, possibly envy. Try to specify some of these abilities that you yourself seem to lack. Why does the other have these abilities and you do not?

Further Reading

Two basic sources are Gumperz (1971) and Hymes (1974). Scherer and Giles (1979) is a useful collection of articles on social markers in speech. See Patrick (2002) for speech communities, Milroy (2002) for social networks, and Meyerhoff (2002) for communities of practice.

Part II Inherent Variety

Variety is the spice of life.

William Cowper

He [John Milton] pronounced the letter R very hard – a certain sign of satirical wit.

John Aubrey

He likes the country, but in truth must own,
Most likes it, when he studies it in town.

William Cowper

Nothing is permanent but change.

Heraclitus

Since 'tis Nature's law to change,
Constancy alone is strange.

John Wilmot, Earl of Rochester

Forward, forward let us range,
Let the great world spin for ever down the ringing grooves of change.

Alfred, Lord Tennyson

6 Language Variation

As we have seen in previous chapters, languages vary in many ways. One way of characterizing certain variations is to say that speakers of a particular language sometimes speak different dialects of that language. Although I have already noted how difficult it is to define *dialect*, we may still find it useful to use the term in our work in sociolinguistics, and even to extend its use from studies of regional variation to those of social variation. In this way it would be possible to talk about both *regional dialects* and *social dialects* of a language. Just as a regional dialect marks off the residents of one region from those of other regions, a social dialect would be a variety associated with a specific social class or group, marking that class or group off from other classes or groups. However, if this further differentiation of varieties is to be successful, it will require us to be able to find linguistic features which are associated with differences in classes or groups and, of course, to define what we mean by these latter terms.

Sociolinguists today are generally more concerned with social variation in language than with regional variation. However, if we are to gain a sound understanding of the various procedures used in studies of social variation, we should look at least briefly at previous work in regional dialectology. That work points the way to understanding how recent investigations have proceeded as they have. Studies of social variation in language grew out of studies of regional variation. It was largely in order to widen the limits and repair the flaws that were perceived to exist in the latter that investigators turned their attention to social-class variation in language. As we will see, there may still be certain limitations in investigating such variation but they are of a different kind. It is also important to note that even if there are limitations to this kind of work, many sociolinguists regard it as being essentially what sociolinguistics is – or should be – all about (see pp. 14–15). In this view the study of language variation tells us important things about languages and how they change. This chapter and the two that follow deal with such matters.

Regional Variation

The mapping of dialects on a regional basis has had a long history in linguistics
(see Petyt, 1980, Chambers and Trudgill, 1998, and Wakelin, 1977). In fact, it
is a well-established part of the study of how languages change over time, i.e.,
of *diachronic* or *historical linguistics*. Traditionally, *dialect geography*, as this
area of linguistic study is known, has employed assumptions and methods drawn
from historical linguistics, and many of its results have been used to confirm
findings drawn from other historical sources, e.g., archeological findings, population studies, written records. In this view languages differentiate internally as
speakers distance themselves from one another over time and space; the changes
result in the creation of dialects of the languages. Over sufficient time, the resulting dialects become new languages as speakers of the resulting varieties become
unintelligible to one another. So Latin became French in France, Spanish in
Spain, Italian in Italy, and so on.

In this model of language change and dialect differentiation, it should always
be possible to relate any variation found within a language to the two factors
of time and distance alone; e.g., the British and American varieties, or dialects,
of English are separated by over two centuries of political independence and by
the Atlantic Ocean; Northumbrian and Cockney English are nearly 300 miles
and many centuries apart. In each case, linguists working in this tradition try to
explain any differences they find with models familiar to the historical linguist,
models which incorporate such concepts as the 'family tree' (Latin has 'branched'
into French, Spanish, and Italian), phonemic 'split' (English /f/ and /v/ are now
distinctive phonemes whereas once they were phonetic variants, or allophones,
of a single phoneme) or phonemic 'coalescence' (English *ea* and *ee* spellings, as
in *beat* and *beet*, once designated different pronunciations), the 'comparative
method' of reconstruction (English *knave* and German *Knabe* come from the
same source), and 'internal reconstruction' (though *mouse* and *mice* now have
different vowel sounds, this was not always the case).

Dialect geographers have traditionally attempted to reproduce their findings
on maps in what they call *dialect atlases*. They try to show the geographical
boundaries of the distribution of a particular linguistic feature by drawing a line
on a map. Such a line is called an *isogloss*: on one side of the line people say
something one way, e.g., pronounce *bath* with the first vowel of *father*, and on
the other side they use some other pronunciation, e.g., the vowel of *cat*. Quite
often, when the boundaries for different linguistic features are mapped in this
way the isoglosses show a considerable amount of criss-crossing. On occasion,
though, a number coincide; i.e., there is a *bundle of isoglosses*. Such a bundle
is often said to mark a *dialect boundary*. One such bundle crosses the south
of France from east to west approximately at the 45th parallel (Grenoble to
Bordeaux) with words like *chandelle*, *chanter*, and *chaud* beginning with a *sh*
sound to the north and a *k* sound to the south. Quite often, that dialect boundary coincides with some geographical or political factor, e.g., a mountain ridge, a
river, or the boundary of an old principality or diocese. Isoglosses can also show
that a particular set of linguistic features appears to be spreading from one

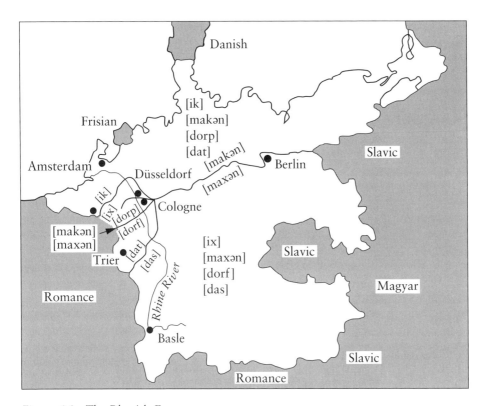

Figure 6.1   The Rhenish Fan

location, a *focal area*, into neighboring locations. In the 1930s and 1940s Boston and Charleston were the two focal areas for the temporary spread of *r*-lessness in the eastern United States. Alternatively, a particular area, a *relic area*, may show characteristics of being unaffected by changes spreading out from one or more neighboring areas. Places like London and Boston are obviously focal areas; places like Martha's Vineyard – it remained *r*-pronouncing in the 1930s and 1940s even as Boston dropped the pronunciation – in New England and Devon in the extreme southwest of England are relic areas. Wolfram (2004) calls the dialect of such an area a *remnant dialect* and, in doing so, reminds us that not everything in such a dialect is a relic of the past for such areas also have their own innovations. Huntley, a rural enclave in Aberdeenshire, Scotland, where Marshall worked (2003, 2004) is also a relic area (see p. 211).

The Rhenish Fan is one of the best-known sets of isoglosses in Europe, setting off Low German to the north from High German to the south. The set comprises the modern *reflexes* (i.e., results) of the pre-Germanic stop consonants *p, *t, and *k. These have remained stops [p,t,k] in Low German but have become the fricatives [f,s,x] in High German (i.e., Modern Standard German), giving variant forms for 'make' [makən], [maxən]; 'that' [dat], [das]; 'village' [dorp], [dorf]; and 'I' [ik], [ix]. Across most of Germany these isoglosses run virtually together from just north of Berlin in an east–west direction until they reach the Rhine. At that point they 'fan', as in figure 6.1. Each area within the fan has a different

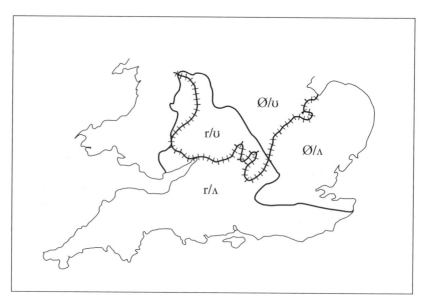

Figure 6.2   Intersecting isoglosses

incidence of stops and fricatives in these words, e.g., Düsseldorf has [ix], [makən], [dorp], and [dat], and Trier has [ix], [maxən], [dorf], and [dat]. The boundaries within the fan coincide with old ecclesiastical and political boundaries. The change of stops to fricatives, called the Second German Consonant Shift, appears to have spread along the Rhine from the south of Germany to the north. Political and ecclesiastical frontiers along the Rhine were important in that spread as were centers like Cologne and Trier. The area covered by the fan itself is sometimes called a *transition area* (in this case, between Low and High German) through which a change is progressing in contrast to either a focal or relic area.

Very often the isoglosses for individual phonological features do not coincide with one another to give us clearly demarcated dialect areas. For example, in England the isogloss that separates *stood* or *come* pronounced with [ʊ] rather than [ʌ] runs roughly east and west (with [ʊ] to the north). It intersects the isogloss that separates *farm* pronounced with or without the [r], which runs roughly northwest to southeast (with [r] to the west, except for pockets of [r] pronunciation in the West Midlands and Northeast). This gives us the four distinct areas illustrated in figure 6.2: [r] and [ʊ]; [r] and [ʌ]; Ø, i.e., nothing and [ʊ]; and Ø and [ʌ]. These two quite different distributions, i.e., the 'criss-cross' pattern, are just about impossible to explain using traditional 'family-tree' type models of linguistic change. We should also note that the [ʊ] and [r] pronunciations are 'retreating' before those with [ʌ] and Ø, which are more and more associated with the standard variety of the language. Isoglosses do cross and bundles of them are rare. It is consequently extremely difficult to determine boundaries between dialects in this way and dialectologists acknowledge this fact. Hudson (1996, p. 39) draws a somewhat negative conclusion: 'isoglosses need not delimit varieties, except in the trivial sense where varieties each consist of just one item; and if we cannot rely on isoglosses to delimit varieties, what can we use?' However, if we look at Trudgill's book (1999) on English dialects we can see the many positive results of this kind of work.

Dialect-atlas type approaches such as Trudgill's take a particular linguistic feature, which we will soon call a *linguistic variable* (see following section), and show its distribution geographically. They also attempt to relate that distribution to the historical development of the language, both internally, i.e., linguistically, and externally, i.e., politically, socially, and culturally.

Because dialect studies grew out of historical studies of languages, it should also come as no surprise that they have focused almost exclusively on rural areas. Rural areas were regarded as 'conservative' in the sense that they were seen to preserve 'older' forms of the languages under investigation. Urban areas were acknowledged to be innovative, unstable linguistically, and difficult to approach through existing survey techniques. When the occasional approach was made, it was biased toward finding the most conservative variety of urban speech. Ignoring towns and cities may be defensible in an agrarian-based society; however, it is hardly defensible in the heavily urbanizing societies of today's world as the only way to study the language variation that exists there. An alternative approach is called for.

One basic assumption in dialect geography is that regional dialects are really quite easy to sample: just find one or two people in the particular location you wish to investigate, people who are preferably elderly and untraveled, interview them, and ask them how they pronounce particular words, refer to particular objects, and phrase particular kinds of utterances. A sampling of such people from various locations throughout a wide geographical area will allow the dialect geographer to show where particular sounds, forms, and expressions are used, and where boundaries can be drawn around these so that area A may be described as an area in which linguistic feature X occurs (or is used) whereas area B has no instances of that feature. If there are sufficient differences between the linguistic features employed in areas A and B, then we may say that we actually have two dialects, A and B, of the particular language in question.

While this kind of study of regional varieties of languages has a long and respected history, it also has serious limitations. As I have said, it tends to ignore densely populated areas, specifically large sprawling urban areas, because of the complexities of both sampling and data evaluation. The selection of informants also tends not to be very well controlled, often reflecting no more than the judgment of the person collecting the data that a particular individual is 'representative' of the area being sampled. It certainly lacks the kind of scientific rigor that sociologists have come to insist on in sampling any population. For example, the informants chosen for the *Linguistic Atlas of the United States and Canada* were of three types (Kurath, 1939, p. 44), chosen as follows:

Type I: Little formal education, little reading, and restricted social contacts
Type II: Better formal education (usually high school) and/or wider reading and social contacts
Type III: Superior education (usually college), cultured background, wide reading, and/or extensive social contacts

Each of these three types was then sub-categorized as follows:

Type A: Aged, and/or regarded by the field worker as old-fashioned
Type B: Middle-aged or younger, and/or regarded by the field worker as
          more modern

We should also note that it was the field worker for the *Atlas* who decided exactly where each informant fitted in the above scheme of things. A certain circularity is obviously involved: the *Atlas* studies were intended partly to find out how speech related to social class, but speech was itself used as one of the criteria for assigning membership in a social class. The field worker alone judged whether a particular informant should be used in the study, and Type IA informants were particularly prized as being most representative of local speech.

In England, the Survey of English Dialects carried out between 1950 and 1961 with informants from 313 localities in England and Wales employed similar criteria (Orton et al., 1978, p. 3):

> The selection of informants was made with especial care. The fieldworkers were instructed to seek out elderly men and women – more often men, since women seemed in general to encourage the social upgrading of the speech of their families – who were themselves of the place and both of whose parents were preferably natives also. They were to be over 60 years of age, with good mouths, teeth and hearing and of the class of agricultural workers who would be familiar with the subject matter of the questionnaire and capable of responding perceptively and authoritatively.

Once again we see strong emphasis given to traditional speech forms as we might expect in dialect studies which are a direct offshoot of historical, comparative work in linguistics.

Dialect-atlas studies attempted to relate variation in language to settlement history and tended to ignore social-class factors. There was some recognition of the latter, but it was relatively small owing to the inadequate systems of social classification that were employed in most investigations. However, it is still possible to make some observations. For example, in the southern and south Midlands dialects of the United States, a form such as *you-all* is found in use among all social classes, whereas *I might could* and *a apple* are found in use only among speakers in the low and middle classes, and *I seed* and *fistes, postes,* and *costes* (as plurals of *fist, post,* and *cost*) are found in use only among speakers from the low class.

Since most of us realize that it is not only where you come from that affects your speech but also your social and cultural background, age, gender, race, occupation, and group loyalty, the traditional bias toward geographic origin alone now appears to be a serious weakness. Then, too, the overriding model of language change and differentiation is an extremely static one, and one that is reinforced, rather than questioned, by the types of data selected for analysis. Speakers from different regions certainly interact with one another; dialect breaks or boundaries are not 'clean'; and change can be said to be 'regular' only if you are prepared to overlook certain kinds of irregularities as exceptions, relics, borrowings, 'minor' variations, and so on. Furthermore, the varieties of a language spoken within large gatherings of people in towns and cities must influence what happens to other varieties of that language: to attempt to discuss the history of English, French, or Italian while ignoring the influences of London, Paris, or Florence would seem to be something like attempting to produce *Hamlet* without the prince!

All of this is not to say that this kind of individual and social variation has gone unnoticed in linguistics. Linguists have long been aware of variation in the use of language: individuals do speak one way on one occasion and other ways on other occasions, and this kind of variation can be seen to occur within even the most localized groups. Such variation is often ascribed to *dialect mixture*, i.e., the existence in one locality of two or more dialects which allow a speaker or speakers to draw now on one dialect and then on the other. An alternative explanation is *free variation*, i.e., random 'meaningless' variation of no significance. However, no one has ever devised a suitable theory to explain either dialect mixture or free variation, and the latter turns out not to be so free after all because close analyses generally reveal that complex linguistic and social factors appear to explain much of the variation.

There have been some recent developments in this kind of work which hold promise for future discoveries. They result largely from our growing ability to process and analyze large quantities of linguistic data. One, for example, is Kretzschmar's work on the Linguistic Atlas of the Middle and South Atlantic States (LAMSAS). He shows (1996) how it is possible to use quantitative methods to demonstrate the probability of occurrence of specific words or sounds in specific areas. This kind of mapping clearly illustrates that when we call something dialect A and something else dialect B we are dealing with somewhat vague concepts, for the realities are quite fuzzy; any concepts we may have about an 'ideal speaker' or a 'dialect boundary' reside at least as much in our heads as they do in the data. In another approach to dialects, this one focusing on how a specific dialect emerged, Lane (2000) used a variety of economic, demographic, and social data from 3,797 residents of Thyborøn, Denmark, covering the years 1890–1996, to reveal how the local dialect 'is the result of a constant situation that led to the formation of a new dialect as a result of massive in-migration . . . a new system created largely out of materials selected from competing systems in contact and from innovations that indexed the new local linguistic community' (p. 287). It was clearly another triumph for an aspiration to achieve a local identity. We can see a similar emphasis on using traditional dialect materials to help us account for current language varieties in recent writings on new Englishes (see Gordon et al., 2004, Hickey, 2004, and Trudgill, 2004).

I have deliberately not focused at length on dialect geography since it is not one of our major concerns and I have already (in chapter 2) considered certain issues related to dialects. Dialect geography does raise a number of issues, however, which are important to our concerns. One is the kind of variation that we should try to account for in language. Another has to do with sampling the population among which we believe variation to exist. Still another is the collection, analysis, and treatment of the data that we consider relevant. And, finally, there are the overriding issues of what implications there are in our findings for theoretical matters concerning the nature of language, variation in language, the language-learning and language-using abilities of human beings, and the processes involved in linguistic change. It is to these issues that I will now turn, and in doing so, focus on social rather than regional variation in language. The major conceptual tool for investigation of such variation will be the 'linguistic variable.'

Discussion

1. If you are unfamiliar with such concepts as the 'family tree,' 'phonemic split,' the 'comparative method of reconstruction,' and 'internal reconstruction,' you should consult a good introductory text on linguistics or historical linguistics. The traditional concept of 'dialect' depends heavily on an understanding of these concepts from historical linguistics. Try to demonstrate that this is so.
2. Look at how informants were selected for the work that went into the dialect atlases of Germany, France, England, and New England. For example, note that they were nearly always older men. Discuss the merits of this kind of sampling. Look also at the kinds of questions that the informants were asked, and how they were asked them. Do the atlases have any value beyond being some kind of historical record, and a partly 'idealized' one at that?
3. In a discussion of the maps used in dialect atlases Le Page (1997, p. 18) says that the 'dialect areas outlined by the isoglosses on the maps were artifacts of the geographer; they had to be matched against such stereotypes as "southern dialect" or "Alemmanic" or "langue d'oc," concepts which often related in the minds of outsiders to just one or two variables characterizing a complete, discrete system.' How do you relate specific pronunciations, word choices, and usages to certain regions? Are these characteristic of all residents of the regions? Is there, therefore, such a being as a 'typical Cockney,' a 'typical Australian,' and a 'typical Texan' so far as language is concerned? (See Preston, 1989.)
4. You might try to find out what you can about how such matters as free variation and dialect mixture are treated in a variety of introductory texts in linguistics. How might a sociolinguist view the same range of phenomena?
5. Try to list the formative influences on the variety of English you speak and to give relative weights to those influences. You might consider such factors as when and where you learned English, your social and cultural background, the range of occasions on which you use English, and any other relevant matters. A comparison of your set of factors and the weights you assign these with the sets and weights that others propose should prove interesting.

The Linguistic Variable

The investigation of social dialects has required the development of an array of techniques quite different from those used in dialect geography. Many of these derive from the pioneering work of Labov, who, along with other sociolinguists, has attempted to describe how language varies in any community and to draw conclusions from that variation not only for linguistic theory but also sometimes for the conduct of everyday life, e.g., suggestions as to how educators should view linguistic variation (see chapter 14). As we will see, investigators now pay serious attention to such matters as stating hypotheses, sampling, the statistical treatment of data, drawing conclusions, and relating these conclusions to such matters as the inherent nature of language, the processes of language acquisition and language change, and the social functions of variation.

Possibly the greatest contribution has been in the development of the use of the 'linguistic variable,' the basic conceptual tool necessary to do this kind of work (see Wolfram, 1991). As I have just indicated, variation has long been of interest to linguists, but the use of the linguistic variable has added a new dimension to linguistic investigations. Although not all linguists find the concept useful in their work, it has nevertheless compelled most of its severest critics to reconsider just what it is they are theorizing about when they talk of 'language,' of a speaker's 'knowledge' of language, and of the relationship between such knowledge and actual 'use.'

A *linguistic variable* is a linguistic item which has identifiable variants. For example, words like *singing* and *fishing* are sometimes pronounced as *singin'* and *fishin'*. The final sound in these words may be called the linguistic variable (ng) with its two variants [ŋ] in *singing* and [n] in *singin'*. Another example of a linguistic variable can be seen in words like *farm* and *far*. These words are sometimes given *r*-less pronunciations; in this case we have the linguistic variable (r) with two variants [r] and Ø (pronounced 'zero'). Still another example involves the vowel in a word like *bend*. That vowel is sometimes nasalized and sometimes it is not; sometimes too the amounts of nasalization are noticeably different. In this case we have the linguistic variable (e) and a number of variants, [ɛ], [ɛ̃]^1, . . . , [ɛ̃]^n; here the superscripts ^{1} to ^{n} are used to indicate the degree of nasalization observed to occur. We might, for example, find two or even three distinct quantities of nasalization.

There are at least two basically different kinds of variation. One is of the kind (ng) with its variants [ŋ] or [n], or (th) with its variants [θ], [t], or [f], as in *with* pronounced as *with*, *wit*, or *wif*. In this first case the concern is with which quite clearly distinct variant is used, with, of course, the possibility of Ø, the zero variant. The other kind of variation is the kind you find above in (e): [ɛ̃]^1, . . . , [ɛ̃]^n, when it is the quantity of nasalization, rather than its presence or absence, which is important. How can you best quantify nasalization when the phenomenon is actually a continuous one? The same issue occurs with quantifying variation in other vowel variables: quantifying their relative frontness or backness, tenseness or laxness, and rounding or unrounding. Moreover, more than one dimension may be involved, e.g., amount of nasalization *and* frontness or backness. In such cases usually some kind of weighting formula is devised, and when the data are treated it is these weights that are used in any calculations, not just the ones and zeros that we can use in the case of (ng): [ŋ] or [n], where [ŋ] = 1 and [n] = 0.

Linguists who have studied variation in this way have used a number of linguistic variables. The (ng) variable has been widely used. So has the (r) variable. Others are the (h) variable in words like *house* and *hospital*, i.e., (h): [h] or Ø;

the (t) variable in *bet* and *better*, i.e., (t): [t] or [ʔ]; the (th) and (dh) variables in *thin* and *they*, i.e., (th): [θ] or [t] and (dh): [ð] or [d]; the (l) variable in French in *il*, i.e., (l): [l] or Ø; and consonant variables like the final (t) and (d) in words like *test* and *told*, i.e., their presence or absence. Vocalic variables used have included the vowel (e) in words like *pen* and *men*; the (o) in *dog, caught,* and *coffee*; the (e) in *beg*; the (a) in *back, bag, bad,* and *half*; and the (u) in *pull*.

Studies of variation employing the linguistic variable are not confined solely to phonological matters. Investigators have looked at the (s) of the third-person singular, as in *he talks*, i.e., its presence or absence; the occurrence or nonoccurrence of *be* (and of its various inflected forms) in sentences such as *He's happy, He be happy,* and *He happy*; the occurrence (actually, virtual nonoccurrence) of the negative particle *ne* in French; various aspects of the phenomenon of multiple negation in English, e.g., *He don't mean no harm to nobody*; and the beginnings of English relative clauses, as in *She is the girl who(m) I praised, She is the girl that I praised,* and *She is the girl I praised*.

To see how individual researchers choose variables, we can look briefly at three studies. In a major part of his work in New York City, Labov (1966) chose five phonological variables: the (th) variable, the initial consonant in words like *thin* and *three*; the (dh) variable, the initial consonant in words like *there* and *then*; the (r) variable, r-pronunciation in words like *farm* and *far*; the (a) variable, the pronunciation of the vowel in words like *bad* and *back*; and the (o) variable, the pronunciation of the vowel in words like *dog* and *caught*. We should note that some of these have discrete variants, e.g., (r): [r] or Ø, whereas others require the investigator to quantify the variants because the variation is a continuous phenomenon, e.g., the (a) variable, where there can be both raising and retraction of the vowel, i.e., a pronunciation made higher and further back in the mouth, and, of course, in some environments nasalization too.

Trudgill (1974) also chose certain phonological variables in his study of the speech of Norwich: three consonant variables and thirteen vowel variables. The consonant variables were the (h) in *happy* and *home*, the (ng) in *walking* and *running*, and the (t) in *bet* and *better*. In the first two cases only the presence or absence of *h*-pronunciation and the [ŋ] versus [n] realizations of (ng) were of concern to Trudgill. In the last there were four variants of (t) to consider: an aspirated variant; an unaspirated one; a glottalized one; and a glottal stop. These variants were ordered, with the first two combined and weighted as being least marked as nonstandard, the third as more marked, and the last, the glottal stop, as definitely marked as nonstandard. The thirteen vowel variables were the vowels used in words such as *bad, name, path, tell, here, hair, ride, bird, top, know, boat, boot,* and *tune*. Most of these had more than two variants, so weighting, i.e., some imposed quantification, was again required to differentiate the least preferred varieties, i.e., the most nonstandard, from the most preferred variety, i.e., the most standard.

The Detroit study (Shuy et al., 1968) focused on the use of three variables: one phonological variable and two grammatical variables. The phonological variable was the realization of a vowel plus a following nasal consonant as a nasalized vowel, e.g., *bin* realized as [bĩ] rather than [bɪn]. The grammatical variables were multiple negation, which I have already mentioned, and pronominal apposition, e.g., *That guy, he don't care*. In a further study of Detroit speech, Wolfram (1969) considered certain other linguistic variables. These included the pronunciation of final consonant clusters, i.e., combinations of final consonants in words like *test, wasp*, and *left, th* in words like *tooth* and *nothing*, final stops in words like *good* and *shed*, and *r*-pronouncing in words like *sister* and *pair*. So far as grammatical variables were concerned, Wolfram looked at matters such as *he talk/talks, two year/years, she nice/she's nice, he's ready/he ready/he be ready*, and multiple negation as in *He ain't got none neither*.

This brief sample indicates some of the range of variables that have been investigated. The important fact to remember is that a linguistic variable is an item in the structure of a language, an item that has alternate realizations, as one speaker realizes it one way and another a different way or the same speaker realizes it differently on different occasions. For example, one speaker may say *singing* most of the time whereas another prefers *singin'*, but the first is likely to say *singin'* on occasion just as the second may be found to use the occasional *singing*. What might be interesting is any relationship we find between these habits and either (or both) the social class to which each speaker belongs or the circumstances which bring about one pronunciation rather than the other.

Labov (1972b) has also distinguished among what he calls indicators, markers, and stereotypes. An *indicator* is a linguistic variable to which little or no social import is attached. Only a linguistically trained observer is aware of indicators. For example, some speakers in North America distinguish the vowels in *cot* and *caught* and others do not. Whether one distinguishes the vowels or not carries little or no social significance. On the other hand, a *marker* does carry with it social significance. In fact, markers may be potent carriers of social information. People are aware of markers, and the distribution of markers is clearly related to social groupings and to styles of speaking. Pronouncing *car* and *cart* in New York City in their *r*-less varieties marks you as using a type of pronunciation associated with lower-class speech in that city. New Yorkers are conscious of this fact and may vary their use of *r* according to circumstances. A *stereotype* is a popular and, therefore, conscious characterization of the speech of a particular group: New York *boid* for *bird* or *Toitytoid Street* for *33rd Street*; Texas 'drawling' or *Howdy Pardner*; a Northumbrian *Wot-cher* (What cheer?) greeting; the British use of *chap*; or a Bostonian's *Pahk the cah in Hahvahd Yahd*. Often such stereotypes are stigmatized. A stereotype need not conform to reality; rather, it offers people a rough and ready categorization with all the attendant problems of such categorizations. Studies of variation tend therefore to focus on describing the distributions of linguistic variables which are markers; they may explain how stereotypes arise, but they merely note indicators. (See Johnstone, 2004, for a discussion of stereotypes in Pittsburgh speech.)

Discussion

1. The word *shibboleth* is of biblical origin (see Judges 12: 4–6). In this case information from a 'survey' concerning a particular linguistic variable was put to immediate and, for many, drastic use. Explain.

2. Try to devise a scale or some kind of quantification for the variants of the variable (a) found in words like *bat*, *bad*, *back*, *bag*, and *bang*. You will have to note quite fine phonetic differences. What difficulties arise? Try to place your own pronunciations of the vowels in these words on the scale as well as the pronunciations of some other people you know. In doing this kind of task, what social judgments do you yourself make of the variants?
3. Which linguistic variables might be usefully investigated in the part of the world in which you live; that is, what kinds of variation have you noticed around you, and how might you characterize the variation using the concept of the 'linguistic variable'?
4. I have suggested that certain linguistic variables are particularly marked, i.e., speakers and listeners are acutely aware of them. We immediately notice either the presence or absence of something. One consequence is that all a speaker must do is use a single instance of the 'wrong' variant, e.g., drop an *h* when he or she should not, to reveal that the middle-class style being used is actually overlaid on a working-class one. Can you think of other examples of this phenomenon, when someone 'gives himself or herself away' by using a linguistic feature in such a way? (Note that it is also possible to give away your middle-class or upper-class origins while pretending to be working class.)
5. In his Prologue to *The Canterbury Tales*, Chaucer says the following of the Knight:

> He nevere yet no vileyne ne sayde
> In al his lyf unto no maner wight.

This use of multiple negation was common in both Old English and Middle English. Although it still persists, it is now highly marked as nonstandard. Try to find out why this variant of negation has fallen into such disfavor (and who actually disfavors it). See Crystal (1984), Bauer and Trudgill (1998), and Wardhaugh (1999).

Linguistic and Social Variation

Once we have identified the linguistic variable as our basic working tool, the next task becomes one of employing that tool in an effort to see how linguistic variation relates to social variation. An early study of linguistic variation by Gumperz (1958), but one cast in a 'modern' mold, shows some of the intricacies involved in trying to relate linguistic variation to social variation. Because the society he was studying is rigidly stratified on the basis of caste membership, the problems are considerably fewer than those encountered in such cities as New York, Detroit, or even Norwich, but they are still present. Gumperz shows how rather small differences in speech can effectively distinguish sub-groups in society from one another in a study of linguistic usage in the village of Khalapur, eighty miles north of Delhi in India. The social structure of the village is determined by Hindu caste membership with Brahmans at the top, then Rajputs (warriors), Vaishyas (merchants), and several groups of artisans and laborers lower down. At the bottom are three untouchable castes: Chamars (landless laborers), Jatia Chamars (leather workers and shoe makers), and Bhangis (sweepers). The latter are restricted to living in certain neighborhoods and have less freedom to move in the village than do members of the upper castes. Ten percent of the population are not Hindus but Muslims; they are outside the caste system.

So far as language is concerned, certain characteristics of the Khalapur village dialect are clear markers of social-group membership. For example, Bhangis do not make certain phonological contrasts that speakers of all the other castes make. Chamars and Jatia Chamars also lack certain phonological contrasts made by all others, and some, in attempting to make such a contrast, actually *hypercorrect*; that is, they over-extend a particular usage in trying to emulate others. Jatia Chamars have a characteristic pronunciation of words that end in [æ] in all other village varieties. Each of the three untouchable castes therefore has speech characteristics that clearly set it off both from the other two untouchable castes and from the touchable castes in the village. Muslim speech resembles that of the touchable classes.

An anomaly is that the variety of village speech spoken by the lowest caste, the Bhangis, is closest to the dialect of the region in which Khalapur is situated. This fact constrains members of the upper castes in their use of the regional dialect since using it would make them sound like untouchables. In their linguistic usage therefore they are forced to innovate away from the regional variety. Since untouchables apparently try to emulate the touchables, the direction of innovation for all groups in Khalapur is away from the regional variety with the innovations prompted, of course, by different needs: the touchables' need to signal their clear distinction from the untouchables, and the untouchables' attempt to reduce that distinction as much as possible.

This study quite clearly shows a direct relationship between linguistic variation and caste membership. If we know certain things about one, we can predict certain things about the other. It is just such connections or correlations that interest sociolinguists working with the linguistic variable. What they seek are measures of social variation to which they can relate the kinds of linguistic variation they observe. However, caste, with its sharp social stratifications, is useless as a measure of social variation outside a few non-Western societies. Consequently, the problem becomes one of finding factors in society that show a relationship to such matters as whether or not an individual says *singing* or *singin'*, *he go* or *he goes*, or *He doesn't know anything* or *He don't know nothing*.

Once a linguistic variable has been identified, the next issue becomes that of collecting data concerning its variants in such a way that we can draw certain conclusions about the social distribution of these variants. To draw such conclusions, we must be able to relate the variants in some way to quantifiable factors in society, e.g., social-class membership, gender, age, ethnicity, and so on. As we will see, there are numerous difficulties in attempting this task, but considerable progress has been made in overcoming them, particularly as studies have built on those that have gone before in such a way as to strengthen the quality of the work done in this area of sociolinguistics.

While it is fairly easy to relate the occurrences of the variants of a linguistic variable to factors such as gender and age, relating them to factors such as race and ethnicity is somewhat more troublesome since these are much more subjective in nature and less easily quantifiable. But the most complicated factor of all is social-class membership, if we consider 'social class' to be a useful concept to apply in stratifying society – and few indeed would deny its relevance! Sociologists use a number of different scales for classifying people when they attempt to place individuals somewhere within a social system. An occupational scale may divide people into a number of categories as follows: major professionals and executives of large businesses; lesser professionals and executives of medium-sized businesses; semi-professionals; technicians and owners of small businesses; skilled workers; semi-skilled workers; and unskilled workers. An educational scale may employ the following categories: graduate or professional education; college or university degree; attendance at college or university but no degree; high school graduation; some high school education; and less than seven years of formal education. Income level as well as source of income are important factors in any classification system that focuses on how much money people have. Likewise, in considering where people live, investigators must concern themselves with both the type of housing and its location.

In assigning individuals to social classes, investigators may use any or all of the above criteria (and others too) and assign different weights to them. Accordingly, the resulting social-class designation given to any individual may differ from study to study. We can also see how social class itself is a sociological construct; people probably do not classify themselves as members of groups defined by such criteria. Wolfram and Fasold (1974, p. 44) point out that 'there are other objective approaches [to establishing social groupings] not exclusively dependent on socio-economic ranking. . . . An investigator may look at such things as church membership, leisure-time activities, or community organizations.' They admit that such alternative approaches are not at all simple to devise but argue that a classification so obtained is probably more directly related to social class than the simple measurement of economic factors. We should note that there is a current emphasis on 'lifestyle' in classifying people, so obviously patterns of consumption of goods and appearance are important for a number of people in arriving at some kind of social classification.

Alternative approaches to using a somewhat simple social-class scale are, however, still rather infrequent. What we find is that people are assigned to social classes through the use of composite scores derived from various scales which 'measure' some of the factors mentioned above. It is also the case that the actual scales used must necessarily vary from community to community since exactly the same characteristics cannot serve to classify people in England and the United States or in New England and New Mexico. However, as I have indicated, nearly all such scales take into account such matters as educational achievement, professional training, occupation (sometimes parental occupation too), 'blue'- or 'white'-collar work, salary or income level, source of that salary, income, or wage (this difference also being important), gender, age, residential area, race, and ethnicity. Weights are then assigned to each of these and some kind of unitary scale is devised so that individuals can be fitted into slots carrying such designations as 'upper class,' 'middle class,' 'lower working class,' and so on. Sometimes the stratifications, or gradations, are few ('upper' vs. 'middle' class), but at other times they are many ('upper middle' vs. 'middle middle' class). Most work in sociolinguistics has drawn on commonly used unitary scales of this kind to designate the social-class membership of individuals in an attempt to describe the characteristic linguistic behavior of various social classes.

In his study of linguistic variation in New York City, Labov (1966) used the three criteria of education, occupation, and income to set up ten social classes. His class 0, his lower class, had grade school education or less, were laborers, and found it difficult to make ends meet. His classes 1 to 5, his working class, had had some high school education, were blue-collar workers, but earned enough to own such things as cars. His classes 6 to 8, his lower middle class, were high school graduates and semi-professional and white-collar workers who could send their children to college. His highest class 9, his upper middle class, were well educated and professional or business-oriented. In this classification system for people in the United States about 10 percent of the population are said to be lower class, about 40 percent working class, another 40 percent lower middle class, and the remaining 10 percent fall into the upper middle class or an upper class, the latter not included in Labov's study. In his later study (2001) of variation in Philadelphia Labov used a socio-economic index based on occupation, education, and house value.

In his study of linguistic variation in Norwich, England, Trudgill (1974) distinguishes five social classes: middle middle class (MMC), lower middle class (LMC), upper working class (UWC), middle working class (MWC), and lower working class (LWC). Trudgill interviewed ten speakers from each of five electoral wards in Norwich plus ten school-age children from two schools. These sixty informants were then classified on six factors, each of which was scored on a six-point scale (0–5): occupation, education, income, type of housing, locality, and father's occupation. Trudgill himself decided the cut-off points among his classes. In doing so, he shows a certain circularity. His lower working class is defined as those who use certain linguistic features (e.g., *he go*) more than 80 percent of the time. Out of the total possible score of 30 on his combined scales, those scoring 6 or less fall into this category. Members of Trudgill's middle middle class always use *he goes*, and that behavior is typical of those scoring 19 or more. His study is an attempt to relate linguistic behavior to social class, but he uses linguistic behavior to assign membership in social class. What we can be sure of is that there is a difference in linguistic behavior between those at the top and bottom of Trudgill's 30-point scale, but this difference is not one that has been established completely independently because of the underlying circularity.

Shuy's Detroit study (Shuy et al., 1968) attempted to sample the speech of that city using a sample of 702 informants. Eleven field workers collected the data by means of a questionnaire over a period of ten weeks. They assigned each of their informants to a social class using three sets of criteria: amount of education, occupation, and place of residence. Each informant was ranked on a six- or seven-point scale for each set, the rankings were weighted (multiplied by 5 for education, 9 for occupation, and 6 for residence), and each informant was given a social-class placement. Four social-class designations were used: upper middle class, those with scores of 20–48; lower middle class, those with scores of 49–77; upper working class, those with scores of 78–106; and lower working class, those with scores of 107–134.

There are some serious drawbacks to using social-class designations of this kind. As Bainbridge (1994, p. 4023) says:

> While sociolinguists without number have documented class-related variation in speech, hardly any of them asked themselves what social class was. They treated class as a key independent variable, with variations in speech dependent upon class variations, yet they never considered the meaning of the independent variable. In consequence, they seldom attempted anything like a theory of why class should have an impact, and even more rarely examined their measures of class to see if they were methodologically defensible.

Woolard (1985, p. 738) expresses a similar view: 'sociolinguists have often borrowed sociological concepts in an ad hoc and unreflecting fashion, not usually considering critically the implicit theoretical frameworks that are imported.' She adds (p. 739), 'However, to say that our underlying social theories are in need of examination, elaboration, or reconsideration is not to say that the work sociolinguists have done or the concepts we have employed are without merit.' (See also Horvath's comment cited on p. 11.)

Chambers (2003, ch. 2) wrestles with the problem of class as a category and with what he calls the 'fuzziness' inherent in class boundaries. He admits (p. 44) that sociolinguists 'often rely on their intuitions in assigning social classes to individuals in the sample population in their studies,' but avers (p. 44) that any such 'judgment sample' made by an experienced sociolinguist familiar with the region under investigation 'carries few risks.' For Chambers it is apparently enough that the sociolinguist has an intuitive grasp of the social-class composition of the group being investigated and chooses representative (or 'prototypical') individuals using his or her own best judgment. He admits that this is not the preferred sociological method and reveals an 'abyss between the sampling methods of sociolinguistic surveys and the type of survey represented by opinion polls' (p. 45). He claims, however, that the particular sampling methods of sociolinguistic investigation have been justified by their results, adding (p. 54) that the social stratification that interests sociolinguists is 'often crystal clear.'

Chambers' view is an optimistic one. 'Class' is not a transparent concept and 'fuzziness' is ever present (see Ash, 2002, for an extended discussion). Can you clearly assign any John Doe or Jane Doe a class membership? Are the same criteria applicable to all individuals in society, e.g., to both the black and white inhabitants of northern cities in the United States, and to both recent immigrants to London and the residents of Mayfair? Is class structure the same in both the industrialized and non-industrialized parts of the same society? Do the criteria for classification apply equally to John Doe and Jane Doe? Are the different generations fairly treated? Another way of looking at John Doe is to try to specify what kinds of groups he belongs to and then relate his various uses of language to membership in these groups. The obvious disadvantage of such an approach is the lack of generalizability of the results: we might be able to say a lot about the linguistic behavior of John Doe *vis-à-vis* his membership in these groups, but we would not be able to say anything at all about anyone else's linguistic behavior. We can contrast this result with the statements we can make from using the aforementioned social-class designations: they say something about the linguistic usage of the 'middle middle class' without assuring us that there is really such an entity as that class; nor do they guarantee us that we can ever find a typical member.

One of the major problems in talking about social class is that social space is multi-dimensional whereas systems of social classification are one-dimensional. As we have seen, at any particular moment, an individual locates himself or herself in social space according to the factors that are relevant to him or her at that moment. While he or she may indeed have certain feelings about being a member of the lower middle class, at any moment it might be more important to be female, or to be a member of a particular church or ethnic group, or to be an in-patient in a hospital, or to be a sister-in-law. That is, self-identification or role-playing may be far more important than some kind of fixed social-class labeling. There need not, of course, be serious conflict between the two approaches. Certain kinds of self-identification and roles to be played may correlate quite closely with certain social-class labels, and they may be more 'real' and immediate to people, in the sense of accounting more accurately for their behavior from moment to moment.

The work of Labov, Trudgill, and others tries to describe the speech characteristics of members of social groups, that is, various *sociolects*. Traditionally, linguists have been interested in *idiolects*, the speech characteristics and linguistic behavior of individuals. They have also maintained that, once free variation is taken into account, an idiolect is highly representative of the linguistic behavior of all the speakers of that language. In fact, that is usually the approach linguists adopt in studying an exotic language: they find a speaker who is willing to serve as an *informant*, and they attempt to describe that speaker's language using appropriate *field methods*. They usually show little hesitation in generalizing their statements about that speaker's linguistic behavior to all speakers of the language. Sociolects, however, are statements about group norms arrived at through counting and averaging. To the extent that the groups are real, that is, that the members actually feel that they do belong to a group, a sociolect has validity; to the extent that they are not, it is just an artifact. In the extremely complex societies in which most of us live, there must always be some question as to the reality of any kind of social grouping: each of us experiences society differently, multiple-group membership is normal, and both change and stability seem to be natural conditions of our existence. We must therefore exercise a certain caution about interpreting any claims made about 'lower working-class speech,' 'upper middle-class speech,' or the speech of any other social group designated with a class label – or any label for that matter.

Distinguishing among social classes in complex modern urban societies is probably becoming more and more difficult. We are far removed from the caste system described by Gumperz (1958) in his village of Khalapur in India, or the clearly differentiated societies so often described by anthropologists. We are also considerably distanced from the rural societies favored by dialect geographers. Cities like New York and London continue to change, and some would argue that the process of change itself has actually speeded up – certainly the process of social change has. If such is the case, the very usefulness of 'social class' as a concept that should be employed in trying to explain the distribution of particular kinds of behavior, linguistic or otherwise, may need rethinking.

It was for reasons not unlike these that Milroy (1987a) preferred to explore network relationships and the possible connection of these to linguistic variation, rather than to use the concept of 'social class.' In her work, Milroy found that it was the network of relationships that an individual belonged to that exerted the most powerful and interesting influences on that individual's linguistic behavior. When the group of speakers being investigated shows little variation in social class, however that is defined, a study of the network of social relationships within the group may allow you to discover how particular linguistic usages can be related to the frequency and density of certain kinds of contacts among speakers. Network relationships, however, tend to be unique in a way that social-class categories are not. That is, no two networks are alike, and network structures vary from place to place and group to group, e.g., in Belfast and Boston, or among Jamaican immigrants to London and Old Etonians. But whom a person associates with regularly may be more 'real' than any feeling he or she has of belonging to this or that social class. I will have more to say in the following chapter about this use of network structure in the study of linguistic variation. We will also see how the concept of 'communities of practice' will be helpful in understanding differences in language behavior.

Discussion

1. How would you try to place individuals according to their social position in the community in which you live? What factors would you consider to be relevant, and how would you weight each? What class designations would seem appropriate? Where would you place yourself?

2. Sociolinguists who have looked at variation in children's speech often assign each child to a social class. In doing so, they have almost always used measures pertaining to the father rather than to the mother: his occupation, income, education, and so on. Corresponding characteristics of the mother may be used for classification only if they produce a demonstrably higher rating for the child than those of the father. Would you recommend any changes? If so, what changes and for what reasons?

3. For his study of certain varieties of American English, Fries (1940) differentiated his subjects into social classes. Examine the criteria that Fries used and discuss their adequacy for the purposes he had in mind. Was this study by Fries also a study of linguistic variation?

4. Is there an upper working class (or any other class) because a number of people exhibit similar patterns of behavior, and is this a suitable designation for them within society as a whole, or because these same people have a particular view of their place in that society and behave accordingly? That

is, is social structure continuously created and re-created out of the behavior of individuals, or is individual behavior fashioned to meet the requirements of an ongoing social structure? Or is this just a riddle best left to philosophers?

Data Collection and Analysis

Once an investigator has made some decision concerning which social variables must be taken into account and has formed a hypothesis about a possible relationship between social and linguistic variation, the next task becomes one of collecting data that will either confirm or refute that hypothesis. In sociolinguistics, this task has two basic dimensions: devising some kind of plan for collecting relevant data, and then collecting such data from a representative sample of speakers. As we will see, neither task is an easy one.

An immediate problem is one that I have previously referred to (p. 19) as the 'observer's paradox.' How can you obtain objective data from the real world without injecting your own self into the data and thereby confounding the results before you even begin? How can you be sure that the data you have collected are uncontaminated by the process of investigation itself? This is a basic scientific quandary, particularly observable in the social sciences where, in almost every possible situation, there is one variable that cannot be controlled in every possible way, namely, the observer/recorder/analyst/investigator/theorist himself or herself. If language varies as much as it does, the presence of an observer will have some effect on that variation. How can we minimize this effect? Even data recorded by remote means, e.g., by hidden cameras and sound recorders, may not be entirely 'clean' and will require us to address additional ethical issues. We know, too, that observations vary from observer to observer and that we must confront the issue of the reliability of any observations that we make. Sociolinguists are aware that there are several serious issues here, and, as we will see, they have attempted to deal with them.

The usual kind of data collection device is a questionnaire designed to elicit data illustrative of the use of the variable or variables that are being investigated. Since experience has shown that the different variants of a variable occur in different circumstances, the questionnaire must be designed to elicit data in a variety of circumstances. Many studies have made a four-fold distinction in categorizing those circumstances: (1) a casual situation, with sub-categories such as speech outside the formal interview, or conversation with a third party (i.e., not the person doing the interviewing), or responses to general questions, or recall of childhood rhymes, or the narration of a story about feeling one's life to be in peril; (2) an interview situation; (3) the reading aloud of a story; and (4) the reading aloud of lists of words and of pairs of words like *den* and *then*. A questionnaire which elicits these various kinds of linguistic behaviors will cover very casual speech (the casual situation), more formal speech (the interview situation), and the most formal speech of all (the different reading tasks). A person who says *shootin'* when explaining how he at some time felt himself to be in mortal danger may well read the same word presented on a list as *shooting*, and someone who pronounces *caught* and *court* as homophones during an interview may well distinguish them in some way when the words appear in contrast with each other on a list of pairs of words.

In his work in New York City, Labov (1966) investigated both careful and casual speech. His four types of careful speech, from most to least careful, were: reading lists of close pairs (e.g., *den* and *then*), reading lists of words, reading a prose passage, and participating in a formal interview. His five types of casual speech came from situations such as speech outside the formal interview, conversation with a third party, responses to questions, telling childhood rhymes, and recounting an incident which might have proved fatal. This classification gave Labov a total of nine *contextual styles* for analysis in his work. He also insisted that each style had to be accompanied by appropriate *channel cues*. In particular, casual style had to be marked by such cues. These cues involved changes of speech pitch, volume, and rate of breathing, and perhaps such things as outbursts of laughter. Labov regarded speech not accompanied by one or more of these cues as formal rather than spontaneous and casual. Such cues most often accompanied either the subject's breaking away from the topic of the recorded interview to deal with some situation in the immediate environment, e.g., a family interruption, or a change of topic, particularly a change brought about by Labov's asking subjects to talk about a narrow escape from death. Labov also included what he called a *subjective reaction test* in his questionnaire, requiring subjects to react to taped samples of speech containing the five variables he was concerned with in his study. In this way he was able to compare what informants said about their own and others' usage with their actual usage, note differences between the two, and hypothesize about the consequences for such matters as linguistic change.

Trudgill's questionnaire (1974, pp. 195–201) required his subjects to answer certain questions, e.g., 'What different parts of Norwich have you lived in?' and 'Which schools did you go to?' It also required that subjects read word lists aloud 'as naturally as you can,' and later 'as rapidly as you can,' and also to read pairs of words. The word lists contained words like *paper*, *baker*, *silly*, *you*, *avoid*, and *girl*; the pairs lists contained pairs like *boot–boat*, *hair–here*, *bust–burst*, *daze–days*, and *moon–moan*. Questions about individual local words were also asked, e.g., 'Do you know what a "dwile" is?' and questions about Norwich itself, e.g., 'What do you think of Norwich as a place to live?' Trudgill then asked his subjects to read aloud a short story 'as naturally as you can,' to make judgments about Norwich speech ('Do you like the way people in Norwich speak?'), to listen to certain pronunciations of words and judge whether or not they themselves used those pronunciations, and to judge ten paired sets of words in order to 'tick which way you think is correct, and then . . . underline the way you say it yourself, either if it's the same or different.'

The other part of the linguist's task is sampling: finding a representative group of speakers. The conclusions we draw about the behavior of any group are only as good as the sample on which we base our conclusions. If we choose the sample badly, we cannot generalize beyond the actual group that comprised the sample. If we intend to make claims about the characteristics of a population, we must either assess every member of that population for those characteristics or sample the whole population in some way. Sampling a population so as to generalize concerning its characteristics requires considerable skill. A genuine sample drawn from the population must be thoroughly representative and completely unbiased. All parts of the population must be adequately represented, and no part should be overrepresented or underrepresented, thereby creating bias of some kind.

The best sample of all is a *random sample*. In a random sample everyone in the population to be sampled has an equal chance of being selected. In contrast, in a *judgment sample* the investigator chooses the subjects according to a set of criteria, e.g., age, gender, social class, education, and so on. Sometimes, too, it is the investigator who judges each of these categories, e.g., to which social class a subject belongs. A judgment sample is obviously less adequate than a random sample. However, it is the kind of sample preferred in most sociolinguistic studies (see Chambers, 2003, pp. 44–5).

In sampling the speech of the Lower East Side in New York City, Labov did not use a completely random sample because such a sample would have produced subjects who were not native to the area, e.g., immigrants from abroad and elsewhere in the United States. He used the sampling data from a previous survey that had been made by Mobilization for Youth, a random sample which used 1,000 informants. Labov's own sample size was eighty-nine. He employed a *stratified sample*, i.e., one chosen for specific characteristics, from that survey. He also wanted to be sure that he had representatives of certain groups which he believed to exist on the Lower East Side. When he could not, for various reasons, interview some of the subjects chosen in the sample, he tried to find out by telephoning the missing subjects if his actual sample had been made unrepresentative by their absence. He was able to contact about half of his missing subjects in this way and, on the basis of these brief telephone conversations, he decided that his actual sample was unbiased and was typical of the total population he was interested in surveying.

The Detroit study (Shuy et al., 1968) initially collected data from 702 informants in the city. However, the data used for the actual analysis came from only thirty-six informants chosen from this much larger number. In selecting these thirty-six, the investigators wanted to be sure that each informant used had been a resident of Detroit for at least ten years, was 'representative,' had given a successful interview, and had provided an adequate amount of taped material for analysis. In other words, to any initial biases that might have been created in choosing the first set of 702 informants was added the possibility of still further bias by choosing non-randomly from the data that had become available. This is not to suggest that any such biases vitiate the results: they do not appear to do so. Rather, it is to point out that the kinds of concerns sociolinguists have about data and sources of data have not necessarily been the same as those of statisticians.

Wolfram (1969) chose forty-eight black informants from those interviewed in the Detroit study. These informants were evenly divided into four social classes used in that study. Each group of twelve was further divided into three age groups: four informants in the 10–12 age group, four in the 14–17 age group, and four in the 30–55 age group. Wolfram also selected twelve white informants from the highest social class in the Detroit project, again by age and sex. Wolfram's study therefore used a total of sixty informants: twenty-four (twelve white and twelve black) from the upper middle class and thirty-six who were black and were members of the working classes, with equal numbers in each such class. Such a sample is very obviously highly stratified in nature.

Studies employing the linguistic variable are essentially *correlational* in nature: that is, they attempt to show how the variants of a linguistic variable are related to social variation in much the same way that we can show how children's ages, heights, and weights are related to one another. We must distinguish between *dependent variables* and *independent variables*. The linguistic variable is a dependent variable, the one we are interested in. We want to see what happens to language when we look at it in relation to some factor we can manipulate, the independent variable, e.g., social class, age, gender, ethnicity, and so on: as one of these changes, what happens to language? As Chambers (2003, p. 26) expresses it, '*Socially significant linguistic variation requires correlation*: the dependent (linguistic) variable must change when some independent variable changes. It also requires that the change be orderly: the dependent variable must stratify the subjects in ways that are socially or stylistically coherent.'

This kind of sociolinguistic investigation is often called *quantitative sociolinguistics* and it is, as I have indicated previously, for some sociolinguists the 'heart of sociolinguistics' (Chambers, 2003, p. xix). Quantitative studies must therefore be statistically sound if they are to be useful. Investigators must be prepared to employ proper statistical procedures not only in their sampling but also in the treatment of the data they collect and in testing the various hypotheses they formulate. They must be sure that what they are doing is both valid and reliable. In our case the issue of validity, that is, whether or not the sociolinguist is really measuring what he or she is claiming to be measuring, hardly ever arises. Such work certainly meets Lepper's criterion (2000, p. 173): 'the researcher must show that what is being described is accurately "named" – that is, that the research process has accurately represented a phenomenon which is recognizable to the scientific community being addressed.' However, the issue of reliability, that is, how objective and consistent the measurements of the actual linguistic data are, is a real and pressing one. There are well-known procedures for making sure that the data we gather have been collected reliably, and there are approved tests of that reliability. However, in some sociolinguistic investigations little attention is paid to this issue. We are simply presented with sums of informants' responses or averages of one kind or another, and given little or no account of how confident we can be concerning the actual items summed or averaged. If only one person collected the data, how consistent was that person in the actual collection? If two or more were involved, how consistently and uniformly did they employ whatever criteria they were using? Bailey and Tillery (2004, pp. 27–8) have identified a cluster of such issues, e.g., the effects of different interviewers, elicitation strategies, sampling procedures, and analytical strategies, and pointed out that these can produce significant effects on the data that are collected and, consequently, on any results that are reported. Therefore, there may still be room for improving the reliability of our results.

Serious empirical studies also require experimental hypotheses to be stated *before* the data are collected, and suitable tests to be chosen to decide whether these hypotheses are confirmed or not and with what degree of confidence. Such tests often require that the data collected be treated quantifiably, so that the variation in the actual distribution of the various responses is taken into account in each category. It is not enough just to calculate simple means or averages. The *standard deviation*, that is, the actual distribution of the various measurements around those means, is critical if we wish to compare different means, which is a standard procedure in sociolinguistics. Peculiar kinds of variations around means, e.g., skewing or bi-modal distributions, must also be noted.

Petyt (1980, pp. 188–90) points out how the kinds of figures that sociolinguists use in their tables may be misleading in a very serious way. Sociolinguists stratify society into sub-groups, the members of which are measured in certain ways, and then these measurements are pooled. Individual variation is eliminated. Petyt (p. 189) provides the data given in table 6.1. The data come from an investigation of *h*-dropping in West Yorkshire, and the table shows the means for five sub-groups, i.e., social classes. Petyt points out that, if the range of variation within each sub-group is also acknowledged to be of consequence, there is a considerable overlap among the performances of individuals, so that 'it is not the case that this continuum can be divided in such a way that the members of each social class fall within a certain range, and members of other classes fall outside this.' He indicates the range of individual scores in table 6.2, and adds that 'in the case of Classes II and V the bracketed figures indicate what the range would have been had there not in each case been one individual whose speech was markedly "status incongruent." If these two individuals had not formed part of the sample the figures would look more "regular," but there would still not be "discrete groups which are relatively unified in their linguistic behavior."' There is considerable overlap.

In cases like this it is quite obvious that if we look only at means we are tempted to say one thing, whereas if we consider the distribution of responses

Table 6.1 H-dropping: means for five social groups

I	II	III	IV	V
96	64	43	21	17

Source: Petyt (1980, p. 189)

Table 6.2 H-dropping: within-group ranges for five social groups

I	II	III	IV	V
81–100	7–100 (40–100)	2–100	0–86	0–80 (0–37)

Source: Petyt (1980, p. 189)

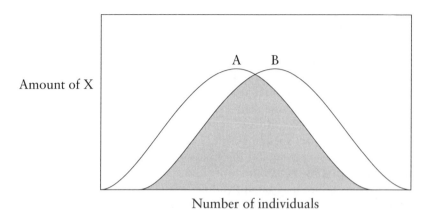

Figure 6.3 X for two groups, A and B

within each class we may draw some other conclusion. But the overriding issue is that there are approved procedures to help investigators to decide how far they can be confident that any differences that they observe to exist among the various classes, that is, among the various means, are due to something other than errors in measurement or peculiarities of distribution. Such procedures require an investigator not only to calculate the means for each class, but also to assess the amount of variation in the responses within each class, and then to test pairs of differences of means among the classes using a procedure which will indicate what likelihood there is that any difference found occurs by chance, e.g., one chance in twenty.

Most social scientists employing statistical procedures regard this last *level of significance* as a suitable test of a hypothesis. In other words, unless their statistical procedures indicate that the same results would occur by chance in fewer than one case in twenty, they will *not* say that two groups differ in some respect or on a particular characteristic; that is, they insist that their claims be significant at what they call the 0.05 level of significance. We are also much more likely to find two means to be significantly different if they are obtained from averaging a large number of observations than a small number.

Figure 6.3 provides a further illustration of the problems inherent in comparing populations in this way. The two groups A and B that are compared there for characteristic X produce different mean scores and that difference may even be statistically significant. However, there is an enormous overlap among individuals in groups A and B – the shaded area. The majority of individuals in the two groups overlap in their X-ness, whatever that may be. It would be very unsafe indeed to make claims about the X-ness of the next person you meet from either group A or group B.

Whenever you look at results reported by sociolinguists, you should keep in mind the above-mentioned issues concerning the formulation of hypotheses and the collection, analysis, and interpretation of data. Statisticians certainly keep them in mind in assessing the claims they make. In examining individual sociolinguistic investigations, therefore, you must ask what exactly are the hypotheses;

how reliable are the methods used for collecting the data; what is the actual significance of results that are reported on a simple graph or histogram; and what do the findings tell us about the initial hypotheses. Anyone who attempts to do serious work in sociolinguistics must address himself or herself to such issues. Likewise, anyone who wishes to draw conclusions about either the structure of language or how language varies within groups or between groups must ask the same questions of data that someone presents to support this or that conclusion. Some sociolinguists have tended not to be very rigorous in their statistical treatments, but this has not stopped them from drawing very strong conclusions, which seem 'obvious' and 'interesting' to them; whether these conclusions are 'significant' in the sense of having met an appropriate statistical test of a well-stated hypothesis may not be a concern.

Milroy and Gordon (2003, p. 168) are aware that there may be problems here. However, they ask: 'should we equate failure to achieve statistical significance with sociolinguistic irrelevance?' Their answer is that 'statistical tests, like all quantitative procedures are tools to provide insight into patterning in variation. They must be used critically.' Dealing with a critic of Labov's work, Milroy (1992, p. 78) says:

> It is not surprising that an anti-quantitative linguist should advocate confirmatory statistical testing, but it is very important to understand the proposition put forward here is simply wrong. If Labov's interpretations were suspect (and of course they are not), this would not arise from the fact that he failed to test for significance. There was no reason for him to do so because the claims he wished to make were quite simple . . . and because in his analysis the same patterns were repeated for every variable studied.

According to Milroy, since this kind of sociolinguistic inquiry is 'exploratory' in nature, it can be likewise 'exploratory' in its quantitative approach. Labov's most recent work (2001) is still exploratory in nature but it is also extremely sophisticated in its sampling, data collection, and hypothesis-testing. Sociolinguists now make increasing use of VARBRUL, a set of computer programs specifically designed to deal with the kinds of problems encountered in studies of variation (see Bayley, 2002, particularly pp. 124–34).

Discussion

1. Look at the sampling techniques employed in studies of linguistic variation in large cities. How different is the sampling from the dialect-atlas type studies? What weaknesses, if any, still exist? Look particularly at the work of such investigators as Labov, Trudgill, Shuy, Wolfram, and Fasold. You might also care to look at Sivertsen's study (1960) of 'Cockney phonology,' using mainly four old ladies, Viereck's study (1966) of the English of Gateshead-upon-Tyne, using mainly a dozen old men, and DeCamp's study (1958–9) of San Francisco English, using a 'judgment' rather than a random sample.
2. Sankoff (1974, p. 22) has described the problem of sampling in sociolinguistic surveys as follows:

Table 6.3 Percentage of non-RP forms for three consonants

	(ng):[n]	(t):[ʔ]	(h):Ø
MMC	31	41	6
LMC	42	62	14
UWC	87	89	40
MWC	95	92	59
LWC	100	94	61

Source: Trudgill (1995, p. 36)

> A speech community sample need not include the large number of individuals usually required for other kinds of behavioural surveys. If people within a speech community indeed understand each other with a high degree of efficiency, this tends to place a limit on the extent of possible variation, and imposes a regularity (necessary for effective communication) not found to the same extent in other kinds of social behaviour. The literature as well as our own experience would suggest that, even for quite complex speech communities, samples of more than about 150 individuals tend to be redundant, bringing increasing data handling problems with diminishing analytical returns. . . . It is crucial, however, that the sample be well chosen, and representative of all social subsegments about which one wishes to generalize.

Keeping these words in mind, how might you go about trying to sample the population of some town or city with which you are familiar so that you will be able to account for any linguistic variation that exists there?

3. Wells (1982, pp. xviii–xix) provides the following set of 24 'keywords' for use in dialect studies in either Britain or North America: *kit, dress, trap, lot, strut, foot, bath, cloth, nurse, fleece, face, palm, thought, goat, goose, price, choice, mouth, near, square, start, north, force,* and *cure*. All the sounds in these words are relevant. Foulkes and Docherty (1999) add *happy, letter, horse,* and *comma* to this list but only for their final unstressed vowels. Ask people you know who come from different parts of the English-speaking world to pronounce these words and record the different pronunciations you find.

4. Given information of the kind contained in table 6.3, and no supporting explanations of how each mean (expressed as a percentage) was determined, what can you say with confidence about the linguistic behavior of members of each of the groups mentioned and about the reported differences in behavior between the various groups? Can you be more confident of some conclusions than of others? You might consider questions such as the following: How important are the differences among the various working classes (UWC, MWC, and LWC)? Between the middle classes (MMC and LMC)? Between the middle classes as a whole and the working classes as a whole? Between the LMC and the UWC? How does performance on the (h) variable appear to be different from performance on the (ng) and (t)

variables in all social classes? Is there any difference in performance on the (ng) and (t) variables? What other kinds of information would you require to strengthen any conclusions you would wish to draw?

Further Reading

Highly recommended for coverage of issues discussed in this chapter and the two following chapters are Chambers et al. (2002), Milroy and Gordon (2003), and Chambers (2003). Linn (1998) is also useful and Wolfram and Schilling-Estes (1998) contains a very useful appendix on American English entitled 'An Inventory of Socially Diagnostic Structures.' For the use of statistics in linguistics see Sankoff (1978, 1985).

7 Some Findings and Issues

Having looked briefly at some of the problems investigators face in using the concept of the 'linguistic variable' to examine linguistic variation in society, I can now turn to some representative quantitative studies. I will look at only a few, and then at only certain of their findings; to deal with all such studies at length would require several book-length treatments. I will comment on various parts of the studies selected to show something of the range of concerns that investigators have had and to indicate the kinds of problems they have faced. I will also look at certain claims that have been made concerning the relevance these studies have to achieving a better understanding of the structure of language and of its acquisition and use.

An Early Study

One of the earliest studies of variation was Fischer's study (1958) of the (ng) variable, i.e., pronunciations like *singing* [ŋ] versus *singin'* [n]. We should observe that there is a long history of both the [ŋ] and [n] variants in the language, that stigmatization of the [n] variant is a phenomenon of the nineteenth and twentieth centuries, and that even today in some circles in the United Kingdom, necessarily privileged ones, people still go *huntin'*, *shootin'*, and *fishin'*, not *hunting*, *shooting*, and *fishing*.

As part of a study of child-rearing practices in a New England community, Fischer conducted interviews with young children, twelve boys and twelve girls, aged 3–10. He noted their use of [ŋ] and [n] in a very formal situation during the administration of the Thematic Apperception Test, in a less formal interview, and in an informal situation in which the children discussed recent activities. Table 7.1 shows that boys used more *-in'* forms than girls in the most formal situation.

Fischer also compared the use of [ŋ] and [n] of a boy described by his teachers as a 'model' boy with that of a boy described as a 'typical' boy. The model boy worked well in school and was described as being popular, thoughtful, and considerate; the typical boy was described as being strong, mischievous, and apparently unafraid of being caught doing something he should not be doing.

Table 7.1 Preferences for *-ing* and *-in'* endings, by sex

	-ing > *-in'*	*-ing* < *-in'*
Boys	5	7
Girls	10	2

Source: Fischer (1958, p. 48)

Table 7.2 Preferences of two boys for *-ing* and *-in'* endings

	-ing	*-in'*
'Model' boy	38	1
'Typical' boy	10	12

Source: Fischer (1958, p. 49)

Table 7.3 Preferences for *-ing* and *-in'* endings, by formality of situation

	Most formal	*Formal interview*	*Informal interview*
-ing	38	33	24
-in'	1	35	41

Source: Fischer (1958, p. 50)

In the most formal situation these two boys produced the numbers of instances of *-ing* and *-in'* reported in table 7.2. However, Fischer further observed that the model boy also used *-in'* more as the formality of the situation decreased, as can be seen in table 7.3. He observed several more interesting facts. As children relaxed in the most formal situation they produced more instances of *-in'*. Such usage was also associated with specific verbs, so that verbs like *hit, chew, swim,* and *punch*, i.e., verbs describing everyday activities, were much more likely to be given *-in'* endings than more 'formal' verbs like *criticize, correct, read,* and *visit*. Fischer's conclusion (p. 51) is that 'the choice between the *-ing* and the *-in'* variants appears to be related to sex, class, personality (aggressive/ cooperative), and mood (tense/relaxed) of the speaker, to the formality of the conversation and to the specific verb spoken.'

Fischer's study, then, is a very simple account of the common linguistic variable (ng). It covers very few subjects, and employs very informal, even casual, methods of data collection. There is also no attempt to subject the findings to statistical testing. But there is also, of course, no attempt to make any profound claims!

Discussion

1. If you were interested in the same phenomenon as Fischer, the (ng) variable among young children, how would you design an investigation so that you would be in a position to make much stronger claims than Fischer was able to make?
2. What particular difficulties do you think there are in investigating children's language that do not exist in investigating adults' language? How might you try to get around these difficulties?
3. Do you see any problems with the concepts of a 'model' boy and a 'typical' boy; e.g., do you see some danger of circularity in the definitions?

New York City

Labov's work in New York City is usually regarded as setting the pattern for quantitative studies of linguistic variation. Labov raised many of the issues that are still addressed and devised many methods for tackling these issues. One of his earliest studies of linguistic variation was a small-scale investigation of the (r) variable (Labov, 1966). Labov believed that *r*-pronunciation after vowels was being reintroduced into New York speech from above, was a feature of the speech of younger people rather than of older people, was more likely to occur as the formality level in speech increased, and would be more likely at the ends of words (*floor*) than before consonants (*fourth*). He set out to test these hypotheses by walking around three New York City department stores (Saks, Macy's, and S. Klein), which were rather clearly demarcated by the social-class groups to which they catered (high, middle, and low, respectively), and asking the location of departments he knew to be situated on the fourth floor. When the shop assistant answered, Labov would seek a careful repetition of 'fourth floor' by pretending not to hear the initial response.

Table 7.4 shows the incidence of *r* use that Labov found among individuals employed in the three stores (Labov, 1972b, p. 51). The table shows that 32 and 31 percent of the personnel approached in Saks and Macy's respectively used *r* in all possible instances but only 17 percent did so in S. Klein; 79 percent of the seventy-one employees in S. Klein who were approached did not use *r* at all, but only 38 percent of the sixty-eight employees approached in Saks and 49 percent of the 125 employees approached in Macy's were *r*-less.

So far as the position of occurrence of *r*-pronunciation was concerned (i.e., before consonant vs. word final, and first response vs. repeated response), Labov found the distribution reported in figure 7.1. This figure shows that *r*-pronunciation was favored in Saks to a greater extent than in Macy's but much less so in S. Klein. Careful repetition of the utterance nearly always increased *r*-pronunciation, and pronunciation of the *r* was found more often in *floor* than

Table 7.4 Percentage of *r*-use in three New York City department stores

	Saks (%)	Macy's (%)	S. Klein (%)
All [r]	32	31	17
Some [r]	30	20	4
No [r]	38	49	79
Number	68	125	71

Source: based on Labov (1972b, p. 51)

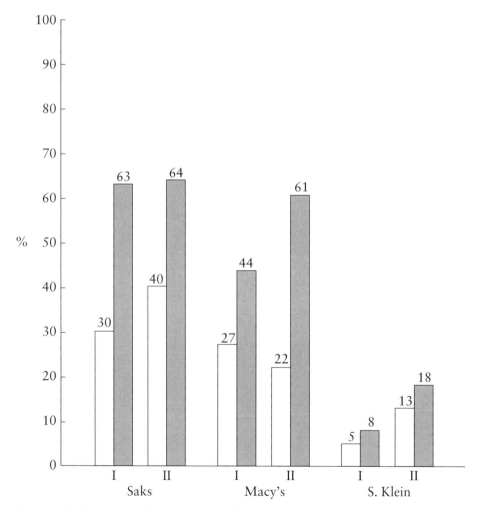

Figure 7.1 Percentage of (r); [r] in first (I) and second (II) utterances of *fourth* (white) and *floor* (solid) in three New York City department stores
Source: based on Labov (1972b, p. 52)

in *fourth* in all circumstances. Labov did not test his findings for statistical significance but the data clearly reveal the patterns I have just mentioned.

A further analysis of the department store data showed that in Saks it was older people who used r-pronunciation less. However, the data from S. Klein on this point were quite inconclusive, and the results from Macy's pointed in a direction completely opposite to that predicted: r-pronunciation actually increased with age. This fact led Labov to conclude that members of the highest and lowest social groups tend not to change their pronunciation after it becomes fixed in adolescence but members of middle social groups sometimes do, possibly because of their social aspirations. He tested this last hypothesis later in a more comprehensive study of New York City speech and found good confirmation for it.

Labov claims that today in New York City pronunciations of words like *car* and *guard* with the r pronounced are highly valued. They are associated with the upper middle class even though members of that class do not always use such pronunciations, nor do they use them on all occasions. We should note that r-pronunciation has not always been highly valued in New York City. New York City was r-pronouncing in the eighteenth century but became r-less in the nineteenth, and r-lessness predominated until World War II. At that time r-pronunciation became prestigious again, possibly as a result of large population movements to the city; there was a shift in attitude toward r-pronunciation, from apparent indifference to a widespread desire to adopt such pronunciation.

This desire is clearly demonstrated on subjective reaction tests carried out in the 1960s. These tests required subjects to evaluate speech with and without r-pronunciation by asking subjects to judge the job prospects of people who differed only in their pronunciation of words containing r, and to say which of two pronunciations they used of words containing r. The tests showed that New Yorkers in the upper middle class and under the age of 40 almost unanimously approved r-pronunciation even though fewer than half actually used r in all possible instances. People below the age of 20 also used more r-pronunciation than people between the ages of 20 and 40, a fact that would suggest r-pronunciation to be on the increase. Above the age of 40, approval fell off to about 60 percent and use showed a dramatic decline to less than 10 percent. Other classes exhibited much the same pattern of approval and use, though, in all cases except one, at much lower levels. In one case – that of the lower middle class – the use of r actually exceeded such use in the upper middle class in certain circumstances. Not only did lower middle-class speakers approve of r-pronunciation, but they also tended to exceed what appear to be the norms for its use in the next highest class in reading word lists and in pronouncing minimal pairs of words.

We should look at this last finding in more detail because Labov makes particularly strong claims concerning it. Figure 7.2 shows the use of r by various social classes in different styles of speech, from the most casual type of speech (e.g., telling about a narrow escape from death) to the most formal type (e.g., reading aloud a list of pairs of words like *bit* and *bid* and *pa* and *par*) (Labov, 1966, p. 240). As we can see, the amount of r use increases by social class and by formality of style. But there is one noticeable exception: Labov's lower middle-class speakers out-perform his upper middle-class speakers on word lists

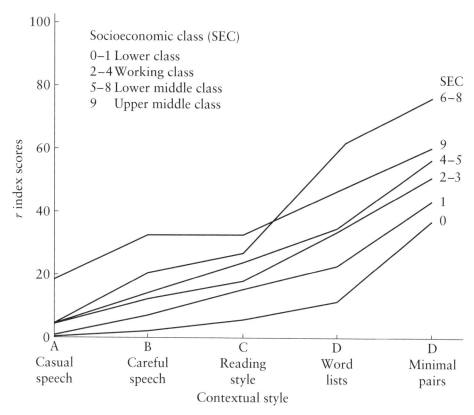

Figure 7.2 R-pronunciation in New York City by social class and style of speech
Source: Labov (1966, p. 240)

and pairs. This is the finding I mentioned in chapter 6. Labov calls this a *cross-over* in the graph and explains it as an instance of *hypercorrection*. Hypercorrection occurs when individuals consciously try to speak like people they regard as socially superior but actually go too far and overdo the particular linguistic behavior they are attempting to match. Here, lower middle-class speakers know how prestigious *r*-pronunciations are and, in reading word lists and lists of pairs, i.e., when they are placed in situations which require them to monitor their speech closely, they out-perform their reference group, in this case the next highest social class, the upper middle class.

Labov makes much of this phenomenon of hypercorrection, particularly because it appears to relate to changes that are taking place in the language. However, a word of caution is necessary (see earlier remarks on pp. 157–8). Such displays as we find in figure 7.2 are displays of group means. We have no information about the amount of variance about the means so we cannot be sure how comparable they are. We do know they are based on quite small numbers of informants in each case. In addition, we cannot be sure that any two means which differ do so significantly in the statistical sense. The cross-over shown in figure 7.2 could, theoretically at least, be the result of the way the data have been treated. However, the fact that it occurs for both word lists and pairs provides us with some assurance of the correctness of Labov's claims.

(If you need to be convinced that using group means drawn from small groups can lead to claims that may not always be valid, consider what you could possibly say about two groups, each of five subjects, who produced the following scores on some test or other: scores of 30, 70, 75, 80, and 85 in the one case and of 75, 76, 77, 78, and 79 in the other. The first group mean is 68 and the second 77. It would be very dangerous indeed to make any claims about overall group behavior other than that the performance of the members of the second group appears to be more homogeneous, i.e., to contain less variance, than the performance of members of the first.)

Labov also investigated the (th) variable in New York City, focusing on the pronunciation of the initial consonants in words like *thing* and *three*. There are three possible variants: [t], [tθ], and [θ], the last being the standard pronunciation, the first being the most nonstandard (something like *ting* and *tree*), and the middle an intermediate variant. Labov shows the distribution of scores on what he calls the *(th) index*, our figure 7.3. The higher the index score, the greater the incidence of nonstandard usage in the particular style of speech. Labov (1972b, pp. 238–40) observes that in every context members of the speech community are differentiated by the use of the variable, but nevertheless every group behaves in the same way, as indicated by the parallel slope of style-shifting. However, individuals are not consciously aware of this general pattern for all groups because each individual is limited in his or her social contacts. The same linguistic variable signals both social and stylistic stratification.

Finally, what is impressive is the striking regularity of the overall pattern, which emerges from samples with as few as five individuals in any sub-group, using no more than five or ten utterances in a given style for each individual. Labov adds that other variables show similar distributions, e.g., the (dh) variable in New York City, i.e., the pronunciation of the initial consonants in words like *this* and *then*, and the distribution of the (ng) variable in a variety of studies. He also adds that the (th) variable indicates that there is a sharp break in linguistic behavior between working-class groups and middle-class groups, as we can see in figure 7.2. He calls a distribution with such a sharp break in the pattern *sharp stratification*.

Discussion

1. In both the United States and the United Kingdom it is possible to hear pronunciations of words like *cart* and *car* with or without the *r* pronounced. However, *r*-pronunciation (or the lack of it) is differently valued on the two sides of the Atlantic. Explain some of the complexities, linguistic and social, of *r*-pronunciation in the two countries. Consider where *r* is found in the two countries, how *r*s are actually pronounced (and by whom), and also such pronunciations as *Shah(r) of Iran*, *idea(r) of it*, *cah* but *car is*, and the different pronunciations of the *r* in *very*. You might also refer, if you can,

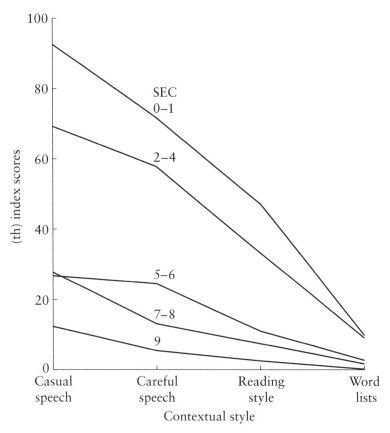

Figure 7.3 Stylistic and social stratification of (th) in *thing, three*, etc., in New York City. SEC as in figure 7.2
Source: Labov (1966, p. 260)

to the same phenomenon in other parts of the English-speaking world, e.g., Canada and Australia.

2. Labov's major study of New York City is based on a sample from the Lower East Side. Labov (1966, pp. 4–5) claims that this area 'exemplifies the complexity of New York City as a whole with all its variability and apparent inconsistencies.' Try to assess this claim.

3. Labov has been criticized for what some see as a simplistic approach to quantification. For example, Hudson (1996, p. 181) criticizes Labov's method of studying variation because:

> it loses too much information which may be important. Information about the use of individual variants is lost when they are merged into variable scores, and information about the speech of individuals is also lost if these are included in group averages. At each stage the method imposes a structure on the data which may be more rigid than was inherent in the data, and to that extent distorts the results – discrete boundaries are imposed on non-discrete

phonetic parameters, artificial orderings are used for variants which are related in more than one way, and speakers are assigned to discrete groups when they are actually related to each other in more complex ways.

(See also Davis, 1983, pp. 97–101.) How justified are such criticisms? For Labov's views, see Labov (1969, p. 731): 'We are not dealing here with effects which are so erratic or marginal that statistical tests are required to determine whether or not they might have been produced by chance.'

4. *Hypercorrect* linguistic behavior is not at all unusual. What examples do you know of? Who gives evidence of such behavior, and on what occasions?

Norwich and Reading

Trudgill (1974) investigated sixteen different phonological variables in his work in Norwich, England. He demonstrates, in much the same way as Labov does in New York City, how use of the variants is related to social class and level of formality. Trudgill's analysis of the variables (ng), (t), and (h) shows, for example, that the higher the social class the more frequent is the use of the [ŋ], [t], and [h] variants in words like *singing*, *butter*, and *hammer* rather than the corresponding [n], [ʔ], and Ø variants. However, whereas members of the lower working class almost invariably say *singin'*, they do not almost invariably say *'ammer*. Moreover, although members of the lower working class say *singin'* when they are asked to read a word list containing words ending in *-ing*, they pronounce the (ng) with the [ŋ] variant on the majority of occasions. The data also suggest that, so far as the (ng) variable is concerned, its variant use is related not only to social class but also to gender, with females showing a greater preference for [ŋ] than males, regardless of social-class membership.

Trudgill (1995, pp. 93–4) uses data such as those in table 7.5 to demonstrate two very important points: first, when style is kept constant, the lower the social class the greater the incidence of the nonstandard variant; second, when class is kept constant, the less formal the style the greater the incidence of the nonstandard variant. The figures therefore increase in table 7.5 in every column from top to bottom and in every row from left to right. Some increases are negligible and some are considerable. For example, middle middle-class speakers always avoid *-in'* pronunciations in the two most formal styles but 'relax' considerably more in casual style. Upper working-class speakers make a very sharp differentiation between the two reading styles and the two speaking styles. Lower working-class speakers make no real distinction between the two speaking styles and use *-in'* pronunciations almost exclusively in both; however, just like middle working-class speakers, they are conscious that *-ing* pronunciations are used in reading styles and do manage to introduce them on many occasions.

In an investigation of linguistic variation in Reading, England, Cheshire (1978) focused on the (s) variable in the speech of three groups of boys and girls. The (s) variable in this case is the extension of third-person singular verb marking to all other persons, e.g., *I knows*, *you knows*, *we has*, and *they calls*. The

Table 7.5 Percentage use of *-in'* in four contextual styles of speech in Norwich

	Style[b]			
Social class[a]	WLS	RPS	FS	CS
MMC	0	0	3	28
LMC	0	10	15	42
UWC	5	15	74	87
MWC	23	44	88	95
LWC	29	66	98	100

[a] Social class: MMC (middle middle class), LMC (lower middle class), UWC (upper working class), MWC (middle working class), LWC (lower working class).
[b] Style: WLS (word list), RPS (reading passage), FS (formal), CS (casual).
Source: based on Trudgill (1995, p. 94)

subjects were thirteen boys and twelve girls aged 9–17. They came from three groups of friends: an all-male group (Orts Road boys), a small group of three boys (Shinfield boys), and an all-female group (Shinfield girls). Members of all groups used nonstandard forms with verbs like *know* and *call* on just over half of the possible occasions for use. They used the nonstandard *has*, e.g., *we has* on about a third of the possible occasions and the nonstandard *does* on just under a quarter of the possible occasions for use. The situation with *do* and *does* is complicated by the fact that the nonstandard *he do* is slightly preferred over *he does*. With *have*, Cheshire found that the *has* form occurred only as a full verb ('We has a muck around in there') or before an infinitive ('I has to stop in') but never as an auxiliary (so 'I have got,' not 'I has got').

Further investigation showed that, if a verb took a finite complement, i.e., if it was followed by a clause in which the verb is marked for tense, then there was no use of this *-s* ending with persons other than third-person singular. Consequently, we find 'Oh, I forget what the place is called' and 'I suppose they went to court' in contrast to 'I just lets her beat me' and 'I knows how to stick in the boot.' Moreover, 'vernacular' verbs, i.e., commonly used verbs, like *go*, *kill*, *boot*, and *learn*, were much more likely to take the *-s* ending in all forms than other verbs, to the extent that use of *goes*, *kills*, *boots*, and *learns* is almost mandatory with such verbs. Cheshire calls these two conditions *constraints on usage* and points out that they work in opposite directions. Consequently, a verb stem always takes the *-s* when it is used in the third-person singular, the *-s* ending is favored in all persons when the verb is a 'vernacular' verb, but the *-s* is not used at all if the verb has a complement in which the verb in the complement is marked for tense (Cheshire, 1978, p. 62).

Some social factors operate, too, in the pattern of variation. Cheshire devised an index based on ambition, degree of 'toughness' (as indicated by such things as ability to fight and steal), and peer-group status in order to assess the strength of an individual's membership in the boys' vernacular culture. She found that high frequencies of *-s* usage went with high index scores and low frequencies with low index scores. Girls' vernacular culture had to be defined differently because the girls had different interests from the boys. Girls used the *-s* ending as much as boys, but did not exhibit the same correlation between frequency of use and index scores. They also shifted their use of the (s) variable toward Standard English norms in formal situations to a greater extent than the boys. Cheshire concluded (p. 68) that 'variation is controlled by both social and linguistic factors. In boys' speech, variation is governed by norms that are central to the vernacular culture, and are transmitted through the peer group. Variation in the girls' speech appears to be a more personal process, and less rigidly controlled by vernacular norms.' She added that both boys and girls 'are subject to two linguistic constraints on the form of regular present-tense verbs, of which one favours the use of the non-standard verb form, and the other favours the use of the standard form.' Nonstandard forms are not without their attraction; they are said to have *covert prestige* in contrast to the obvious overt prestige of standard forms. They signal that those who use them have no hesitation in identifying with the local community through laying claim to local loyalties. Not for them the attractions of some other identity, which the use of standard forms might indicate.

Cheshire further observes that 'variation in the forms of *have* and *do* appears to be due to linguistic changes in progress.' In the next chapter I will have more to say on this last point and on how studies of variation have been used to indicate not just how much variation exists in a language, but also how such variation can be interpreted to show changes that are occurring.

Discussion

1. Table 7.6 is based on a similar table in Trudgill (1974, p. 94). The table shows us how his sixty subjects in Norwich performed on the (ng) variable. A score of 000 indicates exclusive use of [ŋ] pronunciation, e.g., *singing*, whereas a score of 100 indicates exclusive use of [n] pronunciations, e.g., *singin'*. What kinds of conclusions might you be tempted to draw from this kind of display? How confident can you be about your conclusions? Trudgill himself finds the 017 recorded under casual style for male lower middle-class speakers hard to explain. Why do you think he has this difficulty?
2. What similarities and differences do you find in the work of Fischer and Cheshire?
3. In what ways is Cheshire's study more focused than those of Labov and Trudgill that are reported here? What advantages and disadvantages result from narrowing the focus of investigation?

A Variety of Studies

The Detroit study (Shuy et al., 1968) and Wolfram's follow-up to that study (1969) have some findings which are worthy of comment in the present context. For

Table 7.6 The (ng) variable in Norwich

Social class[a]	Style[b] No.	Sex	WLS	RPS	FS	CS
MMC	6	M	000	000	004	031
		F	000	000	000	000
LMC	8	M	000	020	027	017
		F	000	000	003	067
UWC	16	M	000	018	081	095
		F	011	013	068	077
MWC	22	M	024	043	091	097
		F	020	046	081	088
LWC	8	M	066	100	100	100
		F	017	054	097	100

[a] Social class: MMC (middle middle class), LMC (lower middle class), UWC (upper working class), MWC (middle working class), LWC (lower working class).
[b] Style: WLS (word list), RPS (reading passage), FS (formal), CS (casual).
Source: based on Trudgill (1974, p. 94)

example, the Detroit study investigated the use of multiple negation as a linguistic variable in that city. The study showed that there is a very close relationship between the use of multiple negation and social class. Whereas upper middle-class speakers used such negation on about 2 percent of possible occasions, the corresponding percentages for the other three social classes were as follows: lower middle class, 11 percent; upper working class, 38 percent; and lower working class, 70 percent. From such figures we can make a further observation: it is not that members of the upper middle class *always* avoid multiple negation and members of the lower working class *always* employ it; it may be our impression that such is the case, but the facts do not confirm that impression. No class uses one variant of the variable to the exclusion of the other, regardless of circumstances. Speech in any social class, therefore, is inherently variable, just as it is in society as a whole. However, the analyses of the different variables that were investigated in Detroit clearly show that, although individuals exhibit a certain amount of inconsistency in their linguistic behavior, there is nevertheless a pattern to that behavior. For example, as the situation becomes more formal, an individual's linguistic usage comes closer to standard usage, and the higher the social class of the speaker, the more standard too is the speaker's behavior. Moreover, children are less standard in their linguistic behavior than adults with similar social backgrounds, and males are less standard than females.

Wolfram's study was an attempt to show how the distribution of linguistic variables correlated with such factors as social class, gender, age, and racial origin in Detroit. Wolfram wanted to identify varieties of speech which might be associated with specific social groups in the city, e.g., upper middle-class

Table 7.7 Informants used in Wolfram's (1969) study

Social class	Age	White Male	White Female	Black Male	Black Female
Upper middle	10–12	2	2	2	2
	14–17	2	2	2	2
	30–55	2	2	2	2
Lower middle	10–12			2	2
	14–17			2	2
	30–35			2	2
Upper working	10–12			2	2
	14–17			2	2
	30–35			2	2
Lower working	10–12			2	2
	14–17			2	2
	30–35			2	2

whites or lower working-class blacks. His work is based on data collected from forty-eight black subjects drawn from 702 subjects used initially in the Detroit study, plus another twelve white subjects. They were selected to conform as closely as possible to the criteria shown in table 7.7.

Having identified his groups, Wolfram then attempted to show characteristic differences in linguistic behavior. He investigated four phonological variables: word final consonant cluster simplification; medial and final *th*, as in *nothing* and *path*; syllable final *d*; and the occurrence of *r* after vowels. He also investigated four grammatical variables: the zero copula, as in *He tired*; invariant *be*, as in *He be tired*; the *-s* suffixes, as in *girls*, *boy's*, and *goes*; and multiple negation. Figure 7.4, for example, shows group means for the absence of the third-person singular tense-marking (z). A close inspection of the figure shows that, whereas it is quite possible that the differences between the two groups at each of the ends, i.e., between the upper middle and the lower middle classes and between the upper working and the lower working classes, may not be significant, there being only twelve subjects in each group, the difference between the top two groups as a whole and the bottom two groups as a whole, i.e., between the middle class and the working class, almost certainly is, and probably at a very high level of significance. There does therefore appear to be a great difference in usage of the (z) between middle-class and working-class people in Detroit.

We can contrast this graph with another from the same study, this one concerned with (r) absence (Wolfram, 1969, p. 110). Figure 7.5 gives us the information we need. Here we find a progressive step-like set of differences. However, without statistical testing we cannot be sure that there is a significant difference between adjacent means, particularly when the groups are small (twelve subjects) and the difference in means is of the order of 61.3 and 71.7 percent. That

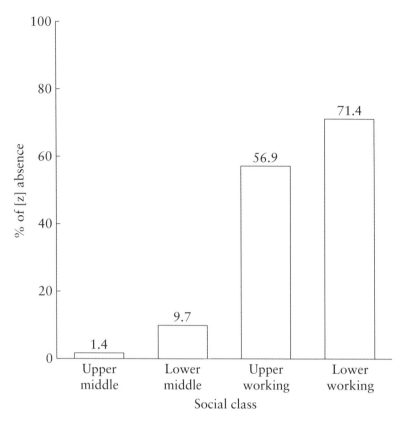

Figure 7.4 Percentage of (z) absence in third-person singular present tense agreement in Detroit black speech
Source: based on Wolfram (1969, p. 136)

there is a significant difference between the two groups at each end does seem very likely, but we cannot be sure of the significance of the difference between any adjacent pairs. The data do, however, fall into a very clear pattern and it is such patterns that sociolinguists seek to explain.

Wolfram and Fasold (1974, pp. 80–1) argue that in the case of (r) absence in figure 7.5 we have an example of what they call *gradient stratification*, i.e., a regular step-like progression in means which matches social groupings. In the previous case of (z) we have *sharp stratification*, i.e., a clear break between a particular pair of social groupings. The first kind of stratification is said to be typical of the distribution of phonological variables; the second kind to be typical of grammatical variables.

Wolfram's general findings in Detroit were that social status was the single most important variable correlating with linguistic differences, with the clearest boundary being between the lower middle and upper working classes. In each class, however, females used more standard-language forms than males. Older subjects also used fewer stigmatized forms than did younger subjects. Finally, reading style showed the fewest deviations of all from standard-language forms.

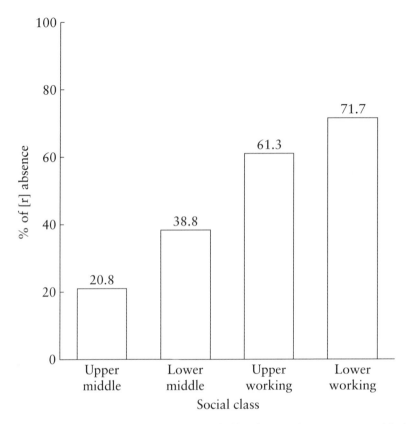

Figure 7.5 Percentage of (r) absence in words like *farm* and *car* in Detroit black speech
Source: based on Wolfram (1969, p. 110)

So far I have mentioned several factors that correlate with linguistic variation: social class, age, and gender. Another study which looked at all of these is Macaulay's study (1977) of five variables in Glasgow: the vowels in words such as *hit, school, hat*, and *now* and the occurrence of glottal stops as replacements for [t] in words like *better* and *get*. Macaulay surveyed sixteen adults, sixteen 15-year-olds, and sixteen 10-year-olds, with equal numbers of males and females represented in each group. His forty-eight subjects were equally divided among four social classes: professional and managerial; white-collar; skilled manual; and semi-skilled and unskilled manual. In the case of children, the occupation of the father was used unless the mother was (or had been) in a 'higher' occupational group. Macaulay counted equal numbers of occurrences of each variable from each speaker as a further control for volubility.

Macaulay found a clear correlation between variation and social class, but in addition he was able to make certain further interesting observations. He found his two lowest classes to be much alike in behavior. With males, the greatest difference between classes was between his top class (professional and managerial) and the second-highest class (white-collar), whereas with females the greatest difference was between the two intermediate classes (white-collar and skilled manual). Increase in age also seemed to be associated with an increase in the difference between social classes, this difference showing itself to be clearly established in the 15-year-olds surveyed (but apparent also in the 10-year-olds). Finally, Macaulay found that, when individual rather than group behavior was plotted for each variable, a continuum of behavior was exhibited in each case. That is, there was considerable variation within each of the four classes, with the behavior of certain individuals in each class overlapping the behavior of individuals in neighboring classes; however, the means for most classes, except the two lowest as noted above, were clearly different from each other.

We can conclude from Macaulay's study that the linguistic behavior of individuals forms a continuum in the same way that social organization is continuous. Social classes are constructs imposed on this continuum. If linguistic variation is correlated with the 'average' behavior of individuals in these classes, it will show class differences. This is what we should expect, and it is what happens. However, the linguistic behavior of certain individuals in one class will overlap the linguistic behavior of certain individuals in neighboring classes. What is important in this view is that there is still a certain homogeneity of behavior within the classes. The majority of speakers within the various classes behave like one another even though some individuals do not. This behavior has its own distinctive quality, and its characteristics are not just the result of some individuals behaving like individuals 'above' them and other individuals behaving like individuals 'below' them in the social hierarchy. That is, the members of each social class exhibit certain ranges of behavior on the linguistic variables and, even though the ranges overlap, each social class has a distinctive range for each variable.

Kiesling's research (1998) on the use of the (ng) variable among a small group of fraternity men at a university in the United States shows how it might be possible to account for individual differences in usage. He recorded conversations in a variety of settings and found, predictably, that the use of *-in'* was closely related to the type of activity: 75 percent in socializing, 53 percent in interviews, 47 percent in meetings, and 54 percent in reading aloud. The big difference here is between the first activity and the other three. Kiesling focused on the two extremes, socializing and meetings, and was drawn to try to account for the language behavior of three participants who diverged from the usual pattern of decreasing their use of *-in'* as the social situation became more formal, i.e., the difference between casual socializing on the one hand and a formal meeting on the other. He concluded that each of the individuals achieved a personal objective in using *-in'* so frequently: for 'Speed' the use of *-in'* symbolized, among other things, values such as hard work, practicality, and freedom as well as a certain rebelliousness and independence; for 'Waterson' its use was likewise emblematic of hard work but was also an appeal to camaraderie and a claim to shared physical power; for 'Mick' the use of *-in'* made the same claim to hard work but also served as an expression of authority and power. Kiesling says that the (ng) variable is here being used to create identity. Although these men are college students they look to working-class modes of behavior in order to express themselves as 'hard working,' 'rebellious,' 'casual,' or 'confrontational,' and they do this through their language choices.

Two studies of the French spoken in Montreal are of interest because they suggest some of the complexities we face in trying to describe the distribution of variants of a variable in one case and the persistence of a rare variant in another. The first study is by Sankoff and Cedergren (1971), who report on the (l) variable in Montreal French, i.e., the presence or absence of [l] in expressions such as 'he does,' [il fɛ] or [i fɛ], and 'he is,' [il e] or [y e]. They found that in 94 percent of the cases when the (l) was followed by a consonant or a glide it was not produced phonetically, but it went phonetically unrealized in only 57 percent of the cases when it was followed by a vowel. Therefore, before a consonant or glide the (l) is generally not pronounced, but it is pronounced before vowels about two times out of five. However, there is a further constraint. When the (l) is part of an impersonal pronoun, e.g., the *l* in *il pleut* ('it's raining') or *il y a* ('there is/are'), that (l) is almost never realized before a consonant or glide; in contrast, a personal *il* ('he') in the same circumstances finds the (l) not realized phonetically about 80 percent of the time. What we find here is that the distribution of the variants of the (l) variable in Montreal French is related to both phonological and grammatical factors, not just social ones. The (l) is affected by its relationship to the following phonological segment and whether it occurs in either a personal or impersonal pronoun, when these are even of identical form, i.e., *il*.

The second example from Montreal French is Sankoff and Vincent's study (1977) of the use of the negative particle *ne*. They found that *ne* is very rarely used at all in Montreal; in fact, it is not used in about 99.5 percent of the cases in which it would be required in formal written French. This same deletion is also found in Standard Continental French with estimates from Paris, where the phenomenon is also advanced, running between 25 and 86 percent for deletions. The deletion phenomenon is even more advanced in Montreal, for among the sixty subjects whose speech was analyzed, the woman who deleted least still realized only 8 percent of the *ne*s required by 'standard' treatments of French. However, *ne* has not disappeared entirely from Montreal French. Its use is characteristic of a certain style or effect that speakers wish to achieve. Sankoff and Vincent observe (p. 303) that '*ne* appears in contexts where speakers are most likely to be aware of speech itself, and to be monitoring their own speech. The topics of language, instruction, discipline, and religion tend to spirit people back to a normative world in which "proper language" becomes very salient.' When speakers do use *ne*, they also tend to use other forms that are rare in Montreal French, e.g., *nous* instead of *on* as a subject; *alors* rather than *donc* or *ça fait que* as a conjunction; and nonreduced forms of *elle* and *elles*. Sankoff and Vincent claim that *ne* persists in Montreal French as a syntactic and stylistic resource which speakers can employ as they see fit. Although many linguists seem to believe that, when a linguistic change has progressed to the point that *ne* deletion has progressed in Montreal, it is best to regard it as lost altogether, Sankoff and Vincent do not agree, claiming that, even at its present extremely low level of use in Montreal, *ne* still has a function to serve. It is still, therefore, a variable feature of Montreal French. Today, when you learn French as a foreign language, you learn to use *ne*. You must use it in writing French. However, as you become increasingly skilled in listening to spoken French, you will

Table 7.8 Percentage of vowels assimilated in casual speech in Teheran Persian

Education	Male				Female			
	Univ.	Second.	Prim.	None	Univ.	Second.	Prim.	None
Scores	7	24	46	71	5	21	33	55
	12	28	48	77	5	22	38	60
	13	32	53	81	6	23	39	67
	14	36	56	81	6	28	43	68
	18	41	57	82	6	29	48	73
Average	13	32	52	78	6	24	40	65
Standard deviation	3	6	4	4	0	3	5	6

Source: Hudson (1996, p. 179); based on a study by Jahangiri (1980)

find that you rarely hear *ne*. Your own *je ne sais pas* is likely to give way to *je sais pas* as you become more and more confident about any 'French' identity you take on as you learn the language.

The investigation of some variables occasionally produces results which appear to verge on the amazing. For example, Hudson (1996, pp. 178–80) reports on a study (Jahangiri, 1980) of the pronunciation of certain words in Teheran Persian. In such words, e.g., /bekon/'Do!', the vowel in the first syllable varies between [e] and [o] as it assimilates to the second vowel, i.e., comes to resemble it in pronunciation. In this study forty speakers, divided equally between males and females and assigned to groups on the basis of amount of education, produced the individual percentages of assimilated vowels in casual speech shown in table 7.8. In this table the average (i.e., mean) for each group is given as well as the measure of the amount of internal variation within each group, the standard deviation. The latter indicates how homogeneous each group is. What is re-markable here is how little overlap there is between groups. There is no overlap within a particular gender grouping, so that all members of the university-educated male group use less assimilation than all members of the next group, those with secondary education, and those, in turn, less than the men with primary education, and so on. The same situation is true of females. The figures show overlap between the genders, but even here the pattern is entirely consistent in that males always overlap the next lowest group of females. That is, if vowel assimilation is dispreferred, being associated with low educational attainment, males show the consequences of this just a little less than do females. The display in figure 7.6 reorganizes the data of table 7.8 to show this effect. In the following chapter we will see that this situation is more complicated still because assimilation can also be shown to depend on the actual word in question, so that although it may occur in /bekon/'Do!' it need not necessarily occur in /bebor/'Cut!'

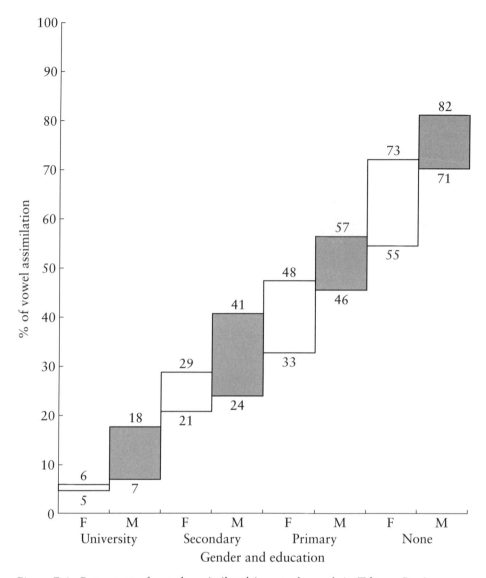

Figure 7.6 Percentage of vowels assimilated in casual speech in Teheran Persian

Discussion

1. In his study in Glasgow, Macaulay found that social-class differences in linguistic behavior seemed to increase with age, i.e., the group means grew further apart as the age of the subjects increased. What might this suggest to you about the social structure of Glasgow, about the process of social-ization there, and about the process of language acquisition?
2. Evidence exists from studies of language behavior in various communities that forms found in local and lower-class speech are used to signal solidarity.

Labov's work in New York City and Trudgill's in Norwich, England, certainly show this. But it has also been a common finding among such diverse groups as speakers of Canadian French in Quebec, Lowland Scots, and Catalan in Spain, to cite but a few examples. In an era of language standardization, which has the support of many public agencies and the mass media, there is a remarkable persistence of both regional and lower-class speech used to demonstrate group solidarity and antipathy toward outside influences. What do you see as the implications, if any, of this phenomenon for public education?

3. Assuming you have learned Standard French 'by the book,' what kinds of unlearning would you have to undergo if you had as your goal 'speaking Montreal French like a native'? What kinds of abilities would be involved in the 'unlearning' process?

4. I have described the study of vowel assimilation in Teheran Persian as producing results which 'verge on the amazing.' Look at table 7.8 and figure 7.6 and make several predictions about how different speakers in Teheran will pronounce /bekon/ and what you can tell about the educational attainment of a speaker if you hear him or her pronounce /bekon/ a number of times. Note the kind of certainty claimed for these predictions. Does it seem to be justified? (You should note that Hudson (1996, p. 184) voices some caution about these findings: 'the words and speakers were specially selected in order to illustrate this point as clearly as possible, and . . . the pattern for the research as a whole . . . is much messier.' See also pp. 216–17.)

Belfast

The Milroys took a rather different approach to variation in their study (Milroy and Milroy, 1978, and Milroy, 1980, 1987a) of certain aspects of speech in three working-class areas in Belfast, Northern Ireland. Many studies conducted in Northern Ireland (and elsewhere) stress the importance of *social networks*. Such networks, which originate in kinship ties, determine an individual's access to employment and to other resources. People develop close and continuing relationships with each other, and they help one another, first their kin and then their co-religionists. Belfast has been called an assemblage of urban villages in which the inhabitants see a need for strong ties because of the external threats they perceive to exist. Furthermore, in spite of other differences, Protestants and Catholics are alike in the importance they place on networks of relationships.

The Milroys were able to show how a stable set of linguistic norms emerges and maintains itself in a community. Lesley Milroy calls these *vernacular norms*, norms which are 'perceived as symbolizing values of solidarity and reciprocity rather than status, and are not publicly codified or recognized' (1980, pp. 35–6). These norms contrast with middle-class norms, the ones most of us would view as being characteristic of any wide social standard. Consequently, the Milroys looked at working-class speech in three stable inner-city working-class communities in Belfast: Ballymacarrett, in East Belfast, a Protestant area with little male unemployment (because of the stability provided by work in the local shipyard), close male relationships, and a sharp differentiation between men's and women's activities with men working within the area and women working outside; the Hammer, in West Belfast, also a Protestant area; and the Clonard, also in West Belfast, a Catholic area. In both the Hammer and the Clonard there was considerable male unemployment (about 35 percent), male relationships were less close than in Ballymacarrett, and there was no sharp differentiation between men's and women's activities. Consequently, both the Hammer and the Clonard exhibited less strong social networks within them than did Ballymacarrett, particularly for males.

The Milroys used a modified participant-observer technique, i.e., Lesley Milroy became part of the system she studied, being introduced into it as 'a friend of a friend,' and the analysis is based on data collected from forty-six working-class speakers of both sexes with approximately one-third from each community. Being interested in social networks, the Milroys tried to place each informant on a six-point scale which characterized that person's participation in networks. All speakers did so participate, because each of the communities exhibited a pattern of dense and multiplex ties. As I indicated on p. 129, *dense* refers to the fact that many people share the same social contacts, and *multiplex* to the fact that people are linked to one another in several ways simultaneously, e.g., as kin, neighbors, or fellow employees. The Milroys' six-point scale for scoring individual network strength used the following factors: membership in a high-density, territorially based cluster; kinship in the immediate neighborhood; working with at least two people of the same sex from the same area; and voluntary leisure-time association with workmates.

The Milroys examined eight linguistic variables and found significant correlations between network strength and linguistic usage on five of these, two at $p < .01$ (i.e., there is less than one chance in a hundred that there is no such relationship) and three at $p < .05$ (i.e., there is less than one chance in twenty that there is no such relationship). The two strongest correlations were with the vowel in words like *hat*, *man*, and *grass* (with the vowel being pronounced rather like that of *father*) and the deletion of the fricative *th* [ð] in *mother* and *brother*. The less strong correlations were with the vowel in words like *pull*, *shove*, and *foot* (with the vowel being pronounced rather like that of *but* and *shut*), and the vowel in either monosyllabic words like *peck*, *bet*, and *went* or in the accented syllables of polysyllabic words like *accént* and *sécond*.

However, a closer inspection of the results by community showed that, with one exception, it was only in Ballymacarrett that there was a significant correlation between the variables and network strength. The greater the network strength, the greater the incidence of the variants identified with the Belfast vernacular. There was also in Ballymacarrett a significant difference between men and women in their use of the vernacular, with men showing a much greater incidence of vernacular usage. The two other communities showed no similar significant differences between men's and women's usage, both ranking below those found in Ballymacarrett, with one exception: young women in the Clonard seemed to prefer certain vernacular variants and seem to be in the vanguard of extending vernacular norms into that sub-group.

What we see in these working-class communities in Belfast, then, is that the stronger the social network, the greater the use of certain linguistic features of the vernacular. The results support Milroy's (1980, p. 43) hypothesis that 'a closeknit network has the capacity to function as a norm enforcement mechanism; there is no reason to suppose that linguistic norms are exempted from this process. Moreover, a closeknit network structure appears to be very common . . . in low status communities.' She adds that 'the closeknit network may be seen as an important social mechanism of vernacular maintenance, capable of operating effectively in opposition to a publicly endorsed and status-oriented set of legitimized linguistic norms.' Once again, we see how low-status varieties of a language maintain themselves in the face of heavy competition from 'above': they enable those who use them to show their solidarity with one another and achieve some kind of group identity.

Discussion

1. Milroy (1987a) says: 'In modern urban society, large socially and geographically mobile sections of the population will lack the conditions necessary for the formation and maintenance of reciprocity networks . . . individual mobility produces inequality of wants, as well as a collapse of well established territorial rights.' What limit does this statement suggest that there might be to the use of networks in the study of linguistic variation? How might you try to make allowances for these?
2. People use language to unify and band together. Try to find some common words with variant pronunciations and attempt to show how individuals may use these variants to identify themselves with others. Here are a few words you might begin with: *breathing, buoy, data, falcon, herb, kiln, mischievous,* and *relevant.*
3. Speakers have been observed to modify their speech to make it more like that of their listeners (see Bell, 1984, and Trudgill, 1986, pp. 8–9). Can you find some examples? How might this phenomenon of 'accommodation' complicate work in sociolinguistics?

Controversies

In a previous section I noted that linguistic variables may show correlations not only with social variables but also with other linguistic features, i.e., they may be linguistically constrained too, as with the deletion of *l* in Montreal. In their discussion of linguistic variation, Wolfram and Fasold (1974, pp. 101–5) present data from an earlier study by Fasold (1972) to show that it is possible to state how two or more factors, or *constraints*, interact to affect the distribution of a variable. In this case they are concerned with deletion of final stops in clusters, e.g., the *d* in a word like *cold*, in speech among blacks in Washington, DC. The data showed that the parenthesized stops were deleted as follows: *san(d)*

Table 7.9 Final cluster simplification among black speakers in Washington,
DC

% deleted	Example	Environment
83.3	*san(d) castle*	after sonorant, before non-vowel
68.8	*fas(t) car*	after non-sonorant, before non-vowel
34.9	*wil(d) elephant*	after sonorant, before vowel
25.2	*lif(t) it*	after non-sonorant, before vowel

Source: based on Wolfram and Fasold (1974, p. 102)

castle, 83.3 percent deletion; *fas(t) car*, 68.8 percent deletion; *wil(d) elephant*, 34.9 percent deletion; and *lif(t) it*, 25.2 percent deletion. If we look closely at the environments of these stops, we will find that sometimes the stop is preceded by a sonorant (a nasal or *l*) and sometimes by a non-sonorant (a stop or a fricative), and it is followed sometimes by a vowel and sometimes by a consonant (or non-vowel). We can see this distribution more clearly in table 7.9. Wolfram and Fasold point out that the constraint of appearing before a non-vowel has a greater effect than the constraint of appearing after a sonorant, i.e., appearance of the stop before a non-vowel leads to a greater amount of deletion than appearance after a sonorant. When both constraints are present we find the highest percentage of deletions: 83.3 percent in *san(d) castle*. When neither constraint is present we have the least: 25.2 percent in *lif(t) it*. In the intermediate cases, appearing before a non-vowel is more important than appearing after a sonorant. Wolfram and Fasold, therefore, call appearing before a non-vowel a *first-order constraint* and appearing after a sonorant a *second-order constraint*. That is, the former exercises a greater influence on a person's linguistic behavior than does the latter.

Constraints may also mix phonological and grammatical features. Wolfram (1969, pp. 59–69) explains a situation in Detroit in which black speakers also delete final stops in clusters, but in this case make a distinction according to the grammatical function of the stop. In the final cluster in *cold* the *d* has no independent grammatical function – it is part of a single unit of meaning – but in *burned* it marks past tense and is grammatically the *-ed* ending, and therefore has its own meaning. The data are distributed as in table 7.10. In this variety of English the first-order constraint is once again appearance before a vowel or non-vowel (here consonant). Appearance before a vowel inhibits cluster simplification in all cases and appearance before a consonant encourages it. The second-order constraint is appearance as the *-ed* ending. That is, such appearance has a lesser effect than whether or not the following sound is a vowel or consonant. Consequently, the greatest loss of [d] in these examples occurs when the following sound is a vowel and the [d] does not represent the *-ed* grammatical ending. The least loss occurs when the [d] is followed by a vowel and it is the *-ed* ending. This situation is the same for all social classes, but the actual amounts of deletion vary from class to class.

Table 7.10   Final cluster simplification among black speakers in Detroit

Social class

Upper middle	Lower middle	Upper working	Lower working	Example	Environment
0.07	0.13	0.24	0.34	*burn(ed) up*	-*ed*, before vowel
0.28	0.43	0.65	0.72	*col(d) out*	not -*ed*, before vowel
0.49	0.62	0.73	0.76	*burn(ed) coal*	-*ed*, before consonant
0.79	0.87	0.94	0.97	*col(d) cuts*	not -*ed*, before consonant

Source: based on Wolfram (1969, pp. 59–69)

Table 7.11   Final cluster simplification among black youth in New York City

Simplification (%)	Example	Environment
24	*pass(ed) eleven*	-*ed*, before vowel
59	*pas(t) eleven*	not -*ed*, before vowel
74	*pass(ed) five*	-*ed*, before non-vowel
91	*pas(t) five*	not -*ed*, before non-vowel

Source: based on Labov (1972b, p. 222)

Further study of this phenomenon by Labov (1972b, p. 222) showed that different sub-groups in society may order two constraints differently. Among black speakers in New York City, Labov found that, whereas more adolescent groups order the above constraints in the way reported in table 7.10, upper working-class adults reverse the order. With most adolescents the situation is as in table 7.11; however, with upper working-class adults we have the situation shown in table 7.12. In this example the first-order constraint is the status of the [t]: whether or not it represents the -*ed* ending; the second-order constraint is the next phonological segment: whether or not it is a vowel. Whereas adolescents are inhibited in their simplification of final clusters, first by whether the following segment is a vowel and only then by the nature of the [t], adults are inhibited in their simplification first by the status of the [t], i.e., they are reluctant to omit it if it represents -*ed*, and only then by the presence of a following vowel.

Using information similar to the kind just presented, Wolfram and Fasold (1974, pp. 133–4) go on to show how it is possible to take a phenomenon like cluster simplification and predict certain kinds of linguistic behavior. They distinguish between speakers of Standard English (SE), white nonstandard English (WNS), and what they call *Vernacular Black English* (VBE). They consider four

Table 7.12 Final cluster simplification among black upper working-class adults in New York City

Simplification (%)	Example	Environment
9	*pass(ed) eleven*	*-ed*, before vowel
19	*pass(ed) five*	*-ed*, before non-vowel
40	*pas(t) eleven*	not *-ed*, before vowel
90	*pas(t) five*	not *-ed*, before non-vowel

Source: based on Labov (1972b, p. 222)

Table 7.13 Final cluster simplification in several varieties of English

Variety of English	Cluster simplification			
SE	sometimes *tes' program*	always *test idea*	always *testing*	always *risking*
Most VBE and some WNS speakers	usually or always *tes' program*	sometimes *tes' idea*	always *testing*	always *risking*
Some WNS Some VBE speakers	always *tes' program*	always *tes' idea*	always *testing*	always *risking*
Some WNS Some VBE speakers	always *tes' program*	always *tes' idea*	usually or always *testing*	usually or always *risking*
Some VBE speakers (especially Deep South children)	always *tes' program*	always *tes' idea*	always *tessing*	always *rissing*

Source: Wolfram and Fasold (1974, p. 134)

environments in which cluster simplification can occur: (1) before a word beginning with a consonant (*test program*); (2) before a word beginning with a vowel (*test idea*); (3) before a suffix such as *-ing* (*testing*); and (4) involving a final consonant other than *t* (e.g., *k*) before a suffix such as *-ing* (*risking*). They report their findings (p. 134) as in table 7.13, with 'always,' 'sometimes,' and 'usually' in that table referring to the pronunciation which they predict will occur. According to such a display, *tes' idea* (for *test idea*) is not a feature of SE; there is a considerable overlap between features found in WNS and VBE; but it is only in the latter that you find *tessing* (for *testing*) and *rissing* (for *risking*). *Tes' program* (for *test program*), however, is found in all varieties of English but with a different incidence of usage: only 'sometimes' in SE, but 'usually' or 'always' in the other varieties.

From the foregoing discussion we can see that it may be possible to predict certain kinds of linguistic behavior if we know the various constraints that operate in connection with a particular variable and the relationships between that variable and factors such as social class, level of formality, age, gender, and race. Labov has suggested that we should attempt to state what we know by writing *variable rules*. A variable rule is a modified version of the kind of rule found in grammars modeled on Chomsky's ideas. It recasts such a rule in the form of a statement that introduces probabilities: do this or that at a certain frequency or frequencies according to the presence or absence of factors *a, b, c, ... n*. Wolfram and Fasold (1974, p. 110) actually hypothesize that speakers 'can identify variable rules, which linguistic factors favor rule operation, the hierarchical order in which they are ranked, the extent to which higher-order constraints are stronger than lower-order ones, and the probabilities toward rule operation contributed by each.'

In practice we face considerable difficulties in trying to write even a single variable rule. For example, what kind of rule could cover all instances of the variable (h)? Some people nearly always say *happen* and *after*, while instances of *'appen* are rare indeed. Others show considerable use of *'appen*, and still others never say anything but *'appen*. None of these say *hafter* for *after*. Not a few say *'appen* and *after*, but occasionally some of these say *happen* and also *hafter*. That is, there are *h*-pronouncers, *h*-droppers, and *h*-inserters. Yet one variable rule is supposed to cover all speakers; either that, or there are two variable rules which interact. But this latter proposal would suggest that people communicate not through the same set of rules but through intersecting sets. It would therefore raise still other issues.

One very serious criticism is that, while the concept of 'probability' is often useful in life in explaining the chances of certain things happening, it offers no guide to conduct in specific instances. Categorical rules, i.e., rules which say 'if X then Y,' do offer a guide to, and therefore an explanation of, conduct, but variable rules do not and cannot. They do no more than summarize general trends, tendencies, or probabilities found within groups. Variable rules are statistical generalizations based on surveys of language use and they indicate trends or norms in populations.

Additional concerns have been voiced about the concept of 'variability' as some kind of rule-governed behavior that can also be ascribed to individuals. We must ask what kinds of mental processes would be necessary to handle that kind of statistical information and how children could acquire it during their language learning (see Kay and McDaniel, 1979). More recently, Fasold (1991, p. 9) has admitted that, 'Variable rules were proposed as a way of understanding how variation works within a theory of human language.' He adds (p. 18) that in reality the variable rule 'was never any more than a display device.' In recent years there has been throughout linguistics a general decline in rule-writing; sociolinguistics has seen much less of it too.

Bailey (1973) and Bickerton (1971) have been particularly critical of such attempts to use variable rules. They acknowledge variability in language but insist that it can be explained if we look closely at the environments in which variation occurs and are prepared to relate the environments to one another using some kind of scale. We must note, of course, that they are concerned with individual speech behavior, what they call the *isolect*, whereas Labov and others have been concerned with group behavior, the *sociolect*, insisting that such behavior is important in studies of how people actually use language not only to communicate verbally but for a variety of other purposes too.

Bailey and Bickerton have proposed that each individual controls an isolect of the language, an individual array of linguistic usages which others may or may not share. Each isolect is a *lect*. The lects of a language differ from one another along a continuum, which forms a *polylectal* or *panlectal* grid such that there is an implicational relationship among the various lects: that is, if lect A has feature X, then it will also have features Y and Z, but if lect B has feature Y but not feature X, it will still have feature Z. Lect C may have only feature Z and it could not acquire feature X until it first acquired feature Y. As Petyt (1980, p. 190) points out, if a Yorkshireman pronounces *grass* with the first vowel of *father* [aː], he will pronounce *cut* with [ʌ]. According to the theory, this 'dynamic' view of language structure is valid both synchronically, i.e., as a description of the structure of a language at any specific moment in its history, and diachronically, i.e., over an extended period of time. It is a new variation of the old *wave theory* of linguistic change, but one that incorporates synchronic matters.

The theory proposed by Bailey and Bickerton tries to reduce the amount of variation in language that linguists must consider by requiring an investigator to look at individual lects and consider all linguistic behavior as categorical, i.e., fully determined by this or that factor or set of factors. They claim that, when the linguistic behavior of an individual is graphed for a particular linguistic variable, that behavior is far more likely to show an 'all-or-none' characteristic, i.e., to be categorical in nature, than to show some kind of statistical distribution around a mean, i.e., to be variable in nature, if the particular circumstances that occasion the behavior are known. Individual lects may then be arranged on various continua that can be related implicationally to one another. At any moment it should also be possible to say exactly what the status of any linguistic variable is, i.e., how speakers are using it over a period of time, in regional or social space, and along various dimensions of the latter, i.e., according to social class, age, gender, ethnicity, and so on. Such panlectal grammars therefore would account for variation; moreover, Bailey and Bickerton suggest that much of the variation that sociolinguists actually talk about is a creation of the methods they employ, i.e., is a methodological artifact.

Bailey and Bickerton also appear to be making a claim which Labov does not make. Their dynamic model suggests that all variation in language results from changes in progress: variation is the mark of linguistic change. On the other hand, Labov does not regard every bit of linguistic variation as being associated with changes in progress. While some variation is associated with changes in progress, he regards variation as an inherent property of language, i.e., you cannot have language without variation but only part of that variation 'goes somewhere,' i.e., results in change.

The kinds of variation we have seen raise important issues about the very nature of language itself. Labov and others have argued that the kinds of grammars preferred by Chomsky and his associates must be modified to recognize variation and, particularly, that the famous (or notorious) *competence–performance* distinction (see pp. 2–3) made in such grammars must be reformulated, weakened, or abandoned. Chomsky himself has never appeared to find much value in Labov's work: for him it is a study of linguistic performance and has very little to offer to a better understanding of language.

There is no denying, however, that recent studies employing the linguistic variable have added an important new dimension to our understanding of language. It is now well documented that variation is a linguistic fact and that it is not haphazard. Previously, dialect geographers had amply documented the differential but systematic distribution of linguistic forms, and the new techniques of investigation have revealed similar patterns that can be related to a variety of social and even linguistic factors. It is also apparent that people are aware, sometimes consciously and sometimes not, that certain variants have more (or less) prestige than others. They are also able to modify their speech to reflect changing circumstances, and do so quite systematically.

The distribution of the variants of variables also seems to be clearly related to changes that languages undergo. No longer is it possible to separate synchronic and diachronic matters into two mutually exclusive domains; descriptive and historical matters are interrelated. Moreover, some findings, such as Labov's discovery of the cross-over phenomenon, appear to indicate not only the direction of change but possibly also some of its motivation. We will turn our attention to some of these matters in the chapter that follows.

Discussion

1. Try to devise a small-scale study focusing on the pronunciations of final clusters before words beginning with vowels and consonants and controlling for the grammatical function of the final stop in the cluster, e.g., *past five, passed five*; *past eleven, passed eleven*. Try to collect data from subjects having different social backgrounds and attempt to vary the formality of usage. Do your results correspond in any way to those reported in this chapter?

2. In comparison with sociologists, linguists who have studied linguistic variation have used very simple ways of determining the social-class membership of individuals. They have argued that more sophisticated approaches are hardly necessary since the results they have achieved have been 'very satisfactory' (see Chambers and Trudgill, 1998, p. 49, and Chambers, 2003, pp. 47–54). How justified is such a claim about their methodology in general? In thinking through your answer, consider how linguists are inclined to treat specialists in other disciplines who treat linguistic data with a similar elementary approach.

3. The rule that tells you to pronounce the *t* at the beginning of *top* with a little puff of air, as [tʰ], is a categorical rule, as is the rule that tells you to

pluralize *man* as *men*; such a rule always operates. The rule that allows you to pronounce the first vowel in *either* to resemble that in *beet* or in *bite* is an optional rule. However, the rule that allows you to say *singing* on one occasion and *singin'* on another is a variable rule. Try to clarify the concept of 'rule' in each case. Look for other kinds of behavior in which the same kinds of distinction can be made. Try to assess the compatibility of these different notions of 'rule' within a single theory of behavior.

Further Reading

The journals *Language in Society*, *Journal of Sociolinguistics*, and *Language Variation and Change* often report studies conducted in this 'quantitative' tradition.

8 Change

Recent work in sociolinguistics has raised once again a long-standing question: can linguistic change be observed while it is actually occurring? In modern linguistics the answer to that question has usually been a resounding negative. Following the example of two of the founders of the modern discipline, Saussure (1959) and Bloomfield (1933), most linguists have maintained that change itself cannot be observed; all that we can possibly hope to observe are the consequences of change. The important consequences are those that make some kind of difference to the structure of a language. At any particular time, it certainly may be possible for linguists to observe variation in language, but that variation is of little importance. Such variation must be ascribed either to dialect mixture, that is, to a situation in which two or more systems have a degree of overlap, or to free variation, that is, to unprincipled or random variation. Linguists therefore attached little or no theoretical importance to variation. Only in recent decades have some of them seen in it a possible key to understanding how languages change.

The Traditional View

In what I will call the traditional view of language change, the only changes that are important in a language are those that can be demonstrated to have structural consequences. Consequently, over a period of time a distinction between two sounds may be lost in a language, as occurred historically in most varieties of English in the vowels of *meet* and *meat* or *horse* and *hoarse*. In most dialects these vowels have fallen together (or coalesced). Alternatively, a distinction may be gained where there was none before, as in *a house* with an [s] but *to house* with a [z], or finally in *thin* and *thing*, the [n] and [ŋ]. In each of these cases a single phonological unit became two: there was a structural split. So we can find instances of *phonemic coalescence*, situations in which a contrast existed at one time but later was lost, and instances of *phonemic split*, situations in which there was no contrast at one time but a contrast developed. According to this view of change, that is all we can really say because it is structural considerations alone that are all-important (i.e., do units A and B contrast or do they not?).

Variation is either controlled by circumstances, e.g., allophonic (as when the *p* in *pin* is aspirated but the *p* in *spin* is not), or it is free, i.e., random. Internal change in a language is observed through its consequences.

Such change, of course, is not restricted to phonology. The morphology and syntax of a language change in the same way. It is possible, therefore, to write *internal* histories of languages showing the structural changes that have occurred over periods of time through use of this principle of 'contrast vs. lack of contrast.'

A second kind of change in a language is *external* in nature. This is change brought about through borrowing. Changes that occur through borrowing from other dialects or languages are often quite clearly distinguishable, for a while at least, from changes that come about internally. They may be somewhat idiosyncratic in their characteristics or distribution and appear, for a while at least, to be quite 'marked' in this way, e.g., the *schl* and *schm* beginnings of *Schlitz* and *schmuck*, or *Jeanne* with the *J* pronounced like *zh*. There are often good social or cultural reasons for borrowing, and the items that are borrowed are usually words used to describe 'exotic' objects, e.g., *pajamas*, *tea*, *perfume*, and *kangaroo*, or learned or scientific words.

Speakers of different languages may have different views about borrowing. English speakers borrow almost indiscriminately from other languages, but speakers of French, German, Modern Hebrew, and Icelandic are far more discriminating. Speakers of Hindi, cultivated ones at least, look to Sanskrit for borrowings, and speakers of Urdu look to Arabic. As we will see in the following section, there is also some borrowing – or spread, at least – of phonological and grammatical items through certain areas, but this phenomenon is much more limited – and undoubtedly much harder to explain – than the borrowing of words to describe objects.

Of these two kinds of change, internal and external, linguists view the former as being far more important even though it is the latter that is inclined to come to public attention, as when efforts are made to 'purify' languages. People tend to react to the consequences of external change by complaining about 'falling language standards,' resisting new usages, and trying to constrain variation. The traditional linguistic approach to change has not been very helpful when controversies have arisen. An approach which says that it is languages that change and not speakers that change languages has little to contribute to a better public awareness of what is happening. As we will see too, it may also be an unrewarding approach to take.

The traditional view of language change also favors a 'family tree' account of change and of the relationships among languages. Linguists tend to reconstruct the histories of related languages or varieties of a language in such a way that sharp differentiations are made between those languages or varieties, so that at one point in time one thing (that is, a language itself, or a variety, or even a specific linguistic item) splits into two or more, or is lost. More rarely, there is coalescence. The alternative 'wave' account of change and relationships is much less easy to work with. In this approach the various changes that occur must be seen as flowing into and interacting with one another. It is not at all easy to reconcile the need to find contrasts with the desire to maintain a certain fluidity in boundaries. A variant of this latter view of change is that particular changes diffuse throughout a language, sometimes in rather idiosyncratic ways. One extreme version of this last view is the claim that 'each word has its own history,' a claim that would seem to reduce historical linguistics to *etymology*, the science of tracing the origins of individual words.

It is in the last view of change, through use of the concepts of 'wave' and 'diffusion,' that we see the possibilities that the study of variation opens up to us for understanding the process of change. The 'family tree' view focuses on the consequences of change and, particularly, on internal change. But if we believe that languages are changing all the time – and all linguists do hold that belief – we should also be able to see change in progress *if we can recognize it*. If we can interpret the variation we see, or some of it at least, as a wave of change going through a language, and if we can see changes apparently diffusing through sets of similar linguistic items, we may also want to recast or even abandon the traditional Saussurean and Bloomfieldian view of language. To do so, however, we will have to be sure that what we are observing is change and not just random fluctuation. That will be our major concern in the rest of this chapter.

Discussion

1. The English language has changed considerably during its history, as even a cursory glance at the language of the Anglo-Saxon Chronicle, Chaucer, Shakespeare, and T. S. Eliot will confirm. But you might look at a few details to get an indication of some precise changes. For example, why do we say *cat* and *cats* but *wife* and *wives* and *goose* and *geese*? Why do we have voiced sounds at the beginning of *this*, *then*, and *there* but voiceless ones at the beginning of *thin*, *through*, and *think*? How alive is the subjunctive in Modern English? What did the following words once mean: *cunning*, *stench*, *earl*, *meat*, *doctor*, *lord*, and *lady*? From which languages have we borrowed the following words: *tea*, *biology*, *sauerkraut*, *pajamas*, *perfume*, *sputnik*, *muskrat*, *blitz*, and *aria*? What can you say about changes in the relative and personal pronouns since the time when the beginning of the Lord's prayer was translated as 'Our Father, which art in Heaven, Hallowed be Thy name'?

2. Much recent attention has been focused on the adverb *hopefully*, particularly on its 'misuse' in sentences such as *Hopefully, he won't succeed*. Try to find out what is happening here. Is this a small linguistic change in progress? You will have to look at similar adverbs (e.g., *personally*, *interestingly*, *confidentially*), at the function that *hopefully* has in the overall pattern of adverb use, and at the possibility that people select items to stigmatize somewhat arbitrarily (see Crystal, 1984, and Wardhaugh, 1999).

3. Are you aware of any special pronunciations or other linguistic usages which seem to be 'creeping in' to the language? If you are, are they approved or disapproved? Does that approval (or disapproval) depend at all on who is using the linguistic item in question?

Figure 8.1   Northern Cities Shift

Changes in Progress

Before discussing changes in language, we must distinguish between variation and change for not all variation is a sign of, or leads to, change. There is what Labov (2001, p. 85) calls 'long-term stable variation,' e.g., the distribution of the (ng), (th), and (dh) variables previously discussed and such alternatives as the *ask–aks* alternation, the latter as old as the language. Schools sometimes devote considerable time and effort – very often wasted – in attempts to eradicate nonstandard variants of stable variables (see Wolfram and Schilling-Estes, 1998, for a list of examples from American English). Socio-economic class, age, and gender in that order appear to be the factors that affect the distributions of these variables and they continue to operate over long periods of time. Labov adds that his work in Philadelphia showed that the 'primary determinant of the stable sociolinguistic variables is . . . social class: the higher the position of a speaker in the social scale, the smaller . . . the frequency of nonstandard forms' (p. 112). However, Dubois and Horvath (1999, p. 298) warn that their work among Cajuns in Louisiana showed that a 'set of variables cannot be prejudged to be stable sociolinguistic variables because they happen to be stable in the English language as a whole or even in a surrounding dialect.' What appears to be an instance of a stable linguistic variable may actually be a local innovation.

In contrast, change has a direction, being both progressive and linear. For example, the Great Vowel Shift in English took centuries and is still incomplete, and the Northern Cities Shift (NCS) in the United States has lasted several generations and shows no sign of weakening (see Gordon, 2002, pp. 254–64). This last change is a vowel change found in cities settled in a westward movement of people from New York State, and centered in places such as Buffalo, Detroit, Chicago, and spreading to smaller urban centers. A major part of it involves a chain shift in vowels apparently set in motion by the raising of the vowel in words like *bag* to resemble the vowel in *beg*. The vowel in *hot* fronts to resemble the vowel in *hat* and the vowel in *caught* lowers to resemble the vowel in *cot*, as in figure 8.1. The NCS proceeds in a very narrow band as it moves east to west. While its effects are apparent in Detroit, Windsor in Canada across the river is unaffected. Likewise, barely thirty miles to the west of Detroit, Ypsilanti is also largely unaffected because of its large population of migrants from Appalachia. The resultant 'tight Appalachian social network in Ypsilanti serves as an inhibitor to adopting features of the NCS' (Evans, 2004, p. 162). Not participating in the NCS appears to be potent identity marker in each case.

Labov points out that language change can be readily observed today: 'In spite of the expansion and homogenization of the mass media, linguistic change is proceeding at a rapid rate ... so that the dialects of Boston, New York, Chicago, Birmingham, and Los Angeles are more different from each other than they were a century ago' (p. xii). The problem therefore is one of identifying changes that are occurring and then of trying to account for them: what sets them in motion; how they spread; and how they are maintained. These issues have been his concern in his two most recent books (1994, 2001).

Various linguists have observed and reported on what they consider to be changes in progress. For example, Chambers and Trudgill (1998, pp. 170–5) describe the spread of uvular *r* in western and northern Europe. All the languages of this part of the world once had either an apical (i.e., tongue-tip), trilled, or flap *r*, but from the seventeenth century on a uvular *r* spread from Paris to replace these other varieties. This new *r* crossed language boundaries, so that it is now standard in French, German, and Danish, and is also found in many varieties of Dutch, Swedish, and Norwegian. It did not cross the Channel into England, nor has it penetrated into Spain or Italy. What you find, though, when you plot the progress of uvular *r*, is the importance of cities in its spread. Uvular *r* seems to be adopted initially by city dwellers, e.g., residents of Bergen and Kristiansand in Norway, The Hague in the Netherlands, Cologne and Berlin in Germany, and Copenhagen in Denmark, and then the new use diffuses outwards. Therefore, the strong internal links in the uvular *r* area are those between cities, which form a kind of network. Apparently, uvular *r* spreads from city to city and later into the countryside surrounding each city.

Another phonetician, Gimson (1962, pp. 83–5) observed that in mid-twentieth-century Received Pronunciation (RP) the first part of the diphthong in a word like *home* was tending to become increasingly centralized and the whole diphthong itself monophthongized. He found such pronunciations mainly among the younger members of fairly exclusive upper-class social groups, but they also appeared in less exclusive varieties of RP, e.g., in the variety favored by BBC announcers of that era. Numerous observers of late twentieth-century speech in England (see particularly Foulkes and Docherty, 1999, 2000) have pointed out the spread of such pronunciations as *dwink* for *drink*, *be'er* for *better*, *bruvver* for *brother*, and *'appy* for *happy*. Such pronunciations apparently originated in southeast England among younger non-RP speakers but are now found in most urban areas and across a wide spectrum of social groups. Bailey (1973, p. 19) has pointed out that in the western United States the distinction between the vowels in such pairs of words as *naughty* and *knotty*, *caught* and *cot*, and *Dawn* and *Don* is disappearing. For many young speakers the vowel distinction is almost entirely gone, so that even *hawk* and *hock* are homophonous on many occasions. For older speakers, there may be complete loss of the vowel distinction before *t* followed by a vowel, but there is less likely to be such loss before a word final *t* or *n*, and most such speakers still preserve it in the *hawk–hock* pair, i.e., before the velar *k*. There is good reason to believe that this merger is now widespread in North America.

Zeller (1997) has described a sound change apparently now in progress in and around Milwaukee, Wisconsin: many speakers pronounce words like *haggle* and *bag* to rhyme with *Hegel* and *beg*, and *bank* like *benk*. This is another instance of the NCS. Zeller's investigation showed how it is both age- and gender-related. The younger speakers she recorded, both male and female, have shifted completely and have lost the vowel contrast in such words. Older males and females are also participating in the change with older females leading so that older males are more likely to retain the vowel contrast than older females. The evidence strongly suggests a change in progress: the loss of a contrast in these vowels before a voiced velar stop or nasal.

All the above are instances of a change diffusing through space. (See Britain, 2002, for a general discussion.) Density of population and the influence of large population centers appear to be important factors. This gravity model of diffusion holds that large, culturally important cities influence smaller cities they dominate and eventually changes filter down to surrounding rural areas through even smaller towns and communities. A change may even spread directly from one city to another leapfrogging, as it were, for a while at least, smaller intervening communities. The actual scale may vary, for it is the relative densities of the various places that are important not their absolute size, i.e., city > town > village, with later filling of gaps. For example, Britain (pp. 612–16) describes how in the Fens of England such a model explains the diffusion pattern in an area in which there are only two towns, King's Lynn and Wisbech, with populations over 20,000 and only fourteen miles apart. These towns influence the areas that surround them because of the road, rail, and waterway infrastucture and the social services they provide to rural residents. There is actually a dialect divide between the two areas because there are still physical barriers to prevent spatial diffusion.

A physical barrier such as a river or a range of hills can prevent diffusion. (Of course, a river can also become an axis for diffusion.) National boundaries may also act as barriers. The NCS meets a national boundary in Detroit; it does not cross the river to Windsor in Canada. Boberg (2000) has shown that so far as vowel systems are concerned, 'Windsor is just as Canadian as Toronto' (p. 13). Chambers (2003) points to one very interesting consequence of a national border as a barrier to diffusion. He reports that even though children in southern Ontario (and Toronto) may call the final letter of the alphabet 'zee' for a while (influenced no doubt by pre-school television broadcasts originating in the United States), they give up this pronunciation for 'zed' by the time they reach adulthood and this 'declining use of "zee" as people grow older repeats itself in succeeding generations' (p. 207). A triumph of Canadian identity over gravity!

In some of the examples just cited the factor of age seems to be important: younger speakers are observed to use the language differently from older speakers. We might consider such differential use as offering us the key we seek if we want to understand how languages change. But, as we will see, age differences of this kind may be quite misleading. We must be sure that something we view as linguistic change because older people say one thing and younger people say something else is not just the phenomenon of *age-grading*, of using speech appropriate to your age group. How can we be sure that in each of the examples given above the younger people will not change their linguistic ways as they get older, with those changes being in the direction of the use of the groups which are presently described as being older? The just cited use of 'zee–zed' in Canada is clearly an instance of age-grading. There are at least two ways of answering that question. The first way is to survey the same younger people twenty to thirty years later when they become middle-aged to see if they maintain the innovations and really stay quite unlike the present older people; this would be a *panel* study. If there was no change in behavior we could be sure that we had eliminated age-grading as an explanation. The second way is to survey carefully chosen samples drawn from the same population at periods of twenty to thirty years to see if comparable groups have changed their behavior; this would be a *trend* study. As Eckert (1997, p. 153) says:

> Community studies of variation frequently show that increasing age correlates with increasing conservatism in speech. With just the evidence from apparent time, it is ambiguous whether the language patterns of the community are changing over the years or whether the speakers are becoming more conservative with age – or both. Without evidence in real time, there is no way of establishing whether or not age-stratified patterns of variation actually reflect change in progress.

(See also Bailey et al., 1991, Chambers 2003, pp. 212–25, Chambers and Trudgill, 1998, pp. 149–51, and Labov, 1994, pp. 76–7, for various points of view on these issues.)

One study which was able to make use of roughly comparable sets of data from two periods of time is Labov's study (1963) of certain sound changes in progress on Martha's Vineyard. In this work Labov found that the survey conducted for the *Linguistic Atlas of New England* thirty to forty years before provided him with rich sources of data about the phenomena in which he was interested. The data collection methods of the two surveys, the *Linguistic Atlas* survey and Labov's, differed, but it was possible for Labov to make allowances for these differences in order to achieve the necessary measure of comparability. Although Labov would have preferred to have worked with sound recordings, that possibility did not exist. (However, it does now for future work.)

Martha's Vineyard is a small island lying three miles off the coast of Massachusetts. At the time of Labov's investigation it had a small permanent population of about 6,000 people, but each summer many more thousands came to stay for varying periods of time. Most of the permanent residents lived in the eastern part of the island, the Down-island part, but this area was also the one most favored by the summer visitors. The western part of the island, the Up-island part, was still quite rural with its center Chilmark. The permanent population consisted of Yankees, Portuguese, and native peoples (i.e., Amerindians). The Yankees were descendants of early settlers; the Portuguese were fairly recent newcomers in comparison with the Yankees but had been on the island for several generations; the native peoples, who lived on a remote headland, Gay Head, were descended from the original occupants of the island.

Labov concentrated his attention on the way native Vineyarders pronounced the vowels in the two sets of words: *out, house,* and *trout* and *while, pie,* and

Table 8.1 Degree of centralization of (ay) and (aw) by age level on
Martha's Vineyard

Age	(ay)	(aw)
75+	25	22
61–75	35	37
46–60	62	44
31–45	81	88
14–30	37	46

Source: Labov (1972b, p. 22)

night. He observed that the first parts of the diphthongs in such words were
being centered: [aʊ] to [əʊ] and [aɪ] to [əɪ], with that centering more noticeable
in the first set of words than in the second. He called the variable in the first
set the (aw) variable ([aʊ] or [əʊ]) and the variable in the second set the (ay)
variable ([aɪ] or [əɪ]). He set out to collect a large quantity of (aw)s and (ay)s
to find out who used the variants of each. He plotted his findings from his sixty-
nine natives of Martha's Vineyard on various graphs to examine the relationships between the degree of centralization and such factors as age, ethnicity,
occupation, and place of residence. The survey conducted in the 1930s for the
Linguistic Atlas of New England provided Labov with data for the earlier linguistic situation on the island.

By age level, Labov (1972b, p. 22) found the distribution of the centralized
variants shown in table 8.1. This table shows that centralization is most obvious
in the 31–45 age group. The change was also a little more advanced in those
of Yankee descent than among those in the other two groups with which Labov
was concerned, but not by much. It was more advanced among those who made
a living from fishing than among those who worked in occupations and businesses
serving the summer visitors. It was also much more typical of Up-island speech,
particularly around Chilmark, the center of the fishing industry, than Down-
island speech, as table 8.2 shows. The change was therefore most advanced in people
in their thirties and early forties who were fishermen living in the Up-island area.

The explanation that Labov offers is that the change was merely an exaggeration of an existing tendency to centralize the first part of the diphthong. This
exaggeration is particularly characteristic of those who identified most closely with
the island. At the time of the survey for the *Linguistic Atlas*, it appeared that
this centralizing tendency was being eliminated. It was virtually extinct in (aw)
and in only moderate use in (ay). What had happened apparently was that,
instead of eliminating the tendency, residents exaggerated it to show their solidarity and their difference from the summer population. The more you identified
with the island, the more you centralized the first part of the diphthong. As
Labov says (1972b, p. 36): 'When a man says [rəit] or [həus], he is unconsciously
establishing the fact that he belongs to the island: that he is one of the natives to
whom the island really belongs.' As further evidence of this fact, Labov divided

Table 8.2 Geographical distribution of centralization on Martha's Vineyard

	(ay)	*(aw)*
Down-island	35	33
Edgartown	48	55
Oak Bluffs	33	10
Vineyard Haven	24	33
Up-island	61	66
Oak Bluffs	71	99
N. Tisbury	35	13
West Tisbury	51	51
Chilmark	100	81
Gay Head	51	81

Source: Labov (1972b, p. 25)

Table 8.3 Degree of centralization and orientation toward Martha's Vineyard

Persons		*(ay)*	*(aw)*
40	Positive	63	62
19	Neutral	32	42
6	Negative	09	08

Source: Labov (1972b, p. 39)

his informants into three groups according to their feelings about the island: positives, negatives, and neutrals. He found a very striking relationship between such feelings and centralization (p. 39), as shown in table 8.3.

If we go back to the original distinction by age, which showed the 31–45 age group in the vanguard of this change, we can see that it is they who had most to gain by identifying with the island. Many of the young were still ambivalent in their feeling: some wanted to leave (and were not inclined to centralize) and some wanted to stay (and did centralize). The very old followed older ways, which did not involve as much centralization. But a person between 31 and 45 was likely to have had to come to terms with life quite recently. That coming to terms quite often meant staying on Martha's Vineyard and showing that commitment by exaggerating centralization, even to the extent of pushing centralizing in (aw) to surpass that in (ay). There was also some evidence that those who had been to the mainland and had returned to the island to live were among the strongest centralizers. Centralization indicated 'Islander' status and local loyalty and solidarity. It had also been fixed on by the Portuguese and native peoples, but in their case as marking some kind of equality with the

Yankees. Here we can quite clearly see the social motivation of a sound change; in this case, the change is one motivated by a desire to show loyalty to a particular place and solidarity with the people who live there.

Blake and Josey (2003) replicated Labov's study forty years later and, in doing so, took 'into account recent methodological and theoretical developments, both acoustic and social, that have been incorporated into sociophonetic studies' (p. 452): specifically, they measured formant frequencies and used the VARBRUL statistical package. They found that Martha's Vineyard had become an even more popular recreational destination so that the locals had become almost entirely dependent on tourism. Fishing had declined in importance. As they became wealthier, the locals no longer sought to separate themselves from tourists and /ay/ lost its earlier meaning as a local social identifier. Locals are now willing to sound just like tourists.

A situation similar to the one Labov found in Martha's Vineyard in the 1960s exists still on Ocracoke Island off the coast of North Carolina (Wolfram, 1997, pp. 116–17, Wolfram and Schilling-Estes, 1995, 1997). In this case a local 'poker game network' consisting of a small, indigenous group of men who meet twice a week to play poker project their 'island' identity by employing largely symbolic choices such as *hoi toide* for *high tide*, words like *dingbatter* 'outsider' and *mommuck* 'to annoy,' and expressions like *She was a-fishing*. Not all islanders behave in this way. Middle-aged men, particularly those who socialize together on a daily basis, provide strongest evidence of this island 'brogue.' Their wives, the young, and even the old are less frequent users of these dialect features. Change is occurring and the dialect is being lost, but those with strong island identity resist the encroachment of the outside world by emphasizing use of the traditional 'brogue.' They mark themselves off in this way from tourists and all other outsiders. The difference here though is that these speakers cling to traditional speech ways, sometimes even exaggerated, in order to resist changes being introduced from outside the older island community.

One goal of Labov's work on the (r) variable in the speech of New York City was to achieve some understanding of sound change there. Labov (1994, pp. 86–94) tells how in 1986 Fowler replicated Labov's earlier study in three stores (actually substituting May's for S. Klein since S. Klein had gone out of business). Fowler's trend study revealed that the stratification of the (r) variable was stable. The figures for *r*-use were actually somewhat higher in 1986, indicating that a real change was occurring and could be shown in all classes, age groups, and styles. Labov concludes (p. 91) that, 'Under the pressure of the new *r*-pronouncing norm, New York City speech is changing slowly.' His earlier study had led him to conclude that lower middle-class speakers cross-over, i.e., behave *hypercorrectly*, so far as the use of *r* is concerned. That is, they tend to 'over-produce' *r* sounds when they try to emulate what they perceive to be the kinds of pronunciation favored by those they aspire to equal. Within this lower middle-class behavior it is also the middle-aged who are at the leading edge of this hypercorrective behavior with women rather than men in the vanguard. Labov had expected that such hypercorrect behavior would hasten the process of sound change. Fowler's findings, however, lead him to conclude (1994, p. 91) that, 'Contrary to what I originally expected, the hypercorrect behavior of the lower middle class, reflected in the pattern of Macy's employees, has not resulted in any sudden advance of *r*-pronunciation as a whole.'

Labov (1981, p. 185) points out that, when found, such behavior is a characteristic of the second-highest status group in a society. It is found in that group when its members adopt a formal style, and it is also found when they self-report their linguistic usage, and respond to subjective reaction tests that require them to evaluate their own and others' linguistic usages. Such tests seem to tap what speakers believe are the norms that operate in society. Moreover, women usually out-perform men in their tendency to adopt or support 'correct' behavior; according to Labov, they do this because, in relation to men, 'women are considered a second highest status group.'

As we have observed, *r*-pronunciation has always been present to some extent in New York City speech. What has happened in New York City recently is that for various reasons *r*-pronunciation in words like *farm* and *car* has become prestigious (or, alternatively, that pronunciation of such words without the *r* has become stigmatized). New Yorkers often try to abandon stigmatized features, for New York speech is often considered to be a 'sink of negative prestige,' not just by outsiders but also by those who live there. There has therefore been a recent re-evaluation of *r*-pronunciation along the eastern seaboard of the United States; whereas in England it is *r*-less pronunciation which is in the ascendancy, in the United States it is the *r*-full variety that is on the increase. What is important is that it is the women of a particular social class who seem to be in the vanguard of change so far as *r* is concerned in New York City. In this case, the change seems to be motivated by a desire to be like those who have higher social prestige.

Trudgill's (1972) work in Norwich, England, also shows certain changes in progress. For example, Trudgill found that the distribution of the variants of the (ng) variable showed that there were very marked differences between the usage of working-class males and working-class females: males favored the [n] variant (i.e., pronunciations such as *singin'* rather than *singing*) much more than did females. He found similar results with other variables, with women showing much stronger preferences for standard forms than men.

Trudgill offers (pp. 182–3) several possible explanations for women using forms associated with the prestige standard more frequently than men. He suggests that women may be more status-conscious because they are less secure and have less well-developed social networks than men. Their social position is usually inferior to men and they are usually subordinate to them. Men are also judged by what they do, whereas women are rated on how they appear, and an important part of that appearance is their speech. Women have a much greater need to use language to signal their social status than do men. Another important factor in this differential usage is that working-class speech has connotations of 'masculinity' and women often want to dissociate themselves from it for that reason, preferring types of speech which are regarded as more refined. Consequently, Trudgill devoted a considerable part of his research effort to investigating working-class speech and what he calls the 'hidden values associated with non-standard speech [which may be] particularly important in explaining the sex differentiation of linguistic variables' (p. 183).

Table 8.4 Percentages of informants overreporting and underreporting variants in Norwich

	(er)			(ō)			(ā)		
	Total	Male	Female	Total	Male	Female	Total	Male	Female
Overreport	43	22	68	18	12	25	32	22	43
Underreport	33	50	14	36	54	18	15	28	0
Accurate	23	28	18	45	34	57	53	50	57

Source: based on Trudgill (1972, p. 187)

Trudgill employed a self-evaluation test to find out what residents of Norwich thought about speech in the city. He asked his informants whether or not they used certain pronunciations and compared the responses they gave him with the actual pronunciations that his informants used. He reports on three variables: (er) as in *ear, here, idea*; (ō) as in *road, nose, moan*; and (ā) as in *gate, face, name*. His findings are shown in table 8.4. In that table 'overreporting' refers to informants claiming to use a prestige variant more often than they are actually observed to use it; 'underreporting' is, of course, the opposite. The percentages show that for two of the variables, (er) and (ā), speakers in Norwich overreport their usage; they underreport (ō). However, although the percentages differ for each variable, in all three cases men tend to underreport and women tend to overreport their usages. A further analysis showed that both middle-class and working-class speakers produced very much the same levels of under- and over-reporting, so the phenomenon appears to be gender-linked rather than social-class-linked. The same kinds of results appeared when people were asked to make judgments about two pronunciations of *better* ([bɛtə] or [bɛʔə]); in this case women showed a stronger preference than men for the standard pronunciation.

Trudgill maintains that linguistic changes in a direction away from the standard norms are led by men from the upper working class and middle working class, at least in Norwich. In the working class, too, young females aged 10–29 underreported their use in some cases, particularly on the (ō) variable. His general conclusion, therefore, is that nonstandard working-class speech forms are highly valued by males, and by females under 30, but these values are expressed covertly rather than overtly; that is, people may tell you they do one thing but they actually do something else. Trudgill emphasizes that, though it may be correct that in certain communities middle-aged middle-class women and the young are in the forefront of change toward the standard norm, 'in Norwich, at least, there appears to be a considerable number of young WC [working-class] men marching resolutely in the other direction' (p. 194). They find a certain 'covert prestige,' their own form of solidarity, in such behavior. (For somewhat similar behavior among young people in Japan, see Haig, 1991.)

A further instance of younger women behaving like men in their use of nonstandard linguistic forms comes from Chambers and Trudgill (1998, p. 86).

They report on a piece of research carried out in Trondheim, Norway. In Norwegian it is nonstandard usage to stress loan words on the first syllable rather than on the last (i.e., to use *ávis* rather than *avís*, 'newspaper'); this use of stress is associated with lower-class behavior. However, whereas Trondheim men of all ages instance approximately two-thirds nonstandard usages of such words, the percentages of such usages in Trondheim women vary directly with age: women over 63 use less than 10 percent; between 37 and 62 about 25 percent; and younger women almost 60 percent, a percentage not significantly different, it would appear, from men of the same – or of any – age. These figures do not unequivocally indicate that there is a change in progress, for it is quite possible that the women's linguistic behavior is age-graded, i.e., a behavior that changes with age. But certainly young women, in Trondheim at least, have a different attitude from older women toward such linguistic behavior. It remains to be seen if that attitude will change, that is, if the behavior is age-graded, or if it stays unchanged, and is therefore indicative of a linguistic change in progress.

Trudgill (1995, pp. 77–9) notes an interesting case which, on the surface at least, goes counter to the principle that, in a social setting of the kind exemplified by Norwich, women generally lead the way in changes toward the standard and men tend to march in the opposite direction. He observes that working-class men exhibit higher scores than working-class women in the use of RP-like vowels in words like *top*, *hot*, and *dog*. He points out that in Norwich it is middle-class women who usually introduce RP vowels. The vowel being introduced by the men is actually not an RP vowel, but one from the neighboring area of Suffolk and used there in working-class speech. It happens to have the same quality as the RP vowel but is introduced as a working-class solidarity marker and not at all in imitation of RP. As a working-class solidarity marker, it is not very acceptable to working-class women, who prefer the unrounded non-RP local vowel, so appearing to be less receptive to the RP vowel than they actually are.

We must accept Trudgill's explanation cautiously. He presents only raw percentages of use in support of his claim and the actual differences are small. For example, the different percentages of usage of the standard vowel in the lower working class are 20 percent for men and 17 percent for women and in the middle working class they are 30 percent for men and 29 percent for women. Even in the upper working class the differences are only 56 percent for men and 32 percent for women. There is certainly an 'interesting' difference here, but not a conclusive one.

Trudgill (1988) reports on a follow-up in 1983 of his earlier study of variation in Norwich. He replicated his original study as far as he could with seventeen additional informants born between 1958 and 1973 and therefore aged between 10 and 25 in 1983. This follow-up study showed that certain changes he had noted earlier had progressed: the vowels in *beer* and *bear* had merged entirely; *gate* and *face* were pronounced with [æi] rather than [e:]; a new variety of *r* had emerged; and words like *thin* and *fin* were no longer always distinguished, both being pronounced like *fin* by about 30 percent of younger people. Trudgill also reports (1986, pp. 35–7) that only children born in Norwich with parents who were also born in Norwich produce a particular local distinction between the vowels of *moan* and *mown*. This learning constraint is extremely difficult to explain; it is also one that seriously restricts the 'heritability' of this particular distinction.

Young people are sometimes found to speak somewhat differently from their parents and the surrounding community. Williams and Kerswill (1999), for example, investigated the speech of preadolescent children in Milton Keynes, a fast-growing new town in England within easy reach of London, Oxford, Cambridge, Coventry, and Leicester. The town has a young, mobile population drawn mainly from southeast England, is socially fluid, and lacks close networks. Children born in Milton Keynes speak neither like their parents nor like people from the surrounding area. Their speech provides strong evidence for dialect leveling as they produce distinctive local forms that tend toward standard pronunciation but at the same time show the influence of the fairly widespread youth culture of southeast England. While it is not clear how lasting such changes will be, they do clearly serve to differentiate the young in Milton Keynes from all others.

Cheshire's (1978) finding in Reading, England, that lower-class boys use more nonstandard syntax than lower-class girls, further supports the thesis that change may be motivated by a desire for identity and solidarity. The 'tougher' the boy, the more nonstandard his use of the *-s* ending on verbs in the present tense. Boys who were not regarded as tough produced a lesser incidence of such nonstandard use. With girls, the more conformist to middle-class values, the lesser the incidence of *-s* endings where they are not found in Standard English. What Reading boys appear to have done is take a particular nonstandard usage in their language, one that actually has a long history in the local dialect but a history which shows that it is being replaced by the usage found in Standard English, and make it into a solidarity marker.

We might actually argue that what we see here is not so much a change in progress but an unconscious resistance to a change being brought in from Standard English. Lacking real-time data, that is, evidence concerning the same phenomenon gathered at two distinct points in time, we cannot be absolutely sure that we are seeing no more than the latter. Cheshire herself acknowledges such a possibility, being prepared to go no further than to say (p. 58) that: 'Patterns of variation in the forms of the present tense *have* and *do* show that variation in the use of these forms may reflect on-going linguistic changes in the morphology of the verbs.' She adds that whatever change has occurred, it has apparently progressed further with *have* than with *do*.

Even if some groups march in the opposite direction or fight rearguard actions, there seems to be a consensus among investigators that linguistic change often seems to originate in the lower middle class, with women in the vanguard of such change. This is the social group that tries to emulate its 'betters.' In addition, because of their roles as mothers and sometimes as teachers, women in this group tend to have an influence far beyond their numbers. However, there is a strong countervailing force: the nonstandard speech of lower-class males has its own appeal to many men and sometimes even to young women. We cannot ignore this factor of solidarity. It is also apparent in Milroy's account (1980, 1987a) of how the vernacular is maintained in Belfast, where the stronger the network, the greater is the influence of the vernacular, and the weaker the network, the greater the influence of outside factors, especially non-working-class norms. What is especially interesting is that in the working class it is apparently males of all ages and sometimes young females who choose solidarity, whereas older females opt often for prestige.

'Linguistic marketplace' forces may also be at work here: what do individuals want and what will they accept or reject linguistically to satisfy these wants? As the introduction to Bourdieu (1991) says:

> Linguistic utterances or expressions are always produced in particular contexts or markets, and the properties of these markets endow linguistic products with 'value.' On a given linguistic market, some products are valued more highly than others; and part of the practical competence of speakers is to know how, and to be able, to produce expressions which are highly valued on the markets concerned.

The linguistic marketplace refers to how language is used in the give-and-take of social interaction. Language is not just a neutral medium of exchange; its uses take on symbolic value. Some uses are highly valued and others are lowly valued. These values are assigned through the various power relationships that exist. RP in England had (and may still have) a high symbolic value. Standard English is more highly valued than nonstandard varieties. High language forms are valued highly in diglossic situations and low language forms are valued not at all. Traditionally, male language uses have been valued more highly than female language uses. (There are many other such marketplaces that we are involved in as humans, e.g., accommodations, dress, food and drink preferences choices of entertainment, and so on.) As we will see in chapter 14, proponents of critical discourse analysis question the legitimacy of the power relationships that exist in all of the above.

Labov (1981, p. 184) makes an interesting observation about the role that women play in linguistic change. He points out that, whenever there is stratification by style and class in linguistic usage, you can also expect differences between men and women, with women showing higher values for preferred variants than men, that is, a preference for forms that have more prestige in society. He adds the following corollary: '[it is] important to bear in mind that this shift of women toward higher prestige forms . . . is limited to those societies where women play a role in public life.' He adds that studies in Teheran and India showed a reverse tendency. Apparently, then, if a woman's status is fixed unalterably, she has no motivation to change linguistically; only in a society in which status can be changed does the necessary motivation exist. Returning to the just mentioned concept of the 'linguistic marketplace,' we can say that in such cases there are simply no market pressures to change so the status quo is maintained.

We can actually see what happens when traditions change in a society and women begin to take a more assertive role in what goes on. For example, in a study of how the inhabitants of Oberwart, a Hungarian enclave in Austria since 1921, are shifting from a pattern of stable bilingualism in German and Hungarian to the sole use of German, Gal (1978, 1979) showed how young women are in the forefront of the change there. As Oberwart, about 100 kilometres south of Vienna, grew from a village of 600 to a town of over 5,000 inhabitants, the indigenous bilingual population decreased as a fraction to about a quarter of the total, and many of these, at least until recently, were peasant farmers. German has become the language of social opportunity and social status, and it is the young women from the bilingual community who have shown most willingness to participate in social change. Hungarian is symbolic of peasant status, and most young people do not want to be peasants. Young bilinguals want to pass as monolingual Germans, and children of mixed marriages – in this case, of a bilingual parent and a monolingual German-speaking parent – do not learn to speak Hungarian.

An analysis of language use in Oberwart shows that Hungarian is most likely to be used by older people in networks involving many peasant contacts. As the number of peasant contacts decreases and the participants become younger, the amount of German used increases. German is now used in more situations in which Hungarian was once used, and it is also used more and more, even by older bilinguals. Young men with strong peasant networks still use Hungarian a great deal, but young women with similar strong peasant networks use German even within these networks. They reject the use of Hungarian, for it is a clear indicator of peasant status in the community. Young peasant women also prefer not to marry peasant men. They prefer non-peasant, German-speaking workers as spouses. But the effect of this is to force the bilingual peasant men also to marry German-speaking peasant women from neighboring villages. The offspring of both kinds of marriage are German-speaking children. However, it is the young women's desire to participate in the social change that is occurring in Oberwart and seek the higher status which the use of German alone seems to offer that is hastening the change from bilingualism to monolingualism in the community.

In a similar study involving a Spanish community, Holmquist (1985) describes how women show preferences for a standard variety of a language rather than a nonstandard one and for marital partners who speak that standard variety. In Ucieda, a small village near Santander in Spain, the women opt for prestigious Castilian pronunciations and look for men who use them as possible husbands. Consequently, local men cannot find women in the village to marry and must look for Castilian-speaking wives. Both kinds of marriage erode the Uciedan dialect.

What we have seen in all of the above studies are attempts made to isolate the kinds of changes that appear to be occurring in specific places. A close examination of the social context of each change also reveals the particular segment of the community which is most involved in that change and possible motivation for the involvement. These motivations can be various: to try to be like a 'higher' social group or less like a 'lower' one; to mark yourself off from 'outsiders'; to achieve a feeling of 'solidarity' with others; or to react to the pressures of the 'linguistic marketplace.' Women may be more active participants than men in some changes, but the situation may be reversed in others. Although the young are usually in the vanguard of most changes, in some it is the not-so-young who lead. In the next section we will look more closely at the issue of motivation and the actual process of change.

Table 8.5 Differences between men's and women's speech

	UMC	LMC	UWC	LWC
Percentage of multiple negation in Detroit speech				
Male	6.3	32.4	40.0	90.1
Female	0.0	1.4	35.6	58.9
Percentage of non-prevocalic /r/ in Detroit Negro speech				
Male	66.7	52.5	20.0	25.0
Female	90.0	70.0	44.2	31.7
Percentage of *-in'* forms in Norwich speech				
Male	4	27	81	100
Female	0	3	68	97

Source: based on Trudgill (1995, pp. 69–70)

Discussion

1. Table 8.5 shows three instances of differences between men's and women's speech in Detroit and Norwich. What relevance, if any, have data such as these to understanding any aspect of linguistic change?
2. For a very different view of the pronunciation of final *-ing*, see Mathisen (1999), who reports on the incidence of the actual pronunciation of the final *g* in Sandwell, West Midlands. Young women are leaders but this time in the pronunciation of a nonstandard form with local prestige status. Are such pronunciations of final *g*s likely to survive the twenty-first century?
3. Individuals who shift from one geographic area to another or who are upwardly mobile (or both) often provide striking evidence of change in progress. Can you apply any of the observations made in this chapter to account for the changing linguistic usage of any such individual who is familiar to you? Can we learn anything about linguistic change in general from looking at individuals in this way?
4. What consequences, if any, might recent emphases on equality between men and women have for linguistic change? This is necessarily a speculative question, but, in that it asks you to address the issue that certain linguistic changes arise from social differences, it has wider implications than gender differences alone.
5. Much of the language instruction provided in schools attended by working-class children is directed toward changing aspects of the language that these children bring with them to school. Most teachers of young children are women, many of them of lower middle- and upper working-class origin. Do you see any potential for conflict here? How might you deal with such conflict?

The Process of Change

In an early study of linguistic change in Kannada, a language of the Indian sub-continent, Bright (1960) examined the Brahman and non-Brahman caste dialects, which originate from the same historical source, Old Kannada, and, though mutually intelligible, exhibit both obvious differences and some of the same historical changes. His examination revealed that the Brahman dialect seems to have undergone unconscious change, that is, changes in phonology and morphology. Bright hypothesizes that, although 'conscious' linguistic change originates among members of the higher social strata, 'unconscious' change is natural in all strata where the literacy factor does not intervene. He looks to the interaction between social dialects for an understanding of linguistic change. He suggests that the upper classes appear to originate sound change at the phonetic level and that, in their chase to imitate such phonetic changes, the lower classes bring about change at the phonemic level, that is, changes which eventually have structural consequences for the language. In other words, we might say that change is somehow initiated at the highest social levels but carried through at the lower levels. As we will see, this explanation is a partial one at the best. Such a view of linguistic change is too simple to account for all the situations we have encountered. However, it might be the case that this is indeed what happens when the social distribution of the variants is caste-based rather than class-based.

Labov (1981) has pointed out how difficult it is to get the right kinds of data on which to base claims about linguistic change in progress and how easy it is to make either false claims or incorrect predictions, giving several instances of the latter from Switzerland, Paris, and Philadelphia (pp. 177–8). He stresses the importance of having good data on which to base claims. Such data can come from studies of a community conducted at different times. However, it is often the case that only a single study is done and the different responses of various age groups are compared and conclusions drawn about changes. Such studies are *apparent-time* studies and require real-time confirmation. Since linguistic usage tends to vary according to the age of the individual, such *age-grading* must also be taken into account, as we saw, for example, on p. 196 with reference to Canadian uses of 'zee' and 'zed'. Hibya (1996) showed how real-time data can confirm apparent-time data. He was interested in the denasalization of the velar nasal stop in Tokyo Japanese, i.e., the use of [g] for [ŋ]. Figure 8.2 shows how he was able to plot this use in 1986 to the left of the vertical broken line by year of birth for informants. There is an almost completely linear decrease in such use from older speakers to younger ones. But is the loss age-graded? Hibya also had recordings made thirty to forty years earlier of speakers aged between 60 and 80 at that time. Their usage is shown to the right of the vertical broken line: virtually 100 percent use of [ŋ]. Since in 1986 60- to 80-year-old speakers used [ŋ] between 10 and 40 percent of the time, the change to [g] is confirmed as a real change.

Labov insists that the best studies of change in progress look for different kinds of data sources, are very much concerned with assessing the accuracy of

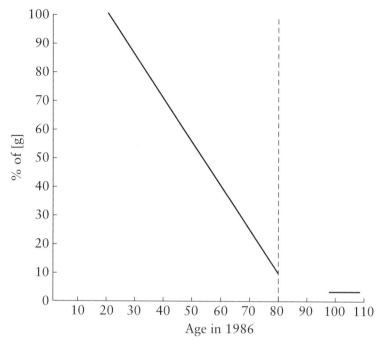

Figure 8.2 Age and use of [g] in Tokyo
Source: based on Hibya (1996)

these sources, and are quite cautious in the claims they make. However, he adds that careful surveys of the current state of affairs also enable 'a good deal of the past [to] be reconstructed from the present if we look into the matter deeply enough' (p. 196). That is, the relationship between diachronic (historical) matters and synchronic (descriptive) ones is a two-way relationship. There is what Labov calls a 'dynamic dimension' to synchronic structure, so that the past helps to explain the present and the present helps to explain the past.

After conducting a number of investigations of sound changes in progress, Labov (1972b, pp. 178–80) suggests that there are two basic kinds of change: *change from below*, i.e., change from below conscious awareness, and *change from above*, i.e., change brought about consciously. Change from below is systematic, unconscious change, whereas change from above is sporadic, conscious, and involves issues of prestige. Since change from above is conscious change, we might expect such change to involve a movement toward standard linguistic norms. Change from above may not actually be initiated within the highest social group in society. This group is a kind of reference group to groups lower down in the social scale, and it is among these groups, particularly slightly lower ones, that such change begins. Change from below is unconscious and away from existing norms. Some observers believe that in societies such as ours women may be in the vanguard of the first kind of change and men in the vanguard of the second, because women and men have different motives. In this view, women are motivated to conform to, and cooperate with, those who are socially more powerful whereas men are more inclined to seek solidarity with peers. Women, therefore, consciously look 'up,' whereas men do not, preferring instead, though they may not be conscious of it, the solidarity they find in the 'masculinity' and 'toughness' of peers and even of those they regard as being 'below' them in society. However, recent work by Labov in Philadelphia (2001) would suggest that such a view is much too simplistic.

It is Labov's view (1994, p. 23) that 'cities have always been at the center of linguistic innovation.' He decided, therefore, to examine the situation in Philadelphia to see if he could further clarify how and where change begins. He chose Philadelphia because 'it appeared that almost all of the Philadelphia vowels were in motion' (1980, pp. 254–5). He was particularly interested in the fronting and raising of (aw) in words like *out* and *down*, the fronting and raising of (ey) in checked syllables in words like *made* and *pain*, and the centralization of (ay) before voiceless consonants in words like *right* and *fight*. Labov's data came from a telephone survey of the whole city together with intensive network studies of the speech behavior of thirty-six individuals in a few selected neighborhoods. He found that 'the speakers who are most advanced in the sound changes are those with the highest status in their local community . . . [have] the largest number of local contacts within the neighborhood, yet . . . [have] the highest proportion of their acquaintances outside the neighborhood' (p. 261). In Philadelphia the leaders in change were upper working-class women, and men lagged by a generation. He concluded (p. 262):

> The identification of the innovators of these sound changes allows us to rule out some of the explanations that have been offered in the past for the phenomenon of sound change. Their advanced social position and the high esteem they hold in the local community rule out the traditional charge of careless ignorance of the norms of society. Their reputation as vigorous and effective users of the language, combined with the nature of the vowel shifts themselves, makes any discussion of the principle of least effort beside the point. The central position that they hold in local networks of communication gives new life to the principle of local density, though we cannot project any discontinuity between these speakers and the exponents of the upper middle-class standard that they are leaving behind in their development of local sound changes. Once we are willing to refine our notion of prestige to give full weight to the local prestige associated with the Philadelphia dialect . . . we must be ready to recognize that such a local prestige, which appears primarily in behavior and rarely in overt reactions, is powerful enough to reverse the normal flow of influence, and allow the local patterns to move upward to the upper middle class and even to the upper class.

Labov's general conclusion (2001) is that the changes that occur essentially arise from the nonconformity of certain upwardly mobile individuals who influence others to adopt their behavior, thus affecting the behavior of the wider community. He adds that his conclusions are valid only for Philadelphia and then only for the speech of non-blacks there. Blacks do not use this vowel system at all, preferring instead that of African American Vernacular English (AAVE). According to Labov, the non-black vowel system in Philadelphia gains much of its vitality from recent immigration to the city, with an accompanying renewed emphasis on local identification and assertion of local rights and privileges, together with a resistance to allowing the large black population to have its share of opportunities in the city. He suggests that the future direction of change in the vowel system in Philadelphia will depend very much on social changes that are occurring in the city.

Further work in Philadelphia led Labov and Harris (1986, p. 20) to conclude that:

> The Philadelphia speech community is separating into two distinct speech communities: white and black. They share a large part of the general English language, and a number of local words as well. . . . But the number of differences between them in grammar and pronunciation seems to be growing steadily greater.

In particular they note black speakers' preference for -*s* as a 'mark of the narrative past,' a feature that white speakers lack entirely. (I will have more to say about this possible divergence of AAVE on pp. 344–5.)

The Milroys (Milroy, 1992, and Milroy and Milroy, 1992) are two other linguists who are interested in how change begins. For them the key lies in network ties: with strong ties change is slow but weak ties can lead to rapid change. New forms are adopted by innovators with weak ties to more than one group. Some of these innovations are taken up by core members of the groups. Change results. Milroy and Milroy (1992, p. 9) say that 'groups linked internally mainly by relatively weak ties are susceptible to innovation' and add that 'innovations between groups are generally transmitted by means of weak rather than strong network ties (e.g., through casual acquaintances rather than kin, close friends, or workmates).' They point out (p. 17) that their conclusion that change begins therefore in the middle of the social-class hierarchy 'is entirely consistent with Labov's finding that innovating groups are located centrally in the class structure, characterized by him as upper-working or lower-middle class. . . . For in British and American society at least, close-knit, territorially based, kin-oriented networks are located most clearly in the lowest classes, but upper-class networks are in some respects structurally similar, being relatively dense.' Marshall's work (2004) in northeast Scotland also showed that the most revealing factor in determining how individuals changed their speech behavior was the group to which they oriented: 'Those with the most positive orientation to the local rural group resist change.' He adds that those 'who have a higher degree of mental urbanisation, or an attitude of openness to supra-local norms, . . . are at the forefront of change' (p. 217).

Many observers have noted the weakening of network ties as social and geographic mobility increased in the late twentieth century. Social contacts increased but became shallower. One consequence for language has been the fairly rapid spread of innovation. Some, like slang, are ephemeral. Others, like accent change, produce more lasting effects. In England the old regional dialects have been much affected. Local varieties adopted linguistic features from influential centers often with women, particularly younger women, in the vanguard. The results have been the creation of various non-localized norms interposed between the local vernaculars to which many older and less educated speakers still cling and standard RP, itself gradually atrophying.

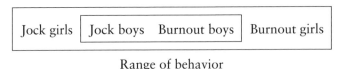

Range of behavior

Figure 8.3   Jock and burnout behavior

Eckert's findings (1988, 1989, 1991, 2000, 2004) from her study of what she calls 'jocks' and 'burnouts' in an almost exclusively white suburban Detroit high school further complicates matters. 'Lifestyle' also seems to be a factor in change. Jocks are either middle-class students or students with middle-class aspirations, and burnouts are either working-class students or students who wish to identify themselves as such. Jocks tend to be college-bound and white-collar-oriented; burnouts will leave school for the blue-collar workplace. Jocks willingly participate in the activities of the school; burnouts find activities outside school more attractive. We must note that only about one-third of the students readily identified themselves as either jocks or burnouts but the in-betweens, the majority, leaned one way or the other. In general, on the linguistic variables that were examined (Eckert and McConnell-Ginet, 1999) girls ranged far more widely than boys. That is, the difference between jock and burnout girls was greater than that between jock and burnout boys, as in figure 8.3. It would appear that, linguistically, girls were required to do more than boys, i.e., to adopt more extreme behaviors in order to establish their places. They developed different practices within the communities within which they functioned. As Eckert says (2000, p. 35), 'A community of practice is an aggregate of people who come together around some enterprise. United by this common enterprise, people come to develop and share ways of doing things, ways of talking, beliefs, values – in short, practices – as a function of their joint engagement in activity.' The jocks and burnouts had entirely different social networks and norms of behavior because of the practices of their communities.

The jock–burnout allegiance showed no relationship to social class and gender. It was clearly some kind of ideological allegiance. Eckert found that burnouts were much more active than jocks in participating in the NCS (see p. 194), with the most burned-out burnouts clearly in the lead. They see themselves as part of the developing local urban landscape and are linguistically engaged in it. Jocks, on the other hand, have a wider horizon but also one that leads them to linguistic conservatism. Eckert (2000, pp. 1–2) comments as follows: 'Ultimately, the social life of variation lies in the variety of individuals' ways of participating in their communities – their ways of fitting in, and of making their mark – their ways of constructing meaning in their own lives.' Variation arises from what individuals do with the language as they attempt to come to terms with their surroundings.

Whenever a change begins and whatever its causes, it is not an instantaneous event for the language as a whole. It has to establish itself. A number of linguists (see Wang, 1969, 1977) have proposed a theory of change called *lexical diffusion*. According to this theory, a sound change spreads gradually through the

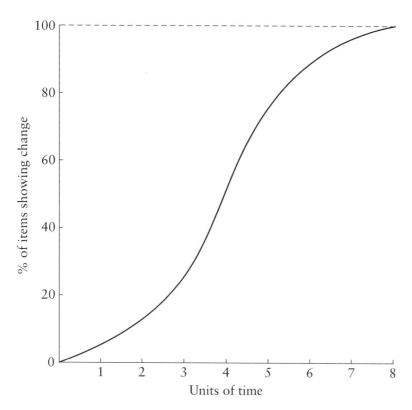

Figure 8.4 Lexical diffusion over time
Source: based on Bailey (1973)

words in which the change applies. For example, a change in vowel quality is not instantaneous, affecting at some specific point in time all words in which that vowel occurs, as if you went to bed one night with vowel quality A in those words and got up next morning with vowel quality B. Instead, only some words that have the vowel will be affected initially, then others, then still others, and so on until the change is complete.

According to this view, change does not proceed at a uniform rate throughout the affected vocabulary. Instead, there is an S-curve effect. That is, there is an initial period of slow change in which as few as 20 percent of the relevant words undergo the change, then a shorter period of time of rapid change in which about 60 percent of the affected words show the change, and a final period, again of much the same length as the initial period, in which all or most – there is often a residue – of the remaining 20 percent of relevant words show the change. Figure 8.4 shows this process of lexical diffusion over time.

This hypothesis allows us to make certain predictions. If a sound change is observed to be occurring in less than a quarter of a set of words which have the necessary conditions for changes, we are probably witnessing the beginning of the process or, of course, the end if the rest of the words already show the change to have occurred. If individual speakers vary in the pronunciation of the

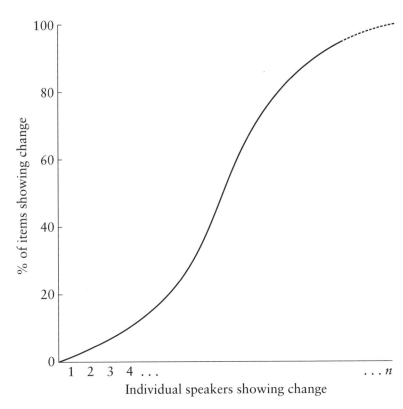

Figure 8.5 Lexical diffusion by individual speakers
Source: based on Bailey (1973)

words in question with a large proportion pronouncing most of the words one way, an equally large proportion pronouncing most of the words the other way, and a third, but smaller, proportion showing a more even distribution of choices, then we have a change in progress and that change has reached its mid-point. If we plot the distributions of the pronunciations of the individual vocabulary items by individual speakers, we will see much the same phenomenon if there is a change in progress; for example, if it is a sound change, some words will be pronounced by almost everyone with the change, some others without the change, again by almost everyone, and another set will show both variants. Figure 8.5 shows how such a process will appear at its mid-point. We can see that at that point in the process half the speakers evidence the change in half the words. (Note the similarity of figure 8.5 to figure 8.4.)

The theory of lexical diffusion has resemblances to the wave theory of language change: a wave is also a diffusion process. We can see, for example, that the Rhenish Fan (see p. 137) shows how the diffusion of the Second German Consonant Shift stopped for different sounds in different places. Figure 8.6 uses the data from figure 6.1 (p. 137) to illustrate how sound change diffuses from south to north in the affected sounds in four different words. Here the diffusion is over geographical space. However, after reviewing S-curve type diffusion as an

North

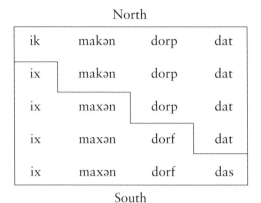

South

Figure 8.6 Second German Consonant Shift

attempt to account for different changes that have occurred in English, Denison (2003) cautions that: 'The S-curve is neither as simple nor as uniform a phenomenon as it is sometimes assumed. Given too the simplistic picture of variation it sometimes reflects (and requires), the S-curve should not be seized on too readily as *the* general shape of language change' (p. 68).

The wave theory of change and the theory of lexical diffusion are very much alike. Each attempts to explain how a linguistic change spreads through a language; the wave theory makes claims about how people are affected by change, whereas lexical diffusion makes claims concerning how a particular change spreads through the set of words in which the feature undergoing change actually occurs: diffusion through linguistic space. That the two theories deal with much the same phenomenon is apparent when we look at how individuals deal with such sets of words. What we find is that in individual usage the change is introduced progressively through the set, and once it is made in a particular word it is not 'unmade', i.e., there is no reversion to previous use. What is remarkable is that, with a particular change in a particular set of words, speakers tend to follow the same order of progression through the set; that is, all speakers seem to start with the same sub-set of words, have the same intermediate sub-set, and extend the change to the same final sub-set. For example, in Belfast the change from [ʊ] to [ʌ] in the vowel in words like *pull*, *put*, and *should* shows a 74 percent incidence in the first word, a 39 percent incidence in the second, and only an 8 percent incidence in the third (Hudson, 1996, p. 182). In East Anglia and the East Midlands of England a sound change is well established in *must* and *come* but the same change is found hardly at all in *uncle* and *hundred* (Chambers and Trudgill, 1998, p. 161). This diffusion is through social space.

Devitt (1989) shows how five features of Standard English diffused into Scots English between 1520 and 1659. She examined 121 different texts written by Scottish writers for the incidence of English and Scots features: *which* and *quhilk* as a relative-clause marker; *-ed* and *-it* as a preterite inflection; *no* and *na* as a negative particle; *an* and *ane* as an indefinite article; and *-ing* and *-and* as a

Table 8.6   Vowel assimilation in Teheran Persian in six words read by seven speakers

	Assimilation by seven speakers reading word list							Assimilation in free speech by all speakers	
	A	B	C	D	E	F	G	% assimilated	Total
/bekon/'Do!'	+	+	+	+	+	+		91	331
/bedo/'Run!'	+	+	+	+	+			78	23
/bexan/'Read!'	+	+	+	+				40	139
/begu/'Tell!'	+	+	+					22	132
/bekub/'Hit!'	+	+						4	122
/bebor/'Cut!'	+							3	124

Source: Hudson (1996, p. 184), based on Jahangiri (1980)

present participle ending. All the texts showed an increase in the use of the English feature from about 15 percent to 90 percent during this period, with *-ing* leading the way followed by *no*. Devitt's study supports the S-curve view of diffusion; she says that although her sources showed only the middle part of the process, 'The general pattern of anglicization, recurring across all five variables, appears to be the S-curve; the changes spread slowly at first, then spread very rapidly before slowing down again at the end' (p. 46). She adds that the S-curve also applied to the different genres of writing although at different rates; religious texts led the way in anglicization, followed by official correspondence, private records, personal correspondence, and, in last place, national public records.

Hudson (1996, p. 184) produces data from Teheran Persian (based on Jahangiri, 1980) which show an even more remarkable pattern. Vowel assimilation in the first syllable of words like /bekon/'Do!' is apparently progressing through a set of words in such a way that, if you hear a speaker assimilate the first vowel in a word like /begu/'Tell!', you can predict that the speaker also assimilates the first vowel in /bexan/'Read!', /bedo/'Run!', and /bekon/'Do!' The data are given in table 8.6. They are interesting because the behavior of individuals is *implicational*; that is, if speaker X assimilates the vowel in /bebor/'Cut!', that speaker also assimilates the vowel in all the other words in the set. But that behavior also corresponds to group norms; that is, 91 percent of all speakers assimilate the vowel in /bekon/'Do!' but only 3 percent assimilate the vowel in /bebor/'Cut!'. The data also suggest that a closer analysis might show an S-curve here, since the two highest percentages are so high (91 and 78 percent) and the two lowest almost non-existent (3 and 4 percent). It appears that the change began with words like /bekon/ and /bedo/ and is now thoroughly established in these, that it is progressing through words like /bexan/ and /begu/, and that only in the most innovative speakers has it reached as far as words like /bekub/ and /bebor/. I should add that Hudson (1996) points out (p. 184) that data from ten speakers concerning sixty words in all produced 'much messier' results, so that a simple hypothesis of the uniform diffusion of change through the lexicon might require modification.

Further messiness is found in the results reported by Hansen (2001) from a study of lexical diffusion in relation to an ongoing change in French nasal vowels, which appear to be undergoing a clockwise chain shift. She found that this chain shift is indeed in progress, but it is not at all a simple one since 'both a vowel's prosodic position and its phonetic surroundings in the spoken chain are relevant' (p. 227). The changes also vary by lexical item, found not at all in occurrences of *sans* but in better than 75 percent of occurrences of *avant* and *moment* (p. 235). Word frequency was not a factor in change but word class appeared to be one. 'The type of sound change considered here mixes facets of typical Neogrammarian and typically lexically diffused sound change' (p. 284). However, the overall mix appears to resist easy explanation.

Labov's view of lexical diffusion is that it has only a very limited role to play in change. He says (1994, p. 501), 'There is no evidence ... that lexical diffusion is the fundamental mechanism of sound change.' It happens but is only a complement – and a small one at that – to regular sound change. The most important factors in linguistic change appear to be long-standing trends in the language, internal variation, and social forces among speakers. These interact and the result is change. According to Labov, the key problem in explaining that change is ascertaining the relevant data in both language and society, and then integrating the resulting observations into a theory of change which will allow us to see how and why change is occurring and plot its course.

As I previously indicated, a number of sociolinguists hold the view that such endeavors are really what sociolinguistics is all about. If I agreed with them these would be the final words of this book. They are not. There are still many more interesting connections between language and society that deserve our attention.

Discussion

1. Labov (1972b, p. 226) says of *g*-dropping, i.e., saying *singin'* for *singing*, that 'we observe listeners reacting in a discrete way. Up to a certain point they do not perceive the speaker "dropping his g's" at all; beyond a certain point, they perceive him as always doing so.' How would you propose to test this claim? If the claim is correct, what does it suggest about the way in which people react to language and to changes that occur in a language?
2. Radio, movies, and television show a preponderant use of standard forms. Such media might be expected to exert a considerable influence on linguistic change. Do they, in fact? Try to state a few testable hypotheses on this matter. Note the word *testable*. You may find it quite easy to come up with a number of hypotheses, but the problem is how to test these rather than just assert them to be obvious truths or well-held beliefs.

3. Not every innovation takes root in a language. In fact, you can argue that most innovations go nowhere. Note that the kinds of changes discussed in this chapter seem to build on something that already exists in a language, that is, some existing variant that is put to use. What kinds of linguistic innovations have you observed to go nowhere? In what way or ways do such innovations fail to meet the various requirements for 'taking root' that are discussed in this chapter?

Further Reading

Labov's views are most clearly expressed in his 1994 and 2001 books. For changes occurring in British English, see Foulkes and Docherty (1999). For an account of vocabulary change in twentieth-century English, decade by decade, see Ayto (1999).

Part III Words at Work

Language grows out of life, out of its needs and experiences.

Annie Sullivan

The limits of my language mean the limits of my world.

Ludwig Wittgenstein

Oaths are but words, and words but wind.

Samuel Butler

He [Lord Macaulay] had occasional flashes of silence, that made his
conversation perfectly delightful.

Sydney Smith

My never-failing friends are they,
With whom I converse day by day.

Robert Southey

And, when you stick on conversation's burrs,
Don't strew your pathway with those dreadful *urs*.

Oliver Wendell Holmes

9 Words and Culture

The exact nature of the relationship between language and culture has fascinated, and continues to fascinate, people from a wide variety of backgrounds. That there should be some kind of relationship between the sounds, words, and syntax of a language and the ways in which speakers of that language experience the world and behave in it seems so obvious as to be a truism. It would appear that the only problem is deciding the nature of the relationship and finding suitable ways to demonstrate it. But, as we will see, what is 'obvious' need not necessarily be 'true': the sun does not rotate around the earth, nor is the earth at the center of the universe! When we do try to specify any such relationship, we run into problems that are no less formidable than those just mentioned: we may be misled by the 'obvious.' In this chapter we will look at various ways in which language and culture have been said to be related. As we will see, some of the resulting claims are unprovable, others are intriguing, but only one or two are potentially of great interest.

A few words are necessary concerning what I mean by 'culture.' I do not intend to use the term *culture* in the sense of 'high culture,' i.e., the appreciation of music, literature, the arts, and so on. Rather, I intend to use it in the sense of whatever a person must know in order to function in a particular society. This is the same sense as in Goodenough's well-known definition (1957, p. 167): 'a society's culture consists of whatever it is one has to know or believe in order to operate in a manner acceptable to its members, and to do so in any role that they accept for any one of themselves.' That knowledge is socially acquired: the necessary behaviors are learned and do not come from any kind of genetic endowment. Culture, therefore, is the 'know-how' that a person must possess to get through the task of daily living; only for a few does it require a knowledge of some, or much, music, literature, and the arts.

Whorf

One long-standing claim concerning the relationship between language and culture is that the structure of a language determines the way in which speakers of that language view the world. A somewhat weaker version is that the structure does not determine the world-view but is still extremely influential in predisposing speakers of a language toward adopting a particular world-view. This claim has intrigued many anthropologists and linguists and there is a fairly extensive literature concerning it. The opposite claim would be that the culture of a people finds reflection in the language they employ: because they value certain things and do them in a certain way, they come to use their language in ways that reflect what they value and what they do. In this view, cultural requirements do not determine the structure of a language – the claim is never that strong – but they certainly influence how a language is used and perhaps determine why specific bits and pieces are the way they are. A third, 'neutral,' claim would be that there is little or no relationship between language and culture.

The claim that the structure of a language influences how its speakers view the world is today most usually associated with the linguist Sapir and his student Whorf, a chemical engineer by training, a fire prevention engineer by vocation, and a linguist by avocation. However, it can be traced back to others, particularly to Humboldt in the nineteenth century. Today, the claim is usually referred to as the Linguistic relativity hypothesis, Sapir–Whorf hypothesis, or the *Whorfian hypothesis*. I will use the latter term since the claim seems to owe much more to Whorf than it does to Sapir.

Sapir acknowledged the close relationship between language and culture, maintaining that they were inextricably related so that you could not understand or appreciate the one without a knowledge of the other. The passage which most clearly summarizes his views (1929b, p. 207) is as follows:

> Human beings do not live in the objective world alone, nor alone in the world of social activity as ordinarily understood, but are very much at the mercy of the particular language which has become the medium of expression for their society. It is quite an illusion to imagine that one adjusts to reality essentially without the use of language and that language is merely an incidental means of solving specific problems of communication or reflection. The fact of the matter is that the 'real world' is to a large extent unconsciously built up on the language habits of the group. . . . We see and hear and otherwise experience very largely as we do because the language habits of our community predispose certain choices of interpretation.

Whorf extended these ideas, going much further than saying that there was a 'predisposition'; in Whorf's view, the relationship between language and culture was a deterministic one.

One of Whorf's strongest statements is the following (Carroll, 1956, pp. 212–14):

> the background linguistic system (in other words, the grammar) of each language is not merely a reproducing instrument for voicing ideas but rather is itself the shaper of ideas, the program and guide for the individual's mental activity, for his analysis of impressions, for his synthesis of his mental stock in trade. Formulation of ideas is not an independent process, strictly rational in the old sense, but is part of a particular grammar, and differs, from slightly to greatly, between different grammars. We dissect nature along lines laid down by our native languages. The categories and types that we isolate from the world of phenomena we do not find

there because they stare every observer in the face; on the contrary, the world is presented in a kaleidoscopic flux of impressions which has to be organized by our minds – and this means largely by the linguistic systems in our minds. We cut nature up, organize it into concepts, and ascribe significances as we do, largely because we are parties to an agreement to organize it in this way – an agreement that holds throughout our speech community and is codified in the patterns of our language. The agreement is, of course, an implicit and unstated one, *but its terms are absolutely obligatory*; we cannot talk at all except by subscribing to the organization and classification of data which the agreement decrees.

Although this view is a deterministic one, Whorf actually twice uses the word *largely*. He does not go all the way to say that the structure of a language completely determines the way its speakers view the world. However, he does go on to add (p. 214):

This fact is very significant for modern science, for it means that no individual is free to describe nature with absolute impartiality but is constrained to certain modes of interpretation even while he thinks himself most free. The person most nearly free in such respects would be a linguist familiar with very many widely different linguistic systems. As yet no linguist is in any such position. We are thus introduced to a new principle of relativity, which holds that all observers are not led by the same physical evidence to the same picture of the universe, unless their linguistic backgrounds are similar, or can in some way be calibrated.

In this view different speakers will therefore experience the world differently insofar as the languages they speak differ structurally, and not even the most sophisticated linguist aware of all the subtleties of structural differences among languages can escape to see the world as it is rather than as it is presented through the screen of this language or that.

On several occasions Fishman (particularly 1960 and 1972c) has written about the Whorfian hypothesis concerning the kinds of claims it makes. One claim is that, if speakers of one language have certain words to describe things and speakers of another language lack similar words, then speakers of the first language will find it easier to talk about those things. We can see how this might be the case if we consider the technical vocabulary of any trade, calling, or profession; for example, physicians talk easily about medical phenomena, more easily than you or I, because they have the vocabulary to do so. A stronger claim is that, if one language makes distinctions that another does not make, then those who use the first language will more readily perceive the differences in their environment which such linguistic distinctions draw attention to. If you must classify camels, boats, and automobiles in certain ways, you will perceive camels, boats, and automobiles differently from someone who is not required to make these differentiations. If your language classifies certain material objects as long and thin and others as roundish, you will perceive material objects that way; they will fall quite 'naturally' into those classes for you.

This extension into the area of grammar could be argued to be a further strengthening of Whorf's claim, since classification systems pertaining to shape, substance, gender, number, time, and so on are both more subtle and more pervasive. Their effect is much stronger on language users than vocabulary differences alone. The strongest claim of all is that the grammatical categories available in a particular language not only help the users of that language to perceive the world in a certain way but also at the same time limit such perception. They act as blinkers: you perceive only what your language allows you, or predisposes you, to perceive. Your language controls your 'world-view.' Speakers of different languages will, therefore, have different world-views.

Whorf's ideas were based on two kinds of experience. One was acquired through his work as a fire prevention engineer for the Hartford Fire Insurance Company; the other was acquired through his linguistic work, as Sapir's student, on Amerindian languages, principally on the Hopi language of Arizona. In his work investigating the origins of fires, Whorf found that speakers of English would use the words *full* and *empty* in describing gasoline drums but only in relation to their liquid content; consequently, they would smoke beside 'empty' gasoline drums, which were actually 'full' of gas vapor. He found other examples of such behavior and was led to conclude that 'the cue to a certain line of behavior is often given by the analogies of the linguistic formula in which the situation is spoken of, and by which to some degree it is analyzed, classified, and allotted its place in that world which is "to a large extent unconsciously built up on the language habits of the group"' (Carroll, 1956, p. 137).

However, it was his work on Amerindian languages that led Whorf to make his strongest claims. He contrasted the linguistic structure of Hopi with the kinds of linguistic structure he associated with languages such as English, French, German, and so on, that is, familiar European languages. He saw these languages as sharing so many structural features that he named this whole group of languages *Standard Average European* (SAE). According to Whorf, Hopi and SAE differ widely in their structural characteristics. For example, Hopi grammatical categories provide a 'process' orientation toward the world, whereas the categories in SAE give SAE speakers a fixed orientation toward time and space so that they not only 'objectify' reality in certain ways but even distinguish between things that must be counted, e.g., trees, hills, waves, and sparks, and those that need not be counted, e.g., water, fire, and courage. In SAE events occur, have occurred, or will occur, in a definite time, i.e., present, past, or future; to speakers of Hopi, what is important is whether an event can be warranted to have occurred, or to be occurring, or to be expected to occur. Whorf believed that these differences lead speakers of Hopi and SAE to view the world differently. The Hopi see the world as essentially an ongoing set of processes; objects and events are not discrete and countable; and time is not apportioned into fixed segments so that certain things recur, e.g., minutes, mornings, and days. In contrast, speakers of SAE regard nearly everything in their world as discrete, measurable, countable, and recurrent; time and space do not flow into each other; sparks, flames, and waves are things like pens and pencils; mornings recur in twenty-four-hour cycles; and past, present, and future are every bit as real as gender differences. The different languages have different obligatory grammatical categories so that every time a speaker of Hopi or SAE says something, he or she must make certain observations about how the world is structured because of the structure of the language each speaks. (We should note that Malotki (1983) has pointed out that some of Whorf's claims about the grammatical structure of Hopi are either dubious or incorrect, e.g., Hopi, like SAE, does have verbs that are inflected for tense.)

In the Whorfian view, language provides a screen or filter to reality; it determines how speakers perceive and organize the world around them, both the natural world and the social world. Consequently, the language you speak helps to form your world-view. It defines your experience for you; you do not use it simply to report that experience. It is not neutral but acts as a filter. Romaine (1999) states the position as follows: 'No particular language or way of speaking has a privileged view of the world as it "really" is. The world is not simply the way it is, but what we make of it through language. The domains of experience that are important to cultures get grammaticalized into languages . . . [and] no two languages are sufficiently similar to be considered as representing the same social reality.'

Those who find this hypothesis attractive argue that the language a person speaks affects that person's relationship to the external world in one or more ways. If language A has a word for a particular concept, then that word makes it easier for speakers of language A to refer to that concept than speakers of language B who lack such a word and are forced to use a circumlocution. Moreover, it is actually easier for speakers of language A to perceive instances of the concept. If a language requires certain distinctions to be made because of its grammatical system, then the speakers of that language become conscious of the kinds of distinctions that must be referred to: for example, gender, time, number, and animacy. These kinds of distinctions may also have an effect on how speakers learn to deal with the world, i.e., they can have consequences for both cognitive and cultural development.

Data such as the following are sometimes cited in support of such claims. The Garo of Assam, India, have dozens of words for different types of baskets, rice, and ants. These are important items in their culture. However, they have no single-word equivalent to the English word *ant*. Ants are just too important to them to be referred to so casually. German has words like *Gemütlichkeit*, *Weltanschauung*, and *Weihnachtsbaum*; English has no exact equivalent of any one of them, *Christmas tree* being fairly close in the last case but still lacking the 'magical' German connotations. Both people and bulls have *legs* in English, but Spanish requires people to have *piernas* and bulls to have *patas*. Both people and horses *eat* in English but in German people *essen* and horses *fressen*. Bedouin Arabic has many words for different kinds of camels, just as the Trobriand Islanders of the Pacific have many words for different kinds of yams. The Navaho of the Southwest United States, the Shona of Zimbabwe, and the Hanunóo of the Philippines divide the color spectrum differently from each other in the distinctions they make, and English speakers divide it differently again. English has a general cover term *animal* for various kinds of creatures, but it lacks a term to cover both *fruit* and *nuts*; however, Chinese does have such a cover term. French *conscience* is both English *conscience* and *consciousness*. Both German and French have two pronouns corresponding to *you*, a singular and a plural. Japanese, on the other hand, has an extensive system of honorifics. The equivalent of English *stone* has a gender in French and German, and the various words must always be either singular or plural in French, German, and English. In Chinese, however, number is expressed only if it is somehow relevant. The Kwakiutl of British Columbia must also indicate whether the stone is visible or not to the speaker at the time of speaking, as well as its position relative to one or another of the speaker, the listener, or possible third party. Some Japanese sentences are almost completely the reverse of corresponding English sentences in their word order.

Lucy (1992a, 1996) tried to test Whorf's ideas. He used the grammatical category of number in English and in Yucatec Maya, a language of Mexico. Both languages mark nouns for plural. English, however, has a contrast between 'count' nouns like *tree* and *book* and 'mass' nouns like *water* and *sugar* (we say *trees* and *books* but not *waters* and *sugars*, except in very marked circumstances). Yucatec pluralization is optional and then only for nouns denoting animates. Lucy hypothesized that English speakers would be more conscious of the numbers of objects they see than Yucatec speakers and would also see more objects as countable. He asked speakers of the two languages to look at pictures of ordinary village life and, using a cleverly devised non-verbal test requiring sorting and recall, found that the two groups did differ in the predicted directions:

> In remembering and classifying, English speakers were sensitive to numbers for animate entities and objects but not for substances. By contrast, Yucatec speakers were sensitive to number only for animate entities . . . the two groups had very similar patterns of response for the animate and substance referents where the two languages roughly agree in structure, but . . . they differed with respect to ordinary object referents, that is, where the grammars of the two languages are in maximal contrast.
> (1996, pp. 49–50)

Other tests produced similar results. Some evidence, therefore, does exist for the kind of claims Whorf made.

Given such evidence, we are faced with the task of drawing defensible conclusions. Those conclusions are generally different from the ones that Whorf drew. For example, the words *fist*, *wave*, *spark*, and *flame* are nouns in English, so we tend to see the events or actions they name as having some kind of existence as 'things.' But we also know that this existence is of a different kind from that of houses, rocks, cats, and trees. We can, therefore, understand that words for the same events or actions can appear as verbs in Hopi: we know that houses and rocks comprise a different order of 'things' from fists and waves. One language refers to certain characteristics of the real world in terms of one possible sub-set of characteristics; another favors a different sub-set. However, speakers of both languages may still be aware of all the characteristics. They are not required to refer to all of them.

Syntactic evidence can also mislead investigators. Much of the evidence is provided by literal translation, as though *breakfast* were understood as a 'break in a fast,' or *cats* as 'cat' plus 'plural,' as though in a group of cats one cat were noticed independently of, and before, the presence of the other cats. Over-literal translation is very dangerous, particularly of metaphoric language. English, for example, is full of metaphors: 'I see what you mean,' 'He grasped the idea,' 'You're behind the times,' and so on. At best, the syntactic evidence suggests that languages allow their speakers to make certain observations more easily in some cases than others. An obligatory grammatical category, for example tense-marking in English verbs, will lead to certain things being said in English that need not be said, for example in Chinese. Periodically, scholars meet to examine Whorf's ideas but the results (e.g., Pütz and Verspoor, 2000, and Enfield, 2002) tend to be either disappointing or inconclusive. There continues to be little agreement as to exactly what Whorf meant, how the hypothesis associated with his name can be tested, and what any 'results' might indicate.

Pinker (1994, pp. 59–67) has no patience at all for any of Whorf's ideas. He says that Whorf's claims were 'outlandish,' his arguments were circular, any evidence he gave for them was either anecdotal or suspect in some other way, and all the experiments conducted to test the ideas have proved nothing. However, Whorf's ideas still exert their fascination. Do different languages produce different world-views? That question is certainly behind many linguists' belief that endangered languages should be protected (see, for example, Dixon, 1997, p. 144, and Nettle and Romaine, 2000). It is also, as we will see in chapter 14, behind the idea that teaching a standard language to a child who speaks some nonstandard variety is essentially a liberating, empowering act. These are but two examples.

Broader attempts to relate types of language structure to patterns of social organization have also met with failure. One problem has been trying to characterize languages by structural types. Language typology is an interesting topic in its own right (see Comrie, 1989), but it is somewhat doubtful that there is any close relationship between the particular types of language, no matter how these are defined, and the cultures of the people who speak them. Boas (1911) long ago pointed out that there was no necessary connection between language and culture or between language and race. People with very different cultures speak languages with many of the same structural characteristics, e.g., Hungarians, Finns, and the Samoyeds of northern Siberia; and people who speak languages with very different structures often share much the same culture, e.g., Germans and Hungarians, or many people in southern India, or the widespread Islamic culture. Moreover, we can also dismiss any claim that certain types of languages can be associated with 'advanced' cultures and that others are indicative of cultures that are less advanced. As Sapir himself observed on this last point (1921, p. 219), 'When it comes to linguistic form, Plato walks with the Macedonian swineherd, Confucius with the head-hunting savage of Assam.'

Finally, the claim that it would be impossible to describe certain things in a particular language because that language lacks the necessary resources is only partially valid at best. We must assume that all languages possess the resources that any speaker might require to say anything that he or she might want to say in that language. Some languages, like English, Russian, French, and Chinese, for example, have had these resources developed in a tremendous variety of ways. But there is no reason to suppose that any other language is incapable of similar development. It might be difficult currently to discuss advanced nuclear physics in Tukano or Basque, but should a compelling necessity arise in the Tukano-speaking and Basque-speaking communities for people to become experts in nuclear physics and use Tukano and Basque to do so, the two languages should prove quite adequate. No society has rejected such modern 'advances' as television, computers, and sophisticated weaponry because its people lacked the linguistic resources to use them. As recent events in many parts of the world have shown, one can go from camels and abacuses to Mercedes and computers in but a few short years.

The most valid conclusion concerning the Whorfian hypothesis is that it is still unproved. It appears to be quite possible to talk about anything in any language provided a speaker is willing to use some degree of circumlocution. However, some concepts may be more 'codable,' that is, easier to express, in some languages than in others. A speaker, of course, will not be aware of such circumlocution in the absence of familiarity with another language that uses a more succinct means of expression. Every natural language not only provides its speakers with a language for talking about every other language, that is, a *metalanguage*, but also provides them with an entirely adequate system for making any kinds of observations that they need to make about the world. If such is the case, every natural language must be an extremely rich system, one that allows its users to overcome any predispositions that exist and to do this without much difficulty.

Discussion

1. Sapir (1921, pp. 92–3) makes the following observation about the equivalents in Chinese and Kwakiutl, an Amerindian language, of the English sentence, 'The farmer kills the duckling':

    > In the Chinese sentence 'Man kill duck,' which may be looked upon as the practical equivalent of 'The man kills the duck,' there is by no means present for the Chinese consciousness that childish, halting, empty feeling which we experience in the literal English translation. The three concrete concepts – two objects and an action – are each directly expressed by a monosyllabic word. . . . Definiteness or indefiniteness of reference, number, personality as an inherent aspect of the verb tense, not to speak of gender – all these are given no expression in the Chinese sentence. . . . Nothing has been said . . . as to the place relations of the farmer, the duck, the speaker, and the listener. Are the farmer and the duck both visible or is one or the other invisible from the point of view of the speaker, and are both placed within the horizon of the speaker, the listener, or of some indefinite point of reference 'off yonder'? In other words, to paraphrase awkwardly certain latent 'demonstrative' ideas, does this farmer (invisible to us but standing behind a door not far away from me, you being seated yonder well out of reach) kill that duckling (which belongs to you)? or does that farmer (who lives in your neighborhood and whom we see over there) kill that duckling (that belongs to him)? This type of demonstrative elaboration is foreign to our way of thinking, but it would seem very natural, indeed unavoidable, to a Kwakiutl Indian.

    What inferences might you want to draw from Sapir's examples about the different cultures that are represented? How confident can you be about these inferences?

2. A language like English makes use of 'natural gender'; German and French employ 'grammatical gender'; and Chinese does without either. What do such facts tell us about the 'world-views' of those who speak English, German, French, and Chinese?

3. Many people in the world are completely bilingual or even multilingual in languages with very different structures. Consider this fact in relation to the Whorfian hypothesis. What are some of the implications? How might you attempt to test these experimentally?

Kinship

One interesting way in which people use language in daily living is to refer to various kinds of kin. It is not surprising, therefore, that there is a considerable literature on kinship terminology, describing how people in various parts of the world refer to relatives by blood (or descent) and marriage. Kinship systems are a universal feature of languages, because kinship is so important in social organization. Some systems are much richer than others, but all make use of such factors as gender, age, generation, blood, and marriage in their organization. One of the attractions that kinship systems have for investigators is that these factors are fairly readily ascertainable. You can therefore relate them with considerable confidence to the actual words that people use to describe a particular kin relationship.

There may be certain difficulties, of course. You can ask a particular person what he or she calls others who have known relationships to that person, for example, that person's father (Fa), or mother's brother (MoBr), or mother's sister's husband (MoSiHu), in an attempt to show how individuals employ various terms, but without trying to specify anything concerning the semantic composition of those terms: for example, in English, both your father's father (FaFa) and your mother's father (MoFa) are called *grandfather*, but that term includes another term, *father*. You will find, too, in English that your brother's wife's father (BrWiFa) cannot be referred to directly; *brother's wife's father* (or *sister-in-law's father*) is a circumlocution rather than the kind of term that is of interest in kinship terminology.

This kind of approach sometimes runs into serious difficulties. It is often virtually impossible to devise an exhaustive account of a particular system. You may also be unable to account for the many instances you may find of terms which are very obviously kinship terms but are used with people who are very obviously not kin by any of the criteria usually employed, e.g., the Vietnamese use of terms equivalent to English *sister*, *brother*, *uncle*, and *aunt* in various social relationships. Such an approach also misses the fact that certain terms recur to mark different relationships; for example, English *uncle* is used to designate FaBr, MoBr, FaSiHu, and MoSiHu, and also non-kin relationships, as when children are sometimes taught to use it for close friends of their parents. A rather different approach to kinship terminology is therefore often employed.

In this latter approach, an investigator seeks to explain why sometimes different relationships are described by the same term, e.g., why Spanish *tío* is
equivalent to both English *uncle* and either father's or mother's male cousin,
and why similar relationships are described by different terms. Burling (1970,
pp. 21–7) describes the kinship system of the Njamal, a tribe of Australian abori-
gines, in this way. To understand why the Njamal use the terms they do, you
must know that every Njamal belongs to one of two 'moieties,' that of his (or
her) father; the mother belongs to the other moiety. Marriage must be with
someone from the other moiety so that husbands and wives and fathers and
mothers represent different moiety membership. This fact, and the need also to
indicate the generation, and sometimes the sex, of the reference or ego (i.e., the
person from whom the relationship is expressed), and occasionally the other's
age relative to the ego (i.e., as being younger or older), provide the keys to
understanding the Njamal system.

One consequence is that a young Njamal man calls by the same name, *njuba*,
his mother's brother's daughter (MoBrDa) and his father's sister's daughter
(FaSiDa), which are both English *cousin*. But he uses *turda* for his father's
brother's daughter (FaBrDa) and his mother's sister's daughter (MoSiDa) when
both are older than he is. He calls any such daughters who are younger than
he is *maraga*. All of these are *cousins* in English. He may marry a *njuba*, since
a cross-cousin is of the opposite moiety, but he cannot marry a *turda* or a
maraga, a parallel cousin of the same moiety. Moiety membership is the overriding consideration in the classification system, being stronger than sex.
For example, a term like *maili* is marked as 'male,' e.g., FaFa, FaMoHu, or
FaMoBrWiBr when used to refer to someone in an ascending generation and
in the same moiety. In a descending generation, however, *maili* is also used to
designate membership in the same moiety, but in this case it can be applied to
both males and females, to DaDaHu, BrSoDa, and DaSoWiSi.

In such an approach, we collect the various kinship terms in use in a particular
society and then attempt to determine the basic components of each term. We
may go even further. For example, as Hudson (1996, pp. 85–6) points out, in
various societies, including the Seminole Indians of Florida and Oklahoma and the
Trobriand Islanders of the Pacific, a single term may refer to a very different type
of relationship, e.g., father (Fa), father's brother (FaBr), and so on to include even
father's father's sister's son's son (FaFaSiSoSo), but to exclude father's father (FaFa).
Hudson points out that the key to understanding such a system is to assume
that there is some typical concept as 'father' and that there are certain 'equiva-
lence rules' such that (a) a man's sister is equivalent to his mother; (b) siblings
of the same sex are equivalent to each other; and (c) half-siblings are equivalent
to full siblings. Since same-sex siblings are equivalent, 'father's brother' equals
'father.' The complicated 'father's father's sister's son's son' reduces to the term
for 'father,' as can be seen in table 9.1. In this system the same term is used for
all the relationships shown in the table. We might feel it strange that one should
refer to so many different kinds of relationship with a single term, but this is
because we live in very different circumstances, in which not knowing who your
father's father's sister's son's son is may be more usual than knowing this information. Then too, having to use such a potent term as *father* to refer to that person,

Table 9.1 Relationships and equivalences in a kinship system

Relationship	Equivalences
father's father's *sister's* son's son	
↓	(a) sister = mother
father's father's *mother's son's* son	
↓	(c) mother's son = brother
father's *father's brother's* son	
↓	(b) father's brother = father
father's *father's son*	
↓	(c) father's son = brother
father's brother	
↓	(b) father's brother = father
father	

Source: based on Hudson (1996, p. 86)

who may well be younger than oneself, would cause us additional concern. Some people do, of course, use *father* to people other than their male biological parents, e.g., to in-laws, adoptive parents, and priests; but these usages tend to be marked, i.e., rather special, in ways that the above usage is not.

It is important to remember that when a term like *father*, *brother*, or *older brother* is used in a kinship system, it carries with it ideas about how such people ought to behave toward others in the society that uses that system. Fathers, brothers, and older brothers are assumed to have certain rights and duties. In practice, of course, they may behave otherwise. It is the kinship system which determines who is called what; it is not the behavior of individuals which leads them to be called this or that.

As social conditions change, we can expect kinship systems to change to reflect the new conditions. The profound social change in Russian society in the last century produced certain changes in Russian kinship designation. At one time it was very important to identify certain in-laws. There were separate words for your wife's brother, *shurin*, and for your brother's wife, *nevestka*. In modern Russian these unitary terms are no longer used. Instead, the phrases *brat zheny* 'brother of wife' and *zhena brata* 'wife of brother' are used. Likewise, *yatrov* 'husband's brother's wife' has totally disappeared, and the term *svoyak* is now used to refer to any male relative by marriage when previously it could be used only for your wife's sister's husband. It is now no longer necessary to refer constantly to such relatives or to be so precise as to a particular relationship. Changing family structures have removed them from daily contact. The new longer phrasal terms also indicate the current lack of importance given to certain kinship relationships, in keeping with a general linguistic principle that truly important objects and relationships tend to be expressed through single words rather than through phrases.

Discussion

1. Look at the English kinship system, particularly your own version of it, and consider the various relationships covered by terms such as *great grandfather, uncle, niece, cousin, step-sister, half-brother, second cousin once removed,* and *father-in-law.* Where are distinctions made to do with such factors as gender, generation, blood, and marriage? Where are such distinctions not made? Is *godson* part of the system?
2. Terms such as *uncle, father, mother, sister, brother, son,* and *cousin* are sometimes used outside the English kinship system. Describe these uses and try to account for them.
3. Family structures are changing: in many parts of the world the extended family is becoming less and less important as the nuclear family grows in importance; divorce results in one-parent families; remarriage results in mixed families. What are some of the consequences for kinship terminology? For example, whereas you can have an *ex-wife,* can you have an *ex-father-in-law*? Are two people who live together necessarily *husband* and *wife*? If not, what are they? In a remarriage do his children, her children, and their children learn to distinguish whose *cousins, uncles,* and so on are whose?
4. If a language uses a term equivalent to English *mother* to cover MoSi, MoBrDa, and MoBrSiDa, and a term equivalent to English *sister* to cover FaBrDa, FaFaSi, and FaSi, what hypotheses might you be tempted to make concerning differences between the family structure of speakers of such a language and your own family structure?

Taxonomies

The above discussion of kinship terminology shows how basic are certain systems of classification in language and society. Language itself has its own classes of units: vowels and consonants; nouns and verbs; statements and questions; and so on. People also use language to classify and categorize various aspects of the world in which they live, but they do not always classify things the way scientists do; they often develop systems which we call *folk taxonomies* rather than scientific classifications. A folk taxonomy is a way of classifying a certain part of reality so that it makes some kind of sense to those who have to deal with it. Typically, such taxonomies involve matters like naturally occurring flora and fauna in the environment, but they may also involve other matters too (see Berlin, 1992).

One of the best-known studies of a folk taxonomy is Frake's account (1961) of the terms that the Subanun of Mindanao in the southern Philippines use to describe disease. There is a considerable amount of disease among the Subanun and they discuss it at length, particularly diseases of the skin. Effective treatment of any disease depends on proper diagnosis, but that itself depends on recognizing the symptoms for what they are. Much effort, therefore, goes into discussing symptoms. As Frake says (pp. 130–1):

> The 'real' world of disease presents a continuum of symptomatic variation which does not always fit neatly into conceptual pigeonholes. Consequently the diagnosis of a particular condition may evoke considerable debate: one reason a patient normally solicits diagnostic advice from a variety of people. But the debate does not concern the definition of a diagnostic category, for that is clear and well known; it concerns the exemplariness of a particular set of symptoms to the definition.

The Subanun have a variety of categories available to them when they discuss a particular set of symptoms. These categories allow them to discuss those symptoms at various levels of generality. For example, *nuka* can refer to skin disease in general but it can also mean 'eruption.' A *nuka* may be further distinguished as a *beldut* 'sore' rather than a *meŋabag* 'inflammation' or *buni* 'ringworm,' and then the particular *beldut* can be further distinguished as a *telemaw* 'distal ulcer' or even a *telemaw glai* 'shallow distal ulcer.' What we have is a hierarchy of terms with a term like *nuka* at the top and *telemaw glai* at the bottom. For example, in this case a *telemaw glai* contrasts with a *telemaw bilgun* 'deep distal ulcer.' As Frake says (p. 131):

> Conceptually the disease world, like the plant world, exhaustively divides into a set of mutually exclusive categories. Ideally, every illness either fits into one category or is describable as a conjunction of several categories. Subanun may debate, or not know, the placement of a particular case, but to their minds that reflects a deficiency in their individual knowledge, not a deficiency in the classificatory system. As long as he accepts it as part of his habitat and not 'foreign,' a Subanun, when confronted with an illness, a plant, or an animal, may say he does not know the name. He will never say there is no name.

Diagnosis is the process of finding the appropriate name for a set of symptoms. Once that name is found, treatment can follow. However, we can see that the success of that treatment depends critically not only on its therapeutic value but on the validity of the system of classification for diseases: that last system is a 'folk' one, not a scientific one.

Burling (1970, pp. 14–17) has applied this same kind of analysis of part of the vocabulary of a language to the pronoun system in Palaung, a language spoken in Burma. There are eleven pronouns altogether, and these can be plotted as in table 9.2, using the components shown in that table. Such an analysis indicates that we can associate certain phonological features we find in the pronoun system to components of meaning: *-ar* 'duality,' *-ɛ* 'more than two,' and the initial *y-*, *p-*, and *g-* related to various combinations of 'inclusion' and 'exclusion' of 'speaker' and 'hearer.' The analysis also shows us that pronouns referring to a single person (*ɔ*, *mi*, and *ʌn*) exist as a separate phonological set.

Analyses into taxonomies and components are useful in that they help us to organize data in ways that appear to indicate how speakers use their languages to organize the world around them. The analyses show how systematic much of that behavior is and do so in a rather surprising way. A folk

Table 9.2   Palaung pronouns

Speaker included	Hearer included	One person	Two persons	More than two persons
✓	✓		ar (you and I)	ɛ (you, I, and others)
✓	✗	ɔ (I)	yar (I and another but not you)	yɛ (I and others, but not you)
✗	✓	mi (you)	par (you and another)	pɛ (you and others)
✗	✗	ʌn (he/she)	gar (he/she and another but not you)	gɛ (he/she and others but not you)

you = you alone
Source: based on Burling (1970, pp. 14–17)

taxonomy of disease is something that develops with little or no conscious attention. That it can be shown to have a complex hierarchical structure is therefore a rather surprising finding. That the Palaung pronoun system is also as 'neat' as it is in the way it makes use of its various components is also intriguing. Evidently, language and culture are related very closely, and much of the relationship remains hidden from view to most of us. Only rarely do we get glimpses of it, and even then we may not know quite what to make of our discoveries.

Discussion

1.   How do you discuss an illness, injury, or disease with others? What kinds of terms do you use? Do they fall into any kind of hierarchy? Do you ever experience difficulty because your terms and the terms that another (e.g., your physician) uses fail to match?
2.   Devising a taxonomy for a set of apparently related phenomena can be a very demanding task. What difficulties do you encounter in trying to devise taxonomies for each of the following: buildings, meals, drinks, rooms in houses, flowers, and popular music?
3.   In a discussion of the various classificatory systems that speakers of different languages employ, Loveday (1982, p. 39) gives the following example:

> The Kwaio of the Solomon Islands label fresh water as one substance, salt water as another; they place birds and bats in one category in contrast to moths, butterflies and the like; they class fish and marine mammals together; and they label with a single term colours westerners call blue and black (Keesing and Keesing 1971). Is this primitive science, or simply a different set of contrasts to carve up the world of meaning with?

How would you answer Loveday's question?

Color

Our world is a world of color but the amount of color varies from place to place and time to time. A January flight from Acapulco, Mexico, to Toronto, Canada, takes one from a sun-drenched array of colors to a gray drabness. Except to those blinded to it, color is all around but it is not everywhere treated in the same way. The terms people use to describe color give us another means of exploring the relationships between different languages and cultures. The color spectrum is a physical continuum showing no breaks at all. Yet we parcel it out in bits and pieces and assign names to the various component parts: *green*, *blue*, *yellow*, *red*, and so on. We also find that we sometimes cannot directly translate color words from one language to another without introducing subtle changes in meaning, e.g., English *brown* and French *brun*. An interesting issue is how colors are referred to in different languages. Are color terms arbitrary, or is there a general pattern? If there is a pattern, what are its characteristics and why might it exist? Berlin and Kay (1969) tried to answer questions such as these, drawing on data from a wide variety of languages.

All languages make use of basic color terms. A basic color term must be a single word, e.g., *blue* or *yellow*, not some combination of words, e.g., *light blue* or *pale yellow*. Nor must it be the obvious sub-division of some higher-order term, as both *crimson* and *scarlet* are of *red*. It must have quite general use; i.e., it must not be applied only to a very narrow range of objects, as, for example, *blond* is applied in English almost exclusively to the color of hair and wood. Also, the term must not be highly restricted in the sense that it is used by only a specific sub-set of speakers, such as interior decorators or fashion writers.

According to Berlin and Kay, an analysis of the basic color terms found in a wide variety of languages reveals certain very interesting patterns. If a language has only two terms, they are for equivalents to *black* and *white* (or *dark* and *light*). If a third is added, it is *red*. The fourth and fifth terms will be *yellow* and *green*, but the order may be reversed. The sixth and seventh terms are *blue* and *brown*. Finally, as in English, come terms like *gray*, *pink*, *orange*, and *purple*, but not in any particular order. In this view there are only eleven basic color terms (although Russian is acknowledged to have twelve since it has two in the blue region: *sinij* 'dark blue' and *goluboj* 'light blue'). All other terms for colors are combinations like *grayish-brown*, variations like *scarlet*, modifications like *fire-engine red*, and finally the kinds of designations favored by paint and cosmetic manufacturers.

An attempt has been made to relate the extent of color terminology in specific languages with the level of cultural and technical complexity of the societies in which these languages are spoken. There is some reason to believe that communities that show little technological development employ the fewest color terms; e.g., the Jalé of New Guinea have words corresponding to *dark* and *light* alone. On the other hand, technologically advanced societies have terms corresponding to all eleven mentioned above. Societies in intermediate stages have intermediate numbers: for example, the Tiv of Nigeria have three terms; the Garo of Assam and the Hanunóo of the Philippines have four; and the Burmese have seven.

One approach to investigating color terminology in languages is predicated on the scientific fact that the color spectrum is an objective reality: it is 'out there,' waiting to be dealt with and, moreover, we know that humans possess rods and cones in their retinas specifically dedicated to color perception. Consequently, if you ask speakers of a language to name chips from the Munsell array of color chips you can access their knowledge of what color means to them. The claim here is that human cognition is so alike everywhere that everyone approaches the spectrum in the same way. Moreover, as cultural and technological changes occur, it becomes more and more necessary for people to differentiate within the color spectrum. Instead of picking bits and pieces of the spectrum at random as it were and naming them, people, no matter what languages they speak, progressively sub-divide the whole spectrum in a systematic way. The similar naming practices appear to follow from human cognitive needs that are the same everywhere.

Lucy (1997) is highly critical of the above claim, declaring that you cannot find out what 'color' means to speakers by simply asking them to label Munsell color chips. He says (p. 341): 'color is not "out there" in the light but in our perceptual interpretation of light, . . . communicatively relevant encodings of visual experience do not lie "in there" in the biology but in socially anchored linguistic systems.' In this alternate view, color systems are social constructions rather than biologically determined ones. The issue is still unresolved.

We do know that if speakers of any language are asked to identify the parts of the spectrum, they find one system of such identification much easier to manipulate than another. They find it difficult to draw a line to separate that part of the spectrum they would call *yellow* from that part they would call *orange*, or similarly to separate *blue* from *green*. That is, assigning precise borders, or marking discontinuities, between neighboring colors is neither an easy task for individuals nor one on which groups of individuals achieve a remarkable consensus. However, they do find it easy, and they do reach a better consensus, if they are required to indicate some part of the spectrum they would call *typically orange*, *typically blue*, or *typically green*. That is, they have consistent and uniform ideas about 'typical' colors. Speakers of different languages exhibit such behavior, always provided that the appropriate color terms are in their languages. As we will see in the following section, we can use this idea that people can and do classify in such a way to propose still another approach to relating language and culture.

Discussion

1. Try to account for the often reported finding that, for English at least, males usually display less ability than females in dealing with matters having to do with color, including the actual use of color terminology.

2. What are some of the more esoteric color designations you have encountered recently? Where did you find them? Who used them? What appears to be their purpose?

3. Two other naturally occurring phenomena capable of sub-division are years and days. How is each divided? Be careful since systems of division may

depend on a variety of factors: geographical, climatic, religious, academic, and so on. Note that in each case, unlike the color spectrum, there is a need to choose an arbitrary beginning (or end) point.

Prototypes

Rosch (1976) has proposed an alternative to the view that concepts are composed from sets of features which necessarily and sufficiently define instances of a concept. Rosch proposes that concepts are best viewed as prototypes: a 'bird' is not best defined by reference to a set of features that refer to such matters as wings, warm-bloodedness, and egg-laying characteristics, but rather by reference to typical instances, so that a 'prototypical bird' is something more like a robin than it is like a toucan, penguin, ostrich, or even eagle. This is the theory of *prototypes*. As we saw in the preceding section, individuals do have ideas of typical instances of colors, and these ideas are remarkably similar among various cultural groups. Such similarity in views, however, is found not only in reference to birds and colors.

A variety of experiments has shown that people do in fact classify quite consistently objects of various kinds according to what they regard as being typical instances; for example, (1) furniture, so that, whereas a chair is a typical item of furniture, an ashtray is not; (2) fruit, so that, whereas apples and plums are typical, coconuts and olives are not; and (3) clothing, so that, whereas coats and trousers are typical items, things like bracelets and purses are not (Clark and Clark, 1977, p. 464). The remarkably uniform behavior that people exhibit in such tasks cannot be accounted for by a theory which says that concepts are formed from sets of defining features. Such a theory fails to explain why some instances are consistently held to be more typical or central than others when all exhibit the same set of defining features.

Hudson (1996, pp. 75–8) believes that prototype theory has much to offer sociolinguists. He believes it leads to an easier account of how people learn to use language, particularly linguistic concepts, from the kinds of instances they come across. He says (p. 77) that:

> a prototype-based concept can be learned on the basis of a very small number of instances – perhaps a single one – and without any kind of formal definition, whereas a feature-based definition would be very much harder to learn since a much larger number of cases, plus a number of non-cases, would be needed before the learner could work out which features were necessary and which were not.

Moreover, such a view allows for a more flexible approach to understanding how people actually use language. In that usage certain concepts are necessarily 'fuzzy,' as the theory predicts they will be, but that very fuzziness allows speakers to use language creatively.

According to Hudson, prototype theory may even be applied to the social situations in which speech occurs. He suggests that, when we hear a new linguistic item, we associate with it who typically seems to use it and what, apparently, is the typical occasion of its use. Again, we need very few instances – even possibly just a single one – to be able to do this. Of course, if the particular instance is atypical and we fail to recognize this fact, we could be in for some discomfort at a later time when we treat it as typical.

Prototype theory, then, offers us a possible way of looking not only at how concepts may be formed, i.e., at the cognitive dimensions of linguistic behavior, but also at how we achieve our social competence in the use of language. We judge circumstances as being typically this or typically that, and we place people in the same way. One person appears to be a 'typical' teacher, jock, burnout, teenager, or American, etc., while another does not. We then attempt to use language appropriate to the other as we perceive him or her and to the situation we are in. As we will see in chapter 12, there is considerable merit to such an approach to attempting to understand how conversations, for example, proceed.

Discussion

1. Which of the following are most and least typical instances of the initial 'concept' (and which might you even want to exclude): 'fruit' – apple, coconut, plum, tomato, olive, strawberry, fig, banana, lemon, melon, pumpkin; 'game' – soccer, chess, golf, poker, hide-and-seek, boxing, horse-racing, baseball, skiing, snakes-and-ladders; 'profession' – stockbroker, priest, undertaker, soldier, dentist, photographer, boxer, politician, professor, lawyer; 'vegetable' – potato, carrot, pea, rhubarb, rice, spinach, watercress, tomato, mint, cabbage, beans, squash?
2. Can you give some typical instances of each of the following and some not-so-typical instances: 'breakfast,' 'war movie,' 'party,' 'lecture,' 'assignment,' 'request from a stranger for directions or for money,' and 'excuse'?
3. Can you explain how prototype theory offers some insight into why speakers occasionally say such things as 'Technically, a whale is a mammal' or 'Strictly speaking, now that he's eighteen he's an adult'?

Taboo and Euphemism

In one sense this chapter has been about 'meaning,' specifically about how cultural meanings are expressed in language. But language is used to avoid saying certain things as well as to express them. Certain things are not said, not because they cannot be, but because 'people don't talk about those things'; or, if those things are talked about, they are talked about in very roundabout ways. In the first case we have instances of linguistic *taboo*; in the second we have the employment of *euphemisms* so as to avoid mentioning certain matters directly.

Taboo is the prohibition or avoidance in any society of behavior believed to be harmful to its members in that it would cause them anxiety, embarrassment, or shame. It is an extremely strong politeness constraint. Consequently, so far as language is concerned, certain things are not to be said or certain objects can be referred to only in certain circumstances, for example, only by certain people, or through deliberate circumlocutions, i.e., euphemistically. Of course, there are always those who are prepared to break the taboos in an attempt to show their own freedom from such social constraints or to expose the taboos as irrational and unjustified, as in certain movements for 'free speech.'

Tabooed subjects can vary widely: sex; death; excretion; bodily functions; religious matters; and politics. Tabooed objects that must be avoided or used carefully can include your mother-in-law, certain game animals, and use of your left hand (the origin of *sinister*). Crowley (1992, pp. 155–6) describes how in the Kabana language of Papua New Guinea people typically have personal names that also refer to everyday objects. However, there is also a strong restriction against saying the names of one's in-laws. What happens, therefore, when you want to refer to the actual thing that your in-law is named after even though you are not using the word as a personal name? For such cases the language has a set of special words which are either words in the Kabana language itself (but with different meanings) or words copied from neighboring languages with the same meanings. For example, the Kabana word for a particular kind of fish is *urae*, so if your in-law is called Urae this fish must be referred to as *moi*, the Kabana word for 'taro'. The Kabana word for 'crocodile' is *puaea* but you cannot use this word if your in-law is called Puaea and you must refer to the crocodile as *bagale*, a borrowing from a neighboring language.

English also has its taboos, and most people who speak English know what these are and observe the 'rules.' When someone breaks the rules, that rupture may arouse considerable comment, although not perhaps quite as much today as formerly, as when Shaw's use of *bloody* in *Pygmalion* or the use of *damn* in the movie *Gone with the Wind* aroused widespread public comment. Standards and norms change. Linguistic taboos are also violated on occasion to draw attention to oneself, or to show contempt, or to be aggressive or provocative, or to mock authority – or, according to Freud, on occasion as a form of verbal seduction, e.g., 'talking dirty.' The penalty for breaking a linguistic taboo can be severe, for blasphemy and obscenity are still crimes in many jurisdictions, but it is hardly likely to cost you your life, as the violation of certain non-linguistic taboos, e.g., incest taboos, might in certain places in the world.

Haas (1951) has pointed out that certain language taboos seem to arise from bilingual situations. She cites the examples of the Creeks of Oklahoma, whose avoidance of the Creek words *fákki* 'soil,' *apíswa* 'meat,' and *apíssi* 'fat' increased as they used more and more English. A similar avoidance can sometimes be noticed among Thai students learning English in English-speaking countries. They avoid Thai words like *fag* 'sheath' and *phrig* '(chili) pepper' in the presence of anglophones because of the phonetic resemblance of these words to certain taboo English words. Thai speakers also often find it difficult to say the English words *yet* and *key* because they sound very much like the Thai words *jed*, a vulgar word for 'to have intercourse,' and *khîi* 'excrement.' In certain circumstances, personal names may even be changed as a speaker of one language finds that his or her name causes embarrassment in a different linguistic framework, e.g., the Vietnamese name *Phuc* in an anglophone group.

The late twentieth century may have seen a considerable change in regard to linguistic taboo – in the English-speaking world at least – as certain social constraints have loosened. However, that decline may have been more than matched by the marked increase in the use of euphemistic language, the 'dressing up' in language of certain areas in life to make them more presentable, more polite, and more palatable to public taste. Euphemistic words and expressions allow us to talk about unpleasant things and disguise or neutralize the unpleasantness, e.g., the subjects of sickness, death and dying, unemployment, and criminality. They also allow us to give labels to unpleasant tasks and jobs in an attempt to make them sound almost attractive. Euphemism is endemic in our society: the glorification of the commonplace and the elevation of the trivial. We are constantly renaming things and repackaging them to make them sound 'better'; we must remember that Orwell's version of the future relied heavily on characterizing the inhabitants of that future world as having fallen victim to its euphemisms, its renaming of reality to fit a new order of society. It is even possible to argue that 'politically correct' language is euphemism in a new guise.

In a series of publications Nadel (particularly 1954) has described how the Nupe of West Africa must be among the most prudish people in the world, distinguishing sharply between expressions that are suitable for polite conversation and those that are not. They constantly resort to circumlocutions and euphemisms in order to avoid direct mention of matters pertaining to parts of the body, bodily functions, sex, and so on. At the same time, however, they show an intense fascination with language and are prepared to discuss various linguistic complexities at length. It seems that they are quite aware of what they are doing when they use circumlocutions and euphemisms. As Nadel says (p. 57), 'When they employ metaphors or otherwise manipulate expressions, they are always fully aware of the semantic implications.' Apparently, the Nupe have developed indirect ways of referring to tabooed matters, ways they can employ on those occasions when it is possible to free themselves from normal constraints, e.g., in certain kinds of story-telling or on specific festive occasions.

Taboo and euphemism affect us all. We may not be as deeply conscious of the effects as are the Nupe, but affect us they do. We all probably have a few things we refuse to talk about and still others we do not talk about directly. We may have some words we know but never – or hardly ever – use because they are too emotional for either us or others. While we may find 'some thoughts too deep for words' – something hard to prove – others we definitely take care not to express at all even though we know the words, or else we express ourselves on them very indirectly. Each social group is different from every other in how it constrains linguistic behavior in this way, but constrain it in some such way it certainly does. Perhaps one linguistic universal is that no social group uses language quite uninhibitedly. If so, it would be intriguing to hypothesize why this is the case. What useful function does such inhibition serve?

Discussion

1. Death and dying is still a heavily tabooed area in Western life. Show that this is the case by finding out what words are avoided? What euphemisms do you find? Good sources of data are obituary notices and almost anything that comes from the various people whose occupation it is to arrange for the disposal of the dead.
2. All of the following expressions can be said to be euphemistic: *pest control officer*; *building engineer*; *comfort station*; *socially deviant behavior*; *seasonal adjustment in employment*; *culturally deprived children*. Try to explain why such expressions arise. Do they have any useful social function to perform? Do you know any other similar expressions?
3. Do taboo and euphemism serve any socially useful purpose? Or are they just 'relics of the Dark Ages'?
4. Is there a useful distinction to be made between 'euphemistic' language and 'politically correct' language?

Further Reading

Some basic books on language and culture are Foley (1997), Duranti (1997), Shaul and Furbee (1998), and Brenneis and Macaulay (1996). See Lucy (1992a), Lee (1996), Gumperz and Levinson (1996), and Pütz and Verspoor (2000) for more on the linguistic relativity hypothesis. A basic collection of Whorf's writings is Carroll (1956). There is an extensive literature on kinship systems, e.g., Tyler (1969); Burling (1970) provides a good brief introduction. Hudson (1996) discusses prototype theory and Blount (1995) and Tsohatzidis (1990) are useful collections of papers. Berlin and Kay (1969) is a basic source for color terminology. Taboo and euphemism are also widely discussed: Farb (1974) and Mencken (1919) are well worth consulting. See Lakoff and Johnson (1980) on metaphors we live by.

The *Journal of Linguistic Anthropology* is a useful publication.

10 Ethnographies

Speech is used in different ways among different groups of people. As we will see, each group has its own norms of linguistic behavior. A particular group may not encourage talking for the sake of talking, and members of such a group may appear to be quite taciturn to outsiders who relish talk, or they may feel overwhelmed by the demands made on them if those others insist on talking. In contrast, in another group talk may be encouraged to the extent that it may even appear to be quite disorderly to an observer who has internalized a different set of 'rules' for the conduct of talk. Listening to thunder or stones, as in the Ojibwa examples mentioned earlier (see pp. 3–4), may appear to be bizarre, even to those who 'listen to their consciences' as a matter of course. We must try to understand how different groups of people use their language (or languages) if we are to achieve a comprehensive understanding of how that language (or those languages) is related to the society that uses it. A society that encourages a wide variety of kinds of talk is likely to be rather different in many nonlinguistic ways from one in which speakers are expected neither to waste words nor to use words lightly. In this chapter, therefore, I will look at how we can talk about the various ways in which people communicate with one another, in an attempt to see what factors are involved.

However, I will also be concerned with the fact that much of that communication is directed toward keeping an individual society going; that is, an important function of communication is social maintenance. Language is used to sustain reality. Consequently, a second purpose of this chapter is to look at ways in which individuals cooperate with one another to sustain the reality of everyday life and at how they use language as one of the means to do so.

Varieties of Talk

It is instructive to look at some of the ways in which various people in the world use talk, or sometimes the absence of talk, i.e., silence, to communicate. For example, Marshall (1961) has indicated how the !Kung, a bush-dwelling people of South West Africa, have certain customs which help them either to avoid or to reduce friction and hostility within bands and between bands. The !Kung lead a very harsh life as hunters and gatherers, a life which requires a considerable amount of cooperation and the companionship of a larger group if survival is to be guaranteed. Many of the customs of the !Kung support their social need for cooperativeness and the individual need for personal acceptance. The !Kung are talkative people. Talk keeps communication open among them; it offers an emotional release; and it can also be used to alert individuals that they are stepping out of bounds, so heading off potentially dangerous conflicts between individuals.

The !Kung talk about all kinds of things, but principally about food and gift-giving. However, they avoid mentioning the names of their gods aloud, and men and women do not openly discuss sexual matters together. Such subjects are taboo. They have their own styles of joking, and story-telling, but, in the latter case, they do not 'make up' stories, finding no interest at all in that activity. They have one kind of talk to resolve disputes; another, which Marshall calls a 'shout,' to resolve the kinds of tension that arise when some sudden, dangerous event occurs, such as the burning down of a grass hut in a village; and still another, a repetitive trance-like type of speech, to indicate a feeling of some kind of deprivation concerning food. According to Marshall, speech among the !Kung helps to maintain peaceful social relationships by allowing people to keep in touch with one another about how they are thinking and feeling. It helps the !Kung to relieve their tensions, and it prevents pressures from building up and finding their release in aggression.

We can contrast the need the !Kung have to talk in order to ensure that tensions do not build up with the Western Apache view of silence (Basso, 1972). Whereas the !Kung speak to prevent uncertainty in human relationships, the Western Apache of east-central Arizona choose to be silent when there is a strong possibility that such uncertainty exists. They are silent on 'meeting strangers,' whether these are fellow Western Apache or complete outsiders; and strangers, too, are expected to be silent. The Western Apache do not easily enter into new social relationships, and silence is deemed appropriate to a new relationship, because such a relationship is felt to be inherently uncertain.

Children returning from government boarding schools are greeted with silence and the children themselves are expected to be silent. Silence is maintained until each person once again becomes accustomed to the presence of the others. When one is 'cussed out,' i.e., disciplined verbally, silence is again the appropriate response, even though the cussing out may be undeserved; the Western Apache believe that responding will make matters worse. The initial stages of courting behavior also require silence; in this case, silence is taken to be a proper indication of the shyness that is expected between two people attempting to enter into a close relationship. They regard talkativeness in such a situation, especially in the female of the pair, as immodest.

Silence is also used as a kind of sympathizing device after someone dies: you are silent in the presence of 'people who are sad,' and you should not further disturb those who are already disturbed by grief. Silence is also required during curing ceremonials if you are not to be considered disrespectful or to be interfering either with the curing process or with the person conducting the ceremonial. According to Basso, the Western Apache resort to silence when they are confronted with ambiguity and uncertainty in their social relationships: they do not try to talk their way out of difficulty or uncertainty as people with other cultural backgrounds sometimes try to do.

Silence is often communicative and its appropriate uses must be learned. Among other things it can communicate respect, comfort, support, disagreement, or uncertainty. In many societies people do not talk unless they have something important to say. As Gardner (1966) has observed, the Puliyanese of south India are neither particularly cooperative nor competitive, and individuals tend to do their own thing. They do not find much to talk about, and by the time they are 40 or so they hardly seem to talk at all. The Aritama of Colombia are described as being not only taciturn, but also, when they do speak, deliberately evasive. Several reports have recounted how Danes appreciate silence, being able to sit in one another's presence for long periods of time without feeling any need to talk and, indeed, finding visitors who insist on talking constantly too demanding. They feel no urge to fill up silences with idle chatter. In other societies, e.g., among certain aboriginal peoples in North America, an acceptable social visit is to arrive at someone's house, sit around for a while, and then leave with hardly a word spoken all the while. If you have nothing to say, you do not need to speak, and there is no obligation to make 'small talk.'

In contrast, other people talk for the sheer pleasure of talking. Fox (1974) has described how the Roti, the residents of the southwestern tip of the island of Timor in eastern Indonesia, consider talk one of the great pleasures of life – not just idle chatter, but disputing, arguing, showing off various verbal skills, and, in general, indulging in verbal activity. Silence is interpreted as a sign of some kind of distress, possibly confusion or dejection. So social encounters are talk-filled. The Bella Coola of British Columbia are said to talk constantly and to prize wittiness. Among the Araucanians of Chile the men take great pride in their oratorical skills, but women maintain silence in the presence of their husbands. Even communities located physically quite near each other can be quite different in this respect. In his *Laws*, Plato described how the Athenians were great talkers whereas the Spartans were known for their brevity and the Cretans were reputed to have more wit than words.

The social situation in Antigua in the West Indies requires another kind of indulgence in talk. Talk is expected of people. Reisman (1974, p. 113) describes what happens when someone enters a casual group:

> no opening is necessarily made for him; nor is there any pause or other formal signal that he is being included. No one appears to pay any attention. When he feels ready he will simply begin speaking. He may be heard, he may not. That is, the other voices may eventually stop and listen, or some of them may not; eyes may or may not turn to him. If he is not heard the first time he will try again, and yet again (often with the same remark). Eventually he will be heard or give up.
>
> In such a system it is also true that there is no particular reason to find out what is going on or who is talking before one starts oneself. There is little pressure to relate one's subject to any state of the group. Therefore it is also quite reasonable to arrive talking, so to speak, and the louder one does so the greater the chances that one is heard.

In Antigua a conversation is multi-faceted in that it freely mixes a variety of activities that in certain other groups would be kept quite apart. Reisman points out (p. 114) how, 'in a brief conversation with me, about three minutes, a girl called to someone on the street, made a remark to a small boy, sang a little, told a child to go to school, sang some more, told a child to go buy bread, etc., all the while continuing the thread of her conversation about her sister.' In Antigua people speak because they must assert themselves through language. They do not consider as interruptions behavior that we would consider to be either interruptive or even disruptive. Reisman says (p. 115) that in Antigua 'to enter a conversation one must assert one's presence rather than participate in something formalized as an exchange.' In a restaurant or store:

> one says aloud what one wants, nobody asks you. Neither is any sign given that your request has been heard. If you feel your request is not getting attention you may repeat it (how often depending on your character, how big a noise you like to make generally). But one must not assume in the remarks one makes that one has *not* been heard the first time or one will be rebuked. One is listened to.

Talk in Antigua is therefore quite a different kind of activity from talk in Denmark. Nor can one kind be said to be 'better' than the other. Each arises from certain needs in the society and each responds to those needs.

As a final example of another special use of languages, I can mention the importance of a certain kind of talk among the Subanun of the Philippines, who employ certain kinds of speech in drinking encounters. Such encounters are very important for gaining prestige and for resolving disputes. Frake (1964) has described how talk, what he calls 'drinking talk,' proceeds in such encounters, from the initial invitation to partake of drink, to the selection of the proper topics for discussion and problems for resolution as drinking proceeds competitively, and finally to the displays of verbal art that accompany heavy, 'successful' drinking. Each of these stages has its own characteristics. Those who are the most accomplished at drinking talk become the *de facto* leaders among the Subanun because successful talk during drinking may be used to claim or assert social leadership. It gives one a certain right to manipulate others, because it is during such talk that important disputes are settled, e.g., disputes which in other societies would have to be settled in the courts. Drinking talk among the Subanun is therefore far removed from 'cocktail party chatter,' as many Westerners know the latter: it is serious business.

I have used these various examples to provide some insight into how speech, or talk, is used in certain societies very differently from the ways we might be accustomed to hearing it used. Those ways, of course, derive entirely from the norms we have internalized or from others with which we have become familiar. We should be prepared to acknowledge that some of our own uses of language would undoubtedly strike a !Kung, a Western Apache, an Antiguan, or a Subanun as strange, if not bizarre. Just think how often we talk about the weather but to no consequence! What we need is some kind of general scheme, or framework, to help us make systematic observations about the different ways people use talk. In the next section we will consider such a framework.

Discussion

1. From what I have said about the various peoples just mentioned, e.g., the Rotinese, Western Apache, !Kung, Antiguans, and so on, we might predict that children learn different ways of speaking in different societies. Samarin reports (1969, p. 323) that, among the Gbeya of the Central African Republic:

    > Gbeya parents and other adults focus little attention on the speech of children. No serious attempt is made to improve their language. In fact, a child only uncommonly takes part in a dyadic speech event with an adult. . . . Among the Gbeya, 'children are seen and not heard.' Finally, there appears to be very little interest in reporting how a person speaks, particularly when psychological motivations are implied.

    We can contrast this kind of upbringing with the Anang of Nigeria (Messenger, 1960, p. 229):

    > The Anang take great pride in their eloquence, and youth are trained from early childhood to develop verbal skills. This proverb riddle instructs young people to assume adult duties and responsibilities as early as possible, even if doing so is difficult and unpleasant at times. As the vine must struggle to escape growing into the pit [the riddle], so must the child strive to overcome his shyness and insecurity and learn to speak publicly, as well as perform other adult roles.

    How would you describe your own linguistic upbringing in similar terms? Do you know others who have had a different kind of upbringing? Are there any social or cognitive consequences to 'the way one learns to speak' in this broad sense?
2. Is there any justification for the claim that different ethnic and social groups in society sometimes exhibit quite different ways of speaking, even that a bilingual person may sometimes behave quite differently, depending on which language he or she is using? If there are such differences, are there any consequences for that society as a whole?
3. In some speech communities there are special occasions and special places for certain kinds of speech. Bauman (1972, pp. 340–1) has described such a special place, the local store, for people in a community in Nova Scotia:

    > What is apparently going on in the culture of the La Have Islanders is that, within the whole range of speech situations making up the speech economy of the islanders, the session at the store is singled out as special, isolated from the others and enjoyed for its own sake, because talking there may be enjoyed for its own sake and not as a part of another activity or for some instrumental purpose. In other words, the fact that this situation is set aside for sociability, pure and simple, makes it special.

    Do you know of any equivalent occasions or places within your own social group? Or any occasions or places in which 'normal rules' are suspended?

4. The Subanun have prescribed rituals they follow for correct 'drinking' behavior. What rituals do we observe when we dine out, e.g., at an elegant restaurant or at a formal banquet?
5. Exchanging greetings with others seems to be an unremarkable activity. However, once you begin to ask questions about what is happening you discover that it may not be so unremarkable after all. Why speak at all? When do you greet others? Who do you greet? Who speaks first? What can (and cannot) be said? What else is involved in an exchange of greetings?

The Ethnography of Speaking

Hymes (1974) has proposed an ethnographic framework which takes into account the various factors that are involved in speaking. An *ethnography* of a communicative event is a description of all the factors that are relevant in understanding how that particular communicative event achieves its objectives. For convenience, Hymes uses the word SPEAKING as an acronym for the various factors he deems to be relevant. We will now consider these factors one by one.

The *Setting* and *Scene* (S) of speech are important. Setting refers to the time and place, i.e., the concrete physical circumstances in which speech takes place. Scene refers to the abstract psychological setting, or the cultural definition of the occasion. The Queen's Christmas message has its own unique setting and scene, as has the President of the United States' annual State of the Union Address. A particular bit of speech may actually serve to define a scene, whereas another bit of speech may be deemed to be quite inappropriate in certain circumstances. Within a particular setting, of course, participants are free to change scenes, as they change the level of formality (e.g., go from serious to joyful) or as they change the kind of activity in which they are involved (e.g., begin to drink or to recite poetry).

The *Participants* (P) include various combinations of speaker–listener, addressor–addressee, or sender–receiver. They generally fill certain socially specified roles. A two-person conversation involves a speaker and hearer whose roles change; a 'dressing down' involves a speaker and hearer with no role change; a political speech involves an addressor and addressees (the audience); and a telephone message involves a sender and a receiver. A prayer obviously makes a deity a participant. In a classroom a teacher's question and a student's response involve not just those two as speaker and listener but also the rest of the class as audience, since they too are expected to benefit from the exchange.

Ends (E) refers to the conventionally recognized and expected outcomes of an exchange as well as to the personal goals that participants seek to accomplish on particular occasions. A trial in a courtroom has a recognizable social end in view, but the various participants, i.e., the judge, jury, prosecution, defense, accused, and witnesses, have different personal goals. Likewise, a marriage ceremony serves a certain social end, but each of the various participants may have his or her own unique goals in getting married or in seeing a particular couple married.

Act sequence (A) refers to the actual form and content of what is said: the precise words used, how they are used, and the relationship of what is said to the actual topic at hand. This is one aspect of speaking in which linguists have long shown an interest, particularly those who study discourse and conversation, and it is one about which I will have more to say in chapter 12. Others too, e.g., psychologists and communication theorists concerned with content analysis, have shown a similar interest. Public lectures, casual conversations, and cocktail party chatter are all different forms of speaking; with each go different kinds of language and things talked about.

Key (K), the fifth term, refers to the tone, manner, or spirit in which a particular message is conveyed: light-hearted, serious, precise, pedantic, mocking, sarcastic, pompous, and so on. The key may also be marked nonverbally by certain kinds of behavior, gesture, posture, or even deportment. When there is a lack of fit between what a person is actually saying and the key that the person is using, listeners are likely to pay more attention to the key than to the actual content, e.g., to the burlesque of a ritual rather than to the ritual itself.

Instrumentalities (I) refers to the choice of channel, e.g., oral, written, or telegraphic, and to the actual forms of speech employed, such as the language, dialect, code, or register that is chosen. Formal, written, legal language is one instrumentality; spoken Newfoundland English is another; code-switching between English and Italian in Toronto is a third; and the use of Pig Latin is still another. In Suriname a high government official addresses a Bush Negro chief in Dutch and has his words translated into the local tribal language. The chief does the opposite. Each speaks this way although both could use a common instrumentality, Sranan. You may employ different instrumentalities in the course of a single verbal exchange of some length: first read something, then tell a dialect joke, then quote Shakespeare, then use an expression from another language, and so on. You also need not necessarily change topic to do any of these.

Norms of interaction and interpretation (N) refers to the specific behaviors and properties that attach to speaking and also to how these may be viewed by someone who does not share them, e.g., loudness, silence, gaze return, and so on. For example, there are certain norms of interaction with regard to church services and conversing with strangers. However, these norms may vary from social group to social group, so the kind of behavior expected in congregations that practice 'talking in tongues' or the group encouragement of a preacher in others would be deemed abnormal and unacceptable in a 'high' Anglican setting. Likewise, an Arab and an Anglo-Saxon meeting for the first time are unlikely to find a conversational distance that each finds comfortable.

Genre (G), the final term, refers to clearly demarcated types of utterance; such things as poems, proverbs, riddles, sermons, prayers, lectures, and editorials. These are all marked in specific ways in contrast to casual speech. Of course, in the middle of a prayer, a casual aside would be marked too. While particular genres seem more appropriate on certain occasions than on others, e.g., sermons inserted into church services, they can be independent: we can ask someone to stop 'sermonizing'; that is, we can recognize a genre of sermons when an instance of it, or something closely resembling an instance, occurs outside its usual setting.

What Hymes offers us in his SPEAKING formula is a very necessary reminder that talk is a complex activity, and that any particular bit of talk is actually a piece of 'skilled work.' It is skilled in the sense that, if it is to be successful, the speaker must reveal a sensitivity to and awareness of each of the eight factors outlined above. Speakers and listeners must also work to see that nothing goes wrong. When speaking does go wrong, as it sometimes does, that going-wrong is often clearly describable in terms of some neglect of one or more of the factors. Since we acknowledge that there are 'better' speakers and 'poorer' speakers, we may also assume that individuals vary in their ability to manage and exploit the total array of factors.

Ethnographies are based on first-hand observations of behavior in a group of people in their natural setting. Investigators report on what they see and hear as they observe what is going on around them. As Duranti (1997, p. 85) says, 'an ethnography is the written description of the social organization, social activities, symbolic and material resources, and interpretive practices characteristic of a particular group of people.' Ethnographers ask themselves what is happening and they try to provide accounts which show how the behavior that is being observed makes sense within the community that is being observed. As Johnstone (2004, p. 76) says, ethnography 'presupposes . . . that the best explanations of human behavior are particular and culturally relative' rather than general and universal. Such studies are also qualitative rather than quantitative. In ethnographies of speaking the focus is on the language the participants are using and the cultural practices such language reflects. They very often deal with issues of identity and power.

Three illustrative book-length ethnographic studies are those of Sherzer (1983), Hill and Hill (1986), and Lindenfeld (1990). Sherzer describes how the Kuna of Panama use language: their public language of the gathering house, and their use of language in curing and music, in rites and festivities, and in everyday conversation. He points out that the Kuna wait very patiently to take their turns in speaking so that interruptions and overlaps in conversation are rare events. Hill and Hill describe how the Malinche of Central Mexico use language in their daily lives and continuing struggle, and Lindenfeld offers an account of the language of a dozen long-standing urban marketplaces in Paris, Rouen, and Grenoble: the talk of vendors, vendor–customer talk, politeness routines, small talk, jokes, insults, etc. She shows how such talk helps to sustain the markets as places where goods are bought and sold while at the same time allowing people to associate with one another, an important function in an increasingly urbanizing society in which interpersonal relationships appear to be difficult to maintain.

Hazen's (2002) study of speech in Warren County, North Carolina, required a year and a half of residence in the community as well as visits over a seven-year period. This participation in the community enabled Hazen to look closely at factors affecting the cultural identity of residents and their expression of that identity through linguistic choices. He looked at three local groups (African Americans, European Americans, and Native Americans) and whether speakers identified only with Warren County or with both Warren County and areas outside the county. He called this their cultural identity. Hazen concludes that while 'linguistic variation in Warren County correlates with several categories, including gender, age, and ethnicity... the cultural identity of speakers should be considered for both large-scale studies of social factors and more ethnographic studies of individual speakers' (p. 253). Cultural identity – a qualitative factor – turned out to be the one that most clearly accounted for the linguistic behaviors that Hazen observed. (The studies by Gal (see pp. 205–6), the Milroys (pp. 181–3), Eckert (p. 212), Kiesling (p. 177), and Marshall (p. 211) also have major ethnographic components.)

An alternative approach to devising ethnographies is to attempt to describe the different functions of language in communication. Various linguists have proposed different categorizations of the functions of language, e.g., Jakobson (1960), Halliday (1973), and Robinson (1972). Halliday's list covers the following functions: instrumental (satisfying some material need); regulatory (regulating the behavior of people); interactional (maintaining social relationships); personal (expressing personality); heuristic (investigating the environment); imaginative (playing and creating); and representational (expressing propositions). Robinson's list (pp. 50–1) covers many of the same functions but names them differently and, of course, divides them differently: avoidance, conformity to norms, aesthetics, encounter regulation, performative, regulation (of self and others), affective, marking of emitter (e.g., emotional state, personality, or identity), role relationship marking, referential, instruction, inquiry, and metalanguage functions.

What is clear from any such list is that there is more to understanding how language is used than describing the syntactic composition of sentences or specifying their propositional content. When you learn to use a language, you learn how to use it in order to do certain things that people do with that language. The term *communicative competence* is sometimes used to describe this kind of ability. Gumperz (1972, p. 205) explains that term as follows: 'Whereas linguistic competence covers the speaker's ability to produce grammatically correct sentences, communicative competence describes his ability to select, from the totality of grammatically correct expressions available to him, forms which appropriately reflect the social norms governing behavior in specific encounters.'

Working with an ethnographic or functional approach, we may attempt to specify just what it means to be a competent speaker of a particular language. It is one thing to learn the language of the Subanun, but quite another to learn how to ask for a drink in Subanun. To do the first you need a certain linguistic competence; to do the latter you need communicative competence. As Saville-Troike (1996, p. 363) says:

> Communicative competence extends to both knowledge and expectation of who may or may not speak in certain settings, when to speak and when to remain silent, whom one may speak to, how one may talk to persons of different statuses and roles, what nonverbal behaviors are appropriate in various contexts, what the routines for turn-taking are in conversation, how to ask for and give information, how to request, how to offer or decline assistance or cooperation, how to give commands, how to enforce discipline, and the like – in short, everything involving the use of language and other communicative dimensions in particular social settings.

Hymes (1972, p. 279) has argued that, in learning a language, children must learn not only how to construct sentences in that language but also must 'acquire knowledge of a set of ways in which sentences are used. From a finite experience of speech acts and their interdependence with sociocultural features, they develop a general theory of the speaking appropriate in their community, which they employ, like other forms of tacit cultural knowledge (competence), in conducting and interpreting social life.' Hymes provides some examples of the kinds of learning that are involved:

> They come to be able to recognize, for example, appropriate and inappropriate interrogative behavior (e.g., among the Araucanians of Chile, that to repeat a question is to insult; among the Tzeltal of Chiapas, Mexico, that a direct question is not properly asked (and to be answered 'nothing'); among the Cahinahua of Brazil, that a direct answer to a first question implies that the answerer has not time to talk, a vague answer, that the question will be answered directly the second time, and that talk can continue).

Another often-cited example is the different ways in which American and Japanese children are indoctrinated into appropriate language use (see Tobin et al., 1989). In contrast to the American encouragement of individual assertiveness the Japanese favor developing social awareness and 'harmony.' A misbehaving Japanese child will be told *hito ni warawareru* 'you'll be laughed at by others' and instructed in polite ways of declining and, especially, of avoiding categorical refusals. Such behavior is appropriate within Japanese culture and it is learned very early in life.

In learning to speak we are also learning to 'talk,' in the sense of communicating in those ways appropriate to the group in which we are doing that learning. These ways differ from group to group; consequently, as we move from one group to another or from one language to another, we must learn the new ways if we are to fit into that new group or to use that new language properly. Communicative competence is therefore a key component of social competence.

Discussion

1. Explain how considerations of *when* and *how* are deeply involved in doing each of the following: giving bad news; asking for a date (or a loan); leaving a party rather early; changing your mind about something important; and breaking off a relationship.
2. Part of the deliberate instruction we give to children about language is instruction in when and how it is appropriate to speak and when you should not speak at all: e.g., 'Don't talk to strangers'; 'Say "Thank you"'; and 'Keep your voice down.' Find some other examples.
3. Question-and-answer behavior is not as simple as it might appear to be. When are indirect questions preferred to direct ones, and vice versa? Must you always answer a question? Can you insist on the answer? When is it appropriate to ask for an answer to be repeated or for you to repeat another's

answer? Are some questions not meant to be answered at all and to be entirely rhetorical? If so, what are these like? How do you recognize them as such? How does the situation control the possibilities that exist for questioning?

4. Your opportunity to respond positively, critically, or even at all to the speech of others is governed by circumstances. Are responses appropriate, and, if so, in what way, in the following circumstances: a judge's pre-sentencing remarks to someone who has just been convicted; a parent's 'dressing down' of a child; a preacher's sermon to a congregation; a politician's speech while electioneering; a pupil's reading aloud to a class; cheerleaders' calls to spectators; and a prime minister's or president's address to the nation to someone watching that address on television?

5. Attempt to specify the essential defining characteristics of each of the following bits of behavior, focusing specifically on the linguistic characteristics: gossiping; heckling; making a speech; giving a poetry reading; passing the time of day; refereeing; debating; and preaching.

Ethnomethodology

While it is possible to investigate talk, the various factors that enter into it, and the variety of its functions, and make many sound observations, this does not by any means exhaust all we might want to say on the subject. As indicated at the beginning of the chapter, talk itself is also used to sustain reality and is itself part of that reality. We can therefore look at talk as a phenomenon in its own right. *Ethnomethodology* is that branch of sociology which is concerned, among other things, with talk viewed in this way.

Ethnomethodologists are interested in the processes and techniques that people use to interpret the world around them and to interact with that world. They are interested in trying to discover the categories and systems that people use in making sense of the world. Therefore, they do not conduct large-scale surveys of populations, devise sophisticated theoretical models of social organization, or hypothesize that some social theory or other will adequately explain social organization. Instead, they focus on the phenomena of everyday existence, actually on various bits and pieces of it, in an attempt to show how those who must deal with such bits and pieces go about doing so. As Leiter (1980, p. 5) states, 'the aim of ethnomethodology . . . is to study the processes of sense making (idealizing and formulizing) that members of society . . . use to construct the social world and its factual properties (its sense of being ready-made and independent of perception).' Another view is that of Fairclough (1989, p. 9):

> Ethnomethodologists investigate the production and interpretation of everyday action as skilled accomplishments of social factors, and they are interested in conversation as one particularly pervasive instance of skilled social action.

Ethnomethodologists are interested in such matters as how people interact, solve common problems, maintain social contacts, perform routine activities, and show that they know what is going on around them and communicate that knowledge to others.

We can use a simple linguistic example to show that we cannot hope to understand others if we do not share certain background assumptions with those others. Only when there is such sharing is communication possible. In unpublished work, Sacks gives the following example of a two-sentence sequence to illustrate this point: 'The baby cried. The mommy picked it up.' How do we understand these two sentences from a child? How do they communicate? We understand that *mommy* in the second sentence refers to the mother of *baby* in the first, but there is nothing in the structure of the sentences themselves to tell us this. All we have is a connection between *baby* and *mommy* achieved through mention in successive sentences. Sacks claims that in such cases there are what he calls *membership categorization devices* which allow us to assign certain meanings to words like *baby* and *mommy*. In this case, we put the words into a set like *baby, mommy, daddy* rather than one like *baby, child, adult*; consequently, we understand that it is the baby's mother who is involved in the second sentence.

Note that we interpret the following relationship quite differently: 'The baby cried. The adult picked it up.' One assumption we apparently share with others who use such sentences (and with the child who used the original pair) is that the world is ordered in such a way that there are certain categories of relationships that are expressed through language. To interpret particular sentences or sets of sentences, we must have some knowledge of the categories that speakers find relevant (Sacks, 1972a, 1972b). This knowledge of membership categorization devices is socially acquired. It is also the kind of knowledge in which ethnomethodologists are interested.

We constantly use such categorizations. They are not unlike labels such as 'jocks' and 'burnouts' discussed earlier (p. 212) except that they tend to be covert rather than overt. We constantly label people, places, and events around us and come to rely on such labels to help us deal with what is going on. Such labeling systems must be learned. What exactly is a 'jock,' a 'convenience store,' a 'rave'? 'Correct' labeling enables us to negotiate our way in society; 'incorrect' labeling is likely to lead to misunderstanding or possibly even to psychiatric care. If X is indeed a jock and you have correctly identified him as such, you have some idea of what to expect of each other. Misidentification in either direction is likely to produce disorder. If both parties know what a convenience store is and how people usually ask for and give directions, you may be directed to the nearest one. A late-night rave may be more difficult to find since it is both a less widely known category and one often transient as to location.

Ethnomethodologists adopt what is called a phenomenological view of the world; that is, the world is something that people must constantly keep creating and sustaining for themselves. In this view, language plays a very significant role in that creating and sustaining. Ethnomethodologists regard 'meaning' and 'meaningful activity' as something people accomplish when they interact socially. They focus on what people must do to make sense of the world around them, and not on what scientists do in trying to explain natural phenomena. Since much of human interaction is actually verbal interaction, they have focused much of their attention on how people use language in their relationships to one another. They have also focused on how in that use of language people employ what ethnomethodologists call *commonsense knowledge* and *practical reasoning*.

Commonsense knowledge refers to a variety of things. It is the understandings, recipes, maxims, and definitions that we employ in daily living as we go about doing things, e.g., knowing that thunder usually accompanies lightning; knowing how houses are usually laid out and lived in; knowing how to make a telephone call; knowing that bus drivers do not take cheques; knowing that there are 'types' of people, objects, and events, e.g., students and professors, classrooms and libraries, and lectures and laboratory sessions. These types help us to classify and categorize what is 'out there' and guide us in interpreting what happens out there. This stock of commonsense knowledge is acquired through experience; but since each person's experience is different from that of everyone else, the knowledge varies from person to person. We also know that it varies, and that some people know more about certain things and others less. The stock itself is not systematic; in fact, it is quite heterogeneous, and often parts of it are inconsistent with other parts – at times even contradictory – but that fact does not usually prove very bothersome to most individuals. In particular circumstances, we draw on the bits and pieces that seem useful; in other circumstances, we look elsewhere in the stock for help and guidance.

Commonsense knowledge also tells us that the world exists as a factual object. There is a world 'out there' independent of our particular existence; moreover, it is a world which others as well as ourselves experience, and we all experience it in much the same way. That world is also a consistent world. Situations and events in it not only occur, they re-occur. Things do not change much from day to day. Knowledge acquired yesterday and the day before is still valid today and will be valid tomorrow. We can take that world for granted, for our experience tells us it is there and so apparently does the experience of others. Philosophers may question that reality, and psychologists may wonder how we can ever make contact with what may be out there, but our experience of ordinary living raises none of the same doubts in us. However, at any one time only bits and pieces of what is out there are relevant to our immediate concerns. We are not required to deal with everything all at once; rather, we must ignore what is irrelevant and focus on what is immediately at issue.

Practical reasoning refers to the way in which people make use of their commonsense knowledge and to how they employ that knowledge in their conduct of everyday life: what they assume; what they never question; how they select matters to deal with; and how they make the various bits and pieces of commonsense knowledge fit together in social encounters so as to maintain 'normal' appearances. It is quite different from logical thinking or the formation and testing of scientific hypotheses, both of which we usually learn in formal settings and have very specialized goals.

As I have just observed, practical reasoning is not the same kind of thing as scientific reasoning. People do not think through the problems of everyday life the same way that trained scientists go about solving problems. Scribner (1977), for example, surveyed a number of pieces of research that looked at how people in different parts of the world reason. Evidently, people with very little or no formal education rely entirely on their own experience in solving problems and do not, or cannot, employ 'logical' thinking. For example, a number of people in a rural tribe in Liberia in West Africa were presented with the following problem:

> All people who own houses pay a house tax.
> Boima does not pay a house tax.
> Does Boima own a house?

The problem proved too difficult for many of the people asked, or, if they did manage to solve it, they could not explain their reasoning. If they said, for example, that Boima did not own a house, they might offer the explanation that it was because he was too poor to pay a house tax. This is not, of course, how the above logical problem works, but is instead a practical commonsense interpretation of the material contained within it *and* of the people's own experience with house-owning and taxes, that is, with the realities of daily living.

In an interesting series of studies, Garfinkel (1972) showed how we conduct our everyday existence in ways that clearly demonstrate how we do not question the kinds of assumptions mentioned above. He did this by creating situations in which his subjects, in this case his students, were not allowed to take certain things for granted; rather, they were required to violate or to question matters which they would normally accept 'routinely.' Needless to say, language was involved in every case.

For example, Garfinkel asked his students to report a conversation and state how the participants understood what they were talking about. To do so, it was necessary not only to interpret what was actually said but also to contrast the said with the unsaid, i.e., that which was implied or that which could possibly be inferred, and to make hypotheses about how the various bits and pieces of the conversation fitted together as they did. Each party necessarily had to know a lot about the other party, about the topic, and about the kind of exchange the conversation was; each also had to tolerate considerable inexplicitness in what was actually said. For example, in part of one reported conversation between a husband and wife, the wife's question, 'Did you take him [our son] to the record store?' leads to the following exchange with her husband (p. 4), with the words actually spoken on the left and the husband's interpretation of these words given on the right:

Husband:	No, to the shoe repair shop.	No, I stopped at the record store on the way to get him and stopped at the shoe repair shop on the way home when he was with me.
Wife:	What for?	I know of one reason why you might have stopped at the shoe repair shop. Why did you in fact?
Husband:	I got some new shoe laces for my shoes.	As you will remember, I broke a shoe lace on one of my brown oxfords the other day, so I stopped to get some new laces.

| Wife: | Your loafers need new heels badly. | Something else you could have gotten that I was thinking of. You could have taken in your black loafers which need heels badly. You'd better get them taken care of pretty soon. |

Garfinkel points out that in such exchanges matters not mentioned or only partially mentioned are still understood, that understanding itself develops as the conversation develops, and that understanding depends on the willingness of each party to work with the other to develop a common scheme of interpretation for what is being talked about. There is common agreement that we have to 'make sense' of what we hear. The shared assumption is that the participants are engaged in a 'normal' social interaction; that assumption will hold until they find very strong contradictory evidence.

When subjects were asked to take part in conversations and to insist that others clarify casual remarks made in those circumstances, the usual reaction of those others was one of either suspicion or hostility. Garfinkel cites (pp. 6–7) two cases that show these consequences quite clearly:

Case 1

S: Hi, Ray. How is your girl friend feeling?
E: What do you mean, how is she feeling? Do you mean physical or mental?
S: I mean how is she feeling? What's the matter with you? (He looked peeved.)
E: Nothing. Just explain a little clearer what do you mean?
S: Skip it. How are your Med School applications coming?
E: What do you mean. How are they?
S: You know what I mean.
E: I really don't.
S: What's the matter with you? Are you sick?

Case 2

On Friday night my husband and I were watching television. My husband remarked that he was tired. I asked, 'How are you tired? Physically, mentally, or just bored?'

S: I don't know, I guess physically, mainly.
E: You mean that your muscles ache, or your bones?
S: I guess so. Don't be so technical.
     (*After more watching.*)
S: All these old movies have the same kind of old iron bedstead in them.
E: What do you mean? Do you mean all old movies, or some of them, or just the ones you have seen?
S: What's the matter with you? You know what I mean.
E: I wish you would be more specific.
S: You know what I mean! Drop dead!

Apparently, conversation proceeds on the assumption that a certain vagueness is normal, that ordinary talk does not require precision, and that many expressions that are used in conversation are not to be taken literally. This vague, imprecise, and non-literal nature of ordinary talk is deemed to be entirely reasonable, and for someone to question it is to act unreasonably.

Garfinkel demonstrated this same non-literal quality in still another set of situations in which subjects were asked to question things they normally did not question, that is, to refuse to accept either 'ordinary' appearances or 'ordinary' uses. In this case, they were asked to behave as though the other person or persons had hidden motives; they were to seek these out and, to that extent, be distrustful of others. This was not an easy task, because students found it difficult to sustain and carry through this distrustful attitude. One student asked a bus driver constantly for reassurances that the bus would pass a certain street and received the following rebuke: 'Look lady, I told you once, didn't I? How many times do I have to tell you!' (p. 13).

In still another task, students were asked to perform as 'cultural dopes,' i.e., to behave as if they were not aware of the social rules that pertained to specific situations; for example, they were asked to try to bargain for standard-priced merchandise. In this case, the greatest problem was that of making the initial move; since you do not bargain for such merchandise, it is difficult to begin the bargaining process because it involves violating a rule of normative behavior. What many students found, though, was that, once this norm was violated, it was possible to bargain in many cases, and that the actual bargaining could be both enjoyable and rewarding (p. 25).

What is apparent from these various reports is that much of what we take for granted in our dealings with others depends on our accepting the appearances those others try to project. In other words, we accept the world for what it is, and most of what we hear we accept in good faith, and what we doubt we may find hard to confront openly. We accept certain norms; we realize that these vary from occasion to occasion so that different ones may apply in specific instances, but norms do apply. It is our job to find or negotiate the ones appropriate to an occasion – in fact, it is everyone's job!

Ethnomethodologists have found that naturally occurring conversations provide them with some of their most interesting data. Such conversations show how individuals achieve common purposes by doing and saying certain things and not doing and saying others. They obey certain rules of cooperation, trust, turn-taking, and so on, and they usually do not confront others openly, doubt them, insist they be always 'logical,' or refuse to do their own part in 'sustaining reality.' I will have more to say on such matters in chapter 12. For the moment it suffices to say that people use language not only to communicate in a variety of ways, but also to create a sense of order in everyday life.

Discussion

1. Ethnomethodology is concerned with 'cultural know-how,' i.e., with what people must know in order to survive in a culture. Explain what kinds of 'know-how' are involved in each of the following situations: being a student

or teacher in a classroom; buying an automobile; attending a wedding reception or a funeral; declining an invitation; acting 'absentmindedly'; flirting. Focus specifically on the linguistic aspects of this 'know-how.'

2. We all have a sense of the 'usual' and the 'normal' against which we judge the 'unusual' and the 'abnormal.' What might mark each of the following as 'unusual' or 'abnormal': bad service in a restaurant; a bad day at the office; strange behavior on the street; 'What's up with Fred today?'; avant-garde theater?

3. Teachers and students must cooperate to sustain the 'reality' of the classroom. What are some of the ways in which a teacher and a class that you know cooperate? What particular patterns of behavior and types of language recur? If you have noticed any violations, how can these be described in terms of these recurrent patterns, i.e., what norms were violated?

4. Gumperz (1972, p. 218) recounts the following joke originally told by a black student to Gumperz's colleague, Alan Dundes:

    > Governor W. died and went to heaven. When he knocked on the door, a voice answered: 'Who dat?' He said, 'Never mind, I'll go to the other place.'

    Use whatever cultural 'know-how' you have to explain how this joke works.

5. One kind of cultural 'know-how' we assume that others have is a store of knowledge about people and places in the world, e.g., the Pope, J. F. Kennedy, the Beatles, Napoleon, Grand Central Station, Paris, Hyde Park, and so on. Of course, we assume that different people have different stores. Do you remember any incidents in which you drew on what you thought was a common store of knowledge only to find that the other person did not know what you were talking about? Have you ever been surprised to find a large common store? Why is communication so much easier in the latter case?

6. Find some examples of linguistic 'know-how,' i.e., of things which it is apparently appropriate to say on specific occasions; for example, 'Excuse me, do you have a light?' or 'I'm sorry to hear that.' What were some completely inappropriate remarks that you either heard or used? Why were they inappropriate?

7. What kinds of cultural and linguistic 'know-how' are necessary to do each of the following:

    a. to telephone a movie theater to ask someone there if a parcel you left has been retrieved?
    b. to get a malfunctioning household appliance fixed?
    c. to get a day off work (i) to go to the races, (ii) to go to a funeral, or (iii) to go for an interview for a position with a rival firm?
    d. to find out as much as you can about the English poet Isaac Rosenberg (1890–1918)?

Further Reading

Johnstone (2000) provides an excellent introduction to the research methods of non-quantitative sociolinguistics. Agar (1996) is a useful introduction to ethnography, and Saville-Troike (1989, 1996) are respectively book- and article-length introductions to the ethnography of communication. Philipsen and Carbaugh (1986) is a useful bibliography of ethnographic studies.

Basic books on ethnomethodology are Heritage (1984), Leiter (1980), and Turner (1974). Cicourel (1973) provides another perspective. Button (1991), Garfinkel (1967), Psathas (1979), and Sudnow (1972) are collections of articles.

See Lepper (2000) for a discussion of categorization.

11 Solidarity and Politeness

When we speak, we must constantly make choices of many different kinds: what we want to say, how we want to say it, and the specific sentence types, words, and sounds that best unite the *what* with the *how*. How we say something is at least as important as what we say; in fact, the content and the form are quite inseparable, being but two facets of the same object. One way of looking at this relationship is to examine a few specific aspects of communication: namely, pronominal choice between *tu* and *vous* forms in languages that require a choice; the use of naming and address terms; and the employment of politeness markers. In each case we will see that certain linguistic choices a speaker makes indicate the social relationship that the speaker perceives to exist between him or her and the listener or listeners. Moreover, in many cases it is impossible to avoid making such choices in the actual 'packaging' of messages. We will also see that languages vary considerably in this respect, at least in regard to those aspects we will examine.

Tu and *Vous*

Many languages have a distinction corresponding to the *tu–vous* (T/V) distinction in French, where grammatically there is a 'singular you' *tu* (T) and a 'plural you' *vous* (V) but usage requires that you use *vous* with individuals on certain occasions. The T form is sometimes described as the 'familiar' form and the V form as the 'polite' one. Other languages with a similar T/V distinction are Latin (*tu/vos*), Russian (*ty/vy*), Italian (*tu/Lei*), German (*du/Sie*), Swedish (*du/ni*), and Greek (*esi/esis*). English, itself, once had such a distinction, the *thou/you* distinction.

According to Brown and Gilman (1960), the T/V distinction began as a genuine difference between singular and plural. However, a complication arose, which they explain as follows (p. 25):

> In the Latin of antiquity there was only *tu* in the singular. The plural *vos* as a form of address to one person was first directed to the emperor, and there are several theories . . . about how this may have come about. The use of the plural to the

emperor began in the fourth century. By that time there were actually two emperors; the ruler of the eastern empire had his seat in Constantinople and the ruler of the west sat in Rome. Because of Diocletian's reforms the imperial office, although vested in two men, was administratively unified. Words addressed to one man were, by implication, addressed to both. The choice of *vos* as a form of address may have been in response to this implicit plurality. An emperor is also plural in another sense; he is the summation of his people and can speak as their representative. Royal persons sometimes say 'we' where an ordinary man would say 'I.' The Roman emperor sometimes spoke of himself as *nos*, and the reverential *vos* is the simple reciprocal of this.

The consequence of this usage was that by medieval times the upper classes apparently began to use V forms with each other to show mutual respect and politeness. However, T forms persisted, so that the upper classes used mutual V, the lower classes used mutual T, and the upper classes addressed the lower classes with T but received V. This latter asymmetrical T/V usage therefore came to symbolize a power relationship. It was extended to such situations as people to animals, master or mistress to servants, parents to children, priest to penitent, officer to soldier, and even God to angels, with, in each case, the first mentioned giving T but receiving V.

Symmetrical V usage became 'polite' usage. This polite usage spread downward in society, but not all the way down, so that in certain classes, but never the lowest, it became expected between husband and wife, parents and children, and lovers. Symmetrical T usage was always available to show intimacy, and its use for that purpose also spread to situations in which two people agreed they had strong common interests, i.e., a feeling of solidarity. This mutual T for solidarity gradually came to replace the mutual V of politeness, since solidarity is often more important than politeness in personal relationships. Moreover, the use of the asymmetrical T/V to express power decreased and mutual V was often used in its place, as between officer and soldier. Today we can still find asymmetrical T/V uses, but solidarity has tended to replace power, so that now mutual T is found quite often in relationships which previously had asymmetrical usage, e.g., father and son, and employer and employee. Brown and Gilman's study of how upper-class French, German, and Italian youth described their use of T/V forms clearly indicates the importance of solidarity over power. They observe as follows (pp. 263–4):

> The many particular differences among the three languages are susceptible of a general characterization. Let us first contrast German and French. The German T is more reliably applied within the family than is the French T; in addition to the significantly higher T scores for grandfather and elder brother's wife, there are smaller differences showing a higher score for the German T on father, mother, wife, married elder brother, and remote male cousin. The French T is not automatically applied to remote relatives, but it is more likely than the German pronoun to be used to express the camaraderie of fellow students, fellow clerks, fellow countrymen abroad, and fellow soldiers. In general it may be said that the solidarity coded by the German T is an ascribed solidarity of family relationships. The French T, in greater degree, codes an acquired solidarity, not founded on family relationships but developing out of some sort of shared fate. As for the Italian T,

it very nearly equals the German in family solidarity and it surpasses the French in camaraderie. The camaraderie of the Italian male, incidentally, is extended to the Italian female; unlike the French or German student, the Italian says T to the co-ed almost as readily as to the male fellow student.

Because solidarity is so important, it sometimes falls on one party to initiate the use of T. Brown and Gilman explain how such a change may be initiated, i.e., the change from asymmetrical T/V or polite V/V to mutual T (p. 260):

> There is an interesting residual of the power relation in the contemporary notion that the right to initiate the reciprocal T belongs to the member of the dyad having the better power-based claim to say T without reciprocation. The suggestion that solidarity be recognized comes more gracefully from the elder than from the younger, from the richer than from the poorer, from the employer than from the employee, from the noble than from the commoner, from the female than from the male.

It has been observed that Germans who have come to know each other quite well often make almost a little ceremony (*Brüderschaft trinken*) of the occasion when they decide to say *du* to each other rather than *Sie*. One French speaker will also sometimes propose to another that they *tutoyer* each other. Usually, on such occasions it is the superior in the relationship who initiates the change. Once a pair of speakers decide on mutual T, it is also impossible to go back to either T/V or V/V usage without changing the social relationship.

Brown and Gilman's study of T/V usage led them to make the following observation (p. 272):

> There is enough consistency of address to justify speaking of a personal-pronoun style which involves a more or less wide use of the solidary T. Even among students of the same socioeconomic level there are differences of style, and these are potentially expressive of radicalism and conservatism in ideology. A Frenchman could, with some confidence, infer that a male university student who regularly said T to female fellow students would favor the nationalization of industry, free love, trial marriage, the abolition of capital punishment, and the weakening of nationalistic and religious loyalties.

This is an interesting claim, that you could at the time of writing listen to a young French male of a certain class and from his T/V usage predict certain opinions he would be likely to hold. As we will see, another study confirmed much the same predictive value for T/V usage among a corresponding social group in Italy.

Lambert and Tucker (1976) pointed out that all French communities and all groups within a community are not alike in their T/V usage. For example, children in Montreal and certain rural parts of Quebec, in the small city of Laval, in Mayenne, France, and in the sparsely populated French islands of Saint-Pierre et Miquelon lying just off the south coast of Newfoundland, Canada, exhibit different T/V usage. In the last two places children use *tu* with all kin and godparents, but in Quebec, especially in rural areas, they still use a considerable amount of *vous* within the family, particularly as distance in age and relationship increases. Children themselves receive *tu* in all three places: in Quebec this use is almost universal for adults to children and young men, regardless of circumstance. In both Saint-Pierre and Laval, however, either some acquaintanceship or some familiarity is necessary before *tu* is used reciprocally in most circumstances beyond the family. Quebec appears to be the most conservative in T/V usage, with *vous* expected by strangers and older people. When a young person uses *tu* to someone who might expect *vous*, that violation is noted even though it may not lead to comment.

Ager (1990, p. 209) points out that in an advertising agency in Paris everybody uses *tu* except to the owner and the cleaning woman. He adds that in general *tu* is used with intimate acquaintances and people considered to be extremely subordinate, commenting that, 'There is nothing intimate or friendly in the *tu* used by the policeman who is checking the papers of a young person or an immigrant worker.' However, upper-class social leaders still use *vous* widely with intimates: President Giscard d'Estaing in the 1970s used *vous* in talking to everybody in his household – wife, children, and dogs included – and at the time of writing the well-connected wife of President Chirac addresses her husband with *vous* but he uses *tu* to almost everyone.

A book published in France entitled *Savoir-vivre en France* (Vigner, 1978) gives the following advice to foreigners on the current use of *tu* and *vous* there. *Tu* should be used between spouses, between brothers and sisters regardless of age, between parents and children, between close relatives, between young people living or working closely together or older people engaged in some common endeavor, and between adults who have a friendship of long standing, particularly adults of the same gender. *Vous* should be used between strangers, between those who have no ties of any kind, and between inferior and superior. According to Vigner, *tu* is customary in certain types of work relationships and among the young, but there are no precise rules for its use. You should not, however, use *tu* indiscriminately, since such behavior will seem excessively familiar and will not be appreciated. Since there is no precise rule for shifting from *vous* to *tu*, it is best to wait until the other person uses it to address you before you use it to address him or her. This last bit of advice has a certain logic to it: if you cannot judge who has power, settle for politeness and wait until the other indicates solidarity. However, the inescapable linguistic fact is that *tu* continues to replace *vous* everywhere; the historical progression is clearly toward *égalité* and *fraternité* and away from *pouvoir*.

Tamil also has a T/V distinction. One study showed that in one caste-based Tamil-speaking village, the lower the caste, the greater the T usage. In the upper castes there was considerable symmetrical V usage but also instances of asymmetrical T/V usage. It seems that in such circumstances symmetrical T usage is quite non-prestigious and the greater the V usage, the more prestige. In an attempt to explain this phenomenon, Brown and Levinson (1979, pp. 332–3) postulate that 'T/V usage is tied primarily to kinds of social relationship, and the association of T-exchange with low-status groups in stratified societies is due to the way that stratification affects the nature of intra-group social relations.' They believe that people in the lower strata in such societies are necessarily quite interdependent, so that 'relations of equality and solidarity are likely to arise between adults, appropriately symbolized by mutual T-exchange.' Social networks among the upper strata are much more fragmented, people are more independent, and social distance is more normal. Hence the V-exchange found in such groups. Family relationships are also more hierarchical and that also precludes the use of T-exchange.

Bolivia is a Spanish-speaking country with two-thirds of its inhabitants of indigenous descent, mainly Aymara and Quechua. While Spanish is the language of La Paz, many inhabitants prefer to dress in ways that show their indigenous affiliation. Placencia (2001) looked at what happened when such people participated in a variety of service encounters in public institutions, such as hospitals, a government agency, and a city hall, with the service providers being either whites or indigenous people (white mestizos) who had adopted a Spanish identity in order 'to move up the social ladder' (p. 199). She was particularly interested in the use of the familiar *tú* and *vos*, and the formal *usted* and *ustedes*. Across a variety of different encounters, such as making requests for information and receiving instructions or requests for payment or to move up in a waiting line, she found that in contrast to white mestizos seeking similar services, 'indigenous persons were generally addressed with the familiar form *tú* or *vos*, were not the recipients of titles or politeness formulas, and, in certain interactions were asked for information or were directed to perform actions with more directness than were their white-mestizo counterparts' (pp. 211–12). Placencia says that social discrimination was quite obviously at work. She adds that 'the use of the familiar form in address to indigenous persons seems to be so ingrained in the linguistic behavior of white-mestizos that they are not even aware of it' (p. 123). While they thought they were being polite, actual observations showed they were not. Inequality was ingrained beyond the reach of social consciousness.

Let us return to a more 'democratic' Europe and look at some class differences there in T/V usage. There is some evidence (Bates and Benigni, 1975) to suggest that T/V usage in Italy is continuing to evolve. A survey of such usage among 117 Italian residents of Rome aged between 15 and 35, and 45 and 65 revealed that symmetrical address was the norm in most circumstances, with difference in age the only factor likely to bring about asymmetrical usage. However, upper-class youth and lower-class youth tended to behave differently. On the whole, lower-class youth were more formal in their choices than upper-class youth, who behaved much as they did in the Brown and Gilman study. One reason for the different behaviors may be that lower-class youth aspire to what they consider to be the practices current among higher social groups, and upper-class youth, who quite often show radical tendencies, attempt to imitate what they consider to be the style of the 'people.' Informal observation tended to confirm this interpretation. An upper-class youth faced with the problem of addressing a lower-class youth can use *tu* for solidarity, but *tu* is also a traditional asymmetrical form. The polite *Lei* is safe. The result sometimes is that with certain upper-class youth there is an almost complete reversal in the use of *tu* and *Lei*, with *Lei* used for attempts to achieve solidarity with members of the lower classes, e.g., waiters and servants, and *tu* used to address professors and employers. But the distinction may be no less rigid in practice than the use of *tu* and *Lei* before the reversal occurred.

Bates and Benigni also comment (pp. 280–1) on the following claim that Brown and Gilman (1960, p. 175) make concerning the previously quoted political views of a young upper-class French male: 'A Frenchman could, with some confidence, infer that a male university student who regularly said T to female fellow students would favor the nationalization of industry, free love, trial marriage, the abolition of capital punishment, and the weakening of nationalistic and religious loyalties.' They agree that the claim is valid for upper-class Italian youth, but for that class alone: 'One could not, with any confidence, predict the political philosophy of a young blue-collar worker upon hearing him address a young female as *tu*' (Bates and Benigni, 1975, p. 281). While upper-class youth appear to be reversing the traditional pattern of T/V usage without necessarily changing the system, change is apparent in other groups in society, particularly a change toward symmetrical usage. Today, most Italians are likely to expect to receive the same address form that they give. For a similar update on German usage, see Clyne (1984, pp. 124–8), who notes a recent move back toward more conservative, i.e., earlier, usage. Braun (1988, p. 30) tells, for example, of an incident in Germany in 1977. A German greengrocer, a woman, used *du* to a policeman, who found such use offensive and took her to court for it. The judge agreed with him and fined the greengrocer 2,250 German marks even though she claimed that in her rural dialect such use of *du* was not offensive.

There is considerable evidence that power is no longer as important as it once was in determining T/V usage; there has been a dramatic shift in recent years to solidarity. However, many local variations still remain. For example, solidarity in the French Revolution called for symmetrical T usage but in the Russian Revolution, symmetrical V usage. Symmetrical T usage has always been characteristic of lower-class relationships, so it may be avoided in certain circumstances to deny any semblance of lower-class membership in a quest for politeness. On the other hand, T forms have sometimes exerted a very special appeal to those of upper-class origin as they have attempted to give their speech a deliberately democratic flavor. We can expect different societies to devise different ways of handling the T/V distinction, and this is indeed what we find, with T/V forms being differently employed currently in Germany, France, and Italy. Moreover, that T/V usage is constantly evolving. It may not even be the case that the evolution is always toward solidarity and away from power. Power is still very much part of modern social structure, and it would be surprising if all traces of its effect were quite suddenly to vanish from T/V pronominal usage. For example, Keevallik (1999) provides an interesting account of how school children in Estonia learn to use the T/V system of that language: *sa* (or *sina*) vs. *te* (or *teie*). There is considerable variety of usage within the system as factors such as age, town vs. country, formality, and changing power relationships are involved. There are also avoidance strategies but these are not always available. The result is that 'singular and plural address in Estonian is actively and creatively used for establishing and maintaining the character of social relations as well as for accomplishing various activities, such as degrading, condemning, or nagging' (p. 143).

English, of course, has no active T/V distinction. The use of T forms by such groups as Quakers is very much limited, but these T forms are a solidarity marker for those who do use them. The T/V use that remains in English is archaic, found in fixed formulas such as prayers or in use in plays written during the era when the T/V distinction was alive or in modern works that try to recapture aspects of that era. It is still possible, however, for speakers of English to show power and solidarity relationships through language; they just have to use other means. As we will see, speakers of English, just like speakers of other languages, can use address terms for that purpose.

Discussion

1. Languages such as Ainu, Tagalog, Tamil, and Turkish also have a T/V distinction. How does that strengthen or weaken Brown and Gilman's claims about the origin of the distinction?
2. Explain the distinction between *you* and *you all* as these are used in parts of the southern United States. Is this a T/V distinction of the kind discussed in this chapter?
3. In a novel based on his experiences and entitled *Men in Prison*, Victor Serge (1977) describes the use of *tu* in a French prison at the beginning of the twentieth century as follows (p. 21):

> Once inside prison walls, the use of the familiar *tu* is practically a rule among inmates. At the house of detention, where crowds of transients are always coming and going – in that sudden physical indignity of arrest which is so much harder on new prisoners than on underworld 'regulars' – the guards call almost everyone *tu*. Elsewhere, after a rapid process of classification by social categories, they reserve this vulgarly familiar address for inmates who command no respect or consideration. One of my first observations – the accuracy of which was confirmed many times later on – was that this use of the familiar form by guards to inmates, or by policemen to criminals, is an instinctive recognition of a common existence and a common mentality. Guards and inmates live the same life on both sides of the same bolted door. Policemen and crooks keep the same company, sit on the same barstools, sleep with the same whores in the same furnished rooms. They mold each other like two armies fighting with complementary methods of attack and defense on a common terrain.

Comment on Serge's explanation of the guards' use of *tu*. In a review of Andrei Amalrik's *Notes of a Revolutionary* in *The New Yorker* (March 26, 1984, p. 130), William Maxwell reports the following bit of behavior by Amalrik in a Soviet prison:

> To the prison officials who addressed him by the familiar – and, in the circumstances, insulting – second-person singular, he replied by calling them 'ty' also; whereupon they instantly switched to the polite form.

Explain what the officials and the prisoner were attempting to do through their choices of T/V forms on such occasions.

4. In Shakespeare's *Twelfth Night*, Sir Toby Belch urges Andrew Aguecheek to send a challenge to the disguised Viola as follows: 'Taunt him with the license of ink, if thou thou'st him some thrice, it shall not be amiss.' At Sir Walter Raleigh's trial for treason in 1603 Sir Edward Coke attacked him as follows: 'All that he did, was at thy instigation, thou viper; for I thou thee, thou traitor.' Explain why in each case T forms are used instead of V forms.

Address Terms

How do you name or address another? By title (T), by first name (FN), by last name (LN), by a nickname, by some combination of these, or by nothing at all, so deliberately avoiding the problem? What factors govern the choice you make? Is the address process asymmetrical; that is, if I call you *Mr Jones*, do you call me *John*? Or is it symmetrical, so that *Mr Jones* leads to *Mr Smith* and *John* to *Fred*? All kinds of combinations are possible in English: *Dr Smith*, *John Smith*, *Smith*, *John*, *Johnnie*, *Doc*, *Sir*, *Mack*, and so on. Dr Smith himself might also expect *Doctor* from a patient, *Dad* from his son, *John* from his brother, *Dear* from his wife, and *Sir* from a police officer who stops him if he drives too fast, and he might be rather surprised if any one of these is substituted for any other, e.g., 'Excuse me, dear, can I see your licence?' from the police officer.

In looking at some of the issues involved in naming and addressing, let us first examine practices among an 'exotic' people to distance ourselves somewhat from English. A brief look at such a different system may possibly allow us to gain a more objective perspective on what we do with our own language and in our own culture. That objectivity is not just useful; it is quite necessary if we are to avoid conclusions distorted by ethnocentricity.

The Nuer, a Sudanese people, have very different naming practices from those with which we are likely to be familiar (Evans-Pritchard, 1948). Every Nuer has a personal or birth name, which is a name given to the child by the parents shortly after birth and retained for life. A personal name may be handed down, particularly to sons, for a son may be called something equivalent to 'son of [personal name].' Nuer personal names are interesting in what they name, e.g., *Reath* 'drought,' *Nhial* 'rain,' *Pun* 'wild rice,' *Cuol* 'to compensate,' *Mun* 'earth,' and *Met* 'to deceive.' Sometimes the maternal grandparents give a child a second personal name. The consequence is that a child's paternal kin may address the child by one personal name and the child's maternal kin by another. There are also special personal names for twins and children who are born after twins. Males are addressed by their personal names in their paternal villages during boyhood, but this usage shifts in later years when senior males are addressed as *Gwa* 'father' by less senior males, who themselves receive *Gwa* from much younger males. Children, however, call everyone in the village by their personal names, older people and parents included.

Every Nuer child also has a clan name, but this name is largely ceremonial so that its use is confined to such events as weddings and initiations. Use of the clan name between females expresses considerable formality as when a woman uses it to address her son's wife. The clan name may also be used by mothers to their small children to express approval and pleasure. Clan names are also used when one is addressed outside one's local tribal area by people from other tribes.

In addition to personal names, which are given, and clan names, which are inherited, the Nuer also have ox names, that is, names derived from a favored ox. A man may choose his own ox name. This is a name which a man uses in the triumphs of sport, hunting, and war, and it is the name used among age-mates for purposes of address. Women's ox names come from the bulls calved by the cows they milk. Women's ox names are used mainly among women. Occasionally, young men will address young girls by their ox names as part of flirting behavior or their sisters by these names if they are pleased with them. Married women replace the ox names with cow names taken from the family herds, and men do not use these names at all.

Evans-Pritchard points out a number of further complications in naming and addressing, having to do with the complicated social arrangements found in Nuer life. A person's name varies with circumstances, for each person has a number of names which he or she can use. In addressing another, the choice of name which you use for the other depends both on your knowledge of exactly who that other is (e.g., his or her age and lineage) and on the circumstances of the meeting. (For another fascinating account of naming practices, this time among the Giriama, a coastal people of Kenya, see Parkin, 1989.)

Having taken this brief glance at Nuer name and addressing practices, we can now turn our attention to English usage. Brown and Ford's study (1961) of naming practices in English was based on an analysis of modern plays, the naming practices observed in a business in Boston, and the reported usage of business executives and children in the mid-western United States and in 'Yoredale' in England. They report that the asymmetric use of title, last name, and first name (TLN/FN) indicated inequality in power, that mutual TLN indicated inequality and unfamiliarity, and that mutual FN indicated equality and familiarity. The switch from mutual TLN to FN is also usually initiated by the more powerful member of the relationship. Other options exist too in addressing another: title alone (T), e.g., *Professor* or *Doctor*; last name alone (LN), e.g., *Smith*; or multiple naming, e.g., variation between *Mr Smith* and *Fred*. We should note that in such a classification, titles like *Sir* or *Madam* are generalized variants of the T(itle) category, i.e., generic titles, and forms like *Mack*, *Buddy*, *Jack*, or *Mate* are generic first names (FN), as in 'What's up, Mate?' or 'Hey, Mack, I wouldn't do that if I were you.'

Address by title alone is the least intimate form of address in that titles usually designate ranks or occupations, as in *Colonel*, *Doctor*, or *Waiter*. They are devoid of 'personal' content. We can argue therefore that *Doctor Smith* is more intimate than *Doctor* alone, acknowledging as it does that the other person's name is known and can be mentioned. Knowing and using another's first name is, of course, a sign of considerable intimacy or at least of a desire for such intimacy. Using a nickname or pet name shows an even greater intimacy. When someone uses your first name alone in addressing you, you may feel on occasion that that person is presuming an intimacy you do not recognize or, alternatively, is trying to assert some power over you. Note that a mother's *John Smith* to a misbehaving son reduces the intimacy of first name alone, or first name with diminutive (*Johnny*), or pet name (*Honey*), and consequently serves to signal a rebuke.

We can see some of the possible dangers in cross-cultural communication when different relationships are expressed through what appears, superficially at least, to be the same address system. The dangers are even greater if you learn the terms in a new address system but fail to appreciate how they are related to one another. Ervin-Tripp (1972, p. 231) provides the following example:

> Suppose the speaker, but not the listener, has a system in which familiarity, not merely solidarity, is required for use of a first name. He will use TLN in the United States to his new colleagues and be regarded as aloof or excessively formal. He will feel that first-name usage from his colleagues is brash and intrusive. In the same way, encounters across social groups may lead to misunderstandings within the United States. Suppose a used-car salesman regards his relation to his customers as solidary, or a physician so regards his relation to old patients. The American . . . might regard such speakers as intrusive, having made a false claim to a solidary status. In this way, one can pinpoint abrasive features of interaction across groups.

I might add that the use of a person's first name in North America does not necessarily indicate friendship or respect. First names are required among people who work closely together, even though they may not like each other at all. First names may even be used to refer to public figures, but contemptuously as well as admiringly.

The asymmetric use of names and address terms is often a clear indicator of a power differential. School classrooms are almost universally good examples; *John* and *Sally* are likely to be children and *Miss* or *Mr Smith* to be teachers. For a long time in the southern states of the United States, whites used naming and addressing practices to put blacks in their place. Hence the odious use of *Boy* to address black males. The asymmetrical use of names also was part of the system. Whites addressed blacks by their first names in situations which required them to use titles, or titles and last names, if they were addressing whites. There was a clear racial distinction in the practice. According to Johnson (1943, p. 140), one consequence of this practice was that:

> middle- and upper-class Negro women never permit their first names to be known. . . . The wife of a well-to-do Negro business man went into a department store in Atlanta to enquire about an account. The clerk asked her first name and she said 'Mrs William Jones.' The clerk insisted on her first name, and when she refused to give it declared that the business could not be completed without it. It was a large account; and the manager, to whom appeal was made, decided that 'Mrs' was simply good business and not 'social equality.'

In this case 'good business' overrode the desire to reinforce the social inequality that would have resulted from the woman's giving the sales-clerk the information requested and then the inevitable use of that first name alone by the clerk in addressing the customer.

Bharati Mukherjee's novel *Jasmine* (1989) is the story of an Indian woman Jyoti, who early in life marries a 'modern' man Prakash (p. 77):

> He wanted me to call him by his first name. 'Only in feudal societies is the woman still a vassal,' he explained. 'Hasnapur is feudal.' In Hasnapur wives used only pronouns to address their husbands. The first months, eager and obedient as I was, I still had a hard time calling him Prakash. I'd cough to get his attention, or start with 'Are you listening?' Every time I coughed he'd say, 'Do I hear a crow trying human speech?' Prakash. I had to practice and practice (in the bathroom, in the tarped-over corner of the verandah which was our kitchen) so I could say the name without gagging or blushing in front of his friends. He liked to show me off. His friends were like him: disrupters and rebuilders, idealists.

Prakash is opposed to the feudalistic traditions which surround them and asymmetrical naming, being one of them, must go. Jyoti also becomes Jasmine and has to struggle with these new ways and the new identity the name gives her. Such an asymmetrical system between spouses is not at all unusual. In Java a wife may address her husband as *mas* 'elder brother' and get her first name, a nickname, or *dhik* 'younger sibling' from him, a reflection of the traditional difference in status between husband and wife.

Dickey (1996, 1997a, 1997b) examined 11,891 address terms in Greek prose writers over more than six centuries (approximately 450 BCE to 160 CE) plus 1,683 other terms from other sources. In this upper-class Athenian society names – and these Greeks had only a single name, a given name – were commonly used in addressing others, e.g., by free adult males to address each other. Slaves were usually addressed as *paî* 'child'; they in turn addressed their masters and mistresses as *déspota* 'master' or *déspoina* 'mistress,' although they sometimes used names too. Men addressed women by either name or *gúnai* 'woman,' and women and children addressed men by name. Children addressed parents as either *pater* 'father' or *mêter* 'mother,' and parents addressed children as *huié* 'son,' *thúgater* 'daughter,' or *paî* 'child.' Siblings used names or *ádelphe* 'brother' or *adelphé* 'sister.' Husbands usually addressed their wives by *gúnai* and their mistresses by name. A wife used either her husband's name or *áner* 'husband.' Dickey says (1997b, p. 8) that 'there was, to all intents and purposes, only one way to address a man by name in Athens.'

In English, when we are in doubt as to how to address another we can actually avoid the difficulty by not using any address term at all. We can say *Good morning* as well as *Good morning, Sir/Mr Smith/Susie*. In other languages such avoidance may be either impolite or deficient. In France, you cannot say *Bonjour*, *Au revoir*, *Merci*, or *Pardon* without attaching an address term. So the French say *Bonjour, Monsieur* or *Merci, Pierre*, whereas we can say simply *Good morning* or *Thank you*.

In English we therefore have the possibility of the avoidance of an address term, that is, Ø use, or of a choice between familiar and polite. One simple test for distinguishing familiar, informal address terms from polite, formal ones in English is to look at them in conjunction with informal and formal greetings and leave-takings, e.g., *Hi*, *Bye*, and *So long* in comparison with *Good morning* and *Goodbye. Hi, Sally*; *Bye, Honey*; and *So long, Doc* are possible, just as are *Good morning, Mr Smith* and *Goodbye, Sir*. However, there is something peculiar about *Hi, Colonel Jones*; *Bye, Professor*; *Good morning, Mate*; and *Goodbye, Pussykins*. (See McConnell-Ginet, 2003, for a discussion of naming and addressing in relation to issues of gender.)

As you age and your family relationships change, issues of naming and addressing may arise. For example, knowing how to address your father-in-law (or mother-in-law) has often been a problem for many people: *Mr Smith* is sometimes felt to be too formal, *Bill* too familiar, and *Dad* pre-empted or even 'unnatural.' The arrival of grandchildren is sometimes seen as a way out, it being easier to call a father-in-law *Grandad* than *Dad*. Such a move may also be accompanied in some families with a switch of address for your own parents, so that your mother is addressed as *Grandma* rather than *Mom*; sometimes this appears to be intended only as a temporary help to the grandchildren in learning the right terms of address, but it can easily become a permanent change so that *Grandad* and *Grandma* come to replace *Dad* and *Mom*. In some cases *Grandma* may be used for the maternal grandmother and *Gran* or *Nana* for the paternal one, or vice versa.

Some languages actually employ what we regard as kinship terms for use as address terms. We saw the equivalent of English *father* so used among the Nuer. Luong (1990) describes how Vietnamese makes extensive use of kinship terms as forms of address, e.g., *cháu* 'grandchild,' *bà* 'grandmother,' and *bác* 'senior uncle/aunt.' The kinship system itself is generation- and age-oriented with terms for both the paternal and maternal sides. It also gives more weight to males than females. Children are also ordered, for example as 'sibling two,' 'sibling three,' etc. – there is no 'sibling one' – and a term like *anh* can be used for both 'elder brother' and 'male cousin, same generation.' Bare English translation of Vietnamese terms into English words like *aunt*, *cousin*, etc., always seems deficient to Vietnamese; as Luong says, 'linguistic forms . . . play a vital instrumental role in the structuring of sociocultural reality' (p. 166) so that the English equivalents fall far short of Vietnamese understanding of social relationships. As a further instance, Pham (2002) says that 'Between married couples, *mình* ["body"] is used to address the spouse, by either the husband or wife. If the speaker is the husband, he uses *anh* "elder brother" for self-reference. If the speaker is a wife, she uses *em* "younger sibling" for self-reference' (p. 295). However, times are changing and in 'urban settings now, if husbands are younger than their wives, wives – particularly educated ones – consider the term *em* for self-reference to be either humorous or embarrassing. In this case, proper names come to the rescue: wives refer to their husbands and to themselves by proper names, or they use *anh* "elder brother" to address their husbands and their own proper names to refer to themselves' (p. 308). Vietnamese address non-relatives using various such kinship terms because neither names (patronyms, middle names, and personal names) find extensive use nor do personal pronouns, the latter tending to express non-solidarity or used typically only by children or certain less favored social groups. (See Oyetade, 1995, for still another example of the use of kinship terms to address strangers, this time among the Yoruba of Nigeria.) Dickey (1997a, p. 272) hypothesizes that such systems of terms originated in the tendency of adults to take the perspective of small children in referring to older relatives in order to teach the children how to address these relatives 'correctly.'

One additional peculiarity of systems of naming and addressing is that people sometimes give names to, and address, non-humans as well as humans. In a society where people keep a lot of pets of different kinds, there is likely to be a considerable variety of names and forms of address used depending on the kind of pet, e.g., horse, cat, or gerbil, and the circumstances, e.g., whether you are alone with the pet or in public view, feeding it, or reprimanding it. It is sometimes said that you can learn a lot about other people from the pets they keep; if this is so, part of that 'keeping' is how those pets are treated linguistically. We should not be surprised that people who view animals very differently are sometimes mystified by our treatment of animals and the way we talk to them, quite often in ways that resemble the way we employ with very young children.

If we look at what is involved in addressing another, it seems that a variety of social factors usually governs our choice of terms: the particular occasion; the social status or rank of the other; gender; age; family relationship; occupational hierarchy; transactional status (i.e., a service encounter, or a doctor–patient relationship, or one of priest–penitent); race; or degree of intimacy. The choice is sometimes quite clear; when racial or caste origin is important in society, that is likely to take preference; when family ties are extremely strong, that is likely to be preferred; and so on. In societies which claim to be egalitarian there may be some doubt as to what is the appropriate address term, and consequently none at all may be used between, say, husband and wife's mother; son who is learning a lowly job in a company and father who is the company president; police officer and young male offender; and older male and much younger feminist. There also seems to be an ordered relationship, something like the steps in courting behavior; you proceed to greater and greater familiarity with no back-tracking! When one party insists on stopping at a point both have previously gone beyond, this is likely to signal a reduction in familiarity and to indicate and be perceived as a kind of violation.

One consequence is that choosing the right terms of address to use in a hierarchical organization may not always be easy. Not many organizations are as rigidly organized as the military, for example, but even here there are occasional difficulties, since soldiers must not only maintain a clear chain of command but sometimes must live together, occasionally in very dangerous circumstances requiring solidarity, for long periods of time. The business world is also hierarchically organized, though generally less rigidly than the military. One unpublished study (Staples, 1971) showed that in a large department store employees had a very good idea of how they should address others and be addressed by them. Relative rank in the organizational structure was the key factor in determining how two employees would address each other, with status in the organization overriding any age difference. However, younger employees tended to be less formal than older employees in their choice of address terms, and informal situations produced greater familiarity in address than formal ones. What is apparent too is that, in such a hierarchical structure, those at the bottom seek to minimize their difference in status from those at the top and those at the top seek to maximize that difference. In trying to do this, members of each group

Table 11.1   Uses of *Tóngzhì* in China

Combination	Example
Ø + Title	*Tóngzhì* 'Comrade'
Given name + Title	*Wéigúo Tóngzhì* 'Comrade Weiguo'
Modifier + Title	*Lǎo Tóngzhì* 'Old Comrade'
	Xiǎo Tóngzhì 'Young Comrade'
Ø + Title + Title	*Zhǔrèn Tóngzhì* 'Comrade Director'
Family name + Title	*Wáng Tóngzhì* 'Comrade Wang'
Family name + Given name + Title	*Wáng Wéigúo Tóngzhì* 'Comrade Wang Weiguo'
Modifier + Family name + Title	*Lǎo Wáng Tóngzhì* 'Old Comrade Wang'

Source: based on Scotton and Wanjin (1983, pp. 484–5)

use address terms as a resource in the resulting power struggle, with those at the bottom preferring the most familiar terms they can manage to use and those at the top the most formal ones.

We can also note that the terms we use to address others are not necessarily the same as those we use to refer to them when speaking to others. However, Dickey (1997a, p. 268) indicates that when A speaks to B about C there is often 'a close relationship between the way that person A addresses person C and the way that A refers to C.' She adds that this is another example of accommodation, specifically of convergence behavior, i.e., the need to gain another's social approval.

A society undergoing social change is also likely to show certain indications of such change if the language in use in that society has (or had) a complex system of address. One such society is modern China (Scotton and Wanjin, 1983, and Fang and Heng, 1983). The Communist Party of China has promoted the use of *tóngzhì* 'comrade' to replace titles for owners and employers, e.g., *lǎobǎn* 'proprietor,' and also honorific titles, e.g., *xiān·sheng* 'mister.' The party wants to put everyone on an equal footing through encouraging the use of an address form that implies no social or economic differences and unites all politically. Titles, however, have not entirely disappeared from use. Professional titles are still used, e.g., *lǎoshī* 'teacher' and *dài-fu* 'doctor,' and skilled workers prefer to be addressed as *shī-fu* 'master.' Table 11.1 shows that *tóngzhì* can be used in a variety of ways (Scotton and Wanjin, 1983, pp. 484–5). However, there are clear differences among the choices. *Tóngzhì* is used in situations that are somewhat neutral, i.e., when there are no clear indications of power or solidarity and no familiarity between the parties, e.g., to an unknown stranger or to someone whose occupation carries with it no title. *Tóngzhì* can also be used deliberately to keep another at arm's length, as it were. For example, a superior may use *tóngzhì* rather than an inferior's title before offering a rebuke. It can also be used in the opposite direction, from inferior to superior, to remind the superior of shared interests, or between equals if such sharing is deemed to be more important on a particular occasion than some other difference which could be acknowledged through choice of another term.

However, many Chinese still prefer the use of a title to the use of *tóngzhì*, e.g., *zhǔ rèn* 'director' or *zhǎng* 'chief.' There is also widespread use of *lǎo* 'old' and *xiǎo* 'little' in conjunction with last names as polite forms not only between intimates but also to mark social distinctions between non-intimates. An inferior may therefore address a superior by either *Lǎo* + LN or LN + title, with practice varying according to location (Fang and Heng, 1983, p. 499), the first variant being preferred in big cities like Beijing and Shanghai, the second in less egalitarian medium and small towns. Still another form of address used to elderly officials and scholars and showing great deference is LN + *Lǎo*, e.g., *Wáng Lǎo*. Some old titles are still used but mainly to accommodate non-Chinese, e.g., *tàitai* 'Mrs.' The Chinese address form for a spouse is usually *àiren* 'lover.' The old *xiānsheng* 'Mr' is now applied only to certain older scholars; young teachers are called *lǎoshī* or, if they are professors, *jiàoshòu*. Fang and Heng conclude as follows (p. 506): 'The address norms in China are indeed extremely complicated. ... What we have discussed ... [are] ... some of the changes in address norms brought about by the Revolution. Taken as a whole, changes in address modes in today's China are unique and drastic. Few countries in the world, we believe, have been undergoing such drastic changes in this respect.' In a later report on the same phenomenon, Ju (1991) points out that *shī-fu* has become somewhat devalued through overextension to those not originally deserving it and that *xiānsheng* has lost its previous derogatory connotations, especially among young people. He concludes (p. 390), 'China is changing as are its political and cultural systems. Predictably, there will be further changes in its use of its address terms.' Keshavarz (1988) reports on a somewhat similar situation in Iran. The revolution there that led to the flight of the Shah resulted in the choice of address terms indicating solidarity; however, the old honorifics were also retained. Consequently, the need to express solidarity led to greater use of terms like /bæradær/ 'brother' and /xahær/ 'sister' and honorifics have been reinterpreted as indicators of humility and politeness rather than of flattery.

One interesting hypothesis about address terms (Robinson, 1972, p. 129) is that, in those societies in which a person's status derives from his or her achievements, few distinctions in address are made. In such societies people may use only one basic form of address; they rely on other means for signaling the variety of relationships that we must presume still exist. However, in societies where status is ascribed, i.e., derived from birth into a particular social group, we are much more likely to find sets of finely graded address terms. Such sets reflect the social structures of those societies. Data from the English of North America and from a highly stratified society like Java seem to illustrate the two extremes; data on address forms from Japan and Korea would also suggest that these societies are much more stratified and that social position within them is more ascribed than earned in contrast to the situations in either North America or the United Kingdom. Undoubtedly, some social theorists would strongly disagree, pointing out that in the last two cases it is still birth rather than ability which makes the greater contribution to your life chances. Consequently, no matter how intriguing the thesis is, it remains unproved.

Discussion

1. English naming practices are not quite as simple as they might appear to be. Comment on each of the following: the initial acquisition of a name or names; changing your name on marriage; legal changes of name; adopting a new name when made a peer or becoming an actor, singer, or entertainer; incorporation; trade names; blaspheming; naming pets; signing your name to a document; aliases and pseudo-names; personation; memorializing; and 'keeping your good name.'

2. How do you address a stranger? Does the form of address depend in any way on factors such as that person's gender, age, ethnicity, dress, perceived role, physical well-being, or behavior? Is it true to say that the primary consideration in addressing strangers is 'be polite' and therefore 'be deferential'?

3. A black physician, Dr Poussaint, gave the following account of being stopped a number of years ago by a white policeman in a southern town in the United States:

    > 'What's your name, boy?' the policeman asked. . . .
    > 'Dr Poussaint. I'm a physician.'
    > 'What's your first name, boy?'
    > 'Alvin.'

    Explain why Dr Poussaint reports himself to have experienced a feeling of 'profound humiliation' because of this treatment.

4. *Sir* has two corresponding terms for females: *Madam* or *Ma'am* (occasionally *Mrs*), and *Miss*. What brings about the distinction in the terms for females? These terms are used both 'up,' to those who are of higher standing, and (in some cases) 'down.' Find examples of both kinds of usage.

5. In what circumstances might a specific individual be addressed as *Smith*, *Mr Smith*, *Professor Smith*, *Smithie*, *John Smith*, *John*, *Johnnie*, *Honey*, *Sir*, *Mack*, *You*, and by no term at all?

6. A waiter who serves a woman and says 'Here's your drink, my dear,' or a waitress who asks 'What'll you have, dearie?' might give offense in some circumstances. Why?

7. How do you attract the attention of another, e.g., someone who has dropped something on the street or left something behind on a bus? You might want to call this form of address a 'summons'; it would also include addressing a waiter or waitress.

8. Murphy (1988) reports that in a North American university setting a number of factors influenced the choice among various combinations of titles and names when a speaker referred to a third person. Among these were the level of intimacy between the speaker and that person, between the addressee and that person, and between any non-participating audience and that person. In addition, the relationship between the speaker and the addressee also affected the choice. Do your observations of similar situations agree with Murphy's?

9. How do you refer to a third party? ('I've come to see Mr Smith'; 'Is the lady of the house at home?')

10. Comment on each of the following address practices. What is your own practice, if relevant, in each case? Teacher–student: TLN/FN; FN/FN. Physician–patient: T/FN; TLN/TLN; FN/FN. Father–son: T(*Dad*)/FN; FN/FN. Salesperson–customer: TLN/TLN; TLN/FN; FN/FN. Apartment dweller–building superintendent: TLN/TLN; TLN/FN; FN/FN; T(*Sir*)/TLN; TLN/T(*Sir*). Older person who lives next door to you: TLN/TLN; FN/FN; TLN/FN.

11. How do you or your parents address in-laws?

12. One aspect of naming is how people are referred to in accounts in broadcasts, newspapers, and magazines, e.g., 'John Smith, 49, a retired policeman' or 'Smith's daughter, Sarah, a junior at Vassar.' Examine such practices. Do you find any evidence that men and women are treated differently?

13. Ervin-Tripp (1972, p. 242) says that 'one cannot say to a stranger on the street, "My name is George Landers. What time is it?" or "Hello, sir. Where is the post office?".' Explain why these are not possible and mark off the speaker as in some way unfamiliar with correct English usage.

Politeness

Through our choice of pronominal forms when a T/V distinction exists and of address terms, we can show our feelings toward others – solidarity, power, distance, respect, intimacy, and so on – and our awareness of social customs. Such awareness is also shown through the general politeness with which we use language. Politeness itself is socially prescribed. This does not mean, of course, that we must always be polite, for we may be quite impolite to others on occasion. However, we could not be so if there were no rules of politeness to be broken. Impoliteness depends on the existence of standards, or norms, of politeness.

The concept of 'politeness' owes a great deal to Goffman's original work (1955, 1967) on 'face.' In social interaction we present a face to others and to others' faces. We are obliged to protect both our own face and the faces of others to the extent that each time we interact with others we play out a kind of mini-drama, a kind of ritual in which each party is required to recognize the identity that the other claims for himself or herself. The consequence is, as Scollon and Scollon (2001) tell us: 'One of the most important ways in which we reduce the ambiguity of communication is by making assumptions about the people we are talking to' (p. 44). They add: 'Any communication is a risk to face; it is a risk to one's own face, at the same time it is a risk to the other person's. We have to carefully project a face for ourselves and to respect the face rights and claims of other participants. . . . "*There is no faceless communication*"' (p. 48).

In discussing 'politeness,' the concept of interest to them, Brown and Levinson (1987, p. 61) define *face* as 'the public self-image that every member wants to claim for himself.' They also distinguish between positive face and negative face.

Positive face is the desire to gain the approval of others, 'the positive consistent self-image or "personality" ... claimed by interactants' (p. 61). *Negative face* is the desire to be unimpeded by others in one's actions, 'the basic claim to territories, personal preserves, rights to non-distraction ... freedom of action and freedom from imposition' (p. 61). Positive face looks for solidarity; negative face, however, is more problematic for it requires interactants to recognize each other's negative face, i.e., the need to act without giving offense.

When we interact with others we must be aware of both kinds of face and therefore have a choice of two kinds of politeness. *Positive politeness* leads to moves to achieve solidarity through offers of friendship, the use of compliments, and informal language use: we treat others as friends and allies, do not impose on them, and never threaten their face. On the other hand, *negative politeness* leads to deference, apologizing, indirectness, and formality in language use: we adopt a variety of strategies so as to avoid any threats to the face others are presenting to us. Symmetric pronominal use is a good example of positive politeness and asymmetric T/V use of negative politeness. This approach to politeness has been quite revealing when applied to many Western societies. However, it has been criticized (Mills, 2003) for encapsulating stereotypical, white, middle-class (and largely female) language behavior. It may also not work so well in other cultures. We will look at two examples: Java and Japan.

Some languages seem to have built into them very complex systems of politeness. Javanese, one of the principal languages of Indonesia, is a language in which, as Geertz (1960, p. 248) says 'it is nearly impossible to say anything without indicating the social relationships between the speaker and the listener in terms of status and familiarity.' Before one Javanese speaks to another, he or she must decide on an appropriate speech style (or *styleme*, in Geertz's terminology): high, middle, or low. Such a decision is necessary because for many words there are three distinct variants according to style. For example, the equivalent to the English word *now* is *samenika* in high style, *saniki* in middle style, and *saiki* in low style. You cannot freely shift styles, so the choice of *saiki* will require the speaker to use *arep* for the verb equivalent to *go* rather than *adjeng* or *bade*, which would be required by the choices of *saniki* and *samenika*, respectively.

But there is still another level of complication. Javanese has a set of honorifics, referring to such matters as people, body parts, possessions, and human actions. These honorifics can be used to further modulate two of the style levels, the high and the low. There are both high honorifics, e.g., *dahar* for *eat*, and low honorifics, e.g., *neda* for *eat*. Only high honorifics can accompany high style, but both high and low honorifics can accompany low style. We can also use the equivalent of English *eat* to show a further complication. *Neda* is found in the high style with no honorifics, the middle style (which cannot have honorifics), and the low style with low honorifics. *Dahar* for *eat* always signals high honorifics in either high or low style. In low style without honorifics *eat* is *mangan*. We can see the various combinations that are possible if we combine the various equivalents of *eat* and *now*, as in table 11.2. In addition, table 11.3 shows the equivalent of the English sentence, 'Are you going to eat rice and cassava now?' in the six levels that are possible in Javanese. Geertz adds a further interesting observation: as you move from low to high style, you speak more slowly and

Table 11.2   Levels in Javanese

Speech level	Example	
	eat	*now*
3a high style, high honorifics	ḍahar	samenika
3 high style, no honorifics	neḍa	samenika
2 middle style, no honorifics	neḍa	saniki
1b low style, high honorifics	ḍahar	saiki
1a low style, low honorifics	neḍa	saiki
1 low style, no honorifics	mangan	saiki

Level names: 3a krama inggil (high style, high honorifics)
              3   krama biasa (high style, no honorifics)
              2   krama madya (middle style, no honorifics)
              1b ngoko sae (low style, high honorifics)
              1a ngoko madya (low style, low honorifics)
              1   ngoko biasa (low style, no honorifics)
Source: Geertz (1960)

Table 11.3   Level differences in a Javanese sentence

	Are	*you*	*going*	*to eat*	*rice*	*and*	*cassava*	*now?*
3a	menapa	pandjenengan	baḍé	ḍahar	sekul	kalijan	kaspé	samenika
3	menapa	sampéjan	baḍé	neḍa	sekul	lan	kaspé	samenika
2	napa	sampéjan	adjeng	neḍa	sekul	lan	kaspé	saniki
1b	apa	pandjenengan	arep	ḍahar	sega	lan	kaspé	saiki
1a	apa	sampéjan	arep	neḍa	sega	lan	kaspé	saiki
1	apa	kowé	arep	mangan	sega	lan	kaspé	saiki

Source: Geertz (1960, p. 250)

softly and more evenly in terms of rhythm and pitch, so that the highest levels, 'when spoken correctly, have a kind of stately pomp which can make the simplest conversation seem like a great ceremony' (p. 173).

   It is not at all easy to specify when a particular level is used. As Geertz says (pp. 257–8):

   A thorough semantic study of the contexts within which the different levels are employed would in itself be a complex and extended investigation, for the number of variables specifically determining the selection of a particular level are very numerous. They include not only qualitative characteristics of the speakers – age, sex, kinship relation, occupation, wealth, education, religious commitment, family background – but also more general factors: for instance, the social setting (one would be likely to use a higher level to the same individual at a wedding than in the street); the content of the conversation (in general, one uses lower levels when speaking of commercial matters, higher ones if speaking of religious or aesthetic matters); the history of social interaction between the speakers (one will tend to speak rather high, if one speaks at all, with someone with whom one has quarreled); the presence of a third person (one tends to speak higher to the same individual if others are listening). All these play a role, to say nothing of individual idiosyncratic attitudes. Some people, particularly, it seems, wealthier traders and self-confident village chiefs, who tend to think the whole business rather uncomfortable and somewhat silly, speak *ngoko* to almost everyone except the very high in status. Others will shift levels on any pretext. A complete listing of the determinants of level selection would, therefore, involve a thorough analysis of the whole framework of Javanese culture.

Irvine (1998, p. 56) points out that 'the higher ... levels are considered to be governed by an ethic of proper order, peace, and calm. In them one "does not express one's own feelings".... The "lower" levels ... are the language one loses one's temper in.' The levels are addressee-focused: 'polite conduct toward a respected addressee is conduct that is stylized, depersonalized, and flat-affect ... use of "high" deferential styles also implies the speaker's own refinement, as shown by the speaker's ability to efface emotion, sensitivity to the equanimity of others, and pragmatic delicacy.' Overall, those of the highest social rank control the widest range of styles and all the subtleties of the highest of those, while those of low rank employ only a small range at the low end.

It is possible to state a few principles that seem to operate. Highest style is used among the old aristocrats or by anyone at the highest levels of society who wants to give the appearance of elegance. Middle style is used by town-dwellers who are not close friends, or by peasants addressing superiors. Village-dwellers would also use this level with very high superiors since they cannot be expected to have any knowledge of high style. Low level is the style all children learn first regardless of social-class origin, and everyone uses it on some occasion, even close acquaintances of the highest classes. It is also used to clear inferiors, e.g., by high government officials to peasants and perhaps even to townspeople. Low honorifics added to low style indicate a lack of intimacy and mark a certain social distance but not much. It is mainly the aristocracy who use the low level with high honorifics but townspeople might use it too; such use seems to indicate a need to express both intimacy through the use of the low style and respect through the use of the honorifics, a kind of compromise solution. Men and women are also required to speak differently. Women are expected to be more talkative than men and to err on the side of being over-polite in their word choices. Javanese men, on the other hand, are required to be extremely careful in manipulating the styles of speech because nuanced speech is highly prized. Moreover, it is just such a difference that maintains men's dominance in public life and reserves the domestic realm for women.

Geertz's caveat still applies: there are many personal and local variations so that the total system is extremely complex and the possibilities for making wrong choices abound. As Java has modernized, certain changes have occurred. One important change has been the spread of the national language, Bahasa Indonesia, a more 'democratic' language. Bahasa Indonesia already dominates the political life of Java because it enables people to talk about issues without having to choose a particular level of speech which necessarily conveys attitudes they might not want to convey. However, there is no reason to assume that Javanese itself will change and that the various levels will disappear. Rather, the spread of Bahasa Indonesia in Java may best be seen as offering a choice to those who know both Javanese and Bahasa Indonesia. As Geertz says (p. 259), Bahasa Indonesia 'seems destined, at least in the short run, to become part of the general Javanese linguistic system, to become one more type of sentence among those available, to be selected for use in certain special contexts and for certain special purposes.'

One thing that is not clear in the above analysis is just which aspects of usage come from the requirements of positive politeness and which from the requirements of negative politeness. There is reason to believe that many choices in Javanese are determined by a wider need to maintain the existing social arrangement rather than by any individual's need to address his or her momentary wants. Japan offers us another example.

The Japanese are also always described as being an extremely polite people. Martin (1964) has summarized some of the ways in which the Japanese use language to show this politeness: honorific forms incorporating negatives (analogous to English 'Wouldn't you like to . . . ?') are more polite than those without negatives; the longer the utterance the more polite it is felt to be; utterances with local dialect in them are less polite and those with a few Chinese loan words in them are more polite; you are more polite to strangers than to acquaintances; your gender determines your use of honorifics, with men differentiating more than women among the available honorifics; whereas knowledge of honorifics is associated with education, attitudes toward using them vary with age; politeness is most expected when women address men, the young address the old, and members of the lower classes address members of the upper classes, with the last, i.e., class differences, overriding the first two; and, although people may say that it is inappropriate to use honorifics with your relatives, they still use them. Martin says that there are four basic factors at work here: in choosing the proper, or polite, address term for another, a Japanese considers out-groupness, social position, age difference, and gender difference in that order. Martin observes that anyone who comes to such a complicated system of politeness and address from a simple one may get 'the feeling that Japanese conversation is all formula, with no content' (p. 407). To the argument that such a complicated system must necessarily give way 'as feudalism is replaced by democracy,' Martin replies that 'we shall probably have speech levels in Japanese . . . as long as we have plurals in English' (p. 412).

The Japanese are very polite. But how much of that politeness is negative politeness? According to Matsumoto (1989) and Ide (1989), perhaps not a great deal. Both argue that the concept does not offer the best explanation of what is happening. The Japanese are always very much aware of the social context of every utterance they use. They are brought up to use *wakimae* 'discernment,' i.e., how to do the right thing socially, so personal face requirements, if any, are pushed into the background. The evidence to support this claim and a similar claim by Nwoye (1992) concerning the Igbo of Nigeria is suggestive rather than conclusive. However, it does remind us that while people must be polite everywhere they are not necessarily polite in the same way or for the same reasons. For example, a recent study (Sreetharan, 2004) of the use of a nonstandard variety of Japanese by men in the Kansai (western) region of Japan revealed that in all-male situations while young men between the ages of 19 and 23 preferred to use forms of speech that are stereotypically masculine, older men between 24 and 68 tended to avoid such language. Indeed, the older they were, the greater the preference for polite, traditionally feminine forms. They thereby cultivated a polite image, no longer needing to project their masculinity (and the power associated with that) through their language.

We can turn to a European language, French, to show still another aspect of politeness. In *Savoir-vivre en France* (Vigner, 1978) we find some examples that clearly illustrate how longer utterances are considered to be more polite than shorter ones in certain circumstances. For example, in asking someone to pick you up at three o'clock, you can say each of the following (pp. 77–8):

A trois heures, avec votre voiture.
'At three o'clock, with your car.'

Vous voudriez bien venir me prendre à trois heures avec votre voiture.
'You should come and get me at three o'clock with your car.'

Pourriez-vous venir me prendre à trois heures avec votre voiture?
'Could you come and get me at three o'clock with your car?'

The first sentence is not at all polite; in the last sentence there is a further softening through choice of the question format. Asking a stranger on the street the way to the Gare de Lyon, you can say (pp. 79–80):

La Gare de Lyon?
'Lyon Station?'

Pour aller à la Gare de Lyon, s'il vous plaît?
'The way to Lyon Station, please?'

Pourriez-vous m'indiquer le chemin pour me rendre à la Gare de Lyon?
'Could you tell me which way I should go for Lyon Station?'

Auriez-vous l'obligeance de bien vouloir m'indiquer le chemin pour me rendre à la Gare de Lyon?
'Would you be so obliging as to want to inform me which way I should go for Lyon Station?'

Whereas the first request is almost certainly too abrupt, the last is almost certainly too obsequious. Finally, you enter an office and must disturb someone who is working there to find out where exactly you should go (pp. 80–1):

Le service des bourses?
'The Finance Office?'

Pardon, le service des bourses, s'il vous plaît?
'Excuse me, the Finance Office, please?'

Je m'excuse de vous déranger, mais pourriez-vous m'indiquer le service des bourses, s'il vous plaît?
'I'm sorry for disturbing you, but would you tell me where the Finance Office is, please?'

According to Vigner (p. 88), this French politeness formula is made up of three components: (1) an initial mitigating component (which can be short, e.g., *Pouvez-vous*, or long, e.g., *Est-ce que vous voudriez bien*) or its absence; (2) the central request or order component; and (3) a final component, the presence or absence of something like *s'il vous plaît*. You can therefore have each of the following:

$$\text{Ø} - \text{request} - \text{Ø}$$
$$\text{Ø} - \text{request} - \text{final}$$
$$\text{short mitigator} - \text{request} - \text{final}$$
$$\text{long mitigator} - \text{request} - \text{final}$$

Requests made in the form Ø – request – Ø are therefore power-loaded, or impolite, or both; requests made in the form, long mitigator – request – final, may be so polite as to appear to be overdone. Notice that a request by a superior to an inferior put in this last form is likely to be interpreted as sarcastic: 'Would you mind, Mr Smith, if I asked you to try occasionally to get to work on time, please?'

Politeness is a very important principle in language use; we must consider others' feelings. The next chapter will again take up the issue of politeness and try to place it in a still broader context.

In using a language, we make use of the devices that the language employs to show certain relationships to others and our attitudes toward them. Indeed, to use the language properly, we must do so. In using French, we cannot avoid the *tu–vous* distinction; in communicating in English, we must refer to others and address them on occasion; in speaking Javanese or Japanese, we must observe the conventions having to do with the correct choice of speech level and honorifics. It is quite possible that we may not like what we must do and find the demands made either onerous or undemocratic, or both. It is also possible that such systems will change over a period of time, but that kind of change is slow and, when it does occur, as we saw with the example from China, not at all easy. There seems to be little doubt that language use and certain aspects of social structure are intimately related. The exact nature of that relationship may continue to intrigue us. That is, do speakers of Javanese and Japanese behave the way they do because their languages *require* them to do so, or do their linguistic choices follow inevitably from the social structures they have developed, or is it a bit of both? Was Whorf right, wrong, or partly right? I will, of course, leave these questions unanswered once more.

Discussion

1. Martin states a number of principles that govern politeness in Japanese. Do we have anything at all equivalent in English?
2. Refer back to Martin's observation concerning Japanese speech levels and English plurals. How valid is Martin's point? Look at what is actually said in such a long polite utterance as 'Would I be bothering you awfully if I asked you to move over one seat?' What makes it so polite? Give some other examples. Contrast these polite utterances with some impoliteness.
3. Record a conversation. Note all the signs of politeness. Take them out. What are you left with? How does the resulting conversation sound, i.e., what is its effect? Alternatively, record an impolite exchange and try to specify exactly why it is impolite.
4. If more polite utterances tend to be longer than less polite ones, how do you account for the fact that people who live and work very closely with each other often communicate effectively (and politely) with very few words? Refer to the concept of 'phatic communion' (see pp. 286–7).
5. Observe how young children address each other and try to describe their 'rules of politeness.' Contrast these rules with those of their parents. How do you learn to be polite?
6. Try to work out some of the difficulties one might experience in giving and receiving compliments, particularly the 'power' and 'solidarity' issues. In what ways do compliments given in symmetrical relationships differ from those given in asymmetrical relationships?
7. It has been said that an apology is a special kind of politeness device that addresses the face needs of a hearer or hearers when some kind of offense has been given. Analyze some offenses and apologies from this perspective.

Further Reading

In addition to the sources cited in the text, Friedrich (1972) provides interesting data on the T/V distinction in Russian, and Mühlhäusler and Harré (1990) examine T/V usage at length. Adler (1978) offers an overview of naming and addressing, and Braun (1988) deals with terms of address. Parkinson (1986) discusses address in Egyptian Arabic. For additional information on Javanese see Errington (1988) and on Japanese honorifics see Coulmas (1992), Ide (1982), Neustupný (1986), and Shibamoto (1985). For other views of politeness see Meier (1995) and particularly Eelen (2001), Watts (2003), and Mills (2003), and for a bibliography see DuFon et al. (1994).

12 Talk and Action

In speaking to one another, we make use of sentences, or, to be more precise, utterances. We can attempt to classify these utterances in any one of a variety of ways. We can try to classify them by length, e.g., by counting the number of words in each utterance, but that appears to be of little interest except to those who believe that shorter utterances are more easily understood than longer ones. We can try to classify them by grammatical structure along a number of dimensions, e.g., their clausal type and complexity: active–passive; statement–question–request–exclamatory; various combinations of these; and so on. We may even try to work out a semantic or logical structure for each utterance. But it is also possible to attempt a classification in terms of what sentences do, i.e., to take a 'functional' approach, but one that goes somewhat beyond consideration of such functions as stating, questioning, requesting, and exclaiming. In recent years a number of philosophers have had interesting things to say about what utterances do as well as mean, observing that part of the total meaning is this very doing.

As soon as we look closely at conversation in general, we see that it involves much more than using language to state propositions or convey facts. We also very rarely use language monologically and such uses are clearly marked. The unmarked use is dialogical, i.e., with another or others in various kinds of verbal give-and-take which we call conversation (see also p. 114). Through conversation we establish relationships with others, achieve a measure of cooperation (or fail to do so), keep channels open for further relationships, and so on. The utterances we use in conversation enable us to do these kinds of things because conversation itself has certain properties which are well worth examining. Our concern in this chapter is therefore twofold: we will be concerned both with what utterances do and how they can be used, and, specifically, with how we use them in conversation.

Speech Acts

One thing that many utterances do is make *propositions*: they do this mainly in the form of either statements or questions but other grammatical forms are also possible. Each of the following is a proposition: 'I had a busy day today,' 'Have you called your mother?,' and 'Your dinner's ready!' Such utterances are connected in some way with events or happenings in a possible world, i.e., one that can be experienced or imagined, a world in which such propositions can be said to be either true or false. They have been called *constative utterances*.

A different kind of proposition is the ethical proposition, e.g., 'Big boys don't cry,' 'God is love,' 'Thou shalt not kill,' 'You must tell the truth,' and even 'Beethoven is better than Brahms.' Just like an ordinary proposition, an ethical proposition may be true or false, although not in the same sense. But truth and falsity are not the real purpose of ethical propositions; their real purpose is to serve as guides to behavior in some world or other. 'Big boys don't cry' is obviously value-laden in a way in which 'Your dinner's ready!' definitely is not. Another kind of utterance is the 'phatic' type, e.g., 'Nice day!,' 'How do you do?,' and 'You're looking smart today!' We employ such utterances not for their propositional content but rather for their affective value as indicators that one person is willing to talk to another and that a channel of communication is either being opened or being kept open. Phatic utterances do not really communicate anything; rather, their use allows communication to occur should there be anything of consequence to say. I will have a little more to say on this matter shortly.

Austin (1975), a philosopher, distinguished still another kind of utterance from these, the *performative utterance*. In using a performative utterance, a person is not just saying something but is actually doing something if certain real-world conditions are met. To say 'I name this ship "Liberty Bell"'' in certain circumstances is to name a ship. To say 'I do' in other circumstances is to find oneself a husband or a wife – or a bigamist. To hear someone say to you 'I sentence you to five years in jail' in still other circumstances is to look forward to a rather bleak future. Such utterances perform acts: the naming of ships, marrying, and sentencing in these cases. A speech act changes in some way the conditions that exist in the world. It does something, and it is not something that in itself is either true or false. Truth and falsity may be claims made about its having been done, but they cannot be made about the actual doing.

Austin pointed out that the 'circumstances' mentioned above can be prescribed. He mentions certain *felicity conditions* that performatives must meet to be successful. First, a conventional procedure must exist for doing whatever is to be done, and that procedure must specify who must say and do what and in what circumstances. Second, all participants must properly execute this procedure and carry it through to completion. Finally, the necessary thoughts, feelings, and intentions must be present in all parties. In general, the spoken part of the total act, the actual *speech act*, will take the grammatical form of having a first-person subject and a verb in the present tense; it may or may not also include the word *hereby*. Examples are 'I (hereby) name,' 'We decree,' and 'I swear.' This kind of utterance is explicitly performative when it is employed in a conventional framework, such as naming ships, making royal proclamations, and taking an oath in court.

There are also less explicit performatives. Declarations like 'I promise,' 'I apologize,' or 'I warn you' have many of the same characteristics as the previously mentioned utterances but lack any associated conventional procedure; for anyone can promise, apologize, and warn, and there is no way of specifying the circumstances quite so narrowly as in naming ships, proclaiming, or swearing an oath. It is also on occasion possible to use other grammatical forms than the combination of first person and present tense. 'Thin ice,' 'Savage dog,' 'Slippery when wet,' and 'Loitering is forbidden' are all very obviously warnings, so to that extent they are performatives. What we can observe, then, is that, in contrast to constative utterances, that is, utterances which are often used to assert propositions and which may be true or false, they are used either appropriately or inappropriately and, if used appropriately, their very utterance is the doing of the whole or part of an action.

Austin divides performatives into five categories: (1) *verdictives*, typified by the giving of a verdict, estimate, grade, or appraisal ('We find the accused guilty'); (2) *exercitives*, the exercising of powers, rights, or influences as in appointing, ordering, warning, or advising ('I pronounce you husband and wife'); (3) *commissives*, typified by promising or undertaking, and committing one to do something by, for example, announcing an intention or espousing a cause ('I hereby bequeath'); (4) *behabitives*, having to do with such matters as apologizing, congratulating, blessing, cursing, or challenging ('I apologize'); and (5) *expositives*, a term used to refer to how one makes utterances fit into an argument or exposition ('I argue,' 'I reply,' or 'I assume').

Once we begin to look at utterances from the point of view of what they do, it is possible to see every utterance as a speech act of one kind or other, that is, as having some functional value which might be quite independent of the actual words used and their grammatical arrangement. These acts may not be as explicit or direct as 'Out!,' 'I do,' or 'We hereby seek leave to appeal' but there can be little dispute that even to say something like 'I saw John this morning' is an act; at the simplest level it is an act of telling the truth (or what you believe to be the truth) or not. There is also no reason to assume that every language has the same performatives. Although it is unlikely that a language will be without performatives for ordering, promising, and challenging, it is quite easy to see it doing without those for baptizing, naming ships, passing jail sentences, and making bets. Performativity almost certainly varies by culture.

We can now return to expressions like 'Nice day!,' 'How do you do?,' and 'You're looking smart today.' A specific kind of speech is the kind we have referred to previously as *phatic communion*. According to Malinowski (1923, p. 315), phatic communion is a type of speech in which ties of union are created by a mere exchange of words. In such communion words do not convey meanings. Instead, 'they fulfill a social function, and that is their principal aim.' What, therefore, is the function of apparently aimless gossip? Malinowski answers as follows:

> It consists in just this atmosphere of sociability and in the fact of the personal communion of these people. But this is in fact achieved by speech, and the situation in all such cases is created by the exchange of words, by the specific feelings which form convivial gregariousness, by the give and take of utterances which make up ordinary gossip. The whole situation consists in what happens linguistically. Each utterance is an act serving the direct aim of binding hearer to speaker by a tie of some social sentiment or other. Once more, language appears to us in this function not as an instrument of reflection but as a mode of action.

Malinowski himself uses the word *act* in this explanation. In phatic communion, therefore, we have still another instance of language being used to do something, not just to say something. (See also Cheepen, 1988, pp. 14–19.)

According to Searle (1969, pp. 23–4), we perform different kinds of acts when we speak. The utterances we use are *locutions*. Most locutions express some intent that a speaker has. They are *illocutionary acts* and have an *illocutionary force*. A speaker can also use different locutions to achieve the same illocutionary force or use one locution for many different purposes. Schiffrin (1994, ch. 3) has a very good example of the latter. She shows how one form, 'Y'want a piece of candy?' can perform many functions as a speech act, including question, request, and offer. In contrast, we can see how different forms can perform a single function since it is quite possible to ask someone to close the door with different words: 'It's cold in here,' 'The door's open,' and 'Could someone see to the door?' Illocutions also often cause listeners to do things. To that extent they are *perlocutions*. If you say 'I bet you a dollar he'll win' and I say 'On,' your illocutionary act of offering a bet has led to my perlocutionary uptake of accepting it. The *perlocutionary force* of your words is to get me to bet, and you have succeeded.

Searle (1999, pp. 145–6) says that illocutionary acts must be performed 'intentionally.' In order to communicate something in a language that will be understood by another speaker of that language as an utterance it must (1) be correctly uttered with its conventional meaning and (2) satisfy a truth condition, i.e., if it is 'It is raining' it must indeed be raining, and the hearer should recognize the truth of (1) and (2): 'if the hearer knows the language, recognizes my intention to produce a sentence of the language, and recognizes that I am not merely uttering that sentence but that I also mean what I say, then I will have succeeded in communicating to the hearer that it is raining.' Searle also recasts Austin's five categories of performative (here repeated in parentheses) by what he calls their point or purpose: assertives (expositives), which commit the hearer to the truth of a proposition; directives (verdictives), which get the hearer to believe in such a way as to make his or her behavior match the propositional content of the directive; commissives (commissives), which commit the speaker to undertake a course of action represented in the propositional content; expressives (behabitives), which express the sincerity conditions of the speech act; and declaratives (exercitives), which bring about a change in the world by representing it as having been changed.

If we look at how we perform certain kinds of acts rather than at how particular types of utterances perform acts, we can, as Searle (1975) has indicated, categorize at least six ways in which we can make requests or give orders even indirectly. There are utterance types that focus on the hearer's ability to do something ('Can you pass the salt?'; 'Have you got change for a dollar?'); those that focus on the speaker's wish or desire that the hearer will do something ('I would like you to go now'; 'I wish you wouldn't do that'); those that focus on the hearer's actually doing something ('Officers will henceforth wear ties at dinner'; 'Aren't you going to eat your cereal?'); those that focus on the hearer's willingness or desire to do something ('Would you be willing to write a letter of recommendation for me?'; 'Would you mind not making so much noise?');

those that focus on the reasons for doing something ('You're standing on my foot'; 'It might help if you shut up'); and, finally, those that embed one of the above types inside another ('I would appreciate it if you could make less noise'; 'Might I ask you to take off your hat?'). As Searle says (1999, p. 151), 'one can perform one speech act indirectly by performing another directly.'

Searle has concentrated his work on speech acts on how a hearer perceives a particular utterance to have the force it has, what he calls the 'uptake' of an utterance. In particular, what makes a promise a promise? For Searle there are five rules that govern promise-making. The first, the *propositional content rule*, is that the words must predicate a future action of the speaker. The second and third, the *preparatory rules*, require that both the person promising and the person to whom the promise is made must want the act done and that it would not otherwise be done. Moreover, the person promising believes he or she can do what is promised. The fourth, the *sincerity rule*, requires the promiser to intend to perform the act, that is, to be placed under some kind of obligation; and the fifth, the *essential rule*, says that the uttering of the words counts as undertaking an obligation to perform the action.

If this view is correct, it should be possible to state the necessary and sufficient conditions for every illocutionary act. Many of these require that the parties to acts be aware of social obligations involved in certain relationships. They may also make reference to certain other kinds of knowledge we must assume the parties have if the act is to be successful. For example, a command such as 'Stand up!' from A to B can be felicitous only if B is not standing up, can stand up, and has an obligation to stand up if A so requests, and if A has a valid reason to make B stand up. Both A and B must recognize the validity of all these conditions if 'Stand up!' is to be used and interpreted as a proper command. We should note that breaking any one of the conditions makes 'Stand up!' invalid: B is already standing up, is crippled (and A is not a faith healer!), outranks A, or is at least A's equal, or A has no reason that appears valid to B so that standing up appears unjustified, unnecessary, and uncalled for.

These kinds of conditions for illocutionary acts resemble what have been called *constitutive rules* rather than *regulative rules* (Rawls, 1955). Regulative rules are things like laws and regulations passed by governments and legislative bodies: they regulate what is right and wrong and sometimes prescribe sanctions if and when the rules are broken, e.g., 'Trespassing is forbidden' or 'No parking.' Constitutive rules, on the other hand, are like the rules of baseball, chess, or soccer: they actually define a particular activity in the form of 'doing X counts as Y' so that if, in certain prescribed circumstances, you strike a ball in a particular way or succeed in moving it into a certain place, that counts as a 'hit' or a 'goal.' The rules constitute the game: without them the game does not exist. In the same way, speech acts are what they are because saying something counts as something if certain conditions prevail. As Schiffrin (1994, p. 60) says, 'Language can do things – can perform acts – because people share constitutive rules that create the acts and that allow them to label utterances as particular kinds of acts.'

In contrast to Austin, who focused his attention on how speakers realize their intentions in speaking, Searle focuses on how listeners respond to utterances, that is, how one person tries to figure out how another is using a particular utterance. Is what is heard a promise, a warning, an assertion, a request, or something else? What is the illocutionary force of a particular utterance? What we see in both Austin and Searle is a recognition that people use language to achieve a variety of objectives. If we want to understand what they hope to accomplish, we must be prepared to take into account factors that range far beyond the actual linguistic form of any particular utterance. A speaker's intent, or perceived intent, is also important, as are the social circumstances that apparently determine that, if factors X, Y, and Z are present, then utterance A counts as an example of P, but if X, Y, and W are present, then the same utterance counts as an example of Q. We can see that this is the case if we consider promises and threats: these share many of the same characteristics, but they must differ in at least one essential characteristic or there would be no distinction.

Discussion

1. Austin specified certain *felicity conditions* if performatives are to succeed. He says that if either of the first conditions is not met we have a *misfire*, but if the third is not met we have an *abuse*. Why do you think he chose those terms? Can you give some examples from your own experience of misfires and abuses?

2. Standing by the side of a swimming pool, you say to a small girl 'Can you swim?' expecting either 'Yes' or 'No' as an answer. However, she jumps into the water instead. Explain how she interpreted your words. Does the same explanation hold for the reply 'I'll bring you one in a minute' rather than 'Yes, we don't need any' to the question, 'Is there any beer in the fridge?'

3. Why may each of the following be said to fail in some way as a performative?

   a. I sentence you to five years of misery.
   b. I promise you I'll kill you.
   c. I baptize this dog 'Fido.'
   d. I pronounce you husband and wife (said by the captain of the Dover–Calais ferry somewhere in the English Channel).
   e. I order you to stop (small boy to dog).
   f. I congratulate you for your failure to win the cup.
   g. I order you to resume breathing.

4. What observations can you make about the relationship of grammatical form and speaker's intent from data such as the following?

   a. Have you tidied up your room yet?
   b. When do you plan to tidy up your room?
   c. Don't you think your room's a mess?
   d. Are you planning to do anything about your room?
   e. Can you go upstairs and tidy up your room?
   f. Would you mind tidying up your room?

    g.   Wouldn't it be a good idea to tidy up your room?
    h.   Go and tidy up your room.
    i.   Your room needs tidying up.
    j.   If you don't tidy up your room, you don't go out.
    k.   Tidy up your room and you can have some ice cream.
    l.   Upstairs, and tidy up your room right now.
    m.   Kids who can't keep their rooms tidy don't get ice cream.

5.   Searle says that neither of the following is a promise: a teacher says to a lazy student, 'If you don't hand in your paper on time, I promise you I will give you a failing grade in the course'; a person accused of stealing money says 'No, I didn't, I promise you I didn't.' Why does Searle adopt this view even though in each case we have an instance of *I promise*? He also says that a happily married man who promises his wife that he will not desert her in the next week is likely to provide more anxiety than comfort. Again, why is this the case?

6.   Gordon and Lakoff (1975, p. 85) argue that a listener will not understand the following sentences as requests to take out the garbage. Why not? How might a listener understand each sentence? Why?

    a.   Are you likely to take out the garbage?
    b.   I suppose you're going to take out the garbage.
    c.   Must you take out the garbage?
    d.   Ought you to take out the garbage?

7.   Austin and Searle appear to be making a claim about all languages, i.e., that every language will be like every other language in the range of 'speech acts' it permits. However, Wittgenstein (1958, p. 11) claims that 'new types of language, new language-games, as we may say, come into existence, and others become obsolete and get forgotten.' What kinds of evidence would be necessary to test between these claims?

Cooperation

We can view utterances as acts of various kinds and the exchanges of utterances that we call conversations as exchanges of acts, not just exchanges of words, although they are this too. However, we may well ask how we can make such exchanges without achieving some prior agreement concerning the very principles of exchange. In fact, we do not. According to philosophers such as Grice, we are able to converse with one another because we recognize common goals in conversation and specific ways of achieving these goals. In any conversation, only certain kinds of 'moves' are possible at any particular time because of the constraints that operate to govern exchanges. These constraints limit speakers as to what they can say and listeners as to what they can infer.

Grice (1975, p. 45) maintains that the overriding principle in conversation is one he calls the *cooperative principle*: 'Make your conversational contribution such as is required, at the stage at which it occurs, by the accepted purpose or direction of the talk exchange in which you are engaged.' You must therefore act in conversation in accord with a general principle that you are mutually engaged with your listener or listeners in an activity that is of benefit to all, that benefit being mutual understanding.

Grice lists four maxims that follow from the cooperative principle: quantity, quality, relation, and manner. The maxim of *quantity* requires you to make your contribution as informative as is required. The maxim of *quality* requires you not to say what you believe to be false or that for which you lack adequate evidence. *Relation* is the simple injunction: be relevant. *Manner* requires you to avoid obscurity of expression and ambiguity, and to be brief and orderly. This principle and these maxims characterize ideal exchanges. Such exchanges would also observe certain other principles too, such as 'Be polite.'

Grice points out (p. 47) that these maxims do not apply to conversation alone. He says:

> it may be worth noting that the specific expectations or presumptions connected with at least some of the foregoing maxims have their analogs in the sphere of transactions that are not talk exchanges. I list briefly one such analog for each conversational category.
>
> 1. *Quantity*. If you are assisting me to mend a car, I expect your contribution to be neither more nor less than is required; if, for example, at a particular stage I need four screws, I expect you to hand me four, rather than two or six.
> 2. *Quality*. I expect your contributions to be genuine and not spurious. If I need sugar as an ingredient in the cake you are assisting me to make, I do not expect you to hand me salt; if I need a spoon, I do not expect a trick spoon made of rubber.
> 3. *Relation*. I expect a partner's contribution to be appropriate to immediate needs at each stage of the transaction; if I am mixing ingredients for a cake, I do not expect to be handed a good book, or even an oven cloth (though this might be an appropriate contribution at a later stage).
> 4. *Manner*. I expect a partner to make it clear what contribution he is making, and to execute his performance with reasonable dispatch.

What we can observe, therefore, is that the maxims are involved in all kinds of rational cooperative behavior: we assume the world works according to a set of maxims or rules which we have internalized, and we generally do our best to make it work in that way. There is nothing special about conversation when we view it in such a way.

Of course, everyday speech often occurs in less than ideal circumstances. Grice points out that speakers do not always follow the maxims he has described, and, as a result, they may *implicate* something rather different from what they actually say. They may violate, exploit, or opt out of one of the maxims, or two of the maxims may clash in a particular instance. Grice offers the following examples (pp. 51–3). In the first set he says that no maxim is violated, for B's response in each case is an adequate response to A's remark:

A: I am out of petrol.
B: There is a garage round the corner.

A: Smith doesn't seem to have a girlfriend these days.
B: He has been paying a lot of visits to New York lately.

He gives further examples, however, in which there is a deliberate exploitation of a maxim. For example, a testimonial letter praising a candidate's minor qualities and entirely ignoring those that might be relevant to the position for which the candidate is being considered flouts the maxim of quantity, just as does protesting your innocence too strongly. Other examples are ironic, metaphoric, or hyperbolic in nature: 'You're a fine friend' said to someone who has just let you down; 'You are the cream in my coffee'; and 'Every nice girl loves a sailor.' What we do in understanding an utterance is to ask ourselves just what is appropriate in terms of these maxims in a particular set of circumstances. We assess the literal content of the utterance and try to achieve some kind of fit between it and the maxims. Consequently, the answer to the question, 'Why is X telling me this in this way?' is part of reaching a decision about what exactly X is telling me. To use one of Grice's examples (p. 55), if, instead of Smith saying to you that 'Miss X sang "Home Sweet Home,"' he says 'Miss X produced a series of sounds that corresponded closely with the score of "Home Sweet Home,"' you will observe that Smith's failure to be brief helps damn Miss X's performance.

The theory of implicature explains how, when A says something to B, B will understand A's remarks in a certain way because B will recognize that A said more than was required, or gave a seemingly irrelevant reply, or deliberately obfuscated the issue. B will interpret what A says as a cooperative act of a particular kind in the ongoing exchange between A and B, but that cooperation may be shown somewhat indirectly. B will have to figure out the way in which A's utterance is to be fitted into their ongoing exchange, and B's operating assumption will be that the utterance is coherent, that sense can be made of it, and that the principles necessary to do so are available. The task is never an unprincipled one: Grice's maxims provide the necessary interpretive framework within which to establish the relevance of utterances to each other because these 'principles operate even when being flouted' (Levinson, 2001, p. 141). What is left unsaid may be just as important as what is said.

However, when we try to apply any set of principles, no matter what kind they are, to show how utterances work when sequenced into what we call conversations, we run into a variety of difficulties. Ordinary casual conversation is possibly the most common of all language activities. We are constantly talking to one another about this or that. Sometimes the person addressed is an intimate friend, at other times a more casual acquaintance, and at still other times a complete stranger. But we still manage conversation. Because it is such a commonplace activity, we tend not to think about conversation from the point of view of how it is organized, i.e., how particular conversations 'work' is beneath our conscious awareness unless we are one of those who have tried to 'improve' our conversational ability by taking courses in self-improvement or by reading certain books on the topic. Such courses and books have their own focus: they tend to concentrate on the subject matter of talk, on 'correct' pronunciation, diction, and grammar, and on matters of personal taste and behavior. They very rarely tell us anything very informative about how we actually manage conversations, i.e., what makes a particular conversation work. They are examples of what Cameron (1995) calls 'verbal hygiene' (see p. 53).

A commonplace activity is one that occurs frequently and is easily recognizable. It must also conform to certain principles which we may or may not be able to state explicitly. Many activities are commonplace by this definition: eating, sleeping, going to work, passing one another in the street, shopping, and, of course, conversing, to cite but a few. We also recognize that in many cases some people are more successful than others in dealing with the commonplace aspects of life. So far as conversation is concerned, we recognize the fact that some people are better conversationalists than others, but at the same time we may find it difficult to say what makes some better and others worse. In addition, most of us are sensitive to bizarre conversational behavior in others, but we may not always be able to say why a particular piece of speaking strikes us as odd. It is only by attempting to state explicitly the principles that appear to operate in conversations that we can explain these various judgments and reactions.

Above all, conversation is a cooperative activity in the Gricean sense, one that depends on speakers and listeners sharing a set of assumptions about what is happening. If anything went in conversation, nothing would happen. The whole activity would be entirely unpredictable and there would be too much uncertainty to make conversations either worthwhile or pleasant. Not anything goes; indeed, many things do not occur and cannot occur because they would violate the unconscious agreement that holds between speakers and listeners that only certain kinds of things will happen in a normal conversation and that both speakers and listeners will hold to that agreement. Conversation makes use of the cooperative principle; speakers and listeners are guided by considerations of quantity, quality, and so on, and the process of implicature which allows them to figure out relationships between the said and the unsaid. Grice's principles, therefore, form a fundamental part of any understanding of conversation as a cooperative activity. (See Sperber and Wilson, 1995, for an interesting extension of many of these ideas into a cognitively oriented theory of 'relevance' and Clark (1996) for an approach which has as its thesis that language use is a form of joint action located within social activities.)

Conversation is cooperative also in the sense that speakers and listeners tend to accept each other for what they claim to be: that is, they accept the face that the other offers (see p. 276). That face may vary according to circumstances, for at one time the face you offer me may be that of a 'close friend,' on another occasion a 'teacher,' and on a third occasion a 'young woman,' but it is a face which I will generally accept. I will judge your words against the face you are presenting, and it is very likely that we will both agree that you are at a particular moment presenting a certain face to me and I am presenting a certain face to you. We will be involved in *face-work*, the work of presenting faces to each other, protecting our own face, and protecting the other's face. We will be playing out a little drama together and cooperating to see that nothing mars the performance. That is the norm.

Of course, one party may violate that norm. I can refuse to accept you for what you claim to be, deny your right to the face you are attempting to present, and even challenge you about it. I may also regard your face as inappropriate or insincere, but say nothing, reserving my judgments about your demeanor and words to myself. The second course of action is the more usual; challenging someone about the face he or she is presenting is generally avoided, and those who make a regular practice of it quickly find themselves unwelcome almost everywhere – even to each other! Conversation therefore involves a considerable amount of role-playing: we choose a role for ourselves in each conversation, discover the role or roles the other or the others are playing, and then proceed to construct a little dramatic encounter, much of which involves respecting others' faces. All the world *is* a stage, and we *are* players!

We do get some help in trying to decide what face another is presenting to us and what role is being attempted, but it requires us to have certain skills. As Laver and Trudgill (1979, p. 28) observe, 'Being a listener to speech is not unlike being a detective. The listener not only has to establish what it was that was said, but also has to construct, from an assortment of clues, the affective state of the speaker and a profile of his identity.' The last two phrases, 'the affective state of the speaker' and 'a profile of his identity,' are much the same as what I have called 'face,' for they are concerned with what the speaker is trying to communicate about himself or herself on a particular occasion. Laver and Trudgill add that, 'Fortunately, the listener's task is made a little easier by the fact that the vocal clues marking the individual physical, psychological, and social characteristics of the speaker are numerous.' In other words, there is likely to be a variety of linguistic clues to help the listener. Obviously, listeners will vary in their ability to detect such clues, just as speakers will vary in their ability to present or maintain faces. Consequently, we find here one area of human activity in which there may be a wide range of human abilities so that, whereas X may be said to be 'sensitive' to others, Y may appear 'insincere,' and Z may be completely 'deviant,' and all because of the 'faces' they present to the world and the amount of success they achieve in their chosen roles.

Conversation is cooperative in at least one further way. As we saw in chapter 10, ethnomethodologists are concerned with how human beings interact with the world around them in dealing with the mundane phenomena of human existence. They insist that human beings make use of commonsense knowledge, which is different in kind from scientific knowledge, and that they employ principles of practical reasoning, which are again somewhat different from scientific principles. Moreover, all humans share this orientation and thus cooperate to deal with the world in much the same way. Consequently, we do *not* do certain kinds of things – insist on the literal interpretations of remarks, constantly question another's assumptions, refuse to take things for granted, attack received wisdom, require logical proofs in all reasoning, and so on. There is an unwritten agreement to deal with the world and matters in the world in certain ways; consequently, we put ourselves in serious peril of misunderstanding if we violate that agreement. As we will see in the following section, there is also a considerable measure of agreement about how conversations are organized, and once more we will see that we violate these principles of organization at our peril.

Discussion

1. What might happen if you said to a friend, 'completely out of the blue,' each of the following? Why?

   a: Your husband/wife is still faithful.
   b: The sun did rise this morning.
   c: Your shoes are clean today.
   d: I'm the happiest person in the world.
   e: Tomorrow's [Friday].
   f: Love makes the world go round.

2. Here are several ways of offering someone some tea. When, and with whom, might you prefer one way of offering rather than another? Why?

   a: Should I make (us) some tea?
   b: Would you like (me to make) some tea?
   c: Can I make you some tea?
   d: Let's have a cup of tea.
   e: How about a nice cup of tea?
   f: I could make you a cup of tea.
   g: Do you drink tea?

3. For each of the following, explain a set of circumstances that might exist to bring about your using the *why* question-form. Explain the various functions of this question-form.

   a: Why are you crying?
   b: Why cry about it?
   c: Why paint it?
   d: Why don't you paint it?
   e: Why are you painting the room blue?
   f: Why don't you paint the room?

4. Part of a professional face is being able to handle the language and tools of a particular calling with assurance. How does each of the following callings show some of its face through the particular types of language its practitioners employ: medicine, preaching, disk-jockeying, linguistics, auctioning, and sports commentating?

5. Face involves more than demeanor, i.e., how one appears. It involves what we project about, and claim for, ourselves. How is each of the following faces projected or claimed linguistically: anger, contentment, suffering, sorrow, excitement, decisiveness, meekness, and contrition?
6. Why is B's response odd in each case?

> A: I wonder what time the sun rises tomorrow.
> B: The sun doesn't rise; the earth rotates.
>
> A: Have a nice day.
> B: What's a *nice day*?

7. The reaction of most people to finding out that a conversation they have had with another has been recorded in some way is nearly always one of betrayal or suspicion. How do you account for this reaction?
8. In an article entitled 'Questions and Non-Answers', Pride (1986) points out nine different kinds of non-answers to questions: an outright lie; three kinds of refusal (unqualified, objection-raising, and remedied or mitigated); and four kinds of evasion (not answering, implicit response, delayed response, and forestalling or heading-off). This schema takes into account the motive of the responder, i.e., the non-answerer. Try to use it to examine a variety of question-and-answer encounters.

Conversation

Speech can be planned or unplanned (Ochs, 1979). We should note that a lot of speech has a certain amount of planning in it: it may not be all thought out and carefully planned and even rehearsed, as, for example, is the welcoming speech of a visiting head of state, but parts may be pre-planned to a greater or lesser extent. Unplanned speech is talk which is not thought out prior to its expression. Unplanned speech has certain characteristics: repetitions; simple active sentences; speaker and listener combining to construct propositions; stringing of clauses together with *and* or *but* or the juxtapositioning of clauses with no overt links at all; deletion of subjects and referents; and use of deictics, e.g., words such as *this*, *that*, *here*, and *there*. It may also be filled with equivocations (or *hedges*), i.e., words and expressions such as *well*, *like*, *maybe*, *but*, *sort of*, *you know*, *I guess*, etc. The syntax of unplanned conversation is also not at all that of formal, edited written prose. It is composed of utterances that are often fragmented and overlapping. They are not the complete, non-overlapping sentences which we carefully organize into larger units like the paragraphs, sections, and chapters of a book such as this one. It is the rare person indeed who 'speaks in paragraphs.' Unplanned speech, however, is not unorganized speech. Unorganized speech would be speech in which anything goes. We saw in the first part of this chapter a number of overriding constraints on what we say. We obviously cannot say anything to anyone at any time. Nor, as we will now see, can we say what we say in any way that we please. There are specific procedures we must follow as we indulge in the give-and-take of conversation. We ignore or violate these at our peril. A very simple illustration should suffice. You find yourself lost in a large city and need to seek help. Who do you approach, what do you say, and what limits are there to any subsequent verbal exchanges?

Analysts working in the ethnomethodological tradition described in the previous chapter have paid close attention to conversation. They have examined how people manage conversations, how talk proceeds in turns, how one utterance relates to another often in some kind of pair relationship, how topics are introduced, developed, and changed, and so on. Their concern is the very orderliness of talk; they regard conversation as skilled work in which we necessarily participate. Their goal is to explain that order and those skills. The data they use are 'closely transcribed examples of actual talk recorded in naturally occurring settings' (Hutchby and Wooffitt, 1998, p. 5) '. . . produced for the specific people present at the time, whether face to face or on the other end of a telephone line . . . [and] what we have to do is look to see how the recipient(s) of such utterances interpreted them' (p. 16) '. . . [because] talk-in-interaction can be treated as an object of analysis in its own right, rather than simply as a window through which we can view other social processes or broader sociological variables' (p. 21).

When we look at how actual speech or conversation is organized, we begin to appreciate how complex it is as soon as we try to devise any kind of system for talking about the various bits and pieces that occur and recur. If a conversation is 'interesting,' it is largely so because of the unpredictability of its content, so classifying by content is likely to be an impossible task. However, finding the organizational principles used offers us some hope. Even the most unpredictable of conversations is likely to make use of such principles; in fact, we might argue that something is a conversation not so much by reason of *what* was said but by reason of *how* it was said, i.e., by the use of certain principles that we employ time and time again to structure what we want to say. What speakers and listeners have is a set of such principles; what they do in a particular conversation is draw on that set. It is also sometimes said that conversations are *locally managed*, i.e., they actually proceed without any conscious plan and the participants simply rely on using the principles that are available to them to achieve any wider objectives they have.

One particularly important principle used in conversation is the *adjacency pair*. Utterance types of certain kinds are found to co-occur: a greeting leads to a return of greeting; a summons leads to a response; a question leads to an answer; a request or offer leads to an acceptance or refusal; a complaint leads to an apology or some kind of rejection; a statement leads to some kind of confirmation or recognition; a compliment leads to acceptance or rejection; a farewell leads to a farewell; and so on. This basic pairing relationship provides the possibilities of both continuity and exchange in that it enables both parties to say something and for these somethings to be related. It also allows for options in the second member of each pair and for a kind of chaining effect. A question can lead to an answer, which can lead to a comment, which can lead to an acknowledgment, and so on. The ring of a telephone (summons) can lead to a response ('Hello') with the rising intonation of a question, which thus requires an answer, and so on. These are purely linear chains. But there can be other types of chain, as when a question–answer or topic–comment routine is included as a sub-routine into some other pair.

It has proved possible to plot the structure of many conversations using these ideas of pairing and chaining in order to show how dependent we are on them. We can also show this same dependence by acknowledging what happens when there are violations: not responding to a question; not offering a comment when one is solicited; not acknowledging a request; not exchanging a greeting; and so on. These violations tend to disrupt conversations or to require explanations. For example, if your telephone keeps ringing when I dial your number, I will tend to assume that you are out rather than that my summons is being ignored.

There is actually some controversy over whether there is such a basic two-part exchange. Another view holds that a basic 'exchange' has three parts: 'initiation,' 'response,' and 'feedback.' In this view, unless some form of feedback occurs the total exchange is incomplete (see Stubbs, 1983). Tsui (1989) also argues for such a three-part exchange in which a following move of some kind closes out the sequence: 'a potentially three-part exchange, which may contain nonverbal component parts, is more adequate than an adjacency pair as a basic unit of conversational organization' (p. 561).

Conversation is a cooperative activity also in the sense that it involves two or more parties, each of whom must be allowed the opportunity to participate. Consequently, there must be some principles which govern who gets to speak, i.e., principles of *turn-taking*. Turn-taking in conversation is much more complex than it might appear because we engage in it so easily and skillfully. Utterances usually do not overlap other utterances, and the gaps between utterances are sometimes measurable in micro-seconds and on average are only a few tenths of a second. Turn-taking also applies in a variety of circumstances: between as few as two participants and upward of a score; on the telephone as well as in face-to-face interaction; and regardless of the length of particular utterances or how many people want to take a turn. It seems that there must be some system of 'traffic rules' which we are aware of since we manage the taking of turns so well. It is very rare indeed to see turn-taking spelled out in advance, e.g., in ceremonials or formal debates in which turns are pre-allocated. Ordinary conversation employs no such pre-allocation: the participants just 'naturally' take turns. We will see, however, that we can offer some account of what actually occurs.

In most conversations – Schegloff (2000, pp. 47–8) admits that there may be exceptions – only one person speaks at a time and that person is recognized to be the one whose turn it is to speak. At the conclusion of that turn another may speak, and, as I have indicated, there may also be slight overlapping of speaking during the transition between turns. The existence of adjacency pairing assures that there will be turns; however, it does not assure that these turns will be of any particular length. Once a speaker gets a turn to speak, he or she may be reluctant to give up that turn and may employ any one or more of a variety of devices to keep it: avoidance of eye contact with listeners; stringing utterances together in a seamless manner; avoiding the kinds of adjacency pairings that require others to speak; employing gestures and a posture that inhibit others from speaking; and so on. In these ways a speaker can exploit a turn, but such exploitation can be dangerous if carried to the extreme of 'hogging' the conversation, turning it into a speech or a monolog, or just simply boring the listeners by not allowing them the opportunity to participate or possibly even to escape. You must be prepared to give others a turn if you expect to take a turn yourself.

Turn-taking may actually vary by cultural group. Tannen (1987) identifies a New York conversational style which she labels (p. 581) as 'conversational overlap.' She claims that New Yorkers like a lot of talk going on in casual conversation to the extent that they talk while others are talking. In a later book (1994) she calls this kind of simultaneous speech 'cooperative overlapping' (p. 62). She adds that it is 'supportive rather than obstructive, evidence not of domination but of participation, not power, but the paradoxically related dimension, solidarity.' It is speech motivated by high involvement rather than disruption. She does admit, though, in the earlier discussion that those unfamiliar with this habit may well consider themselves to be constantly interrupted or even talked into silence, their turn-taking principles having been violated.

There are also certain linguistic and other signals that go with turn-taking. Speakers may signal when they are about to give up a turn in any one of several ways, or by some combination (Duncan, 1972, 1974). The final syllable or final stressed syllable of an utterance may be prolonged. The pitch level of the voice may signal closure, for example, by dropping in level on the final syllable. An utterance may be deliberately closed syntactically to achieve a sense of completeness. Words or expressions like 'you know' or 'something' can also be used to indicate a turn-point. Finally, the body itself, or part of it, may signal closure: a relaxing of posture; a gesture with a hand; or directing one's gaze at the listener. Such cues signal completion and allow the listener to take a turn. They signal what has been called a 'transition relevant place.' We must be alert to such places if we want to take a turn. Of course, such places also offer the speaker the opportunity to select the next speaker. When there are several listeners present, a speaker may attempt to address the cues to a specific listener so as to select that listener as next speaker. Speaking is not always a matter of self-selection; sometimes a specific person is clearly being called upon to speak, even on the most informal of occasions. A speaker's use of gaze, i.e., looking at a specific individual, or of a name ('honey,' or 'John,' or 'coach') or even a plain 'you' may suffice, but such usage varies widely by group and situation (Lerner, 2003). Sometimes, when there is no such selection, there is often an embarrassing pause, and, since conversationalists (certainly English conversationalists!) abhor silence, someone will usually try to take up the turn as soon as possible.

If pairing and turn-taking are integral parts of all conversations, they are so by virtue of the fact that we can identify a certain kind of language activity as conversation and particular instances as specific conversations. Conversations must also have ways of getting started, have some recognizable core or substance to them, i.e., topic or topics, and be concludable. Each conversation must be recognizable as an instance of the genre; however, what makes each recognizable is not its content but rather its form.

The beginning of a conversation will generally involve an exchange of greetings (see Schegloff, 1986). A telephone conversation may involve an exchange of 'Hello's; a meeting between strangers might require an exchange of 'How do you do's followed by some kind of self-identification; a meeting between very intimate acquaintances who spend much time together may have its own special ritualistic beginning. Much of this preliminary part of a conversation is highly prescribed by cultural setting: how you answer the telephone varies from group to group; greeting exchanges involving the use of names or address terms vary enormously, as we saw in chapter 11; who speaks first, what a suitable reply is, and even what variety of language is employed may also be tightly constrained by circumstances.

To return briefly to the subject of answering the telephone, I can illustrate a little of the variety we find. In Japan, it is the caller who speaks first on the telephone, and, in doing so, identifies himself or herself. In the Netherlands and Sweden (Lindström, 1994) people usually answer the telephone by identifying themselves. In France, a telephone call is an intrusion, so the caller feels some obligation to verify the number, identify himself, and be excused for intruding (Godard, 1977). We can see the process of verification at work when the caller says such things as *Allô, c'est toi Nicole?*, *Allô, je suis bien chez M. Thibault?*, or *Allô, la Mairie?* and then proceeds to identify himself (*Ici, Jacques*), because, according to one source (Vigner, 1978), the rule is *Dire très rapidement qui vous êtes et indiquer aussi la raison de votre appel* ('Say very quickly who you are and also state the reason for your call'). In North America, telephone calls are not regarded as intrusive to the same extent. They quite routinely interrupt other activities. People seem to find it difficult not to answer the telephone, and apologies for calling are rarely offered or are not taken very seriously, except at strange hours, e.g., a wrong number dialed at 4 a.m. (For how Greeks have taken to the telephone and integrated its use into their culture, see Sifianou, 1989.) As telephone technology changes with the addition of screening systems and answering devices it will be interesting to see how calls are managed to reflect these new ways of answering the telephone. When you call someone you are choosing the time and topic and are exercising some degree of power. When you return someone's call you are choosing the time if not the topic but you are not unprepared. If you do not return the call you have exercised some power of your own, little though that may be. (See also Hopper, 1992, ch. 9.)

Once a conversation has been initiated and the opening forms have been exchanged, it will be necessary to establish a topic or topics on which to talk. One party may have something he or she wishes to convey to, or discuss with, the other. In a telephone conversation, for example, you assume that it is the caller who has a definite topic in mind. If a telephone caller does not have a specific topic in mind, he or she must quickly mention this fact in some way. If the caller attempts to complete the call without either bringing up a topic or explaining that it was a call without a pre-designated topic, the party called is likely to feel somewhat bewildered.

Most investigators are agreed that what actually constitutes a *topic* in a conversation is not at all clear. Brown and Yule (1983, pp. 89–90) discuss this issue as follows:

it is a feature of a lot of conversation that 'topics' are not fixed beforehand, but are negotiated in the process of conversing. Throughout a conversation, the next 'topic' of conversation is developing. Each speaker contributes to the conversation in terms of both the existing topic framework and his or her personal topic. It is clear . . . that some elements in a speaker's personal topic do not become salient elements in the conversation if neither the other participant nor the speaker herself mentions them again. . . . Characterising the individual speaker's topic as 'what I think we're talking about' incorporates both that element which the conversational analyst tends to abstract as the 'topic of conversation' for the participants ('What we're talking about') and the individual speaker's version ('I think'), as he/she makes a conversational contribution. That speakers do introduce what they want to say via some form of personal reference has a noticeable effect on the structure of contributions in conversational discourse. . . .

From what we have proposed as speakers' topics in conversational discourse, it must occasionally happen that there are at least two versions of 'What I think we're talking about' which are potentially incompatible. It is a noticeable feature of co-operative conversational discourse, however, that this potential incompatibility rarely leads to conflict over the topic of conversation. What typically happens is that, in the negotiation process, one speaker realises that his version is incompatible with what the other appears to be talking about and makes his contributions compatible with 'what I think *you* (not we) are talking about'.

In one sense, then, the topic is obviously the thing that is talked about, but each of the talkers may have quite different views from the others concerning exactly what was talked about. Moreover, since parts of some conversations and sometimes the whole of others may be mainly phatic in intent, what exactly was talked about may be less important than the fact that talk itself occurred. It is also often possible to give a better account of what topics were discussed after a conversation than during it because topics work themselves out in the process of talking. It is very rare indeed, usually only on very special and, therefore, highly marked occasions, that speakers and listeners work systematically through a topic. What they are much more likely to do is *talk topically*, and in doing so exhibit a considerable degree of tolerance for unclarity, ambiguity, inexplicitness, and even incoherence in the expectation that all, or at least those parts that are necessary for proper understanding, will eventually be revealed.

Speaking around and about a topic requires what has been called *floor management*, i.e., ensuring that everyone gets to make the contribution he or she wishes to make. Speakers may overlap one another so that simultaneous talk will occur, there will be *back-channel* cues given and taken (often verbal encouragements), and almost certainly some synchronicity of movements and gestures. Hayashi (1996) compared English and Japanese conversations using groups of university students, four of which were English-speaking Americans and four Japanese-speaking Japanese, with each group divided equally by gender. She found that whereas Japanese males held the floor to a greater extent than Japanese females, American males and females shared the floor equally. The Japanese showed a greater preference for back-channeling than did the Americans. The Japanese women were generally quiet listeners who tended to support men rather than interact with them as equals. Itakura and Tsui (2004) used conversations produced by eight mixed-gender pairs of Japanese university students to look at issues of turn-taking and dominance, i.e., who gets to control the floor in conversation. They found that 'male speakers' self-oriented conversational style and female speakers' other-oriented conversational style are complementary and mutually reinforcing rather than competing. In other words, male dominance is not something predetermined and imposed on female speakers. It is instead mutually constructed by the two parties' (p. 244). While topic management and floor management may employ the same devices everywhere, they do not always produce the same results.

Since topics in conversation are usually not well defined, they may be fairly easily changed. One topic exhausts itself so a new one is introduced. However, if most of the conversationalists are fully engaged with a topic and one person tries to force such a change before the point of exhaustion, that attempt is likely to be resisted. It may be successful only if the person trying to force the change has some special power in the group, that is, if he or she is a leader, boss, or teacher, for example. A premature change in topic may be regarded as an interruption, and when the interruption is dealt with, as when the new topic is dropped or the person with power moves away, the original topic may be resumed. Sometimes a topic exhausts itself and there appears to be no new topic available to the group; in such circumstances silence is likely to result with some attempt made to fill it. If the attempt to fill the silence is unsuccessful, the group may disband.

Alternatively, there may be competition among two or more new topics and speakers, with some consequent overlap until one topic gets established and the other or others are dropped or shelved for a while. If all participants regard that new topic as a suitable one, it will be developed; if not, they may drop it quite quickly, particularly if one of the shelved topics now appears to be more interesting, a fact which need not have been immediately obvious to the group.

Once a topic is established, speakers can keep it going by employing many of the same devices they use as individuals to keep their turns going. They can link utterances together thematically, syntactically, or logically. A wide variety of devices is available to achieve such continuity. In the case of an individual turn these devices can prevent interruption in that they can be used to show that the speaker is not finished and that the turn will not be completed until it is properly marked as completed. So far as continuing a topic is concerned, the same types of device serve to link utterance to utterance. One speaker can link remarks to another speaker's remarks, overlap another's remarks, or even deliberately adopt or adapt the devices the other is employing. *Feedback*, an important element in warranting the continuation of a turn, can also lend approval to the continuation of a topic. The nods of approval or other gestures of listeners, 'mhm's and 'yes's, and other empathetic signals indicate to a speaker that the floor is still his or hers and the topic is of interest. When such feedback (or *back-channeling*) ceases, both turn and topic are put at risk. (See Schiffrin, 1987, for a general discussion of 'discourse markers.')

Speakers are sometimes interrupted or even interrupt themselves. A skillful speaker may try to lessen the chances of the first kind of interruption by structuring his or her remarks in such a way as to lessen the possibilities of interruption, controlling the amount and kind of gaze used between self and others, and ensuring that the kinds of signals that tend to indicate that a turn is being relinquished are not allowed to occur by accident. But interruptions may still occur: there may be a knock at the door, the telephone may ring, someone may knock over a glass, and so on. What sometimes occurs then is a kind of *insertion sequence* (Schegloff, 1968), a piece of conversational activity with its own structure but a piece completely unrelated to the ongoing conversation and inserted within it. The word *inserted* is used because in most such instances the original conversation tends to be resumed where it broke off, sometimes without indication that anything at all has happened, particularly if it is some kind of ritual that is involved, or with the most minor kind of acknowledgment: 'Now where were we? Oh, yes.' Here is an example of such an insertion:

> A: . . . and as I was saying (telephone rings) Mary, get the phone.
> C: Okay.
> A: . . . as I was saying, it should be next week.
> B: I see.

On the other hand, a *side sequence* (Jefferson, 1972) serves as a kind of clarification:

> A: You'll go then?
> B: I don't have to wear a tie?
> A: No!
> B: Okay, then.

The above BA sequence is a side sequence within the initial-final AB sequence of 'You'll go then?' and 'Okay, then.' Wootton (1975, p. 70) gives the following interesting example of such a sequence used in a conversation between a patient and a therapist:

> *Patient*: I'm a nurse, but my husband won't let me work.
> *Therapist*: How old are you?
> *Patient*: Thirty-one this December.
> *Therapist*: What do you mean, he won't let you work?

In this case we can see that the therapist's question about the patient's age is directed toward clarifying the patient's claim that her husband will not let her work. Apparently, the therapist considers that at 31 years of age the patient should realize that she can exercise more control over her life than she seems prepared to exercise.

Sometimes side sequences act as *repairs*. Repairs are corrections of some kind of 'trouble' that arises during the course of conversation, that trouble coming from any one of a variety of factors. 'Excuse me' is sometimes interjected by a listener into a speaker's words in an attempt to seek some kind of clarification: this is other-initiated repair. Self-repair occurs when the speaker seeks to clarify in some way what is being said and not being understood. Egbert (1996) reports on an interesting example of other-directed repair, the use of *bitte* 'pardon' in German. *Bitte* initiates repair but only when there is no mutual gaze between the parties. This use of *bitte* carries over to the telephone where there can be no such mutual gaze. Egbert points out (p. 608) that this use of '*bitte* indexes the fact that no mutual gaze is established during the delivery of the trouble-source turn,' i.e., the place in the conversation where there is some breakdown in communication.

Conversations must also be brought to a close (see Aston, 1995). Quite often the close itself is ritualistic, e.g., an exchange of 'Goodbye's. But such rituals do not come unannounced: they are often preceded by clear indications that closings are about to occur. All topics have been exhausted and nothing more remains to be said, but it is not quite the time to exchange farewells. It is into such places that you fit *pre-closing signals* which serve to negotiate the actual closing. Such signals can involve an expression like 'Well, I think that's all,' or a brief, deliberate summary of some earlier agreement, or a personal exchange like 'Give my regards to your wife,' or they may take the form of a gesture or a physical movement such as rising from a chair or adjusting your posture in some way. Such signals indicate that the conversation is being closed with final closure waiting only for a ritual exchange. Once conversationalists arrive at the pre-closing stage, specific acknowledgment of that fact must be made if somehow the conversation does not actually proceed to close: 'Oh, by the way; I've just remembered,' or 'Something else has just occurred to me.'

An actual closing may involve several steps: the closing down of a topic, e.g., 'So that's agreed' or 'One o'clock, then' repeated by the other party or acknowledged in some form; then possibly some kind of pre-closing exchange, e.g., 'Okay-Okay'; a possible further acknowledgment of the nature of the exchange, e.g., 'Good to see you,' 'Thanks again,' or 'See you soon'; and finally an exchange of farewells, e.g., 'Bye-Bye.' The following is an example of such a closing:

    A: So, that's agreed?
    B: Yep, agreed.
    A: Good, I knew you would.
    B: Yes, no problem really.
    A: Thanks for the help.
    B: Don't mention it.
    A: Okay, I'll be back soon.
    B: Okay, then, Bye. Take care.
    A: Bye.

Pre-closing signals may indeed be regarded as a sub-variety of *mitigating expressions* used in conversation. Such expressions serve the twofold function of keeping conversation going in a systematic manner and doing so while allowing the conversationalists to preserve either the reality or the appearance of cooperation. For example, a pre-request to a secretary might take the following form:

    A: Are you doing anything important right now?
    B: No, not really.
    A: Okay, then, can you do this letter for me? I need it in a hurry.

Consequently, we ask if we can make a request; or we negotiate a closing; or we question someone's veracity, but, in doing so, we carefully tone down our doubts about the truthfulness of what we are being told. We observe the decencies of linguistic behavior, choosing our words to match the circumstances. Those circumstances tell us that a particular conversation is but one in a long stream of conversations that will fill our lives. If we want to keep that stream flowing, and most of us do, we have to work with others and constantly address issues of face and politeness.

Boxer (2002, p. 51) provides a very short conversation that illustrates many of the points just made. Two female students pass each other on campus on the way to class:

A: Hey, how are you doing?
B: Fine, how about you? Going to class?
A: Calculus, I hate it! (keeps moving)
B: Ugh! Well, catch you later.
A: Yeah, see you at the meeting.

Here we have various pairings, including a greeting and a farewell, and a topic briefly raised and dealt with, and all this done in a mutually supportive way. As Boxer says, this 'sequence, despite being on the run, does important interactional work for these interlocutors' (p. 52).

The characteristics I have just discussed are some of the more interesting ones that have been observed in ordinary everyday conversation. Almost any conversation will provide examples of some of them, and any long conversation will probably provide instances of just about all. What will be remarkable is that none of the conversations will strike you as being unusual in any respect, but without the kinds of organizing principles I have described they would not exist at all. Strange or unusual conversations may be so described because of the way in which they violate, fail to employ, or exploit one or more of the principles mentioned above. For example, a monolog does not allow for turn-taking; talking to oneself involves turn-taking without the usual accompanying exchange of speaker and listener; and an aside in a speech within a play is a particular kind of side-sequence employed as a stage convention.

However, there are conversational settings that are unusual in still other ways. Because of the way in which certain of the principles are used, particular types of conversation may be given quite specific names: for example, teaching, interviewing, or interrogating. That is, in certain circumstances some of the principles we customarily use in conversation are not used at all, or are used in special ways, or are used in an 'abnormal' manner.

The use of language in the classroom by teachers and students provides a good example. Most teaching involves a lot of talk, but classroom talk is dominated by the teacher, who selects topics, sees that participants stick to the chosen topics, and decides how these will be discussed and who will be allowed, even nominated, to discuss them. The teacher has special rights and also has the power to control much of what happens in the classroom. As Coulthard (1977, p. 101) says,

Verbal interaction inside the classroom differs markedly from desultory conversation in that its main purpose is to instruct and inform, and this difference is reflected in the structure of the discourse. In conversation, topic changes are unpredictable and uncontrollable, for . . . a speaker can even talk 'on topic' without talking on the topic intended by the previous speaker. Inside the classroom it is one of the functions of the teacher to choose the topic, decide how it will be subdivided into smaller units, and cope with digressions and misunderstandings.

Moreover, the teacher gets to ask most of the questions, and, on the whole, these questions are of a very special kind: they are usually questions to which the teacher already has the answer. The questions are quite often addressed to a whole group of listeners and individuals in that group are required to bid for the right to answer. Furthermore, when someone is chosen to answer the question, the whole answering ritual is gone through for the benefit of all participants, not just for the benefit of the one who asked the question. Finally, the questioner actually evaluates the answer as one which is not only right in providing the information that was sought but also right in relation to how the teacher is seeking to develop the topic. The conversation can also be made topical, as responses can be judged for their quality, quantity, and appropriateness (or lack of it). Classroom conversational activity is very highly marked, for any of the above activities carried over to ordinary everyday conversation would result in strong objections by 'innocent' parties in such conversation: they would feel that they were being manipulated.

Classroom conversation is different from ordinary conversation in the sense that the teacher may be said to 'own' the conversation, whereas in ordinary conversations such ownership may be said to be shared. You own a conversation when you control such matters as topic selection, turn-taking, and even beginnings and endings. In such circumstances there is also a reduction of local management, that is, the need to work things out in conversation as you proceed. Classroom conversations have officially appointed managers, just like coronations, parliamentary debates, religious services, court hearings, and so on.

Teachers actually get to comment on the contributions of others with the intent of making such contributions fit a predetermined pattern. We can try to imagine what would happen if we attempted to manage an ordinary conversation in such a manner: if we insisted on selecting topics and saw that others keep to them and to our definitions of them; decided who was to speak and for how long, and interrupted as we felt the urge; began or ended the talk to meet our own goals or external demands, such as bells and recesses; and told X that what he said was irrelevant, Y that what she said was just repeating W, and asked Z to summarize what A and B said, and then expressed our approval (or disapproval) of the result. Children must learn about such ownership, and that learning may not be at all easy.

Doctor–patient or lawyer–client interviewing is also full of questioning behavior, but in this case the questions are asked for the purposes of double-checking and eliciting anything that might be relevant to deciding on a particular course of action. Such questioning may also be used for the purpose of classification: the name of a disease given to symptoms that have been elicited; a course of therapy indicated as a result of psychiatric assessment; or a particular plea to be made or position to be adopted by a client in a legal case. In each case the conversation is directed toward establishing relevant 'facts' at a level of certainty that one would never tolerate in ordinary discussion of what happened or is happening. The extreme of this behavior is the investigative or interrogative process which a person in custody or a witness in the witness box sometimes undergoes, with its goal the establishing of what happened, 'the truth,' 'guilt,' or 'innocence.' Special rules often exist to control just what kinds of question can be asked in such circumstances.

In these various circumstances there is an important evaluative component: the question and answering is conducted so that someone, not always the questioner, can make a judgment of some kind. Ordinary conversation too involves evaluation, but not at the same level of intensity. A 'good' patient, witness, or even candidate being interviewed for a job realizes how important such evaluation is and acts accordingly, tailoring responses to fit this known requirement and, in that respect, reacting differently than he or she would toward similar questions asked in less marked circumstances. To fail to do so in certain circumstances, as when you have sworn in court to tell the truth, may lead to a charge of perjury. Likewise, in an interview for a job, a refusal to play along to some extent with the conventions of interviewing may lead to a failure to acquire the desired position. We should also be aware that not everyone possesses the same knowledge of the conventions that apply in such circumstances.

One consequence is that verbal exchanges which involve people from different cultural backgrounds can more easily go wrong than those that involve people who share the same cultural background (Gumperz and Cook-Gumperz, 1982, p. 14):

> Many of the meanings and understandings, at the level of ongoing processes of interpretation of speaker's intent, depend upon culturally specific conventions, so that much of the meaning in any encounter is indirect and implicit. The ability to expose enough of the implicit meaning to make for a satisfactory encounter between strangers or culturally different speakers requires communicative flexibility.

Not everyone has such communicative flexibility, this ability to cross cultural boundaries. Consequently, when the cross-cultural exchange involves some important matter, e.g., a trial, an interview for a position, or a disagreement between employer and employee, there can be a serious breakdown in communication from the lack of such flexibility, as one party finds the other to be 'evasive,' 'confrontational,' 'irrelevant,' 'angry,' 'aloof,' or 'indifferent.' We tend to rely very heavily on our own cultural background in interpreting the talk of others, and it may not be at all easy to understand how this can create difficulties when the others are either complete strangers or come from quite different cultural backgrounds.

As Fairclough (1989) points out, many such situations are also asymmetric insofar as power is concerned. When the parties to an exchange have both different norms of behavior and claims to power, their intentions toward each other must be our concern. Farfán (2003) recounts a very good example of such inequalities in power between a Mestizo professional middleman buyer and a poor female Hñahñu occasional seller in a marketplace in Mexico. The buyer has better control of Spanish and the money that she needs for goat skins she must sell to survive. The convention is that they should bargain to reach a fair price for the skins because they are 'equal' parties. However, in addition to the inequalities in language, gender, and power, there is consistent violation of the linguistic conventions of buying and selling. The buyer takes control of the opening exchange, manipulates the turn-taking, cuts short the seller's responses, and, in fact, produces what might better be described as a monolog. For the buyer this strategy maximizes his profits; for the seller it provides further confirmation of her oppression. The language use testifies to the fundamental social asymmetry that exists. In the chapters that follow we will look further at certain other possible asymmetries in the distribution of power, and at the views of Fairclough and others like him that sociolinguists should do more than just report on the imbalances they find: they should seek to reduce them.

Discussion

1. Gumperz (1982a, p. 1) cites the following conversation recorded in a small office:

   A: Are you gonna be here for ten minutes?
   B: Go ahead and take your break. Take longer if you want to.
   A: I'll just be outside on the porch. Call me if you need me.
   B: OK, don't worry.

   What can you say about the people, the situation, and their relationship from this brief exchange? (Gumperz discusses the conversation after he cites it.) Examine the following conversation in the same way (Levinson, 1983, p. 48):

   A: So can you please come over here right now.
   B: Well, I have to go to Edinburgh today sir.
   A: Hmm. How about this Thursday?

   (Levinson also discusses what one might reasonably say about it.)

2. Here are three more conversations with a few details you might need for interpretation (Wardhaugh, 1985). Try to explain how each remark in the conversation relates to what has gone before and what follows.

   a. This is a simple home-coming routine. Speaker B is in the house as Speaker A enters and takes off his coat. Charlie is a cat.

      A: (*Loudly*) Hi, Sue!
      B: (*Loudly*) Hi, John!
      A: (*Quietly*) Hi, Charlie! Had your dinner?
      B: (*Quite loudly*) I've fed the animals already.
      A: (*Walks to kitchen*) Been home long?

B: Just a few minutes. I was out in a school all afternoon.
A: Ah. We eating at home?
B: Could I suppose.
A: No. Let's go out. I've got to look for a book.
B: OK. Give me a few minutes to get changed. By the way...
A: Yes?
B: Oh, nothing. Chinese food?
A: Yeah. If you want. I'll take the dog out for a walk while you
     get ready. (*Loudly*) Rufus!

b.   In this conversation the setting is a neighborhood convenience store
     and the time 11 p.m. Speaker A is a woman in one of the two lines
     to the cash registers. These lines are quite closely packed because there
     is not much space in the area in front of the registers. Speaker B, a
     man, is directly behind A in the same line. He is looking around at
     shelves and others in the store but is paying no particular attention to
     the woman in front of him – she is just one of those 'others.'

     A: (Looks directly at B) Would you like to get in front of me?
     B: (Surprised) No!
     A: You know I can feel your tension.
     B: (Edges back) I'm sorry but I'm not aware of it. (Turns away,
          raises his eyebrows, and shrugs his shoulders, directing these
          last two actions toward the next one in line, C, who has over-
          heard the brief exchange.)
     C: (Similar shrugging behavior)

c.   This conversation involves an encounter between complete strangers. The
     setting is a park adjacent to a university, one frequented by students
     and also by the general public. It is small, tree-filled, and pleasant.
     The time is a fine autumn afternoon and the park is well populated.
     Speaker B is sitting on a park bench. She is dressed in the style favored
     by students. There is an open book on her lap and some books on the
     bench beside her. Speaker A approaches her. He is a young man dressed
     in jeans and a black leather jacket, not a style of dress favored by
     students. As A approaches B, he speaks.

     A: You look a little lonely.
     B: Not at all.
     A: You smoke hash?
     B: I don't want to buy any, and I don't have any to sell.
     A: How about coke?
     B: Look! I'm not bothering anyone and I *was* quite content until...
     A: Two's company.
     B: *You're* a crowd.
     A: Don't get fresh with me.
     B: (Stands up, picks up books, leaves)

3. Here are some conversational openers. When might each be suitable?

    a: What time is it, please?
    b: Gotta match?
    c: Do you have the time?
    d: The bus is sure late!
    e: What a mess!
    f: Can I help you?
    g: Did you see that?
    h: Sorry!
    i: You seem lonely.
    j: Are you looking for Mr Jones?

    Which of the above would be improved by an introductory 'Excuse me'?
4. Account for the 'Oh!' in the following conversation:

    A: Hello, John, how are you today?
    B: Awful. I've got a horrible cold, my dog's sick, and work's just piling up all around me.
    A: Oh!

5. You are at a party and you approach a group of strangers, one of whom says 'Hello, we were just talking about the news from the Middle East.' What do you consider to be the purpose of such a remark?
6. What is the function of 'Yes' in the following two exchanges?

    Teacher: So which is the dependent variable?
    Student: Age.
    Teacher: Yes.

    Physician: How often do you get this itching?
    Patient: Often, just about every night.
    Physician: Yes.

    Would you expect the two utterances of 'Yes' to be alike in loudness and pitch? Who would speak next? What might be said?
7. Try to formulate what you consider to be the characteristics of a 'good' conversationalist and of a 'poor' conversationalist. Be as specific as you can in trying to assess such matters as fluency, style of speech adopted, special mannerisms, types of expressions used, and so on.
8. People seem to be reluctant to leave messages on answering machines. Can you think of any reasons why this should be so? What kinds of instructions to potential answerers seem to help?
9. Edwards (1981, p. 303) contrasts 'relatively "open"' and '"typical" classrooms' as follows:

    In relatively 'open' classrooms, the greater range of semantic options available to pupils may be evident in more overlapping talk, more pupil-selected next speakers, more self-selected next speakers, more interruptions by pupils, fewer pauses, fewer invited stories and fewer but more tentative and more widely distributed formulations. In short, more of the speech exchange system will be locally managed, and pupils too will be able to direct speakership in a creative way. . . . In 'typical' classrooms, the point of persistent reference is the authority of the teacher as expert, which provides a more or less continuous interpretive context. A basic presupposition of teacher knowledge and pupil ignorance is a main resource from which both teacher and pupils accomplish mutually comprehensible talk. Where the teacher's authority has been partly relinquished or eroded, then the resulting interplay of alternative frames of reference and relevance will be evident in the discourse.

Record some examples of student–teacher linguistic interaction in a classroom (or classrooms) with which you are familiar and use them to justify a claim that they reveal an 'open' situation rather than a 'typical' one, or vice versa.

10. 'You know' and 'like' are two expressions (hedges) that often pepper certain conversations; they seem to be spread all over. Try to figure out some of the uses of either (or both). (See Dailey-O'Cain, 2000, for 'like.')

11. Much of the humor in movies featuring the Marx Brothers comes from their crazy conversations as they violate many of the principles discussed in this chapter. Find some examples and try to explain what is going on.

Further Reading

The best general book on topics in this chapter is Schiffrin (1994). Two other basic books are Coulthard (1977) and Wardhaugh (1985). Blakemore (1992), Yule (1996), Mey (1993), and Levinson (1983) provide good treatments of pragmatics, and Davis (1991) and Tsohatzidis (1994) are useful collections of papers. There are numerous books on conversation and discourse: Brown (1996), Brown and Yule (1983), Coulmas (1981), Drew (1994), Eggins and Slade (1997), Ford et al. (2002), Geis (1995), Gumperz (1982a), Have (1999), Hutchby and Wooffitt (1998), Jaworski and Coupland (1999), McLaughlin (1984), Sacks (1992), Schenkein (1978), Stenström (1994), Stubbs (1983), Taylor and Cameron (1987), and Wilson (1989). See Silverman (1998) for more on Sacks. Goffman (1981) provides still another approach to talk and Carston and Uchida (1998) updates 'relevance' theory.

Part IV Understanding and Intervening

Her voice was ever soft,
Gentle and low, an excellent thing in woman.

William Shakespeare

It is hard for a woman to define her feelings in language which is
chiefly made by men to express theirs.

Thomas Hardy

Men have had every advantage of us in telling their own story.
Education has been theirs in so much higher a degree; the pen has
been in their hands.

Jane Austen

The awful shadow of some unseen Power
Floats, tho' unseen, amongst us.

Percy Bysshe Shelley

Power takes as ingratitude the writhing of its victims.

Rabindranath Tagore

Zeus does not bring all men's plans to fulfilment.

Homer

13　Gender

A major topic in sociolinguistics is the connection, if any, between the structures, vocabularies, and ways of using particular languages and the social roles of the men and women who speak these languages. Do the men and women who speak a particular language use it in different ways? If they do, do these differences arise from the structure of that language, which would therefore be one kind of confirmation of the Whorfian hypothesis (chapter 9), or, alternatively, do any differences that exist simply reflect the ways in which the sexes relate to each other in that society, whatever the reason? May it be possible to describe a particular language as 'sexist,' or should we reserve such a description for those who use that language? If the answer to either question is affirmative, what could and should be done?

These issues generated a considerable amount of thought and discussion in the last decades of the twentieth century and many are still unresolved. They are also very emotional issues for many who have chosen either to write on them or to discuss them, and that they should be so is quite understandable. The literature on these issues is now vast; it has been one of the biggest 'growth' areas within sociolinguistics in recent years. In this chapter I will attempt to see what some of the underlying facts are and to avoid the kinds of rhetoric and dialectic that characterize much of the discussion of 'sexism in language,' a topic which often seems to invite 'large' arguments based on 'small' data.

I should note too that in certain earlier editions of this book I entitled this chapter 'Language and Sex' rather than 'Language and Gender' or just simply 'Gender,' the current title. I said then that I preferred not to use the word *gender* because it was a technical term in linguistics (see Corbett, 1991) and many of the issues dealt with in the chapter focused on claims about 'sexism.' I think that statement is still true. However, the current vogue is to use *gender* rather than *sex* as the cover word for the various topics discussed in this chapter and I have therefore adopted it here. Sex is to a very large extent biologically determined whereas gender is a social construct (but still one heavily grounded in sex, as we can see in recent publications that use the term 'sexuality,' e.g., Kulick, 2003, and Cameron and Kulick, 2003) involving the whole gamut of genetic, psychological, social, and cultural differences between males and females. Wodak (1997b, p. 13) says that gender is 'not . . . a pool of attributes "possessed" by a person, but . . . something a person "does." ' Elsewhere (1997a, p. 4) she adds that 'what it means to be a woman or to be a man [also] changes from one generation to the next and . . . varies between different racialized, ethnic, and religious groups, as well as for members of different social classes.' In such a view, gender must be learned anew in each generation. Cameron (1998b, pp. 280–1) states that view in a slightly different way:

> Men and women . . . are members of cultures in which a large amount of discourse about gender is constantly circulating. They do not only learn, and then mechanically reproduce, ways of speaking 'appropriate' to their own sex; they learn a much broader set of gendered meanings that attach in rather complex ways to different ways of speaking, and they produce their own behavior in the light of these meanings. . . .
> Performing masculinity or femininity 'appropriately' cannot mean giving exactly the same performance regardless of the circumstances. It may involve different strategies in mixed and single-sexed company, in private and public settings, in the various social positions (parent, lover, professional, friend) that someone might regularly occupy in the course of everyday life.

Gender is also something we cannot avoid; it is part of the way in which societies are ordered around us, with each society doing that ordering differently. As Eckert and McConnell-Ginet (2003, p. 50) say: 'The force of gender categories in society makes it impossible for us to move through our lives in a nongendered way and impossible not to behave in a way that brings out gendered behavior in others.' Gender is a key component of identity.

We will look at some of the evidence that there are gender differences in language use. One purpose will be to evaluate that evidence: just how good is it? However, the main purpose is to try to discover, when indeed there is good evidence, what it is good evidence of. That languages can be sexist? That those who use languages may be sexist? That language-learning is almost inevitably tied to gender-learning? That such learning is almost always skewed in such a way as to favor one gender over the other? That change is not only desirable but possible? It is issues such as these that will be our concern.

Differences

That there are differences between men and women is hardly a matter of dispute. Females have two X chromosomes whereas males have an X and a Y; this is a key genetic difference and no geneticist regards that difference as unimportant. On average, females have more fat and less muscle than males, are not as strong, and weigh less. They also mature more rapidly and live longer. The female voice usually has different characteristics from the male voice, and often females and males exhibit different ranges of verbal skills. However, we also know that many of the differences may result from different socialization practices (see Philips et al., 1987). For example, women may live longer than men because of the different roles they play in society and the different jobs they tend to fill. Differences in voice quality may be accentuated by beliefs about what men and women *should* sound like when they talk, and any differences in verbal skills may be explained in great part through differences in upbringing. (It has often been noted that there is far more reading failure in schools among boys than girls, but it does not follow from this fact that boys are inherently less well equipped to learn to read, for their poor performance in comparison to girls may be sociocultural in origin rather than genetic.) There is also an important caveat concerning all such studies showing differences between groups, and the two genders are just groups like any other; it is one I made earlier (p. 158) and will repeat here. For many in the two groups under comparison there will be no difference at all: the next person you meet on the street may be male or female, tall or short, long-lived or short-lived, high-voiced or low-voiced, and so on, with not one of these characteristics being predictable from any other. (Given a thousand or more such encounters some tendencies may emerge, but even knowing what these are would not help you with the very next person you meet.)

Numerous observers have described women's speech as being different from that of men (see Baron, 1986, Arliss, 1991, pp. 44–112, and pp. 162–207 of this book). I should also observe that there is a bias here: men's speech usually provides the norm against which women's speech is judged. We could just as well ask how men's speech differs from that of women, but investigators have not usually gone about the task of looking at differences in that way. For example, in discussing language change in Philadelphia, Labov (2001, pp. 281–2) deliberately recasts his statement that 'Women conform more closely than men to sociolinguistic norms that are overtly prescribed, but conform less than men when they are not' to read that men 'are less conforming than women with stable linguistic variables, and more conforming when change is in progress within a linguistic system.' He does this so as to avoid appearing to bias his findings.

Any view too that women's speech is trivial (see the denial in Kipers, 1987), gossip-laden, corrupt, illogical, idle, euphemistic, or deficient is highly suspect; nor is it necessarily more precise, cultivated, or stylish – or even less profane (see De Klerk, 1992, and Hughes, 1992) – than men's speech. Such judgments lack solid evidentiary support. For example, apparently men 'gossip' just as much as women do (see Pilkington, 1998); men's gossip is just different. Men indulge in a kind of phatic small talk that involves insults, challenges, and various kinds of negative behavior to do exactly what women do by their use of nurturing, polite, feedback-laden, cooperative talk. In doing this, they achieve the kind of solidarity they prize. It is the norms of behavior that are different.

In the linguistic literature perhaps the most famous example of gender differentiation is found in the Lesser Antilles of the West Indies among the Carib Indians. Male and female Caribs have been reported to speak different languages, the result of a long-ago conquest in which a group of invading Carib-speaking men killed the local Arawak-speaking men and mated with the Arawak women. The descendants of these Carib-speaking men and Arawak-speaking women have sometimes been described as having different languages for men and women because boys learn Carib from their fathers and girls learn Arawak from their mothers. This claim of two separate languages is now discounted. What differences there are actually do not result in two separate or different languages, but rather one language with noticeable gender-based characteristics (Baron, 1986, pp. 59–63, and Taylor, 1951b).

Phonological differences between the speech of men and women have been noted in a variety of languages. In Gros Ventre, an Amerindian language of the northeast United States, women have palatalized velar stops where men have palatalized dental stops, e.g., female *kjatsa* 'bread' and male *djatsa*. When a female speaker of Gros Ventre quotes a male, she attributes female pronunciations to him, and when a male quotes a female, he attributes male pronunciations to her. Moreover, any use of female pronunciations by males is likely to be regarded as a sign of effeminacy. In a northeast Asian language, Yukaghir, both women and children have /ts/ and /dz/ where men have /tj/ and /dj/. Old people of *both* genders have a corresponding /čj/ and /ǰj/. Therefore, the difference is not only gender-related, but also age-graded. Consequently, in his lifetime a male goes through the progression of /ts/, /tj/, and /čj/, and /dz/, /dj/, and /ǰj/, and a female has a corresponding /ts/ and /čj/, and /dz/ and /ǰj/. In Bengali men often substitute /l/ for initial /n/; women, children, and the uneducated do not do this. Likewise, in a Siberian language, Chukchi, men, but not women, often drop /n/ and /t/ when they occur between vowels, e.g., female *nitvaqenat* and male *nitvaqaat*. In Montreal many more men than women do not pronounce the *l* in the pronouns *il* and *elle*. Schoolgirls in Scotland apparently pronounce the *t* in words like *water* and *got* more often than schoolboys, who prefer to substitute a glottal stop. Haas (1944) observed that in Koasati, an Amerindian language spoken in southwestern Louisiana, among other gender-linked differences, men often pronounced an *s* at the end of verbs but women did not, e.g., male *lakáws* 'he is lifting it' and female *lakáw*. What was interesting was that this kind of pronunciation appeared to be dying out, because younger women and girls do not use these forms. That older speakers recognized the distinction as gender-based is apparent from the fact that women teach their sons to use the male forms and men narrating stories in which women speak employ female forms in reporting their words. This practice is in direct contrast to the aforementioned situation in Gros Ventre, where there is no such changeover in reporting or quoting.

There is also a very interesting example from English of a woman being advised to speak more like a man in order to fill a position previously filled only by men. Margaret Thatcher was told that her voice did not match her position as British Prime Minister: she sounded too 'shrill.' She was advised to lower the pitch of her voice, diminish its range, and speak more slowly, and thereby adopt an authoritative, almost monotonous delivery to make herself heard. She was successful to the extent that her new speaking style became a kind of trademark, one either well-liked by her admirers or detested by her opponents.

In the area of morphology and vocabulary, many of the studies have focused on English. In a paper which, although it is largely intuitive, anecdotal, and personal in nature, is nevertheless challenging and interesting, Lakoff (1973), claims that women use color words like *mauve, beige, aquamarine, lavender,* and *magenta* but most men do not. She also maintains that adjectives such as *adorable, charming, divine, lovely,* and *sweet* are also commonly used by women but only very rarely by men. Women are also said to have their own vocabulary for emphasizing certain effects on them, words and expressions such as *so good*, *such fun*, *exquisite*, *lovely*, *divine*, *precious*, *adorable*, *darling*, and *fantastic*. Furthermore, the English language makes certain distinctions of a gender-based kind, e.g., *actor–actress*, *waiter–waitress*, and *master–mistress*. Some of these distinctions are reinforced by entrenched patterns of usage and semantic development. For example, *master* and *mistress* have developed quite different ranges of use and meaning, so that whereas Joan can be described as *Fred's mistress*, Fred cannot be described as *Joan's master*. Other pairs of words which reflect similar differentiation are *boy–girl*, *man–woman*, *gentleman–lady*, *bachelor–spinster*, and even *widower–widow*. In the last case, whereas you can say 'She's Fred's widow,' you cannot say 'He's Sally's widower.' Lakoff cites numerous examples and clearly establishes her point that 'equivalent' words referring to men and women do have quite different associations in English. A particularly telling example is the difference between 'He's a professional' and 'She's a professional.' Other investigators have documented the same phenomenon in other languages, for example in French uses of *garçon* and *fille*.

One of the consequences of such work is that there is now a greater awareness in some parts of the community that subtle, and sometimes not so subtle, distinctions are made in the vocabulary choice used to describe men and women. Consequently, we can understand why there is a frequent insistence that neutral words be used as much as possible, as in describing occupations e.g., *chairperson*, *letter carrier*, *salesclerk*, and *actor* (as in 'She's an actor'). If language tends to reflect social structure and social structure is changing, so that judgeships, surgical appointments, nursing positions, and primary school teaching assignments are just as likely to be held by women as men (or by men as women), such changes might be expected to follow inevitably. This kind of work does two things: it draws our attention to existing inequities, and it encourages us to make the necessary changes by establishing new categorizations (e.g., *Ms*), and suggesting modifications for old terms (e.g., changing *policeman* to *police officer* and *chairman* to *chairperson*). However, there is still considerable doubt that changing *waitress* to either *waiter* or *waitperson* or describing Nicole Kidman as an actor rather than as an actress indicates a real shift in sexist attitudes. Reviewing the evidence, Romaine (1999, pp. 312–13) concludes that 'attitudes toward gender equality did not match language usage. Those who had adopted more gender-inclusive language did not necessarily have a more liberal view of gender inequities in language.'

One particular bit of sexism in languages that has aroused much comment is the gender systems that so many of them have, the *he–she–it* 'natural' gender system of English or the *le–la* or *der–die–das* 'grammatical' gender systems of French and German. The possible connections between gender systems (masculine, feminine, neuter) and gender differences (male, female, neither) are various. See Romaine (1999) for some observations and claims concerning these connections, e.g., her claim (p. 66) that 'ideological factors in the form of cultural beliefs about women . . . enter into gender assignment in [grammatical] systems that are supposedly purely formal and arbitrary.' In English such connections sometimes create problems for us in finding the right pronoun: compare the natural 'Everybody should hand in their papers in five minutes' to the apparently biased 'No person in his right mind would do that.' Again, *he–she* distinctions can often be avoided – sometimes clumsily, to be sure – so it probably does not follow that languages with gender distinctions must be sexist, which would also be a clear argument in support of the Whorfian hypothesis (see pp. 221–8). It is the people who use languages who are or who are not sexist; Chinese, Japanese, Persian, and Turkish do not make the kinds of gender distinctions English makes through its system of pronouns, but it would be difficult to maintain that males who speak these languages are less sexist than males who speak English!

There certainly are gender differences in word choice in various languages. Japanese women show they are women when they speak, for example, by the use of a sentence-final particle *ne* or another particle *wa*. In Japanese, too, a male speaker refers to himself as *boku* or *ore* whereas a female uses *watasi* or *atasi*. Whereas a man says *boku kaeru* 'I will go back' in plain or informal speech, a woman says *watasi kaeru wa* (Takahara, 1991). Children learn to make these distinctions very early in life. However, Reynolds (1998, p. 306) points out that 'the use of *boku* . . . by junior high school girls has recently become quite common in Tokyo. Girls who were interviewed in a TV program explain that they cannot compete with boys in classes, in games or in fights with *watasi*. . . . The use of *boku* and other expressions in the male speech domain by young female speakers has escalated to a larger area and to older groups of speakers.' In polite conversation a female speaker of Thai refers to herself as *dichǎn* whereas a man uses *phǒm*. In Thai, too, women emphasize a repeated action through reduplication, i.e., by repeating the verb, whereas men place a descriptive verb, *mak*, after the verb instead.

Different languages do seem to prescribe different forms for use by men and women. To cite another example, according to Sapir (1929a), the Yana language of California contains special forms for use in speech either by or to women. However, very few are like the language of the Dyirbal people of North Queensland, Australia, who have a special language which is gender-differentiated in a rather novel way (Dixon, 1971). The normal everyday language, Guwal, is used by both genders; but, if you are a man and your mother-in-law is present, or if you are a woman and your father-in-law is present, you use Dyalŋuy, a 'mother-in-law' variety. This variety has the same phonology and almost the same grammar as Guwal but its vocabulary is entirely different. However, both genders have access to both varieties.

Another Australian aboriginal language, Yanyuwa, spoken by approximately 90 to 150 people, has gender-differentiated dialects. The dialects use the same word stems but there are different class-marking prefixes on nouns, verbs, and pronouns. According to Bradley (1998), men use one dialect among themselves and women use the other. Men also use men's dialect to speak to women and women use women's dialect to speak to men. Children are brought up in women's dialect with boys required to shift – not always done easily – to men's dialect as they are initiated into manhood. Bradley adds (p. 16) that: 'If individuals wish to speak Yanyuwa then they are expected to speak the dialect which is associated with their sex – there is no other alternative.' A person can use the other sex's dialect only in very well-defined circumstances such as story-telling, joking, and certain singing rituals. The Yanyuwa find all of this perfectly normal and natural.

In the Dyirbal example cited above we may find an important clue as to why there are sometimes different varieties for men and women. One variety may be forbidden to one gender, i.e., be taboo, but that gender is apparently nearly always the female gender. (See pp. 238–40.) This phenomenon has been noted among the Trobriand Islanders, various aboriginal peoples of Australia, Mayans, Zulus, and Mongols, to cite but a few examples. The taboos often have to do with certain kinship relationships or with hunting or with some religious practice and result in the avoidance of certain words or even sounds in words. They derive from the social organization of the particular group involved and reflect basic concerns of the group. Such concerns quite often lead to women being treated in ways that appear inimical to egalitarian-oriented outsiders.

When we turn to certain grammatical matters in English, we find that Brend (1975) claims that the intonation patterns of men and women vary somewhat, women using certain patterns associated with surprise and politeness more often than men. In the same vein, Lakoff says that women may answer a question with a statement that employs the rising intonation pattern usually associated with a question rather than the falling intonation pattern associated with making a firm statement. According to Lakoff, women do this because they are less sure about themselves and their opinions than are men. For the same reason, she says that women often add tag questions to statements, e.g., 'They caught the robber last week, didn't they?' These claims about tag questions and insecurity have been tested by others (Dubois and Crouch, 1975, Cameron et al., 1989, and Brower et al., 1979) and found wanting: experimental data do not necessarily confirm intuitive judgments. The latter investigators did find, however, that the gender of the addressee was an important variable in determining how a speaker phrased a particular question.

We have already seen at other places in this book instances of language behavior varying according to gender. Many of these are quantitative studies in which sex is used as one of the variables that are taken into account. As Milroy and Gordon (2003, p. 100) say, 'Strictly speaking . . . it makes sense . . . to talk of sampling speakers according to sex, but to think of gender as the relevant social category when interpreting the social meaning of sex-related variation.' I will remind you of a few of these studies. Fischer's work (see pp. 162–3) showed how very young boys and girls differ in certain choices they make, as did Cheshire's work in Reading (pp. 170–2) in an older group. Labov's studies in New York (pp. 164–8) and Philadelphia (pp. 209–11) also revealed noticeable gender differences in adult speech. These led him to make some interesting claims about what such differences indicated, e.g., about women's role in language change. The Milroys' study exploring network relationships (pp. 181–3) showed certain characteristics of men's and women's speech: how they were alike in some ways but different in others. Jahangiri's study in Teheran (pp. 179–80) is of interest because of the very clear differences he reported between the speech of males and females. Finally, Gal's study in the Oberwart of Austria (pp. 205–6) showed how it is not only what women say but who they are willing to say it to that is important. We have also noted that there are often different politeness requirements made of men and women.

Still other gender-linked differences are said to exist. Women and men may have different paralinguistic systems and move and gesture differently. The suggestion has been made that these often require women to appear to be submissive to men. Women are also often named, titled, and addressed differently from men. Women are more likely than men to be addressed by their first names when everything else is equal, or, if not by first names, by such terms as *lady*, *miss*, or *dear*, and even *baby* or *babe*. Women are said to be subject to a wider range of address terms than men, and men are more familiar with them than with other men. Women are also said not to employ the profanities and obscenities men use, or, if they do, use them in different circumstances or are judged differently for using them. (However, the successful American television series 'Sex and the City' might seriously challenge that idea!) Women are also sometimes required to be silent in situations in which men may speak. Among the Araucanian Indians of Chile, men are encouraged to talk on all occasions, but the ideal wife is silent in the presence of her husband, and at gatherings where men are present she should talk only in a whisper, if she talks at all.

Some writers are not impressed with the kinds of findings reported in the preceding paragraphs. These findings come from quantitative, variationist studies of the kind I discussed in chapters 6–8. For example, Cameron (1998a, pp. 945–6) says that these findings 'belong to the tradition of empirical sex difference studies that do no more than set out to find statistically significant differences between women's and men's behavior. This research formula has proved as durable as it is dubious (not to say dull).' She adds that this kind of work 'deals in arcane sound changes presented through complex statistics.' In this view, merely to observe, count, and graph linguistic phenomena is not enough. An investigator needs some kind of theory about such behavior and some ideas to test before beginning an investigation. And, possibly, as we will see, some kind of ideology to suggest the 'right' theory.

In setting out a list of what she calls 'sociolinguistic universal tendencies,' Holmes (1998) does offer some testable claims. There are five of these:

1. Women and men develop different patterns of language use.
2. Women tend to focus on the affective functions of an interaction more often than men do.
3. Women tend to use linguistic devices that stress solidarity more often than men do.
4. Women tend to interact in ways which will maintain and increase solidarity, while (especially in formal contexts) men tend to interact in ways which will maintain and increase their power and status.
5. Women are stylistically more flexible than men.

It is through testing claims such as these that we are likely to refine our understanding of those matters that interest us.

There are differences in gendered speech, some undoubtedly real but others almost certainly imaginary. Any differences that do exist surely also must interact with other factors, e.g., social class, race, culture, discourse type, group membership, etc. In the next section we will look more closely at some possible explanations for them. We will also try to avoid examining women's speech in relation to men's speech as though the latter provides the norm. (To show just how 'normal' that is, the paragraph on p. 322 beginning 'Still other gender-linked . . .' was deliberately written in that way. You might try to recast it using women's language behavior as the norm.)

Discussion

1. Lakoff (1973, pp. 50–2) says that, in each of the following pairs, it is quite clear which utterance is used only by females:

    1a. Oh dear, you've put the peanut butter in the refrigerator again.
    1b. Shit, you've put the peanut butter in the refrigerator again.

    2a. What a terrific idea!
    2b. What a divine idea!

    What is your opinion? How do you explain any difference in usage?
2. When do you use the words *boy(s)* and *girl(s)* to refer to members of your own sex or of the other sex? Are there any uses of these words that you hear but refuse to employ yourself? Why? Has this always been the case? If not, why not?
3. How do you use the words *lady* and *woman*? Do you ever use combinations such as *lady doctor* or *woman executive*? Do you use *cleaning lady*, *cleaning woman*, or some other term? Are *lady* and *woman* synonymous?
4. Whereas a young man may sometimes be referred to as a *stud, dude,* or *guy*, a young woman may be referred to as a *broad, chick, dame, doll, fox,* or *dog*. You might know some other terms too. Are there any fairly clear semantic differences between the two sets? If there are, what would you say they indicate?
5. How do you address men and women who hold equivalent positions? Do you make any kind of distinction by gender? How do such people address you? Is there a difference according to whether they are male or female? Do they address someone of the same age as yourself but of different gender in the same manner?
6. Check the etymologies of the following words: *lady, lord, woman, female, spinster, witch, housewife*. Any conclusions?
7. What are your views of proposed new words like *chairperson, anchor-person, spokesperson, craftsperson, personslaughter, personhandle,* and *personhood*?
8. In March, 1991, Mayor David Dinkins of New York City referred to military personnel returning from the Gulf War as 'our heroes and she-roes.' Any comment?
9. Are words like *masterpiece, masterful, mastery,* and *to master* sexist?
10. Sex and grammatical gender are different. What do the following French words refer to: *la sentinelle, un mannequin, la recrue,* and *un laideron*?

11. Holborow (1999, p. 192) offers the following criticism of gender studies: 'it is cooperation between men and women for social purposes not competition that has . . . been decisive historically, and . . . social divisions are more significant than sexual ones.' She claims that differences associated with gender are not the same as those arising from social class. The latter are far more important than the former. Indeed, concentration on gender differences may undermine our understanding of how language really functions in our lives, men and women alike. How tenable is such a view?

12. There are many magazines oriented toward a specific gender. Can you distinguish a magazine's orientation by its linguistic choices alone?

13. Some newspapers and magazines carry columns devoted to men and women seeking other men and women for a variety of purposes. How do those using such columns label themselves and those they seek? What do such labels reveal about any of the issues discussed in this chapter?

14. Check the definitions of *person*, *man*, and *woman* in a variety of dictionaries, including as many old ones as you can find. Are you uncomfortable with any of them?

Possible Explanations

When we turn to matters having to do with how men and women use language in a wider sense, that is, in social interaction and to achieve certain ends, we find clues to possible explanations for the differences we encounter. One analysis of how women are presented in a set of cartoons produced some interesting findings (Kramer, 1974). The cartoons were taken from thirteen issues of *The New Yorker* magazine published between February 17 and May 12, 1973. The analysis showed that, when both genders were represented in the cartoon, men spoke twice as much as women. In the cartoons men and women also spoke on different topics, with men holding forth on such topics as business, politics, legal matters, taxes, and sports, and women on social life, books, food and drink, life's troubles, and lifestyle. Women spoke less forcefully than men, and men swore much more than women. Men were also more blunt and to the point in their speaking. There was also some evidence that the use of words like *nice* and *pretty* was gender-linked. Although such cartoons are not actual records of what happens in speech, they must be based on what people think happens if they are to be effective. They make use of the stereotypes we have about the speech of men and women. Let us look at some better evidence freed from such stereotyping.

In conversations involving both men and women many researchers agree that men speak more than women do. One also found that when men talked to men, the content categories of such talk focused on competition and teasing, sports, aggression, and doing things. On the other hand, when women talked to women, the equivalent categories were the self, feelings, affiliation with others, home, and family. Women are also reported to use more polite forms and more compliments than men. In doing so, they are said to be seeking to develop solidarity with others in order to maintain social relationships. On the other hand, men are likely to use talk to get things done. However, these are tendencies only; men also try to bond and women also try to move others to action.

Mills (2003) contests the view that women are more polite than men. She says that 'politeness' is not a property of utterances; it is rather 'a set of practices or strategies which communities of practice develop, affirm, and contest' (p. 9). Politeness requirements vary by situation and there is no overall imperative to be polite to others; we can be impolite too and other views of politeness are incorrect (see p. 276). While there may be a stereotypical, white, middle-class (and largely female) idea of what politeness is, it is not widely shared (although it is extremely influential in the literature on politeness). 'For some women, this stereotype may be important, but for others it may be something which they actively resist and reject' (p. 214). Politeness 'is clearly a resource which interactants use to structure their relations with others, and they are able to be self-reflexive about their own and others' use of politeness and impoliteness' (pp. 245–6).

When the two genders interacted, men tended to take the initiative in conversation, but there seemed to be a desire to achieve some kind of accommodation so far as topics were concerned: the men spoke less aggressively and competitively and the women reduced their amount of talk about home and family. A thorough review of the literature by James and Drakich (1993) showed inconsistency in the findings when fifty-six studies of talk either within or between genders were examined. What was important in determining who talked was 'the context and the structure of the social interaction within which gender differences are observed' (p. 281). James and Drakich add (pp. 302–3):

> women are expected to use and do use talk to a greater extent than men to serve the function of establishing and maintaining personal relationships (this is not surprising, as the responsibility for interpersonal relationships primarily rests with women); for example, as we have observed, women, to a greater extent than men, are expected to talk, and do talk, simply in order to keep the interaction flowing smoothly and to show goodwill toward others, and they are expected to talk, and do talk, about personal feelings and other socioemotional matters relevant to interpersonal relationships to a greater extent than men . . . what is particularly important in female friendships is the sharing of intimate feelings and confidences through talk, whereas in male friendships the sharing of activities is more important.

Another interesting claim is that in cross-gender conversations men frequently interrupt women but women much less frequently interrupt men (Zimmerman and West, 1975). James and Clarke (1993) looked at fifty-four studies that addressed the claim that men are much more likely than women 'to use interruption as a means of dominating and controlling interactions' (p. 268). They report that the majority of studies have found no significant differences between genders in this respect and both men and women interrupt other men and women. However, according to James and Clarke, 'A small amount of evidence exists that females may use interruptions of the cooperative and rapport-building type to a greater extent than do males, at least in some circumstances' (p. 268).

Still another claim is that there is evidence that in cross-gender conversation women ask more questions than men, encourage others to speak, use more back-channeling signals like *mhmm* to encourage others to continue speaking, use more instances of *you* and *we*, and do not protest as much as men when they are interrupted. On the other hand, men interrupt more, challenge, dispute, and ignore more, try to control what topics are discussed, and are inclined to make categorical statements. Such behaviors are not characteristic of women in conversations that involve both men and women. In other words, in their interactional patterns in conversation, men and women seem often to exhibit the power relationship that exists in society, with men dominant and women subservient.

If different behaviors are sometimes found in cross-gender communication, what do we find within same-gender groups? Coates (1996) discusses conversation among women friends. She analyzed over nineteen hours of recorded conversation among women interacting socially in small groups. Coates admits that she is no longer a 'dispassionate investigator' of language. She is a middle-class woman and feminist, and an ethnographer who puts women at the center of her work. She says (p. 39) that her work shows that among the groups she looked at 'friendships with women are a constant in women's lives.' In such conversations women tell and exchange stories, constantly hedge what they say, use questions to invite others to talk, i.e., for conversational maintenance, and often repeat what others say. Such talk is collaborative and establishes a feeling of solidarity among those who use it.

In still another study, this time one that used an experimental setting, Freed and Greenwood (1996) recorded and analyzed the casual conversations of approximately thirty-five minutes each of eight same-sex pairs of friends, four male and four female. They focused particularly on the use of *you know* and questions. The setting of each of the 35-minute conversations was manipulated so that each conversation provided a period of 'spontaneous' talk, one of 'considered' talk, and finally one of 'collaborative' talk. Freed and Greenwood found no differences in the use of *you know* and questions: 'Women and men of the same speech community, speaking in same-sex pairs in the same conversational context, with equal access to the conversational floor, do not differ either in the frequency of the use of *you know* or in the number of questions uttered' (p. 3). Women and men also use *you know* and questions for the same purposes. It is the linguistic task or the speaking situation that determines the style of speaking not the gender of the speaker. They add (p. 22) that 'just as the communicative style of women has been overly stereotyped as cooperative, so too the verbal style of men has been overgeneralized as competitive and lacking in cooperativeness.'

When we do observe gender differences in language behavior we are confronted with the task of trying to explain them. One explanation is that languages can be sexist. I will have a little more to say about this idea later. For now, three other claims are of interest. The first claim is that men and women are biologically different and that this difference has serious consequences for gender. Women are somehow predisposed psychologically to be involved with one another and to be mutually supportive and non-competitive. On the other hand, men are innately predisposed to independence and to vertical rather than horizontal relationships. There appears to be little or no evidence for this claim; it seems rather to be a clear case of stereotyping, which offers no more than a facile solution to a difficult problem.

The second claim is that social organization is best perceived as some kind of hierarchical set of power relationships. Moreover, such organization by power may appear to be entirely normal, justified both genetically and evolutionarily, and therefore natural and possibly even preordained. Language behavior reflects male dominance. Men use what power they have to dominate each other and, of course, women, and, if women are to succeed in such a system, they must learn to dominate others too, women included. Men constantly try to take control, to specify topics, to interrupt, and so on. They do it with each other and they do it with women, who, feeling powerless, let them get away with it, preferring instead to seek support from other women. Consequently, since women are relatively powerless they opt for more prestigious language forms to protect themselves in dealing with the more powerful. At the same time the use of such forms serves to mark them off from equally powerless males of the same social class. Women may also have weaker social networks than men but they show a greater sensitivity to language forms, especially standard ones.

Lakoff (1975) adopts the position that men are dominant and women lack power. Women may have to behave more like men if this unequal relationship is to be changed. Others share Lakoff's view. For example, DeFrancisco (1997, p. 39) proposes that 'power be placed at the centre of [feminist] analysis and that gender, race, ethnicity, social class, age, sexual orientation, and other social categories be examined as political tools of oppression.' Crawford (1995) is another who declares that power relations best explain what happens when men and women interact linguistically. Her explicit goal is 'to create a feminist social science for all women' (p. 8). Talbot (1998, pp. 133–4) sounds a cautionary note: 'A major determinant [of the dominance framework] is that male dominance is often treated as though it is pan-contextual. But . . . all men are not in a position to dominate all women.' Furthermore, anthropologists have pointed out that women are never without power and effectively control some societies. Dominance clearly fails as a universal explanation of gendered language differences.

The third claim, which does not actually deny the second claim, is that men and women are social beings who have learned to act in certain ways. Language behavior is largely learned behavior. Men learn to be men and women learn to be women, linguistically speaking. Society subjects them to different life experiences. This is often referred to as the *difference* (sometimes also *deficit*) view as opposed to the *dominance* view just mentioned.

Maltz and Borker (1982) propose that, in North America at least, men and women come from different sociolinguistic sub-cultures. They have learned to do different things with language, particularly in conversation, and when the two genders try to communicate with each other, the result may be miscommunication. The *mhmm* a woman uses quite frequently means only 'I'm listening,' whereas the *mhmm* a man uses, but much less frequently, tends to mean 'I'm agreeing.' Consequently, men often believe that 'women are always agreeing with them and then conclude that it's impossible to tell what a woman really thinks,' whereas 'women . . . get upset with men who never seem to be listening' (p. 202). They conclude that women and men observe different rules in conversing and that in cross-gender talk the rules often conflict. The genders have different views of what questioning is all about, women viewing questions as part of conversational maintenance and men primarily as requests for information; different conventions for linking; different views of what is or is not 'aggressive' linguistic behavior, with women regarding any sign of aggression as personally directed, negative, and disruptive, and men as just one way of organizing a conversation; different views of topic flow and topic shift; and different attitudes toward problem-sharing and advice-giving, with women tending to discuss, share, and seek reassurance, and men tending to look for solutions, give advice, and even lecture to their audiences. (See also Preisler, 1986.)

Tannen (1990, 1993, 1994, 1998) is undoubtedly the best-known proponent of the claim that women and men have been raised to live in different sub-cultures. Consequently, 'cross-cultural communication,' Tannen's words, can be difficult. In various interesting and entertaining accounts, Tannen has tried to show how girls and boys are brought up differently. Part of the socialization process is learning not only gender-related activities and attitudes but gender-related language behavior. We saw earlier in Fischer's study (pp. 162–3) how very young children show that they have learned to act 'like boys and girls.' Gender differences in language become established early and are then used to support the kinds of social behavior males and females exhibit. It is mainly when males and females interact that the behavior each uses separately becomes noticeable. As Holmes (1992, p. 330) says,

> The differences between women and men in ways of interacting may be the result of different socialisation and acculturation patterns. If we learn the ways of talking mainly in single sex peer groups, then the patterns we learn are likely to be sex-specific. And the kind of miscommunication which undoubtedly occurs between women and men will be attributable to the different expectations each sex has of the function of the interaction, and the ways it is appropriately conducted.

One consequence of such differences is that women's speech has often been devalued by men, for, as Tannen rightly observes, her difference approach in no way denies the existence of male dominance (1993, p. 9). Tannen's solution is an interesting one, although one not without its critics. She believes that men and women should try to understand why they speak as they do and try to adapt to each other's styles. However, the self-help nature of her 1990 book *You Just Don't Understand* might seem to thrust much of such work onto the shoulders (or tongues?) of women rather than men. Although by no means as big a best-seller as John Gray's *Men are from Mars, Women are from Venus* (1992), Tannen's book was widely acclaimed, so its message obviously spoke to many people, women in particular. As Talbot (1998) observes of the book, with its appearance of objectivity and neutrality and its stress on differences and equality, Tannen's approach provides a 'comfortable explanation' (p. 139) for some troublesome issues.

A variation of the third claim is found in the concept of 'community of practice.' According to Eckert and McConnell-Ginet (1998), gender issues are essentially complex and not easy to separate from other issues. They deplore (p. 485) the fact that too often,

> Gender is abstracted whole from other aspects of social identity, the linguistic system is abstracted from linguistic practice, language is abstracted from social action, interactions and events are abstracted from community and personal history, difference and dominance are each abstracted from wider social practice, and both linguistic and social behavior are abstracted from the communities in which they occur.

In order to understand what is happening when people acquire and use language, we must try to understand the various communities of practice in which people function. They explain this concept as follows (p. 490):

> A community of practice is an aggregate of people who come together around mutual engagement in some common endeavor. Ways of doing things, ways of talking, beliefs, values, power relations – in short, practices – emerge in the course of their joint activity around that endeavor. A community of practice is different as a social construct from the traditional notion of community, primarily because it is defined simultaneously by its membership and by the practice in which that membership engages. Indeed, it is the practices of the community and members' differentiated participation in them that structures the community socially.

They add that various kinds of differences arise in such circumstances, including gender differences: 'gender is . . . produced and reproduced in differential forms of participation in particular communities of practice. . . . The relations among communities of practice when they come together in overarching communities of practice also produce gender arrangements' (p. 491). Individuals participate in various communities of practice and these communities interact in various ways with other communities. Since these processes of participation and interaction are constantly changing, there is also constant reshaping of both individual identity and any kind of group identity, including gender identity. You must learn to be a jock or a burnout, a particular kind of man or a particular kind of women, and, as we will see shortly (p. 332), any other kind of socially categorized or gendered person. Individual identity is created through interaction with others and, as interactants change, so may identity.

If either of the last two claims is correct, we must be prepared to acknowledge the limits of proposals that seek to eliminate 'sexist' language without first changing the underlying relationship between men and women. Many of the suggestions for avoiding sexist language are admirable, but some, as Lakoff points out with regard to changing *history* to *herstory*, are absurd. Many changes can be made quite easily: *early humans* (from *early man*); *salesperson* (from *salesman*); *ordinary people* (from *the common man*); and *women* (from *the fair sex*). But other aspects of language may be more resistant to change, e.g., the *he–she* distinction. Languages themselves may not be sexist. Men and women use language to achieve certain purposes, and so long as differences in gender are equated with differences in access to power and influence in society, we may expect linguistic differences too. For both men and women, power and influence are also associated with education, social class, regional origin, and so on, and there is no question in these cases that there are related linguistic differences. Gender is still another factor that relates to the variation that is apparently inherent in language. While we may deplore that this is so, variation itself may be inevitable. Moreover, we may not be able to pick and choose which aspects of variation we can eliminate and which we can encourage, much as we might like to do so.

As still another example that gender differences in language may be social in origin rather than linguistic we can look at a study of norms and norm-breaking in Malagasy (Keenan, 1974). Among the Malagasy, men do not put others into situations in which they may lose face. They use language subtly, try to maintain good communication in their relationships, and avoid confrontations. They are discreet, they prefer indirectness as an expression of respect, and they are considered to be able speechmakers: men's 'requests are typically delayed and inexplicit, accusations imprecise, and criticisms subtle' (p. 141). We should note that many of these characteristics of men's speech might be associated with women's speech in another society. Therefore, how do women speak in Malagasy?

Women do not operate with the same set of rules. They openly and directly express anger toward others. They also criticize and confront, and men use them to do this. They can be direct and straightforward, and because they can be so, they perform tasks, such as interacting with strangers, buying and selling when these require negotiating a price, and reprimanding children, which men prefer not to perform. In this society, then, it is the men who are indirect and the women (and children) who are direct. But the most interesting fact is that it is indirectness of speech which is prized in Malagasy society and regarded as 'traditional' and it is the men who employ it. On the other hand, 'direct speech . . . is associated with a loss of tradition, with contemporary mores' and it is found among women and children (p. 142). Women are definitely inferior to men in this society too, for 'where subtlety and delicacy [which are prized characteristics] are required in social situations, men are recruited,' but 'where directness and explicitness [necessary at times but not prized characteristics] are desired in social situations, women are recruited' (p. 143). Consequently, once more we can see how the speech of the genders reflects their relationship within the total society.

The kinds of evidence we have looked at strongly suggests that men and women differ in the kinds of language they use because men and women often fill distinctly different roles in society. We may expect that the more distinct the roles, the greater the differences, and there seems to be some evidence to support such a claim, for the greatest differences appear to exist in societies in which the roles of men and women are most clearly differentiated. Since boys are brought up to behave like men in those societies and girls to behave like women, the differences are also perpetuated.

In societies that are less rigidly stratified and in which men's and women's roles are less clearly differentiated, we may expect to find a reflection of this situation in the language that is used and also, if change in society is occurring, change in the language too. This is, indeed, what we do find, as we saw in chapters 7 and 8: men and women, and even boys and girls, exhibit certain differences in language use in such cities as New York, Norwich, Reading, and Belfast. Most of those differences can be explained by the different positions men and women fill in society. Men have more power and may be more assertive; women tend to be kept 'in their place' but aspire quite often to a different and 'better' place. Women therefore appear to be more conscious of uses of language which they associate with their 'betters' in society, that is, those they regard as being socially superior. They therefore direct their speech toward the models these provide, even to the extent in some cases of hypercorrection, as in the example from New York City (p. 167). Women, therefore, tend to be in the vanguard of change toward the norms of the upper classes, and lower middle-class women are at the very front.

One consequence is that sometimes we view the speech of certain women as being hypercorrect. That too is a normative-laden concept. It assumes a correct male norm and characterizes the female norm as deviant. Once again difference rather than deviance might be a better characterization, with the difference arising from the different experiences that females and males have of the world.

Men have power, even lower-class men. They are less influenced linguistically by others and, in the case of the lower working class, may seek solidarity through the 'toughness' that nonstandard varieties of the language seem to indicate. If they lead in any kind of change, such change may well be away from the norm (p. 202). Again, as I indicated earlier (pp. 205–6), women may not find appropriate the kinds of solidarity that men seek through the use of a particular language or certain kinds of language. The peasant women of Oberwart in Austria seek not Hungarian-speaking peasant husbands, but German-speaking worker husbands and, in doing so, lead the traditionally bilingual peasant population away from Hungarian–German bilingualism toward German monolingualism. Women are not without solidarity; it is just a different kind of solidarity from that of men and just as normal.

All deliberate attempts to change or modify languages to free them of perceived sexism or make them gender-neutral are a form of language planning. Sometimes the goal appears to be to force language to catch up to social change, and at other times it seems designed to bring about social change through mandating language change. Whatever it is, it requires us to accept a very Whorfian view of the interrelationship of language and culture and is subject to all the difficulties of interpretation and implementation that we saw in chapter 9. Here is Pauwels' (1998, p. 228) statement of a similar position:

> The aims of many feminist LP [langage planning] efforts are to expose the inequalities in the linguistic portrayal of the sexes which reflect and contribute to the unequal positions of women and men in society and to take action to rectify this linguistic imbalance. Language action . . . is social action, and to bring about linguistic change is to effect social change.

(See Pauwels, 2003, on attempts at language reform in a variety of countries.)

Some feminists want to go further than 'cleaning up' the language and even deny any possibility of 'neutrality.' Their expressed mission is to 'reclaim' language for themselves (see especially Lakoff, 1990, Penelope, 1990, Sellers, 1991, and Spender, 1985). Spender adopts a Whorfian view of language (see pp. 221–8), declaring (p. 3) that: 'Language helps form the limits of our reality. It is our means of ordering and manipulating the world. It is through language that we become members of a human community, that the world becomes comprehensible and meaningful, that we bring into existence the world in which we live.' However, she goes much further than Whorf, asserting (p. 12) that 'the English language has been literally man-made and . . . is still primarily under male control' and that males, as the dominant group, have produced language, thought, and reality. Penelope argues that women should be aware of 'the lies of the fathers' tongues' and of the 'Patriarchal Universe of Discourse.' Her view is that women should in a sense reinvent language for their own purposes, and many feminists have indeed tried to develop their own linguistic conventions, e.g., non-competitive, non-interruptive speech, in order to 'liberate' women. However, other feminists such as Cameron (1992) do not hold such strong views. They would require intervention into language use on a grand scale. Any such intervention would have to be based not on any rational view of language behavior but entirely on ideology.

Language and gender studies have seen an interesting development in recent years, known by such terms as *queer linguistics* and *lavender linguistics*. These studies deal with the language of non-mainstream groups such as gays, lesbians, bisexuals, the transgendered, etc., and focus on 'sexuality' rather than sex or gender. In fact, a major claim is that the focus on sex or gender may have been misdirected. In their book-length treatment of sexuality, Cameron and Kulick (2003) adopt a postmodern aproach heavily dependent on the ideas of Derrida, Foucault, and Lacan, and argue that a concept they call 'desire' should play a central role in trying to understand human behavior since ' "desire" encompasses more than just the preference for partners of the same or the other sex: it also deals with the non-intentional, non-conscious and non-rational dimensions of human sexual life. The unconscious and irrational aspects of sexuality may not be manifested on the surface of people's behaviour in the same way that their behaviour displays the sexual identities they have consciously chosen ("gay," "lesbian," "straight," etc.)' (p. 140). They argue that the issues of identity and power are less important, an argument that Bucholtz and Hall (2004) reject, claiming that 'desire' is much too vague a concept to be useful and that issues of identity and power are not only relevant but essential in any research on such language varieties. Just what the ultimate significance to the subject matter of this chapter this concern for 'marginalized' groups will have is difficult to predict. The research has produced some findings of interest to us, e.g., Barrett's study discussed on p. 117, and to ignore such findings would be to fall into the trap of appearing to use 'power' oppressively. However, only time will tell if this will ultimately prove to be a significant development.

It is also apparent, as Freed has indicated (2003, p. 706), that 'despite the enormity of our research results, the public representation of the way women and men speak is almost identical to the characterization provided thirty years ago.' Too often researchers talk only to each other, research results are either ignored or misrepresented, and stereotyped views continue to influence how people think and behave.

My own view is that men's and women's speech differ because boys and girls are brought up differently and men and women often fill different roles in society. Moreover, most men and women know this and behave accordingly. If such is the case, we might expect changes that make a language less sexist to result from child-rearing practices and role differentiations which are less sexist. Men and women alike would benefit from the greater freedom of choice that would result. However, it may be utopian to believe that language use will ever become 'neutral.' Humans use everything around them – and language is just a thing in that sense – to create differences among themselves. Speech may well be gendered but there actually may be no easy solution to that problem.

Discussion

1. Kramer's analysis of cartoons (see p. 324) may be worth replicating. What do you find in some other set? You can also apply the same approach to illustrations in children's books, comic books, and other similar sources.
2. Women are usually expected to react differently from men to jokes, particularly risqué jokes. Describe any differences you have observed between men and women, not only in reactions to jokes but also to various other kinds of boisterous or playful linguistic behavior. Account for the differences.
3. Graffiti tend to be a commonplace of modern life. You and someone of the opposite gender might try to collect graffiti from a couple of neighboring locations, one frequented by males and the other by females, e.g., adjacent washrooms. A comparison of the language used and the themes covered might prove to be very interesting.
4. A set of guidelines issued by an educational publishing house (Scott, Foresman and Company, 1972), one of many such sets issued by publishers and professional groups during the late twentieth century, e.g., the Linguistic Society of America in 1995, advises substitutions of the kinds indicated below to avoid sexist language and role-stereotyping in publications. How effective are such suggestions – another is King (1991) – likely to be? (See Krosroshahi, 1989, Rubin, 1986, Ehrlich and King, 1994, and Pauwels, 1998.)

Change	To
early man	early humans
Man and His World	*World History*
mailmen	mail carriers
the common man	ordinary people
the motorist . . . he	the motorist . . . he or she
the farmer and his wife	a farm couple
Mary Smith is a highly successful woman executive	Mary Smith is a highly successful executive
the fair sex	women
The captain is John Smith. His beautiful first officer is Joan Porter.	The captain is John Smith and the first officer is Joan Porter.

5. How likely is it that certain child-rearing practices encourage different kinds of linguistic behavior in young boys and girls? Consider, for example, the fact that girls are often encouraged to participate with mothers in non-competitive domestic activities in which language is very important; on the other hand, boys may be expected to be more competitive, to play outside more, and to be engaged in physical rather than social activity. They may also have less contact with their fathers than their sisters have with their mothers. Can you think of any specific examples of linguistic usage that may be explained in this way?

6. Smith (1979, p. 138) makes the following observation about the relationship between language and gender:

    > we must beware of relegating speech to the role of the 'symptom' of social relations. Speech and language use itself may play an active role in the development of the subjective aspects of gender identity and hence in the development and use of language itself.

    What opinions do you have on this matter, and what evidence seems to you to support those opinions?

7. In Shaw's *Pygmalion*, Professor Higgins goes about transforming Eliza Doolittle by teaching her to talk like a lady. Colonel Pickering treats her like a lady and ignores her talk. Eliza observes that any success she has is attributable to Pickering's approach rather than to Higgins! Is there anything we can learn about the relationship of language to behavior from Eliza's observation?

8. There is an ongoing debate about the desirability of single-sex classes within schools and of single-sex schools. Which arguments for and against seem to you to be the strongest and which the weakest?

Further Reading

Gender is one of the great 'growth' areas in sociolinguistics and there is an abundant literature. Holmes and Meyerhoff (2003) provide very useful comprehensive coverage, and other useful books are Baron (1986), Coates (1993, 1996), Eckert and McConnell-Ginet (2003), Graddol and Swann (1989), Holmes (1995), Key (1996), Lakoff (1975), Pauwels (1998), Romaine (1999), Smith (1985), and Talbot (1998). Some recent collections of papers are Bergvall et al. (1996), Cameron (1998c), Coates (1998), Hall and Bucholtz (1995), Kotthoff and Wodak (1997), and Cheshire and Trudgill (1998). See Swann (1993) for the language of boys and girls, Johnson and Meinhof (1997) for 'language and masculinity,' Coates (2002) for the language of men, and Cameron and Kulick (2003), Livia and Hall (1997), and Leap (1996) for still other 'gendered' varieties of language.

14   Disadvantage

As we have seen, each language exists in a number of different varieties, and individuals vary in their language use according to occasion. Not every individual will necessarily command the same range of varieties as every other person. Throughout the total linguistic community there will be a considerable overlap, a situation which seems necessary if there is to be good communication. However, as we saw in chapter 2, such differences may exist within the total community that the variety (or varieties) spoken by one group may be quite unlike the variety (or varieties) spoken by some other group, while both groups may still be said to be speaking the *same* language. In such circumstances we may appreciate why a variety spoken by a group that has a favored position in society is likely to be accorded more prestige – and hence often comes to be used as a model for speakers of other varieties – than one spoken by a group that is less favored. In this way, as we also saw in chapter 2, one variety may eventually be promoted to serve as a standard for the whole community and become the norm against which all other varieties are judged.

We should observe that linguists are agreed that no variety of a language is inherently better than any other. They insist that all languages and all varieties of particular languages are equal in that they quite adequately serve the needs of those who use them. The only exceptions they recognize are pidgins, which are by definition restricted varieties, or the varieties we associate with people who are impaired in some way, e.g., certain mentally or physically handicapped people. A standard variety of a language is 'better' only in a social sense: it has a preferred status; it gives those who use it certain social advantages; and it increases their life chances. Nonstandard varieties tend to produce the opposite effect. These are some of the consequences that follow from elevating one variety and denigrating others, but there is no reason to suppose that any one of the varieties is intrinsically more worthy than any other. If the capital cities of England and France had been York and Avignon respectively, Standard English and Standard French today would be quite different from what they actually are, and speakers of RP and Parisian French would in such circumstances be regarded rather differently, as speaking somewhat peculiar local dialects that would not be very helpful 'if you want to get on in the world.'

This attitude that linguists have toward different languages and their different varieties is not one that everyone else shares. Many people believe that some languages or varieties *are* better than others, e.g., that some languages are particularly 'beautiful,' others 'primitive,' some dialects more 'expressive,' others 'deficient,' and so on. In other words, it is widely believed that you can be advantaged or disadvantaged not just socially or esthetically, but also cognitively, i.e., intellectually, by the accident of which language or variety of a language you happen to speak.

In this chapter I will look at two different linguistic situations which have been widely discussed in terms of such disadvantage. One of these concerns certain social class differences in the use of language in England; the other is the variety of English found in the United States that is now usually referred to as *African American Vernacular English*. In each case, one or more investigators have pointed out important social and educational consequences of the linguistic differences that they believe to exist. We will attempt to look at some of the basic facts and issues and to assess the various claims that have been made about both those linguistic differences and the consequences that are said to follow.

Codes Again

The work of Bernstein, a British sociologist concerned with educational matters, has been very influential, particularly in the United Kingdom and Germany. Bernstein's interest is socialization, i.e., how a child acquires a specific cultural identity and responds to that identity. In particular, he has been interested in the role of language in socialization. Bernstein's work and theories have been widely discussed and both misconstrued and misrepresented, so it is not always easy to determine whether he actually said what he is said to have said. He has not always helped his own case either, for his writings are often obscure and some-times ambiguous. Certain North Americans have been particularly critical of Bernstein, as we will see, but he has not gone uncriticized on his own side of the Atlantic either.

Bernstein's views of the relationship between language and culture are heavily influenced by his reading of Whorf (see chapter 9). On more than one occasion he has pointed out how Whorf alerted him to what he calls the deep structure of linguistically regulated communication. Bernstein regards language as something which both influences culture and is in turn influenced by culture. A child growing up in a particular linguistic environment and culture learns the language of that environment and that culture and then proceeds to pass on that learning to the next generation. Bernstein believes that there is a direct and reciprocal relationship between a particular kind of social structure, in both its establishment and its maintenance, and the way people in that social structure use language. Moreover, this relationship is a continuing one in that it is handed down from generation to generation. For Bernstein, a particular kind of social structure leads to a particular kind of linguistic behavior and this behavior in turn reproduces the original social structure. Consequently, a cycle exists in which certain social patterns produce certain linguistic patterns, which in turn repro-duce the social patterns, and so on.

Individuals also learn their social roles through the process of communication. This process differs from social group to social group, and, because it is different in each social group, existing role differences are perpetuated in society. What is of particular concern to Bernstein, therefore, are the quite different types of language that different social groups employ. He claims that there are two quite distinct varieties of language in use in society. He calls one variety *elaborated code* (originally *formal code*) and the other variety *restricted code* (originally *public code*). According to Bernstein, these codes have very different characteristics. For example, elaborated code makes use of accurate – in the sense of standard – grammatical order and syntax to regulate what is said; uses complex sentences that employ a range of devices for conjunction and subordination; employs prepositions to show relationships of both a temporal and logical nature; shows frequent use of the pronoun *I*; uses with care a wide range of adjectives and adverbs; allows for remarks to be qualified; and, according to Bernstein (1961, p. 169), 'is a language use which points to the possibilities inherent in a complex conceptual hierarchy for the organizing of experience.' In contrast, restricted code employs short, grammatically simple, and often unfinished sentences of poor – in the sense of nonstandard – syntactic form; uses a few conjunctions simply and repetitively; employs little subordination; tends toward a dislocated presentation of information; is rigid and limited in the use of adjectives and adverbs; makes infrequent use of impersonal pronoun subjects; confounds reasons and conclusions; makes frequent appeals to 'sympathetic circularity,' e.g., *You know?*; uses idioms frequently; and is 'a language of implicit meaning.'

It is Bernstein's view that every speaker of the language has access to the restricted code because all employ this code on certain occasions; e.g., it is the language of intimacy between familiars. However, not all social classes have equal access to the elaborated code, particularly lower working-class people and their children, who are likely to have little experience with it. According to Bernstein (1972b, p. 173), the consequences of this unequal distribution are considerable. In particular, children from the lower working class are likely to find themselves at a disadvantage when they attend school, in which extensive use is made of the elaborated code. He says:

> the different focusing of experience through a restricted code creates a major problem of educability only where the school produces discontinuity between its symbolic orders and those of the child. Our schools are not made for these children; why should the children respond? To ask the child to switch to an elaborated code which presupposes different role relationships and systems of meaning without a sensitive understanding of the required contexts must create for the child a bewildering and potentially damaging experience.

According to Bernstein, therefore, there are serious consequences for the children of the lower working class when they come to school because elaborated code is the medium of instruction in schooling. When schools attempt to develop in children the ability to manipulate elaborated code, they are really involved in trying to change cultural patterns, and such involvement may have profound social and psychological consequences for all engaged in the task. Educational failure is likely to be the result.

Bernstein's theories have been employed in a variety of studies. A typical study is one by Henderson (1972), who investigated the language used by 100 mothers to their 7-year-old children. The mothers were divided into a middle-class (MC) group and a working-class (WC) group. Henderson reports that, relative to working-class mothers, middle-class mothers report they favor the use of abstract definitions, explicit rather than implicit definitions, and information-giving strategies in answering children's questions, and they use language to transmit moral principles and to indicate feelings. In contrast to a child from the working class, a child from the middle class is oriented through language to principles as these relate to objects and persons and is given access to the systems through which knowledge is acquired. Henderson's findings appear to support Bernstein's theory that social classes differ in their use of language and pass these differences on from generation to generation. Henderson points out (p. 329) the consequences such findings have so far as education is concerned:

> It should be apparent that the linguistic socialization of the MC child is critically relevant to his ability to profit from the educational experience as this is *currently* defined. There is little discontinuity between the symbolic orders of the school and those to which he has been socialized through his family. Whereas for the working-class child there is a hiatus between the symbolic orders of the school and those of his family. He is less oriented towards the meta-languages of control and innovation and the pattern of social relationships through which they are transmitted. The genesis of educational failure, according to our findings, may well be found in the pattern of communication and control which are realizations and thus transmitters of specific subcultures.

The important word here is *hiatus*: there is a gap between what the lower working-class child brings to school and what happens in school. Moreover, present types of schooling do not close the gap, and child-rearing practices continue to ensure that it exists in subsequent generations.

Bernstein (1972b, pp. 174–6) also shows his concern with what he calls *position-oriented* and *person-oriented* families. In position-oriented families language use is closely related to such matters as close physical contact among members, a set of shared assumptions, and a preference for implicit rather than explicit meaning in communication. On the other hand, in person-oriented families language use depends less on these factors, and communication is more explicit and more context-free, that is, less dependent for interpretation on such matters as the physical surroundings. According to Bernstein, position orientation leads to a strong sense of social identity with some loss of personal autonomy, whereas person orientation fosters personal autonomy but at the expense of social identity. We can easily note how these two orientations relate to Bernstein's restricted and elaborated codes, for position orientation appears to require less complexity and elaboration in language use than person orientation. Ammon (1994) likewise relates the use of restricted code to the closed, multiplex social networks typical of members of the working class or lower social classes in general because 'for want of other resources [they are] more dependent on mutual assistance in everyday life, which also explains why solidarity usually ranks high as a value among them' (p. 579). Such people, he says, are also more status-oriented (i.e., position-oriented) than person-oriented.

Other investigators, many undoubtedly influenced by Bernstein's ideas, have commented on the different ways in which adults in various social classes respond linguistically to their children. Cook (1971) found that lower working-class mothers used more commands to their young children than did middle-class mothers, who preferred to point out to their children the consequences of what they were doing, particularly the consequences to the mother's feelings; e.g., 'Now you've broken that cup and I am very angry.' Cook also found that lower working-class mothers often relied on their positional authority to get their way, by saying things like 'I'm your mother' and 'I'm telling you to do that.' Other investigators, e.g., Newson and Newson (1970), found that working-class mothers invoke authority figures such as police officers in threatening their children. Robinson and Rackstraw (1967) found that middle-class mothers, far more often than lower working-class mothers, tried to answer their children's *Wh*-questions, i.e., information-seeking questions, with genuine explanations rather than with answers like 'Because I say so' or 'Because they do.' Such explanations would involve causes, consequences, analogies, and so on. Similar evidence is reported from studies in the United States, e.g., Hess and Shipman (1965). In this study, middle-class mothers and lower working-class mothers, faced with the task of helping their 4-year-old children in either block-sorting tasks or the use of an Etch-a-Sketch, revealed important differences in behavior, with middle-class mothers far better able to help or instruct their children than lower working-class mothers, who were unable to offer much assistance to their children. In a discussion of their results, Hess and Shipman (1967, p. 79) point out how frustrated the child of a lower working-class mother must feel in such circumstances. The child is often required to do things without any explanation being given, without adequate instructions, and without models for the desired behavior; moreover, rewards and punishments seem quite random and, when these do occur, punishments are usually more frequent and intense than rewards. These views are in accord with Bernstein's. It is his view that people in the middle class much more so than those in the working class employ language to discuss cause and effect, and moral principles and their application in bringing up children. They are more likely to encourage verbal interaction, less likely to avoid answering difficult questions and employ coercion, and more likely to employ language to induce desired behavioral changes.

Bernstein believes that the British social-class system does not allow the lower working class easy access to the elaborated code. Members of that class most frequently use restricted code, which limits the intellectual horizons of its speakers. We should note that in Bernstein's view it is the *lower* working class, not the whole of the working class, who are penalized in this way; too often his work is interpreted as a claim about the working class as a whole. Of course, Bernstein and his followers must accept much of the responsibility for this misunderstanding since they generally omit the word *lower* and appear to be discussing the whole of the working class. Among critics, however, Rosen (1972) has criticized Bernstein on the ground that he has not looked closely enough at working-class life and language and that many of the key terms in his work are quite inadequately defined, e.g., *code*, *class*, *elaborated*, and so on. Many of the arguments also appear to be circular in nature and the hypotheses weak.

Labov (1972a) has echoed many of these criticisms and added a few of his own. He has argued that one cannot reason from the kinds of data presented by Bernstein that there is a qualitative difference between the two kinds of speech Bernstein describes, let alone a qualitative difference that would result in cognitive and intellectual differences. For example, he says (1970, p. 84): 'The cognitive style of a speaker has no fixed relation to the number of unusual adjectives or conjunctions that he uses.' A quantitative difference does not establish a qualitative one, particularly if the functions of language are ignored or down-played. Many linguists would agree with Labov that it is not the range of devices that is found in a particular variety of language that is important so much as the way in which speakers actually use whatever devices exist. For example, the English of a thousand years ago, Old English, lacked certain devices that Modern English has, but it would surely be false to claim that King Alfred was considerably less 'smart' than your next door neighbor as a consequence of this apparent 'deficiency.'

For his part, Bernstein has tried to refute some of Labov's criticisms. He says (1990, p. 115) that the story told by Larry (see pp. 345–6) could bear a different interpretation from that offered by Labov, i.e., that it shows good logical reasoning. Bernstein points out that Larry needs five probes to structure his argument. This example and another that Labov uses really show 'interchanges which are embedded in different social bases and thus founded upon different rules and competences' (p. 117). Bernstein adds that what is needed is 'less *ad hoc* ideology and interpretation and a more systematic, general understanding of the social basis of modalities of communication and their distributive principles and differential outcomes' (p. 118), which is what he is trying to gain through his work.

Bernstein is, of course, aware that not all of the language differences between working-class children and middle-class children are advantageous to the latter. He has acknowledged that young middle-class children do not tend to respond as uninhibitedly as their working-class counterparts in certain activities, for example role-playing. Apparently, they often want to know what the rules are before they will play in this way because they want to avoid doing the wrong thing. There may also be an additional constraint at work in the use of elaborated code: you tailor your language to fit the social occasion and particularly the expectations that others have of you. Therefore, when you are unsure of, or concerned with, those expectations, you may react by saying little and saying that very carefully. In certain circumstances it will even be the case that users of the restricted code will be the more verbal, since they are unlikely to be as concerned with the impression they are making on others.

In his work Bernstein has opened up an interesting area of investigation into the varieties of language used by children. His views have been dismissed far too readily by many linguists, who tend to reject all his claims because a few appear to be untenable. The kinds of data that Bernstein has presented raise important issues. Linguists generally approach these issues differently but it cannot really be said that they have been any more successful than Bernstein in dealing with them.

Discussion

1. Try to elicit some examples of speech from several children. You should try to vary a number of factors. For example, you might try younger and older children; spontaneous conversation, story-telling, and playing games with them; formal and informal settings; individual and group activities; home and out-of-the-home settings; and so on. Try to determine as far as you can do so how the different approaches affect what you can say about children's language. Are there any characteristics which seem easier than others to assess, and, if so, why? You might also like to compare the techniques you employ with the kinds of techniques for eliciting children's language that are described in books published for use by teachers, language consultants, speech therapists, child psychologists, and so on. You should also look at the advice that is often given in such sources about the significance of certain results. Is any such advice questionable? And, if so, for what reasons?

2. Try to design an experiment that will either confirm (or disconfirm) the existence of restricted and elaborated codes. You might look at Bernstein (1972a, 1972b) for some guidance in this matter. You might also try to use certain other possible measures of language differences if you can isolate two (or more) discrete varieties of speech, e.g., counting word production, measuring clause and/or sentence length and/or complexity, and so on. You might also investigate some other sources for data concerning how different social groups use forms of speech which might be called 'codes' of the kind that interest Bernstein. Written sources might be useful, e.g., plays, short stories, and novels. It may be important, however, to assess the accuracy of the presentation of characters in such sources since stereotyping is a distinct possibility.

3. According to Bernstein, education proceeds through the use of elaborated code, although, of course, there are also many instances of the use of restricted code in classrooms. Try to apply Bernstein's concept of the two codes to classroom activity to see how useful they are. Do you find any instances of misunderstanding which might be explained as failure to deal adequately with a particular code?

4. Bernstein has been criticized for saying that lower working-class speech has certain characteristics and then going out to find confirmation of his claims. Another approach might be to go out and collect data concerning such speech before making any hypotheses at all. How might you attempt to organize such a collection of linguistic data? What problems do you think might arise in your work?

5. Try to observe mothers controlling, disciplining, or explaining things to very young children. Try to find a 'naturalistic' method for collecting your data, because Hess and Shipman's study has been criticized on the ground that it used an experimental, hypothetical situation rather than a natural one, therefore raising doubts about the generalizations you can make from it. What kinds of language do mothers use and what kinds of strategies do

they employ? Do there appear to be differences that you can associate with class or with other factors?

African American Vernacular English

Linguists who have described the speech that is characteristic of many black residents of the northern United States have noticed how uniform that speech is in many respects. In other words, blacks who live in New York City, Boston, Chicago, Detroit, and Seattle speak very much alike, whereas the same cannot be said of non-blacks who live in the same cities. The speech of blacks in these cities also resembles the speech of blacks in southern states in many respects. In one respect this similarity is the result of the relatively recent migrations of blacks out of the south; in another, it is one reflection of long-standing patterns of racial segregation only now slowly changing, patterns which have tended to separate the population of the United States along color lines. Linguists have referred to this variety of speech as *Black English*, *Black Vernacular English*, and *Afro-American Vernacular English*. Today, the most-used term is *African American Vernacular English* (AAVE) but *Ebonics* (a blend of *Ebony* and *phonics*) has also recently achieved a certain currency.

AAVE has certain phonological, morphological, and syntactic characteristics. Words like *thing* and *this* may be pronounced as *ting* and *dis*. *Bath* may sound like *baff*, *brother* like *bruvver*, *nothing* like *nuffin*, and *thread* like *tred*. Still other examples are *bik* for *big*, *kit* for *kid*, and *cup* for *cub*, as final stops are devoiced. Others may be lost. *Test*, *desk*, and *end* may be pronounced without their final consonants. The plural of *test* may actually be *tess* or *tesses*, depending on how an individual forms the plural. *Carol*, *Paris*, *protect*, and *from* may show loss of *r*, and *car* and *cart* will nearly always show loss of *r*. As a result, *your brother* may become identical to *you brother*. *Cold* may show loss of the final *d* (*col'*) or even loss of both *l* and *d* (*co'*), because *l* after a vowel is often deleted. The result may be that *bold* and *bowl* become homophonous with *bow*.

One result of such losses is that there are likely to be quite different homophones in AAVE and in standard varieties of the language. Vowels may be nasalized and nasal consonants lost: *run* and *end* may just be in the first case an *r* followed by a nasalized vowel and in the second case a simple nasalized vowel with no pronunciation at all of the final *nd*. The diphthongs in words like *find* and *found* may be both monophthongized and nasalized, and the words may lack any pronunciation of the final *nd*. Consequently, *find*, *found*, and even *fond* may become homophonous, all pronounced with an *f* and a following nasalized vowel.

In morphology, because final *t* and *d* are often unpronounced, there may be no overt signaling of the past tense, so that *I walked* sounds just like *I walk*. There may also be no signaling of the third-person singular in the present tense of the verb, resulting in a form like *he go*. *Tesses* as a pronunciation of *tests* would also indicate that there is no final *t* at all in the speaker's basic form of the word, which has become for that speaker a word just like *dress*, with its plural *dresses*.

Syntactically, AAVE has special uses of *be*, or lack of *be* (the zero copula), as in a contrast between 'He nice' ('He is nice right now') and 'He be nice' ('He is nice sometimes'). The negatives of these sentences would also be 'He ain't nice' and 'He don't be nice,' respectively. 'You tired' may be an equivalent of the standard 'You're tired.' AAVE also employs constructions such as 'I asked Joe what can he do,' 'Can't nobody do that' (as a statement), and 'It ain't no heaven for you to go to,' in which *it* functions like *there* in Standard English (or SE). *Ain't* is used frequently, as is multiple negation, and there are also special auxiliary verb uses of *done* and *been*, as in 'He done told me' and 'I been washing it.'

One of the most interesting characteristics of AAVE is the above-mentioned use of the zero copula. As Labov (1969) has explained, the rule for its use is really quite simple. If you can contract *be* in SE, you can delete it in AAVE. That is, since 'He is nice' can be contracted to 'He's nice' in SE, it can become 'He nice' in AAVE. Likewise, 'But everybody's not black' can become 'But everybody not black.' However, 'I don't know where he is' cannot be contracted to 'I don't know where he's' in SE and, consequently, it cannot become 'I don't know where he' in AAVE, nor can 'That's the way it is here' become 'That's the way it here.' The latter can become 'That the way it is here' (or even 'That the way it be here,' depending on whether the observation is being made only about the present moment – *it is* – or about a habitual condition – *it be*). In both SE and AAVE the verb *be* must be realized in the last example.

We should note that the zero copula is very rarely found in the speech of whites, even poor southern whites. Not all blacks use it, either. Labov (1972a) shows, for example, that zero copula use can be correlated with strength of group membership among certain black youths in Harlem, members of a gang called the Jets. His work revealed that the gang had core members, secondary members, and peripheral members. Outside were non-members, who were called *lames* by the members. Zero copula use diminished as strength of group membership decreased: core members had 45 percent zero copula use; secondary members 42 percent; peripheral members 26 percent; and lames 21 percent. Even the lames, those black youths who are least closely associated with black culture, use the zero copula 21 percent of the time: they show their 'blackness' through such use. However, they use it much less than those who might be regarded as more typical examples of both black culture and black linguistic usage. Obviously, then, certain characteristics of AAVE indicate solidarity; indeed, the use of AAVE itself may be regarded as a strong solidarity marker for this ethnic group in the United States. As Labov (1972a, p. 258) says, 'It is only by virtue of being available and on the city street every day that anyone can acquire the deep familiarity with local doings and the sure command of local slang that are needed to participate in vernacular culture.'

The above are some of the more frequently noted characteristics of AAVE. Linguists, however, disagree on how AAVE relates to other varieties of English in the United States. Some, such as Kurath (1949, p. 6) and McDavid (1965, p. 258), argue that it has no characteristics which are not found in other varieties of English, particularly nonstandard varieties spoken by Americans of any color in the south. This is sometimes called the Anglicist hypothesis of origin. In this view, AAVE is just another dialect of American English (see Wolfram and Schilling-Estes, 1998, pp. 175–8). That black speakers may produce greater quantities of certain nonstandard usages is merely a peculiarity of the style of speaking they have adopted. This claim that AAVE is a variety of southern United States English is also quite compatible with another claim that is sometimes made: that the speech of blacks in the southern states has had a considerable influence on the speech of whites living there, e.g., in the latter's borrowing of such words as *goober* ('peanut'), *buckra* ('white man'), *gumbo* (a type of soup), and perhaps *jazz* and *banjo*. Wolfram (2003) and Wolfram and Thomas (2002) take a slightly different position, favoring a neo-Anglicist hypothesis that early African Americans maintained certain features of the languages they brought with them while at the same time accommodating to the local dialects of English. Wolfram and Thomas say that the substrate influence of the African languages still persists in AAVE, certainly in the variety they examined in Hyde County, North Carolina.

Diametrically opposed to this view is the view of the creolists, e.g., Stewart (1967), Dillard (1972), and Rickford (1977, 1997, 1999a), who maintain that AAVE is of creole origin (see chapter 3), and therefore a variety of English which originated quite independently of SE. In this view, AAVE has features that are typical of creoles, particularly the zero copula, some residual Africanisms, and certain styles of speaking (such as rapping, sounding, signifying, rifting, and fancy talk), which look back to an African origin. AAVE, therefore, is not a dialect of English but a creolized variety of English which still, for many people, has certain profound differences from the standard variety, differences which must be acknowledged if we are to make wise decisions in matters affecting the education of children. Ewars (1996) adopts a somewhat intermediate position that the characteristics of AAVE are neither those of a variety of English of creole origin nor those related to a specific variety of English. AAVE may have 'taken a development of its own' (p. 227). (See also Poplack, 2000.)

A third view, that of linguists such as Labov (1972a), is that the issue of whether or not AAVE originated as a creole is now moot. Labov claims that every feature that you might be tempted to regard as unique to AAVE can be related 'by rule' to SE. What speakers of AAVE possess is basically the same grammar that all speakers of English possess. Just as speakers of Cockney English and Newfoundland English have special rules to produce their unique varieties, so speakers of AAVE have their special rules; however, the core rules are alike for all. In this view, AAVE is just another variety of English.

Another issue that intrigues linguists is whether or not AAVE and SE are converging or diverging. Bailey and Maynor (1989) say that they are diverging in the Brazon Valley in Texas, with only black speakers using constructions like 'He always be tryin' to catch up' and resisting the adoption of post-vocalic *r* in words like *farm*. In this view the English of blacks and whites is diverging in certain parts of the United States. Butters (1989) argues that there is no solid evidence to support such a claim, pointing out that there are both divergent and convergent features. He says that AAVE is just like any other dialect of English;

it has its own innovations but remains strongly influenced by the standard variety. Wolfram (1990) also discusses the idea that these varieties are diverging and concludes that the evidence is 'flimsy' (p. 131). However, another review of the evidence (Spears, 1992) finds some substance. There may actually, as just stated, be both convergence and divergence, for as Wolfram and Thomas say (p. 24), 'it is quite possible for particular structures, or structures on one level of language organization, to show convergence at the same time that other structures indicate divergence.' Rickford (1999a, pp. 274–7) also points to evidence of both convergence and divergence in East Palo Alto, California, with black adults showing evidence of convergence and black teenagers of divergence although whether the latter is mainly an age-graded phenomenon is not at all clear.

Whatever theory about origins is correct and however opinions differ concerning the direction of change, we can be sure that there is such a variety of English as AAVE in the United States. Labov (2001, pp. 506–8) says that it is almost identical in cities such as Boston, New York, Detroit, Chicago, San Francisco, and Los Angeles and shows none of the changes that are occurring in the white populations of these cities. Nor do blacks readily participate in the NCS (see p. 194). Those who speak AAVE recognize that what they speak is something different from the varieties employed by most non-blacks. Most Americans are prepared to categorize someone who contacts them by telephone as either black or non-black using speech alone as the criterion, and most such categorizations are correct. In cases of mis-categorization, it is usually because of special circumstances: a black person has been brought up among non-blacks, or a non-black has been brought up among blacks.

Discussion

1. As an example of both AAVE and the logic that can be expressed in AAVE, Labov (1972a, pp. 214–15) cites the following conversation between Larry, a 15-year-old core member of the Jets, a Harlem gang, and JL, an interviewer:

JL:	What happens to you after you die? Do you know?
Larry:	Yeah, I know.
JL:	What?
Larry:	After they put you in the ground, your body turns into – ah – bones, an' shit.
JL:	What happens to your spirit?
Larry:	Your spirit – soon as you die, your spirit leaves you.
JL:	And where does the spirit go?
Larry:	Well, it all depends . . .
JL:	On what?
Larry:	You know, like some people say if you're good an' shit, your spirit goin' t'heaven . . . 'n' if you bad, your spirit goin' to hell. Well, bullshit! Your spirit goin' to hell anyway, good or bad.
JL:	Why?

> *Larry*: Why? I'll tell you why. 'Cause, you see, doesn' nobody really
> know that it's a God, y'know, 'cause I mean I have seen black
> gods, pink gods, white gods, all color gods, and don't nobody
> know it's really a God. An' when they be sayin' if you good, you
> goin' t'heaven, tha's bullshit, 'cause you ain't goin' to no heaven,
> 'cause it ain't no heaven for you to go to.

What characteristics of AAVE are there in Larry's speech and how logical
is his argument?

2.   The United Kingdom and Canada each contain a significant minority black
population. In what ways does the speech of these people correspond to
AAVE? In what way is it different? How relevant are statements and claims
made about AAVE to the situations that exist in the United Kingdom and
Canada?

3.   To what extent might the relationship between AAVE and SE be characterized
as a *diglossic* one? (Refer back to chapter 4.)

Consequences for Education

There has been widespread misunderstanding in the United States of AAVE,
both of its characteristics and of how it is used (see Mufwene et al., 1998). This
misunderstanding has had a number of unfortunate consequences. Many educators regarded the various distinguishing characteristics of AAVE as deficiencies: black children were deficient in language ability because their language did
not have certain features of the standard, and the consequence of that deficiency
was cognitive deficiency. This is sometimes called the Deficit hypothesis. For
example, Bereiter and Engelmann (1966, p. 39) state that such children show 'a
total lack of ability to use language as a device for acquiring and processing
information. Language for them is unwieldy and not very useful.' In the late
1960s, this view led to certain proposals to teach black children the standard
variety of the language. To remedy the deficiencies they believed to exist, Bereiter
and Engelmann proposed a program designed to teach black children how to
speak: e.g., how to make statements, to form negatives, to develop polar concepts ('big' and 'little'), to use prepositions, to categorize objects, and to perform
logical operations. In this view, black children suffered from 'verbal deprivation'
or 'had no language,' and it was the duty and responsibility of educators to
supply them with one. This view also found support among many African
Americans who looked down on AAVE. Lippi-Green (1997, p. 200) has observed
that 'It cannot be denied that some of the most scornful and negative criticism
of AAVE speakers comes from other African Americans,' and from all walks of
life (see Rickford, 2004).

  Labov and others have been severely critical of such views, believing that they
completely misrepresent the linguistic abilities of black children. These children
speak a variety of English which is different from the standard favored by

educators, but it is neither deficient nor unsystematic. Indeed, the variety is both systematic in itself and is also related systematically to the standard. Moreover, black children live in a rich verbal culture in which linguistic ability is highly prized and in which many opportunities are offered for competition in verbal skill. To assume that such children cannot affirm, negate, categorize, or think logically because they perform poorly in certain extremely inhibiting testing situations is absurd. They must use language all the time in order to get by, and any fair test of linguistic ability shows them to be as skilled as any other children. In addition, black children have a rich store of verbal games (e.g., sounding, signifying, toasts, rifting, louding, and so on) which encourage them to develop their verbal skills. That such children need 'compensatory education' for their lack of linguistic ability is a complete misinterpretation of the facts. They may need some help in adjusting to certain middle-class values about how language is used in education, but that is a different matter and is a problem for many non-black children too. Such views also assume that a major function of schooling is to indoctrinate working-class children into middle-class ways, with language central to this process.

In questioning Bereiter and Engelmann's claim that black children appear to have no language at all, 'the myth of verbal deprivation,' Labov (1972a) points out that, if you put a black child in front of an adult white interviewer who then proceeds to fire questions at that child, you may expect few responses (p. 185): 'The child is in an asymmetrical situation where anything he says can literally be held against him. He has learned a number of devices to avoid saying anything in this situation, and he works very hard to achieve this end.' Perhaps nowhere are the inadequacies of Bereiter and Engelmann's program more clearly illustrated than in the following incident recounted by Fasold (1975, pp. 202–3):

> A film showing the corrective program developed by a team of educational psychologists for children alleged to have these language deficiencies was screened for linguists at the 1973 Linguistic Institute in Ann Arbor, Michigan. It contained the following sequence:
> Earnest White teacher, leaning forward, holding a coffee cup: 'This-is-not-a-spoon.'
> Little Black girl, softly: 'Dis not no 'poon.'
> White teacher, leaning farther forward, raising her voice: 'No, This-is-not-a-spoon.'
> Black child, softly: 'Dis not a 'poon.'
> White teacher, frustrated: 'This-is-not-a-spoon.'
> Child, exasperated: 'Well, dass a cup!'
> The reaction of the linguists, after they had finished applauding and cheering for the child, was a mixture of amusement, incredulity, and anger.

It is quite apparent from the child's final frustrated response that children may be much smarter than adults believe them to be, and sometimes, as in this case, smarter than those who would help them.

African Americans are aware that African American children perform poorly in schools. Rickford (1999a, p. 305) paints a bleak picture of the school performance of black third- and fourth-graders in East Palo Alto, California between

1989 and 1993. Green (2002, pp. 28–9) shows how in a national study conducted as part of the National Assessment of Educational Progress about two-thirds of African American fourth-graders in inner city schools were found to be reading below their grade level in the 1990s, and even in the twelfth grade the proportion exceeded two-fifths. (The corresponding rates for white students were 29 percent and 17 percent.) Even for those who regard AAVE as a genuine and inherently non-limiting variety of English, there still remains the problem of how to deal with that variety in the classroom (see Smitherman, 1999). One approach is to attempt to eradicate AAVE and replace it with SE: AAVE may not limit its users cognitively but it certainly limits them socially, and one of the purposes of education is the achievement of social equality. This is the traditional attitude that educators have toward nonstandard dialects. (You do not have to be a speaker of AAVE to experience this opinion of your speech, as any Cockney, Scouse, Geordie, or New Yorker knows who has been told his speech sounds poor, slovenly, ugly, bad, or lazy!) But this approach has not been particularly effective. Great solidarity can be gained by effectively resisting acquisition of the standard variety; as we saw in chapter 7, Labov, Trudgill, Cheshire, and others have amply documented such resistance. We should note that among black youths in New York City the less standard the variety of English spoken, the more successfully formal education appears to have been resisted, e.g., Labov's comments on the Jets reported in the previous section (see p. 343). Likewise, some adolescents of Caribbean descent in cities like London are deliberately recreolizing (see p. 85) their speech as a solidarity marker when they find they do not fit into the wider society.

An alternative approach has been called the approach through bidialectalism. Speakers of AAVE should be taught to speak SE, but no attempt should be made to eradicate AAVE. Indeed, in the early stages of instruction AAVE itself should be used as the language of instruction. For example, in recommending that reading materials written for black children should recognize the existence of AAVE, Stewart (1969, pp. 185–6) advocates the use of transitional materials. He says that in the very first stage of reading, such children would meet a sentence like 'Charles and Michael, they out playing.' Later, after they had learned to use the copula, they would see 'Charles and Michael, they are out playing.' Finally, they would meet the standard 'Charles and Michael are out playing.'

This attempt to use transitional reading materials written in AAVE proved a complete failure. Those who advocated the use of such materials saw them as providing a kind of bridge into readers written in SE. They argued that black children had enough problems when they entered school without facing the additional barrier of learning to read from readers written in an alien dialect. They could learn to read in their own dialect and make a later transition to books written in the standard. Blacks themselves led the opposition to such a move, and teachers, parents, and black activists united to oppose it. (In England, many parents of Caribbean descent have shown a similar resistance to any use of 'creole' in the classroom – see Sebba, 1997, pp. 78–83.) Their motives were various: some felt that such readers would disadvantage their children; others denied the validity of the variety of language itself; still others resisted the notion that there should be any differences at all made in teaching white and black children; and still others insisted that the problem, if there was one, was ascribable to attitudes, i.e., was a problem of racism, and not a linguistic problem at all.

Race and language were united, however, in two important incidents affecting the schooling of blacks in the United States. The by-now famous 'Ann Arbor Decision' of 1979 is an example of a successful claim that AAVE is a *bona fide* dialect that schools must recognize. The parents of eleven African American children attending Martin Luther King School in Ann Arbor, Michigan, sued the school board in federal court saying that their children had been denied the 'equal opportunity' to which they were entitled on account of the variety of English they spoke. The judge in the case agreed and ordered the board to take appropriate action to teach the children to read. If that action required the school system to recognize that the children did speak a different variety of the language from that used elsewhere in the school system then the school system had to adjust to the children and not the children to the school system. Although this was not quite a decision in favor of using both AAVE and SE, it did give both legal and public recognition to AAVE as an issue that educators could not shy away from.

The second decision involved *Ebonics*, a term particularly popular among those who believe that there are strong connections between AAVE and African languages, specifically Niger-Congo languages (see Williams, 1975). On December 18, 1996, the Oakland School Board in California decided to recognize, maintain, and use Ebonics in the classroom so that black children would eventually acquire fluency in SE. In effect, the board declared Ebonics to be a separate language from English, one moreover that was 'genetically based,' whatever that meant. This decision was supported by a unanimous vote of the Linguistic Society of America at its annual meeting on January 7, 1997, as being 'linguistically and pedagogically sound' without that organization giving any kind of endorsement to the idea that Ebonics was indeed 'genetically based.' Elsewhere it produced a very strong negative reaction (see Perry and Delpit, 1998, Adger et al., 1999, Rickford, 1999a, 1999b, 2004, Lakoff, 2000, and Baugh, 2000). For example, it led to a United States Senate sub-committee hearing in January, 1997, and strong opposition from both prominent African Americans (e.g., Jesse Jackson, until he changed his mind after taking time to reconsider the issues) and white conservatives (e.g., Rush Limbaugh). The resulting furore caused the board to drop the word *Ebonics* from its proposal in April, 1997. If nonstandard varieties of English were to have a place in Oakland classrooms, they would have to enter through the back door rather than the front door. (There is now a considerable literature on Ebonics, little of which is very illuminating, for what is said is often just as confusing as the term itself, what happened in Oakland, and ideas about what people should do next time something similar happens.)

Many linguists believe that language should not be an issue at all in education. They regard all varieties of a language as equal, so what we should be doing is teaching everyone to be tolerant and accepting of other varieties (Trudgill, 1995, pp. 186–7). This is a perhaps hopelessly utopian view. The inescapable reality is that people do use language as a discriminator in just about every sense of that word. Milroy and Milroy (1999) state that what actually happens is that although public discrimination on the grounds of race, religion, and social class is not now publicly acceptable, it appears that discrimination on linguistic grounds is publicly acceptable, even though linguistic differences may themselves be associated with ethnic, religious, and class differences. Varieties of a language do exist, and people do use these varieties for their own purposes, not all of them to be applauded. As linguists we may deplore this fact, but we would be naive to ignore it. It may not be something we can do anything about, for it may well be the case that this is an inevitable use people make of language, and in that sense some kind of linguistic (or social) universal.

Fairclough (1995) goes even further in his criticism of any kind of live-and-let-live solution. He criticizes the 'language awareness' approach advocated in various government reports in England in which students are taught SE but asked to recognize the legitimacy of other varieties for certain purposes. He says (p. 225) that this is a doubtful bit of 'social engineering,' that 'passing on prestigious practices and values such as those of standard English without developing a critical awareness of them . . . implicitly legitim[izes] them,' that it 'dress[es] up inequality as diversity.' Moreover, 'attributing the stigmatization of varieties to individual prejudice papers over the systematic, social legitimized stigmatization of varieties.' It does so because 'it puts linguistics . . . in the position of helping to normalize and legitimize a politically partisan representation, and turns a social scientific discipline into a resource for hegemonic struggle' (p. 250). In Fairclough's view, when linguists say that they should not take sides, they are actually taking sides, having been ideologically co-opted – though unwittingly – into the struggle about language and power in society.

I have said that there may be a certain solidarity to be found in the use of AAVE and also that Bernstein has argued that the characteristic language of the lower working class successfully perpetuates itself. In neither case are the users of these two varieties unfamiliar with SE. Nor are they unaware that SE has a prestige which their variety lacks. It is quite easy to document such familiarity and awareness. For example, some of the studies reported in chapter 7 clearly indicate that speakers know that certain varieties are preferred but they do not necessarily choose to use these varieties. One 15-year-old Glasgow boy had this to say on that subject to Macaulay (1977): 'I don't think I would change the way I speak. I wouldn't like to have an English accent. I think it's a very daft one. They pronounce words correctly but they don't sound very nice. In your own environment you'd feel out of place. If you live in Glasgow you must talk like a Glaswegian.'

A number of other studies have clearly demonstrated that adolescents and even very young children are quite aware of language differences and some of the consequences of such differences. Giles and Powesland (1975, p. 102) report on one study in which an investigator who could speak in either a Birmingham accent or RP spoke to two groups of 17-year-olds about psychology, using one accent with one group and the other with the other. When the students were asked certain questions after the two talks, it was apparent that the investigator was rated higher in his RP guise so far as his intelligence was concerned. Moreover, students wrote more to him and about him in this guise than in his Birmingham guise. Apparently, even though many students themselves do not use an RP accent, and may say they do not like it, they are still willing to ascribe certain virtues to those who speak it, whether or not these are deserved, as this use of the matched-guise technique (see pp. 112–13) effectively demonstrates. RP speakers are judged more competent, intelligent, and industrious, but non-RP speakers are judged to have greater personal integrity, to be better-humored, and to be more socially attractive.

In still another study the same investigators (p. 31) found that, although 12-year-olds knew which accents have social prestige and which accents lack such prestige, they tend not to judge their own accents reliably, many considering that they use an RP accent when in fact they actually use a strong local accent. Such studies may have interesting consequences for those who attempt to match teachers and pupils, for it is quite likely that the various possible mixes of RP and local accents, and standard and local varieties, will produce differential results as teachers and students view each other differently and react accordingly.

Perhaps the most interesting study of all is Rosenthal's study (1974) of attitudes toward two kinds of speech using 136 schoolchildren between the ages of 3 and 6, ninety upper-class white children and the rest lower-class black children. Each child saw two identical cardboard boxes, and each box contained a cassette-tape recorder and a present hidden from the child's view. Each box represented a 'head,' and the 'voice' in each head described the present in the box. One voice spoke AAVE and the other SE. Each child was asked to choose which of the two presents he or she preferred and to answer certain questions. Asked which voice spoke better, 79 percent of the children chose the speaker with the standard voice, and 73 percent said they expected a better present from the box that contained this voice. So far as accent was concerned, 92 percent of the white children identified one voice as belonging to a black person and 72 percent the other as belonging to a white person. The corresponding percentages for the black children's identifications were 73 and 59 percent. Black children said they liked the AAVE voice more than the other and almost half (46 percent) opted to take the present from its box. This study clearly shows that even very young children have learned that people speak differently and that such differences have social consequences.

Children very quickly learn to associate certain types of speech with race, class, gender, and so on. Reviewing work on language disadvantage done during the 1980s, Edwards (1989, p. 149) reports that 'Recent studies of language attitudes indicate that problems associated with speech perceptions and speech stereotyping continue.' He adds that nonstandard varieties continue to be disfavored, even by those who use them. His conclusion (p. 151) is that

> while the logical course of action, given unfavourable attitudes to certain varieties, is to alter the attitudes, this is at best a long-term strategy and, at worst simply utopian. Besides, social needs quite reasonably dictate a common standard which, while not the maternal variety of everyone, can at least be presented to all through education, particularly in the more formal domains of reading and writing.

It was just such a view that was behind the British government's 'Better English' campaign of 1995 designed to improve spoken English: there was to be a war on 'communication by grunt,' i.e., nonstandard English.

It is the social consequences of the use of nonstandard English and the need for a common standard that Honey (1983, 1989, 1997) has tried to address. In Honey's view, the schools would be doing a disservice to students if they did not teach SE. For Honey, all varieties of English are *not* equal because people do not view them as equal. (Honey himself does not believe that all varieties of the language are equal. He is quite sure that SE and RP are the 'best.') He says (1989, p. 174):

> There is a simplistic argument which says that rather than requiring the child to adapt to society, we should change society to accommodate the characteristics of the child. Those who use this argument to deny children access to any awareness of the implications of speaking with one accent rather than another are doing them an obvious disservice, if they cannot also guarantee that society's attitudes will have changed in time for that generation of children to benefit.

In Honey's view, schools should provide students with advantages. One of these is to be 'well-spoken,' well-spokenness being 'an attribute of human dignity' (p. 176). Finally, he adds (p. 177) that, 'Whether we like it or not, the ability to handle one of the most widely acceptable accents [presumably RP] has become an important indicator of an individual's ability to control the world around him.' Discussing SE, he says (1997, p. 42) that 'causing children to learn standard English is an act of empowerment which will give them access to a whole world of knowledge and to an assurance of greater authority in their dealings with the world outside their own homes, in a way which is genuinely liberating.' Honey's views have not been popular among sociolinguists because they feel that many of his statements misrepresent the positions linguists hold, or lack any evidence to support them, or are just plain wrong. However, they do appeal to those who seek simple solutions to complex problems.

The advantages of adopting styles of speech associated with the middle class and giving up those of the working class often seem to teachers to be too obvious to be questioned. They seem directly related to social mobility, which is a 'good thing.' Many teachers have actually gone through this process, at least to some extent, themselves. However, for many working-class children, perhaps a large majority, the advantages are not at all obvious. Many see no advantage to buying what the educational system is trying to sell because they find no value in what is being sold: only promises too often broken. As we saw earlier (chapter 7), many members of the working class, including children, find much to be gained from hanging on to their language and resisting attempts that others make to change it. They find solidarity in working-class speech. The prestige it has may be negative and covert, but it is not without its comforts. Moreover, they may be quite aware of what it means to change: almost certain alienation from their peers without necessarily acceptance by social superiors. Attempting to 'speak posh' in Newcastle or Liverpool is almost certain to bring about your social isolation if you attend a local state school. Eckert's work (1989) with jocks and burnouts (see p. 212) clearly shows how important identifying with the local area is for the latter group. In London, Sebba (1993, p. 33) found that London Jamaican was 'a sign of ethnic identity and solidarity, and [provided] an in-group language for adolescents.' An instructive account of some of the pressures and consequences of making any such change is contained in Hoggart's account (1970) of moving from a working-class childhood to a middle-class, intellectually oriented adulthood. All that may happen from teachers' exhortations to children to adopt a 'better' variety of language is an increase in any linguistic insecurity the children have. The consequences may therefore be quite negative for many children.

While linguists may try to offer what they regard as correctives to views associated with Bernstein and to false and misleading statements about the language abilities of many blacks in the United States, they may not necessarily be able to provide any solutions to these problems. For example, Alim (2005) describes how difficult it is to deal with the issue of teaching standard English to black youths in Haven High, a high school in a small American city in which opportunities for blacks are constantly decreasing. Teachers have a poor knowledge of the language of black youths and do not understand why they resist 'white cultural and linguistic norming' (p. 195), what Alim calls attempts to 'gentrify' their language. His view is that some kind of balance must be found between the two language varieties; however, he offers no suggestions as to how such a balance might possibly be achieved. Perhaps that is not surprising since the problem has proved to be intractable everywhere it has been identified.

We must take seriously certain observations by Goody and Watt (1972), who warn against ignoring the oral transmission of knowledge and all that goes with such transmission. They say (pp. 342–3):

> If . . . we return to the reasons for the relative failure of universal compulsory education to bring about the intellectual, social, and political results that James Mill expected, we may well lay a major part of the blame on the gap between the public literate tradition of the school, and the very different and indeed often directly contradictory private oral traditions of the pupil's family and peer group . . . there seem to be factors in the very nature of literate methods which make them ill-suited to bridge the gap between the street-corner society and the blackboard jungle. . . . In a literate society . . . the mere fact that reading and writing are normally solitary activities means that, in so far as the dominant cultural tradition is a literate one, it is very easy to avoid. . . . and even when it is not avoided its actual effects may be relatively shallow. Not only because, as Plato argued, the effects of reading are intrinsically less deep and permanent than those of oral converse; but also because the abstractness of the syllogism and of the Aristotelian categorizations of knowledge do not correspond very directly with common experience. The abstractness of the syllogism, for example, of its very nature disregards the individual's social experience and immediate personal context; and the compartmentalization of knowledge similarly restricts the kind of connections which the individual can establish and ratify with the natural and social world. The essential way of thinking of the specialist in literate culture is fundamentally at odds with that of daily life and common experience; and the conflict is embodied in the long tradition of jokes about absent-minded professors.

Such a view of education places both AAVE and Bernstein's views concerning the linguistic socialization of children into a much broader framework than the one within which linguists usually work. We should also remind ourselves that the problems that educators must deal with in their work are extremely complex, and, while linguists may make a contribution toward solving some of these problems, that contribution may not be a particularly large one. Language is but one factor among many that we must consider when we try to solve pressing social problems. A total solution must take other factors into account too. Linguists must be prepared to recognize that fact.

Discussion

1. As we saw in the previous section, there are at least three quite different views of the relationship between AAVE and SE: (1) AAVE is a dialect (probably best considered a nonstandard one rather than a regional one) of SE; (2) AAVE is a creolized variety of English and its speakers use it in a creole continuum; and (3) AAVE is a variety of English related systematically to all other varieties of English. What do you see as the educational consequences of each of these views?

2. How would you propose to deal with each of the following in the classroom:

   a. AAVE in Detroit?
   b. West Indian Creole in London?
   c. South Asian (i.e., Indian) English in Toronto?
   d. Scouse in Liverpool?

   What kinds of factors would be important to you in your decision-making?

3. 'People often say one thing but do another' is an observation that is not infrequently made about human behavior. How might such an observation apply to the linguistic beliefs and practices of children, parents, members of different social classes and ethnic groups, and teachers? What are some of those beliefs and practices?

4. Goody and Watt (1972, p. 353) comment on the persistence of the oral tradition in Western civilization as follows:

   > in our civilization, writing is clearly an addition, not an alternative, to oral transmission. Even in our *Buch und Lesen* culture, childrearing and a multitude of other forms of activity both within and outside the family depend upon speech; and the relationship between the written and the oral traditions must be regarded as a major problem in Western cultures.

   If their claim is correct, what implications do you find in it for language education?

5. Stubbs (1980, p. 156) makes the following observation concerning the work of Bernstein and Labov: 'The two bodies of work are . . . not directly comparable in terms of either data or theory.' To what extent do Bernstein and Labov seem to address the same issues? To the extent that they do address the same issues, who seems to make the greater contribution to understanding?

To the extent that they address different issues, who seems to have more to say to linguists, sociolinguists, and educators?

6. Sociolinguists sometimes appear as 'expert witnesses' in cases before the courts. Try to find some examples of their testimony. Why was it helpful/ unhelpful, accepted/disregarded?

Further Reading

For a brief overview of the topics dealt with here, see Edwards (1994). An excellent book-length treatment, more broadly based, is McKay and Hornberger (1996). For Bernstein's basic ideas, see Bernstein (1971–5, 1972b, and particularly 1990), parts of Robinson (1972), and especially Atkinson (1985). For more about AAVE, see Burling (1973), Dillard (1972), Mufwene et al. (1998), Rickford (1999a), pp. 4–9 of which contain an excellent list of the distinguishing characteristics of AAVE, and especially Green (2002, 2004). For Caribbean varieties of English in the United Kingdom, see Cropley (1983), Edwards (1979), Hewitt (1986), Roberts (1988), Sutcliffe (1982), and especially Sebba (1993). Trudgill (1975), Stubbs (1980), Lippi-Green (1997), and McWhorter (1998) discuss various educational consequences of language differences. Rickford et al. (2004) is an excellent bibliographical resource.

15 Planning

As a final topic I want to turn attention to some of the numerous attempts that have been made to change a particular variety of a language, or a particular language, or some aspect of how either of these functions in society. Such changes are usually described as instances of *language planning*. According to Weinstein (1980, p. 56), 'Language planning is a government authorized, longterm, sustained, and conscious effort to alter a language's function in a society for the purpose of solving communication problems.' It may involve assessing resources, complex decision-making, the assignment of different functions to different languages or varieties of a language in a community, and the commitment of valuable resources. As we will see, language planning can take a variety of forms and produce many different kinds of results. It is also not without its controversies.

Language planning has become part of modern nation-building because a noticeable trend in the modern world is to make language and nation synonymous. Deutsch (1968) has documented the tremendous increase within Europe during the last thousand years in what he calls 'full-fledged national languages.' A millennium ago these numbered six: Latin, Greek, Hebrew, Arabic, Anglo-Saxon (i.e., Old English), and Church Slavonic. By 1250 this number had increased to seventeen, a number that remained fairly stable until the beginning of the nineteenth century with, of course, changes in the actual languages, as Hebrew, Arabic, Low German, Catalan, and Norwegian either were submerged or became inactive, and languages like English, Dutch, Polish, Magyar, and Turkish replaced them in the inventory. In the nineteenth century the total number of fully fledged national languages increased to thirty. According to Deutsch, it showed a further increase to fifty-three by 1937, and it has further increased since then. Each 'new' country wanted its own language, and language became a basic expression of nationalistic feeling, as we see in such examples as Finnish, Welsh, Norwegian, Romanian, Bulgarian, Ukrainian, Irish, Breton, Basque, Georgian, and Hebrew. Consequently, governments have had to plan to develop or promote certain languages and sometimes to hinder or demote others, and a demand for 'language rights' is often one of the first demands made by a discontented minority almost anywhere in the world.

I will discuss some of the ideas that have gone into planning efforts made on behalf of some of these languages and, in doing so, mention briefly what planning has meant for certain other languages. I will also comment on the 'global' nature of English at the beginning of the third millennium.

Issues

Language planning is an attempt to interfere deliberately with a language or one of its varieties: it is human intervention into natural processes of language change, diffusion, and erosion. That attempt may focus on either its status with regard to some other language or variety or its internal condition with a view to changing that condition, or on both of these since they are not mutually exclusive. The first focus results in *status planning*; the second results in *corpus planning*.

Status planning changes the function of a language or a variety of a language and the rights of those who use it. For example, when speakers of a minority language are denied the use of that language in educating their children, their language has no status. Alternatively, when a government declares that henceforth two languages rather than one of these alone will be officially recognized in all functions, the newly recognized one has gained status. Status itself is a relative concept; it may also be improved or reduced by degrees, and usually is. So far as languages and their varieties are concerned, status changes are nearly always very slow, are sometimes actively contested, and often leave strong residual feelings. Even relatively minor changes or proposals for changes can produce such effects, as the residents of many countries, e.g., Norway, Belgium, Canada, and India, are well aware.

Corpus planning seeks to develop a variety of a language or a language, usually to standardize it, that is, to provide it with the means for serving every possible language function in society (see Clyne, 1997, for a collection of recent papers). Consequently, corpus planning may involve such matters as the development of an orthography, new sources of vocabulary, dictionaries, and a literature, together with the deliberate cultivation of new uses so that the language may extend its use into such areas as government, education, and trade. Corpus planning has been particularly important in countries like Indonesia, Israel, Finland, India, Pakistan, and Papua New Guinea. These two types of planning often co-occur, for many planning decisions involve some combination of a change in status with internal change. As one particular language in Papua New Guinea is developed, all other languages are affected, whether or not the effects are recognized officially. We must also note then that, just as planning may either be deliberate or proceed somewhat haphazardly, even accidentally, so its results may be deliberately intended or not at all as intended. Even though it is possible to recognize most of the relevant parameters, language planning is still far from being any kind of exact science. Linguists have also been quite involved in many planning activities and surrounding controversies. A few take another position, e.g., Calvet, 1998, maintaining that all such activities, since they are prescriptive in nature, necessarily conflict with the basic tenets of linguistics, which is essentially descriptive in its focus.

Cobarrubias (1983) has described four typical ideologies that may motivate actual decision-making in language planning in a particular society: these are *linguistic assimilation*, *linguistic pluralism*, *vernacularization*, and *internationalism*.

Linguistic assimilation is the belief that everyone, regardless of origin, should learn the dominant language of the society. Examples are easy to find. France applied this policy to various peoples within its borders. The United States also applied the policy both internally to immigrants and externally in a possession, Guam, where Chamorro was suppressed until 1973, and in the Philippines, where instruction in the schools had to be in English throughout the period in which the United States ruled that country; a similar assimilationist ideology prevailed in Puerto Rico until the 1940s. Linguistic assimilation is practiced widely and in a wide variety of forms, e.g., policies of Hellenization of Macedonian in Greece and of Russification in the former Soviet Union.

Linguistic pluralism, the recognition of more than one language, also takes a variety of forms. It can be territorially based or individually based or there may be some combination of the two. It can be complete or partial, so that all or only some aspects of life can be conducted in more than one language in a society. Examples are countries like Belgium, Canada, Singapore, South Africa, and Switzerland. Vernacularization is the restoration or elaboration of an indigenous language and its adoption as an official language, e.g., Bahasa Indonesia in Indonesia; Tok Pisin in Papua New Guinea; Hebrew in Israel; Tagalog (renamed Filipino) in the Philippines; and Quechua in Peru.

Internationalization is the adoption of a non-indigenous language of wider communication either as an official language or for such purposes as education or trade, e.g., English in Singapore, India, the Philippines, and Papua New Guinea. The languages that have been most internationalized in this sense are English and French with English much more so than French. (Currently France is seeking to develop *La Francophonie* as an organization to further French in the world.) I will have more to say about English later in this chapter.

As a result of planning decisions, a language can achieve one of a variety of statuses (Kloss, 1968). A language may be recognized as the sole official language, as French is in France or English in the United Kingdom and the United States. This fact does not necessarily mean that the status must be recognized constitutionally or by statute; it may be a matter of long-standing practice, as it is with English in the two cases cited above. Two or more languages may share official status in some countries, e.g., English and French in Canada and in Cameroon; French and Flemish in Belgium; French, German, Italian, and Romansh (even though the latter has very few speakers and is actually only a 'national' language) in Switzerland; English and Afrikaans in South Africa; and English, Malay, Tamil, and Chinese in Singapore, although in this case Malay has an additional 'national-language' status.

A language may also have official status but only on a regional basis, e.g., Igbo, Yoruba, and Hausa in Nigeria; German in Belgium; and Marathi in Maharashtra, India. A language may be a 'promoted' language, lacking official status, but used by various authorities for specific purposes, e.g., many languages in Canada. A tolerated language is one that is neither promoted nor proscribed or restricted, e.g., Basque in France, many immigrant languages in western Europe, and Amerindian languages in North America. Finally, a discouraged or proscribed language is one against which there are official sanctions or restrictions, e.g., Basque in the early years of Franco's regime in Spain; Scots Gaelic after the

1745 rising; Macedonian in Greece; until recently many immigrant and native languages in areas like North America and Australia, particularly in schools for the children of such people; and the Norman French patois of the Channel Islands during the German occupation in World War II. Kurdish is today largely proscribed in Turkey. The language cannot be used for writing anything, but since 1991 it can be used in speaking and singing!

Planning decisions will obviously play a very large role in determining what happens to any minority language or languages in a country (Cobarrubias, 1983, pp. 71–3). They can result in deliberate attempts to eradicate such a language, as with Franco's attempt to eliminate Basque from Spain by banning that language from public life. Official neglect may result in letting minority languages die by simply not doing anything to keep them alive. This has been the fate of many Amerindian languages and is likely to be the fate of many more. In France Basque was neglected; in Spain it was virtually proscribed. One interesting consequence is that, while once there were more speakers of Basque in France than in Spain, now the situation is reversed. Instead of neglect there may be a level of tolerance, so that if a community with a minority language wishes to keep that language alive, it is allowed to do so but at its own expense. In 1988 the Council of Europe adopted a Charter on Regional or Minority languages that gave some recognition to such languages but really allowed each country to do as it pleased with them.

Two other issues are worthy of comment. The first has to do with what language rights immigrants to a country should have in an era of widespread immigration motivated by a variety of concerns but within a system of states which often equates statehood or nationhood with language and sometimes with ethnicity. It is not surprising, therefore, that what language rights immigrants should have is a controversial issue almost everywhere. One view is that immigrants give up their rights to their languages and their cultures by migrating. The opposite view is that no one should be required to give up a mother tongue by reason of such movement, and that this is particularly regrettable in a world in which population movement is either encouraged, e.g., nineteenth-century migration to the Americas, or enforced, e.g., by persecutions. Both UNESCO and the United Nations have declared that ethnic groups have the right to maintain their languages. However, it is not at all clear that immigrants to countries like the United States, Canada, and Australia, or the families of European 'guest workers' are covered by such declarations. Indigenous populations clearly are, but there may be disagreement as to what constitutes an indigenous group, as various people have learned, sometimes fatally, in places like the former Yugoslavia, Rwanda and Burundi, and Sri Lanka to cite but a few examples.

The second issue concerns the problem of identifying the right kinds of data that must go into planning decisions. Planning must be based on good information, but sometimes the kinds of information that go into planning decisions are not very reliable. Census-takers, for example, may have considerable difficulty in determining just who speaks what languages when and for what purposes. The census of India has always had this problem. The issues are complex, and gatherers of such information may have great difficulty in getting answers even to simple questions. You also get different answers according to the way you phrase your questions. What is your mother tongue? What was the first language you learned? What languages do you speak? What language do you speak at home? What languages are you fluent in? Do you speak Spanish (French) (German)? And so on. Moreover, the questions and how they are answered may be politically motivated. The different answers are also subject to a variety of interpretations.

Furthermore, it is easier to elicit particular kinds of information at certain times than at other times. During World War II many people in North America apparently suppressed information concerning either a German ethnicity or any ability to speak German. By the 1960s and 1970s the ability to speak Spanish was something to be proud of in the United States, just as was the ability to speak French in Canada. Recent Canadian censuses show more and more people claiming bilingual ability in English and French, but little assessment is made of such self-reported claims; it is apparently enough that people should wish to make them! Consequently, we must always exercise caution in interpreting untreated data from censuses.

Questions asked at ten-year periods may also produce different answers, partly because there have been objective quantifiable changes but also because less quantifiable and more subjective psychological changes have occurred. A particularly telling example is the so-called 're-discovery' of ethnicity in the United States in the late twentieth century. We must remember that we cannot ignore the feelings that people have about who they are, what they speak, and what rights they should have. Such feelings are real. For example, as mentioned earlier, speakers of Cantonese and Mandarin insist they speak the same language even though linguists deny that they do; such a feeling of 'sameness' is every bit as important in language planning as is the linguists' fact of 'difference.'

Discussion

1. Refer back to pp. 358–9 to the examples given of languages which may be described as official, joint official, regional official, promoted, tolerated, and proscribed. Find further examples for as many of these categories as you can.
2. Some people are minorities everywhere so far as language is concerned, e.g., Basques, Lapps, Kurds, and most aboriginal peoples. What linguistic 'rights' do you consider such minorities to possess?
3. Can you find any instances in your own community of languages that enjoy different statuses? That is, how many different languages do you come across, and how must, or how do, those in authority deal with people who use these languages?
4. The Maori language of New Zealand has been described as an endangered language. Virtually every Maori speaks English, and, while many young Maori are bilingual, an increasing number do not speak any Maori at all. In fact, Maori is used as an everyday language only in some rural areas. Education is conducted in English, English is the language of towns and cities in which the Maori increasingly prefer to live, and Maori itself is

used more and more only by older speakers on ceremonial occasions, with attempts to teach it as a subject in many secondary schools so far showing few signs of success. Do you know of any situations which appear to be analogous to the situation with the Maori? How would you plan to preserve Maori language and culture?

5. Gaelic was not allowed to be taught in Scottish schools until 1918, and then only as a subject of instruction. It took a further forty years for it to become used as a language of instruction. The Welsh gained the same right to use Welsh as a language of instruction only in 1953. Some would argue that 'progress' has been made; others, 'regress.' Why are there such conflicting views?

6. There are different kinds of migrants in the modern world, e.g., permanent 'voluntary' migrants, 'guest workers,' refugees, and temporary residents. How are the language rights, if any, of such people viewed in different countries?

A Variety of Situations

In this section we will look at a variety of linguistic situations in the world to see some instances of planning. In the following section we will look at a number of countries chosen because they show some of the variety of issues that states engaged in planning face as they continue to make changes. Many other examples could be cited; I have chosen these to illustrate certain points. Doubtless other examples would have served just as well, for it is probably true to say that nowhere in the world can you find a country where nothing is being done, either directly or by default, concerning the language or languages of that country.

France serves as a good example of a country which has a single national language and does little or nothing for any other language. Most inhabitants simply assume that French is rightly the language of France. Consequently they virtually ignore other languages so that there is little national interest in any move to try to ascertain exactly how many people speak Provençal or Breton or to do anything for, or against, Basque. Likewise, if an immigrant group to France, e.g., Algerians or Vietnamese, wants to try to preserve its language, it must try to do so in its own time and with its own resources, for it is widely assumed that French is the proper language of instruction in schools in France. (The only major exception is that German is taught in Alsace.) This situation is little different from the one that existed in the old colonial days, in which it was assumed that the French language and the curriculum of Metropolitan France were entirely appropriate in the *lycées* of colonies such as Algeria and Indo-China (now Vietnam) attended by the more fortunate local children, who might then aspire to higher education in France. France is a highly centralized country with Paris its dominant center even to the extent that when traveling in France you often see signposts indicating exactly how far you are from Paris (actually from the cathedral of Notre Dame, its symbolic center). It has been so since the time of Richelieu. France and the French language are inseparable. Regional languages such as Breton, Basque, Occitan, Flemish, Catalan, Corsican, and Franco-Provençal persist, get varying amounts of state support, and provide local identities to those who maintain them. Such languages may be tolerated but they cannot be allowed to threaten a state unified around French. The French, of course, are not alone in seeing their country as essentially a monolingual one; the English just across the Channel and the Japanese right across the world are like them in this respect.

Adjacent to France we have in one direction the multilingualism of Switzerland and in another the bilingualism of Belgium, but it is the second of these to which I will refer. Today, French and Flemish (Dutch) coexist in a somewhat uneasy truce in Belgium. The struggle between the French and Flemish in that country has a long history. In 1815 the politically and socially ascendant French in Belgium found themselves returned at the end of the Napoleonic Wars to Dutch rule. William of Holland proceeded to promote Dutch interests and language and limit the power of the French, the Walloons. He was also a strong Calvinist, and in 1830 both Flemish and Walloon Catholics rebelled and gained independence for Belgium. However, this religious unity between the Flemish Catholics and the Walloon Catholics soon gave way to cleavage along linguistic lines, language proving in this case to be a stronger force for divisiveness than religion for cohesion. The new state became French-oriented and Flemish was banned from the government, law, army, universities, and secondary schools. French domination was everywhere, and it was not until the twentieth century that the Flemish, who are actually a majority of the population, were able to gain a measure of linguistic and social equality. Today's equality, however, is still colored by memories of past discrimination based on language. The Belgians have tried to settle their differences by separating the languages on a territorial basis and regarding Brussels as a bilingual city, even though it is clearly French-dominant. Periodically, however, linguistic differences surface in Belgium to create tensions between the Walloons and the Flemish, just as they do, as we will see, in Canada.

In Spain the recent revival of Catalan is of interest. The Catalans have had a long and proud history, traditionally regarding themselves as more prosperous and progressive than the Castilians and constantly having to assert themselves to see that they were not exploited, e.g., by revolts in 1640 and 1705, and through expressing their displeasure with the mismanagement that led to the loss of Cuba at the beginning of the twentieth century. But Catalan, a language which resembles French as much as it does Spanish, itself was a dying language by the end of the nineteenth century, spoken monolingually only in the villages and giving way to Castilian even in Barcelona. However, a group of intellectuals and poets succeeded in reviving the language in the early twentieth century in conjunction with a movement to promote Catalan nationalism. When this movement failed in 1923, an era of repression began, which led to a further reform movement culminating in the founding of the Republic of Spain and its consequence, the Spanish Civil War. Catalonia suffered dreadfully during that war. One of the war's results was, again, the suppression of Catalan, and this was not effectively ended until after Franco's death and the restoration of a democratic system of government. As a result of the decrees of King Juan Carlos, it is now once more possible to worship in Catalan, to be educated in Catalan, and to use the language freely without being suspected of disloyalty. Similar rights were given to the Basques, another linguistically persecuted group in Spain during Franco's time. Catalan has once more achieved a considerable amount of the status it once enjoyed in the Spanish peninsula, and Basque now enjoys a measure of status long denied to it. There is even some evidence of a kind of backlash against any kind of exclusivity for Catalan in Catalonia. O'Donnell (1996) reports that many Catalonians fear recent changes may have gone a bit too far: they are happy to be able to use Catalan without restriction but they also want to retain their Castilian-language ability and its wider Spanish connection.

Turkey provides a good example of very deliberate language planning designed to achieve certain national objectives and to do this very quickly. When Kemal Atatürk (*ata* 'father'), the 'father of the Turks,' established the modern republic of Turkey, he was confronted with the task of modernizing the language. It had no vocabulary for modern science and technology, was written in an unsuitable Arabic orthography, and was strongly influenced by both Arabic and Persian. In 1928 Atatürk deliberately adopted the Roman script for his new modern Turkish. This effectively cut the Turks off from their Islamic past and directed their attention toward both their Turkish roots and their future as Turks in a modern world. Since only 10 percent of the population was literate, there was no mass objection to the changes. It was possible to use the new script almost immediately in steps taken to increase the amount of literacy in the country.

In the 1930s Atatürk promoted a further move away from Arabic and Persian in the development of the new vocabulary that the language required in order to meet the needs of science and technology. The 'Sun Language Theory' was developed, a theory which said that Turkish was the mother tongue of the world and that, when Turkish borrowed from other languages, it was really taking back what had originally been Turkish anyway. Some deliberate attempts were made to purify the language, but these were not very successful, and today Turkish is full of borrowings, particularly from English, French, and other European languages. Corpus planning was very effective for a while in bringing about a modernizing, secular-oriented Turkey. However, it stagnated in the last decades of the twentieth century as problems arose with defining a new Turkish identity: secular or religious, European or Asian, Western or Islamic. (See Lewis, 1999, and Doğançay-Aktuna, 2004, together with the rest of that issue of the *International Journal of the Sociology of Language* for assessments of recent developments.)

In the former Soviet Union there was a great amount of language planning dating from its very founding, though not all of it was coherent or consistent. One of the most important policies was Russification. Needless to say, in a state as vast as the Soviet Union, composed of approximately 100 different nationalities, each with its own language or variety of a language, there were several different aspects to such a policy. One of these was the elevation of regional and local dialects into 'languages,' a policy of 'divide and rule.' Its goal was to prevent the formation of large language blocks and also allow the central government to insist that Russian be used as a lingua franca. It also led to the large number of languages that flourished in the Soviet Union.

In addition, the Cyrillic script was extended to nearly all the languages of the Soviet Union. This orthography further helped to cut off the Muslim peoples of central Asia from contact with Arabic, Turkish, and Persian influences. In the 1930s these people were actually provided with Romanized scripts, but Atatürk's Romanization of Turkish posed a threat in that it made the Turkish world accessible to the Soviet peoples of central Asia. Consequently, Romanization was abandoned in 1940, Cyrillic alphabets were reimposed, and deliberate attempts were made to stress as many differences as possible among the various languages of the area (e.g., by developing special Cyrillic characters for local pronunciations) as part of the policy of divide and rule. Russification also required the local languages of the Soviet Union to borrow words from Russian when new words were needed. Population migrations, not necessarily voluntary, also spread Russian (and Russians) throughout the country as a whole, e.g., into Kazakhstan where Kazakhs became a minority, and into the Baltic republics, particularly Latvia and Estonia.

While many local and regional languages were actively encouraged in the Soviet Union, so that Russian itself could be legitimized as a lingua franca, a number of languages were banned from support, e.g., Arabic, Hebrew, and German, since it was not deemed to be in the interests of the state to support these. Russian was also promoted as a universal second language and as a language of instruction in the schools. However, there was resistance in such areas as Georgia, Armenia, Azerbaijan, and the Baltic republics.

When the Soviet Union eventually fell into disarray at the end of the 1980s such policies had interesting consequences. The Soviet Union had been organized internally by republics constructed primarily on language and ethnicity. It proceeded to divide that way. For example, Ukraine, even though the language itself and the people had been heavily Russified, became a separate state. The Baltic republics of Estonia, Latvia, and Lithuania went their ways too. Moldavia became Moldova and its Moldavian language was finally acknowledged to be what it was, Romanian, and was renamed Moldavian–Romanian. Georgia, Armenia, and Kazakhstan separated too and proclaimed Georgian, Armenian, and Kazakh as their national languages, even though in the last case only 40 percent of the population were Kazakhs and 37 percent were Russians. The Turkic-speaking republics, deliberate creations within the Soviet Union, also separated and found their main linguistic problem to be how closely they should identify with Turkey itself. Their abandonment of the Cyrillic script and choice of Roman scripts rather than Arabic-Persian ones appears to indicate a close but secular relationship.

Finland is a very close, and sometimes uncomfortable, neighbor of both Russia and Sweden. In the nineteenth century the Finns developed their language to differentiate themselves from both the Russians and the Swedes by turning what was essentially an unwritten spoken language into one with a writing system, literature, and the full panoply of uses that signify a standard language. This deliberate bit of corpus planning gave them a distinct language and reinforced the differences they felt to exist between them and both Russians and Swedes, differences further accentuated by the fact that Finnish belongs to an entirely different language family (Finno-Ugric) from the other two languages (Indo-European).

In a more general vein, we can observe that there was a marked difference in the twentieth century in the way in which the old European and central Asian empires broke up and the way in which imperial bonds were loosened elsewhere in South and Southeast Asia and in Africa. When the Austro-Hungarian, Russian, and Ottoman Empires broke up, the result was the emergence of nation-states based primarily on claims about language with a consequent complete redrawing of boundaries. This redrawing did not suit everyone, since many former minorities proved to be no more tolerant of smaller 'captive' language groups than their previous oppressors once they had achieved political recognition as nation-states. When European imperialism was finally effectively removed from Asia and Africa, however, there was no such redrawing of political boundaries. The previous colonies, often peculiar amalgams of language and ethnic groups, since conquest rather than language or ethnicity had accounted for their origins, became independent whole states except in a few cases, such as Pakistan, Burma, and Sri Lanka, when there was successful separation in contrast to Biafra's unsuccessful attempt to secede from Nigeria and Katanga's from Zaïre. Many of the resultant states have no common language, no common ethnicity, and strong internal linguistic and ethnic rivalries, making national planning and consensus difficult to achieve at the best.

One important consequence is that the new states of Africa and Asia are often multilingual but, as a result of their histories, have elites who speak a European language such as English or French. This language not only serves many as an internal working language but is also still regarded as the language of mobility. It is both the language that transcends local loyalties and the one that opens up access to the world outside the state. It is unlikely that in these circumstances such outside languages will disappear; rather, it is likely that they will continue to be used and that positions of leadership will continue to go only to those who have access to them, unless present conditions change.

An attempt is sometimes made to find a 'neutral' language, that is, a language which is not English and which gives no group an advantage. In 1974 President Kenyatta of Kenya decreed that Swahili was to become the language of the country, the language of national unity, even though most Kenyans did not speak the language; it was not the language of the major city, Nairobi; it was spoken in a variety of dialects and pidgins; the majority of those who did speak it did not speak it well; and English was better known in the higher echelons of government, the professions, and so on. Both Swahili and English were to remain as official languages, however. Swahili was chosen over one of the local languages, e.g., the president's own Kikuyu, a language spoken by about 20 percent of the population, because the ethnic composition of the country made any other choice too difficult and dangerous. In that respect, Swahili was a neutral language. It was for much the same reason – that it was a neutral unifying language in a state with over 100 indigenous languages – that Swahili was also chosen in Tanzania as the national language, although in this case it was spoken fairly widely as a trade language along the coast and also in the capital, Dar es Salaam. The consequence of the 1974 decree in Kenya is that Swahili is now used much more than it was, but it has not by any means replaced English in those areas of use in which English was previously used.

Although the use of Swahili in Kenya has become a matter of national pride, this does not mean that its extension into certain spheres of life goes unresisted. One consequence has been that Kenyans have developed their own version, or versions, of the language. Like Tanzanians, they speak 'bad' Swahili, according to many of those for whom it is an ancestral language. The Kenyan and Tanzanian varieties are also different. National pride may cause even further differentiation to emerge, with the Kenyan variety of Swahili eventually becoming somewhat different from the original coastal variety of the language on which it is based and different from the Tanzanian variety standardized on the speech of Zanzibar: Kenya's variety is likely to be based on the speech of Mombasa. Currently, Tanzania has moved much further than Kenya in the use of Swahili. However, full social mobility in both countries requires a citizen to be able to use Swahili, English, and one or more local vernaculars since each has appropriate occasions for use.

India, with more than a billion people, is another country which has had to face similar problems. In this case the solution has been to promote Hindi in the Devanagari script as the official language that unites the state, but more than a dozen other languages, including Sanskrit, are recognized as official languages in the nation's constitution. However, there are serious obstacles to the spread of Hindi in India. There is a considerable difference between literary Hindi and the various regional and local spoken varieties (see chapter 2). Gandhi tried to emphasize building Hindi on popular speech so as to bridge the gap between the literary and colloquial varieties and also to unify the regions. In an attempt to overcome some of the difficulties, the Indian government established various groups to develop scientific terminology, glossaries, dictionaries, and an encyclopedia. One noticeable development has been the way in which those entrusted with such tasks, usually the Hindi elite, have looked to Sanskrit in their work: they have followed a policy of Sanskritization in their attempts to purify Hindi of English and also increasingly to differentiate Hindi from Urdu, the variety of the language used in Muslim Pakistan. The effects have been particularly noticeable in literary Hindi, which has possibly grown further away from the evolving colloquial varieties as a result of such activities. There has been some periodic dissatisfaction with what has happened (Gumperz, 1971, pp. 146–7), for example with teaching Hindi in the same way as Sanskrit has been taught traditionally.

The linguistic situation in India is further complicated today in a way it was not complicated at the partition of the subcontinent into India and Pakistan (and then later into a third state, Bangladesh). India came into existence as a unitary state. However, local opposition to such centralization was strong and the country was quickly reorganized by states, the first being the Telugu-speaking Andhra state in 1953. Now India has two important levels of government, the central one in New Delhi looking after common interests, and the other, the state level with each state government looking after that state's interests and, more importantly, doing so in the language of that state and not in the Hindi or English of the central government.

Hindi is often viewed in India as giving northern Indians unwarranted advantages over Indians elsewhere. This feeling is particularly strong in the south of India, where various Dravidian languages are spoken. To that extent, English continues to offer certain advantages. Its use spread throughout the upper social strata everywhere in India in the former imperial regime; now it can be viewed as quite neutral even though, of course, its use may be opposed strongly at an official level, where it is recognized only as an 'auxiliary' language (Inglehart and Woodward, 1967). English is used in the higher courts, as a language of parliamentary debate, as a preferred language in the universities, and as a language of publication in learned journals. Although Hindi is promoted as the unifying language of India, many Indians now see such promotion to be at the expense of some other language they speak, or a set of religious beliefs, or the opportunity to acquire a world language like English. Language planning in India, however, is largely confined to elites: the masses, whose needs are more immediate, are largely unaffected. Like any other kind of planning in India, it seems fraught with difficulties, dangers, and unforeseen consequences.

Finally, if we return to the English-speaking world, or rather to a country which is assumed to be thoroughly committed to English, we can observe how it too must confront a number of issues to do with language. Language planning has become a serious concern in the United States in recent years, particularly as a result of a recognition that there is a large indigenous Spanish-speaking population and because of continued immigration into the country (see Fishman, 1966, and Veltman, 1983). Recent censuses have shown that as many as one in six people in the United States do not have English as their mother tongue, that the majority of these are native-born Americans and that the proportion is growing, particularly in the southwest, i.e., Texas, New Mexico, Arizona, and California, and along parts of the eastern seaboard (Waggoner, 1981). A recent source (Huntington, 2004) points out that Hispanics comprised 12 percent of the population in 2000, that their proportion in the total population exceeded that of black Americans in 2002, and that it is estimated that by 2040 25 percent of the total population will be of Hispanic origin (p. 224). In recent years, too, more and more languages from Asia, Southeast Asia, and the Middle East are represented in the population.

Not only is a language other than English the mother tongue of a great number of residents of the United States, but many do not speak English at all or speak it with difficulty. There is obviously a vast resource of languages in the United States, but the traditional policy of assimilation is still widely pursued. English is very much the language of the mainstream, and even though languages such as Spanish may be in widespread use in some areas and have certain official approval there, this use is motivated by pragmatic concerns alone. We can note that only two of the states are officially bilingual: New Mexico, with the other language being Spanish, and Hawaii, with the other language being Hawaiian. It is of interest to note too that in 1993 Puerto Ricans restored English as an official language in the Commonwealth after an earlier 1991 law made Spanish the sole official language. English had become part of Puerto Rican identity (Morris, 1996, Velez and Schweers, 1993).

Fishman (1981) has pointed out that Americans regard English as something to be used rather than something that they necessarily must take pride in. Moreover, this view spreads to other languages too, with one consequence being that, since most Americans are monolingually English, little effort is expended on preserving other languages. Indeed, as Fishman observes (p. 517), 'The greatest American linguistic investment by far has been in the Anglification of its millions of immigrant and indigenous speakers of other languages.' The Bilingual Education Act, he insists, was primarily 'an act for the Anglification of non-English speakers and not an act for *bilingualism*,' but rather an act against bilingualism. Bilingualism is seen as potentially divisive in the United States as 'Quebecization' or 'Balkanization,' in Fishman's words. Bilingual education, therefore, is expediency. It is transitional education designed to ease those who do not speak English into the mainstream of English. As Fishman says (p. 522), 'Language maintenance in the USA is not part of public policy because it is rarely recognized as being in the public interest,' being regarded as divisive and incompatible with progress, modernity, and efficiency.

The United States actually has no official language but, as Schiffman (1996, p. 213) says, the language policy of the United States:

> is not neutral, it FAVORS the English language. No statute or constitutional amendment or regulatory law is necessary to maintain this covert policy – its strength lies in the basic assumptions that American society has about language. These basic assumptions range from simple communicative competence in English to deeply held prejudices, attitudes, biases (often supported by religious belief), and other 'understandings' that constitute what I call American linguistic culture, which is the locus of covert policy in this (or any) polity.

There has even been a move in Congress in recent years to amend the constitution in order to make English the official language and many individual states have enacted legislation giving English official status within them (see Adams and Brink, 1990, Baron, 1990, Crawford, 1992a, 1992b, and Schmid, 2001). Those in favor of this move believe that the increasing use of other languages than English in the United States, and in particular the increasing use of Spanish, poses some kind of internal threat. Rickford (2004) has even gone so far as to claim that some of the hostility shown to Ebonics (see p. 349) arose from this same source: fear of recognizing any other language than Standard English. Proponents of English only have pointed to Canada as an example of a country where bilingualism has not worked in their argument for making the United States officially monolingual in English. That official bilingualism may have actually been Canada's salvation seems not to have occurred to them, nor does the fact that the two countries have had entirely different, though not necessarily unrelated, histories.

In the United States there is a growing awareness that the country is not unilingual and that either an attempt must be made to make it so or there must be some recognition that it is not so (see Dicker, 1996). Huntington (2004), a prominent American political scientist, says that Americans are currently experiencing a crisis of identity. For nearly two centuries they upheld the 'American creed,' some of the components of which were the English language, Christianity, religious commitment, the rule of law, the importance of individual rights, Protestant values of individualism, and a strong work ethic (p. xvi). According to Huntington, this creed provided Americans with a national identity that began to erode in the 1960s and continues to do so still under an influx of immigrants, a tolerance of multilingualism, the encouragement of bilingualism, the rise of group identities based on race, ethnicity, and gender, the growing commitment of elites to cosmopolitan identities and globalization (a commitment not shared by the population at large), and after the late 1980s no perceived external enemy (until 2001). He says that English-only moves, hostility to group rights and bilingual education, and the growing religiosity of the American population can all be explained as a reaction to this perceived decreased commitment to a national identity. Huntington ends by suggesting that the new century requires a reaffirmation of the traditional identity but it is clear that this will not be an easy task.

Discussion

1. As we saw in chapter 2, it is not at all easy to define *language* and to distinguish it from *dialect*. There may be strong political and other considerations for creating numerous distinctions where few originally existed, or for doing the opposite. Supply examples where differences have deliberately been created between varieties of a language or between languages themselves to accentuate differences. Supply examples of the opposite kind too, that is, of deliberate attempts to minimize differences.

2. Discussing the origins of Flemish, Dutch, German, and Afrikaans, Deutsch (1968, pp. 602–3) remarks as follows: 'It was not at first these languages that made history; it was history that made these languages.' What do you understand by this remark? If Deutsch's observation is correct, what are its implications for emerging nations?

3. The Polish, Czech, and Romanian alphabets were Romanized in the nineteenth century and Cyrillic alphabets were abandoned. How might you account for such changes?

4. Many new Asian and African states are multilingual and multi-ethnic. They are nearly all subject to the same pressures which led to the foundation of European-type nation-states founded on linguistic and ethnic groupings, pressures which could result in their break-up. What kinds of planning activities appear to be necessary if these new states are to evolve in a different way from those owing their origin to linguistic and ethnic separatism? What kinds of planning appear to be necessary in the latter both to reduce national rivalries and deal with 'captive' minorities?

5. Hebrew has been successfully revived in Israel, but the Irish have been unsuccessful in their attempts to revive Irish Gaelic in Ireland. Today, Gaelic is spoken by less than 5 percent of the population and then only in small pockets, mainly along the west coast. What factors seem to explain success in one case and failure in the other?

6.   The United States has nearly always been characterized as a 'melting-pot' so far as its linguistic treatment of immigrants and even of minorities has been concerned. To what extent has the myth been based on fact? Is it still valid to any extent? You might also compare this myth with that of the 'cultural mosaic' said to be favored by its neighbor Canada, and ask the same two questions about that country and its myth.

Further Examples

Some further examples of kinds of planning decisions that have been made in a number of countries in different parts of the world will show how difficult at times planning can be. The first example is Papua New Guinea, a nation of 700 or more indigenous languages, some, possibly more than a third, with fewer than 500 speakers, and this in a total population of approximately 4 million. Papua New Guinea has three official languages which are all second languages to the vast majority of its people: Hiri Motu, Tok Pisin, and English. The first two are pidgin-based languages. Of the three, Tok Pisin is becoming more and more the first language of many young people, particularly city dwellers. Although all children learn English in school and most parents feel that knowledge of English brings great advantages to their children, very little use is made of English outside certain formal contexts, e.g., in schools and in certain occupations such as the legal profession. Tok Pisin is now used almost exclusively for purposes of debate in the House Assembly, which is the parliament of Papua New Guinea. It is also frequently used in broadcasting, even to report on and discuss matters of considerable complexity, and increasingly in the press and in education, particularly at the lower levels. One representative view of the importance of Tok Pisin to Papua New Guinea is the following (Wolfers, 1971, pp. 418–19):

> [Tok Pisin], then, whatever one may argue as to its intrinsic merits, has revolutionized New Guinea society. It has broken down old barriers, and allowed for direct inter-racial and inter-language-group communication where this was not previously possible. It has made a national radio news-service feasible, and a newspaper, the *Nu Gini Toktok*, available to the relatively unsophisticated. The pidgin has been one of the most important elements in the Territory's slow and hesitant groping towards nationhood. Its very history, its origins on the plantations and in European employ generally, have allowed for, if not encouraged, the growth of that common set of experiences and attitudes from which a nation grows.

Tok Pisin is a pidgin-based language; consequently, it must be developed to meet the various new needs it must serve. Such growth is not without its difficulties. One particular development that has met with negative reaction from a number of linguists is that, for pragmatic reasons, vocabulary expansion has taken place through large-scale borrowing from English, rather than through the exploitation of native resources, e.g., words such as *amenmen, ekspendisa, eleksen, komisin, mosin, praim minista, privilij,* and *spika.* English exerts a powerful influence on Tok Pisin. Anglicized varieties of the language may show not only borrowings of English words but also the occasional English plural *-s*, use of English subordination patterns and the English counting system, and so on. At the moment, in spite of certain Anglicizations that are apparent in some varieties, Tok Pisin is still so distinct from English that there is no evidence of a continuum between Tok Pisin and English. However, there is a real danger that a continuum could develop with Standard English at the 'top' and local varieties of Tok Pisin at the 'bottom,' much as in Jamaica (see p. 81), with all the attendant problems.

Tok Pisin has also developed a number of sub-varieties, particularly in urban areas, so that it is now not as uniform as it once was. There is some risk that, without a deliberate effort to standardize the language, it will not remain as efficient a lingua franca as it has been. Deliberate language planning rather than *ad hoc* developments seem increasingly necessary. It is also in the country's interest that the variety that should be developed is the rural variety, the less Anglicized, more stable variety recognized by the people themselves as the 'good' variety of Tok Pisin.

Hiri Motu is the other pidgin-based official language of Papua New Guinea. It is identified with Papua and Papuan languages are quite different from those in New Guinea. Many people there take great pride in using Hiri Motu, the descendant of Police Mutu, a native-based, pidgin language of the area, rather than Tok Pisin to show local loyalties. The result has been a dramatic increase in the use of Hiri Motu in Papua New Guinea, particularly among separatist-minded Papuans.

As we can see, then, each of the three official languages of Papua New Guinea confers advantages of certain kinds to its speakers. However, it seems still too early to predict the future pattern of coexistence for the three languages and, of course, for those who speak them.

Our second example is Singapore (see also pp. 101–2), an independent republic of approximately 3 million people (see Kuo, 1977). It is also a small island, situated at the tip of the Malayan peninsula with another large Malay-speaking nation, Indonesia, to its south. The 2000 census showed its population to be approximately 77 percent Chinese, 14 percent Malays, 8 percent Indians, and just over 1 percent others, e.g., Eurasians, Europeans, and Arabs. Five major languages are spoken in Singapore (Malay, English, Mandarin, Tamil, and Hokkien) and three minor ones (Teochew, Cantonese, and Hainanese). At the time of independence four of these languages were given official status: Malay, Mandarin, Tamil, and English. The first three represented Singapore's traditions; the last was deliberately chosen because of its international status, particularly important because of Singapore's position as a trading nation. Officially, it is a language of convenience only, a neutral language dissociated from issues of ethnicity (Lee, 2002).

Of the four official languages, Malay is also the national language because of Singapore's position in the Malay world, not because more people in Singapore speak or understand Malay better than any other language. However, English has become the working language of Singapore: it is the language of the government bureaucracy, the authoritative language of all legislation and court judgments, and the language of occupational mobility and social and economic advancement (see Foley, 1988). It is also the language of banking, work in government offices, public transportation, hotels and tourism, and much non-food shopping. All schoolchildren are required to learn English (Gupta, 1994) and another of the official languages, although the first language of instruction can be any one of the four official languages. However, the majority of parents choose English-medium schools for their children.

One result of these decisions has been that English is now understood by more than half the population, even though only a much smaller percentage speak it comfortably. 'English is becoming the dominant language; it already is the *de facto* national language of intra- and inter-communication' (Foley, 1988, p. xvi). Although the major Chinese language in Singapore is Hokkien, it is Mandarin, the language that unites Singapore to China, that is taught in schools. There has been a dramatic increase in recent years, therefore, in the percentage of the population who understand Mandarin. The government also actively supports the use of Mandarin in its 'Speak Mandarin' campaign and seeks to eradicate the other Chinese 'dialects' (Gupta, 1994, Gupta and Yeok, 1995). Malay continues to have a place in everyday life in Singapore but knowledge of Tamil has declined. Consequently, a native of Singapore is likely to understand, and use, with different levels of success, Mandarin, Hokkien, English, Malay, and local varieties of each of these. Truly a multilingual situation!

This multilingualism is particularly prevalent in the younger generation, and, since Singapore is also a country with a large proportion of young people in its population, it is likely to be a change that will accelerate. A survey of 15- to 20-year-olds in 1975 showed them able to understand the major languages as follows: English (87.3 percent), Malay (50.3 percent), Mandarin (72.5 percent), Hokkien (74.0 percent), and Tamil (5.8 percent). A comparison across age-groups showed that young people had a much better knowledge (i.e., understanding) of English and Mandarin than old people, but only a slightly better knowledge of Hokkien, and much less knowledge of Malay and Tamil. In 2004 the Singapore Minister of Education acknowledged that about half of Singapore's ethnic Chinese children use English at home compared with 34 percent in 1994 and that such use of English is increasing: 'There is a clear generational shift in language use at home' (*The Times*, December 18, 2004). Such evidence would appear to confirm that Singapore is basically a Chinese nation somewhat precariously located in a Malay-speaking area and extremely conscious of the fact that its vitality and future lie in preserving a Chinese heritage in a trading world dominated by English.

The language policies pursued by the government of Singapore are not without certain difficulties because they are allied to a policy which says that Singapore itself has no distinctive culture but is a composite of three cultures: Chinese, Malay, and Indian. Each group is forced to distinguish itself culturally from the others to achieve support, yet it must be careful in what it promotes so as not to offend the others and not to appear to be too closely attached to foreign places. Banton (1983, p. 394) has described the consequences as follows:

the policy presses the Chinese to become more Chinese, the Indians more Indian and the Malays more Malay. Each culture turns in upon itself since it has to be Singaporean and cannot develop ties with the original homeland. Secondly, the arts (or 'high' culture) have difficulty obtaining official support and financial backing. Individualistic (and therefore 'non-racial') creations are seen as irrelevant or possibly as examples of decadent foreign influence. Thirdly, the Singaporeans' image of themselves and of their history is distorted to fit the four-category model. Cultural characteristics are assumed to derive from distinctive genetic backgrounds and therefore to change only very slowly indeed. In reality, people of all groups are changing as they adapt to the opportunities provided by a bustling commercial city, and this is the real basis for a commonality of culture which is growing rapidly.

The current plans for language and culture in Singapore may be creating certain paradoxes, even contradictions, which may require at some point still another round of planning and considerable changes.

The third example is also that of a small country, this time one with a population of about 4 million people who are faced with the problem of reconciling an internal linguistic split. Modern Norway with its two varieties of one language, or its two languages in some views, has some particularly interesting problems so far as planning is concerned. When, after four centuries of domination, the Norwegians managed to separate themselves politically from Denmark in 1814, the country found itself with a variety of Danish and local dialects but no national language (Haugen, 1966b, 1968). In the nineteenth century therefore attempts were made to develop a Norwegian language. Two attempts were noteworthy, those of Knud Knudsen and Ivar Aasen. The former developed a language which is a modified variety of Standard Danish, known later as Riksmål 'State language' (since 1928 called Bokmål 'Book language'); the latter developed a language based on local Norwegian dialects, known as Landsmål 'Language of the country' (now called Nynorsk 'New Norwegian'). We can see the similarities in the two languages from the following sentences (and their gloss) taken from Haugen (1968, pp. 686–7):

Nynorsk

Det rette heimlege mål i landet er det som landets folk har arva ifrå forfedrene, frå den eine ætta til den andre, og som no om stunder, trass i all fortrengsle og vanvønad, enno har grunnlag og emne til eit bokmål, like så godt som noko av grannfolk-måla.

Bokmål

Det rette heimlige mål i landet er det som landets folk har arvet ifra forfedrene, fra den ene ætt til den andre, og som nå om stunder, trass i all fortrengsle og vanvønad, ennå har grunnlag og emne til et bokmål, like så godt som noe av nabo-målene.

English

The right native tongue in this country is the one that the people of the country have inherited from their ancestors, from one generation to the next, and which nowadays, in spite of all displacement and contempt, still has the basis and material for a written language just as good as any of the neighbors' languages.

During the twentieth century the major planning task has been to unite the two varieties, since, as we can see, they do differ in certain ways in spelling, grammar, and vocabulary. Progress in that unification has been slow as compromises have not been easy to achieve. It is now virtually at a standstill and language reform continues to be a contentious issue in Norway. Although, according to its defenders, Nynorsk is said to be more 'Norwegian' in spirit, many Norwegians find certain aspects of it vulgar and rustic because of its origins in western rural dialects; consequently, they reject it in favor of the more 'civilized' Bokmål. Currently, the proponents of Bokmål are in the stronger position linguistically in that this variety more closely conforms to standard colloquial (i.e., spoken) Norwegian, but 'true' nationalists still insist on Nynorsk, Bokmål still being too 'Danish' for them. Today, Bokmål is the language of the national press and the majority of books, and the instructional medium of five out of every six schoolchildren. Bokmål dominates the towns and cities, but official documents still employ both varieties, and children must learn to use both. The search for a compromise goes on, but it is unlikely that Norwegians will easily agree on one variety to the exclusion of the other while an important regional minority regards Nynorsk as a clear marker of their identity (Vikør, 2002).

Our fourth example of language planning is Canada, a country of 31 million people, which is now, by its new constitution of 1982, a constitutionally bilingual country. However, bilingualism itself continues to be a controversial issue in Canada, as anyone who reads its newspapers or follows political discussions there will know. Canada is a federal country, with its origins in the conquest of the French (of what is now Quebec) by the English in 1759. This conquest was followed by the gradual expansion of the nation to include other British possessions in North America and to fill the prairies to the north of the United States. Although the country dates its 'birth' to 1867 and it was effectively independent from the United Kingdom after that date, its constitution remained an act of the Parliament of the United Kingdom until 1982. Controversies over language rights played a prominent part in discussions leading up to making the constitution entirely Canadian in 1982.

In 1867 the French in Canada seemed assured of opportunities to spread their language and culture throughout the country. Just as English rights in Quebec were protected in the constitution of that year, so French rights outside Quebec seemed to have a strong measure of protection. But that was not to be, as the French soon found in the new province of Manitoba, where French rights were deliberately abrogated. Increasingly, the French in Canada found themselves confined to Quebec, itself dominated by the English of Montreal, and saw the country develop as a country of two nations (or 'two solitudes') with one of them – theirs – in a very inferior position. Today, of the less than 30 percent of Canadians who are of French origin, approximately 80 percent live in the province of Quebec.

The Canadian government appointed a Royal Commission on Bilingualism and Biculturalism in 1963 to look into the resulting situation. The commission's report led to the Official Languages Act of 1969 (reaffirmed in a new form in 1988), which guaranteed the French in Canada certain rights to language everywhere in the country in order to preserve the nation as a bilingual one. The act also appointed an ombudsman, a Commissioner of Official Languages, to report annually to Parliament on progress in implementing new policies. Later, the Constitution Act of 1982 incorporated these language rights guaranteed by statute in 1969 into the patriated constitution. However, if Canada is officially a 'bilingual' country, bilingualism in the two official languages is found mainly in the population of French origin and truly bilingual communities are few, e.g., Montreal, Sherbrooke, and the Ottawa-Hull area.

At the same time as the Government of Canada was guaranteeing French rights throughout Canada, the Government of Quebec took measures to minimize the use of English within the province. While the federal government was trying to extend bilingualism in the rest of Canada, the Government of Quebec was trying to restore French unilingualism within Quebec. They did this because they found that bilingualism led to unilingualism in English. Outside Quebec, the French in Canada were losing French in favor of English as they went over the generations from being unilingual in French, to being bilingual in French and English, and finally to being unilingual in English. There was mounting evidence that this was also happening within Quebec. However, such moves to restrict the use of English in Quebec, e.g., in public education, have come under attack as a violation of rights provided in the new constitution, and in 1984 the Supreme Court of Canada voided those parts of Quebec's Bill 101 of 1977 that restricted certain rights of anglophones in that province. Quebec does have a variety of language laws to protect French in the province and the authorities are vigilant in enforcing them. Some of those who dislike these laws have moved to other provinces. Others, particularly immigrants, often prefer to learn English rather than French, but between 1971 and 2001 governmental measures have increased the proportion of those who learn French from 29 percent to 46 percent. Certain legislation on the statute books in Manitoba for nearly a century has likewise been voided for denying francophone rights in that province, e.g., to have legislation enacted in French.

The basic English–French polarization still exists. The French are still a minority in Canada. Their proportion in the overall population continues to decline, no matter what statistic is used (ethnic origin, mother tongue use, or language of the home), with that decline being over 1 percent between the national censuses of 1971 and 1981. By the 1991 census whereas 73 percent of the population reported English as their first official language only 25 percent reported French and that proportion continues to fall. The decline in the use of French is particularly noticeable outside Quebec. It is not really surprising, therefore, that in recent years the French within Quebec have toyed with 'separatist' notions, believing that, if they cannot guarantee their future within Canada as a whole, they should at least guarantee it within their home province. The separatist desire increased dramatically in 1990 with the failure that year to reach a countrywide agreement – the so-called Meech Lake Accord – on amending the 1982 constitution. A further attempt at some kind of constitutional settlement failed in 1992 when the Charlottetown Agreement was defeated in a national referendum. However, in 1995 a Quebec referendum on separation from Canada also failed, narrowly though, to gain support for such a move.

The language situation is further complicated by the fact that Canada is also a country of immigrants who have flocked mainly to the larger cities. For example, in 1996, 37 percent of the residents of Toronto and 34 percent of the residents of Vancouver had a mother tongue other than English or French. There are large numbers of speakers of Italian, German, Ukrainian, Portuguese, Spanish, Polish, and Chinese. (In 1996, 17 percent of the Canadian population were immigrants in contrast to 8 percent in the United States.) Many of these immigrants face language loss, and some who speak on their behalf say that the French in Canada, particularly the French outside Quebec, should have no privileges, so far as language is concerned, that they themselves do not enjoy. This feeling is particularly strong in many parts of western Canada. The importance of such claims is better understood if one realizes that Canadians of ethnic origins other than French or English now comprise the same proportion of the Canadian population as those of French origin. The French of Quebec are entirely opposed to the idea that they are just another non-English group within Canada. In the view of many they are one of the two founding peoples and a 'nation' with the right to separate whenever conditions are right.

Language planning in Canada is obviously not complete. The ongoing dispute over the constitution and moves to enact various language laws that might be acceptable within the new constitutional framework are but the latest incidents in Canada's continual concern with language planning. Canada's two official languages are increasingly becoming territorially based (like the situation in Switzerland and Belgium). However, the constitution rejects such 'territoriality.' It is not a happy situation.

Our final example is China, a state with 1.3 billion inhabitants. Eight different varieties of Chinese, *Hanyu* (the 'Han' language), are spoken. Linguists call these eight different varieties 'languages' but the Chinese themselves prefer to call them different dialects (*fang yan*) because of the writing system they share. Among those who speak Hanyu, the following percentages are said to speak these varieties: Mandarin 71 percent, Wu 8 percent, Xiang 5 percent, Cantonese 5 percent, Hakka 4 percent, Southern Min (Fukienese) 3 percent, Gan 2 percent, and Northern Min (Fukienese) 1 percent. There are also estimated to be about 5 percent of speakers of non-Chinese languages in China, languages such as Mongolian, Tibetan, and Korean. Although Mandarin is by far the dominant language numerically and geographically, it is only quite recently that it has achieved a political status commensurate with its numbers, since an archaic form of Chinese dominated written usage well into the twentieth century. Language reform and planning has long been a feature of Chinese life, but it has become increasingly important since the founding of the People's Republic of China.

There are plans to change Chinese in three ways: the first is to simplify Chinese characters; the second is to popularize the Beijing variety of Mandarin, *Putonghua* ('the common language'), as it is now referred to; the third is to develop a phonetic alphabet. As we will see, only very limited progress has been made in all three areas, even though the changes advocated by the Committee on Language Reform have the strong support of the State Council of the central government.

The simplification of the estimated 7,000–8,000 Chinese characters has been given top priority, and periodically the Committee on Language Reform publishes lists of new simplifications and recommends that they be used. The goal is to simplify about half of the characters. The recommendations are widely followed, so that all new publications are printed in simplified characters, many public signs employ them, and they are taught in schools. Today, the effect of this simplification is easily observed: Chinese materials printed in China use simplified characters, whereas those produced in Hong Kong and Taiwan and by most overseas Chinese continue to use the unsimplified ones.

Much effort has also gone into extending the use of Putonghua throughout the nation. Putonghua actually uses the pronunciation of Beijing, the grammar of the northern dialects, and the vocabulary of modern literary Chinese. It has become the language of Chinese political life, its use is encouraged on various occasions, and it is increasingly taught in schools. However, in such a vast country as China, the extension of Putonghua is a complex and formidable task that will require a long period of time for completion. At the moment, more and more use of Putonghua is noticeable in large urban areas, e.g., Canton and Shanghai. There is also considerable tolerance for local pronunciations of Putonghua, and those who do not speak it at all do not see it as a threat to the varieties they do speak; instead, Putonghua is acknowledged to be the national language just as some other variety is the local one.

So far as the phoneticization of Chinese writing is concerned, that is, the development of an alphabetic writing system, the current use of Pinyin is merely the latest in a series of attempts to alphabetize; for example, the Wade-Giles system going back to 1859; the proposal for a National Phonetic Alphabet in 1913; the National Language Romanization proposed by Chao and others in 1925–6; and another attempt, *Latinxua* ('Latinization'), to develop a Romanized script for the Chinese living in Russia in 1913. Pinyin is now used as an aid in learning Chinese characters, in certain dictionaries, and in the orthographies for several previously unwritten minority languages, e.g., Zhuang, Miao, Yi, and Dong. Its further use seems to depend on the spread of Putonghua, but not everyone agrees on such use. There is agreement, however, that any spread should be slow.

There is also considerable disagreement concerning whether Pinyin should replace traditional characters or just provide a supplementary system of writing. While Pinyin is taught in early years in elementary schools, it is not used a great deal, it tends to be forgotten since few materials employ it, and the attention of children is quickly directed to learning the more useful Chinese characters. The Chinese are very conscious of their past, have a great reverence for learning, and their traditional writing system provides a strong unifying force; they are unlikely, therefore, easily to abandon it. While there is evidence that more and more Chinese can use Pinyin and do use it for certain purposes in a growing number of places, e.g., on maps and street signs, and in textbooks, the changes are actually very moderate. The plan seems to be to move slowly in this area; simplifying characters and extending the uses of Putonghua are obviously much more important goals in language planning in contemporary China. We must also remember that even fulfilling the simplest of goals becomes an immense task when it involves so many people.

Discussion

1. The size of a country seems to be quite unrelated to the problems in language planning it may face, because both small and large countries can have problems. What seem to you to be the most important factors in creating problems and in resolving them?
2. Statements of the following kind have sometimes been made in an attempt to relate the number of languages spoken in a nation to the 'success' of that nation.

   a. Linguistically homogeneous countries may be rich or poor, but, in general, they are more advanced economically and more stable than linguistically heterogeneous countries.
   b. The latter are always less advanced or less developed in important ways.
   c. Language uniformity is a necessary but not sufficient condition of economic development (see Fishman, 1968b, and Pool, 1972).

   How correct are such observations? Are they basically correct except for one or two notable exceptions, e.g., Switzerland? Or are the observations colored entirely by their authors' value systems?
3. Assess the 'wisdom' of each of the following:

   a. adopting Tok Pisin instead of English in Papua New Guinea;
   b. giving official status to Mandarin rather than Hokkien in Singapore;
   c. trying to effect a compromise solution to the 'two-language' problem in Norway rather than choosing one of the languages;
   d. adopting Pinyin in China;
   e. making Canada a country bilingual in its federal machinery from coast to coast rather than a country of two regional unilingualisms with French in Quebec and English everywhere else.

Winners and Losers

It seems fitting to close a chapter on language planning in various places in the world by indicating some of the facts about languages in general. We live in a world of more than 6 billion people and by the most generous estimate 6,000 languages. Many of these are endangered or even dying (see Dorian, 1981, 1989, 1998, Fase et al., 1992, Grenoble and Whaley, 1998, and Mühlhäusler, 1996). Dixon estimates that there may be actually as few as 4,000 languages spoken today with that number steadily decreasing. He says (1996, p. 199) that:

> Each language encapsulates the world-view of its speakers – how they think, what they value, what they believe in, how they classify the world around them, how they order their lives. Once a language dies, a part of human culture is lost – for ever.
>
> The most important task in linguistics today – indeed, the only really important task – is to get out in the field and describe languages, while this can still be done.

Nettle and Romaine (2000) voice a very similar view, say that as many as 60 percent of all languages are already endangered, and go so far as to claim that some of the endangered languages have much to tell us about the natural world, e.g., invaluable information about ecological matters, and even perhaps about the nature of reality (see the Whorfian hypothesis, pp. 221–8): 'each language . . . [is] a way of coming to grips with the external world and developing a symbolism to represent it so that it can be talked and thought about' (p. 69). Crystal (2000) also deplores the reduction of language diversity brought about by language death.

Estimates of language loss go as high as 95 percent within the new century if nothing is done to stop the decline. It is for just such a reason that the Linguistic Society of America has gone on record as deploring language loss and established a Committee on Endangered Languages and their Preservation to help arrest it. However, we should note that not all linguists agree that they should be out in the field trying to describe – and possibly preserve – threatened languages. Mühlhäusler (1996) goes so far as to argue that linguists are sometimes part of the problem rather than part of the solution. However, no matter what happens the number of languages spoken in the world will almost certainly continue to decline.

In marked contrast to such decline, a few languages thrive, e.g., the Mandarin variety of Chinese, Hindi, Arabic, and Spanish (with its enormous growth potential in South America), and one, English, has spread everywhere in the world (see Wardhaugh, 1987, and Crystal, 2003b, 2004). Languages like French (even when promoted by *La Francophonie*), Russian, German, and Japanese, on the other hand, do not thrive in the same way: they win few converts and, as the world's population grows, they decrease proportionally. As Crystal has pointed out, English spread initially through conquest and then by being in the right place at the right time for use in international relations, the worldwide media, international travel, education, and now communications. He estimates that one-quarter of the world's population have some kind of fluency in the language. Its major appeal is as a lingua franca, a common second language with a certain amount of internal diversity (see Meierkord, 2004). In December 2004, a British Council report estimated that 2 billion more people would begin learning English within a decade and by 2050 there would be over 3 billion speakers of English in the world. The main motivation to learn English would continue to be an economic one and an important consequence would be a great increase in bilingualism/multilingualism in English and one or more other languages. (According to this report, Chinese, Arabic, and Spanish would also become increasingly important languages.)

Huntington (1996, p. 61) puts the case for English as follows:

English is the world's way of communicating interculturally just as the Christian calendar is the world's way of tracking time, Arabic numbers are the world's way of counting, and the metric system is, for the most part, the world's way of measuring. The use of English in this way, however, is *intercultural* communication; it presupposes the existence of separate cultures. A lingua franca is a way of coping with linguistic and cultural differences, not a way of eliminating them. It is a tool for communication not a source of identity and community.

He adds (p. 62):

The people who speak English throughout the world also increasingly speak different Englishes. English is indigenized and takes on local colorations which distinguish it from British or American English and which, at the extreme, make these Englishes almost unintelligible one to the other, as is also the case with varieties of Chinese.

In its spread English has differentiated; there are New Englishes, and English is not just a single language any more. It also lacks a dominant center; English is pluricentric and is used to express various national identities (Schneider, 2003). (See also Kachru, 1992, Fishman et al., 1996, McArthur, 1998, Gordon et al., 2004, Hickey, 2004, and Trudgill, 2004.)

Huntington points out that languages inherently compete with each other and voices the following caution (p. 63):

As the power of the West gradually declines relative to that of other civilizations, the use of English and other Western languages in other societies and for communication between societies will also slowly erode. If at some point in the distant future China displaces the West as the dominant civilization in the world, English will give way to Mandarin as the world's lingua franca.

However, Bruthiaux (2002), after reviewing possible factors that might diminish the current dominance of English, concludes that no other language will 'displace English as the dominant global language in the 21st century' (p. 153).

The spread of English in the world has not gone without critics (see Phillipson, 1992, 2003, Mühlhäusler, 1996, and Pennycook, 1998) who regard the language as a clear expression of political, cultural, and economic imperialism – a kind of dominance – and assail all efforts to promote the further use of English in the world, e.g., by government-sponsored teaching programs. Writing in the tradition of critical theory (or critical discourse analysis; see p. 350), such critics cannot conceive of English as a value-free language. As Pennycook says, there is nothing 'neutral' about English use in Hong Kong: 'this image of English use as an open and borrowing language, reflecting an open and borrowing people, is a cultural construct of colonialism that is in direct conflict with the colonial evidence' (p. 143). Others apply this kind of judgment everywhere English has spread. Mühlhäusler (1996), for example, regards languages like English – others are Bahasa Indonesia and Mandarin Chinese – as 'killer languages' because as national languages of modernization, education, and development they stifle and eventually kill local languages. Dorian (1998, p. 9) states the case unequivocally: 'Europeans who come from polities with a history of standardizing and promoting just one high-prestige form carried their "ideology of contempt" for subordinate languages with them when they conquered far-flung territories to the serious detriment of indigenous languages.'

House (2003) draws a different conclusion concerning the spread of English in the European Union. There, English is spreading because it is an effective lingua franca and she says that this spread may actually strengthen local languages as people seek to maintain local identities. The European Union shows how such a compromise has occurred. Wright (2004, p. 14) comes to a similar conclusion but one not limited to the European Union: 'it is not inconceivable that as intergroup communication happens increasingly in English, speakers from the smaller language groups will move from being bilingual in their own language and the national language to being bilingual in their own language and English. This latter bilingualism might be more stable than the former.'

There is a paradox here: linguists are told that they save languages best by not acting at all; certainly they should do nothing to promote English in the world, or to standardize a language, or possibly to help in any kind of language planning anywhere. Yet, there is no assurance that they will save a single language by not acting. An alternative possibility is that intervention actually slows down decline and loss. However, there is really no hard evidence for either position. Each is essentially ideologically derived: if you believe this you do one thing and if you believe that you do another. We do well to remember that because we are involved in *socio*-linguistic matters, ideology is likely to be at least as potent a factor as science in determining which approach we ultimately adopt. Issues of identity and power will also never be far from the surface.

Discussion

1. Bickerton (1977, p. 197) makes the following observation: 'Where population remains stable, indigenous languages will survive and even flourish under considerable adverse pressure; where a population is abruptly transferred to a new terrain, languages will wither even in the fact of positive effort to keep them alive.' Although Bickerton was addressing himself to pidgins and creoles when he made these remarks, it seems they have a wider applicability. Can you find examples to support what Bickerton says? Are there counter-examples?

2. Latin is a dead language and Hebrew once again a live one. How did Latin die? (Remember it is still very much alive in the sense that French, Italian, Spanish, and Portuguese, i.e., its 'dialects,' are spoken today!) How was Hebrew revitalized? (See Myhill, 2004.)

3. What are some of the difficulties faced in trying to revive a dead language or trying to maintain, even at some minimal level, a dying language? Consider the current situations in Scotland, Wales, and Ireland, or among many native peoples of the Americas, or within minority group languages, either indigenous or immigrant, in large modern states.

4. Try to sketch the best-case and the worst-case scenarios for English as a possible global language during the twenty-first century. What factors must you consider? (See Crystal, 2003b, and Huntington, 1996.)

5. 'An orderly Standard World English, amid the diversity and social disparity of today's world, seems more like a forlorn cry after the horse has bolted than a robust, forcible ideology' (Holborow, 1999, p. 3). What is your view?

Further Reading

There is an extensive literature on language planning. Good introductory books are Cooper (1989), Eastman (1983), Kaplan and Baldauf (1997), Clyne (1997), Spolsky (2004), and Wright (2004). See also Edwards (1985), Jahr (1993), Mansour (1993), and Tollefson (1991). For endangered languages and language decline and 'death,' see Dorian (1981, 1989, 1998), Fase et al. (1992), Fishman (2001), Grenoble and Whaley (1998), and Joseph (2004). On the spread of English, see Crystal (2003b) and Cheshire (1991), and for examples of new Englishes see Melchers (2003). For other languages, see Barbour and Carmichael (2002), Maurais and Morris (2004), and Wardhaugh (1987). Finegan and Rickford (2004) review the current language situation in the United States and Huntington (2004) draws certain conclusions from it. Huntington (1996) provides an insightful view into the current world. The journal *Current Issues in Language Planning* is also useful.

16 Conclusion

Most books that deal with language in society and offer themselves as introductions to sociolinguistics or the sociology of language lack formal conclusions. The reason for such an omission is probably clear by now. Just what can you possibly conclude when the issues are so complex, the data so varied, and the approaches so different? However, I will attempt to say a few words.

Our consideration of various issues has revealed above all how complex a thing a language is, or any variety of a language. Languages are just as complex as societies, and we all know how difficult it is to make generalizations about those. That languages should be so complex is not surprising. Languages and societies are related, and social and linguistic complexity are not unrelated. Just as it is naive to believe that there are societies that possess only very primitive cultures, so it is equally naive to believe that certain peoples speak primitive languages. All cultures and all languages are extremely complex. Some may actually be more complex than others, but we do not as yet have an exhaustive and definitive study of a single culture or of a single language from anywhere in the world, nor are there any immediate prospects of one. If both the culture and language of any group of people almost defy adequate description, then we can be assured that the relationships that certainly exist between the two are not likely to be more transparent, even to well-informed observers.

A further complication is added by the fact that, among the various kinds of complexity we observe in language, one kind must give us considerable concern: that is, the amount of variation that is apparent wherever we look. Language varies in many kinds of ways, and investigations repeatedly show that people are aware of this fact, even though they may not be conscious of precisely what they are doing or how they are reacting to the variants that others use. Variation seems to be an inherent property of language. If it is, it creates a number of theoretical problems for linguists.

Linguists working in the Chomskyan tradition have generally tried not to involve themselves with variation, preferring to adopt a view of language which sees it as homogeneous and describing a *linguistic competence* which they assume all speakers possess. However, if an important part of the linguistic competence of language users is their ability to handle variation and the various uses of language in society, then the competence that needs to be explained is one that encompasses a much wider range of abilities: it is *communicative competence*, of which linguistic competence is but a part. While sociolinguists have talked at length, however, about communicative competence, attempts to specify just what it is have not been very successful, probably because it is so complex and all-encompassing. Furthermore, attempts to use the concept in applied work, e.g., the teaching of foreign languages, have tended to rely more on rhetoric than on substance.

If there is such a thing as communicative competence, and there must surely be in some sense, a further problem arises in trying to explain how it develops in individuals. Just how does an individual learn to use the variants of a linguistic variable, to code-switch, to use sexist language, and so on? Moreover, how does that individual learn to use these in the same way as certain other individuals and in slightly different ways from still other individuals? What are the social forces that bring about such learning, what intellectual abilities are called for, and what survival value follows from the results? These are all very important linguistic and social problems, answers to which will bring us important understanding about human linguistic and social organization.

One of the facts that our various inquiries have certainly shown is that the data we can use in explorations of the relationships between language and society seem boundless. Moreover, there is no shortage of concepts and categories available to use in our attempts to make sense of those data. We have seen various attempts at such organization. We can begin with concepts like 'language' and 'dialect' in an attempt to discover how useful these are. In just about every case, such an approach has revealed shortcomings. While such concepts allow us to organize large amounts of data, they fail us too often to become the building blocks of a comprehensive theory. For example, we cannot adequately define either *language* or *dialect*, nor can we infallibly distinguish the one from the other.

Quantification is another approach that has both its strengths and its weaknesses. We can count instances of certain kinds of language use; we can devise tables, draw graphs, and show trends and correlations; we can even subject the resulting quantities to statistical analysis and claim significance for certain findings. I have referred to numbers and percentages throughout the preceding chapters, but have made special reference to such matters in discussion of the linguistic variable. Quantification is useful in showing what kinds of behavior you may expect to find among groups of people and trends in that behavior across various dimensions such as time, space, gender, age, and social class. But any resulting claims are claims about the behavior we can expect of groups, or of sub-groups. In that respect they are statements about an idealized typical member, whoever he or she might be. In actual fact, individuals are never typical, and certainly their behavior is never ideal by almost any criterion. What is interesting is the particular fit between individuals and such idealizations, and especially the fundamental sociological puzzle of whether people model their behaviors on certain ideals they perceive to exist or whether any ideals that people claim to exist are just idealizations arrived at through emphasizing similarities we believe to exist in people's behavior and down-playing differences. The approach through quantification is therefore not without a whole array of problems, ranging from very simple issues such as collecting data, to profound ones having to do with the nature of social reality.

An approach through language functions may also be indicated by the fact that language is used for so many purposes. As we have seen, there are many ways of trying to deal with language function. We can try an ethnographic approach, we can analyze conversations, we can attempt to distinguish what people do with language as opposed to what they use language to say, as in a speech-acts approach, and so on. Much understanding of language use has been achieved by investigations conducted with such aims. Above all, though, they show how subtle and varied are the differences that exist, yet how easily and confidently speakers (and listeners) handle these subtleties.

One thing that our examination of various issues has revealed though is how important such concepts as 'identity,' 'class,' 'power,' 'solidarity,' 'politeness,' and 'gender' are in trying to make sense of the data we find. Unfortunately, we have no grand theory to unite these. Figueroa concludes her study of sociolinguistic theory in general and specifically the ideas of Labov, Hymes, and Gumperz by saying (1994, p. 179), 'There is no unified theory of sociolinguistics, or even for that matter, a shared metatheory. There is a shared sociolinguistic subject matter – "utterance" – but this would not necessarily delimit sociolinguistics from other types of linguistics.'

Some sociolinguists insist on a narrow view. We may agree with Chambers (2003, pp. 273–4) that:

> we have come to understand how variables function in vernacular and standard dialects. It is time now to go beyond that and ask why. Why do certain variables recur in dialects all around the world? Why is it these particular variables, not others, that persist? Why are they constrained in exactly the same ways in widely separated communities? Why are they embedded so similarly in the social strata?

However, his next sentence, 'This vast, virtually unexplored area lies at the very root of our discipline,' might give us pause. Are there no other roots? Is that all sociolinguistics should be about?

Perhaps the study of language in society is best served by resisting premature urges to declare that it must proceed along certain lines and may not proceed along others. Repeatedly, we have seen the multi-dimensional nature of any issue we have looked at. Even when we took a uni-dimensional approach, we did so knowing full well what we were doing and in the knowledge that another approach or other approaches might cast a different light on the issue. Although people have long been interested in the relationships between language and society, it is only fairly recently that scientific approaches have been adopted. It seems wiser to encourage a variety of scientific approaches and the generation of a range of theories than to put our entire trust and hope into a single way of doing sociolinguistics. That is certainly the way I have gone about looking at how language and society are related. I have not avoided theoretical issues, and I have not avoided looking at data themselves, and not simply in the sense that 'you cannot have data without a theory.' However, I have found it neither useful nor possible to adopt a single theoretical approach.

This, I suggest, is also a correct characterization of current sociolinguistic inquiries; there are numerous theories, vast amounts of data, and important findings, but there is no central doctrine a sociolinguist must adhere to. In no way do I regard the absence of such a doctrine as a fatal flaw; rather, it should serve to encourage us to try to make new discoveries and find new areas to explore in the hope of gaining a still better understanding of both language and society and of the many relationships between the two. Some of us may even be tempted then to try to change some of the relationships we find. I have suggested we use caution if we are so tempted: ideology has too often proved to be a sure path to disaster!

References

Achebe, C. (1975a). *A Man of the People*. London: Heinemann.

Achebe, C. (1975b). *No Longer at Ease*. London: Heinemann.

Adams, K. L. and D. T. Brink (eds.) (1990). *Perspectives on Official English: The Campaign for English as the Official Language of the USA*. Berlin: Mouton de Gruyter.

Adger, C. T., D. Christian, and O. Taylor (eds.) (1999). *Making the Connection: Language and Academic Achievement among African American Students*. Washington, DC: Center for Applied Linguistics.

Adler, M. K. (1978). *Naming and Addressing: A Sociolinguistic Study*. Hamburg: Helmut Buske.

Agar, M. H. (1996). *The Professional Stranger: An Informal Introduction to Ethnography*. 2nd edn. San Diego: Academic Press.

Ager, D. E. (1990). *Sociolinguistics and Contemporary French*. Cambridge: Cambridge University Press.

Aitchison, J. (1991). *Language Change: Progress or Decay?* 2nd edn. Cambridge: Cambridge University Press.

Aitchison, J. (1994). Pidgins and Creoles. In Asher and Simpson (1994).

Alim, H. S. (2005). Hearing What's Not Said and Missing What Is: Black Language in White Public Space. In Kiesling and Paulston (2005).

Allsopp, R. (1958). The English Language in British Guiana. *English Language Teaching*, 12(2): 59–66.

Ammon, U. (1994). Code, sociolinguistic. In Asher and Simpson (1994).

Ammon, U., N. Dittmar, and K. J. Mattheier (eds.) (1987). *Sociolinguistics*. Berlin: Mouton de Gruyter.

Arends, J., P. Muysken, and N. Smith (eds.) (1995). *Pidgins and Creoles: An Introduction*. Amsterdam: John Benjamins.

Arliss, L. P. (1991). *Gender Communication*. Englewood Cliffs, NJ: Prentice-Hall.

Ash, S. (2002). Social Class. In Chambers et al. (2002).

Asher, R. E. and J. M. Simpson (eds.) (1994). *The Encyclopedia of Language and Linguistics*. Oxford: Pergamon.

Aston, G. (1995). Say 'Thank You': Some Pragmatic Constraints on Conversational Closings. *Applied Linguistics*, 16(1): 57–86.

Atkinson, P. (1985). *Language, Structure, and Reproduction*. London: Methuen.

Auer, P. (ed.) (1998). *Code-switching in Conversation: Language, Interaction and Identity*. London: Routledge.

Austin, J. L. (1975). *How to Do Things with Words*. 2nd edn. Oxford: Clarendon Press.

Ayto, J. (1999). *Twentieth-Century Words*. New York: Oxford University Press.

Bailey, B. (2005). The Language of Multiple Identities among Dominican Americans. In Kiesling and Paulston (2005).

Bailey, C.-J. N. (1973). *Variation and Linguistic Theory*. Washington, DC: Center for Applied Linguistics.

Bailey, G. and N. Maynor (1989). The Divergence Controversy. *American Speech*, 64: 12–39.

Bailey, G. and J. Tillery (2004). Some Sources of Divergent Data in Sociolinguistics. In Fought (2004).

Bailey, G., T. Wikle, J. Tillery, and L. Sand (1991). The Apparent Time Construct. *Language Variation and Change*, 3: 241–64.

Bailey, R. W. and M. Görlach (eds.) (1982). *English as a World Language*. Ann Arbor: University of Michigan Press.

Bainbridge, W. S. (1994). Sociology of Language. In Asher and Simpson (1994).

Baker, P. and J. Eversley (eds.) (2000). *Multilingual Capital: The Languages of London's Schoolchildren and Their Relevance to Economic, Social and Educational Policies*. London: Battlebridge.

Bakker, P. (1997). *A Language of Our Own: The Genesis of Michif, the Mixed Cree-French Language of the Canadian Métis*. Oxford: Oxford University Press.

Bakker, P. and R. A. Papen (1997). Michif: A Mixed Language Based on Cree and French. In Thomason (1997).

Banton, M. (1983). *Racial and Ethnic Competition*. Cambridge: Cambridge University Press.

Barbour, S. and C. Carmichael (eds.) (2002). *Language and Nationalism in Europe*. Oxford: Oxford University Press.

Baron, D. E. (1982). *Grammar and Good Taste: Reforming the American Language*. New Haven: Yale University Press.

Baron, D. (1986). *Grammar and Gender*. New Haven: Yale University Press.

Baron, D. (1990). *The English-Only Question: An Official Language for Americans?* New Haven: Yale University Press.

Barrett, R. (1998). Markedness and Styleswitching in Performances by African American Drag Queens. In Myers-Scotton (1998).

Basso, K. H. (1972). 'To Give up on Words': Silence in Western Apache Culture. In Giglioli (1972).

Bates, E. and L. Benigni (1975). Rules of Address in Italy: A Sociological Survey. *Language in Society*, 4: 271–88.

Bauer, L. (1994). *Watching English Change: An Introduction to the Study of Linguistic Change in Standard Englishes in the Twentieth Century*. London: Longman.

Bauer, L. and P. Trudgill (eds.) (1998). *Language Myths*. Harmondsworth, England: Penguin Books.

Baugh, J. (2000). *Beyond Ebonics: Linguistic Pride and Racial Prejudice*. New York: Oxford University Press.

Bauman, R. (1972). The La Have Island General Store: Sociability and Verbal Art in a Nova Scotia Community. *Journal of American Folklore*, 85: 330–43.

Bauman, R. and J. Sherzer (eds.) (1974). *Explorations in the Ethnography of Speaking*. London: Cambridge University Press.

Bayley, R. (2002). The Quantitative Paradigm. In Chambers et al. (2002).

Bell, A. (1984). Language Style as Audience Design. *Language in Society*, 13: 145–204.

Bell, A. (2001). Back in Style: Reworking Audience Design. In Eckert and Rickford (2001).

Bell, R. T. (1976). *Sociolinguistics: Goals, Approaches and Problems*. London: Batsford.

Bereiter, C. and S. Engelmann (1966). *Teaching Disadvantaged Children in the Pre-school*. Englewood Cliffs, NJ: Prentice-Hall.

Bergvall, V. L., J. M. Bing, and A. F. Freed (eds.) (1996). *Rethinking Language and Gender Research: Theory and Practice*. London: Longman.

Berlin, B. (1992). *Ethnobiological Classification: Principles of Categorization of Plants and Animals in Traditional Society*. Princeton, NJ: Princeton University Press.

Berlin, B. and P. Kay (1969). *Basic Color Terms: Their Universality and Evolution*. Berkeley: University of California Press.

Bernstein, B. (1961). Social Structure, Language and Learning. *Educational Research*, 3: 163–76.

Bernstein, B. (1971–5). *Class, Codes and Control*, vols 1–3. London: Routledge & Kegan Paul.

Bernstein, B. (1972a). A Sociolinguistic Approach to Socialization; with Some Reference to Educability. In Gumperz and Hymes (1972).

Bernstein, B. (1972b). Social Class, Language and Socialization. In Giglioli (1972).

Bernstein, B. (1990). *The Structuring of Pedagogic Discourse*, vol. 4: *Class, Codes and Control*. London: Routledge.

Bernsten, J. (1998). Marked versus Unmarked Choices on the Auto Factory Floor. In Myers-Scotton (1998).

Bex, T. and R. J. Watts (eds.) (1999). *Standard English: The Widening Debate*. London: Routledge.

Biber, D. and E. Finegan (eds.) (1994). *Sociolinguistic Perspectives on Register*. Oxford: Oxford University Press.

Bickerton, D. (1971). Inherent Variability and Variable Rules. *Foundations of Language*, 7: 457–92.

Bickerton, D. (1975). *Dynamics of a Creole System*. Cambridge: Cambridge University Press.

Bickerton, D. (1977). Pidginization and Creolization: Language Acquisition and Language Universals. In Valdman (1977).

Bickerton, D. (1981). *Roots of Language*. Ann Arbor: Karoma Publishers.

Bickerton, D. (1983). Creole Languages. *Scientific American*, 249(1): 116–22.

Bickerton, D. (1990). *Language and Species*. Chicago: University of Chicago Press.

Blake, R. and M. Josey (2003). The /ay/ Diphthong in a Martha's Vineyard Community: What Can We Say 40 Years after Labov? *Language in Society*, 32: 451–85.

Blakemore, D. (1992). *Understanding Utterances: An Introduction to Pragmatics*. Oxford: Blackwell.

Blom, J.-P. and J. J. Gumperz (1972). Social Meaning in Linguistic Structure: Code-switching in Norway. In Gumperz (1971) and Gumperz and Hymes (1972).

Bloomfield, L. (1927). Literate and Illiterate Speech. *American Speech*, 2: 432–9. In Hymes (1964a).

Bloomfield, L. (1933). *Language*. New York: Henry Holt.

Blount, B. G. (ed.) (1995). *Language, Culture, and Society: A Book of Readings*. 2nd edn. Prospect Heights, IL: Waveland Press.

Boas, F. (1911). Introduction. *Handbook of American Indian Languages*. Washington, DC: Smithsonian Institution. In Hymes (1964a).

Boberg, C. (2000). Geolinguistic Diffusion and the U.S.–Canada Border. *Language Variation and Change*, 12: 1–24.

Bolinger, D. (1975). *Aspects of Language*. 2nd edn. New York: Harcourt Brace Jovanovich.

Bourdieu, P. (1991). *Language and Symbolic Power*. Cambridge, MA: Harvard University Press.

Boxer, D. (2002). *Applying Sociolinguistics: Domains and Face-to-face Interaction*. Amsterdam: John Benjamins.

Bradley, J. (1998). Yanyuwa: 'Men Speak One Way, Women Speak Another.' In Coates (1998).

Braun, F. (1988). *Terms of Address*. Berlin: Mouton de Gruyter.

Brend, R. (1975). Male–Female Intonation Patterns in American English. In Thorne and Henley (1975).

Brenneis, D. and R. K. S. Macaulay (1996). *The Matrix of Language: Contemporary Linguistic Anthropology*. Boulder, CO: Westview Press.

Bright, W. (ed.) (1992). *International Encyclopedia of Linguistics*. New York: Oxford University Press.

Bright, W. O. (1960). Social Dialect and Language History. *Current Anthropology*, 1 (5–6): 424–5. In Hymes (1964a).

Britain, D. (2002). Space and Spatial Diffusion. In Chambers et al. (2002).

Brower, D., M. Gerritsen, and D. de Haan (1979). Speech Differences between Women and Men: On the Wrong Track? *Language in Society*, 8: 33–50.

Brown, G. (1996). *Speakers, Listeners and Communication*. Cambridge: Cambridge University Press.

Brown, G. and G. Yule (1983). *Discourse Analysis*. Cambridge: Cambridge University Press.

Brown, P. and S. Levinson (1979). Social Structure, Groups and Interaction. In Scherer and Giles (1979).

Brown, P. and S. C. Levinson (1987). *Politeness: Some Universals of Language Use*. Cambridge: Cambridge University Press.

Brown, R. and M. Ford (1961). Address in American English. *Journal of Abnormal and Social Psychology*, 62: 375–85. In Hymes (1964a) and Laver and Hutcheson (1972).

Brown, R. and A. Gilman (1960). The Pronouns of Power and Solidarity. In T. A. Sebeok (ed.), *Style in Language*, New York: John Wiley. In Fishman (1968a), Giglioli (1972), and Laver and Hutcheson (1972).

Bruthiaux, P. (2002). Predicting Challenges to English as a Global Language in the 21st Century. *Language Problems and Language Planning*, 26(2): 129–57.

Bucholtz, M. (1999). You Da Man: Narrating the Racial Other in the Production of White Masculinity. *Journal of Sociolinguistics*, 3(4): 443–60.

Bucholtz, M. and K. Hall (2004). Theorizing Identity in Language and Sexuality Research. *Language in Society*, 33: 469–515.

Burling, R. (1970). *Man's Many Voices: Language in its Cultural Context*. New York: Holt, Rinehart, and Winston.

Burling, R. (1973). *English in Black and White*. New York: Holt, Rinehart, and Winston.

Butters, R. R. (1989). *The Death of Black English: Divergence and Convergence in Black and White Vernaculars*. Frankfurt: Peter Lang.

Button, G. (ed.) (1991). *Ethnomethodology and the Human Sciences*. Cambridge: Cambridge University Press.

Bynon, T. (1977). *Historical Linguistics*. Cambridge: Cambridge University Press.

Calvet, L.-J. (1998). *Language Wars and Linguistic Politics*. Oxford: Oxford University Press.

Cameron, D. (1992). *Feminism and Linguistic Theory*. 2nd edn. London: Macmillan.

Cameron, D. (1995). *Verbal Hygiene*. London: Routledge.

Cameron, D. (1996). The Language–Gender Interface: Challenging Co-option. In Bergvall et al. (1996).

Cameron, D. (1997). Demythologizing Sociolinguistics. In Coupland and Jaworski (1997).

Cameron, D. (1998a). Gender, Language, and Discourse: A Review Essay. *Signs: Journal of Women in Culture and Society*, 23(4): 945–73.

Cameron, D. (1998b). Performing Gender Identity: Young Men's Talk and the Construction of Heterosexual Masculinity. In Coates (1998).

Cameron, D. (ed.) (1998c). *The Feminist Critique of Language: A Reader*. 2nd edn. London: Routledge.

Cameron, D. and D. Kulick (2003). *Language and Sexuality*. Cambridge: Cambridge University Press.

Cameron, D., F. McAlinden, and K. O'Leary (1989). Lakoff in Context: The Social and Linguistic Functions of Tag Questions. In J. Coates and D. Cameron (eds.), *Women in Their Speech Communities*. London: Longman.

Carmichael, C. (2002). 'A People Exists and that People Has its Language': Language and Nationalism in the Balkans. In Barbour and Carmichael (2002).

Carroll, J. B. (ed.) (1956). *Language, Thought, and Reality: Selected Writings of Benjamin Lee Whorf*. Cambridge, MA: MIT Press.

Carston, R. and S. Uchida (eds.) (1998). *Relevance Theory: Applications and Implications*. Amsterdam: John Benjamins.

Cave, G. N. (1973). Some Communication Problems of Immigrant Children in Britain. Unpublished paper.

Chambers, J. K. (2002). Studying Language Variation: An Informal Epistemology. In Chambers et al. (2002).

Chambers, J. K. (2003). *Sociolinguistic Theory: Linguistic Variation and its Social Significance*. 2nd edn. Oxford: Blackwell.

Chambers, J. K. and P. Trudgill (1988). *Dialectology*. 2nd edn. Cambridge: Cambridge University Press.

Chambers, J. K., P. Trudgill, N. Schilling-Estes (eds.) (2002). *The Handbook of Language Variation*. Oxford: Blackwell.

Cheepen, C. (1988). *The Predictability of Informal Conversation*. London: Pinter.

Cheshire, J. (1978). Present Tense Verbs in Reading English. In Trudgill (1978).

Cheshire, J. (ed.) (1991). *English around the World: Sociolinguistic Perspectives*. Cambridge: Cambridge University Press.

Cheshire, J. and P. Trudgill (eds.) (1998). *The Sociolinguistics Reader*, vol. 2: *Gender and Discourse*. London: Arnold.

Chomsky, N. (1965). *Aspects of the Theory of Syntax*. Cambridge, MA: MIT Press.

Cicourel, A. V. (1973). *Cognitive Sociology: Language and Meaning in Social Interaction*. Harmondsworth, England: Penguin Books.

Clark, H. H. (1996). *Using Language*. Cambridge: Cambridge University Press.

Clark, H. H. and E. V. Clark (1977). *Psychology and Language: An Introduction to Psycholinguistics*. New York: Harcourt Brace Jovanovich.

Clyne, M. G. (1984). *Language and Society in the German-speaking Countries*. Cambridge: Cambridge University Press.

Clyne, M. (ed.) (1992). *Pluricentric Languages: Differing Norms in Different Nations*. Berlin: Mouton de Gruyter.

Clyne, M. (ed.) (1997). *Undoing and Redoing Corpus Planning*. Berlin: Mouton de Gruyter.

Coates, J. (1993). *Women, Men and Language*. 2nd edn. London: Longman.

Coates, J. (1996). *Women Talk: Conversation between Women Friends*. Oxford: Blackwell.

Coates, J. (ed.) (1998). *Language and Gender: A Reader*. Oxford: Blackwell.

Coates, J. (2002). *Men Talk: Stories in the Making of the Masculinities*. Oxford: Blackwell.

Coates, J. and D. Cameron (1989). *Women in Their Speech Communities*. London: Longman.

Cobarrubias, J. (1983). Ethical Issues in Status Planning. In J. Cobarrubias and J. A. Fishman (eds.), *Progress in Language Planning: International Perspectives*. The Hague: Mouton Publishers.

Cole, P. and J. L. Morgan (eds.) (1975). *Syntax and Semantics*, vol. 3: *Speech Acts*. New York: Academic Press.

Comrie, B. (1989). *Language Universals and Linguistic Typology: Syntax and Morphology*. 2nd edn. Oxford: Blackwell.

Conklin, H. C. (1959). Linguistic Play in its Cultural Context. *Language*, 35: 631–6. In Hymes (1964a).

Cook, J. (1971). An Inquiry into Patterns of Communication and Control between Mothers and their Children in Different Social Classes. London University PhD Thesis.

Cook, V. J. and M. Newson (1996). *Chomsky's Universal Grammar: An Introduction*. Oxford: Blackwell.

Cooper, R. L. (1982). *Language Spread: Studies in Diffusion and Social Change*. Bloomington: Indiana University Press.

Cooper, R. L. (1989). *Language Planning and Social Change*. Cambridge: Cambridge University Press.

Corbett, G. (1991). *Gender*. Cambridge: Cambridge University Press.

Coulmas, F. (ed.) (1981). *Conversational Routine*. The Hague: Mouton Publishers.

Coulmas, F. (1992). Linguistic Etiquette in Japanese Society. In R. J. Watts, S. Ide, and K. Ehlich (eds.), *Politeness in Language: Studies in its History, Theory and Practice*. Berlin: Mouton de Gruyter.

Coulmas, F. (ed.) (1997). *The Handbook of Sociolinguistics*. Oxford: Blackwell.

Coulmas, F. (1999). The Far East. In J. A. Fishman (ed.), *Handbook of Language and Ethnic Identity*. Oxford: Oxford University Press.

Coulthard, M. (1977). *An Introduction to Discourse Analysis*. London: Longman Group.

Coupland, N. and A. Jaworski (eds.) (1997). *Sociolinguistics: A Reader*. New York: St Martin's Press.

Crawford, J. (1992a). *Hold Your Tongue: Bilingualism and the Politics of 'English Only.'* Reading, MA: Addison-Wesley.

Crawford, J. (1992b). *Language Loyalties: A Sourcebook on the Official English Controversy*. Chicago: University of Chicago Press.

Crawford, M. (1995). *Talking Difference: On Gender and Language*. London: Sage.

Crewe, W. (ed.) (1977). *The English Language in Singapore*. Singapore: Eastern Universities Press.

Cropley, A. J. (1983). *The Education of Immigrant Children*. London: Croom Helm.

Crowley, T. (1992). *An Introduction to Historical Linguistics*. Auckland: Oxford University Press.

Crystal, D. (1984). *Who Cares About English Usage?* Harmondsworth, England: Penguin Books.

Crystal, D. (1997). *The Cambridge Encyclopedia of Language*. 2nd edn. Cambridge: Cambridge University Press.

Crystal, D. (2000). *Language Death*. Cambridge: Cambridge University Press.

Crystal, D. (2003a). *The Cambridge Encyclopedia of the English Language*. 2nd edn. Cambridge: Cambridge University Press.

Crystal, D. (2003b). *English as a Global Language*. 2nd edn. Cambridge: Cambridge University Press.

Crystal, D. (2004). *The Language Revolution*. Cambridge: Polity Press.

Dailey-O'Cain, J. (2000). The Sociolinguistic Distribution and Attitudes Toward Focuser *Like* and Quotative *Like*. *Journal of Sociolinguistics*, 4(1): 60–80.

Davis, L. M. (1983). *English Dialectology: An Introduction*. University, AL: University of Alabama Press.

Davis, S. (ed.) (1991). *Pragmatics: A Reader*. New York: Oxford University Press.

DeCamp, D. (1958–9). The Pronunciation of English in San Francisco. *Orbis*, 7: 372–91; 8: 54–77.

DeCamp, D. (1977). The Development of Pidgin and Creole Studies. In Valdman (1977).

DeFrancisco, V. (1997). Gender, Power and Practice: Or, Putting Your Money (and Your Research) Where Your Mouth Is. In Wodak (1997a).

De Klerk, V. (1992). How Taboo are Taboo Words for Girls? *Language in Society*, 21: 277–90.

Denison, D. Log(ist)ic and Simplistic S-curves. (2003). In R. Hickey (ed.), *Motives for Language Change*. Cambridge: Cambridge University Press.

Deutsch, K. W. (1968). The Trend of European Nationalism – the Language Aspect. In Fishman (1968a).

Devitt, A. J. (1989). *Standardizing Written English*. Cambridge: Cambridge University Press.

Dicker, S. J. (1996). *Languages in America: A Pluralist View*. Clevedon: Multilingual Matters.

Dickey, E. (1996). *Greek Forms of Address: From Herodotus to Lucian*. Oxford: Oxford University Press.

Dickey, E. (1997a). Forms of Address and Terms of Reference. *Journal of Linguistics*, 33: 225–74.

Dickey, E. (1997b). The Ancient Greek Address System and Some Proposed Sociolinguistic Universals. *Language in Society*, 26: 1–13.

Dillard, J. L. (1972). *Black English: Its History and Usage in the United States*. New York: Random House.

Dittmar, N. (1976). *Sociolinguistics: A Critical Survey of Theory and Application*. London: Edward Arnold.

Dixon, R. M. W. (1971). A Method of Semantic Description. In D. D. Steinberg and L. A. Jakobovits (eds.), *Semantics: An Interdisciplinary Reader in Philosophy, Linguistics and Psychology*. Cambridge: Cambridge University Press.

Dixon, R. M. W. (1997). *The Rise and Fall of Languages*. Cambridge: Cambridge University Press.

Doğançay-Aktuna, S. (2004). Language Planning in Turkey: Yesterday and Today. *International Journal of the Sociology of Language*, 165: 5–32.

Dorian, N. C. (1981). *Language Death*. Philadelphia: University of Pennsylvania Press.

Dorian, N. (ed.) (1989). *Investigating Obsolescence: Studies in Language Contraction and Death*. Cambridge: Cambridge University Press.

Dorian, N. (1998). Western Language Ideologies and Small-language Prospects. In Grenoble and Whaley (1998).

Downes, W. (1998). *Language and Society*. 2nd edn. Cambridge: Cambridge University Press.

Drew, P. (1994). Conversation Analysis. In Asher and Simpson (1994).

Dubois, B. L. and I. Crouch (1975). The Question of Tag Questions in Women's Speech: They Don't Really Use More of Them, Do They? *Language in Society*, 4: 289–94.

Dubois, S. and B. Horvath (1999). When the Music Changes, You Can Change Too: Gender and Language Change in Cajun English. *Language Variation and Change*, 11(3): 287–313.

DuFon, M. A., G. Kasper, S. Takahashi, and N. Yoshinaga (1994). Bibliography on Linguistic Politeness. *Journal of Pragmatics*, 21: 527–78.

Duncan, S. (1972). Some Signals and Rules for Taking Speaking Turns in Conversation. *Journal of Personality and Social Psychology*, 23: 283–92.

Duncan, S. (1974). On the Structure of Speaker–Auditor Interaction during Speaking Turns. *Language in Society*, 2: 161–80.

Duranti, A. (1997). *Linguistic Anthropology*. Cambridge: Cambridge University Press.

Duranti, A. (ed.) (2001). *Key Terms in Language and Culture*. Oxford: Blackwell.

Eastman, C. M. (1983). *Language Planning: An Introduction*. San Francisco: Chandler & Sharp.

Eckert, P. (1988). Adolescent Social Structure and the Spread of Linguistic Change. *Language in Society*, 17: 183–207.

Eckert, P. (1989). *Jocks and Burnouts: Social Categories and Identities in the High School*. New York: Teachers College Press.

Eckert, P. (1991). Social Polarization and the Choice of Linguistic Variants. In P. Eckert (ed.), *New Ways of Analyzing Sound Change*. New York: Academic Press.

Eckert, P. (1997). Age as a Sociolinguistic Variable. In Coulmas (1997).

Eckert, P. (2000). *Linguistic Variation as Social Practice: The Linguistic Construction of Identity in Belten High*. Oxford: Blackwell.

Eckert, P. (2004). Variation and a Sense of Place. In Fought (2004).

Eckert, P. and S. McConnell-Ginet (1998). Communities of Practice: Where Language, Gender, and Power All Live. In Coates (1998).

Eckert, P. and S. McConnell-Ginet (1999). New Generalizations and Explanations in Language and Gender Research. *Language in Society*, 28: 185–201.

Eckert, P. and S. McConnell-Ginet (2003). *Language and Gender*. Cambridge: Cambridge University Press.

Eckert, P. and J. R. Rickford (eds.) (2001). *Style and Sociolinguistic Variation*. Cambridge: Cambridge University Press.

Edelsky, C. (1979). Question Intonation and Sex Roles. *Language in Society*, 8: 15–32.

Edwards, A. D. (1981). Analysing Classroom Talk. In P. French and M. Maclure (eds.), *Adult–Child Conversation*. London: Croom Helm.

Edwards, J. (1985). *Language, Society and Identity*. Oxford: Blackwell.

Edwards, J. (1989). *Language and Disadvantage*. 2nd edn. London: Cole and Whurr.

Edwards, J. (1994). Educational Failure. In Asher and Simpson (1994).

Edwards, V. (1986). *Language in a Black Community*. Clevedon: Multilingual Matters.

Edwards, V. K. (1979). *The West Indian Language Issue in British Schools*. London: Routledge and Kegan Paul.

Eelen, G. (2001). *A Critique of Politeness Theories*. Manchester: St Jerome Publishing.

Egbert, M. M. (1996). Context-sensitivity in Conversation: Eye Gaze and the German Repair Initiator. *Language in Society*, 25: 587–612.

Eggins, S. and D. Slade (1997). *Analyzing Casual Conversation*. London: Cassell.

Ehrlich, S. and R. King (1994). Feminist Meaning and the (De)politicization of the Lexicon. *Language in Society*, 23: 59–76.

Enfield, N. J. (ed.) (2002). *Ethnosyntax: Explorations in Grammar and Culture*. Oxford: Oxford University Press.

Errington, J. J. (1988). *Structure and Style in Javanese*. Philadelphia: University of Pennsylvania Press.

Ervin-Tripp, S. (1972). On Sociolinguistic Rules: Alternation and Co-occurrence. In Gumperz and Hymes (1972).

Evans, B. (2004). The Role of Social Network in the Acquisition of Local Dialect Norms by Appalachian Migrants in Ypsilanti, Michigan. *Language Variation and Change*. 16: 153–67.

Evans, S. and C. Green (2001). Language in Post-colonial Hong Kong: The Roles of English and Chinese in the Public and Private Sectors. *English World-Wide*, 22(2): 247–68.

Evans, S. and C. Green (2003). The Use of English by Chinese Professionals in Post-1997 Hong Kong. *Journal of Multilingual and Multicultural Development*, 24(5): 386–412.

Evans-Pritchard, E. E. (1948). Nuer Modes of Address. *The Uganda Journal*, 12: 166–71. In Hymes (1964a).

Ewars, T. (1996). *The Origin of American Black English: Be-forms in the HOO-DOO Texts*. Berlin: Mouton de Gruyter.

Fabricus, A. (2002). Ongoing Change in Modern RP: Evidence for the Disappearing Stigma of t-glottalling. *English World-Wide*, 23(1): 115–36.

Fairclough, N. (1995). *Critical Discourse Analysis*. London: Longman.

Fairclough, N. (2001). *Language and Power*. 2nd edn. London: Longman.

Fang, H. and J. H. Heng (1983). Social Changes and Changing Address Norms in China. *Language in Society*, 12: 495–507.

Farb, P. (1974). *Word Play: What Happens When People Talk*. New York: A. A. Knopf.

Farfán, J. A. F. (2003). 'Al fin que ya los cueros no van a correr': The Pragmatics of Power in Hñahñu (Otomi) Markets. *Language in Society*, 32: 629–58.

Fase, W., K. Jaspaert, and S. Kroon (eds.) (1992). *Maintenance and Loss of Minority Languages*. Amsterdam: John Benjamins.

Fasold, R. W. (1972). *Tense Marking in Black English: A Linguistic and Social Analysis*. Washington, DC: Center for Applied Linguistics.

Fasold, R. W. (1975). Review of J. L. Dillard, *Black English*. *Language in Society*, 4: 198–221.

Fasold, R. W. (1984). *The Sociolinguistics of Society*. Oxford: Blackwell.

Fasold R. (1990). *The Sociolinguistics of Language*. Oxford: Blackwell.

Fasold, R. W. (1991). The Quiet Demise of Variable Rules. *American Speech*, 66(1): 3–21.

Fehlen, F. (2002). Luxembourg, A Multilingual Society at the Romance/Germanic Language Boundary. *Journal of Multilingual and Multicultural Development*, 23(1): 80–97.

Ferguson, C. A. (1959). Diglossia. *Word*, 15: 325–40. In Giglioli (1972) and Hymes (1964a).

Ferguson, C. A. (1972). *Language Structure and Language Use*. Stanford, CA: Stanford University Press.

Ferguson, C. A. (1994). Dialect, Register, and Genre: Working Assumptions about Conventionalization. In Biber and Finegan (1994).

Ferguson, C. A. and S. B. Heath (eds.) (1981). *Language in the USA*. Cambridge: Cambridge University Press.

Figueroa, E. (1994). *Sociolinguistic Metatheory*. Oxford: Pergamon.

Finegan, E. (1980). *Attitudes Toward English Usage*. New York: Teachers College Press.

Finegan, E. and J. Rickford (eds.) (2004). *Language in the USA*. Cambridge: Cambridge University Press.

Finlayson, R., K. Calteaux, and C. Myers-Scotton (1998). Orderly Mixing and Accommodation in South African Codeswitching. *Journal of Sociolinguistics*, 2(3): 395–420.

Fischer, J. L. (1958). Social Influences in the Choice of a Linguistic Variant. *Word*, 14: 47–56. In Hymes (1964a).

Fishman, J. A. (1960). A Systematization of the Whorfian Hypothesis. *Behavioral Science*, 5: 323–39.

Fishman, J. A. (1966). *Language Loyalty in the United States*. The Hague: Mouton.

Fishman, J. A. (ed.) (1968a). *Readings in the Sociology of Language*. The Hague: Mouton.

Fishman, J. A. (1968b). Some Contrasts between Linguistically Homogeneous and Linguistically Heterogeneous Polities. In Fishman, Ferguson, and Das Gupta (1968).

Fishman, J. A. (ed.) (1971–2). *Advances in the Sociology of Language*, 2 vols. The Hague: Mouton.

Fishman, J. A. (1972a). The Relationship between Micro- and Macro-Sociolinguistics in the Study of Who Speaks What Language to Whom and When. In Pride and Holmes (1972).

Fishman, J. A. (1972b). The Sociology of Language. In Giglioli (1972).

Fishman, J. A. (1972c). *The Sociology of Language: An Interdisciplinary Social Science Approach to Language in Society*. Rowley, MA: Newbury House.

Fishman, J. A. (1980). Prefatory Notes. In P. H. Nelde (ed.), *Languages in Contact and Conflict, XI*. Wiesbaden: Steiner.

Fishman, J. A. (1981). Language Policy: Past, Present, and Future. In Ferguson and Heath (1981).

Fishman, J. A. (ed.) (2001). *Can Threatened Languages be Saved? Reversing Language Shift, Revisited: A 21st Century Perspective*. Clevedon: Multilingual Matters.

Fishman, J., A. W. Conrad, and A. Rubal-Lopez (eds.) (1996). *Post-imperial English*. Berlin: Mouton de Gruyter.

Fishman, J. A., C. A. Ferguson, and J. Das Gupta (eds.) (1968). *Language Problems of Developing Nations*. New York: John Wiley.

Fishman, J. A., A. Tabouret-Keller, M. Clyne, B. Krishnamurti, and M. Abdulaziz (eds.) (1986). *The Fergusonian Impact*. Berlin: Mouton de Gruyter.

Foley, J. (ed.) (1988). *New Englishes: The Case of Singapore*. Singapore: Singapore University Press.

Foley, W. A. (1997). *Anthropological Linguistics: An Introduction*. Oxford: Blackwell.

Ford, C. E., B. A. Fox, and S. A. Thompson (eds.) (2002). *The Language of Turn and Sequence*. Oxoford: Oxford University Press.

Fought, C. (ed.) (2004). *Sociolinguistic Variation: Critical Reflections*. New York: Oxford University Press.

Foulkes, P. and G. J. Docherty (eds.) (1999). *Urban Voices: Accent Studies in the British Isles*. London: Arnold.

Foulkes, P. and G. J. Docherty (2000). Another Chapter in the Story of /r/: 'Labiodental' Variants in British English. *Journal of Sociolinguistics*, 4(1): 30–59.

Fox, J. J. (1974). 'Our Ancestors Spoke in Pairs': Rotinese Views of Language, Dialect, and Code. In Bauman and Sherzer (1974).

Frake, C. O. (1961). The Diagnosis of Disease among the Subanun of Mindanao. *American Anthropologist*, 63: 113–32. In Hymes (1964a).

Frake, C. O. (1964). How to Ask for a Drink in Subanun. *American Anthropologist*, 66(6:2): 127–32. In Giglioli (1972) and Pride and Holmes (1972).

Frangoudaki, A. (1992). Diglossia and the Present Language Situation in Greece: A Sociological Approach to the Interpretation of Diglossia and Some Hypotheses on Today's Linguistic Reality. *Language in Society*, 21: 365–81.

Freed, A. F. (2003). Epilogue: Reflections on Language and Gender Research. In Holmes and Meyerhoff (2003).

Freed, A. F. and A. Greenwood (1996). Women, Men, and Type of Talk: What Makes the Difference? *Language in Society*, 25: 1–26.

Friedrich, P. (1972). Social Context and Semantic Feature: The Russian Pronominal Usage. In Gumperz and Hymes (1972).

Fries, C. C. (1940). *American English Grammar*. New York: Appleton-Century-Crofts.

Gal, S. (1978). Peasant Men Can't Find Wives: Language Change and Sex Roles in a Bilingual Community. *Language in Society*, 7: 1–16.

Gal, S. (1979). *Language Shift: Social Determinants of Linguistic Change in Bilingual Austria*. New York: Academic Press.

Gal, S. (1988). The Political Economy of Code Choice. In Heller (1988).

Gardner, P. (1966). Symmetric Respect and Memorate Knowledge: The Structure and Ecology of Individualistic Culture. *Southwestern Journal of Anthropology*, 22: 389–415.

Gardner-Chloros, P. (1991). *Language Selection and Switching in Strasbourg*. Oxford: Oxford University Press.

Gardner-Chloros, P. (1997). Code-switching: Language Selection in Three Strasbourg Department Stores. In Coupland and Jaworski (1997).

Garfinkel, H. (1967). *Studies in Ethnomethodology*. Englewood Cliffs, NJ: Prentice-Hall.

Garfinkel, H. (1972). Studies of the Routine Grounds of Everyday Activities. In Sudnow (1972).

Geertz, C. (1960). *The Religion of Java*. Glencoe, IL: Free Press. Excerpted in Fishman (1968a) and Pride and Holmes (1972).

Geis, M. L. (1995). *Speech Acts and Conversational Interaction*. Cambridge: Cambridge University Press.

Giglioli, P. P. (ed.) (1972). *Language and Social Context: Selected Readings*. Harmondsworth, England: Penguin Books.

Giles, H. and N. Coupland (1991). *Language: Contexts and Consequences*. Buckingham: Open University Press.

Giles, H. and P. F. Powesland (1975). *Speech Style and Social Evaluation*. London: Academic Press.

Giles, H., K. R. Scherer, and D. M. Taylor (1979). Speech Markers in Social Interaction. In Sherer and Giles (1979).

Gimson, A. C. (1962). *An Introduction to the Pronunciation of English*. London: Edward Arnold.

Godard, D. (1977). Same Setting, Different Norms: Phone Call Beginnings in France and the United States. *Language in Society*, 6: 209–19.

Goffman, E. (1955). On Face-work: An Analysis of Ritual Elements in Social Interaction. *Psychiatry*, 18: 213–31. In Laver and Hutcheson (1972).

Goffman, E. (1967). *Interaction Ritual: Essays in Face-to-Face Behavior*. New York: Anchor Books.

Goffman, E. (1981). *Forms of Talk*. Philadelphia: University of Pennsylvania Press.

Goodenough, W. H. (1957). Cultural Anthropology and Linguistics. In P. L. Garvin (ed.), *Report of the Seventh Round Table Meeting on Linguistics and Language Study*. Washington, DC: Georgetown University Press.

Goody, J. and I. Watt (1972). The Consequences of Literacy. In Giglioli (1972).

Gordon, D. and G. Lakoff (1975). Conversational Postulates. In Cole and Morgan (1975).

Gordon, E., L. Campbell, J. Hay, M. Maclagan, A. Sudbury, and P. Trudgill (2004). *New Zealand English: Its Origin and Evolution*. Cambridge: Cambridge University Press.

Gordon, M. J. (2002). Investigating Chain Shifts and Mergers. In Chambers et al. (2002).

Graddol, D. and J. Swann (1989). *Gender Voices*. Oxford: Blackwell.

Gray, J. (1992). *Men are from Mars, Women are from Venus*. New York: HarperCollins.

Green, L. (2004). Research on African American English since 1998. *Journal of English Linguistics*, 32(3): 210–29.

Green, L. J. (2002). *African American English: A Linguistic Introduction*. Cambridge: Cambridge University Press.

Greenberg, R. D. (2004). *Language and Identity in the Balkans: Serbo-Croatian and its Disintegration*. Oxford: Oxford University Press.

Grenoble, L. A. and L. J. Whaley (eds.) (1998). *Endangered Languages: Language Loss and Community Response*. Cambridge: Cambridge University Press.

Grice, H. P. (1975). *Logic and Conversation*. In Cole and Morgan (1975).

Grillo, R. D. (1989). *Dominant Languages*. Cambridge: Cambridge University Press.

Gumperz, J. J. (1958). Dialect Differences and Social Stratification in a North Indian Village. *American Anthropologist*, 60: 668–81. In Gumperz (1971).

Gumperz, J. J. (1968). The Speech Community. *International Encyclopedia of the Social Sciences*. London: Macmillan. In Giglioli (1972) and Gumperz (1971).

Gumperz, J. J. (1971). *Language in Social Groups*. Stanford, CA: Stanford University Press.

Gumperz, J. J. (1972). Sociolinguistics and Communication in Small Groups. In Pride and Holmes (1972).

Gumperz, J. J. (1982a). *Discourse Strategies*. Cambridge: Cambridge University Press.

Gumperz, J. J. (ed.) (1982b). *Language and Social Identity*. Cambridge: Cambridge University Press.

Gumperz, J. J. and J. Cook-Gumperz (1982). Introduction: Language and the Communication of Social Identity. In Gumperz (1982b).

Gumperz, J. J. and D. H. Hymes (eds.) (1972). *Directions in Sociolinguistics: The Ethnography of Communication*. New York: Holt, Rinehart, and Winston.

Gumperz, J. J. and S. C. Levinson (eds.) (1996). *Rethinking Linguistic Relativity*. Cambridge: Cambridge University Press.

Gumperz, J. J. and R. Wilson (1971). Convergence and Creolization: A Case from the Indo-Aryan/Dravidian Border in India. In Gumperz (1971), and Hymes (1971).

Gupta, A. F. (1994). *The Step-Tongue: Children's English in Singapore*. Clevedon: Multilingual Matters.

Gupta, A. F. and S. P. Yeok (1995). Language Shift in a Singapore Family. *Journal of Multilingual and Multicultural Development*, 16: 301–14.

Haas, M. R. (1944). Men's and Women's Speech in Koasati. *Language*, 20: 142–9. In Hymes (1964a).

Haas, M. R. (1951). Interlingual Word Taboos. *American Anthropologist*, 53: 338–44. In Hymes (1964a).

Haig, J. H. (1991). A Phonological Difference in Male–Female Speech among Teenagers. In S. Ide and N. H. McGloin (eds.), *Aspects of Japanese Women's Language*. Tokyo: Kurosio.

Hale, K. (1971). A Note on a Walbiri Tradition of Autonymy. In D. D. Steinberg and L. A. Jakobovits (eds.), *Semantics: An Interdisciplinary Reader in Philosophy, Linguistics and Psychology*. London: Cambridge University Press.

Hall, K. and M. Bucholtz (eds.) (1995). *Gender Articulated: Language and the Socially Constructed Self*. London: Routledge.

Hall, R. A. (1966). *Pidgin and Creole Languages*. Ithaca, NY: Cornell University Press.

Hall R. A. (1972). Pidgins and Creoles as Standard Languages. In Pride and Holmes (1972).

Halliday, M. A. K. (1973). *Explorations in the Functions of Language*. London: Edward Arnold.

Hancock, I. F. (1977). Appendix: Repertory of Pidgin and Creole Languages. In Valdman (1977).

Hansen, A. B. (2001). Lexical Diffusion as a Factor of Phonetic Change: The Case of Modern French Nasal Vowels. *Language Variation and Change*, 13: 209–52.

Haugen, E. (1966a). Dialect, Language, Nation. *American Anthropologist*, 68: 922–35. In Pride and Holmes (1972).

Haugen, E. (1966b). *Language Conflict and Language Planning: The Case of Modern Norwegian*. Cambridge, MA: Harvard University Press.

Haugen, E. (1968). Language Planning in Modern Norway. In Fishman (1968a).

Have, P. ten (1999). *Doing Conversational Analysis: A Practical Guide*. London: Sage.

Hayashi, T. (1996). *Cognition, Empathy, and Interaction: Floor Management of English and Japanese Conversation*. Norwood, New Jersey: Ablex Publishing.

Hazen, K. (2002). Identity and Language Variation in a Rural Community. *Language*, 78(2): 240–57.

Heeringa, W. and J. Nerbonne (2001). Dialect Areas and Dialect Continua. *Language Variation and Change*, 13: 375–400.

Heller, M. (ed.) (1988). *Codeswitching*. Berlin: Mouton de Gruyter.

Heller, M. S. (1982). Negotiations of Language Choice in Montreal. In Gumperz (1982b).

Henderson, D. (1972). Contextual Specificity, Discretion and Cognitive Socialization: With Special Reference to Language. In Pride and Holmes (1972).

Heritage, J. (1984). *Garfinkel and Ethnomethodology*. Oxford: Blackwell.

Hess, R. D. and V. C. Shipman (1965). Early Experience and the Socialization of Cognitive Modes in Children. *Child Development*, 36: 869–86.

Hess, R. D. and V. C. Shipman (1967). Cognitive Elements in Maternal Behavior. In J. P. Hill (ed.), *Minnesota Symposium on Child Psychology*. Minneapolis: University of Minnesota Press.

Hewitt, R. (1986). *White Talk Black Talk*. Cambridge: Cambridge University Press.

Hewitt, R. (1989). Creole in the Classroom: Political Grammars and Educational Vocabularies. In R. Grillo (ed.), *Social Anthropology and the Politics of Language*. Sociological Review Monograph 36. London: Routledge.

Hibya, J. (1996). Denasalization of the Velar Nasal in Tokyo Japanese. In G. R. Guy, C. Feagin, D. Schiffrin, and J. Baugh (eds.), *Towards a Social Science of Language: Papers in Honour of William Labov*. Amsterdam: John Benjamins.

Hickey, R. (2004). *Legacies of Colonial English*. Cambridge: Cambridge University Press.

Hill, J. H. and K. C. Hill (1986). *Speaking Mexicano*. Tucson: University of Arizona Press.

Hoggart, R. (1970). *The Uses of Literacy: Aspects of Working-class Life with Special Reference to Publications and Entertainments*. London: Oxford University Press.

Holborow, M. (1999). *The Politics of English: A Marxist View of Language*. London: Sage.

Holm, J. (1988, 1989) *Pidgins and Creoles*. 2 vols. Cambridge: Cambridge University Press.

Holm, J. (2000). *An Introduction to Pidgins and Creoles*. Cambridge: Cambridge University Press.

Holm, J. (2004). *Languages in Contact: The Partial Restructuring of Vernaculars*. Cambridge: Cambridge University Press.

Holmes, J. (1992). *An Introduction to Sociolinguistics*. London: Longman.

Holmes, J. (1995). *Women, Men and Politeness*. London: Longman.

Holmes, J. (1998). Women's Talk: The Question of Sociolinguistic Universals. In Coates (1998).

Holmes, J. and M. Meyerhoff (eds.) (2003). *The Handbook of Language and Gender*. Oxford: Blackwell.

Holmquist, J. (1985). Social Correlates of a Linguistic Variable: A Study in a Spanish Village. *Language in Society*, 14: 191–203.

Honey, J. (1983). *The Language Trap: Race, Class and the Standard Language Issue in British Schools*. Middlesex: National Council for Educational Standards.

Honey, J. (1989). *Does Accent Matter? The Pygmalion Factor*. London: Faber and Faber.

Honey, J. (1997). *Language is Power: The Story of Standard English and its Enemies*. London: Faber and Faber.

Hopper, R. (1992). *Telephone Conversation*. Bloomington: University of Indiana Press.

Horvath, B. (1998). Some 'Fractious Energy.' *Journal of Sociolinguistics*, 2(3): 446–56.

House, J. (2003). English as a Lingua Franca: A Threat to Multilingualism? *Journal of Sociolinguistics*, 7(4): 556–78.

Hudson, A. (1992). Diglossia: A Bibliographic Review. *Language in Society*, 21: 611–74.

Hudson, R. A. (1996). *Sociolinguistics*. 2nd edn. Cambridge: Cambridge University Press.

Hughes, A. and P. Trudgill (1996). *English Accents and Dialects: An Introduction to Social and Regional Variation in British English*. 3rd edn. London: Edward Arnold.

Hughes, S. E. (1992). Expletives of Lower Working-class Women. *Language in Society*, 21: 291–301.

Huntington, S. P. (1996). *The Clash of Civilizations and the Remaking of World Order*. New York: Simon and Schuster.

Huntington, S. P. (2004). *Who Are We? The Challenges to America's National Identity*. New York: Simon and Schuster.

Hutchby, I. and R. Wooffitt (1998). *Conversation Analysis: Principles, Practices and Applications*. Cambridge: Polity Press.

Hymes, D. H. (1962). The Ethnography of Speaking. In T. Gladwin and W. C. Sturtevant (eds.), *Anthropology and Human Behavior*. Washington, DC: Anthropological Society of Washington. In Fishman (1968a).

Hymes, D. H. (ed.) (1964a). *Language in Culture and Society: A Reader in Linguistics and Anthropology*. New York: Harper & Row.

Hymes, D. H. (1964b). Toward Ethnographies of Communication: The Analysis of Communicative Events. *American Anthropologist*, 66(6:2): 1–34. In Giglioli (1972).

Hymes, D. H. (ed.) (1971). *Pidginization and Creolization of Languages*. Cambridge: Cambridge University Press.

Hymes, D. H. (1972). On Communicative Competence. In Pride and Holmes (1972).

Hymes, D. H. (1974). *Foundations in Sociolinguistics: An Ethnographic Approach*. Philadelphia: University of Pennsylvania Press.

Hymes, D. H. (1980). Commentary. In Valdman and Highfield (1980).

Ide, S. (1982). Japanese Sociolinguistics: Politeness and Women's Language. *Lingua*, 57: 357–86.

Ide, S. (1989). Formal Forms and Discernment: Two Neglected Aspects of Linguistic Politeness. *Multilingua*, 8: 223–48.

Inglehart, R. F. and M. Woodward (1967). Language Conflicts and Political Community. *Comparative Studies in Society and History*, 10: 27–45. In Giglioli (1972).

Irvine, J. T. (1998). Ideologies of Honorific Language. In Schieffelin et al. (1998).

Itakura, H. and A. B. M. Tsui (2004). Gender and Conversational Dominance in Japanese Conversation. *Language in Society*, 33: 223–48.

Jahangiri, N. (1980). A Sociolinguistic Study of Tehrani Persian. London University PhD Thesis.

Jahr, E. H. (ed.) (1993). *Language Conflict and Language Planning*. Berlin: Mouton de Gruyter.

Jakobson, R. (1960). Closing Statement: Linguistics and Poetics. In T. A. Sebeok (ed.), *Style in Language*. New York: John Wiley.

James, D. and S. Clarke (1993). Women, Men, and Interruptions: A Critical Review. In Tannen (1993).

James, D. and J. Drakich (1993). Understanding Gender Differences in Amount of Talk: A Critical Review of Research. In Tannen (1993).

Jaworski, A. and N. Coupland (eds.) (1999). *The Discourse Reader*. London: Routledge.

Jefferson, G. (1972). Side Sequencers. In Sudnow (1972).

Jespersen, O. (1922). *Language: Its Nature, Development and Origin*. New York: W. W. Norton.

Johnson, C. S. (1943). *Patterns of Negro Segregation*. New York: Harper.

Johnson, S. and U. H. Meinhof (eds.) (1997). *Language and Masculinity*. Oxford: Blackwell.

Johnson-Weiner, K. M. (1998). Community Identity and Language Change in North American Anabaptist Communities. *Journal of Sociolinguistics*, 2(3): 375–94.

Johnstone, B. (2000). *Qualitative Methods in Sociolinguistics*. New York: Oxford University Press.

Johnstone, B. (2004). Place, Globalization, and Linguistic Variation. In Fought (2004).

Joos, M. (1962). *The Five Clocks*. Bloomington, IN: Indiana University Research Center in Anthropology, Folklore, and Linguistics.

Joseph, J. E. (1987). *Eloquence and Power*. London: Pinter.

Joseph, J. E. (2004). *Language and Identity*. London: Palgrave Macmillan.

Ju, Z. (1991). The 'Depreciation' and 'Appreciation' of Some Address Terms in China. *Language in Society*, 20: 387–90.

Kachru, B. B. (ed.) (1992). *The Other Tongue*. 2nd edn. Urbana: University of Illinois Press.

Kaplan, R. B. and R. B. Baldauf (eds.) (1997). *Language Planning: From Practice to Theory*. Clevedon: Multilingual Matters.

Kay, P. and C. K. McDaniel (1979). On the Logic of Variable Rules. *Language in Society*, 8: 151–87.

Kaye, A. S. and M. Tosco (2001). *Pidgin and Creole Languages: A Basic Introduction*. Munich: Lincom Europa.

Keenan, E. (1974). Norm-makers, Norm-breakers: Uses of Speech by Men and Women in a Malagasy Community. In Bauman and Sherzer (1974).

Keesing, R. M. and F. M. Keesing (1971). *New Perspectives in Cultural Anthropology*. New York: Holt, Rinehart, and Winston.

Keevallik, L. (1999). The Use and Abuse of Singular and Plural Address Forms in Estonian. *International Journal of the Sociology of Language*, 139: 125–44.

Kennedy, C. (1984). *Language Planning and Language Education*. London: George Allen & Unwin.

Keshavarz, M. (1988). Forms of Address in Post-Revolutionary Iranian Persian: A Socio-linguistic Analysis. *Language in Society*, 17: 565–75.

Key, M. R. (1996). *Male/Female Language*. 2nd edn. Lanham, Maryland: Scarecrow Press.

Kiesling, S. F. (1998). Men's Identities and Sociolinguistic Variation: The Case of Fraternity Men. *Journal of Sociolinguistics*, 2(1): 69–99.

Kiesling, S. F. and C. B. Paulston (eds.) (2005). *Intercultural Discourse and Communication*. Oxford: Blackwell.

King, R. (1991). *Talking Gender: A Guide to Nonsexist Communication*. Toronto: Copp Clark Pitman.

Kipers, P. S. (1987). Gender and Topic. *Language in Society*, 16: 543–57.

Kloss, H. (1968). Notes Concerning a Language–Nation Typology. In Fishman, Ferguson, and Das Gupta (1968).

Kotthoff, H. and R. Wodak (eds.) (1997). *Communicating Gender in Context*. Amsterdam: John Benjamins.

Kramer, C. (1974). Wishy-washy Mommy Talk. *Psychology Today*, 8(1): 82–5.

Kremer, L. (1999). The Netherlands–German National Border as a Subjective Language Boundary. In Preston (1999).

Kretzschmar, W. A., Jr (1996). Quantitative Aerial Analysis of Dialect Features. *Language Variation and Change*, 8: 13–39.

Krosroshahi, F. (1989). Penguins Don't Care, but Women Do: A Social Identity Analysis of a Whorfian Problem. *Language in Society*, 18: 505–25.

Kulick, D. (2003). Language and Desire. In Holmes and Meyerhoff (2003).

Kuo, E. C. Y. (1977). The Status of English in Singapore: A Sociolinguistic Analysis. In Crewe (1977).

Kurath, H. (1939). *Handbook of the Linguistic Geography of New England*. Providence, RI: Brown University Press.

Kurath, H. (1949). *A Word Geography of the Eastern United States*. Ann Arbor: University of Michigan Press.

Labov, W. (1963). The Social Motivation of a Sound Change. *Word*, 19: 273–309. In Labov (1972b).

Labov, W. (1966). *The Social Stratification of English in New York City*. Washington, DC: Center for Applied Linguistics.

Labov, W. (1969). Contraction, Deletion, and Inherent Variability of the English Copula. *Language*, 45: 715–62.

Labov, W. (1970). The Study of Language in its Social Context. *Studium Generale*, 23: 30–87. In Fishman (1971–2, vol. 1), Giglioli (1972), and Pride and Holmes (1972).

Labov, W. (1971). The Notion of 'System' in Creole Studies. In Hymes (1971).

Labov, W. (1972a). *Language in the Inner City: Studies in the Black English Vernacular.* Philadelphia: University of Pennsylvania Press.

Labov, W. (1972b). *Sociolinguistic Patterns.* Philadelphia: University of Pennsylvania Press.

Labov, W. (1980). The Social Origins of Sound Change. In W. Labov (ed.), *Locating Language in Time and Space.* New York: Academic Press.

Labov, W. (1981). What Can Be Learned about Change in Progress from Synchronic Description? In D. Sankoff and H. Cedergren (eds.), *Variation Omnibus.* Edmonton: Linguistic Research Inc.

Labov, W. (1994). *Principles of Linguistic Change, I: Internal Factors.* Oxford: Blackwell.

Labov, W. (2001). *Principles of Linguistic Change, II: Social Factors.* Oxford: Blackwell.

Labov, W. and W. Harris (1986). De Facto Segregation of Black and White Vernaculars. In D. Sankoff (ed.), *Diversity and Diachrony.* Amsterdam: John Benjamins.

Lakoff, G. and M. Johnson (1980). *Metaphors We Live By.* Chicago: University of Chicago Press.

Lakoff, R. (1973). Language and Woman's Place. *Language in Society*, 2: 45–80.

Lakoff, R. (1975). *Language and Woman's Place.* New York: Harper & Row.

Lakoff, R. T. (1990). *Talking Power.* New York: Basic Books.

Lakoff, R. T. (2000). *The Language War.* Berkeley: University of California Press.

Lambert, W. E. (1967). A Social Psychology of Bilingualism. *Journal of Social Issues*, 23: 91–109. In Pride and Holmes (1972).

Lambert, W. E. and G. R. Tucker (1976). *Tu, Vous, Usted: A Social–Psychological Study of Address Patterns.* Rowley, MA: Newbury House.

Lane, L. A. (2000). Trajectories of Linguistic Variation: Emergence of a Dialect. *Language Variation and Change*, 12: 267–94.

Laver, J. and S. Hutcheson (eds.) (1972). *Communication in Face to Face Interaction.* Harmondsworth, England: Penguin Books.

Laver, J. and P. Trudgill (1979). Phonetic and Linguistic Markers in Speech. In Scherer and Giles (1979).

Leap, W. L. (1996). *Word's Out: Gay Men's English.* Minneapolis: University of Minnesota Press.

Lee, L. (2002). When English is not a Mother Tongue: Linguistic Ownership and the Eurasian Community in Singapore. *Journal of Multilingual and Multicultural Development*, 23(4): 282–95.

Lee, P. (1996). *The Whorf Theory Complex: A Critical Reconstruction.* Amsterdam: John Benjamins.

Lefebvre, C. (1998). *Creole Genesis and the Acquisition of Grammar: The Case of Haitian Creole.* Cambridge: Cambridge University Press.

Lefebvre, C. (2004). *Issues in the Study of Pidgin and Creole Languages.* Amsterdam: John Benjamins.

Lehmann, W. P. (ed.) (1975). *Language and Linguistics in the People's Republic of China,* Austin: University of Texas Press.

Leiter, K. (1980). *A Primer on Ethnomethodology.* London: Oxford University Press.

Leith, D. (1997). *A Social History of English.* 2nd edn. London: Routledge.

Le Page, R. B. (1997). The Evolution of a Sociolinguistic Theory of Language. In Coulmas (1997).

Le Page, R. B. and A. Tabouret-Keller (1985). *Acts of Identity.* Cambridge: Cambridge University Press.

Lepper, G. (2000). *Categories in Text and Talk: A Practical Introduction to Categorization Analysis*. London: Sage.

Lerner, G. H. (2003). Selecting Next Speaker: The Context-sensitive Operation of a Context-free Organization. *Language in Society*, 32: 177–201.

Levinson, S. (1983). *Pragmatics*. Cambridge: Cambridge University Press.

Levinson, S. C. (2001). Maxim. In Duranti (2001).

Lewis, G. (1999). *The Turkish Language Reform: A Catastrophic Success*. Oxford: Oxford University Press.

Li, W. (1995). Code-switching, Preference Marking and Politeness in Bilingual Cross-generational Talk: Examples from a Chinese Community in Britain. *Journal of Multilingual and Multicultural Development*, 16(3): 197–214.

Li, W. and L. Milroy (1995). Conversational Code-switching in a Chinese Community in Britain: A Sequential Analysis. *Journal of Pragmatics*, 23: 281–99.

Lilles, J. (2000). The Myth of Canadian English. *English Today*, 16: 3–9, 17.

Lindenfeld, J. (1990). *Speech and Sociability at French Urban Marketplaces*. Amsterdam: John Benjamins.

Lindström, A. (1994). Identification and Recognition in Swedish Telephone Conversation Openings. *Language in Society*, 23: 231–52.

Linn M. D. (ed.) (1998). *Handbook of Dialects and Language Variation*. 2nd edn. San Diego: Academic Press.

Lippi-Green, R. (1997). *English with an Accent: Language, Ideology, and Discrimination in the United States*. London: Routledge.

Livia, A. and K. Hall (eds.) (1997). *Queerly Phrased: Language, Gender, and Sexuality*. New York: Oxford University Press.

Long, D. and D. R. Preston (eds.) (2003). *Handbook of Perceptual Dialectology*, vol. 2. Amsterdam: John Benjamins.

Loveday, L. (1982). *The Sociolinguistics of Learning and Using a Non-native Language*. Oxford: Pergamon Press.

Lucy, J. A. (1992a). *Grammatical Categories and Cognition: A Case Study of the Linguistic Relativity Hypothesis*. Cambridge: Cambridge University Press.

Lucy, J. A. (1992b). *Language Diversity and Thought: A Reformulation of the Linguistic Relativity Hypothesis*. Cambridge: Cambridge University Press.

Lucy, J. A. (1996). The Scope of Linguistic Relativity: An Analysis and Review of Empirical Research. In Gumperz and Levinson (1996).

Lucy, J. A. (1997). The Linguistics of 'Color.' In C. L. Hardin and L. Maffi (eds.), *Color Categories in Thought and Language*. Cambridge: Cambridge University Press.

Luong, H. V. (1990). *Discursive Practices and Linguistic Meanings*. Amsterdam: John Benjamins.

Lyons, J. (ed.) (1970). *New Horizons in Linguistics*. Harmondsworth, England: Penguin Books.

Macaulay, R. K. S. (1977). *Language, Social Class, and Education: A Glasgow Study*. Edinburgh: Edinburgh University Press.

Malinowski, B. (1923). The Problem of Meaning in Primitive Languages. In C. K. Ogden and I. A. Richards, *The Meaning of Meaning*. London: Routledge & Kegan Paul. In Laver and Hutcheson (1972).

Malotki, E. (1983). *Hopi Time: A Linguistic Analysis of the Temporal Concepts in the Hopi Language*. Berlin: Mouton.

Maltz, D. N. and R. A. Borker (1982). A Cultural Approach to Male–Female Miscommunication. In Gumperz (1982b).

Mansour, G. (1993). *Multilingualism and Nation Building*. Clevedon: Multilingual Matters.

Marshall, J. (2003). The Changing Sociolinguistic Status of the Glottal Stop in Northeast Scottish English. *English World-Wide*, 24(1): 89–108.

Marshall, J. (2004). *Language Change and Sociolinguistics: Rethinking Social Networks*. Basingstoke: Palgrave Macmillan.

Marshall, L. (1961). Sharing, Talking and Giving: Relief of Social Tensions among !Kung Bushmen. *Africa*, 31: 231–46. In Fishman (1968a).

Martin, S. (1964). Speech Levels and Social Structure in Japan and Korea. In Hymes (1964a).

Mathiot, M. and P. L. Garvin (1975). Functions of Language: A Sociocultural View. *Anthropological Quarterly*, 48: 148–56.

Mathisen, A. G. (1999). Sandwell, West Midlands: Ambiguous Perspectives on Gender Patterns and Models of Change. In Foulkes and Docherty (1999).

Matsuda, M. J. (1991). Voice of America: Antidiscrimination Law, and a Jurisprudence for the Last Reconstruction. *Yale Law Journal*, 100: 1329–407.

Matsumoto, Y. (1989). Politeness and Conversational Universals – Observations from Japanese. *Multilingua*, 8: 207–22.

Maurais, J. and M. Morris (2004). *Languages in a Globalising World*. Cambridge: Cambridge University Press.

McArthur, T. (ed.) (1992). *The Oxford Companion to the English Language*. Oxford: Oxford University Press.

McArthur, T. (1998). *The English Languages*. Cambridge: Cambridge University Press.

McConnell-Ginet, S. (2003). 'What's in a Name?' Social Labeling and Gender Practices. In Holmes and Myerhoff (2003).

McDavid, R. I. (1965). American Social Dialects. *College English*, 26: 254–60.

McKay, S. L. and N. H. Hornberger (eds.) (1996). *Sociolinguistics and Language Teaching*. Cambridge: Cambridge University Press.

McLaughlin, M. L. (1984). *Conversation*. Beverly Hills: Sage.

McMahon, A. M. S. (1994). *Understanding Language Change*. Cambridge: Cambridge University Press.

McWhorter, J. H. (1995). The Scarcity of Spanish-Based Creoles Explained. *Language in Society*, 24: 213–44.

McWhorter, J. (1998). *The Word on the Street: Fact and Fable about American English*. New York: Plenum.

McWhorter, J. H. (2000). *The Missing Spanish Creoles: Recovering the Birth of Plantation Contact Languages*. Berkeley: University of California Press.

Meier, A. J. (1995). Passages of Politeness. *Journal of Pragmatics*, 24: 381–92.

Meierkord, C. (2004). Syntactic Variation in Interactions across International Englishes. *English World-Wide*, 25(1): 109–32.

Melchers, G. (2003). *World Englishes*. Oxford: Oxford University Press.

Mencken, H. L. (1919). *The American Language*. New York: A. A. Knopf.

Mendoza-Denton, N. (2001). Style. In Duranti (2001).

Messenger, J. (1960). Anang Proverb-riddles. *Journal of American Folklore*, 73: 225–35.

Mesthrie, R. (ed.) (2001). *Concise Encyclopedia of Sociolinguistics*. Amsterdam: John Benjamins.

Mesthrie, R., J. Swann, A. Deumert, and W. L. Leap (2000). *Introducing Sociolinguistics*. Edinburgh: Edinburgh University Press.

Mey, J. (1993). *Pragmatics: An Introduction*. Oxford: Blackwell.

Meyerhoff, M. (2002). Communities of Practice. In Chambers et al. (2002).

Mills, S. (2003). *Gender and Politeness*. Cambridge: Cambridge University Press.

Milroy, J. (1992). *Language Variation and Change*. Oxford: Blackwell.

Milroy, J. (2001). Language Ideologies and the Consequences of Standardization. *Journal of Sociolinguistics*, 5(4): 530–55.

Milroy, J. and L. Milroy (1978). Belfast: Change and Variation in an Urban Vernacular. In P. Trudgill (ed.), *Sociolinguistic Patterns in British English*. London: Arnold.

Milroy, J. and L. Milroy (1999). *Authority in Language*. 3rd edn. London: Routledge.

Milroy, L. (1980). Social Network and Language Maintenance. In Pugh, Lee, and Swann (1980).

Milroy, L. (1987a). *Language and Social Networks*. 2nd edn. Oxford: Blackwell.

Milroy, L. (1987b). *Observing and Analysing Natural Language*. Oxford: Blackwell.

Milroy, L. (2002). Social Networks. In Chambers et al. (2002).

Milroy, L. and M. Gordon (2003). *Sociolinguistics: Method and Interpretation*. Oxford: Blackwell.

Milroy, L. and J. Milroy (1992). Social Networks and Social Class: Toward an Integrated Sociolinguistic Model. *Language in Society*, 21: 1–26.

Milroy, L. and P. Muysken (eds.) (1995). *One Speaker, Two Languages*. Cambridge: Cambridge University Press.

Mishoe, M. (1998). Styleswitching in Southern English. In Myers-Scotton (1998).

Mitford, N. (ed.) (1956). *Noblesse Oblige: An Enquiry into the Identifiable Characteristics of the English Aristocracy*. New York: Harper & Brothers.

Montgomery, M. (1995). *An Introduction to Language and Society*. 2nd edn. London: Routledge.

Morgan, M. (ed.) (1994). *Language and the Social Construction of Identity in Creole Situations*. Los Angeles: Center for Afro-American Studies, UCLA.

Morgan, M. M. (2001). Community. In Duranti (2001).

Morris, N. (1996). Language and Identity in Twentieth Century Puerto Rico. *Journal of Multilingual and Multicultural Development*, 17(1): 17–32.

Mufwene, S. (ed.) (1993). *Africanisms in Afro-American Language Varieties*. Athens, GA: University of Georgia Press.

Mufwene, S. S., J. R. Rickford, G. Bailey, and J. Baugh (eds.) (1998). *African-American English: Structure, History and Use*. London: Routledge.

Mugglestone, L. (1995). *'Talking Proper': The Rise of Accent as Social Symbol*. Oxford: Clarendon Press.

Mühlhäusler, P. (1982). Tok Pisin in Papua New Guinea. In Bailey and Görlach (1982).

Mühlhäusler, P. (1996). *Linguistic Ecology: Language Change and Linguistic Imperialism in the Pacific Region*. London: Routledge.

Mühlhäusler, P. (1997). *Pidgin and Creole Linguistics*. Rev. edn. London: University of Westminster Press.

Mühlhäusler, P. and R. Harré (1990). *Pronouns and People*. Oxford: Blackwell.

Mukherjee, B. (1989). *Jasmine*. New York: Viking.

Murphy, G. L. (1988). Personal Reference in English. *Language in Society*, 17: 317–49.

Murray, S. O. (1998). *American Sociolinguistics: Theorists and Theory Groups*. Amsterdam: John Benjamins.

Myers-Scotton, C. (1993a). *Duelling Languages: Grammatical Structure in Code-Switching*. Oxford: Clarendon.

Myers-Scotton, C. (1993b). *Social Motivation for Code-Switching*. Oxford: Clarendon.

Myers-Scotton, C. (ed.) (1998). *Codes and Consequences: Choosing Linguistic Varieties*. New York: Oxford University Press.

Myhill, J. (2004). *Language in Jewish Society: Towards a New Understanding*. Clevedon: Multilingual Matters.

Nadel, S. F. (1954). Morality and Language among the Nupe. *Man*, 54: 55–7. In Hymes (1964a).

Nettle, D. and S. Romaine (2000). *Vanishing Voices: The Extinction of the World's Languages*. Oxford: Oxford University Press.

Neustupný, J. V. (1986). Language and Society: The Case of Japanese Politeness. In Fishman, Tabouret-Keller, Clyne, Krishnamurti, and Abdulaziz (1986).

Newson, J. and E. Newson (1970). *Four Years Old in an Urban Community*. Harmondsworth, England: Penguin Books.

Newton, G. (ed.) (1996). *Luxembourg and Lëtzebuergesch: Language and Communication at the Crossroads of Europe*. Oxford: Oxford University Press.

Niedzielski, N. and D. R. Preston (1999). *Folk Linguistics*. Berlin: Mouton de Gruyter.

Nishimura, M. (1997). *Japanese/English Code-switching: Syntax and Pragmatics*. New York: Peter Lang.

Nwoye, O. G. (1992). Linguistic Politeness and Socio-Cultural Variations of the Notion of Face. *Journal of Pragmatics*, 18: 309–28.

Ochs, E. (1979). Planned and Unplanned Discourse. In T. Givon (ed.), *Syntax and Semantics*, vol. 12: *Discourse and Syntax*. New York: Academic Press.

O'Donnell, P. E. (1996). 'I'm Catalan but I'm not a Fanatic': Shifting Tides in Catalan Opinion. *Language Problems and Language Planning*, 20(1): 44–52.

Orton, H., S. Sanderson, and J. Widdowson (eds.) (1978). *The Linguistic Atlas of England*. London: Croom Helm.

Oyetade, S. O. (1995). A Sociolinguistic Analysis of Address Forms in Yoruba. *Language in Society*, 24: 515–35.

Parkin, D. (1989). The Politics of Naming among the Giriama. In R. Grillo (ed.), *Social Anthropology and the Politics of Language*. Sociological Review Monograph 36. London: Routledge.

Parkinson, D. B. (1986). *Constructing the Social Context of Communication*. Berlin: Mouton de Gruyter.

Patrick, P. L. (1999). *Urban Jamaican Creole: Variation in the Mesolect*. Amsterdam: John Benjamins.

Patrick, P. L. (2002). The Speech Community. In Chambers et al. (2002).

Paulston, C. B. and G. R. Tucker (eds.) (2003). *Sociolinguistics: The Essential Readings*. Oxford: Blackwell.

Pauwels, A. (1998). *Women Changing Language*. London: Longman.

Pauwels, A. (2003). Linguistic Sexism and Feminist Linguistic Activism. In Holmes and Meyerhoff (2003).

Penelope, J. (1990). *Speaking Freely*. Oxford: Pergamon Press.

Pennycook, A. (1998). *English and the Discourses of Colonialism*. London: Routledge.

Perry, T. and L. Delpit (eds.) (1998). *The Real Ebonics Debate: Power, Language, and the Education of African-American Children*. Boston: Beacon Press.

Petyt, K. M. (1980). *The Study of Dialect: An Introduction to Dialectology*. London: André Deutsch.

Pfaff, C. (1979). Constraints on Language Mixing. *Language*, 55: 291–318.

Pham, H. (2002). Gender in Addressing and Self-reference in Vietnamese: Variation and Change. In M. Hellinger and H. Bussmann (eds.), *Gender Across Languages: The Linguistic Representation of Men and Women*, vol. 2. Amsterdam: John Benjamins.

Philips, S. U., S. Steele, and C. Tanz (eds.) (1987). *Language, Gender and Sex in Comparative Perspective*. Cambridge: Cambridge University Press.

Philipsen, G. and D. Carbaugh (1986). A Bibliography of Fieldwork in the Ethnography of Communication. *Language in Society*, 15: 387–98.

Phillipson, R. (1992). *Linguistic Imperialism*. Oxford: Oxford University Press.

Phillipson, R. (2003). *English-only Europe? Challenging Language Policy*. London: Routledge.

Pike, K. L. (1967). *Language in Relation to a Unified Theory of the Structure of Human Behavior*. Rev. edn. The Hague: Mouton.

Pilkington, J. (1998). 'Don't Try and Make Out that I'm Nice!' The Different Strategies Women and Men Use when Gossiping. In Coates (1998).

Pinker, S. (1994). *The Language Instinct: How the Mind Creates Language*. New York: William Morrow.

Placencia, M. E. (2001). Inequality in Address Behavior at Public Institutions in La Paz, Bolivia. *Anthropological Linguistics*, 43(2): 198–217.

Platt, J. T. and H. K. Platt (1975). *The Social Significance of Speech: An Introduction to and Workbook in Sociolinguistics*. Amsterdam: North-Holland.

Pool, J. (1972). National Development and Language Diversity. In Fishman (1971–2, vol. 2).

Poplack, S. (ed.) (2000). *The English History of African American English*. Oxford: Blackwell.

Preisler, B. (1986). *Linguistic Sex Roles in Conversation*. Berlin: Mouton de Gruyter.

Preston, D. R. (1989). *Perceptual Dialectology*. Dordrecht: Foris.

Preston, D. R. (ed.) (1999). *Handbook of Perceptual Dialectology*, vol. 1. Amsterdam: John Benjamins.

Preston, D. R. (2002). Language with an Attitude. In Chambers et al. (2002).

Pride, J. B. (1986). Questions and Non-Answers. In Fishman, Tabouret-Keller, Clyne, Krishnamurti, and Abdulaziz (1986).

Pride, J. B. and J. Holmes (1972). *Sociolinguistics: Selected Readings*. Harmondsworth, England: Penguin Books.

Psathas, G. (ed.) (1979). *Everyday Language: Studies in Ethnomethodology*. New York: Irvington Publishers.

Pütz, M. and M. H. Verspoor (eds.) (2000). *Explorations in Linguistic Relativity*. Amsterdam: John Benjamins.

Rai, A. (1991). *A House Divided: The Origin and Development of Hindi-Urdu*. Delhi: Oxford University Press.

Rampton, B. (1995). *Crossing: Language and Ethnicity among Adolescents*. London: Longman.

Rampton, B. (2001). Crossing. In Duranti (2001).

Rawls, J. (1955). Two Concepts of Rules. *Philosophical Review*, 64: 3–32.

Reisman, K. (1974). Contrapuntal Conversations in an Antiguan Village. In Bauman and Sherzer (1974).

Reynolds, K. A. (1998). Female Speakers of Japanese in Transition. In Coates (1998).

Rickford, J. R. (1977). The Question of Prior Creolization in Black English. In Valdman (1977).

Rickford, J. R. (1997). Prior Creolization of African-American Vernacular English? Sociohistorical and Textual Evidence from the 17th and 18th Centuries. *Journal of Sociolinguistics*, 1(3): 315–36.

Rickford, J. R. (1999a). *African American Vernacular English*. Oxford: Blackwell.

Rickford, J. R. (1999b). The Ebonics Controversy in my Backyard: A Sociolinguist's Experience and Reflections. *Journal of Sociolinguistics*, 3(2): 267–75.

Rickford, J. R. (2004). Spoken Soul: The Beloved, Belittled Language of Black America. In Fought (2004).

Rickford, J. R., J. Sweetland, and A. E. Rickford (2004). African American English and Other Vernaculars in Education. *Journal of English Linguistics*, 32(3): 230–320.

Roberts, P. A. (1988). *West Indians and Their Language*. Cambridge: Cambridge University Press.

Robinson, W. P. (1972). *Language and Social Behaviour*. Harmondsworth, England: Penguin Books.

Robinson, W. P. and S. J. Rackstraw (1967). Variations in Mothers' Answers to Children's Questions. *Sociology*, 1: 259–79.

Romaine, S. (1988). *Pidgin and Creole Languages*. London: Longman.

Romaine, S. (1999). *Communicating Gender*. Mahwah, NJ: Lawrence Erlbaum.

Romaine, S. (2001). *Language in Society: An Introduction to Sociolinguistics*. 2nd edn. Oxford: Oxford University Press.

Rosch, E. (1976). Classification of Real-world Objects: Origins and Representations in Cognition. In S. Ehrlich and E. Tulving (eds.), *La Mémoire sémantique*. Paris: Bulletin de Psychologie.

Rosen, H. (1972). *Language and Class: A Critical Look at the Theories of Basil Bernstein*. Bristol: Falling Wall Press.

Rosen, H. (1980). *Linguistic Diversity in London Schools*. In Pugh, Lee, and Swann (1980).

Rosenthal, M. (1974). The Magic Boxes: Pre-school Children's Attitudes Toward Black and Standard English. *Florida FL Reporter*, Spring/Fall: 56ff.

Rosewarne, D. (1994). Estuary English – Tomorrow's RP? *English Today*, 10(1): 3–8.

Rubin, J. (1968). *National Bilingualism in Paraguay*. The Hague: Mouton. Excerpted in Pride and Holmes (1972).

Rubin, J. (1986). How Does the Way Women are Referred to and Described Affect Their Participation in Development and Democracy? In Fishman, Tabouret-Keller, Clyne, Krishnamurti, and Abdulaziz (1986).

Sacks, H. (1972a). An Initial Investigation of the Usability of Conversational Data for Doing Sociology. In Sudnow (1972).

Sacks, H. (1972b). On the Analyzability of Stories by Children. In Gumperz and Hymes (1972).

Sacks, H. (1992). *Lectures on Conversation*. Oxford: Blackwell.

Salisbury, R. F. (1962). Notes on Bilingualism and Linguistic Change in New Guinea. *Anthropological Linguistics*, 4(7): 1–13. In Pride and Holmes (1972).

Samarin, W. J. (1968). Lingua Francas of the World. In Fishman (1968a).

Samarin, W. J. (1969). The Art of Gbeya Insults. *International Journal of American Linguistics*, 35: 323–9.

Samarin, W. J. (1973). *Tongues of Men and Angels*. New York: Macmillan.

Sankoff, D. (ed.) (1978). *Linguistic Variation: Models and Methods*. New York: Academic Press.

Sankoff, D. (1985). Statistics in Linguistics. *Encyclopedia of Statistical Sciences*, vol. 5. New York: John Wiley.

Sankoff, G. (1972). Language Use in Multilingual Societies: Some Alternative Approaches. In Pride and Holmes (1972).

Sankoff, G. (1974). A Quantitative Paradigm for the Study of Communicative Competence. In Bauman and Sherzer (1974).

Sankoff, G. and H. Cedergren (1971). Some Results of a Sociolinguistic Study of Montreal French. In R. Darnell (ed.), *Linguistic Diversity in Canadian Society*. Edmonton: Linguistic Research Inc.

Sankoff, G. and D. Vincent (1977). L'Emploi productif du *ne* dans le Français parlé à Montréal. *Le Français Modern*, 45: 243–56.

Sapir, E. (1921). *Language: An Introduction to the Study of Speech*. New York: Harcourt, Brace.

Sapir, E. (1929a). Male and Female Forms of Speech in Yana. In S. W. J. Teeuwen (ed.), *Donum Natalicum Schrijnen*. Nijmegen: Dekker & Van de Vegt.

Sapir, E. (1929b). The Status of Linguistics as a Science. *Language*, 5: 207–14.

Saussure, F. de (1959). *Course in General Linguistics*. New York: McGraw-Hill.

Saville-Troike, M. (1989). *The Ethnography of Communication: An Introduction*. 2nd edn. Oxford: Blackwell.

Saville-Troike, M. (1996). The Ethnography of Communication. In McKay and Hornberger (1996).

Schegloff, E. A. (1968). Sequencing in Conversational Openings. *American Anthropologist*, 70: 1075–95. In Fishman (1971–2, vol. 2), Gumperz and Hymes (1972), and Laver and Hutcheson (1972).

Schegloff, E. (1986). The Routine as Achievement. *Human Studies*, 9: 111–52.

Schegloff, E. A. (2000). Overlapping Talk and the Organization of Turn-taking for Conversation. *Language in Society*, 29: 1–63.

Schenkein, J. (ed.) (1978). *Studies in the Organization of Conversational Interaction*. New York: Academic Press.

Scherer, K. R. and H. Giles (eds.) (1979). *Social Markers in Speech*. Cambridge: Cambridge University Press.

Schieffelin, B. B. and R. C. Doucet (1998). The 'Real' Haitian Creole. In Schieffelin et al. (1998).

Schieffelin, B. B., K. Woolard, and P. V. Kroskrity (eds.) (1998). *Language Ideologies: Practice and Theory*. Oxford: Oxford University Press.

Schiffman, H. (1996). *Linguistic Culture and Language Policy*. London: Routledge.

Schiffrin, D. (1987). *Discourse Markers*. Cambridge: Cambridge University Press.

Schiffrin, D. (1994). *Approaches to Discourse*. Oxford: Blackwell.

Schilling-Estes, N. (2002). Investigating Stylistic Variation. In Chambers et al. (2002).

Schmid, C. L. (2001). *The Politics of Language: Conflict, Identity, and Cultural Pluralism in Comparative Perspective*. Oxford: Oxford University Press.

Schneider, E. W. (2003). The Dynamics of New Englishes: From Identity Construction to Dialect Birth. *Language*, 79(2): 233–81.

Scollon, R. and S. W. Scollon (2001). *Intercultural Communication: A Discourse Approach*. 2nd edn. Oxford: Blackwell.

Scott, Foresman and Company (1972). *Guidelines for Improving the Image of Women in Textbooks*. Glenview, IL: Scott, Foresman.

Scotton, C. M. (1983). The Negotiation of Identities in Conversation: A Theory of Markedness and Code Choice. *International Journal of the Sociology of Language*, 44: 115–36.

Scotton, C. M. (1986). Diglossia and Code Switching. In Fishman, Tabouret-Keller, Clyne, Krishnamurti, and Abdulaziz (1986).

Scotton, C. M. and Z. Wanjin (1983). *Tóngzhi* in China: Language Change and its Conversational Consequences. *Language in Society*, 12: 477–94.

Scribner, S. (1977). Modes of Thinking and Ways of Speaking: Culture and Logic Reconsidered. In P. Johnson-Laird and P. C. Wason (eds.), *Thinking: Readings in Cognitive Science*. Cambridge: Cambridge University Press.

Searle, J. (1969). *Speech Acts: An Essay in the Philosophy of Language*. London: Cambridge University Press.

Searle, J. (1975). Indirect Speech Acts. In Cole and Morgan (1975).

Searle, J. (1999). *Mind, Language and Society: Doing Philosophy in the Real World*. London: Weidenfeld and Nicolson.

Sebba, M. (1993). *London Jamaican: Language Systems in Interaction*. London: Longman.

Sebba, M. (1997). *Contact Languages: Pidgins and Creoles*. London: Macmillan.

Sellers, S. (1991). *Language and Sexual Difference: Feminist Writing in France*. New York: St Martin's Press.

Serge, V. (1977). *Men in Prison*. London: Writers' and Readers' Publishing Cooperative.

Seuren, P. A. M. (2004). *Chomsky's Minimalism*. Oxford: Oxford University Press.

Shaul, D. L. and N. L. Furbee (1998). *Language and Culture*. Prospect Heights, IL: Waveland Press.

Sherzer, J. (1983). *Kuna Ways of Speaking*. Austin: University of Texas Press.

Shibamoto, J. (1985). *Japanese Women's Language*. Orlando: Academic Press.

Shuy, R. W., W. A. Wolfram, and W. K. Riley (1968). *Field Techniques in an Urban Language Study*. Washington, DC: Center for Applied Linguistics.

Siegel, J. (1995). How to Get a Laugh in Fijian: Code-switching and Humor. *Language in Society*, 24: 95–110.

Sifianou, M. (1989). On the Telephone Again! Differences in Telephone Behavior: England versus Greece. *Language in Society*, 18: 527–44.

Silverman, D. (1998). *Harvey Sacks: Social Science and Conversation Analysis*. Oxford: Oxford University Press.

Singh, I. (2000). *Pidgins and Creoles: An Introduction*. London: Arnold.

Sivertsen, E. (1960). *Cockney Phonology*. Oslo: Oslo University Press.

Sledd, J. H. and W. R. Ebbitt (eds.) (1962). *Dictionaries and THAT Dictionary*. Chicago: Scott Foresman.

Smith, N. (1995). An Annotated List of Creoles, Pidgins, and Mixed Languages. In Arends et al. (1995).

Smith, N. (1999). *Chomsky: Ideas and Ideals*. Cambridge: Cambridge University Press.

Smith, P. M. (1979). Sex Markers in Speech. In Scherer and Giles (1979).

Smith, P. (1985). *Language, the Sexes and Society*. Oxford: Blackwell.

Smitherman, G. (1999). *Talkin That Talk: Language, Culture and Education in African America*. New York: Routledge.

Sorensen, A. P. (1971). Multilingualism in the Northwest Amazon. *American Anthropologist*, 69: 670–84. In Pride and Holmes (1972).

Spears, A. K. (1992). Reassessing the Status of Black English (Review Article). *Language in Society*, 21: 675–82.

Spears, A. K. and D. Winford (eds.) (1997). *The Structure and Status of Pidgins and Creoles*. Amsterdam: John Benjamins.

Spender, D. (1985). *Man Made Language*. 2nd edn. London: Routledge & Kegan Paul.

Sperber, D. and D. Wilson (1995). *Relevance*. 2nd edn. Oxford: Blackwell.

Spolsky, B. (1998). *Sociolinguistics*. Oxford: Oxford University Press.

Spolsky, B. (2004). *Language Policy*. Cambridge: Cambridge University Press.

Sridhar, K. K. (1996). Societal Multilingualism. In McKay and Hornberger (1996).

Staples, L. M. (1971). A Study of Address Forms used in an Hierarchical Organization. Unpublished manuscript.

Stenström, A.-B. (1994). *An Introduction to Spoken Interaction*. London: Longman.

Stewart, W. A. (1967). Sociolinguistic Factors in the History of American Negro Dialects. *Florida FL Reporter*, 5(2): 11ff.

Stewart, W. A. (1969). On the Use of Negro Dialect in the Teaching of Reading. In J. C. Baratz and R. W. Shuy (eds.), *Teaching Black Children to Read*. Washington, DC: Center for Applied Linguistics.

Streetharan, C. S. (2004). Students, *Sarariiman* (pl.), and Seniors: Japanese Men's Use of 'Manly' Speech Register. *Language in Society*, 33: 81–107.

Strevens, P. (1972). *British and American English*. London: Collier-Macmillan.

Stubbs, M. (1980). *Language and Literacy. The Sociolinguistics of Reading and Writing*. London: Routledge & Kegan Paul.

Stubbs, M. (1983). *Discourse Analysis: The Sociolinguistic Analysis of Natural Language*. Chicago: University of Chicago Press.

Sudnow, D. (ed.) (1972). *Studies in Social Interaction*. New York: Free Press.

Sutcliffe, D. (1982). *British Black English*. Oxford: Blackwell.

Swann, J. (1993). *Girls, Boys and Language*. Oxford: Blackwell.

Swann, J., A. Deumert, T. Lillis, and R. Mesthrie (2004). *A Dictionary of Sociolinguistics*. Edinburgh: Edinburgh University Press.

Sweetland, J. (2002). Unexpected but Authentic Use of an Ethnically-marked Dialect. *Journal of Sociolinguistics*, 6(4): 514–36.

Takahara, K. (1991). Female Speech Patterns in Japanese. *International Journal of the Sociology of Language*, 92: 61–85.

Talbot, M. M. (1998). *Language and Gender: An Introduction*. Cambridge: Polity Press.

Tannen, D. (1987). Repetition in Conversation: Toward a Poetics of Talk. *Language*, 63: 574–605.

Tannen, D. (1990). *You Just Don't Understand: Women and Men in Conversation*. New York: William Morrow.

Tannen, D. (1993). *Gender and Conversational Interaction*. New York: Oxford University Press.

Tannen, D. (1994). *Gender and Discourse*. New York: Oxford University Press.

Tannen, D. (1998). Talk in the Intimate Relationship: His and Hers. In Coates (1998).

Tanner, N. (1967). Speech and Society among the Indonesian Elite: A Case Study of a Multilingual Community. *Anthropological Linguistics*, 9(3): 15–39. In Pride and Holmes (1972).

Taylor, A. R. (1981). Indian Lingua Francas. In Ferguson and Heath (1981).

Taylor, D. M. (1951a). Structural Outline of Caribbean Creole. *Word*, 7: 43–59.

Taylor, D. M. (1951b). *The Black Carib of British Honduras*. New York: Wenner-Gren Foundation for Anthropological Research.

Taylor, T. J. and D. Cameron (1987). *Analysing Conversation*. Oxford: Pergamon Press.

Thomas, G. (1991). *Linguistic Purism*. London: Longman.

Thomason, S. G. (ed.) (1997). *Contact Languages: A Wider Perspective*. Amsterdam: John Benjamins.

Thomason, S. G. (2001). *Language Contact: An Introduction*. Washington, D.C.: Georgetown University Press.

Thorne, B. and N. Henley (eds.) (1975). *Language and Sex: Difference and Dominance*. Rowley, MA: Newbury House.

Tobin, J. J., D. Y. H. Wu, and D. H. Davidson (eds.) (1989). *Preschool in Three Cultures: Japan, China, and the United States*. New Haven: Yale University Press.

Todd, L. (1990). *Pidgins and Creoles*. New edn. London: Routledge.

Tollefson, J. W. (1991). *Planning Language, Planning Inequality*. London: Longman.

Trudgill, P. (1972). Sex, Covert Prestige and Linguistic Change in the Urban British English of Norwich. *Language in Society*, 1: 179–95.

Trudgill, P. (1974). *The Social Differentiation of English in Norwich*. Cambridge: Cambridge University Press.

Trudgill, P. (1975). *Accent, Dialect and the School*. London: Edward Arnold.

Trudgill, P. (ed.) (1978). *Sociolinguistic Patterns in British English*. London: Edward Arnold.

Trudgill, P. (1986). *Dialects in Contact*. Oxford: Blackwell.

Trudgill, P. (1988). Norwich Revisited: Recent Linguistic Changes in an English Urban Dialect. *English World-Wide*, 9: 33–49.

Trudgill, P. (1995). *Sociolinguistics: An Introduction to Language and Society*. 3rd edn. Harmondsworth, England: Penguin Books.

Trudgill, P. (1999). *The Dialects of England*. 2nd edn. Oxford: Blackwell.

Trudgill, P. (2003). *A Glossary of Sociolinguistics*. Oxford: Oxford University Press.

Trudgill, P. (2004). *New-dialect Formation: The Inevitability of Colonial Englishes*. Oxford: Oxford University Press.

Trudgill, P. and J. Cheshire (eds.) (1998). *The Sociolinguistics Reader*, vol. 1: *Multilingualism and Variation*. London: Arnold.

Trudgill, P. and J. Hannah (2002). *International English: A Guide to the Varieties of Standard English*. 4th edn. Oxford: Oxford University Press.

Tseronis, A. (2002). Diglossic Past and Present Lexicographical Practices: The Case of Two Greek Dictionaries. *Language Problems and Language Planning*, 26(3): 219–52.

Tsohatzidis, S. L. (ed.) (1990). *Meanings and Prototypes: Studies in Linguistic Categorization*. London: Routledge.

Tsohatzidis, S. L. (ed.) (1994). *Foundations of Speech Act Theory. Philosophical and Linguistic Perspectives*. London: Routledge.

Tsui, A. B. M. (1989). Beyond the Adjacency Pair. *Language in Society*, 18: 545–64.

Turner, L. D. (1949). *Africanisms in the Gullah Dialect*. Chicago: University of Chicago Press.

Turner, R. (ed.) (1974). *Ethnomethodology*. Harmondsworth, England: Penguin Books.

Tyler, S. A. (ed.) (1969). *Cognitive Anthropology*. New York: Holt, Rinehart, and Winston.

Upton, C. and J. D. A. Widdowson (eds.) (1996). *An Atlas of English Dialects*. Oxford: Oxford University Press.

Valdman, A. (ed.) (1977). *Pidgin and Creole Linguistics*. Bloomington: Indiana University Press.

Valdman, A. and A. Highfield (eds.) (1980). *Theoretical Orientations in Creole Studies*. New York: Academic Press.

van Dijk, T. A. (1993). Principles of Critical Discourse Analysis. *Discourse and Society*, 4: 249–83. Also in Trudgill and Cheshire (1998).

Velez, J. A. and C. W. Schweers (1993). A U.S. Colony at a Linguistic Crossroads: The Decision to Make Spanish the Official Language of Puerto Rico. *Language Problems and Language Planning*, 17(2): 117–39.

Veltman, C. (1983). *Language Shift in the United States*. Berlin: Mouton Publishers.

Viereck, W. (1966). *Phonematische Analyse des Dialekts von Gateshead-Upon-Tyne, Co. Durham*. Hamburg: Cram & de Gruyter.

Vigner, G. (1978). *Savoir-vivre en France*. Paris: Hachette.

Vikør, L. (1993). *Nordic Languages: Their Status and Interrelations*. Oslo: Novus Press.

Vikør, L. (2002). Northern Europe: Languages as Prime Markers of Ethnic and National Identity. In Barbour and Carmichael (2002).

Waggoner, D. (1981). Statistics on Language Use. In Ferguson and Heath (1981).

Wakelin, M. F. (1977). *English Dialects: An Introduction*. Rev. edn. London: Athlone Press.

Wang, W. S.-Y. (1969). Competing Changes as a Cause of Residue. *Language*, 45: 9–25.

Wang, W. S.-Y. (ed.) (1977). *The Lexicon in Phonological Change*. The Hague: Mouton.

Wardhaugh, R. (1985). *How Conversation Works*. Oxford: Blackwell.

Wardhaugh, R. (1987). *Languages in Competition*. Oxford: Blackwell.

Wardhaugh, R. (1999). *Proper English: Myths and Misunderstandings about Language*. Oxford: Blackwell.

Wassink, A. B. (1999). Historic Low Prestige and Seeds of Change: Attitudes Toward Jamaican Creole. *Language in Society*, 28: 57–92.

Watt, D. J. L. (2000). Phonetic Parallels between the Close-mid Vowels of Tyneside English: Are They Internally or Externally Motivated? *Language Variation and Change*, 12: 69–101.

Watt, D. J. L. (2002). 'I Don't Speak Geordie with an Accent, I Speak, like, the Northern Accent': Contact-induced Levelling in the Tyneside Vowel System. *Journal of Sociolinguistics*, 6(1): 44–63.

Watts, R. J. (2003). *Politeness*. Cambridge: Cambridge University Press.

Webster, G. (1960). Korean Bamboo English Once More. *American Speech*, 35: 261–5.

Weinstein, B. (1980). Language Planning in Francophone Africa. *Language Problems and Language Planning*, 4(1): 55–77.

Wells, J. C. (1982). *Accents of English*. Cambridge: Cambridge University Press.

Whinnom, K. (1971). Linguistic Hybridization and the 'Special Case' of Pidgins and Creoles. In Hymes (1971).

Whiteley, W. H. (1984). Sociolinguistic Surveys at the National Level. In Kennedy (1984).

Widdowson, H. G. (1998). Review Article: The Theory and Practice of Critical Discourse Analysis. *Applied Linguistics*, 19(1): 136–51.

Williams, A. and P. Kerswill (1999). Dialect Levelling: Change and Continuity in Milton Keynes, Reading and Hull. In Foulkes and Docherty (1999).

Williams, G. (1992). *Sociolinguistics: A Sociological Critique*. London: Routledge.

Williams, R. (ed.) (1975). *Ebonics: The True Language of Black Folk*. St Louis: Institute of Black Studies.

Wilson, J. (1989). *On the Boundaries of Conversation*. Oxford: Pergamon Press.

Winford, D. (1997a). Creole Formation in the Context of Contact Languages. *Journal of Pidgin and Creole Language*, 12(1): 131–51.

Winford, D. (1997b). Creole Studies and Sociolinguistics. *Journal of Pidgin and Creole Language*, 12(2): 303–18.

Winford, D. (2003). *An Introduction to Contact Linguistics*. Oxford: Blackwell.

Wittgenstein, L. (1958). *Philosophical Investigations*. 2nd edn. Oxford: Blackwell.

Wodak, R. (ed.) (1997a). *Gender and Discourse*. London: Sage.

Wodak, R. (1997b). Introduction: Some Important Issues in the Research of Gender and Discourse. In Wodak (1997a).

Wolfers, E. (1971). A Report on Neo-Melanesian. In Hymes (1971).

Wolfram, W. (1969). *A Sociolinguistic Description of Detroit Negro Speech*. Washington, DC: Center for Applied Linguistics.

Wolfram, W. (1990). Re-examining Vernacular Black English. *Language*, 66: 121–33.

Wolfram, W. (1991). The Linguistic Variable: Fact and Fantasy. *American Speech*, 66(1): 22–32.

Wolfram, W. (1997). Dialect in Society. In Coulmas (1997).

Wolfram, W. (2003). Reexamining the Development of African American English: Evidence from Isolated Communities. *Language*, 79(2): 282–316.

Wolfram, W. (2004). The Sociolinguistic Construction of Remnant Dialects. In Fought (2004).

Wolfram, W. and R. W. Fasold (1974). *The Study of Social Dialects in American English*, Englewood Cliffs, NJ: Prentice-Hall.

Wolfram, W. and N. Schilling-Estes (1995). Moribund Dialects and the Endangerment Canon: The Case of the Ocracoke Brogue. *Language*, 71: 696–721.

Wolfram, W. and N. Schilling-Estes (1997). *Hoi Toide on the Outer Banks: The Story of Ocracoke Brogue*. Chapel Hill: University of North Carolina Press.

Wolfram, W. and N. Schilling-Estes (1998). *American English: Dialects and Variation*. Oxford: Blackwell.

Wolfram, W. and E. R. Thomas (2002). *The Development of African American English*. Oxford: Blackwell.

Woolard, K. A. (1985). Language Variation and Cultural Hegemony: Toward an Integration of Linguistic and Sociological Theory. *American Ethnologist*, 12: 738–48.

Woolard, K. A. (1989). *Double Talk: Bilingualism and the Politics of Ethnicity in Catalonia*. Stanford, CA: Stanford University Press.

Wootton, A. J. (1975). *Dilemmas of Discourse: Controversies about the Sociological Interpretation of Language*. London: George Allen & Unwin.

Wright, S. (2004). *Language Policy and Language Planning: From Nationalism to Globalisation*. New York: Palgrave Macmillan.

Yau, F. M. (1997). Code Switching and Language Choice in the Hong Kong Legislative Council. *Journal of Multilingual and Multicultural Development*, 8(1): 40–51.

Yule, G. (1996). *Pragmatics*. Oxford: Oxford University Press.

Zeller, C. (1997). The Investigation of a Sound Change in Progress. *Journal of English Linguistics*, 25(2): 142–55.

Zimmerman, D. H. and C. West (1975). Sex Roles, Interruptions and Silences in Conversation. In Thorne and Henley (1975).

Index